Singapore Mandarin Grammar II

As the second volume of a two-volume set that presents a comprehensive syntactical picture of Singapore Mandarin, this title analyses various expressions relating to number, quantity, time and place, composite sentences, and the characteristics and standardisation of Singapore Mandarin.

The first two chapters discuss expressions of number, quantity, time and place in Singapore Mandarin and touch upon the differences in these expressions between Singapore and Chinese Mandarin (Putonghua). Composite sentences are then analysed, covering seven types of compound sentences and eight types of complex sentences, as well as connective words with a focus on conjunctions. The final part of the volume analyses the characteristics of Singapore Mandarin grammar compared with Chinese Mandarin, on the level of phrase, lexicon and sentence. From the perspectives of language contact, political and social contexts and bilingualism, it summarises the possible reasons for the differences between the two varieties of Chinese and points out primary challenges and major concerns in the standardisation of Singapore Mandarin.

With rich and authentic language examples, the book will serve as a must read for learners and teachers of Mandarin Chinese and linguistics scholars interested in global Chinese and especially Singapore Mandarin.

Lu Jianming is a professor and doctoral supervisor in the Chinese Department of Peking University, China. He has been teaching and researching modern Chinese studies for more than 60 years and has served as President of the World Chinese Teaching Association and President of the International Chinese Linguistic Society.

China Perspectives

The *China Perspectives* series focuses on translating and publishing works by leading Chinese scholars, writing about both global topics and China-related themes. It covers Humanities & Social Sciences, Education, Media and Psychology, as well as many interdisciplinary themes.

This is the first time any of these books have been published in English for international readers. The series aims to put forward a Chinese perspective, give insights into cutting-edge academic thinking in China, and inspire researchers globally.

To submit proposals, please contact the Taylor & Francis Publisher for the China Publishing Programme, Lian Sun (Lian.Sun@informa.com)

Titles in linguistics currently include:

Modern Chinese Grammar III
Substitution and Numeration
WANG Li

Modern Chinese Grammar IV
Special Forms and Europeanised Grammar
WANG Li

Singapore Mandarin Grammar I
Lu Jianming

Cognitive Neural Mechanism of Semantic Rhetoric
Qiaoyun Liao, Lijun Meng

Singapore Mandarin Grammar II
Lu Jianming

For more information, please visit www.routledge.com/China-Perspectives/book-series/CPH

Singapore Mandarin Grammar II

Lu Jianming

LONDON AND NEW YORK

This book is published with financial support from the Chinese Fund for the Humanities and Social Sciences.

First published in English 2023
by Routledge
4 Park Square, Milton Park, Abingdon, Oxon OX14 4RN

and by Routledge
605 Third Avenue, New York, NY 10158

Routledge is an imprint of the Taylor & Francis Group, an informa business

© 2023 Lu Jianming

Translated by Peng Guozhen, Yang Xiaodong, Zhao Yiya

The right of Lu Jianming to be identified as author of this work has been asserted in accordance with sections 77 and 78 of the Copyright, Designs and Patents Act 1988.

All rights reserved. No part of this book may be reprinted or reproduced or utilised in any form or by any electronic, mechanical, or other means, now known or hereafter invented, including photocopying and recording, or in any information storage or retrieval system, without permission in writing from the publishers.

Trademark notice: Product or corporate names may be trademarks or registered trademarks, and are used only for identification and explanation without intent to infringe.

English version by permission of The Commercial Press

ISBN: 978-1-032-39546-3 (hbk)
ISBN: 978-1-032-39551-7 (pbk)
ISBN: 978-1-003-35024-8 (ebk)

DOI: 10.4324/9781003350248

Typeset in Times New Roman
by Apex CoVantage, LLC

Contents

	List of translators	vi
	Foreword	vii
1	Expressions of Number and Quantity	1
2	Expressions of Location, Time and Place	107
3	Composite Sentences	180
4	Characteristics of Singapore Mandarin Grammar	282
5	The Standardisation of Singapore Mandarin	392
	Postscript	403
	Appendix 1: English-Chinese Term List	407
	Appendix 2: Translation of Examples and Glossary	414
	Appendix 3: The Sources of Examples	416
	References	421
	Index	424

Translators

Peng Guozhen is a professor of linguistics at Zhejiang University of Technology. Her research interest is linguistic typology and syntax.

Yang Xiaodong is an associate professor of linguistics at Zhejiang University of Technology. His research interest is syntax and corpus linguistics.

Zhao Yiya is a lecturer of linguistics at Zhijiang College of Zhejiang University of Technology. Her research interest is translation studies and language education.

Foreword

Professor Lu Jianming's new book, *Singapore Mandarin Grammar II*, is to be published, and I have been invited to write the foreword for it as I am connected to this work in some ways. Many of my views on language relate to the content of this book. Reading this manuscript in advance not only brings me enjoyment but takes me back to the 1990s. This foreword, therefore, will elaborate upon the intellectual merits of the volume, as well as some pleasant recollections.

I. Recollections of the Past

The late former Prime Minister Lee Kuan Yew was a staunch supporter of the Chinese language during his lifetime, and in 1979 he initiated the Speak Mandarin Campaign.[1] To make it easier for Singaporeans to learn Mandarin and to use it, the authorities also launched the programme "Dial for Mandarin", helping Singaporeans interested in learning Mandarin to do so through telephone calls. At that time, we were using modern Chinese Mandarin as the standard language. As one of the consultants for the course, I was sceptical about the standardness of the expression 贵也贵不到哪里去 *guì yě guì bùdào nǎlǐ qù* 'It won't be too expensive'. Such a sentence is well-formed in dialects, but was it grammatical in Chinese Mandarin? I had no idea because I had never been to China, and there was no explanation about it in any of the grammar texts I could find, including Lü Shuxiang and Zhu Dexi's 《语法修辞讲话》 *Yǔfǎ xiūcí jiǎnghuà* '*Speech on Grammar and Rhetoric*' and Chao Yuen Ren's *A Grammar of Spoken Chinese*. Later, I was relieved to discover such a usage in Lao She's work and thus decided to keep the expression in the textbook for "Dial for Mandarin".

In 1985, the First International Conference on Chinese Language Teaching and Research was held at Xiangshan, Beijing, and I attended the conference with Lu Shaochang, Chen Chongyu, Xie Zewen and Xie Shiya. That was my first visit to Beijing. During the several days I stayed there, I became aware that there were differences between Chinese Mandarin and Singapore Mandarin. But what exactly were the differences? In response to my question, Professor Lu Jianming said, "It is necessary to understand, identify and describe the features of Singapore Mandarin, which will lay the groundwork for its standardization." Only by doing so, these differences may be properly addressed and handled in the teaching of Singapore Mandarin. These are the things I have kept in mind all this time.

Following China's reform and opening up, a large number of Chinese intellectuals arrived in Singapore, bringing a variety of viewpoints about the language used in *Zaobao*. At that time, I was a member of the newspaper's advisory board, so I got the chance to see the expressions that they were critical of. Most of those expressions, with the exception of some clearly incorrect or ill-formed ones, were also used by the majority of Singaporeans. Therefore I advised the then-Prime Minister Lee Kuan Yew that *Zaobao* should engage a language expert to review the journalists' vocabulary. At the same time, I was wondering whether it was necessary for Singapore Mandarin to be entirely normalised according to the standards of Chinese Mandarin.

In 1994, Nanyang Technological University established the Chinese Language and Culture Centre, with myself as the director and Professor Li Yunwei as the deputy director. For linguistic research, we then launched three research programs: (1) a study of Chinese languages in Southeast Asia; (2) a comparative study of Singapore Mandarin and the modern standard Mandarin; (3) a study of language usage of Chinese people in Singapore.

Professor Lu Jianming was our Centre's first visiting faculty. I have always believed that mainland China's first-class intellectuals should receive their due respect. Thus the payment for Professor Lu Jianming at the Centre was the same as that for professors from Europe and the United States. My peers at a Hong Kong tertiary colleges then criticized me, saying, "You have violated the market", for at that time it was the prevailing practice in Hong Kong to give unfair salaries to mainland Chinese specialists and scholars.

Professor Lu Jianming came to the Centre to work on the comparative study of Singapore Mandarin and the modern standard Mandarin, and wrote an article entitled "Characteristics of Singapore Mandarin Grammar". At that time, I was unable to participate in the research due to my heavy administrative responsibilities, but I attended every seminar of the research group and was quite familiar with the research process. Professor Lu's research had a two-fold influence on me. First, it changed my view from regarding Chinese Mandarin as the absolute standard for every aspect of Singapore Mandarin to advocating a normative standard close to Chinese Mandarin for Singapore Mandarin. Second, it led to my advocating the compilation of the 《全球华语词典》 *quánqiú huáyǔ cídiǎn* '*Global Chinese Dictionary*' and 《全球华语大词典》 *quánqiú huáyǔ dà cídiǎn* '*Great Global Chinese Dictionary*', as well as researching Global Chinese Grammar to address issues that arose in global Chinese language communication.

While Professor Lu Jianming was in Singapore we struck up a friendship through our research sessions and daily interactions and communications. From 1994 to the present, over the course of more than two decades, he has become a sincere and real friend for me, a friend I can rely on in Beijing.

Upon returning to China in 1995, he deliberately took with him a number of works by local writers, planning to write a grammar book on the Chinese language in Singapore. Thus *Singapore Mandarin Grammar II* is a description of the grammar features of Singapore Mandarin during the 1980s and 1990s, based on the corpus of written language.

II. Features and Contributions of *Singapore Mandarin Grammar II*

Firstly, the author reviewed the local research on Singapore Mandarin grammar conducted in the 1980s and 1990s and made the following comments: (1) Singaporean scholars paid little attention to the boundaries between the common language and dialects, and tended to regard everything that was different from Chinese Mandarin as characteristics of Singapore Mandarin grammar. In fact, many of the grammatical phenomena discussed were merely dialectal components, not features of Singapore Mandarin as a common language. (2) There were some overgeneralisations about Singapore Mandarin. For instance, in the discussion about the word order of double object constructions, it is stated that due to the influence of Min and Cantonese, the object referring to things (i.e. direct object) precedes the object referring to the person (i.e. indirect object) in Singapore Mandarin (e.g. 他给三本书我 *tā gěi sān běn shū wǒ* 'He gave me three books'). Such a generalisation gives a false impression that this is the only possible word order for double object constructions. The fact is that apart from the order mentioned, the reverse order, in which the indirect object precedes the direct object, is also allowed in Singapore Mandarin (e.g. 给他五块钱 *gěi tā wǔ kuài qián* 'Give him five dollars' or 告诉他一个好消息 *gàosù tā yī gè hǎo xiāoxī* 'Tell him the good news'). In addition, this order is even more prevalent in written texts, while the use of the first order is rather limited. These comments are all quite pertinent. Moreover, the Singapore Mandarin grammatical studies at that time mixed up written and spoken languages and would usually use examples to demonstrate the differences between Singapore Mandarin and Chinese Mandarin. However, none of the researchers spoke Chinese Mandarin nor were familiar with its syntax, and what they were referring to were only grammar books published at that time or before.

Unlike those researchers, Professor Lu lives in a contemporary Chinese Mandarin-speaking environment and has conducted extensive research on the grammar of this language. Having him study Singapore Mandarin grammar, we can avoid the trap of failing to 'make out the true face'.[2] As a result, there are so many findings in the book that we, as Singapore Mandarin speakers, have not been able to discover. Currently, the differences highlighted in the book still exist in Singapore Mandarin.

Secondly, the book mainly examines the written language of Singapore Mandarin, while also taking the spoken language into account. Professor Lu gives the following reasons: (1) Written language is substantially more standardised since it has been modified and refined. (2) The common language of an ethnic group usually contains both spoken and written forms, though with a different historical formation process. Generally speaking, the written language will become the common language before the spoken form does. (3) In the case of Singapore Mandarin, the spoken form has not yet matured into the common language for

Singaporeans. If the spoken language should be the focus of linguistic investigation, one will inevitably include some non-Singapore-Mandarin usages as characteristics of it. Therefore, Professor Lu Jianming chose to investigate the written language of more than 110 works by Singaporean authors and scholars, including novels, dramas, essay collections, travelogues, academic essay collections and Singapore Mandarin textbooks for primary and secondary schools (see Appendix 3, The Origins of Examples). He also examined several Chinese newspapers circulated in Singapore, focusing on *Zaobao* as a representative example, and collected data from some Chinese programmes broadcast on Singapore TV's Channel 8. He made strenuous efforts to make the corpus universal and representative in order to "describe and explain characteristics that are compatible with Chinese Mandarin, and to specify characteristics that are inconsistent with Chinese Mandarin".

I once held the view that the influence of foreign languages on spoken Singapore Mandarin was far greater than that on written forms, since spoken Singapore Mandarin had not developed into a common and mature language as the written language had. This is in line with Professor Lu's view that "spoken Singapore Mandarin is immature". On the other hand, from the perspective of language contact, spoken Singapore Mandarin has more grammatical variations than the written form. Some variations have become conventional and are also found in other Chinese-speaking regions, such as Malaysia. These phenomena need to be studied in the future. If these instances occur in other Chinese-speaking regions as well, can they be labelled as "grammatical features of Singapore Mandarin"?

Thirdly, this book is the first monograph that systematically discusses the grammar of Singapore Mandarin. Readers will learn the grammatical features of Singapore Mandarin, understand the reasons for these features and the detailed differences between Singapore Mandarin and Chinese Mandarin. Meanwhile, they are also learning a whole grammatical system, some aspects of which are listed here.

1 一般上 *yībānshàng* 'in general' is an adverb particularly and frequently used in Singapore Mandarin.
2 In Chinese Mandarin, only *de* 得 'DE' can be used in predicate-state complement constructions, but not 到 *dào* 'DAO'. There is no 使到 *shǐdào* 'make' in Chinese Mandarin either.
3 来 *lái* 'come' is a very unique auxiliary in Singapore Mandarin, which usually follows the predicate-complement structure V 好 *hǎo* 'well'. V 好来 *hǎolái* 'well' is semantically equivalent to V 好 *hǎo* 'well' but with an emphasis of hoping to achieve the desired good results.
4 Unstressed 是 *shì* 'be' is used in adjective predicate sentences, such as 我认为这是不公平 *wǒ rènwéi zhè shì bù gōngpíng* 'I don't think it is fair'. This kind of Europeanised sentence is not found in Chinese Mandarin.
5 Due to the influence of English, the BEI construction is extensively utilised in Singapore Mandarin, not exclusively found in translated works.

The foregoing features make this text particularly well suited as a reference book for those working in the local press and media, as a textbook for Chinese language teacher education in tertiary institutions, and for Chinese language or comparative linguistics courses in Chinese departments. Professor Lu Jianming said modestly that the publication of the monograph was simply a way to leave his mark. As an ex-practitioner in Chinese language teachers' education who has spent my entire career promoting and working on the development and application of Chinese language in Singapore, I replied that this mark was never small.

Finally, I would like to reaffirm Professor Lu Jianming's view on the regulation of Singapore Mandarin. "Of the two, universality and systematicity, universality is primary, and systematicity is ultimately subordinate to universality." It was with this view in mind that I came up with the notion of 大华语 *dà huáyǔ* 'Great Chinese'. I also put forward the principle of "strict teaching and lenient evaluation" in the teaching of Mandarin. "Strict teaching" means that the selection of teaching materials should tilt towards Chinese Mandarin, while "lenient evaluation" means that language usage in Singapore should be taken fully into account in evaluation.

Chew Ching Hai

Notes

1 Translator's note: For detailed discussion about different terms used for Chinese language in Singapore and other Chinese speaking regions, see section 1.2.
2 The author cited a famous Chinese poem by Li Bai here, which goes 不识庐山真面目，只缘身在此山中 'Of Mountain Lu we cannot make out the true face, for we are lost in the heart of the very place' (translated by Xu Yuanchong). It implies that one may not find the real characteristics of a grammar if one is immersed in it.

1 Expressions of Number and Quantity

1.1 Two Types of Numerals

We use numerals to express pure numbers and use a "numeral + classifier" phrase to express quantity.

There are two types of numerals: cardinals and ordinals. Cardinals are to express numbers; one cardinal represents one specific number. For example:

一	三	五	八	十	十二	二十三
yī	*sān*	*wǔ*	*bā*	*shí*	*shí'èr*	*èrshísān*
one	three	five	eight	ten	twelve	twenty-three

Ordinals indicate the order in which things are placed in a sequence; different ordinals represent different orders. For example:

第一	第三	第六	第十	第二十三	. . .
dìyī	*dìsān*	*dìliù*	*dìshí*	*dì'èrshísān*	
first	third	sixth	tenth	twenty-third	

Generally speaking, the smaller ordinals precede the larger ordinals. For example, when it comes to the ranking of a competition, 第一名 *dìyī míng* 'first place' comes first, and 第二名 *dì'èr míng* 'second place' comes after 第一名 *dìyī míng* 'first place', and the next is 第三名 *dìsān míng* 'third place'. If there are ten people in the competition, 第十名 *dìshí míng* 'tenth place' will be last.

The term *numeral*, in its broadest sense, refers to numeral expressions (including cardinals and ordinals), be it a word (such as 一 *yī* 'one', 二 *èr* 'two', 三 *sān* 'three', etc.) or a phrase (such as 十二 *shí'èr* 'twelve', 二十三 *èrshísān* 'twenty-three', 一百二十一 *yībǎi èrshíyī* 'one hundred and twenty-one' and 第一 *dìyī* 'first' 第二十三 *dì'èrshísān* 'twenty-third' and so on). In its narrowest sense, the term *numeral* refers only to the 15 single cardinals and the five magnitudinal numerals, as expounded in Section 1.2.

DOI: 10.4324/9781003350248-1

2 Expressions of Number and Quantity

1.2 About Cardinal Numerals

1.2.1 Single Cardinals and Magnitudinal Numerals

Cardinal numerals can be classified into single cardinals and magnitudinal numerals. Listed below are the 15 single cardinals:

一 *yī* 'one'	二 *èr* 'two'	三 *sān* 'three'	四 *sì* 'four'
六 *liù* 'six'	七 *qī* 'seven'	八 *bā* 'eight'	九 *jiǔ* 'nine'
两 *liǎng* 'two'	半 *bàn* 'half'	几 *jǐ* 'several'	多少 *duōshǎo* 'many'

五 *wǔ* 'five'

十 *shí* 'ten'

零 *líng* 'zero'

These are the five most common magnitudinal numbers.[1]

十 *shí* 'ten'	百 *bǎi* 'hundred'	千 *qiān* 'thousand'
万 *wàn* 'ten thousand'		亿 *yì* 'hundred million'

In Singapore Mandarin, all numerals are represented by these single cardinals, or combinations of these single cardinals and magnitudinal numerals.

1.2.2 A Few Points About Single Cardinals and Magnitudinal Numerals

1   Single cardinals can directly modify classifiers. For example:

(1)

一	位	二	公尺	三	张
yī	*wèi*	*èr*	*gōngchǐ*	*sān*	*zhāng*
one	CL	two	CL	three	CL
'one (person)'		'two metres'		'three pieces'	

四	个	五	支	七	寸
sì	*gè*	*wǔ*	*zhī*	*qī*	*cùn*
four	CL	five	CL	seven	CL
'four (ones)'		'five (ones)'		'seven cuns'	

八	块	九	个	十	岁
bā	*kuài*	*jiǔ*	*gè*	*shí*	*suì*
eight	CL	nine	CL	ten	CL
'eight blocks'		'nine (ones)'		'ten years old'	

两	间	半	句	几	个
liǎng	jiān	bàn	jù	jǐ	gè
two	CL	half	CL	several	CL
'two (rooms)'		'half sentence'		'several (ones)'	

多少	个	零	分
duōshǎo	gè	líng	fēn
how.many	CL	zero	CL
'how many'		'zero score'	

Magnitudinal numerals cannot directly modify classifiers.

2 Originally, 十 *shí* 'ten' was a magnitudinal numeral. However, 一 *yī* 'one' in 一十 *yīshí* 'ten' is often omitted, and thus expressions such as 十个人 *shí gè rén* 'ten people' and 十本书 *shí běn shū* 'ten books' are conventional usages, while * 一十个人 *yīshí gè rén* and * 一十本书 *yīshí běn shū* are ungrammatical. In 十个人 *shí gè rén* 'ten people' and 十本书 *shí běn shū* 'ten books', 十 *shí* 'ten' functions as a single cardinal (because it directly modifies a classifier), while in 二十 *èrshí* 'twenty', 三十 *sānshí* 'thirty', up to 九十 *jiǔshí* 'ninety', it functions as a magnitudinal numeral. Therefore, 十 *shí* 'ten' is now both a magnitudinal numeral and a single cardinal. However, as a single cardinal, 十 *shí* 'ten' is slightly different from other single cardinals in usage (see Section 1.4).

3 Although both 两 *liǎng* 'two' and 二 *èr* 'two' mean 'two', they have different usages.

4 半 *bàn* 'half' is a single cardinal, but it is different from general single cardinals. General single cardinals can modify classifiers as well as magnitudinal numerals, for example:

(2) 三　个　(三 *sān* 'three' modifies the classifier 个 *gè*.)
　　sān　*gè*
　　three　CL

　　三　十　(三 *sān* 'three' modifies the magnitudinal numeral 十 *shí*.)
　　sān　*shí*
　　three　ten

半 *bàn* 'half' can only modify classifiers, such as 半句 *bàn jù* 'half a sentence' (*Tiàowǔ* 35) and 半个 *bàn gè* (*Xúnmiào* 6); it cannot modify magnitudinal numerals.[2] In addition, 半 *bàn* 'half' can be used after a numeral-classifier phrase, such as 一年半 *yī nián bàn* 'a year and a half' (*Fēngzhēng* 215), while other single cardinals are usually not used in this way.

4 Expressions of Number and Quantity

5 几 *jǐ* 'how many/several' and 多少 *duōshǎo* 'how many/many' are both interrogative pronouns and single cardinals. As single cardinals, they both express an uncertain number (more than one) instead of interrogation, for example:

(3) 只   剩下   **几**   个   人，   满   心   好奇地
    zhǐ   shèngxià **jǐ**   gè   rén   mǎn xīn   hàoqíde
    only   remain   **several** CL person full heart curiously

  还   停足   期待。（寻庙 56）
  hái   tíngzú   qīdài
  still stop.foot   look.forward.to

  'Only a couple of people, full of curiosity, still stopped and kept expecting (for something to happen).' (*Xúnmiào* 56)

(4) 在   这   山岭   之间，   莫   说   游客，   即使   是
    zài   zhè   shānlǐng   zhījiān   mò   shuō   yóukè   jíshǐ   shì
    at   this mountain   middle   NEG say   tourist even   SHI

  山民，   也   不   曾   碰见   **多少**   个。（寻庙 47）
  shānmín   yě   bù   céng   pèngjiàn   **duōshǎo**   gè
  mountain.   also NEG   ever   meet   **many**   CL
  people

  'There are not many local people in these mountain ranges, let alone tourists.' (*Xúnmiào* 47)

Both 几 *jǐ* 'several' in sentence (3) and 多少 *duōshǎo* 'many' in sentence (4) represent an uncertain number, but there are still some differences between them in usage. First, as a single cardinal, 几 *jǐ* 'several' can modify magnitudinal numerals just like other single cardinals as in (5), but 多少 *duōshǎo* 'many' cannot. Second, as a single cardinal, 几 *jǐ* 'several' can be used after a magnitudinal numeral like other single cardinals, as in (6), but 多少 *duōshǎo* 'many' cannot.

(5) **几十**   年   的   斗争   总算   告   一   个
    jǐshí   nián   de   dòuzhēng   zǒngsuàn   gào   yī   gè
    several-ten   year   DE   struggle   finally   tell   one   CL

  段落。（金狮奖 40）
  duànluò
  stage

'The struggle that has lasted for decades finally comes to an end.'
(*Jīnshījiǎng* 40)

(6) 摸索   了   二十   几   年， 我们   不但   无法
    mōsuǒ le   **èrshí** **jǐ**   nián   wǒmen   bùdàn   wúfǎ
    grope LE   **twenty** **several** year   1PL   not.only unable

形成   以   英文   为   主流   的   文化   体系
xíngchéng yǐ   yīngwén   wéi   zhǔliú   de   wénhuà   tǐxì
form   by   English   be   mainstream DE   culture   system

也   逐渐   放弃   了   合   各   族
yě   zhújiàn   fàngqì   le   hé   gè   zú
also   gradually abandon   LE   integrate various ethnic.group

文化   为   一   的   想法。（△ 小小鸟 178）
wénhuà   wéi   yī   de   xiǎngfǎ
culture   be   one   DE   idea

'After more than 20 years of exploration, we not only failed to form a cultural system with English as the mainstream, but also gradually gave up the idea of integrating the cultures of all ethnic groups.'
(△*Xiǎoxiǎoniǎo* 178)

几 *jǐ* 'several' in sentences (5) and (6) cannot be replaced by 多少 *duōshǎo* 'many'.

6 As a single cardinal, 零 *líng* 'zero' can be written as '〇'. Sometimes it represents nothing, such as 一减一等于〇 *yī jiǎn yī děngyú líng* 'one minus one equals zero', and sometimes it represents a place value of zero, such as 一百〇八 *yī bǎi líng bā* '108' 一万〇三百 *yī wàn líng sān bǎi* '10300'. Here is another example:

(7) 你   的   能力   只   能   担   一   百   斤，
    nǐ   de   nénglì   zhǐ   néng   dān   yī   bǎi   jīn
    2SG   DE   ability only   can   shoulder   one   hundred CL

而   你   偏要   逞强，   挑   一   百
ér   nǐ   piānyào   chěngqiáng   tiāo   yī   bǎi
but   2SG   insist   flaunt.your.superiority shoulder one   hundred

6 *Expressions of Number and Quantity*

零　　一　　斤，　　无　　异　　　自讨烦恼，
líng　yī　jīn　　wú　yì　　zìtǎofánnǎo
zero　one　CL　NEG　different　ask.for.trouble

不　　失眠　　才　　怪。（八方 120）
bù　shīmián　cái　guài
NEG　lose.sleep　just　strange

'You can only shoulder 50 kg, but you want to flaunt your superiority by shouldering 50.5 kg. You are troubling yourself. So you will definitely lose sleep.' (*Bāfāng* 120)

Different from general single cardinals, 零 *líng* 'zero' cannot modify magnitudinal numerals, but it can modify classifiers, such as 零票 *líng piào* 'zero votes' and 〇分 *líng fēn* 'zero points', so in this sense it can be classified as a single cardinal.

1.3 Categories of Numerals

There are five main types of numerals used in everyday life: integers, fractions, decimals, approximations and multiples. For example:

(1)　转眼间　　　整整　　　八　　年　了。（梦 1）
　　 zhuǎnyǎnjiān　zhěngzhěng　**bā**　nián　le
　　 suddenly　　　whole　　　**eight**　year　LE

'In the blink of an eye eight years has passed.' (*Mèng* 1)

(2)　实际的　支出　　　比　　预算　　减少　　了
　　 shíjìde　zhīchū　bǐ　yùsuàn　jiǎnshǎo　le
　　 actual　spending　than　budget　lessen　LE

四分之一。（报 1995 年 6 月 8 日 12 版）
sìfēnzhīyī
one.fourth

'The actual expenditure was reduced by a quarter compared to the budget.' (*Bào*, June 8, 1995, Issue no. 12)

(3)a　在　　昨天的　　东京　　外汇　　　　市场上，　　　美元
　　　zài　zuótiānde　dōngjīng　wàihuì　　　shìchǎngshàng　měiyuán
　　　at　yesterday　Tokyo　foreign.currency　market　　　US.dollar

汇率　跌　　至　　八十一点二七
huìlǜ　diē　zhì　**bāshíyīdiǎn'èrqī**
rate　fall　to　**eighty.one.point.two.seven**

Expressions of Number and Quantity 7

日元 　　（新视第八波道 1995 年 4 月 18 日晚十点新闻）
rìyuán
Japanese.Yen

'On yesterday's Tokyo stock market the exchange rate of the US dollar fell to 81.27 Japanese Yen.' (*Xīnshìdìbābōdào* (News at 10:00 PM), Apr. 18, 1995)

b　在　　昨天的　　东京　　外汇　　　　市场上，　　美元
　　zài　zuótiānde　dōngjīng　wàihuì　　　shìchǎngshàng　měiyuán
　　at　 yesterday　 Tokyo　 foreign.currency　market　 US.dollar

　　汇率　跌　至　**81.27**　　　　　　　　　日元，
　　huìlǜ　diē　zhì　**bāshíyīdiǎn'èrqī**　　　rìyuán
　　rate　fall　to　eighty.one.point.two.seven　Japanese.Yen

　　接近　　上星期的　　　最　　低点　　　的
　　jiējìn　shàngxīngqīde　zuì　dīdiǎn　　de
　　approach　last.week　 most　low.point　DE

80.15　　　　　　　日元。　　（报 1995 年 4 月 19 日
　　　　　　　　　　　　　　　第 30 版）
bāshíyīdiǎnyīwǔ　rìyuán
eighty.point.one.five　Japanese.Yen

'On yesterday's Tokyo stock market, the exchange rate of the US dollar fell to 81.27 Japanese Yen, approaching last week's lowest point of 80.15 Yen.' (*Bào*, Apr. 19, 1995, p. 30)

(4)a　一般　　住宅　　也　　不过　　**四、　五**　层　　楼。（寻庙 36）
　　　yībān　zhùzhái　yě　bùguò　**sì　wǔ**　céng　lóu
　　　general　residence　also　just　**four　five**　layer　floor

'Generally, residential buildings are only four or five storeys.' (*Xúnmiào* 36)

(4)b　这时，　　人群　　　中　　　有　　**一两**　　声　　尖叫，
　　　zhèshí　rénqún　zhōng　yǒu　**yīliǎng**　shēng　jiānjiào
　　　this.moment　people　middle　have　**one.or.two**　CL　scream

　　　或者　　窃笑　　寻庙　（54）
　　　huòzhě　qièxiào
　　　or　　　chuckle

'At this moment, one or two screams or chuckles appeared among the people.' (*Xúnmiào* 54)

(5) 12   年   来,   讲   英语   的   华族   家庭
    shí'èr nián   lái   jiǎng   yīngyǔ   de   huázú   jiātíng
    12   year   come   speak   English DE   Chinese.people family

增加   了   三   倍。(△ 小小鸟 80)
zēngjiā   le   sān   bèi
increase LE three times

'In the past 12 years, the number of English-speaking Chinese families has increased three times.' (△*Xiǎoxiǎoniǎo* 80)

In example (1), 八 *bā* 'eight' is an integer; in example (2), 四分之一 *sì fēnzhī yī* 'one fourth' is a fraction; 八十一点二七 *bāshíyī diǎn èrqī* 'eighty one point two seven', 81.27 *bāshíyī diǎn èrqī* 'eighty one point two seven', and 80.15 *bāshíyī diǎn yīwǔ* 'eighty point one five' in example (3) are all decimals; in example (4) 四、五 *sìwǔ* 'four or five' and 一两 *yīliǎng* 'one or two' are approximations; 三倍 *sānbèi* 'three times' in example (5) is a multiple.

The concept of numbers is shared by people all over the world, but the ways of expressing them are not necessarily the same in different languages. The following is a demonstration of how each of the five types of numerals are constructed in Singapore Mandarin.

1.4 Integers

1.4.1 Four Types of Integers

In modern standard Mandarin (including Singapore Mandarin), there are four types of integers, as follows:

1   The first type of integer consists of the following single cardinals alone: 一 *yī* 'one', 二 *èr* 'two', 三 *sān* 'three', 四 *sì* 'four', 五 *wǔ* 'five', 六 *liù* 'six', 七 *qī* 'seven', 八 *bā* 'eight', 九 *jiǔ* 'nine', 十 *shí* 'ten' and 两 *liǎng* 'two' (半 *bàn* 'half', 几 *jǐ* 'several' and 多少 *duōshǎo* 'how many' are not included).
2   The second type of integer is expressed by 'single cardinal + magnitudinal numeral' compounds. For example, 二十 *èrshí* 'twenty', 七十 *qīshí* 'seventy', 三百 *sānbǎi* 'three hundred', 五千 *wǔqiān* 'five thousand', 四万 *sìwàn* 'forty thousand', 六亿 *liùyì* 'six hundred million' and so on. This type of compound cardinal can be analysed as a modifier-head phrase, with the single cardinal modifying a magnitudinal numeral. Take 三百 *sānbǎi* 'three hundred' as an example:

三   百   *sānbǎi* 'three hundred'
1   2   (attribute-head endocentric relation)

From the perspective of arithmetic analysis, there is a multiplicative relationship between the single cardinals and magnitudinal numerals in such integers:

二十 èrshí 'twenty' = 2 × 10
三百 sānbǎi 'three hundred' = 3 × 100
五千 wǔqiān 'five thousand' = 5 × 1,000
四万 sìwàn 'forty thousand' = 4 × 10,000
六亿 liùyì 'six hundred million' = 6 × 100,000,000

The single cardinals 半 bàn 'half' 几 jǐ 'several' and 多少 duōshǎo 'how many' cannot be used in this type of compound cardinals.

3 The third type of integer is in the form of the 'magnitudinal numeral + single cardinal' compound, in which the only magnitudinal numeral that comes before other single cardinals can only be 十 shí 'ten', like 十二 shíèr 'twelve', 十六 shíliù 'sixteen' and so on. This type of compound is grammatically a coordinate phrase. For example, 十二 shíèr 'twelve' can be analysed as follows:

十 二 shíèr 'twelve'
1 2 (coordinate relation)

From the arithmetic perspective, there is an additive relationship between the magnitudinal numeral and the single cardinal in such a compound:

十一 shíyī 'eleven' = 10 + 1
十二 shíèr 'twelve' = 10 + 2
十六 shíliù 'sixteen' = 10 + 6

4 The fourth type of integer is formed with a combination of compound cardinals. This combination can be realised by two compound cardinals, like 二百五十 èrbǎiwǔshí 'two hundred and fifty', or by one compound cardinal plus a single cardinal, like 三十一 sānshíyī 'thirty-one'. The combination of compound cardinals is also grammatically a coordinate phrase. These examples can be analysed as follows:

二 百   五 十   èrbǎiwǔshí 'two hundred and fifty'
__1__   __2__   (coordinate relation)
3 4   5 6   (3-4, 5-6 'attribute-head' endocentric relation)

三 十   一   sānshíyī 'thirty-one'
__1__   2   (coordinate relation)
3 4   ('attribute-head' endocentric relation)

10 *Expressions of Number and Quantity*

As for the arithmetical meaning, there is an additive relationship between the constituents of the combination:

二百五十 *èrbǎi wǔshí* 'two hundred and fifty' = 2 × 100 + 5 × 10
三十一 *sānshíyī* 'thirty-one' = 3 × 10 + 1

The number of compound cardinals combined may be more than two. For example, 五万六千七百三十四 *wǔwàn liùqiān qībǎi sānshísì* 'Fifty-six thousand, seven hundred and thirty-four' can be analysed grammatically as in the following:

五	万	六	千	七	百	三	十	四	
__1__		__2__		__3__		__4__		5	*wǔwànliùqiānqībǎisānshísì* '56734' (coordinate relation)
6	7	8	9	10	11	12	13		(6-7, 8-9, 10-11, 12-13, 'attribute-head' endocentric relation)

Its arithmetical meaning can be analysed as:

五万六千七百三十四 *wǔwàn liùqiān qībǎi sānshísì* 'Fifty-six thousand, seven hundred and thirty-four' = 5 × 10,000 + 6 × 1,000 + 7 × 100 + 3 × 10 + 4

1.4.2 Integers Modifying Classifiers

Integers can modify classifiers as illustrated by the following examples:

(1) 三　　个　　孩子，　　　竟　　　　　没有　一　　个　　继承
 sān ***gè*** *háizi* *jìng* *méiyǒu* ***yī*** ***gè*** *jìchéng*
 three **CL** children unexpectedly NEG **one** **CL** inherit

他　　的　衣钵。（牛车水 86）
tā *de* *yībō*
3SG DE legacy

'Unexpectedly, none of the three children could inherit his legacy.' (*Niúchēshuǐ* 86)

(2) 我　　规定　　　自己　　每　　天　　背诵　　二十　　个
 wǒ *guīdìng* *zìjǐ* *měi* *tiān* *bèisòng* ***èrshí*** ***gè***
 1SG stipulate oneself every day recite **twenty** **CL**

生　　　字。（Δ 天长 131）
shēng *zì*
new word

'I make it a rule to recite twenty new words every day.' (Δ*Tiāncháng* 131)

(3) 他们　　合作　　　了　**十二**　**个**　年头　　了。（一心 201）
    tāmen　　hézuò　　le　**shí'èr**　**gè**　niántóu　Le
    they　　 cooperate LE **twelve** **CL** year　　LE
    'They have been cooperating for twelve years.' (*Yīxīn* 201)

(4) 我们　　接到　　了　**五百二十七**　　　　　**封**　投诉　　信，
    wǒmen　jiēdào　 le　**wǔbǎi'èrshíqī**　　　　**fēng**　tóusù　　xìn
    1PL　　receive　LE　**five.hundred.twenty.**　**CL**　complaint　letter
    　　　　　　　　　　　 seven

一千九百三十九　　　　　**通**　投诉　　电话　　　（再见 67）
yīqiānjiǔbǎisānshíjiǔ　**tōng**　tóusù　　diànhuà
one.thousand.nine.　　　**CL**　complaint　call
hundred.thirty.nine

'We received 527 letters of complaint and 1,939 phone calls of complaint.' (*Zàijiàn* 67)

1.4.3 Expressions of Integers

1 In Singapore Mandarin, integers that are less than 'ten thousand' generally adopt the decimal system. Specifically, integers less than 十 *shí* 'ten' are represented by different cardinals, including:

一 *yī* 'one'　二 *èr* 'two'　三 *sān* 'three'　四 *sì* 'four'　五 *wǔ* 'five'
六 *liù* 'six'　七 *qī* 'seven'　八 *bā* 'eight'　九 *jiǔ* 'nine'

九 *jiǔ* 'nine' plus 一 *yī* 'one' amounts to 十 *shí* 'ten'. (Strictly speaking, it should be 一十 *yīshí* 'ten', but it's usually omitted to be 十 *shí* 'ten'.) The numbers from 一 *yī* 'one' to 九 *jiǔ* 'nine' are called the ones digits, and numbers starting from 十 *shí* 'ten' are called the tens digits, which are expressed in the form of (一)十 *(yī)shí* 'ten' followed by the aforementioned ones-digit cardinals, like

(一)十一 *(yī)shíyī* 'eleven'
(一)十二 *(yī)shí'èr* 'twelve'
(一)十三 *(yī)shísān* 'thirteen'
...
(一)十九 *(yī)shíjiǔ* 'nineteen'

(一)十九 *(yī)shíjiǔ* 'nineteen' plus 一 *yī* 'one' carries to 二十 *èrshí* 'twenty', and if more is added, it would carry respectively to 三十 *sānshí* 'thirty' 四十 *sìshí* 'forty' 五十 *wǔshí* 'fifty'... 九十 *jiǔshí* 'ninety'. 九十 *jiǔshí* 'ninety' plus 十 *shí* 'ten' carries to 百 *bǎi* 'hundred', also called 一百 *yībǎi* 'one hundred', meaning ten tens. The numbers carrying to 百 *bǎi* 'hundred' are called hundreds digits. Ten hundreds carry to 千 *qiān* 'thousand' (i.e. 一千 *yīqiān* 'one thousand'), and the numbers carrying to 千 *qiān* 'thousand' are called thousands digits. Ten thousands carry to 万 *wàn* 'ten thousand' (i.e. 一万 *yīwàn* 'ten thousand'), and the numbers carrying to 万 *wàn* 'ten thousand' are called ten-thousand-digit numbers.

2   If the number is greater than ten thousand, the 万进制 *wàn jìnzhì* "ten thousand carrying system" is adopted.[3] That is, when the number reaches 十万 *shíwàn* 'a hundred thousand', it does not carry to a new digit. For example, the following numbers are always expressed in such way:

十万 *shíwàn* 'a hundred thousand'
十六万 *shíliùwàn* 'one hundred and sixty thousand'
五十三万 *wǔshísānwàn* 'five hundred and thirty thousand'

When the number reaches 百万 *bǎiwàn* 'one million', it does not carry to the next digit, either. And those numbers are always expressed as such:

一百七十万 *yībǎi qīshí wàn* 'one million and seven hundred thousand'
四百三十万 *sìbǎi sānshí wàn* 'four million and three hundred thousand'
八百五十六万 *bābǎi wǔshíliù wàn* 'eight million and five hundred and sixty thousand'

Similarly, the number does not carry to the next digit after reaching 千万 *qiānwàn* 'ten million'. And those numbers are always expressed in such a way:

一千二百万 *yīqiān èrbǎi wàn* 'twelve million'
三千八百九十万 *sānqiān bābǎi jiǔshí wàn* 'thirty-eight million and nine hundred thousand'

九千九百九十九万 *jiǔqiān jiǔbǎi jiǔshíjiǔ wàn* 'ninety-nine million, nine hundred and ninety thousand' plus 一万 *yīwàn* 'ten thousand' will carry to 亿 *yì* 'hundred million', that is, ten thousand 万 *wàn* 'ten thousand' equal 亿 *yì* 'hundred million'. In the 1930s and 1940s, there was a saying of 四万万同胞 *sìwànwàn tóngbāo* 'four hundred million compatriots', which is now generally replaced by 四亿 *sìyì* 'four hundred million'.

As mentioned earlier, in Singapore Mandarin, the decimal system is generally used when integers are less than ten thousand. The reason why we use 'generally' here is that ten-thousand-digit numbers can be expressed in two ways in Singapore Mandarin, as influenced by English.

A   The first way is by using the magnitudinal numeral 万 *wàn* 'ten thousand', which is the traditional expression of Singapore Mandarin. For example,

Expressions of Number and Quantity 13

(4) 至少　　　　　一万二！(再见 87)
zhìshǎo　　　　yīwànèr
at.least　　　　twelve.thousand
'At least twelve thousand!' (*Zàijiàn* 87)

(5) 可口可乐　有限公司　　以及　亚洲　　乳酪品　　　私人
kěkǒukělè　yǒuxiàngōngsī　yǐjí　yàzhōu　rǔlàopǐn　sīrén
Coca-Cola　Co., Ltd.　　　and　　Asia　　dairy.product　private

有限公司　　　　各　　捐　　　**2 万 5000**
yǒuxiàngōngsī　gè　　juān　　**èrwànwǔqiān**
Co., Ltd.　　　each　donate　twenty-five.thousand

元。(报 1995 年 3 月 12 日 1 版)
yuán
yuan

'Coca-Cola Co., Ltd. and Asian Cheese Products Co., Ltd. respectively donate twenty-five thousand yuans.' (*Bào*, Mar. 12, 1995, Issue no. 1)

B The second way is to express by 千 *qiān* 'thousand' instead of 万 *wàn* 'ten thousand', which is a usage influenced by English. For example,

(6) 好像　　是　　**二十千**　　　　的　税务　　回扣。(生命 141)
hǎoxiàng　shì　**èrshíqiān**　　　de　shuìwù　huíkòu
seem　　　be　**twenty.thousand**　DE　tax　　　kickback
'It seems to be a tax kickback of twenty thousand.' (*Shēngmìng*, 141)

(7) 小全　　　上礼拜　　　赌马　　　　输　　了　**二十几千**…(吾
　　　　　　　　　　　　　　　　　　　　　　　　　　　　土·小说上 14)
xiǎoquán　shànglǐbài　dǔmǎ　　　　shū　le　**èrshí-jǐ-qiān**
Xiaoquan　last.week　horse.gamble　lose　LE　**twenty-several-thousand**
'Xiaoquan lost about twenty thousand betting on a horse last week.' (*Wútǔ* (novel I), 14)

(8) 准备　　一　炫　　　　自己　这　　装修　　　了
zhǔnbèi　yī　xuàn　　　zìjǐ　zhè　zhuāngxiū　le
prepare　one　show.off　oneself　this　decorate　LE

14 *Expressions of Number and Quantity*

数 十 千 元 的 华屋。(再见 83)
shù shí qiān yuán de huáwū
several ten thousand yuan DE luxurious.house

'(He) prepares to show off this beautiful house that cost thousands of yuans to decorate.' (*Zàijiàn* 83)

(9) 我 看 他 这 一 次 输 了 **几十千，**
wǒ kàn tā zhè yī cì shū le **jǐshíqiān**
1SG look 3SG this one CL lose LE **thousands.of**

大概 是 跑掉 了 吧！(新马 199)
dàgài shì pǎodiào le ba
probably SHI run.away LE SFP

'I guess he has probably run away after losing tens of thousands of dollars this time!' (*Xīnmǎ* 199)

(10) 获 利 **80 千。**(新视第八波道 1995 年 4 月 27 日晚上 10 点新闻)
huò lì **bāshíqiān**
gain profit **eighty.thousand**

'Make a profit of eighty thousand.' (*Xīnshìdìbābōdào* (News at 10:00 PM), Apr. 27, 1995)

(11) 3 房 估价： 新元 **25 千** 到
sān fáng gūjià xīnyuán **èrshíwǔqiān** dào
three room evaluate Singapore.dollar **twenty-five.thousand** to

50 千， 现金。(豪丰产业广告)
wǔshíqiān xiànjīn
fifty.thousand cash

'The estimated price of a three-room apartment: twenty-five thousand to fifty thousand Singapore dollars in cash.' (*Háofēngchǎnyèguǎnggào*)

In example (6), 二十千 *èrshíqiān* means 二万 *èrwàn* 'twenty thousand' (or 两万 *liǎngwàn* 'twenty thousand'). In example (7), 输了二十几千 *shūle èrshíjǐ qiān* indicates the same as 输了两万多 *shūle liǎngwàn duō* 'lose about twenty thousand'. In example (8), 数十千元 *shù shíqiān yuán* is equal to 几万元 *jǐwàn yuán* 'thousands of yuans'.

In Chinese Mandarin, only expression A is acceptable when expressing ten-thousand-digit numbers. That is to say, in Chinese Mandarin, 十 *shí* 'ten' as a single cardinal can modify magnitudinal numerals 万 *wàn* 'ten thousand' and 亿 *yì* 'hundred million', but not 十 *shí* 'ten' 百 *bǎi* 'hundred' or 千 *qiān* 'thousand'. However, in Singapore Mandarin, 十 *shí* 'ten' can modify the magnitudinal numeral 千 *qiān* 'thousand'.

1.5 Fractions

Fractions provide another way to express division. For example, if we use a fraction to express 'ten divided by two' (i.e. 10 ÷ 2), it can be represented as 二分之十 *èr fēnzhī shí* 'ten out of two'. In the representation of fractions, the number before 分之 *fēnzī* 'divided by' (e.g. 二 *èr* 'two') is called a 分母 *fēnmǔ* 'denominator', and the number after 分之 *fēnzhī* 'divided by' (e.g. 十 *shí* 'ten') is called a 分子 *fēnzǐ* 'numerator'; the denominator is the divisor and the numerator is the number being divided.

Fractions are seldom used in daily life; they are occasionally found in written Chinese. For example,

(1) 突尼斯　大约　有　**五分之二**　的　面积　属于
tūnísī　dàyuē　yǒu　wǔfēnzhīèr　de　miànjī　shǔyú
Tunisia　about　have　**two.fifths**　DE　area　belong

沙漠　地带。（△ 一壶 43）
shāmò　dìdài
desert　land

'About two fifths of Tunisia is desert.' (△*Yīhú* 43)

A fraction whose denominator is one hundred is usually called a 百分数 *bǎifēnshù* 'percentage'. In Singapore Mandarin, there are three ways to express percentages.

The first method is to use Arabic numerals plus '%'. This is only used in the written genre and mostly in newspapers. For example:

(2) 根据　　　估计，　　到　公元　　2030　　　年，
gēnjù　　　gūjì　　　dào　gōngyuán　èrlíngsānlíng　nián
according.to　estimation　to　AD　　　twenty.thirty　year

我国　　　的　老人　　将　达　八十二　　万，
wǒguó　　　de　lǎorén　jiāng　dá　bāshíèr　wàn
our.country　DE　elders　will　reach　eighty-two　ten.thousand

16   Expressions of Number and Quantity

占   总   人口   的   22%。（华文教材 2A 143）
zhàn   zǒng   rénkǒu   de   bǎifēnzhīèrshíèr
account   total   population DE   twenty-two.percent

'According to estimations, by 2030 AD, the number of elderly people in our country will reach eight hundred and twenty thousand, accounting for 22% of the total population.' (*Huáwénjiàocái* 2A, 143)

(3) 公积金   局   从   7   月   1   日   起，
    gōngjījīn   jú   cóng   qī   yuè   yī   rì   qǐ
    provident.fund   bureau   from   seven   month   first day start

    调整   公积金   会员   的   存款   利率，
    tiáozhěng   gōngjījīn   huìyuán   de   cúnkuǎn   lìlǜ
    adjust   provident.fund   member   DE   savings   interest.rate

    从   目前   的   3.1%   调   高   到
    cóng   mùqián   de   bǎifēnzhīsāndiǎnyī   tiáo   gāo   dào
    from   current   DE   3.1%   adjust   up   to

    3.82%。（报 1995 年 5 月 13 日 3 版）
    bǎifēnzhīsāndiǎnbāèr
    3.82%

    'The Provident Fund Board has made a decision to adjust the deposit rate for Provident Fund members from the current 3.1% to 3.82%, which will take effect from July 1st.' (*Bào*, May 13, 1995, Issue no. 3)

The second method is to use 百分之 . . . *bǎifēnzhī* '. . . percent', an expression commonly used in radio broadcasting and occasionally in the written genre. For example:

(4) 路税   又   高涨   了，   调   高   百分之 三
                                                           十。（胜利 83）
    lùshuì   yòu   gāozhǎng   le   tiáo   gāo   bǎifēnzhīsānshí
    road.tax   again   rise   LE   adjust   high   thirty.percent

    'The road tax has gone up again, by 30 percent.' (*Shènglì* 83)

(5) 新加坡   来   的   新闻   工作者   有的   说   听
    xīnjiāpō   lái   de   xīnwén   gōngzuòzhě   yǒude   shuō   tīng
    Singapore   come   DE   news   practitioner some   say   listen

Expressions of Number and Quantity 17

懂	**百分之** 十，	有的	说	**百分之** 六十。（平心 116）
dǒng	**bǎifēnzhī**shí	yǒude	shuō	**bǎifēnzhī**liùshí
understand	**ten.percent**	some	say	**sixty.percent**

'Some of the journalists from Singapore said they understood 10 percent, and others said 60 percent.' (*Píngxīn* 116)

The third method is to use numerals plus the word 巴仙 *bāxiān* 'percent' (which is a transliteration of the English word 'percentage'). This is an English-influenced expression commonly used in both the spoken and written genres. In the written genre, the numeral can be written either in Chinese characters or as an Arabic numeral. For example:

(6)
当初	新厂	合	股	...	自己	只	占	四十五
dāngchū	xīnchǎng	hé	gǔ		zìjǐ	zhǐ	zhàn	sìshíwǔ
once	new.factory	joint	stock		self	only	account	45

巴仙	的	股份。（吾土 · 小说上 41）
bāxiān	de	gǔfèn
percent	DE	stock

'When the new factory was first co-founded, I had a mere 45 percent share for myself.' (*Wútǔ* (novel I), 41)

(7)
你们	不是	加	了	五	**巴仙**	薪水	喽？（吾土 · 小说上 31）
nǐmen	bùshì	jiā	le	wǔ	**bāxiān**	xīnshuǐ	lou
2PL	NEG	add	LE	five	**percent**	wages	SFP

'Didn't your salary increase by 5%?' (*Wútǔ* (novel I), 31)

(8)
预备班	所	授	的	课程	60	**巴仙**
yùbèibān	suǒ	shòu	de	kèchéng	liùshí	**bāxiān**
preparatory.class	SUO	teach	DE	course	sixty	**percent**

用	华语，	40	**巴仙**	用	英语
yòng	huáyǔ	sìshí	**bāxiān**	yòng	yīngyǔ
use	Chinese	forty	**percent**	use	English

教，	以	加强	双语	基础。（薪传 154）
jiāo	yǐ	jiāqiáng	shuāngyǔ	jīchǔ
teach	to	strengthen	bilingual	foundation

'The preparatory classes were taught 60% in Chinese and 40% in English, so as to strengthen the bilingual foundation.' (*Xīnchuán* 154)

However, in Chinese Mandarin, only the first two ways of expressions are available.

A fraction with ten as its denominator can also be expressed in the form of "single cardinal + 成 *chéng* 'ten percent'". 十分之一 *shí fēnzhī yī* 'one tenth' is called 一成 *yīchéng*; 十分之二 *shí fēnzhī èr* 'two tenths' is called 两成 *liǎngchéng*; 十分之三 *shí fēnzhī sān* 'three tenths' is called 三成 *sānchéng*; and so on. For example:

(9) 目前， 建筑物质 **八成** 由 格尔木
    mùqián   *jiànzhùwùzhì*   ***bāchéng***   *yóu*   *géěrmù*
    present   building.material   **eighty.percent**   by   Golmud

转运。（南北 75）
zhuǎnyùn
transfer

'At present, 80% of the building materials are transported by Golmud.' (*Nánběi* 75)

(10) 我 看 **八成** 是 虚荣心 在 作祟。（金狮奖 117）
    wǒ   *kàn*   ***bāchéng***   *shì*   *xūróngxīn*   *zài*   *zuòsuì*
    1SG   see   **eighty.percent**   be   vanity   in.process   make.mischief

'I think it's 80 percent because of vanity.' (*Jīnshījiǎng* 117)

(11) 有关 记录 显示, 共 有 **六成** 的
    yǒuguān   *jìlù*   *xiǎnshì*   *gòng*   *yǒu*   ***liùchéng***   *de*
    relative   record   show   total   have   **sixty.percent**   DE

赞助商 没有 按时 交付 赞助捐。（万花筒 9）
zànzhùshāng   *méiyǒu*   *ànshí*   *jiāofù*   *zànzhùjuān*
sponsor   NEG   timely   deliver.pay   sponsorship.donation

'Records show that a total of 60% of the sponsors did not deliver their sponsorship donations on time.' (*Wànhuātǒng*, 9)

However, this usage is not common.

1.6 Decimal Numerals

A decimal numeral is another written form of a decimal fraction. For example, 十分之一 *shí fēnzhī yī* 'one tenth' can be written as 0.1 *líng diǎn yī*; 百分之二十三 *bǎi fēnzhī èrshísān* '23 percent' can be written as 0.23 *líng diǎn èrsān*. In the middle of a decimal numeral, there is a dot '.', called a decimal point, with the integer part on its left and the fractional part on its right. Here are some examples:

(1) 在　　　2030　　　　　年，　　则　　　只　　　有　　　**2.2**　　　　　个
    zài　　*èrlíngsānlíng*　*nián*　*zé*　　*zhǐ*　　*yǒu*　　**èrdiǎnèr**　　*gè*
    in　　　twenty.thirty　　year　　then　　only　　have　　**two.point.two**　CL

    工作者　　　　支持　　　一　　个　　老人　……（风筝 156）
    gōngzuòzhě　*zhīchí*　　*yī*　　*gè*　*lǎorén*
    worker　　　　support　　one　CL　old.people

    'In 2030, there will be only 2.2 workers supporting each elderly person . . .' (*Fēngzhēng* 156)

(2) 他　　是　　一　　个　　十分　　尽职的　　　空中少爷，
    tā　　*shì*　*yī*　*gè*　*shífēn*　*jìnzhíde*　　*kōngzhōngshàoyé*
    3SG　be　　one　CL　very　　　dedicated　　steward

    一点八　　　　米　　　高　　的　　魁梧　　　　体型
    yīdiǎnbā　　　*mǐ*　　*gāo*　*de*　*kuíwú*　　　*tǐxíng*
    one.point.eight　metre　tall　DE　tall.and.strong　figure

    不断地　　　　往　　　来　　　忙碌　　着。（再见 2）
    bùduànde　　*wǎng*　*lái*　　*mánglù*　*zhe*
    continually　　go　　come　busy　　　ZHE

    'He, a 1.8-metres-tall man with a strong build, is a very dedicated steward who is continually busy with his work.' (*Zàijiàn* 2)

(3) 一　　盘　　意大利粉　　　便　　需　　　三　　磅　　　多
    yī　*pán*　*yìdàlìfěn*　　*biàn*　*xū*　　*sān*　*bàng*　*duō*
    one　CL　spaghetti　　then　need　three　pound　much

    每　　　磅　　　合　　　新币　　　**3.4**　　　　　元。（风筝 196）
    měi　*bàng*　*hé*　　*xīnbì*　　**sāndiǎnsì**　　*yuán*
    each　pound　convert　Singapore.　**three.point.**　yuan
    　　　　　　　　　　　　dollar　　　**four**

'A plate of spaghetti costs more than three pounds (each pound is equivalent to 3.4 SGD).' (*Fēngzhēng* 196)

1.7 About Approximations

An approximation, just as its name implies, refers to a rough number. There are four main classes of approximation expressions.

1.7.1 几 Jǐ 'Several' and 多少 Duōshǎo 'Many'

Single cardinals 几 *jǐ* 'several' and 多少 *duōshǎo* 'many' represent approximations. Here are some examples involving the use of 几 *jǐ* 'several':

(1) 在 我 生下 没 **几** 年, 父亲 便 在
zài wǒ shēngxià méi ***jǐ*** nián fùqīn biàn zài
in 1SG be.born NEG **several** year father then in

一 个 深夜 里 莫名其妙地 撇下 我们
yī gè shēnyè lǐ mòmíngqímiào-de piēxià wǒmen
one CL night inside inexplicably leave 1PL

去 了。(太阳 58)
qù Le
go LE

'A few years after my birth, my father inexplicably left us in the middle of the night.' (*Tàiyáng* 58)

(2) 前面 的 一 个 人 用 锄头 打 洞
qiánmiàn de yī gè rén yòng chútóu dǎ dòng
front DE one CL person use hoe dig hole

后面 的 一 个 人 在 每 个 洞 里
hòumiàn de yī gè rén zài měi gè dòng lǐ
back DE one CL person in each CL hole inside

点下　**几**　粒　麦　种。（跳舞 14）
diǎnxià **jǐ**　lì　mài　zhǒng
sow　**several**　CL　wheat　seed

'The person at the front used a hoe to dig holes and the person at the back sowed a few seeds of wheat into each hole.' (*Tiàowǔ* 14)

(3) 我　十　**几**　岁　就　到　马来西亚，　做
wǒ　**shí**　**jǐ**　suì　jiù　dào　mǎláixīyà　zuò
1SG　ten　several　years　then　to　Malaysia　do

割　胶　工人　...（青青 108）
gē　jiāo　gōngrén
cut　rubber　worker

'I went to Malaysia when I was a little over ten years old and worked as a tapping worker...' (*Qīngqīng* 108)

(4) 摸索　了　**二十**　**几**　年，　我们　不但　无法
mōsuǒ　le　**èrshí**　**jǐ**　nián　wǒmen　bùdàn　wúfǎ
grope　LE　**twenty**　**several**　year　1PL　not.only　unable

形成　以　英文　为　主流　的　文化　体系
xíngchéng　yǐ　yīngwén　wéi　zhǔliú　de　wénhuà　tǐxì
form　by　English　be　mainstream　DE　culture　system

也　逐渐　放弃　了　合　各　族　文化
yě　zhújiàn　fàngqì　le　hé　gè　zú　wénhuà
also　gradually　abandon　LE　integrate　various　ethnic.group　culture

为　一　的　想法。（Δ 小小鸟 178）
wéi　yī　de　xiǎngfǎ
be　one　DE　idea

'After more than 20 years of exploration, we not only failed to form a cultural system with English as the mainstream, but also gradually gave up the idea of integrating the cultures of all ethnic groups.' (Δ*Xiǎoxiǎoniǎo* 178)

22 *Expressions of Number and Quantity*

(5) 看　　别人　　中　　　四字　　　　好像　　　很　　容易，
　　kàn　biérén　zhòng　sìzì　　　　hǎoxiàng　hěn　róngyì
　　see　others　win　　four.digit.lottery　seem　　very　easy

　　我　　买　　了　　**几**　　十　　年，　　却　　从来
　　wǒ　　mǎi　le　　**jǐ**　　shí　nián　　què　cónglái
　　1SG　buy　LE　**several**　ten　year　　but　ever

　　没　　中　　过，　你　　说　怪　　不　　怪！(追云 42)
　　méi　zhòng　guò　nǐ　　shuō　guài　bù　　guài
　　NEG　win　　GUO　2SG　say　strange　NEG　strange

　　'It seems that it is very easy for other people to win the lottery, but I have been buying tickets for decades and never won one. Isn't it strange?' (*Zhūiyún* 42)

(6) 工厂　　　　女工　　　有　　什么　　　不好，　　一　　个
　　gōngchǎng　nǚgōng　yǒu　shénme　bùhǎo　　yī　　gè
　　factory　　female.worker　have　what　　bad.points　one　CL

　　月　　有　　**几**　　**百**　　块　　钱　　的　　收入，
　　yuè　yǒu　**jǐ**　　**bǎi**　kuài　qián　de　shōurù
　　month　have　**several**　**hundred**　yuan　money　DE　income

　　好　　过　　分文不进。(吾土·戏剧 87)
　　hǎo　guò　fēnwénbùjìn
　　good　exceed　have.no.income

　　'There's nothing wrong with being a female worker in a factory. Earning hundreds of yuans a month is better than earning nothing.' (*Wútǔ* (drama), 87)

(7) **几**　　**千**　　年　　了，大海　　一直　　让　　自己　　的
　　jǐ　　**qiān**　nián　le　dàhǎi　yīzhí　ràng　zìjǐ　de
　　several　**thousand**　year　LE　sea　always　let　oneself　DE

　　宝藏　　被　　打捞　　起，　而　　丢落　　给　　它　　的
　　bǎozàng　bèi　dǎlāo　qǐ　　ér　　diūluò　gěi　tā　de
　　treasure　BEI　salvage　up　and　throw　give　3SG　DE

也	自己	默默地	收容	起。(扶轮 19)
yě	zìjǐ	mòmòde	shōuróng	qǐ
also	oneself	silently	take.in	up

'For thousands of years, the sea has allowed its treasures to be salvaged, and silently taken in those thrown to it.' (*Fúlún* 19)

As shown in examples (1) and (2), the single cardinal 几 *jǐ* 'several' represents an approximation directly. In examples (3) and (4), 几 *jǐ* 'several' either follows the magnitudinal numeral 十 *shí* 'ten' or the compound cardinal 二十 *èrshí* 'twenty', while in examples (5), (6) and (7), 几 *jǐ* 'several' precedes a magnitudinal numeral to indicate an approximation.

The following examples from (8) to (10) are cases of 多少 *duōshǎo* 'many', indicating an approximation:

(8)
在	这	人世界，	有	**多少**	不幸的	生命，
zài	zhè	rénshìjiè	yǒu	**duōshǎo**	búxìngde	shēngmìng
in	this	world	have	**many**	unfortunate	life

在	饥寒交迫	中	倔强地	成长！(△ 含羞草 38)
zài	jīhánjiāopò	zhōng	juèjiàng-de	chéngzhǎng
in	suffer.hunger.and.cold	midst	resiliently	grow.up

'In this world, there are many unfortunate people who grow up resilient in the midst of hunger and cold.' (△*Hánxiūcǎo* 38)

(9)
对于	我	来	说，	塞车	与否，	也	无
duìyú	wǒ	lái	shuō	sāichē	yǔfǒu	yě	wú
for	1SG	come	say	traffic.jam	or.not	also	NEG

所谓，	反正	迟到	十	分钟	八	分钟，
suǒwèi	fǎnzhèng	chídào	shí	fēnzhōng	bā	fēnzhōng
matter	anyway	late	ten	minute	eight	minute

少	听不了	**多少**	课。(寻庙 35)
shǎo	tīng-bù-liǎo	**duōshǎo**	kè
less	listen-NEG-finish	**many**	lesson

'For me, it doesn't matter whether there is a traffic jam or not. Anyway, even though I'm ten minutes or eight minutes late, I won't miss much of the lesson.' (*Xúnmiào* 35)

24 *Expressions of Number and Quantity*

(10) 出来 谈谈， 要不了 **多少** 时间 的。(大胡子 37)
    chūlái tántán yào-bù-liǎo **duōshǎo** shíjiān de
    come.out talk.talk not.need **many** time DE
    'Come out and talk. It won't take long.' (*Dàhúzi* 37)

When representing an approximation, 多少 duōshǎo 'many' can only be used alone rather than together with a magnitudinal numeral, and it is not as frequently used as 几 jǐ 'several'.

1.7.2 Approximations Represented by Cardinal Phrases

Cardinal phrases with two single cardinals juxtaposed together can also indicate approximation. There are two types of this kind of phrase:

A. The first type of approximation cardinal phrase is a juxtaposition of two adjacent single cardinals, such as 七八年 qībā nián 'seven or eight years' and 一两个 yīliǎng gè 'one or two', as shown in (11)–(13):

(11) 有 **三四** 个 人 涌 上来， 七手八脚地
    yǒu **sān-sì** gè rén yǒng shànglái qīshǒubājiǎode
    have **three.or.four** CL person crowd up hurriedly

    把 他 推开， 为 我 解了围。(石头 30)
    bǎ tā tuīkāi wèi wǒ jiě-le-wéi
    BA 3SG push.away for 1SG rescue
    Three for four people rushed up and hurriedly pushed him away, which rescued me from the trouble.' (*Shítou* 30)

(12) 然后 **七八** 名 同学 拿 着 花束
    ránhòu **qī-bā** míng tóngxué ná zhe huāshù
    then **seven.or.eight** CL student hold ZHE bouquet

    奔 上 了 舞台 ...(寻庙 65)
    bēn shàng le wǔtái
    rush up LE stage
    'Then, seven or eight students rushed onto the stage, holding bouquets of flowers ...' (*Xúnmiào* 65)

(13) 我们　　以　　二三十　　　　年　　　的　　时间　　提升
    wǒmen　yǐ　èr-sān-shí　　　nián　de　shíjiān　tíshēng
    1PL　　by　twenty.or.thirty　year　DE　time　　improve

    了　经济 ...（△ 小小鸟 91）
    le　jīngjì
    LE　economy

    'We have spent twenty or thirty years to improve the economy.'
    (△Xiǎoxiǎoniǎo 91)

In Chinese Mandarin, it is clearly specified that there is no slight-pause mark '、' between two adjacent numbers which are used to express approximate numbers,[4] while in written Singapore Mandarin, the slight-pause mark '、' can be adopted, for example:

(14) 孩子　　大概　　只有　　五、六　　　岁。（寻庙 59）
    háizi　　dàgài　　zhǐyǒu　wǔ-liù　　　suì
    child　　probably　only　five.or.six　year

    'This child is probably only five or six years old.' (Xúnmiào 59)

(15) 日　已　　上　　了　七、八　　　　竿　了。（心情 76）
    rì　yǐ　　shàng　le　qī-bā　　　　　gān　le
    sun　already　up　LE　seven.or.eight　pole　LE

    'The sun is seven or eight poles high.(It is late in the afternoon)'
    (Xīnqíng 76)

(16) 只有　　二、三　　　　千　　　　人。（至性 134）
    zhǐyǒu　èr-sān　　　　qiān　　　rén
    only　　two.or.three　thousand　person

    'There are only two or three thousand people.' (Zhìxìng, 134)

(17) 那　天　　气象　　　报告　　是　华氏　　　　零下
    nà　tiān　qìxiàng　bàogào　shì　huáshì　　　língxià
    that　day　weather　report　be　Fahrenheit　minus

    二十七、八　　　　　　　　　度。（怀旧 34）
    èrshíqī-bā　　　　　　　　　dù
    twenty-seven.or.twenty-eight　degree

    'According to the weather report that day was minus twenty-seven or twenty-eight degrees.' (Huáijiù 34)

It seems arbitrary whether the slight-pause mark '、' is adopted or not. Sometimes, even in one sentence with two approximations of adjacent numbers, one has the slight-pause mark '、', while the other has not, as in (18).

(18) 虽然　　间隔　　**八、九**　　米　　就　　有　　路灯，
　　　suīrán　jiàngé　**bā-jiǔ**　　mǐ　　jiù　yǒu　lùdēng
　　　although　gap　**eight.or.nine**　metre　just　have　streetlight

　　　但　　路上　　仍　　不　　能　　看　　得　　很　　清楚，
　　　dàn　lùshàng　réng　bù　néng　kàn　de　hěn　qīngchǔ
　　　but　street　still　NEG　can　see　DE　very　clear

　　　有　　**一两**　　位　　同学　　便　　因此　　摔　　了
　　　yǒu　**yī-liǎng**　wèi　tóngxué　biàn　yīncǐ　shuāi　le
　　　have　**one.or.two**　CL　student　then　so　fall　LE

　　　一　　跤。(华韵 91)
　　　yī　jiāo
　　　one　CL

'Although there were streetlights just eight or nine metres apart, it was still not very clear on the road, which made one or two students fall.'
(*Huáyùn* 91)

We've carried out a rough statistical analysis of Liu Huixia's collection of essays *Don't Be a Kite with a Broken Line*. It is found that among the 218 pages (big 32mo), there are 60 approximations of adjacent numbers, among which 27 cases are without the slight-pause mark '、', while the other 33 cases are with such mark. The following two groups of examples provide further evidence that the usage of the slight-pause mark '、' is totally arbitrary.

(19)a.　**八九**　　年　　前，　当　　我　　在　　东京　　旅行　　时，
　　　　bā-jiǔ　nián　qián　dāng　wǒ　zài　dōngjīng　lǚxíng　shí
　　　　eight.or.nine　year　ago　when　1SG　at　Tokyo　travel　when

　　　　和　　一　　位　　50　　岁　　的　　日本　　朋友
　　　　hé　yī　wèi　wǔshí　suì　de　rìběn　péngyǒu
　　　　with　one　CL　fifty　year　DE　Japanese　friend

在　　　餐馆　　　相聚。（风筝 144）
zài　　cānguǎn　　xiāngjù
at　　restaurant　gather

'Eight or nine years ago, I met with one 50-year-old Japanese friend at a restaurant when I was traveling in Tokyo.' (*Fēngzhēng* 144)

b. 造成　　　这　　种　　现象　　　有　　两　　个　　原因：
　　zàochéng　zhè　zhǒng　xiànxiàng　yǒu　liǎng　gè　yuányīn
　　cause　　this　type　phenomenon　have　two　CL　reason

一　是　**八、九**　**年**　前　的　人力
yī　shì　**bā-jiǔ**　**nián**　qián　de　rénlì
one　be　**eight.or.nine**　**year**　ago　DE　human.resources

策划　　计算　　　有　　偏差 . . .（风筝 198）
cèhuà　jìsuàn　yǒu　piānchā
plan　calculate　have　deviation

'There are two reasons for such phenomena: one is the deviation in calculation for manpower planning eight or nine years ago . . .' (*Fēngzhēng* 198)

(20)a. 他们　　现在　　已经　　**五六十**　　**岁**　　了，　很　　多
　　　 tāmen　xiànzài　yǐjīng　**wǔ-liù-shí**　**suì**　le　hěn　duō
　　　 3PL　　now　　already　**fifty.or.sixty**　**years**　LE　very　many

已　　　退休　了　或　　行将　　　退休　了。（风筝 100）
yǐ　　　tuìxiū　le　huò　xíngjiāng　tuìxiū　le
already　retire　LE　or　about.to　retire　LE

'Now they are fifty or sixty years old, many of whom have retired or are about to retire.' (*Fēngzhēng* 100)

b. 第二　　群　　人　　是　在　**五、六十**　**年代，**
　　dìèr　qún　rén　shì　zài　**wǔ-liù-shí**　**niándài**
　　second　CL　person　be　at　**fifty.or.sixty**　**years**

因　　　　家境、　　　　　大学　　学位　　短缺　　或
yīn　　　jiājìng　　　　　dàxué　xuéwèi　duānquē　huò
because　family.circumstance　university　degree　shortage　or

28   *Expressions of Number and Quantity*

其他	缘故	错过	了	入	大学	的	机会。（风筝 100）
qítā	yuángù	cuòguò	le	rù	dàxué	de	jīhuì
other	reason	miss	LE	enter	university	DE	opportunity

'The second group of people missed the opportunity of entering universities in the 1950s or 1960s because of family circumstances, lack of academic qualifications, or other reasons.' (*Fēngzhēng* 100)

The two sentences of example (19) appear on different pages, but they contain the same approximation phrase and classifier, one with a slight-pause mark '、', the other without. The two sentences in example (20) involve the same approximation and appear on the same page. The only difference lies in the classifiers, but the slight-pause mark '、' is used in sentence (20b), not in sentence (20a). Ms. Liu Huixia is a well-known educator and also a columnist of *Zǎobào* in Singapore. Her usage of approximations with adjacent numbers (whether to adopt a slight-pause mark '、' or not) is representative of the general trend in Singapore Mandarin.

B. The second type of approximation cardinal phrase contains the cardinal 三 *sān* 'three', including three- phrases, namely 三五 *sān-wǔ* 'three-five', 三几 *sān-jǐ* 'three-several' and 三两 *sān-liǎng* 'three-two'. The two numbers in 三五 *sān-wǔ* 'three-five' are not adjacent, 三几 *sān-jǐ* 'three-several' is a combination of single cardinal 三 *sān* 'three' and the approximation cardinal 几 *jǐ* 'several', and in the phrase 三两 *sān-liǎng* 'three-two' the two adjacent numbers appear in reverse order. The uses of these phrases are shown in the following example:

(21)

说	建筑	吧 ...	**三五**	个	月	便	会	在
shuō	jiànzhù	ba	**sān-wǔ**	gè	yuè	biàn	huì	zài
say	building	TOP	**three-five**	CL	month	then	will	at

校园	不	知道	哪	一	个	角落，	冒	起
xiàoyuán	bù	zhīdào	nǎ	yī	gè	jiǎoluò	mào	qǐ
campus	NEG	know	which	one	CL	corner	emit	up

一	座	不	知道	是	什么	的	房子。（寻庙 78）
yī	zuò	bù	zhīdào	shì	shénme	de	fángzi
one	CL	NEG	know	be	what	DE	house

'Talking about buildings . . . it takes only three or five months for a building, for which no one knows the purpose, to appear somewhere on the campus.' (*Xúnmiào* 78)

(22) 三几   个   鬼头   总   要   谈   呀   谈   的,
     sān-jǐ   gè   guǐtóu   zǒng   yào   tán   ya   tán   de
     three-several CL   little.devils always want   talk   SFP   talk   DE

   谈   到   不能   不   分手   的   时候   才
   tán   dào   bùnéng   bù   fēnshǒu   de   shíhòu   cái
   talk   until   cannot   NEG   goodbye   DE   time   only

   离开。(吾土·小说上 159)
   líkāi
   leave

   'A couple of little devils always talk for a long time, until they have to say goodbye.' (*Wútǔ Novel I*, 159)

(23) 三两   个   月   功夫   就   输   光   了   他
     sān-liǎng gè   yuè   gōngfu   jiù   shū   guāng   le   tā
     three-two   CL   month   time   just   lose   empty   LE   3SG

   几   年   来   辛勤   刻苦   积蓄   下来   的
   jǐ   nián   lái   xīnqín   kèkǔ   jīxù   xiàlái   de
   several year   come   industrious   assiduous   save   down   DE

   一些   银行   存款 ...(Δ 大喜 185)
   yīxiē   yínháng   cúnkuǎn
   some   bank   deposit

   'In just two or three months, he lost all his savings saved over several years of industrious work.' (Δ*Dàxǐ* 185)

Syntactically, the ordinal phrase can be analysed as a coordinate phrase as indicated next. Semantically, they all indicate alternative relation.

七   八 (名)   三   五 (个)
qī   *bā* (*míng*)   *sān*   *wǔ* (*gè*)
1   2   1   2   (coordinate relation)

三   几 (个)   三   两 (下子)
sān *jǐ* (*gè*)   *sān*   *liǎng* (*xiàzi*)
1   2   1   2   (coordinate relation)

1.7.3 Auxiliary Phrase Approximations

Approximations can also be expressed by adding such auxiliary words as 来 *lái* 'about', 多 *duō* 'more', 余 *yú* 'more' or 左右 *zuǒyòu* 'around' after a numeral.⁵

The auxiliary 来 *lái* 'about' generally follows 十 *shí* 'ten' or a compound cardinal to indicate approximation, such as 十来个 *shí lái gè* 'about ten', 五十来个 *wǔshí lái gè* 'about fifty', 二百来个 *èrbǎi lái gè* 'about two hundred'. Other examples are as follows:

(24) 才   十   来   个   自愿   工作者？（青青 108）
     cái   shí   lái   gè   zìyuàn   gōngzuòzhě
     only ten   about   CL   voluntary worker

'Only about ten volunteers?' (*Qīngqīng* 108)

(25) 平时   十   来   分钟   就   到   的   路程，
     píngshí   shí   lái   fēnzhōng   jiù   dào   de   lùchéng
     usual   ten   about   minute   just   arrive DE   routine

    挨   了   半   个   小时   才   "溜"   完。（怀旧 35）
    ái   le   bàn   gē   xiǎoshí   cái   liū   wán
    take   LE   half   CL   hour   just   slide finish

'It took half an hour to finish the journey, which usually takes about ten minutes.' (*Huáijiù* 35)

(26) 铁栏   外   是   一   条   宽   约   二十   来
     tiělán   wài   shì   yī   tiáo   kuān   yuē   èrshí   lái
     metal fence outside be   one   CL   wide   about   twenty   about

    尺   的   水沟。（壁虎 58）
    chǐ   de   shuǐgōu
    chi   DE   ditch

'There is a ditch about twenty chis wide outside the metal fence.' (*Bìhǔ* 58)

Sometimes it can also be attached to numeral-classifier compounds expressing the units of measurements, for example:

(27) 路边   的   积雪   有   一   尺   来   厚。（怀旧 35）
     lùbiān   de   jīxuě   yǒu   yī   chǐ   lái   hòu
     roadside   DE   snow   have   one   chi   about   thick

'The snow by the side of the road is about one chi thick.' (*Huáijiù* 35)

The auxiliary 多 *duō* 'more' can follow 十 *shí* 'ten' or a compound cardinal to convey approximation as well, such as 十多个 *shí duō gè* 'more than ten' and 二十多个 *èrshí duō gè* 'more than twenty'. Other examples are as follows:

(28) 育英　　中学　　　　校园　　　里，　种植　　了　十　多
　　　yùyīng　zhōngxué　　xiàoyuán　lǐ　　zhòngzhí　le　shí　duō
　　　Yuying　middle.school　campus　in　plant　　　LE　ten　more

棵　　　矮种柳树 ...(一心 5)
kē　　　ǎizhǒngliǔshù
CL　　　dwarf.willow

'There are around a dozen dwarf willow trees planted on the campus of Yuying Middle School.' (*Yīxīn* 5)

(29) 你　　说　　你　　学　　相声　　　学　　了　六十　　多
　　　nǐ　　shuō　nǐ　　xué　xiàngsheng　xué　le　liùshí　duō
　　　2SG　say　2SG　learn　crosstalk　　learn　LE　sixty　more

年？（笑眼 2）
nián
year

'You said that you had been learning crosstalk for more than sixty years?' (*Xiàoyǎn* 2)

In Singapore Mandarin, 多 *duō* 'more' can even be attached to bare magnitudinal numerals like 百 *bǎi* 'hundred' and 千 *qiān* 'thousand' as shown in the following examples, a usage not found in Chinese Mandarin:

(30) 他　10　多　　年　　来　　勤奋　　作画，　积累　　　　了
　　　tā　shí　duō　nián　lái　qínfèn　zuòhuà　jīlěi　　　　le
　　　3SG　ten　more　year　about　diligent　paint　accumulate　LE

百　　　　多　　　张　　　画作。(报 1995 年 3 月 15 日副刊 10)
bǎi　　　　duō　　　zhāng　huàzuò
hundred　more　　CL　　　painting

'He has been working hard on painting for more than ten years and has accumulated about a hundred paintings.' (*Bào*, Mar. 3, 1995, Issue no. 10, supplementary edition)

(31) 多可惜， 平白 损失 了 **千** **多**
    duōkěxī *píngbái* *sǔnshī* *le* **qiān** **duō**
    what.a.pity gratuitously lose LE **thousand** **more**

块！（吾土 · 小说上 89）
kuài
yuan

'What a pity! To lose more than a thousand yuans gratuitously!'
(*Wútǔ Novel I*, 89)

Furthermore, the auxiliary 多 *duō* 'more' can follow numeral-classifier compounds, as in (32), for example:

(32) 逼 他 出工 已 **一 年 多** 了。(金狮奖（四）12)
    bī *tā* *chūgōng* *yǐ* **yī** **nián** **duō** *le*
    force 3SG go.to.work already **one** **year** **more** LE

'It has been more than one year since he was forced to go to work.'
(*Jīnshījiǎng* IV, 12)

(33) 当 日本 侵略者 挥军 南下 的 时候，
    dāng *rìběn* *qīnlüèzhě* *huījūn* *nánxià* *de* *shíhòu*
    when Japan invaders command.army southward DE period

于 这 非常的 时期， 我 和 一 位 同事
yú *zhè* *fēichángde* *shíqī* *wǒ* *hé* *yī* *wèi* *tóngshì*
at this special time 1SG and one CL colleague

友人 张君， 就 在 那里 挨过 了
yǒurén *zhāngjūn* *jiù* *zài* *nàlǐ* *áiguò* *le*
friend Mr.Zhang just at there survive LE

二 个 多 月 的 避难 生活。（痕迹 118）
èr **gè** **duō** **yuè** *de* *bìnàn* *shēnghuó*
two **CL** **more** **month** DE refuge life

'During the time when the Japanese invaders commanded their army to the south, a colleague and friend of mine, Mr. Zhang, and I had spent over two months in hiding there.' (*Hénjī* 118)

Another auxiliary that is always attached to the magnitudinal numeral 十 *shí* 'ten' or compound cardinals is 余 *yú* 'more', like 十余斤 *shí yú jīn* 'more than ten *jīn*' and 五十余个 *wǔshí yú gè* 'more than fifty'. Other examples are as follows:

(34) 我　　曾　　为　　一　　家　　商行　　　理账
　　　wǒ　　céng　wèi　yī　　jiā　　shāngháng　lǐzhàng
　　　1SG　once　for　one　CL　firm　　　　manage.account

　　　十　　余　　　年　　之　　久 ...(痕迹 118)
　　　shí　**yú**　nián　zhī　jiǔ
　　　ten　**more**　year　LIG　long

　　　'I had been managing accounts for a firm for more than ten years ...'
　　　(*Hénjì*, 118)

(35) 里里外外，　　　住　　着　　三十　　余　　户　　人家。(金狮
　　　　　　　　　　　　　　　　　　　　　　　　　　　　　　奖（四）2)
　　　lǐlǐwàiwài　　　zhù　zhe　**sānshí**　**yú**　**hù**　rénjiā
　　　inside.and.outside　live　ZHE　**thirty**　**more**　**CL**　family

　　　'There are more than thirty families around here.' (*Jīnshījiǎng* IV, 12)

(36) 其中　　的　　三万　　　　　　余　　个　　标本，
　　　qízhōng　de　**sānwàn**　　　　**yú**　**gè**　biāoběn
　　　therein　DE　**thirty.thousand**　**more**　**CL**　specimen

　　　便　　在　　" 王子　猎场 "　　　　里　　展出。(石头 15)
　　　biàn　zài　wángzǐ　lièchǎng　　　lǐ　　zhǎnchū
　　　then　at　prince　hunting.ground　inside　exhibit

　　　'There are more than thirty thousand specimens exhibited at the Prince's Hunting Ground.' (*Shítou* 15)

The auxiliary 左右 *zuǒyòu* 'around' generally follows numeral-classifier compounds to indicate approximation, for example:

(37) 飞　　离　　地　　才　　一　　公尺　　左右 ...(心情 53)
　　　fēi　　lí　　dì　　cái　　yī　　gōngchǐ　**zuǒyòu**
　　　fly　away　ground　just　one　metre　**around**

　　　'It was only about a metre off the ground ...' (*Xīnqíng* 53)

34 *Expressions of Number and Quantity*

(38) 辜振甫　　的　　讲话　　只有　　十　　分钟　　**左右**。（∆ 小
　　　　　　　　　　　　　　　　　　　　　　　　　　　　　　小鸟 171）
　　　gūzhènfŭ　*de*　*jiǎnghuà*　*zhǐyǒu*　*shí*　*fēnzhōng*　***zuǒyòu***
　　　Koo.Chenfu　DE　speech　only　ten　minute　**around**
　　　'Koo Chenfu's speech lasted for only about ten minutes.' (∆*Xiǎoxiǎoniǎo* 171)

(39) 每　　年　　有　　三千　　　　男孩　　申请，　而
　　　měi　*nián*　*yǒu*　*sānqiān*　*nánhái*　*shēnqǐng*　*ér*
　　　each　year　have　three.thousand　boy　apply　while

　　　被　　录取　　的　　只有　　150　　　　　名　　**左右**…（风
　　　　　　　　　　　　　　　　　　　　　　　　　　　　筝 113）
　　　bèi　*lùqŭ*　*de*　*zhǐyǒu*　*yībǎiwǔshí*　*míng*　***zuǒyòu***
　　　BEI　admit　DE　only　one.hundred.fifty　CL　**around**
　　　'There are three thousand boys applying each year, while only about one hundred and fifty will be admitted.' (*Fēngzhēng* 113)

In Chinese Mandarin, one more auxiliary 上下 *shàngxià* 'around' is often used to express approximations when talking about age. For example:

(40) 年龄　　在　　三十　　岁　　**上下**。（《现代汉语八百词》[6]
　　　　　　　　　　　　　　　　　　　　422 页）
　　　niánlíng　*zài*　*sānshí*　*suì*　***shàngxià***
　　　age　at　thirty　years　**around**
　　　'(His) age is about thirty years old.' (Quoted from *Xiàndài hànyŭ bābǎi cí*, p. 422)

(41) 据　　　　我　　看来，　这　　个　　人　　的　　年龄
　　　jù　　*wǒ*　*kànlái*　*zhè*　*gè*　*rén*　*de*　*niánlíng*
　　　according.to　1SG　see-come　this　CL　person　DE　age

　　　总　　在　　三十　　**上下**。（《现代汉语虚词例释》[7] 383 页）
　　　zǒng　*zài*　*sānshí*　***shàngxià***
　　　always　at　thirty　**around**
　　　'In my opinion, the age of this person may always be about thirty.' (Quoted from *Xiàndàihànyŭxūcílìshì*, 383)

This kind of expression can be found in *The Story of the Stone*, for example:

(42) 寡母　　　　　王氏　　乃　现任　　京营节度使
　　 guǎmǔ　　　　 wángshì　nǎi　xiànrèn　 jīngyíngjiédùshǐ
　　 widowed.mother Ms.Wang　be　incumbent　governor

　　 王子腾　　　之　妹 …　今年　　方　　四十　**上下**
　　 wángzǐténg　 zhī　mèi　　jīnnián　fāng　sìshí　**shàngxià**
　　 Wang.Ziteng　DE　sister　this.year　just　forty　**around**

　　 年纪，　　　只　　有　　薛蟠　　　一　　子。(第四回)
　　 niánjì　　　 zhǐ　 yǒu　 xuēpán　　 yī　　zǐ
　　 age　　　　 only　have　Xue.Pan　　one　 son

　　 'Ms. Wang, a widowed mother, is the sister of the incumbent governor Wang Ziteng. She is about forty years old, and has only one son named Xue Pan.' (Chapter IV)

It seems that 上下 *shàngxià* 'around' is not used for approximation in Singapore Mandarin. It is not found in the written materials I have observed, and during my half-year stay in Singapore, I never heard expressions like 三十岁上下 *sānshí suì shàngxià* 'about thirty years old' or 四十上下 *sìshí shàngxià* 'about forty years old'.

1.7.4 *'Magnitudinal Numeral +* 多 *Duō 'More' +* 二 / 两 *Èr/liǎn 'Two' + Magnitudinal Numeral + Classifier' Construction*

In Singapore Mandarin, 'magnitudinal numeral + 多 *duō* 'more' + 二 / 两 *èr/liǎng* 'two' + magnitudinal numeral + classifier' construction is often used to represent an approximation. For example:

(43) 家才，　　 这　 个　 地方，　　你　　也　　住　　了
　　 jiācái　　　zhè　 gè　 dìfāng　　 nǐ　　 yě　　zhù　 le
　　 Jiacai　　　this　CL　 place　　 2SG　 also　 live　 LE

　　 十　　多　　二　　十　　年　了，
　　 shí　 duō　 èr　　shí　 nián　le
　　 ten　 more　two　 ten　 year　LE

　　 就　　 这么　　 一　　句　　话，
　　 jiù　　 zhème　　yī　　 jù　　huà
　　 just　　such　　 one　 CL　　saying

36 *Expressions of Number and Quantity*

说　　　走　就　　走？　（华文教材　4 B 59）
shuō　　zǒu jiù　zǒu
say　　 go   then go

'Jiacai, you have been living here for more than a decade or two. You're just going to say that and leave?' (*Huáwénjiàocái* 4B, 59)

(44)　(电话卡)　只　　买　了　百　　　多　　二　　百
　　　diànhuàkǎ　zhǐ　mǎi　le　bǎi　　duō　èr　　bǎi
　　　phone.card only buy LE hundred more two hundred

块。　(新视第八波道 1995 年 8 月 25 日晚 10 点新闻)
kuài
CL

'It only cost like one hundred or two hundred yuans to buy a SIM card.' (*Xīnshìdìbābōdào* (News at 10:00 PM), Aug. 25, 1995)

(45)　"一　　套　　多少　　　钱？　这么　小看　　我。"
　　　yī　　tào　duōshǎo　qián　zhème　xiǎokàn　wǒ
　　　one   CL   how.much   money such   belittle   1SG

'How much is one set? Don't belittle me like that.'

"千　　　多　　两　　千　　　块！"（蓝天 50）
qiān　　duō　liǎng　qiān　　kuài
thousand more two   thousand CL

'About one or two thousand yuans.' (*Lántiān*, 50)

十多二十年 *shíduō èrshí nián* in example (42) means 'a decade or two'. The meanings of similar expressions in examples (43) and (44) can also be understood in this way. In addition, in Singapore Mandarin, there is another similar construction of 'classifier + 多 *duō* 'more' + 两 *liǎng* 'two' + classifier' indicating approximation, for example:

(46)　所　　花　　也　　不过　　块　　多　　两　　块　　钱。(风雨 88)
　　　suǒ　huā　yě　bùguò　kuài　duō　liǎng　kuài　qián
　　　SUO   cost   also no.more   CL   more   two   CL   money

'It only costs one or two yuans.' (*Fēngyǔ* 88)

块多两块钱 *kuàiduō liǎngkuài qián* in example (45) means one or two yuans. There is no such expression in Chinese Mandarin.

1.8 Multiples

A multiple can be expressed as 'numeral + 倍 *bèi* "times"'. For example:

(1) 眼看　　着　　同学　　中　　当　　经纪人　　的　　收入
yǎnkàn　zhe　tóngxué　zhōng　dāng　jīnjìrén　de　shōurù
see　　ZHE　classmate　middle　do　manager　DE　income

竟　　超过　　自己　　薪水　　的　　二　　倍。（吾土·小说上 71）
*jìng　　chāoguò　zìjǐ　xīnshuǐ　de　**èr**　**bèi***
unexpectedly　exceed　oneself　income　DE　**two**　**times**

'Some of (my) classmates who work as managers are earning more than twice what I do.' (*Wútǔ* (novel I), 71)

(2) 12　　年　　来，　讲　　英语　　的　　华族
shíèr　nián　lái　jiǎng　yīngyǔ　de　huázú
twelve　year　come　speak　English　DE　Chinese.people

家庭　　增加　　了　　三　　倍。（△小小鸟 80）
*jiātíng　zēngjiā　le　**sān**　**bèi***
family　increase　LE　**three**　**time**

'In the past 12 years, the number of English-speaking Chinese families has tripled.' (△*Xiǎoxiǎoniǎo* 80)

In Chinese Mandarin, another multiple expression, 'numeral + the classifier 番 *fān* "times"', is used only as the object of the verb ' 翻 *fān* increase', as shown in the following:

(3) 今年　　电脑　　的　　销售量　　比　　去年
jīnnián　diànnǎo　de　xiāoshòuliàng　bǐ　qùnián
this.year　computer　DE　sales　than　last.year

翻　　了　　一　　番。
fān　le　yī　fān
increase　LE　**one**　**time**

'Sales of computers this year have doubled compared to that of last year.'

(4) 水产品　　的　　价格　　涨幅　　最　　大，　像
shuǐchǎnpǐn　de　jiàgé　zhǎngfú　zuì　dà　xiàng
aquatic.product　DE　price　increase　most　big　like

甲鱼、	螃蟹	与	去年	同期	相比	几乎
jiǎyú	*pángxiè*	*yǔ*	*qùnián*	*tóngqī*	*xiāngbǐ*	*jīhū*
turtle	crab	with	last.year	same.time	compare	almost

翻	了	**两**	**番**。
fān	*le*	***liǎng***	***fān***
increase	LE	**two**	**time**

'Aquatic products witnessed the biggest price increases. Products like turtles and crabs almost quadrupled compared to the same period last year.'

翻一番 *fān yī fān* means 'doubling the original quantity'; 翻两番 *fān liǎng fān* means 'quadrupling the original quantity', i.e. increase by four times. Thus, in example (3), 销售量比去年翻了一番 *xiāoshòuliàng bǐ qùnián fān le yī fān* means 'the sales doubled that of last year'; in example (4), 价格翻了两番 *jiàgé fān le liǎng fān*, means that 'the current price has quadrupled (i.e. the current price has increased by four times compared to that of the last year)'. However, there is no such expression in Singapore Mandarin.

1.9 Ordinals

1.9.1 Ordinals in the Form of '第 Dì + Integer'

The most commonly seen ordinals are compounds formed by the 第 *dì* and an integer, such as 第一 *dìyī* 'first', 第三 *dìsān* 'third', 第五十六 *dìwǔshíliù* 'fifty-sixth' and so on. Ordinals with 第 *dì* often precedes a classifier, as a modifier.

(1) | **第一** | 天 | 考 | 两 | 场, | **第一** | **场** | 考 | 的 |
|---|---|---|---|---|---|---|---|---|
| ***dìyī*** | *tiān* | *kǎo* | *liǎng* | *chǎng* | ***dìyī*** | ***chǎng*** | *kǎo* | *de* |
| **first** | day | test | two | CL | **first** | **CL** | test | DE |

是	英文,	**第二**	**场**	考	的	是	华文。(跳舞 89)
shì	*yīngwén*	***dìèr***	***chǎng***	*kǎo*	*de*	*shì*	*huáwén*
be	English	**second**	**CL**	test	DE	be	Chinese

'There are two tests on the first day, the first one is English and the second one is Chinese.' (*Tiàowǔ* 89)

(2) | 马来西亚 | 的 | 胡椒 | 产量 | 居 | 世界 | **第 4** | **位** ... |
|---|---|---|---|---|---|---|---|
| | | | | | | | (南北 26) |
| *mǎláixīyà* | *de* | *hújiāo* | *chǎnliàng* | *jū* | *shìjiè* | ***dìsì*** | ***wèi*** |
| Malaysia | DE | pepper | production | rank | world | **fourth** | **CL** |

'Malaysia ranks fourth in the world for pepper production ...' (*Nánběi* 26)

(3) 请   大家   翻开   课本，
    qǐng   dàjiā   fānkāi   kèběn
    please everyone open   textbook

    今天   讲   **第三十二**   页 – (Δ 大喜 20)
    jīntiān   jiǎng   **dìsānshí'èr**   yè
    today   talk   **thirty-second** CL

    'Please open the textbook. Today, we are going to talk about the contents on page 32.' (Δ*Dàxǐ* 20)

Apart from being a modifier, ordinal compounds with 第 *dì* have four other usages.

First, ordinals with 第 *dì* can occur in the subject position, as can been seen in examples (4) to (6):

(4) 要   发展   新加坡文化，   根据   我   的   看法，   有
    yào   fāzhǎn   xīnjiāpōwénhuà   gēnjù   wǒ   de   kànfǎ   yǒu
    want   develop   Singapore.   according.1SG   DE   opinion   have
                     culture   to

    三   方面   值得   留意。   **第一**   是   语言   的   平衡
    sān   fāngmiàn   zhídé   liúyì   **dìyī**   shì   yǔyán   de   pínghéng
    three   aspect   worth   attention   **first** be   language   DE   balanced

    发展 ...   **第二**   是   多元   文化   的   接触   和
    fāzhǎn   **dì'èr**   shì   duōyuán   wénhuà   de   jiēchù   hé
    development   **second** be   multiple   culture   DE   contact   and

    融合 ...   **第三**   是   文化   的   深入   探讨 ...(华文教
                                                                       材 3B, 20 –22)
    rónghé   **dìsān**   shì   wénhuà   de   shēnrù   tàntǎo
    integration   **third**   be   culture   DE   deep   discussion

    'In my opinion, to develop Singaporean culture, three aspects need our attention. The first is a balanced development of languages ... The second is contact among multiple cultures and the integration of them ... The third is a deep discussion of culture ...' (*Huáwénjiàocái* 3B, 20–22)

(5) 让   我   反驳   反方   发言人   所   提出   的   两
    ràng   wǒ   fǎnbó   fǎnfāng   fāyánrén   suǒ   tíchū   de   liǎng
    let   1SG   rebut   the.opposite   spokesman   SUO   raise   DE   two

40 *Expressions of Number and Quantity*

点	意见：	**第一**、	那个	年代	我国	工商业
diǎn	yìjiàn	**dìyī**	nàgè	niándài	wǒguó	gōngshāngyè
CL	opinion	**first**	that	age	our.country	industry.and.commerce

正	处于	大力	发展	的	阶段，	所以	经济
zhèng	chǔyú	dàlì	fāzhǎn	de	jiēduàn	suǒyǐ	jīngjì
just	at	great	develop	DE	stage	so	economy

成长	迅速。	**第二**、	进入	80 年代，	我国
chéngzhǎng	xùnsù	**dìèr**	jìnrù	bāshíniándài	wǒguó
grow	rapid	**second**	enter	the.1980s	our.country

面对	的	竞争	越来越大。	（华文教材 2B 120）
miànduì	de	jìngzhēng	yuèláiyuèdà	
face	DE	competition	increasingly.big	

'Let me rebut two opinions from the spokesman of the opposite side: first, in those years, the industry and commerce in our country was under great development, so we had rapid economic growth; second, the competition that we faced was getting more and more serious in the 1980s.' (*Huáwénjiàocái* 2B, 120)

(6)
三	位	前辈	也	谈及	他们	的	一些
sān	wèi	qiánbèi	yě	tánjí	tāmen	de	yīxiē
three	CL	predecessor	also	talk.about	3PL	DE	some

宝贵	经验：	**第一,**	要	有	献身	教育	的
bǎoguì	jīngyàn	**dìyī**	yào	yǒu	xiànshēn	jiàoyù	de
valuable	experience	**first**	need	have	devote	education	DE

校长	与	教员、	公众人士、	家长	合作无间。
xiàozhǎng	yǔ	jiàoyuán	gōngzhòngrénshì	jiāzhǎng	hézuòwújiàn
chancellor	and	teacher	the.public	parent	cooperate.closely

第二，	校风	要	靠	校长、	教员	的	牺牲
dìèr	xiàofēng	yào	kào	xiàozhǎng	jiàoyuán	de	xīshēng
second	school. spirit	need	depend	chancellor	teacher	DE	endeavour

第三，	...（薪传 109－110）
dìsān	
third	

'Three predecessors also talked about their valuable experience: first, there must be devoted chancellors, teachers, members of the public and parents who may work together closely; second, the school spirit depends on the endeavour of the chancellor and teachers; third, ...' (*Xīnchuán* 109–110)

   If ordinals like 第一 *dìyī* 'first' in the subject position are followed by the copula verb 是 *shì* 'be', there is no pause between them. Otherwise, there should be a pause after the ordinals, which could be indicated by a slight-pause mark or a comma, as exemplified in (5) and (6) respectively.
   Second, ordinals with 第 *dì* can serve as predicates, for example:

(7)
他	深	谙	大卫·林	的	人生	哲学	是
tā	shēn	ān	dàwèilín	de	rénshēng	zhéxué	shì
3SG	deeply	know	David.Lin	DE	life	philosophy	be

"金钱	**第一**，	万事	**第二**"，	他	的	所谓
jīnqián	**dìyī**	wànshì	**dìèr**	tā	de	suǒwèi
money	**first**	everything	**second**	3SG	DE	so.called

"闯天下"	即是	赚	大钱	...（变调 49）
chuǎngtiānxià	jíshì	zhuàn	dàqián	
carve.a.niche	be	make	big.money	

'He clearly knows David Lin's philosophy of life: money comes first, while everything else is second. His so-called carving a niche for himself just means to make big money.' (*Biàndiào* 49)

   Third, ordinals with 第 *dì* can function as objects, for example:

(8)
这	次	比赛，	他	得	了	**第一**，	我	得	了	**第二**。
zhè	cì	bǐsài	tā	dé	le	**dìyī**	wǒ	dé	le	**dìèr**
this	CL	game	3SG	win	LE	**first**	1SG	win	LE	**second**

'In this game, he won the first place, and I won the second.'

42 *Expressions of Number and Quantity*

Fourth, ordinals with 第 *dì* can directly modify nouns; the number of nouns being modified, however, is highly limited. The common ones are 夫人 *fūrén* 'madam', as in 第一夫人 *dìyī fūrén* 'First lady'; and 要素 *yàosù* 'element', as in 第一要素 *dìyī yàosù* 'the most important element'. Here are some other examples:

(9) 第二　　语文　　　　　　第二　　阶段
    dìèr　　yǔwén　　　　　*dìèr*　　jiēduàn
    second　language　　　**second**　stage
    'the second language'　　'the second stage'

    第三　　阶段　　　　　　第二　　语言
    dìsān　jiēduàn　　　　　*dìèr*　　yǔyán
    third　stage　　　　　**second**　language
    'the third stage'　　　　'the second language'

    第十一　　单元
    dìshíyī　dānyuán
    eleventh　unit
    'the eleventh unit'

In our opinion, 第*dì* is an auxiliary word.[8] Grammatically, 第三十二页 *dìsānshíèr yè* 'page 32' in example (3) can be analysed as follows.

第　三　十　二　页
dì　sān　shí　èr　yè

```
      ___1___   _2_        ('attribute-head' endocentric phrase)
  3    ___4___              (auxiliary phrase)
         5   6              (coordinate phrases, compound cardinals)
         _7_ _8_            ('attribute-head' endocentric phrase, compound cardinals)
```

1.9.2 Cardinals Being Used as Ordinals

The meaning of ordinals can also be expressed directly by integer cardinals without any auxiliaries, such as:

(10)　这　　　说明　　　　华文报章　　　　　　同时　　　　　　在　　　　　扮演
　　　zhè　*shuōmíng*　*huáwénbàozhāng*　*tóngshí*　　　　*zài*　　　*bànyǎn*
　　　this　illustrate　　Chinese.newspapers　simultaneously　in.process　act

着	两	种	角色，	一	是	报道	与	评论，	二
zhe	liǎng	zhǒng	juésè	yī	shì	bàodǎo	yǔ	pínglùn	èr
ZHE	two	CL	role	**one**	be	report	and	review	**two**

是	传播	文化。（文艺 41）
shì	chuánbō	wénhuà
be	disseminate	culture

'It means that the Chinese newspapers play two roles simultaneously: the first is reporting and reviewing; the second is disseminating culture.' (*Wényì* 41)

(11)
组成	一	个	国家	有	三	项	要素：
zǔchéng	yī	gè	guójiā	yǒu	sān	xiàng	yàosù
constitute	one	CL	country	have	three	CL	element

一	是	国民，	二	是	领土，	三	是	主权。（伦理·中三 116）
yī	shì	guómín	èr	shì	lǐngtǔ	sān	shì	zhǔquán
one	be	citizen	**two**	be	territory	**three**	be	sovereignty

'There are three major elements that constitute a nation: first, citizens; second, territory; third, sovereignty.' (*Lúnlǐ* III 116)

(12)
华文	知识分子	...	大概	可	分为	三	组：
huáwén	zhīshífènzǐ		dàgài	kě	fēnwéi	sān	zǔ
Chinese	intellectual		probably	can	divide.into	three	group

一、	华文	教学	人员。
yī	huáwén	jiàoxué	rényuán
one	Chinese	teach	staff

二、	华文	专业	工作者。
èr	huáwén	zhuānyè	gōngzuòzhě
two	Chinese	professional	worker

三、	华文	文化	工作者。（风筝 20）
sān	huáwén	wénhuà	gōngzuòzhě
three	Chinese	culture	worker

'Chinese intellectuals can be roughly divided into three groups: first, Chinese language teachers; second, Chinese professionals and third, Chinese cultural workers.' (*Fēngzhēng* 20)

44 *Expressions of Number and Quantity*

In these examples, 一 yī 'one', 二 èr 'two' and 三 sān 'three' are all used as ordinals, meaning the same as 第一 dìyī 'the first', 第二 dìèr 'the second' and 第三 dìsān 'the third'. In written genres, especially in argumentative writing, numbers in Chinese characters and a parenthesis '( )', or an Arabic number plus a dot '.' or a parenthesis '( )', can all indicate the meaning of cardinals, as illustrated by (13), (14) and (15) respectively.

(13) 在   我   看   来，   若是   下列   三   种
      zài   wǒ   kàn   lái   ruòshì   xiàliè   sān   zhǒng
      in   1SG   see   come   if   following three CL

情况   继续   恶化   下去，   很   可能   促使
qíngkuàng   jìxù   èhuà   xiàqù   hěn   kěnéng   cùshǐ
circumstance continue deteriorate down   very   likely   prompt

我们   变成   单语   或   无根的   社会：
wǒmen   biànchéng   dānyǔ   huò   wúgēnde   shèhuì
1PL   become   monolingual or   rootless   society

(一)   母语   社会   地位   日渐   低落。…
yī   mǔyǔ   shèhuì   dìwèi   rìjiàn   dīluò
first mother.tongue society   position   gradually decline

(二)   母语   应用   范围   狭窄。…
èr   mǔyǔ   yìngyòng   fànwéi   xiázhǎi
second mother.tongue application   range   narrow

(三)   母语   水准   继续   下降，   母语
sān   mǔyǔ   shuǐzhǔn jìxù   xiàjiàng mǔyǔ
third mother. level   continue decline   mother.
       tongue   language

终归   变成   口头语。(风筝 4-5)
zhōngguī   biànchéng   kǒutóuyǔ
finally   change.into   colloquialism

'From my perspective, our society may become mono-lingual or rootless if the following three circumstances further deteriorate: first, the social status of the mother tongue gradually declines; second, the mother tongue is used on fewer occasions; third, the mother tongue level continues to decline, and eventually it could be reduced to the level of colloquialism.' (*Fēngzhēng* 4–5)

(14) | 《报告书》 | 列明 | 华文 | 科 | 的 | 主要 | 教学
| bàogàoshū | lièmíng | huáwén | kē | de | zhǔyào | jiàoxué
| Report | specify | Chinese | course | DE | major | teach

目标　　是：
mùbiāo　shì
goal　　be

1.　通过　　语文　　技能，　听、　说、　读　和
yī　tōngguò　yǔwén　jìnéng　tīng　shuō　dú　hé
first　through　Chinese　skill　listen　speak　read　and

写　的　教导，　培养　　学生　　的　语文　　能力；
xiě　de　jiàodǎo　péiyǎng　xuéshēng　de　yǔwén　nénglì
write　DE　instruct　cultivate　student　DE　Chinese　ability

2.　向　　学生　　灌输　　有利　于　建国
èr　xiàng　xuéshēng　guànshū　yǒulì　yú　jiànguó
second　towards　student　instil　beneficial　to　found.a.country

工作　的　亚洲　文化　和　优良的　传统　价值观；
gōngzuò　de　yàzhōu　wénhuà　hé　yōuliángde　chuántǒng　jiàzhíguān
work　DE　Asia　culture　and　good　tradition　value

3.　注重　　发展　　学生　　的　语言　能力，　而
sān　zhùzhòng　fāzhǎn　xuéshēng　de　yǔyán　nénglì　ér
third　emphasise　develop　student　DE　language　ability　but

不是　掌握　　语文　　知识　的　能力。（薪传 180）
bùshì　zhǎngwò　yǔwén　zhīshí　de　nénglì
NEG　grasp　Chinese　knowledge　DE　ability

'*The Report* specifies that the major teaching goals of the Chinese course are as follows: First, cultivate students' language ability through language acquiring skills, listening, speaking, reading, and writing. Second, instil Asian culture in students, which is conducive to nation-founding work, and excellent traditional values. Third, pay attention to the development of students' language ability rather than their capacity to grasp Chinese knowledge.' (*Xīnchuán* 180)

46 Expressions of Number and Quantity

(15) 从　　表　　十　　我们　　可以　　得出　　以下　　的　　结论：
　　　cóng　biǎo　shí　wǒmen　kěyǐ　déchū　yǐxià　de　jiélùn
　　　from　table　ten　1PL　can　get　following　DE　conclusion

　　(1)　从　　双语　　能力　　看，　马来　　组　　的　　学生
　　yī　*cóng　shuāngyǔ　nénglì　kàn,　mǎlái　zǔ　de　xuéshēng*
　　first　from　bilingual　ability　look　Malay　group　DE　student

　　双语　　能力　　最　　好，　其次　　是　　印族　　学生，
　　shuāngyǔ　nénglì　zuì　hǎo,　qícì　shì　yìnzú　xuéshēng,
　　bilingual　ability　most　good　next　be　Indian　student

　　再次　　是　　华族　　学生。
　　zàicì　shì　huázú　xuéshēng.
　　still.next　be　Chinese　student

　　(2)　英语　　能力　　最　　强　　的　　是　　华族　　学生。
　　èr　*yīngyǔ　nénglì　zuì　qiáng　de　shì　huázú　xuéshēng.*
　　second　English　ability　most　strong　DE　be　Chinese　student

　　(3)　母语　　能力　　最　　强　　的　　是　　印族
　　sān　*mǔyǔ　nénglì　zuì　qiáng　de　shì　yìnzú*
　　third　mother.language　ability　most　strong　DE　be　Indian

　　学生，其次　　是　　马来族　学生，　华族　　学生
　　xuéshēng, qícì　shì　mǎláizú　xuéshēng, huázú　xuéshēng
　　student　next　be　Malay　student　Chinese　student

　　母语　　　　能力　　最差。
　　mǔyǔ　　　nénglì　zuìchà.
　　mother.language　ability　the.worst

　　(4)　华英　　　　组　　的　　学生　　是　　唯一　　一　　组
　　sì　*huáyīng　　zǔ　de　xuéshēng　shì　wéiyī　yī　zǔ*
　　fourth　Chinese-English　group　DE　student　be　only　one　group

　　英文　比　母语　　强　的　学生。(华文 18)
　　yīngwén　bǐ　mǔyǔ　qiáng　de　xuéshēng.
　　English　than　mother.tongue　strong　DE　student

'We can conclude from Table Ten: First, students in the Malay group have the best bilingual competence, with Indian students coming off second best, while Chinese students are third. Second, the English proficiency of the Chinese students is the best. Third, Indian students hold the best mother tongue proficiency, followed by Malay students and Chinese students. Fourth, Chinese-English students are the only group where the students' English ability is better than their mother tongue.' (*Huáwén*, 18)

In written genres, ordinals without auxiliaries can also be used after a couple of nouns, like 表 *biǎo* 'table', 图 *tú* 'graph', 练习 *liànxí* 'exercise' and so on. For example:

(16) 表　　二：　　听写　　字形　　　　　　错误　　举例（华文 2）
biǎo　**èr**　　**tīngxiě**　**zìxíng**　　　　**cuòwù**　**jǔlì**
table　two　　dictate　character.pattern　mistake　give.examples
'Table 2: examples of character errors in dictation.' (*Huáwén*, 2)

(17) 练习　　二十一　　（第七　　单元　　总　　　复习）（△ 华文练习 2B 7）
liànxí　**èrshíyī**　　**dìqī**　　**dānyuán**　**zǒng**　**fùxí**
exercise　twenty-one　seventh　unit　　　general　review
'Exercise 21: general review for unit seven.' (△*Huáwénliànxí* 2B, 7)

(18) 单元　　十　（△ 高级练习 2B 63）
dānyuán　**shí**
unit　　　ten
'Unit 10.' (△*gāojíliànxí* 2B, 63)

(19) 附录　　一：　大　旅行家　　来　　叩门（石头 225）
fùlù　**yī**　　dà　lǚxíngjiā　lái　kòumén
appendix　one　big　traveller　come　knock.on.the.door
'Appendix 1: the great traveller comes knocking.' (*Shítou* 225)

In example (16), 表二 *biǎo èr* 'Table 2' means the second table; in example (17), 练习二十一 *liànxí èrshíyī* 'Exercise 21' represents the twenty-first exercise; 单元十 *dānyuán shí* 'Unit 10' in example (18) is the same as the tenth unit; and 附录一 *fùlù yī* 'Appendix 1' in example (19) refers to the first appendix.

In everyday usage the ordinal numbers without auxiliary are usually used in the following cases:

Firstly, they are used to express the exact century, year, month, date and time. For example, 三月 *sānyuè* 'March' does not mean 'three months', but 'the third month in a year'. Actually, to express 'the third month', people never say 第三个月 *dìsān gè yuè*. More examples are shown as follows:

(20) | 我国 | 政府 | 对于 | **21** | **世纪** | 的 | 来临， |
| --- | --- | --- | --- | --- | --- | --- |
| *wǒguó* | *zhèngfǔ* | *duìyú* | **èrshíyī** | **shìjì** | *de* | *láilín* |
| our.country | government | about | twenty-first | century | DE | come |

备有	堂堂的	"新的起点	新的生活,"	的	蓝图，
bèiyǒu	*tángtángde*	*xīnde qǐdiǎn*	*xīnde shēnghuó*	*de*	*lántú*
prepare	impressive	new starting	new life	DE	blueprint

人民	的	生活，	预想	中	可	达到
rénmín	*de*	*shēnghuó*	*yùxiǎng*	*zhōng*	*kě*	*dádào*
people	DE	life	expect	in	may	reach

与	瑞士	比美	的	地步。	（风筝 121）
yǔ	*ruìshì*	*bǐměi*	*de*	*dìbù*	
with	Switzerland	compare	DE	degree	

'Our government has a blueprint entitled "New Beginning, New Life" for the advent of the 21st century, and the life of the people is expected to be comparable to that of Switzerland.' (*Fēngzhēng* 121)

(21) | 相传 | 唐代 | 贞观 | **15 年** |
| --- | --- | --- | --- |
| *xiāngchuán* | *tángdài* | *zhēnguān* | **shíwǔnián** |
| according.to.the.legend | the.Tang.Dynasty | Zhenguan | the.fifteenth.year |

文成公主	与	藏王	松赞干布	联姻。（南北 71）
wénchénggōngzhǔ	*yǔ*	*zàngwáng*	*sōngzàngānbù*	*liányīn*
Princess.Wen.Cheng	and	Tibet.king	Songtsen.Gampo	get.married

'According to the legend, Princess Wen Cheng got married to Songtsen Gampo, the Tibetan king, in the fifteenth year of Zhenguan (641 AD).' (*Nánběi* 71)

(22) | 一九九二年 | 十一月 | 十八日 | 于 | 狮城（怀旧 • 自序） |
| --- | --- | --- | --- | --- |
| *yījiǔjiǔèrnián* | *shíyīyuè* | *shíbārì* | *yú* | *shīchéng* |
| nineteen.ninety.two | November | eighteenth.day | at | Singapore |

In Singapore, Nov. 18, 1992 (*Huáijiù Zìxù*)

(23) 傍晚　　七　　点　　三十　　分，　　许家　　　一　　家
　　 bàngwǎn　qī　　diǎn　sānshí　fēn　　xǔjiā　　　yī　　jiā
　　 dusk　　　seven　hour　thirty　minute　Hsu.family　one　CL

　　 四　　口　　仍然　　杳无踪迹。（再见 24）
　　 sì　　kǒu　réngrán　yǎowúzōngjì
　　 four　CL　still　　no.news.of

'By seven thirty in the evening, there was still no news of the four members of the Hsu Family.' (*Zàijiàn* 24)

Secondly, they are used to express the street number, house number, floor number, room number and postal code of specific locations. For example:

(24) 丧居：　　　　武吉巴督　**34**　　　街　　　大牌
　　 sàngjū　　　wǔjíbādū　**sānshísì**　jiē　　dàpái
　　 being.in.mourn　Bukit.Batok　thirty.four　street　block

　　 348　　　　楼下。（报 1995 年 4 月 19 日 29 版）
　　 sānsìbā　　 lóuxià
　　 three.four.eight　downstairs

'Bereavement: downstairs, Block 348 in Bukit Batok street No. 34.' (*Bào*, Apr. 19, 1995, Issue no. 29)

(25) 报告　　警长，　　案　　发　　地点　　是　　泉州街
　　 bàogào　jǐngzhǎng　àn　　fā　　dìdiǎn　shì　quánzhōujiē
　　 report　sheriff　　crime　happen　location　be　Quanzhou.Street

　　 三十七　　号　　　楼上，　　属于　　谋杀　　性质。（△断
　　　　　　　　　　　　　　　　　　　　　　　　　　　 情剪 35）
　　 sānshíqī　**hào**　lóushàng　shǔyú　móushā　xìngzhì
　　 thirty-seven　**number**　upstairs　belong　murder　nature

'Sheriff, the crime was a murder that happened upstairs at No. 37 Quanzhou Street.' (△*duànqíngjiǎn* 35)

(26) 有时　　　电梯　　坏　　了，　　唉哟哟，　　气喘吁吁地　　爬上
　　 yǒushí　diàntī　huài　le　　āiyōyo　　qìchuǎnxūde　páshàng
　　 sometimes　lift　broken　LE　ouch　　puff.and.pant　climb.up

50 Expressions of Number and Quantity

<table>
<tr><td>十三</td><td>楼，</td><td>再</td><td>汗流浃背的</td><td>踅下</td><td>十三</td><td>楼，</td></tr>
<tr><td>shísān</td><td>lóu</td><td>zài</td><td>hànliújiābèide</td><td>xuéxià</td><td>shísān</td><td>lóu</td></tr>
<tr><td>thirteen</td><td>layer</td><td>then</td><td>sweaty</td><td>walk.down</td><td>thirteen</td><td>layer</td></tr>
</table>

<table>
<tr><td>什么</td><td>赴宴</td><td></td><td>的</td><td>情趣，</td></tr>
<tr><td>shénme</td><td>fùyàn</td><td></td><td>de</td><td>qíngqù</td></tr>
<tr><td>whatever</td><td>attend.a.banquet</td><td></td><td>DE</td><td>happiness</td></tr>
</table>

<table>
<tr><td>都</td><td>破坏殆尽</td><td>了。</td><td>(△ 天长 65)</td></tr>
<tr><td>dōu</td><td>pòhuàidàijìn</td><td>le</td><td></td></tr>
<tr><td>all</td><td>break.down.totally</td><td>LE</td><td></td></tr>
</table>

'Sometimes the lift is broken. Oh no, panting up to the 13th floor and then sweating your way back down totally ruins the happiness of attending a banquet.' (Δ*Dàxǐ* 135)

(27)
<table>
<tr><td>" 那么，</td><td>十</td><td>号</td><td>房</td><td>在</td><td>哪儿？"</td></tr>
<tr><td>nàme</td><td>**shí**</td><td>**hào**</td><td>fáng</td><td>zài</td><td>nǎr</td></tr>
<tr><td>then</td><td>**ten**</td><td>**number**</td><td>room</td><td>at</td><td>where</td></tr>
</table>

<table>
<tr><td>萍妹</td><td>问。(△ 大喜 135)</td></tr>
<tr><td>píngmèi</td><td>wèn</td></tr>
<tr><td>Sister.Ping</td><td>ask</td></tr>
</table>

'"So, where is Room no. 10?" Sister Ping asked.' (Δ*Dàxǐ* 135)

(28)
<table>
<tr><td>当</td><td>他</td><td>重</td><td>回</td><td>产房</td><td>时，</td><td>他</td><td>才</td></tr>
<tr><td>dāng</td><td>tā</td><td>chóng</td><td>huí</td><td>chǎnfáng</td><td>shí</td><td>tā</td><td>cái</td></tr>
<tr><td>when</td><td>3SG</td><td>again</td><td>back</td><td>delivery.room</td><td>when</td><td>3SG</td><td>just</td></tr>
</table>

<table>
<tr><td>知道</td><td>产妇</td><td>已</td><td>被</td><td>转移</td><td>到</td><td>**五**</td><td>**号**</td></tr>
<tr><td>zhīdào</td><td>chǎnfù</td><td>yǐ</td><td>bèi</td><td>zhuǎnyí</td><td>dào</td><td>**wǔ**</td><td>**hào**</td></tr>
<tr><td>know</td><td>mother</td><td>already</td><td>BEI</td><td>transfer</td><td>to</td><td>**five**</td><td>**number**</td></tr>
</table>

<table>
<tr><td>病房</td><td>去</td><td>了。(追云 35)</td></tr>
<tr><td>bìngfáng</td><td>qù</td><td>le</td></tr>
<tr><td>ward</td><td>go</td><td>LE</td></tr>
</table>

'He did not know that the mother had already been sent to the No. 5 ward until he came back to the delivery room.' (*Zhuīyún* 35)

(29)
<table>
<tr><td>报名</td><td>表格</td><td>请</td><td>寄交</td><td>下列</td><td>地址：</td></tr>
<tr><td>bàomíng</td><td>biǎogé</td><td>qǐng</td><td>jìjiāo</td><td>xiàliè</td><td>dìzhǐ</td></tr>
<tr><td>apply</td><td>form</td><td>please</td><td>send.to</td><td>follow</td><td>address</td></tr>
</table>

Expressions of Number and Quantity 51

新城中学　　　　校长
xīnchéngzhōngxué　　xiàozhǎng
Xincheng.Middle.School　headmaster

美名路　　**12**　　号
měimínglù　　**shí'èr**　　hào
Meiming.Road　twelve　number

新加坡　　邮区　　　212525（Δ 高级课本 2B 18）
xīnjiāpō　　yóuqū　　èryī'èrwǔ'èrwǔ
Singapore　postal.district　two.one.two.five.two.five

'Please send the application form to the following address:
Headmaster of Xincheng Middle School
12, Meiming Road
Singapore postal district: 212525' (Δ*Gāojíkèběn* 2B, 18)

Thirdly, the ordinal numbers without auxiliary are used for phone numbers and fax numbers. For example:

(30) " 你　　有　　电话　　吗？"
　　　nǐ　　yǒu　　diànhuà　　ma
　　　2SG　have　phone　　SFP
　　　'Do you have a phone number?'

　　　" 有的！　你　　打　　**22345**　　　　　大洋　　贸易
　　　yǒude　　nǐ　　dǎ　　**èrèrsānsìwǔ**　　dàyáng　màoyì
　　　have　　2SG　call　two.two.three.four.five　Dayang　Trade

　　　公司　　找　　彼德黄　　就　　行了。（Δ 大喜 26）
　　　gōngsī　zhǎo　bǐdéhuáng　jiù　xíngle
　　　Company　find　Peter.Hwang　just　OK
　　　'Yes, I do. You can call 22345 at the Dayang Trade Company and ask for Peter Hwang.' (*Xīnchuán* 247)

(31) Ginvera　美容　　服务　　中心，　　电话：
　　　Ginvera　měiróng　fúwù　　zhōngxīn　diànhuà
　　　Ginvera　beauty　service　centre　　telephone

　　　2960364,
　　　èrjiǔliùlíngsānliùsì
　　　two.nine.six.zero.three.six.four

52 *Expressions of Number and Quantity*

学生　　　热线：　　2980288（薪传　247）
xuéshēng　rèxiàn　　èrjiǔbālíngèrbābā
student　　hotline　two.nine.eight.zero.two.eight.eight
'Beauty Service Centre, telephone: 2960364, student hotline: 2980288.'
(*Xīnchuán* 247)

(32) 和美　　发展　　私人　　有限　　公司　　电话：
　　　héměi　fāzhǎn　sīrén　yǒuxiàn　gōngsī　diànhuà
　　　Hemei　develop　private　limit　company　telephone

7487522,　　　传真：　　**7459167**
　　　　　　　　　　　　　　（报　1995 年 4 月 22 日 18 版）
qīsìbāqīwǔèrèr　*chuánzhēn*　***qīsìwǔjiǔyīliùqī***
seven.four.eight.　fax　　**seven.four.five.nine.one.six.seven**
seven.five.two.two
'Hemei Development Pte Ltd. Telephone: 7487522, Fax: 7459167.'
(*Bào*, Apr. 22, 1995, Issue no. 18)

Fourthly, the ordinal numbers without auxiliary are used to indicate public transportation including flight numbers and bus numbers. For example:

(33) 一月　　六　　日，　他　乘坐　　新加坡　　航空　　公司
　　　yīyuè　liù　rì　tā　chéngzuò　xīnjiāpō　hángkōng　gōngsī
　　　January　sixth　day　3SG　take　Singapore　airline　company

SQ802　航班　　的　　飞机　　到达　　了　　北京。
SQ_bālíng'èr_　hángbān　de　fēijī　dàodá　le　běijīng
SQ802　airline　DE　aeroplane　arrive　LE　Beijing
'On January 6, he took Singapore Airlines flight SQ802 to Beijing.'

(34) 八达　　　控股有限公司　　　文告　　说，　　乌节弯路
　　　bādá,　kònggǔyǒuxiàngōngsī　wéngào　shuō　wūjiéwānlù
　　　Octopus　Holdings.Limited　statement　say　Orchard.Turn

的　新　　停车站　　　昨天　　启用。
de　xīn　tíngchēzhàn　zuótiān　qǐyòng
DE　new　stop　　　yesterday　use

文告　　说，　八达　　　167　　　号　　182　　　号
wéngào　shuō　bādá　yīliùqī　hào　yībāèr　hào
statement　say　Octopus　one.six.seven　CL　one.eight.two　CL

和	952	号	巴士,	市区	短程巴士
hé	jiǔwǔèr	hào	bāshì	shìqū	duǎnchéngbāshì
and	nine.five.two	CL	bus	city	city.bus

3	号	和	5	号,	以及	豪华小巴
sān	hào	hé	wǔ	hào	yǐjí	háohuáxiǎobā
three	CL	and	five	CL	and	luxury.bus

9	号	与	10	号,	将	不会	驶经
jiǔ	hào	yǔ	shí	hào	jiāng	bùhuì	shǐjīng
nine	CL	and	ten	CL	will	not	pass

乌节连路　　的　　停车站。（报 1995 年 5 月 8 日 4 版）
wūjiéliánlù　　de　　tíngchēzhàn
Orchard.Link　DE　stop

The new stop at Orchard Turn opened yesterday, according to a statement from Octopus Holdings Limited. Buses No. 167, 182 and 952, city buses No. 3 and No. 5, and luxury minibuses No. 9 and No. 10 will not pass by the stop on Orchard Link, the statement said. (*Bào*, May 8, 1995, p. 4)

(35)
最后	一	辆	双层的	**七**	**号**	巴士	载
zuìhòu	yī	liàng	shuāngcéng-de	**qī**	**hào**	bāshì	zǎi
last	one	CL	double-deck	**seven**	**number**	bus	load

了	一	群	少年。（青青 32）
le	yī	qún	shàonián
LE	one	CL	teenager

'The last double-decker bus No. 7 carried a group of teenagers.' (*Qīngqīng* 32)

Fifthly, the ordinal numbers without auxiliary are used to indicate general serial numbers. For example:

(36)
在	发掘	的	13	座	墓	中,
zài	fājué	de	shísān	zuò	mù	zhōng
at	excavate	DE	thirteen	CL	tomb	inside

出土的	砖	壁画	共	有	660	幅,...
chūtǔde	zhuān	bìhuà	gòng	yǒu	liùbǎiliùshí	fú
excavated	brick	mural	totally	have	six.hundred.sixty	CL

54 Expressions of Number and Quantity

其中　　6　　号　　墓　　就　　有　　122
qízhōng liù hào mù jiù yǒu yībǎièrshíèr
besides six CL tomb just have one.hundred.twenty.two

幅，　占　　出土　　总数　　的　　百分之二十　(南北 65－66)
fú,   zhàn chūtǔ zǒngshù de bǎifēnzhīèrshí
CL   account excavate total DE twenty.percent

'In the 13 tombs excavated, a total of 660 brick murals were unearthed, ... of which 122 were in Tomb 6, accounting for 20 percent of the total number unearthed.' (*Nánběi* 65–66)

(37) 聘请　　日班　　或　　夜班　　巴士　　司机，　须　　有
     pìnqǐng rìbān huò yèbān bāshì sījī, xū yǒu
     hire day.shift or night.shift bus driver must have

4　　号　　驾驶　　执照　　和　　手牌。
（报 1995 年 4 月 30 日 34 版）
sì hào jiàshǐ zhízhào hé shǒupái
four number drive license and GDL

'Bus drivers for day shift or night shift wanted: a No. 4 driver's licence and GDL are required.' (*Bào*, Apr. 30, 1995, Issue no. 34)

(38) " 报告　警长，　这里　发生　　了　命案！"
     bàogào jǐngzhǎng, zhèlǐ fāshēng le mìng'àn
     report sheriff here take.place LE murder

'Sheriff, I report that there's been a murder here!'

3721　　　　号　　警员　　向　　我　　作　　了
sānqīèryī hào jǐngyuán xiàng wǒ zuò le
three.seven.two.one number policeman to 1SG do LE

报告。（报 1995 年 4 月 30 日 34 版）
bàogào
report

'Policeman No. 3721 made a report to me.' (Δ*duànqíngjiǎn* 34)

(39) 槟城　　赛马　　开彩　　揭晓，　光业　　果然
     bīnchéng sàimǎ kāicǎi jiēxiǎo, guāngyè guǒrán
     Penang horse.race draw announce Kwong.Yip indeed

Expressions of Number and Quantity 55

中	了	万字头奖，	赢得	十	多	千，
zhòng	le	wànzìtóujiǎng	yíngdé	shí	duō	qiān
win	LE	jackpot	win	ten	more	thousand

他	买	的	号码	是	"3 1 0 8"。	(追云 60)
tā	mǎi	de	hàomǎ	shì	sānyīlíngbā	
3SG	buy	DE	number	be	three.one.zero.eight	

'The Penang horse race draw result came out and Kwong Yip indeed won the jackpot, winning more than 10,000. The number he bought is "3 1 0 8".' (*Zhuīyún* 60)

1.9.3 Two Additional Points About Ordinals

Firstly, expressions such as 初一 *chūyī* 'the first day of a lunar month', 初二 *chū'èr* 'the second day of a lunar month' and 初三 *chūsān* 'the third day of a lunar month', used in the Chinese lunar calendar, are not ordinals. The use of such expressions is illustrated in the following examples:

(40)

只有	每	年	在	农历	大年	**初一，**
zhǐyǒu	měi	nián	zài	nónglì	dànián	**chūyī**
only	each	year	on	lunar.calendar	New.Year	**first.day**

才	有	机会	见见	那	衰老的	容颜。(△ 大喜 172)
cái	yǒu	jīhuì	jiàn-jiàn	nà	shuāilǎode	róngyán
only	have	chance	see-see	that	old	complexion

'Only on the first day of each Lunar New Year does (he) get the chance to see that ageing face.' (△*Dàxǐ 172*)

(41)

农历	七月	**初七，**	是	七夕	也
nónglì	qīyuè	**chūqī**	shì	qīxī	yě
lunar.calendar	seventh.month	**seventh.day**	be	Qixi.Festival	also

叫	乞巧节。(报 1995 年 5 月 3 日副刊 2 版)
jiào	qǐqiǎojié
call	Qiqiao.Festival

'The seventh day of the seventh month in the lunar calendar is the Qixi Festival (Chinese Valentine's Day), also known as the Qiqiao Festival.' (*Bào*, May 3, 1995, Issue no. 2, supplementary edition)

初*chū* 'the first' in this case differs from auxiliary 第 *dì* and cannot be regarded as auxiliary indicating ordinals. 初 *chū* here means 'to begin', or 'the first' (see

Modern Chinese Dictionary). Numerals from 一 *yī* 'one' to 十 *shí* 'ten' all appear three times in marking days in a lunar month. Take 七 *qī* 'seven' as an example: It is used three times, as in 七 *qī* 'seven', 十七 *shíqī* 'seventeen' and 二十七 *èrshíqī* 'twenty-seven'. The 七 *qī* 'seven' that appears the earliest is called 初七 *chūqī*, which means the first 'seven'. The same goes with 初一 *chūyī*, 初二 *chūèr* and 初三 *chūsān*, which are different from 第一 *dìyī* 'the first', 第二 *dìèr* 'the second' and 第三 *dìsān* 'the third', so they are not ordinals.

Secondly, some appellations for relatives, like 老二 *lǎoèr* 'the second child' and 三弟 *sāndì* 'the third brother', are not ordinals. See the following examples for such expressions:

(42) 老二　　　刚　踏　入　家　门，
lǎoèr　　　*gāng*　*tà*　*rù*　*jiā*　*mén*
second.child　just　step　into　house　door

就　急不及待地　冲　着　我　说：" 妈 …"
jiù　*jíbùjídài-de*　*chòng*　*zhe*　*wǒ*　*shuō*　*mā*
then　cannot.wait　face　ZHE　1SG　say　mum

'As soon as my second child stepped into the house, [he] couldn't wait to say to me: "Mum."'

(43) 二哥　　　　和　四弟　　　　换　了　衣服
èrgē　　　　*hé*　*sìdì*　　　　*huàn*　*le*　*yīfu*
second.brother　and　fourth.brother　change　LE　clothes

走　出　大　门 …（短篇 62）
zǒu　*chū*　*dà*　*mén*
walk　out　big　door

'The second and fourth brothers changed their clothes and walked out the door …' (*Duǎnpiān* 62)

(44) 我　的　祖父、八叔　　　　一　家　都　葬
wǒ　*de*　*zǔfù*　*bāshū*　　　*yī*　*jiā*　*dōu*　*zàng*
1SG　DE　grandpa　eighth.uncle　one　family　all　bury

于　此！（至性 138）
yú　*cǐ*
at　here

'My grandfather and eighth uncle's family are all buried here!' (*Zhìxìng*, 138)

Expressions such as 老二 *lǎoèr*, 二哥 *èrgē*, 四弟 *sìdì* and 八叔 *bāshū* undoubtedly indicate meanings of ranking, but they themselves are definitely not ordinals. They are only common nouns referring to people. Also, 二 *èr* 'two', 四 *sì* 'four' and 八 *bā* 'eight' here are not ordinals but morphemes indicating numbers.

1.10 Classifiers

We briefly introduced classifiers in Section 3.8 of Volume I. We mentioned that classifiers are units of measurement of things or actions, or of time.

Generally speaking, classifiers that express the measurement of things (including people) are called 名量词 *míngliàngcí* 'nominal classifiers', such as 个 *gè* 'CL', 粒 *lì* 'CL' and 间 *jiān* 'CL'; classifiers that express measurement of actions are called 动量词 *dòngliàngcí* 'verbal classifiers', such as 次 *cì* 'time', 回 *huí* 'time' and 下 *xià* 'bit'; classifiers that express measurement of time are called 时量词 *shíliìngcí* 'temporal classifiers', such as 年 *nián* 'year', 天 *tiān* 'day' and 分钟 *fēnzhōng* 'minute'.

Since classifiers are words that express units of measurement, their most significant grammatical function is to be modified by numerals and thus form numeral-classifier compounds. For example:

三个	*sāngè* 'three (ones)'	(*Tàiyáng* 71)	numeral + nominal classifier
一次	*yīcì* 'one time'	(*Tàiyáng* 54)	numeral + verbal classifier
十年	*shínián* 'ten years'	(*Tàiyáng* 65)	numeral + temporal classifier

Grammatically, this type of numeral-classifier compound is an 'attribute-head' endocentric phrase, with the numeral as the attribute and the classifier as the head (see Sections 8.3 and 8.9 in Volume I).

Classifiers can also be used with demonstrative pronouns, such as 这 *zhè* 'this' or 那 *nà* 'that', and interrogative pronouns such as 哪 *nǎ* 'which'. Take a nominal classifier 个 *gè* as an example:

这个	*zhègè*	'this one'	(*Xiàoyǎn* 13)
那个	*nàgè*	'that one'	(*Xiàoyǎn* 21)
哪个	*nǎgè*	'which one'	(*Xiàoyǎn* 164)

In fact, in these phrases, pronouns 这 *zhè* 'this'/ 那 *nà* 'that'/ 哪 *nǎ* 'which' do not modify the classifier 个 *gè* 'CL', but 一个 *yīgè* 'one- CL', only that numeral 一 *yī* 'one' here is omitted. In other words, 这个 *zhègè* 'this one'/ 那个 *nàgè* 'that one'/ 哪个 *nǎgè* 'which one' are actually abbreviated forms of 这一个 *zhèyīgè* 'this one'/ 那一个 *nàyīgè* 'that one'/ 哪一个 *nǎyīgè* 'which one', as shown in the examples quoted from Tian Liu's *Collection of Crosstalk: A Laughing Eye on Life*:

58 Expressions of Number and Quantity

(1) 个 : a. 给 你 改 了 这 一 **个** 名字,
gè   gěi nǐ gǎi le zhè yī **gè** míngzì
       give 2SG change LE this one **CL** name

   是 最 理想 不过 了。(笑眼 24)
   shì zuì lǐxiǎng bùguò le
   be most ideal not.pass LE
   'I changed this name for you, which cannot be more ideal.' (Xiàoyǎn 24)

   b 这 **个** 姓 不 太 理想 ...(笑眼 22)
   zhè **gè** xìng bù tài lǐxiǎng
   this **CL** family.name NEG too ideal
   'This last name isn't so ideal ...' (Xiàoyǎn 22)

(2) 句 : a 还 是 你 这 一 **句** 话
jù   hái shì nǐ zhè yī **jù** huà
       still SHI 2SG this one **CL** sentence

   比较 有 分量 !(笑眼 34)
   bǐjiào yǒu fènliàng
   comparatively have weight
   'It's your words that carry more weight.' (Xiàoyǎn 34)

   b 这 **句** 话 就 不 合 逻辑 了。(笑眼 112)
   zhè **jù** huà jiù bù hé luójí le
   this **CL** sentence thus NEG match logic LE
   'This sentence doesn't make any sense.' (Xiàoyǎn 122)

(3) 副 : a 就 凭 您 老哥 这 一 **副** 长相,
fù   jiù píng nín lǎogē zhè yī **fù** zhǎngxiāng
       then depend.on 2SG brother this one **CL** appearance

   可 真 是 " 亮 " 得 很 哪 !(笑眼 114)
   kě zhēn shì liàng dé hěn na
   can really SHI shiny DE very SFP
   'With your appearance, you are indeed a shiny person!' (Xiàoyǎn 114)

Expressions of Number and Quantity   59

  b 瞧   你   这   **副** 模样，   才   像
    *qiáo nǐ   zhè **fù** móyàng   cái   xiàng*
    look 2SG this **CL** appearance only like

    个   " 活死人 "！（笑眼 9）
    gè   huósǐrén
    CL   the.living.dead
    'Look at you! You really look like the living dead!' (*Xiàoyǎn* 9)

(4) 首： a 告诉   你，   我   这   一   **首**   是   "无底诗"。
                   （笑眼 41）
 shǒu *gàosù nǐ   wǒ   zhè   yī   **shǒu**   shì   wúdǐshī*
    tell   2SG   1SG   this one   **CL**   be   bottomless.poem
   'I tell you that this poem of mine is a "bottomless poem".'
   (*Xiàoyǎn* 41)

  b 这   **首**   诗谜   的   谜底， 应该   是   风！
                 （笑眼 41）
    *zhè **shǒu** shīmí   de   mídǐ   yīnggāi shì fēng*
    this **CL**   poetic.riddle DE key   should   be   wind
    'The answer to this poetic riddle should be wind!' (*Xiàoyǎn* 41)

(5) 种： a 我   这   一   **种**   在   赌国   里
 zhǒng *wǒ zhè   yī   **zhǒng** zài dǔguó   lǐ*
    1SG this one   **CL**   at   gambling.realm in

   出生   的   "博士"…（笑眼 124）
   chūshēng   de   bóshì
   born   DE   doctor
   'I am this kind of "doctor" in the realm of gambling…'
   (*Xiàoyǎn* 124)

  b 像   阁下   您   这   **种**   "麻将博士"…
               （笑眼 124）
    *xiàng géxià   nín   zhè   **zhǒng** májiāng bóshì*
    like   your.grace 2SG   this **CL**   doctor.of.mahjong
    'A "doctor of mahjong" like your grace…' (*Xiàoyǎn* 124)

(6) 条: a 这   一   **条**   巷   正在   开辟   中 --
            tiáo   zhè   yī   **tiáo**   xiàng   zhèngzài   kāipì   zhōng
                   this one   CL   alley   in.process.of construct middle
                                                                    （笑眼 245）

'This alley is under construction –' (*Xiàoyǎn* 245)

b 你   就   快   要   听   人   提   起
   nǐ   jiù   kuài   yào   tīng   rén   tí   qǐ
   2SG   thus nearly need   listen   people mention up

这   **条**   巷   咯 !（笑眼 245）
zhè   **tiáo**   xiàng   gē
this CL   alley   SFP

'You are about to hear people mention this alley!' (*Xiàoyǎn* 245)

In these examples, a numeral, 一 *yī* 'one', precedes the classifiers in sentence (a), but not in sentence (b). The deletion of 一 *yī* 'one' from sentence (a) or the addition of 一 *yī* 'one' in sentence (b) will not result in any change of the original meanings of these sentences. As for which of the two expressions '这 *zhè* 'this' / 那 *nà* 'that' + classifier' and '这 *zhè* 'this'/ 那 *nà* 'that' + 一 *yī* 'one' + classifier' is more frequent in Singapore Mandarin, though no comprehensive survey is done, the statistics from Tian Liu's *Collection of Crosstalk: A Laughing Eye on Life* (a 258-page book) are provided here for reference:

Structure	Count
这 *zhè* 'this'/ 那 *nà* 'that' + 一 *yī* 'one' + classifier	52 times
这 *zhè* 'this'/ 那 *nà* 'that' + classifier	99 times
哪 *nǎ* 'which' + 一 *yī* 'one' + classifier	25 times
哪 *nǎ* 'which' + classifier	5 times

Many monosyllabic classifiers can be duplicated and convey meanings of 'every' or 'all'. For example:

(7) **个**   **个**   容光焕发,   衣着   鲜   华。(变调 72)
    gè   **gè**   róngguānghuànfā   yīzhuó   xiān   huá
    CL   CL   radiant   clothes   vivid   splendid

'All of them were radiant and well-dressed.' (*Biàndiào* 72)

(8) 有   一阵子,   几乎   **天**   **天**   有   诗。(Δ 自然 106)
    yǒu   yīzhènzi   jīhū   **tiān**   **tiān**   yǒu   shī
    have   a.while   almost   CL   CL   have   poem

'For many days, there were poems almost every day.' (Δ*Zìrán* 106)

Expressions of Number and Quantity

(9) 这些 全 是 "作家" 们 的 **条 条** 财路。（笑眼 122）
zhèxiē quán shì zuòjiāmen de **tiáo tiáo** cáilù
these all be writers DE CL CL means.for.making.money
'These are all the ways for "writers" to make money.' (*Xiàoyǎn* 122)

In examples (7) and (8), the reduplicated classifiers serve as subjects, while in example (9), they are used as an attribute. In example (7), 个个容光焕发 *gè gè róngguānghuànfā* means 'everyone was radiant'; in example (9), 条条财路 *tiáo tiáo cáilù* means 'all the ways of making money'.

In the following, we will make further introductions to nominal, verbal and temporal classifiers.

1.11 Nominal Classifiers

In general, nominal classifiers are unit words used to count or measure things (including people) and can be further divided into the following six subtypes.

1.11.1 Individual Nominal Classifiers

Things that can be counted one by one are usually modified by specific classifiers. For example, books are modified by 本 *běn*, flowers by 朵 *duǒ*, knives by 把 *bǎ* and so on. This type of classifier is called an 'individual nominal classifier', as illustrated by the following examples:

间:	两	**间**	公司		一	**间**	学校
jiān	liǎng	**jiān**	gōngsī		yī	**jiān**	xuéxiào
	two	CL	company		one	CL	school
	'two companies'				'a school'		

幢:	一	**幢**	楼房		一	**幢**	公寓
zhuàng	yī	**zhuàng**	lóufáng		yī	**zhuàng**	gōngyù
	one	CL	building		one	CL	flat
	'a building'				'a flat'		

只:	三	**只**	眼睛		一	**只**	鸡
zhī	sān	**zhī**	yǎnjīng		yī	**zhī**	jī
	three	CL	eye		one	CL	chicken
	'three eyes'				'a chicken'		

条:	一	**条**	尾巴		一	**条**	长裤
tiáo	yī	**tiáo**	wěiba		yī	**tiáo**	chángkù
	one	CL	tail		one	CL	trousers
	'a tail'				'a pair of trousers'		

Expressions of Number and Quantity

个：	一	**个**	男孩		三	**个**	庭院
gè	yī	**gè**	nánhái		sān	**gè**	tíngyuàn
	one	CL	boy		three	CL	backyard
	'a boy'				'three backyards'		

粒：	一	**粒**	石子		一	**粒**	球
lì	yī	**lì**	shízǐ		yī	**lì**	qiú
	one	CL	stone		one	CL	ball
	'a stone'				'a ball'		

张：	一	**张**	脸		一	**张**	白纸
zhāng	yī	**zhāng**	liǎn		yī	**zhāng**	báizhǐ
	one	CL	face		one	CL	white.paper
	'a face'				'a piece of white paper'		

把：	一	**把**	雨伞		一	**把**	刀
bǎ	yī	**bǎ**	yǔsǎn		yī	**bǎ**	dāo
	one	CL	umbrella		one	CL	knife
	'an umbrella'				'a knife'		

朵：	一	**朵**	荷花		一	**朵**	玫瑰
duǒ	yī	**duǒ**	héhuā		yī	**duǒ**	méiguī
	one	CL	lotus		one	CL	rose
	'a lotus'				'a rose'		

棵：	一	**棵**	大树		一	**棵**	椰树
kē	yī	**kē**	dàshù		yī	**kē**	yēshù
	one	CL	big.tree		one	CL	coconut.palm
	'a big tree'				'a coconut palm'		

件：	一	**件**	事		一	**件**	乐器
jiàn	yī	**jiàn**	shì		yī	**jiàn**	yuèqì
	one	CL	thing		one	CL	musical.instrument
	'one thing'				'a musical instrument'		

本：	一	**本**	书		一	**本**	汉语	辞典
běn	yī	**běn**	shū		yī	**běn**	hànyǔ	cídiǎn
	one	CL	book		one	CL	Chinese	dictionary
	'a book'				'a Chinese dictionary'			

Expressions of Number and Quantity

根:	一	根	头发		一	根	棍子
gēn	yī	**gēn**	tóufà		yī	**gēn**	gùnzi
	one	CL	hair		one	CL	stick
	'a hair'				'a stick'		

位:	一	位	教员		一	位	女	作家
wèi	yī	**wèi**	jiàoyuán		yī	**wèi**	nǚ	zuòjiā
	one	CL	teacher		one	CL	female	writer
	'a teacher'				'a female writer'			

片:	两	片	落叶		一	小	片	面包
piàn	liǎng	**piàn**	luòyè		yī	xiǎo	**piàn**	miànbāo
	two	CL	fallen.leaves		one	small	CL	bread
	'two fallen leaves'				'a small slice of bread'			

盏:	一	盏	灯笼		一	盏	灯
zhǎn	yī	**zhǎn**	dēnglóng		yī	**zhǎn**	dēng
	one	CL	lantern		one	CL	light
	'a lantern'				'a light'		

颗:	一	颗	心		一	颗	流星
kē	yī	**kē**	xīn		yī	**kē**	liúxīng
	one	CL	heart		one	CL	meteor
	'a heart'				'a meteor'		

辆:	一	辆	的士		一	辆	坦克
liàng	yī	**liàng**	dīshì		yī	**liàng**	tǎnkè
	one	CL	taxi		one	CL	tank
	'a taxi'				'a tank'		

首:	一	首	歌		4	首	新诗
shǒu	yī	**shǒu**	gē		sì	**shǒu**	xīnshī
	one	CL	song		four	CL	new.style.poem
	'a song'				'four new style poems'		

幅:	一	幅	画		一	幅	宜人的	景象
fú	yī	**fú**	huà		yī	**fú**	yírénde	jǐngxiàng
	one	CL	painting		one	CL	pleasant	scene
	'a painting'				'a pleasant scene'			

64   *Expressions of Number and Quantity*

扇:	一	**扇**	门		几	**扇**	窗
shàn	*yī*	***shàn***	*mén*		*jǐ*	***shàn***	*chuāng*
	one	**CL**	door		several	**CL**	window
	'a door'				'several windows'		

封:	一	**封**	信
fēng	*yī*	***fēng***	*xìn*
	one	**CL**	letter
	'a letter'		

1.11.2 Collective Nominal Classifiers

Classifiers that are used to count or measure things by pairs or groups are generally called 'collective nominal classifiers'. Here are some examples:

(1) 她 低 着 头, 一 **双** 手, 紧张 不安地
tā *dī* *zhe* *tóu* *yī* ***shuāng*** *shǒu* *jǐnzhāng* *bùān-de*
3SG lower ZHE head one **CL** hand nervously restlessly

抓 着 裙子；一 **双** 眼, 惶恐 不安地
zhuā *zhe* *qúnzi* *yī* ***shuāng*** *yǎn* *huángkǒng* *bùān-de*
grab ZHE skirt one **CL** eye in.panic restlessly

瞪 着 地板。(跳舞 72)
dèng *zhe* *dìbǎn*
stare ZHE floor

'She lowered her head, her hands grabbing at her skirts nervously, her eyes staring at the floor in fear.' (*Tiàowǔ* 72)

双 *shuāng* in example (1) is a collective nominal classifier. 一双手 *yīshuāng shǒu* means 'a pair of hands' and 一双眼 *yīshuāng yǎn* refers to 'a pair of eyes'. Some commonly used collective nominal classifiers are as follows:

对:	一	**对**	情侣		一	**对**	耳朵
duì	*yī*	***duì***	*qínglǚ*		*yī*	***duì***	*ěrduo*
	one	**CL**	lovers		one	**CL**	ear
	'a couple of lovers'				'a pair of ears'		

Expressions of Number and Quantity

双: 两 **双** 筷子   一 **双** 运动鞋
shuāng   liǎng **shuāng** kuàizi   yī **shuāng** yùndòngxié
         two   CL   chopstick   one   CL   sport.shoes
         'two pairs of chopsticks'   'a pair of sports shoes'

群: 一 **群** 乌鸦   一 **群** 好友
qún   yī **qún** wūyā   yī **qún** hǎoyǒu
         one   CL   crow   one   CL   friend
         'a flock of crows'   'a group of friends'

批: 一 **批** 年轻人   一 **批** 人马
pī   yī **pī** niánqīngrén   yī **pī** rénmǎ
         one   CL   young.man   one   CL   people
         'a group of young men'   'a group of people'

串: 一 **串** 假 珍珠   一 大 **串** 钥匙
chuàn   yī **chuàn** jiǎ zhēnzhū   yī dà **chuàn** yàoshi
         one   CL   fake   pearl   one   big   CL   key
         'a string of fake pearls'   'a big bunch of keys'

套: 一 **套** 沙发   六 **套** 邮票
tào   yī **tào** shāfā   liù **tào** yóupiào
         one   CL   sofa   six   CL   stamp
         'a sofa set'   'six sets of stamps'

排: 一 **排** 座位   一 **排** 旧式 房屋
pái   yī **pái** zuòwèi   yī **pái** jiùshì fángwū
         one   CL   seat   one   CL   old.style   house
         'a row of seats'   'a row of old style houses'

打: 一 **打** 啤酒   部分: 一 **部分** 车辆
dǎ   yī **dǎ** píjiǔ   **bùfèn**   yī **bùfèn** chēliàng
         one   CL   beer   one   CL   car
         'a dozen beers'   'part of the cars'

66 Expressions of Number and Quantity

系列：	一	**系列**	散文		一	**系列**	行动
xìliè	yī	**xìliè**	sǎnwén		yī	**xìliè**	xíngdòng
	one	CL	prose		one	CL	action
	\'a series of prose pieces\'				\'a series of actions\'		

1.11.3 Measure Words

Classifiers that denote units of measurement are generally called 'measure words', such as 尺 *chǐ* 'chi', 公斤 *gōngjīn* 'kilogram', 公里 *gōnglǐ* 'kilometre' and so on. Classifiers that denote monetary units, such as 元（块）*yuán* (*kuài*) 'yuan', 角（毛）*jiǎo* (*máo*) 'ten cents' and 分 *fēn* 'cent' are also called measure words.[9] Here are some examples:

公里 *gōnglǐ*:   210 公里 *liǎngbǎiyīshí gōnglǐ* '210 kilometres'
　　　　　　　二十一公里 *èrshíyī gōnglǐ* 'twenty-one kilometres'

米 *mǐ*:   三米 *sān mǐ* 'three metres'
　　　　1.6米 *yìdiǎnliù mǐ* '1.6 metres'

公尺 *gōngchǐ*:   一公尺 *yī gōngchǐ* 'a metre'

吋 *cùn*:   十余吋 *shí yú cùn* 'more than ten inches'

里 *lǐ*:   八千里 *bāqiān lǐ* 'eight thousand lis'

丈 *zhàng*:   十丈 *shí zhàng* 'ten zhangs'

尺 *chǐ*:   十二尺 *shíèr chǐ* 'twelve chis'
　　　　一尺 *yī chǐ* 'one chi'

寸 *cùn*:   一寸 *yī cùn* 'one cun'
　　　　二十八寸 *èrshíbā cùn* 'twenty eight cuns'

斤 *jīn*:   三斤 *sān jīn* 'three jins'
　　　　四斤 *sì jīn* 'four jins'

两 *liǎng*:   一两 *yī liǎng* 'one liang'
　　　　二十克 *èrshí kè* 'twenty grams'

元 *yuán*:   五元 *wǔ yuán* 'five yuans'
　　　　一元 *yī yuán* 'one yuan'

磅 *bàng*: 十几**磅** *shíjǐ bàng* 'more than ten pounds'

毛 *máo*: 五**毛** *wǔ máo* 'five maos'

块 *kuài*: 十**块** *shí kuài* 'ten yuans'
一百**块** *yībǎi kuài* 'a hundred yuans'

角 *jiǎo*: 五**角** *wǔ jiǎo* 'five jiaos'
一**角** *yī jiǎo* 'one jiao'

1.11.4 Categorical Nominal Classifiers

There are only two categorical nominal classifiers in Singapore Mandarin: 种 *zhǒng* 'kind' and 类 *lèi* 'class'. These are shown in the following examples:
For 种 *zhǒng* 'kind':

(2) 两 **种** 果子： 日本 梨子 和 台湾 蜜柑。（风雨 11）
liǎng **zhǒng** *guǒzi* *rìběn* *lízi* *hé* *táiwān* *mìgān*
two **CL** fruit Japanese pear and Taiwan tangerine
'There are two kinds of fruit, pears from Japan and tangerines from Taiwan.' (*Fēngyǔ* 11)

(3) 寂寞 是 怎样 一 **种** 苦味 呢？（太阳 12）
jìmò *shì* *zěnyàng* *yī* **zhǒng** *kǔwèi* *ne*
loneliness be how one **CL** bitterness SFP
'What kind of bitter taste is loneliness?' (*Tàiyáng* 12)

For 类 *lèi* 'class':

(4) 现在 还 有 点 时间, 好 不 好
xiànzài *hái* *yǒu* *diǎn* *shíjiān* *hǎo* *bù* *hǎo*
now still have CL time good NEG good
分析 一 下 这 三 **类** 文人 的 丑态？（笑眼 66）
fēnxī *yī* *xià* *zhè* *sān* **lèi** *wénrén* *de* *chǒutài*
analyse one CL this three **CL** literatus DE buffoonery

'Since we still have time now, can we analyse the buffoonery of the three categories of literati?' (*Xiàoyǎn* 66)

(5) 人选   可   分为   两   **类**,   一   是   出钱
     rénxuǎn *kě* *fēnwéi*   *liǎng* **lèi** *yī* *shì* *chūqián*
     candidate can   divide.into two   **CL**   one   be   chip.in

  的   人,   一   是   出力   的   人。（薪传 117）
  de *rén* *yī* *shì* *chūlì*   *de* *rén*
  DE   person one be   give.strength   DE   person

'The candidates fall into two categories: those who give money, and those who give strength.' (*Xīnchuán* 117)

1.11.5 Indefinite Nominal Classifiers

There are only two indefinite nominal classifiers, 些 *xiē* 'some' and 点（儿）*diǎn(er)* 'a bit', which are usually used to express uncertain quantity. The numeral that precedes indefinite classifiers is limited to 一 *yī* 'one'. For example:

些: 一   **些**   朋友   （有）   一   **些**   道理
xiē *yī* **xiē**   *péngyou*   *yǒu*   *yī* **xiē**   *dàolǐ*
       one   **CL**   friend   have   one   **CL**   truth
       'some friends'   '(have) some truth'

点（儿）: （出）   一   **点**   力   （花 了）   一   **点**   时间
diǎn (er) *chū*   *yī* **diǎn**   *lì*   *huā le*   *yī*   **diǎn** *shíjiān*
            use   one   **CL**   strength cost   LE   one   **CL**   time
            '(spent) a little effort'   'take a little while'

In Singapore Mandarin, there is a tendency in the choice of indefinite nominal classifiers: 些 *xiē* 'some' is preferred when it comes to concrete objects, especially for countable things; while for abstract things, 点（儿）*diǎn(er)* 'a bit' is more often used.

1.11.6 Temporary Nominal Classifiers

Some nouns indicating containers can also be temporarily used as classifiers, as their loading capacity can be used as measuring units. These are called temporary nominal classifiers. Please compare the following two groups of examples:

(6)a. 水槽 **碗** 碟 堆积如山， 粘 在 **碗** 碟
shuǐcáo **wǎn** dié duījīrúshān zhān zài **wǎn** dié
basin **bowl** plate pile.like.mountains stick at **bowl** plate

上 的 食物 的 残渣， 干 而 硬 ...(跳舞 6)
shàng de shíwù de cánzhā gān ér yìng
on DE food DE remains dry and hard

'The bowls and plates are piled up like a mountain in the basin, while the dry and hard food remains sticking to them.' (*Tiàowǔ* 6)

b. 她 一 手 拿 **碗**, 一 手 拿 筷子 ...（追云 48）
tā yī shǒu ná **wǎn** yī shǒu ná kuàizi
3SG one hand hold **bowl** one hand hold chopsticks

'She held a bowl in one hand and chopsticks in the other.' (*Zhuīyún* 48)

(7)a. 买 了 一 **碗** 面， 邓文茵 独自 一 人
mǎi le yī **wǎn** miàn dèngwényīn dúzì yī rén
buy LE one **CL/bowl** noodle Deng.Wenyin alone one person

静静地 吃。（跳舞 91）
jìngjìng-de chī
quietly eat

'Deng Wenyin bought a bowl of noodles and ate quietly by herself.' (*Tiàowǔ* 91)

b. 去 中餐馆 吃 一 **碗** 云吞面， 也
qù zhōngcānguǎn chī yī **wǎn** yúntūnmiàn yě
go Chinese.restaurant eat one **CL/bowl** wonton.noodle also

需 三 镑 多 ...（风筝 196）
xū sān bàng duō
need three pound more

'It also costs more than three pounds to have a bowl of wonton noodles in a Chinese restaurant.' (*Fēngzhēng* 196)

In example (6), 碗 *wǎn* 'bowl' is used as a noun that refers to a utensil for serving food. In example (7), it is temporarily borrowed as a nominal classifier to serve as a measuring unit of 面 *miàn* 'noodle' and 云吞面 *yúntūnmiàn* 'wonton noodle'. More examples are shown as follows:

桶： 一 **桶** 水
tǒng *yī* ***tǒng*** *shuǐ*
     one **CL/pail** water
     'a pail of water'

杯： 一 **杯** 白开水
bēi *yī* ***bēi*** *báikāishuǐ*
     one **CL/cup** boiled.water
     'a cup of boiled water'

车： 一 **车** 行李
chē *yī* ***chē*** *xínglǐ*
     one **CL/car** luggage
     'a load of baggage'

盒： 一 **盒** 蛋糕
hé *yī* ***hé*** *dàngāo*
     one **CL/box** cake
     'a box of cake'

箱： 一 **箱** 啤酒
xiāng *yī* ***xiāng*** *píjiǔ*
     one **CL/crate** beer
     'a crate of beer'

篮： 一 **篮** 冰糖糕
lán *yī* ***lán*** *bīngtánggāo*
     one **CL/basket** rock.sugar.cake
     'a basket of rock sugar cake'

壶： 一 **壶** 水
hú *yī* ***hú*** *shuǐ*
     one **CL/kettle** water
     'a kettle of water'

盘： 一 **盘** 炒粿条
pán *yī* ***pán*** *chǎoguǒtiáo*
     one **CL/dish** fried.kway.teow
     'a dish of fried kway teow'

碟： 一 **碟** 炒面
dié *yī* ***dié*** *chǎomiàn*
     one **CL/plate** chow.mien
     'a plate of chow mien'

罐： 半 **罐** 萤火虫
guàn *bàn* ***guàn*** *yínghuǒchóng*
     half **CL/can** glowworm
     'half a can of glowworms'

瓶： 一 **瓶** 金黄色的 酒
píng *yī* ***píng*** *jīnhuángsè-de* *jiǔ*
     one **CL/bottle** golden wine
     'a bottle of golden wine'

桌： 数 十 **桌** 喜宴
zhuō *shù* *shí* ***zhuō*** *xǐyàn*
     several ten **CL/table** the.wedding.banquet
     'dozens of tables of food in the wedding banquet'

缸： 一 **缸** 金鱼
gāng *yī* ***gāng*** *jīnyú*
 one **CL/tank** goldfish
'a tank of goldfish'

The next example contains several temporary nominal classifiers in the same sentence:

(8) 你 说 她 三 天 吃 两 **罐** 炼奶、
nǐ *shuō* *tā* *sān* *tiān* *chī* *liǎng* ***guàn*** *liànnǎi*
2SG say 3SG three day eat two **CL** condensed.milk

一 **瓶** 酒， 五 天 吃 一 **盒** 饼、 三
yī ***píng*** *jiǔ* *wǔ* *tiān* *chī* *yī* ***hé*** *bǐng* *sān*
one **CL** wine five day eat one **CL** cookies three

罐 鸡汁， 谁 又 不 相信 来着？（今后 74）
guàn *jīzhī* *shuí* *yòu* *bù* *xiāngxìn* *láizhe*
CL chicken.bouillon who again NEG believe SFP

'You see, she drank two cans of condensed milk and one bowl of wine every three days, and ate one box of cookies, and three cans of chicken bouillon every five days. Who doesn't believe that?' (*Jīnhòu* 74)

1.11.7 Compound Nominal Classifiers

Apart from the six types of nominal classifiers mentioned earlier, there are also compound nominal classifiers. The most commonly used one is 人次 *réncì* 'person-times'. For example:

(9) 参观者 多 达 1542 **人次**。（报 1995 年 5 月 1 日 5 版）
cānguānzhě *duō* *dá* 1542 ***réncì***
visitor more reach 1542 **CL/person-times**
'The number of visitors is up to 1542.' (*Bào*, May 1, 1995, Issue no. 5)

(10) 每 100 万 **人次**， 只有 1.2 地铁
měi *yībǎiwàn* ***réncì*** *zhīyǒu* *yīdiǎnèr* *dìtiě*
each one.million **CL/person-times** only one.point.two subway

搭客　　　投诉。（报 1995 年 5 月 27 日 20 版）
dākè　　　tóusù
passenger　complain

'On average, only 1.2 out of a million passengers issue complaints for the subway. (*Bào*, May 27, 1995, Issue no. 20)

1.11.8 About 粒 lì 'CL' and 间 jiān 'CL'

Most nominal classifiers in Singapore Mandarin are the same as those in Chinese Mandarin. However, there are still some differences. One significant difference is the wide use of 粒 *lì* 'CL' and 间 *jiān* 'CL' in Singapore Mandarin.

In Singapore Mandarin, 粒 *lì* 'CL' can be used for a wide range of nouns. It can modify nouns indicating not only small granular things like rice and sesame, but also big spherical things like apples, eggs, and watermelon. For example,

(11)　几　　粒　　小　　桃　　　　几　　粒　　榴莲
　　　jǐ　　lì　　xiǎo　táo　　　　jǐ　　lì　　liúlián
　　several　CL　small　peach　　several　CL　durian
　　'some peaches'　　　　　　　'some durian'

　　　一　　粒　　苹果　　　　　　一　　粒　　重重的　　　　西瓜
　　　yī　　lì　　píngguǒ　　　　yī　　lì　　zhòngzhòng-de　xīguā
　　　one　CL　apple　　　　　　one　CL　heavy　　　　　watermelon
　　　'an apple'　　　　　　　　'a heavy watermelon'

　　　一　　粒　　气球　　　　　　一　　粒　　鱼丸
　　　yī　　lì　　qìqiú　　　　　yī　　lì　　yúwán
　　　one　CL　balloon　　　　　one　CL　fish.ball
　　　'a balloon'　　　　　　　　'a fish ball'

　　　一　　粒　　乒乓球　　　　　五　　粒　　鸡蛋
　　　yī　　lì　　pīngpāngqiú　　wǔ　　lì　　jīdàn
　　　one　CL　Pingpong ball　　five　CL　egg
　　　'a pingpong ball'　　　　　'five eggs'

In Chinese Mandarin, the classifier 个 *gè* 'CL' is used instead of 粒 *lì* 'CL' for the preceding examples.

In Singapore Mandarin, 间 *jiān* 'CL' can be applied to modify nouns referring to institutions for business or education or places related to houses. For example,

Expressions of Number and Quantity   73

(12) 两   间   公司   一   间   饭庄
      liǎng jiān gōngsī   yī   jiān   fànzhuāng
      two   CL   company   one   CL   restaurant
      'two companies'   'a restaurant'

      一   间   制衣厂   8   间   工厂
      yī   jiān zhìyīchǎng   bā   jiān   gōngchǎng
      one   CL   clothing.factory eight CL   factory
      'a clothing factory'   'eight factories'

      一   间   商店   这   间   银行
      yī   jiān shāngdiàn   zhè   jiān   yínháng
      one   CL   shop   this   CL   bank
      'a shop'   'this bank'

(13) 一   间   健身院   几十   间   幼稚园
      yī   jiān jiànshēnyuàn   jǐshí jiān   yòuzhìyuán
      one   CL   gym   dozen CL   kindergarten
      'a gym'   'dozens of kindergartens'

      一   间   学院   416   间   托儿所
      yī   jiān xuéyuàn   sìbǎiyīshíliù   jiān   tuōérsuǒ
      one   CL   college   four.hundred.sixteen CL kindergarten
      'a college'   '416 kindergartens'

      某   间   中学   哪   间   学校
      mǒu   jiān zhōngxué   nǎ   jiān   xuéxiào
      some CL   middle.school   which CL   school
      'a certain middle school'   'which school'

(14) 有   课室   5   间
      yǒu   kèshì wǔ   jiān
      have classroom five CL
      'there are five classrooms'

      神庙   有   好   几   间
      shénmiào yǒu   hǎo   jǐ   jiān
      temples   have good   several CL
      'there are a good many temples'

142　　　　　　　间　公寓
yībǎisìshíèr　　　　jiān　gōngyù
one.hundred.and.forty.two　CL　apartment
'142 apartments'

一　间　独立式　洋房
yī　jiān　dúlìshì　yángfáng
one　CL　detached　bungalow
'a detached bungalow'

In Chinese Mandarin, nouns referring to industrial and commercial enterprises are generally counted by 个 *gè* 'CL' or 家 *jiā* 'CL'. For example,

(15)　一　个/家　公司　　　　一　个/家　银行
　　　yī　gè/jiā　gōngsī　　　yī　gè/jiā　yínháng
　　　one　CL/CL　company　　one　CL/CL　bank
　　　'a company'　　　　　　　'a bank'

　　　一　个/家　饭店　　　　一　个/家　工厂
　　　yī　gè/jiā　fàndiàn　　yī　gè/jiā　gōngchǎng
　　　one　CL/CL　restaurant　one　CL/CL　factory
　　　'a restaurant'　　　　　'a factory'

　　　一　个 / 家　商店
　　　yī　gè/jiā　shāngdiàn
　　　one　CL/CL　shop
　　　'a shop'

Nouns relating to cultural and educational institutes are generally modified by 个 *gè* 'CL' or 所 *suǒ* 'CL'. For example,

(16)　一　个 / 所　小学　　　　一　个 / 所　中学
　　　yī　gè/suǒ　xiǎoxué　　　yī　gè/suǒ　zhōngxué
　　　one　CL/CL　primary.school　one　CL/CL　middle.school
　　　'a primary school'　　　　'a middle school'

　　　一　个 / 所　学校　　　　一　个 / 所　学院
　　　yī　gè/suǒ　xuéxiào　　　yī　gè/suǒ　xuéyuàn
　　　one　CL/CL　school　　　one　CL/CL　college
　　　'a school'　　　　　　　　'a college'

一	个 / 所	大学		一	个	托儿所
yī	**gè/suǒ**	dàxué		yī	**gè**	tuōérsuǒ
one	**CL/CL**	university		one	**CL**	nursery

'a university'   'a nursery'

Except for nouns like 屋子 *wūzi* 'house', 卧室 *wòshì* 'bedroom' and 客房 *kèfáng* 'guestroom', which can still be modified by 间 *jiān* 'CL' (also tend to be replaced by 个 *gè* 'CL'), nouns indicating places related to houses are generally modified by 个 *gè* 'CL', and only a few can be modified by other classifiers. For example,

(17)
一	个	课室		一	个	仓库
yī	**gè**	kèshì		yī	**gè**	cāngkù
one	**CL**	classroom		one	**CL**	warehouse

'a classroom'   'a warehouse'

一	个 / 座	公寓		一	个/幢	洋房
yī	**gè/zuò**	gōngyù		yī	**gè/zhuàng**	yángfáng
one	**CL**	apartment		one	**CL**	bungalow

'an apartment'   'a bungalow'

一	个	大厅		一	个 / 座	庙
yī	**gè**	dàtīng		yī	**gè/zuò**	miào
one	**CL**	hall		one	**CL**	temple

'a hall'   'a temple'

1.12 Verbal Classifiers

Verbal classifiers are used to indicate units of measurement for actions. They are often combined with numerals and placed after verbs as quasi-objects, indicating the number of times of actions performed. For example:

(1)
张望	了	一	回,	不	见	动静,	哥哥
zhāngwàng	le	**yī**	**huí**	bù	jiàn	dòngjìng	gēge
look.around	LE	**one**	**CL**	NEG	see	movement	brother

又	蹿	到	另	一	棵	树	下 ... (追云 96)
yòu	cuàn	dào	lìng	yī	kē	shù	xià
again	dart	to	another	one	CL	tree	below

'Looking around, without perceiving any movement, (my) brother rushed under another tree . . .' (*Zhuīyún* 96)

In example (1), 一回 yīhuí 'one time' serves as the quasi-object of the verb 张望 zhāngwàng 'look around', indicating how many times the action is performed, and 回 huí 'time' here is a verbal classifier. We can further divide verbal classifiers into four subtypes.

1.12.1 Specialised Verbal Classifiers

Specialised verbal classifiers are used to indicate the measurement of actions or events. Here are some common examples:

次: 喷   了   五   次（华韵 14）   再   来   一   次（牛车水 29）
cì   pēn   le   wǔ   cì   zài   lái   yī   cì
     sprayed LE five CL   again come one   CL
     'Sprayed five times' (*Huáyùn* 14)   'Do it again.' (*Niúchēshuǐ* 29)

趟: 送   他   一   趟（追云 47）   来   一   趟（跳舞 70）
tàng sòng tā   yī   tàng   lái   yī   tàng
     send 3SG   one   CL   come one   CL
     'Send him on a trip.' (*Zhuīyún* 47)   'Come here.' (*Tiàowǔ* 70)

回: 张望   了   一   回（追云 96） 看   一   回（壁虎 69）
huí zhāngwàng   le   yī   huí   kàn   yī   huí
     look.around LE   one   CL   look one   CL
     'Looked around once.' (*Zhuīyún* 96)   'Looked once.' (*Bìhǔ* 69)

声: 叫   了   我   一   声（Δ大喜 195） 赞叹   了   一   声（独上 70）
shēng jiào le   wǒ   yī   shēng   zàntàn le   yī   shēng
     call LE   1SG   one   CL   praise LE   one   CL
     'Called me once.' (*ΔDàxǐ* 195)   'Praised once.' (*Dúshàng* 70)

场: 闹   了   一   场   大   病   了   一   场
                            （大胡子 44）   （再见 91）
chǎng nào   le   yī   chǎng   dà   bìng le   yī   chǎng
     make.a.fuss LE   one   CL   big   ill   LE   one   CL
     'Someone made a fuss.' (*Dàhúzi* 44) 'Someone was very sick once.'
                                           (*Zàijiàn* 91)

番: 游览   一   番   （晚上 153）
fān yóulǎn   yī   fān
     visit   one   CL
     'Visit somewhere once.'   (*Wǎnshàng* 153)

Expressions of Number and Quantity   77

祭奠				一	番	（太阳 19）
jìdiàn				yī	**fān**	
have.a.memorial.ceremony				one	CL	

'Have a memorial ceremony for someone.' (*Tàiyáng* 19)

顿:	痛	骂	了	自己	一	顿	（扶轮 88）
dùn	tòng	mà	le	zìjǐ	yī	**dùn**	
	sting	scold	LE	oneself	one	CL	

'I harshly scolded myself.' (*Fúlún* 88)

下:	钟	声	刚刚	敲	完	十二	下	（太阳 21）
xià	zhōng	shēng	gānggāng	qiāo	wán	shíèr	**xià**	
	bell	sound	just	strike	finish	twelve	CL	

'The bell has just struck twelve times.' (*Tàiyáng* 21)

遍:	把	全部	旧	作	都	翻阅	过	一	遍	（回忆 28）
biàn	bǎ	quánbù	jiù	zuò	dōu	fānyuè	guò	yī	**biàn**	
	BA	all	old	works	all	browse	GUO	one	CL	

'(He) browsed through all his old works.' (*Huíyì* 28)

1.12.2 Nouns Being Used as Verbal Classifiers

The verbal classifiers of this type are originally nouns that denote instruments by which actions are performed. For example:

(2)
所以,	你	当时	痛	极	生	恨,	索性
suǒyǐ	nǐ	dāngshí	tòng	jí	shēng	hèn	suǒxìng
so	2SG	then	hurt	extreme	generate	hatred	might.as.well

在	陆浩东	中	了	你	行刺	的	三
zài	lùhàodōng	zhòng	le	nǐ	xíngcì	de	sān
at	Lu.Haodong	get	LE	2SG	assassinate	DE	three

两	刀	后,	顺手	就	连连	下	刺
liǎng	**dāo**	hòu	shùnshǒu	jiù	liánlián	xià	cì
two	CL	after	handy	thus	continuous	down	stab

78 Expressions of Number and Quantity

十二 **刀** 之 多。（浮萍 41）
shí'èr **dāo** zhī duō
twelve **CL** LIG much

'So, after Lu Haodong had been stabbed two or three times, you stabbed him again as many as 12 times in a row out of pain and hatred.' (*Fúpíng* 41)

Generally, 刀 *dāo* is a common noun meaning 'knife'. In example (2), it is used as a classifier to measure the number of times of the action indicated by the verb 刺 *cì* 'stab', and semantically it refers to the instrument with which the stabbing action is performed. Thus, 刀 *dāo* here is a noun being used as a verbal classifier. Here are more examples of this kind:

脚： 踢 了 一 **脚**（狮子）
jiǎo tī   le yī **jiǎo**
      kick LE one **CL/foot**
      '(Someone) kicked (him).' (*Shīzi*)

眼： 望 了 一 **眼**（金狮奖 231）
yǎn wàng le yī **yǎn**
      look LE one **CL/eye**
      '(Someone) looked at (somewhere).' (*Jīnshījiǎng* 231)

拳： 揍 了 一 **拳**（扶轮 10）
quán zòu le yī **quán**
      punch LE one **CL/fist**
      '(Someone) punched (someone).' (*Fúlún* 10)

口： 吸 了 一 大 **口**（跳舞 130）
kǒu xī   le yī dà **kǒu**
      sip LE one big **CL/mouth**
      '(I) took a big sip.' (*Tiàowǔ* 130)

刀： 被 人 在 背后 捅 一 **刀** （再见 83）
dāo bèi rén zài bèihòu tǒng yī **dāo**
      BEI person at back stab one **CL/knife**
      '(I) was stabbed in (my) back.' (*Zàijiàn* 83)

Expressions of Number and Quantity   79

枪：	没有	发射	一	枪（痕迹 50）
qiāng	méiyǒu	fāshè	yī	qiāng
	NEG	fire	one	CL/shot

'Without firing a shot.' (*Hénjì* 50)

巴掌：	刮	你	一	巴掌（再见 64）
bāzhǎng	guā	nǐ	yī	bāzhǎng
	slap	2SG	one	CL/hand

'Slap you once.' (*Zàijiàn* 64)

1.12.3 Verbs Being Used as Verbal Classifiers

Verbs that can be temporarily used as verbal classifiers are restricted to monosyllable verbs which are reduplicatable. The only numeral preceding this kind of classifiers is 一 *yī* 'one', and the resulting numeral-classifier phrases can only occur in the object (or quasi-object) position. In this case the verb and the classifier are always in identical form, as evidenced in the following examples:

(3) 先生， 等 一 等。（金狮奖 29）
    xiānshēng **děng** *yī* **děng**
    sir   wait   one CL

'Sir, please wait for a moment.' (*Jīnshījiǎng* 29)

In example (3), the former 等 *děng* 'wait' is a verb, serving as a predicate, while the latter 等 *děng* 'CL' is a verbal classifier. 一等 *yī děng* 'one CL' here serves as a quasi-object of the verb 等 *děng* 'wait'. More similar examples are shown in the following:

(4) 你   也   **说**   一   **说**   吧，   **说**   一   **说**   你
    nǐ   yě   **shuō** *yī* **shuō** ba   **shuō** *yī* **shuō** nǐ
    2SG also talk   one CL   SFP   talk   one CL   2SG

    历史沧桑   的   身世，   **说**   一   **说**   那些   沉淀
    lìshǐcāngsāng   de   shēnshì **shuō** *yī* **shuō** nàxiē chéndiàn
    vicissitude.of.history DE life   talk   one CL   those   settle

在 你 糟蹋的 河床 里 的 许多 故事。
（牛车水 22）
zài nǐ zāotàde héchuáng lǐ de xǔduō gùshi
at 2SG spoiled riverbed inside DE many story
'Tell us a little too, of the vicissitudes of your life, of the many stories that settled in your spoiled riverbed.' (*Niúchēshuǐ* 22)

(5) 雷探长 不动声色地 **按 一 按** 台铃，
léitànzhǎng bùdòngshēngsède **àn yī àn** táilíng
Detective.Lei unemotionally **press one CL** table.bell

两 名 干探 应声而入。(Δ 浮萍 32)
liǎng míng gàntàn yìngshēng'érrù
two CL detective enter.with.the sound

Detective Lei calmly pressed the bell on the desk and two detective entered in response. (Δ*Fúpíng* 32)

(6) 让 我 来 **考 一 考** 你…（笑眼 106）
ràng wǒ lái **kǎo yī kǎo** nǐ
let 1SG come **test one CL** 2SG
'Let me give you a test…' (*Xiàoyǎn* 106)

(7) 她 含 笑 地 往 座位 底下
tā hán xiào de wǎng zuòwèi dǐxià
3SG contain smile DE toward seat underneath

指 了 一 指。（短篇 16）
zhǐ le yī zhǐ
point LE one CL
'She smiled and pointed under the seat.' (*Duǎnpiān* 16)

(8) 杨铭 **呆 了 一 呆，** 有点 吃惊（金狮奖 92）
yángmíng **dāi le yī dāi** yǒudiǎn chījīng
Yang.Ming **stun LE one CL** a.little surprise
'Yang Ming was stunned for a moment, a little surprised.' (*Jīnshīijiǎng* 92)

(9) 张大嫂　　　　把　　话锋　　　　　　**转　　了　　一　　转，**
　　 zhāngdàsǎo　bǎ　huàfēng　　　　　**zhuǎn　le　yī　zhuǎn**
　　 Auntie.Zhang　BA　topic.of.conversation　**turn　LE　one　CL**

　　 有意　　　在　　　炫耀　　　　自己　　的　　得宠。（冰灯 6）
　　 yǒu　　　 zài　　xuànyào　　zìjǐ　 de　déchǒng
　　 intentionally　in.process　show.off　oneself　de　in.one's.great.grace
　　 Auntie Zhang steered the conversation, intentionally showing off the great grace she had. (*Bīngdēng* 6)

1.12.4 Indefinite Verbal Classifiers

There are only two indefinite verbal classifiers, 下 *xià* 'CL' and 通 *tòng* 'CL'. As a verbal classifier, 下 *xià* 'CL' can be both a specialised verbal classifier and an indefinite verbal classifier. When used as a specialised verbal classifier, its meaning is similar to 次 *cì* 'CL/time', indicating the number of times that an action is performed. The numeral preceding this classifier is not limited to 一 *yī* 'one'. As an indefinite classifier, it means 'a little or a bit', indicating that the action is of short and indefinite duration time, and the numeral preceding it is limited to 一 *yī* 'one'. Let's compare:

(10) 当　　　钟　　　声　　　刚刚　　　敲　　　完　　　十二　　**下**　　的
　　　dāng　zhōng　shēng　gānggāng　qiāo　wán　shíèr　**xià**　de
　　　when　clock　sound　just　strike　finish　twelve　**CL**　DE

　　　一瞬间，　　　所有的　　　鞭炮　　　　仿佛　　　约　　　好　　　似的，
　　　yīshùnjiān　suǒyǒu-de　biānpào　fǎngfú　yuē　hǎo　shìde
　　　at.that.moment　all　firecracker　seem　arrange　good　as.if

　　　同时　　　响　　了　　起来。（太阳 21）
　　　tóngshí　xiǎng　le　qǐlái
　　　at.the.same.time　sound　LE　up
　　　'As soon as the bell struck twelve, all the firecrackers went off at the same time, as if by arrangement.' (*Tàiyáng* 21)

(11) 但　　最好　　　还是　　动　　一　　**下**　　手术，
　　　dàn　zuìhǎo　háishì　dòng　yī　**xià**　shǒushù
　　　but　best　still　have　one　**CL**　operation

82   *Expressions of Number and Quantity*

这样	弟弟	日后	就	可以	撑	着
zhèyàng	dìdi	rìhòu	jiù	kéyǐ	chēng	zhe
thus	brother	future	thus	can	support	ZHE

拐杖	走路	了。（太阳 67）
guǎizhàng	zǒulù	le
cane	walk	LE

'But it would be better to have an operation so that in the future my brother can walk with a cane.' (*Tàiyáng* 67)

In example (10), 下 *xià* 'CL' is a specialised verbal classifier. The numeral 十二 *shíèr* 'twelve' before this classifier can be replaced by other numerals. However, in example (11), 下 *xià* 'CL' is an indefinite verbal classifier and the numeral preceding it can only be 一 *yī* 'one'. Here are more examples for 下 *xià* 'CL' as an indefinite verbal classifier:

(12)	你	和	他们	谈谈，	商量	一	下	住
	nǐ	hé	tāmen	tántan	shāngliang	yī	**xià**	zhù
	2SG	and	3PL	talk	discuss	one	**CL**	accommodate

的	问题。（金狮奖 70）
de	wèntí
DE	question

'You'd better have a talk with them about accommodation.' (*Jīnshījiǎng* 70)

(13)	请	队员	互相	照应	一	下…（南北 18）
	qǐng	duìyuán	hùxiāng	zhàoyìng	yī	**xià**
	please	member	each.other	take.care	one	**CL**

'Please take care of each other.' (*Nánběi* 18)

(14)	我	想	把	剧本	修改	一	下…（华文课本 3B 25）
	wǒ	xiǎng	bǎ	jùběn	xiūgǎi	yī	**xià**
	1SG	want	BA	script	revise	one	**CL**

'I want to revise the script.' (*Huáwénjùběn* 3B, 25)

For the other indefinite classifier, 通 *tòng* 'CL', the numeral preceding it is also limited to 一 *yī* 'one', as can be seen in the following example:

(15)	看到	我	那	惊愕的	表情,	乐	得
kàndào	wǒ	nà	jīng'ède	biǎoqíng	lè	de
see	1SG	that	astonished	expression	happy	DE

他们	嘻嘻哈哈地	大	笑	一	**通**。（南北 8）
tāmen	xīxīhāhā-de	dà	xiào	yī	**tòng**
3PL	laughly	big	laugh	one	**CL**

'It was a joy to see my stunned expression and they couldn't stop laughing for a while.' (*Nánběi* 8)

(16)	我	高兴地	奔	上	前	去,	胡	抓
wǒ	gāoxìng-de	bēn	shàng	qián	qù	hú	zhuā
1SG	happily	run	up	front	go	carelessly	grab

一	**通,**	什么	也	抓	不	着。（壁虎 15）
yī	**tòng**	shénme	yě	zhuā	bù	zháo
one	**CL**	what	also	grab	NEG	SFP

'I ran up happily and grabbed around for a while but couldn't catch anything.' (*Bìhǔ* 15)

1.13 Temporal Classifiers

Temporal classifiers are unit words measuring time and can be divided into two subtypes: specialised temporal classifiers and indefinite temporal classifiers.

1.13.1 Specialised Temporal Classifiers

Definite temporal classifiers that are exclusively used to measure time are called 'specialised temporal classifiers'. Listed in the following are such classifiers:

世纪:	展望	二十	**世纪**	的	世界	华文	与
shìjì	zhǎnwàng	èrshí	**shìjì**	de	shìjiè	huáwén	yǔ
	look.forward.to	twenty	**CL/century**	DE	world	Chinese	and

华人	文学（Δ 新华文学 273）
huárén	wénxué
Chinese	literature

'Looking forward to (the development of) Chinese language and Chinese literature in the 20th century' (Δ*Xīnhuáwénxué* 273)

84   *Expressions of Number and Quantity*

年代：	二十	**年代** （△ 中国作家 12）
niándài	*èrshí*	***niándài***
	twenty	**CL/years**

'In the 1920' (△*zhōngguózuòjiā* 12)

年：	数	十	**年** （一心 13）
nián	*shù*	*shí*	***nián***
	several	ten	**CL/year**

'For several decades' (*Yīxīn* 13)

（这	件	绒线衣	我	已经）	织	了	十	**年**。（风雨 8）
zhè	*jiàn*	*róngxiànyī*	*wǒ*	*yǐjīng*	*zhī*	*le*	*shí*	***nián***
this	CL	wool.clothes	1SG	already	knit	LE	ten	**CL/year**

'I've been knitting the woollen sweater for ten years.' (*Fēngyǔ* 8)

载：	同窗		六	**载** （梦 13）
zǎi	*tóngchuāng*		*liù*	***zǎi***
	study.in.the.same.class		six	**CL/year**

'(We) have been classmates for six years.' (*Mèng* 13)

（在	教育	机关）	服务	十	多	**载** （晚上 139）
zài	*jiàoyù*	*jīguān*	*fúwù*	*shí*	*duō*	***zǎi***
at	education	institution	serve	ten	more	**CL/year**

'(I) have been working (in an educational institution) for more than a decade.' (*Wǎnshàng* 139)

月：	去年	十一	**月** （△ 含羞草 11）
yuè	*qùnián*	*shíyī*	***yuè***
	last.year	eleventh	**CL/month**

'Last November' (△*hánxiūcǎo* 11)

天：	工作	了	二十	**天** （短篇 36）
tiān	*gōngzuò*	*le*	*èrshí*	***tiān***
	work	LE	twenty	**CL/day**

'(I) have worked for twenty days.' (*Duǎnpiān* 36)

Expressions of Number and Quantity 85

	十三	天？（青青 20）
	shísān	**tiān**
	thirteen	**CL/day**

'Thirteen days?' (*Qīngqīng* 20)

日：	何曾	有	安宁	的	一	日（金狮奖 15）
rì	hécéng	yǒu	ānníng	de	yī	**rì**
	ever	have	peaceful	DE	one	**CL/day**

'Is there ever a peaceful day?' (*Jīnshījiǎng* 15)

点：	星期天	下午	2	点（南北 27）
diǎn	xīngqītiān	xiàwǔ	liǎng	**diǎn**
	Sunday	afternoon	two	**CL/o'clock**

'2 pm on Sunday' (*Nánběi* 27)

点钟：	九	点钟	有	一	个	关系	到	擢升	的
diǎnzhōng	jiǔ	**diǎnzhōng**	yǒu	yī	gè	guānxì	dào	zhuóshēng	de
	nine	**CL/o'clock**	have	one	CL	relate	to	promotion	DE

会议（再见 5）
huìyì
meeting

'There is a meeting connected with promotion at 9 o'clock.' (*Zàijiàn* 5)

时：	桌	上	的	钟	指	着	二	时	零
shí	zhuō	shàng	de	zhōng	zhǐ	zhe	èr	**shí**	líng
	table	above	DE	clock	point	ZHE	two	**CL/hour**	zero

八 分。（短篇 11）
bā fēn
eight CL/minute

'The clock on the table pointed at eight minutes past two.' (*Duǎnpān* 11)

小时：	一	天	八	小时	全力以赴（青青 149）
xiǎoshí	yī	tiān	bā	**xiǎoshí**	quánlìyǐfù
	one	day	eight	**CL/hour**	go.all.out

'Go all out eight hours a day.' (*Qīngqīng* 149)

86 Expressions of Number and Quantity

分:	只	用	了	9	天	21		小时
fēn	zhǐ	yòng	le	jiǔ	tiān	èrshíyī		xiǎoshí
	only	use	LE	nine	day	twenty.one		hour

42　　**分**（△ 高级课本 2B 108）
sìshíèr　　**fēn**
forty.two　**CL/minute**

'It only takes 9 days, 21 hours and 42 minutes'
(△*Gāojíkèběn* 2B, 108)

分钟:	走	十	**分钟**（石头 203）
fēnzhōng	zǒu	shí	**fēnzhōng**
	walk	ten	**CL/minute**

'Walk for ten minutes.' (*Shítou* 203)

	等	公车	起码	要	二、	三十	**分钟**（怀旧 45）
	děng	gōngchē	qǐmǎ	yào	èr	sānshí	**fēnzhōng**
	wait	bus	at.least	need	two	thirty	**CL/minute**

'waiting for the bus will take at least 20 to 30 minutes.' (*Huáijiù* 45)

秒:	过	了	一	**秒**（青青 127）
miǎo	guò	le	yī	**miǎo**
	pass	LE	one	**CL/second**

'One second has passed.' (*Qīngqīng* 127)

	时间	一	分	一	**秒**	地	过去（课本 3B 20）
	shíjiān	yī	fēn	yī	**miǎo**	de	guòqù
	time	one	minute	one	**CL/second**	DE	pass

'Time passes by minute by minute, second by second.' (*Kèběn* 3B, 20)

秒钟:	在	几	**秒钟**	的	沉思	后（金狮奖 142）
miǎozhōng	zài	jǐ	**miǎozhōng**	de	chénsī	hòu
	at	several	**CL/second**	DE	contemplation	after

'After a few seconds of contemplation' (*Jīnshījiǎng* 142)

	停顿	了	十	来	**秒钟**（△ 浮萍 117）
	tíngdùn	le	shí	lái	**miǎozhōng**
	pause	LE	ten	about	**CL/second**

'There was a pause of about ten seconds.' (△*Fúpíng* 117)

岁 suì 'years old', as a unit of measurement of age, is also classified as a 'specialised temporal classifier', for example:

岁：	七十	**岁**（青青 34）	八九	**岁**（风雨 11）
suì	qīshí	**suì**	bājiǔ	**suì**
	seventy	**CL/years**	eight.or.nine	**CL/years**
	'seventy years old' (Qīngqīng 34)		'eight or nine years old' (Fēngyǔ 11)	

Regarding specialised temporal classifiers, a few more points need to be made:

First, numeral-classifier phrases with such specialised temporal classifiers as 载 zǎi 'year', 天 tiān 'day', 分钟 fēnzhōng 'minute' and 秒钟 miǎozhōng 'second' represent only periods of time rather than points of time, for example:

三载 sān zǎi 'three years' 三年 sān nián 'three years'
三分钟 sān fēnzhōng 'three minutes' 三秒钟 sān miǎozhōng 'three seconds'

Second, numeral-classifier phrases with specialised temporal classifiers like 点 diǎn 'o'clock', 点钟 diǎnzhōng 'o'clock', 时 shí 'hour' and 月份 yuèfèn 'month' represent only points of time rather than periods of time, for example:

三点 sān diǎn 'three o'clock' 三点钟 sān diǎnzhōng 'three o'clock'
三时 sān shí 'three o'clock' 三月份 sān yuèfèn 'March'

Third, numeral-classifier phrases with specialised temporal classifiers like 世纪 shìjì 'century' and 月 yuè 'month' indicate points of time rather than periods of time (e.g. 二十一世纪 èrshíyī shìjì '21st century', 三月 sānyuè 'March'). Nevertheless, if the classifier 个 gè is inserted in the phrases, they can represent periods of time. For example:

(1) 像 送 走 了 一 **个** 世纪， 又 仿佛 只
    xiàng sòng zǒu le yī **gè** shìjì yòu fǎngfú zhǐ
    like send go LE one **CL** century also as.if only

过 了 一 秒。（青青 127）
guò le yī miǎo
pass LE one second

'It seems like that a century has passed by, but it's also like just a second.' (Qīngqīng 127)

88 *Expressions of Number and Quantity*

(2) 毕竟　　我　　在　　这儿　　只　　生活　　了　　**两三**
　　bìjìng　wǒ　zài　zhèr　zhǐ　shēnghuó　le　**liǎngsān**
　　after.all　1SG　at　here　only　live　LE　two.or.three

个　　月。（怀旧 53）
gè　yuè
CL　month

'After all, I've only lived here for two or three months.' (*Huáijiù* 53)

Strictly speaking, 世纪 *shìjì* 'century' and 月 *yuè* 'month' in examples (1) and (2) are no longer classifiers, but nouns. In other words, 世纪 *shìjì* 'century' and 月 *yuè* 'month' are multicategory words: both nouns and classifiers. 世纪 *shìjì* 'century' in 公元三世纪 *gōngyuán sān shìjì* 'the 3rd century AD' and 月 *yuè* 'month' in 三月 *sānyuè* 'March' are classifiers, while in 三个世纪 *sān gè shìjì* 'three centuries' and 三个月 *sān gè yuè* 'three months', they are nouns.

Fourth, both numerals and numeral-classifier compounds can modify 小时 *xiǎoshí* 'hour', and thus formed phrases can represent only periods of time rather than points of time, for example:

(3)a. 整整　　　磨蹭　　　了　　**三十八**　　**小时**，　才　　来到　　这个
　　　zhěngzhěng　mócèng　le　**sānshíbā**　**xiǎoshí**　cái　láidào　zhège
　　　fully　hang.about　LE　thirty.eight　hour　then　arrive　this

人口　　只　　有　　五万　　　的　　中西部　　　小城。
　　　　　　　　　　　　　　　　　　　　　　　　（怀旧 29）
rénkǒu　zhǐ　yǒu　wǔwàn　de　zhōngxībù　xiǎochéng
population　only　have　fifty.thousand　DE　Midwest　small.city

'It took (me) thirty-eight hours to get to this small Midwestern city of 50,000 people.' (*Huáijiù* 29)

b. 比　　　原有的　　　记录　　缩短　　　了　　**38**
　　bǐ　yuányǒude　jìlù　suōduǎn　le　**sānshíbā**
　　than　previous　record　shorten　LE　thirty.eight

小时。（高级课本 2B 108）
xiǎoshí
hour

'(That's) 38 hours shorter than the previous record.' (*Gāojíkèběn* 2B, 108)

(4)a. 如果　忘　了　带　钥匙，　就　得　　在　门口
　　　rúguǒ wàng le dài yàoshi   jiù děi   zài ménkǒu
　　　if　　forget LE take key   then have.to at door

　　等　上　　几　　个　　小时，　或是　　到
　　děng shàng jǐ   gè   xiǎoshí huòshì dào
　　wait　up   several CL hour   or   go.to

　　邻居　　　家　　坐　上　几　　个　　小时 … (△ 南风 12)
　　línjū   jiā   zuò shàng jǐ   gè   xiǎoshí
　　neighbour home sit up   several CL hour

　　'If you forgot your keys, you'd have to wait for hours at the door or sit in a neighbour's house for hours …' (△*Nánfēng* 12)

b.　托儿所　　每天　　都　提供　　三　　个　　小时　的
　　tuōérsuǒ měitiān dōu tígōng   sān   gè   xiǎoshí de
　　nursery　everyday all provide three CL hour   DE

　　学前　　教育　　　呀！（大胡子 102）
　　xuéqián jiàoyù   ya
　　preschool education SFP

　　'The nursery provides three hours of preschool education every day!' (*Dàhúzi* 102)

In example (3), 小时 *xiǎoshí* 'hour' follows numerals, while in example (4), it follows numeral-classifier compounds. Strictly speaking, 小时 *xiǎoshí* 'hour' should also be regarded as both a noun and a classifier. It is a classifier after a numeral and a noun after a numeral-classifier compound.

Fifth, it seems that words like 礼拜 *lǐbài* 'week', 下午 *xiàwǔ* 'afternoon' and 钟头 *zhōngtóu* 'hour' are also unit words used to measure time. However, these words cannot follow numerals directly without the classifier 个 *gè* as shown in the following examples. That is to say, these words can only follow numeral-classifier compounds, which means that they are not temporal classifiers, but nouns.

(5)　足足　　一　个　礼拜　了。（变调 8）
　　zúzú   yī   gè lǐbài le
　　fully   one CL week   LE

　　'(It's) been a whole week.' (*Biàndiào* 8)

90 Expressions of Number and Quantity

(6) 一   整   个   **下午**   或   黄昏,   便   这样
    yī   zhěng gè **xiàwǔ**   huò huánghūn biàn zhèyàng
    one whole CL **afternoon** or   dusk   then such

与   阿花   追逐   着   度   过去   了。（风雨 46）
yǔ   āhuā zhuīzhú zhe dù   guòqù le
with Ahua chase   ZHE spend pass   LE

'A whole afternoon was spent on chasing with Ahua.' (*Fēngyǔ* 46)

(7) 我   回   家   已经   一   个   **钟头**   多   了。
                                                （华文教材
                                                2B 116）

wǒ   huí   jiā   yǐjīng yī   gè   **zhōngtóu** duō le
1SG return home already one CL   hour   more LE

'I have been home for over an hour.' (*Huáwénjiàocái* 2B, 116)

1.13.2 Indefinite Temporal Classifiers

There are three indefinite temporal classifiers in all: 下 *xià* 'moment', 会儿 *huìr* 'while' and 阵 *zhèn* 'while'. Among them, 会儿 *huìr* 'while' and 阵 *zhèn* 'while' are only indefinite temporal classifiers, while 下 *xià* can also be used as a specialised verbal classifier meaning 'time' and an indefinite verbal classifier meaning 'bit/ little' (see Section 1.12) apart from the indefinite temporal classifier usage.

The only numeral that can precede indefinite temporal classifiers is 一 *yī* 'one', and thus formed compounds 一下 *yīxià* 'a moment', 一阵 *yīzhèn* 'a while' and 一会儿 *yīhuìr* 'a while' all represent an uncertain period of time, as shown in the following:

(8) 我   等   一   **下**   来   领,   可以   吗？（跳舞 3）
    wǒ   děng yī   **xià** lái   lǐng   kěyǐ   ma
    1SG wait one **CL** come take   can   SFP

'Can I take it later?' (*Tiàowǔ* 3)

(9) 他   首先   打开   了   书桌   的   中间   抽屉,
    tā   shǒuxiān dǎkāi   le   shūzhuō   de   zhōngjiān chōutì
    3SG first   open   LE   desk   DE   middle   drawer

翻   了   一   **会儿**。（Δ 大喜 110）
fān   le   yī   **huìér**
turn.over LE   one   **CL**

'He first opened the middle drawer of the desk and searched in it for a while.' (Δ*Dàxǐ* 110)

(10) 克斯汀娜　　知道　　没有　　人　　伸出　　援手，
　　 kèsītīngnà　zhīdào　méiyǒu　rén　shēnchū　yuánshǒu
　　 Christina　know　not.have　person　reach.out　aid

　　 哭　一　阵，　喊　一　阵，
　　 kū　yī　zhèn　hǎn　yī　zhèn
　　 cry　one　CL　scream　one　CL

　　 便　　怏怏然地　　　摸索　　着　　站　　了　　起来。（跳舞 144）
　　 biàn　yàngyàngrán-de　mōsuǒ　zhe　zhàn　le　qǐlái
　　 then　unhappily　　　fumble　ZHE　stand　LE　up

　　 Knowing that no one would offer a helping hand, Christina cried and yelled for a while, then groped around and sullenly stood up. (*Tiàowǔ* 144)

In Chinese Mandarin, 儿 *ér* in 一会儿 *yīhuìr* 'a while' cannot be omitted, while in Singapore Mandarin, 儿 *ér* is often omitted in spoken genres and even in some written genres, because there is no rhotacisation in Singapore Mandarin, for example:

(11) 让　我　歇　一　会　吧！（撞墙 15）
　　 ràng　wǒ　xiē　yī　huì　ba
　　 let　1SG　rest　one　CL　SFP
　　 'Let me have a rest!' (*Zhuàngqiáng* 15)

　　 我们　聊　了　一　会。（金狮奖 70）
　　 wǒmen　liáo　le　yī　huì
　　 1PL　chat　LE　one　CL
　　 'We chatted for a while.' (*Jīnshījiǎng* 70)

　　 女主人　把　我　上下　　　看　了　一　会…（万花筒 22）
　　 nǚzhǔrén　bǎ　wǒ　shàngxià　kàn　le　yī　huì
　　 hostess　BA　1SG　up.and.down　look　LE　one　CL
　　 'The hostess looked me up and down . . .' (*Wànghuātǒng*, 22)

Another alternative expression for 一阵 *yīzhèn* 'a while' is 一阵子 *yīzhènzi* 'a while', as in the following examples:

(12) 过　了　一　阵子，　门铃　又　响　了　一　下。（跳舞 2）
　　 guò　le　yī　zhènzi　ménlíng　yòu　xiǎng　le　yī　xià
　　 pass　LE　one　CL　doorbell　again　ring　LE　one　CL
　　 'After a while, the doorbell rang again.' (*Tiàowǔ* 2)

(13) 她 考虑 了 一 **阵子**, 决定 不 去 领 那
    tā kǎolǜ le **yī** **zhènzi** juédìng bù qù lǐng nà
    3SG consider LE **one** **CL** decide NEG go take that

    笔 钱。（华韵 8）
    bǐ qián
    CL money

    'She considered for a while and decided not to get the money.' (*Huáyùn* 8)

(14) 他 回忆 了 一 **阵子** ...（Δ 大喜 102）
    tā huíyì le **yī** **zhènzi**
    3SG recall LE **one** **CL**

    'He recalled for a while . . .' (Δ*Dàxǐ* 102)

Generally speaking, with respect to the time of duration expressed, the duration indicated by 一下 *yīxià* 'a moment' is shorter than that indicated by 一会儿 *yīhuìr* 'a while', which is shorter than that indicated by 一阵（子）*yīzhèn(zi)* 'a while'.

1.14 Numeral-Classifier Phrases and the Expressions of Number and Quantity

As we have discussed in this chapter, the most important grammatical function of classifiers is to be modified by the numeral. The combination of numerals and classifiers is called numeral-classifier phrase, or numeral-classifier compound, which belongs to the 'attribute-head' endocentric phrase (see Sections 3.8 and 8.3 in Volume I and Section 1.10 of this chapter respectively).

1.14.1 The Main Grammatical Functions of Numeral-Classifier Phrases

1   The numeral-classifier phrase can serve as attribute, modifying a head noun. For example:

一 个 **女子**   一 把 **小刀**   一 张 **书签**
yī gè **nǚzǐ**   yī bǎ **xiǎodāo**   yī zhāng **shūqiān**
one CL **woman**   one CL **knife**   one CL **bookmark**
'A woman'   'A knife'   'A bookmark'

The head modified can also be a nominal 的 *de* 'DE' construction (see Section 8.3 in Volume I). For example:

（要）	一	棵	**小**	**的**
yào	yī	kē	**xiǎo**	**de**
want	one	CL	**small**	**DE**

'A small one, please.'

（想起）	两	个	**小**	**的**...
xiǎngqǐ	liǎng	gè	**xiǎo**	**de**
remember	two	CL	**small**	**DE**

'(It reminds me of) the two little ones.'

The head can also be a monosyllabic adjective, provided that the classifier is a measure word (see Section 8.3 in Volume I). For example:

八	尺	宽，	十二	尺	长
bā	chǐ	kuān	shíèr	chǐ	cháng
eight	chi	wide	twelve	chi	long

'Eight *chi* wide and twelve *chi* long'

一点八	米	高
yīdiǎnbā	mǐ	gāo
one.point.eight	CL	tall

'one point eight metres tall'

2   The numeral-classifier phrase can be in the subject position, with a verbal phrase as its predicate. For instance:

(1)
跟	他	同	来	的	有	两	位	比较
gēn	tā	tóng	lái	de	yǒu	liǎng	wèi	bǐjiào
with	3SG	together	come	DE	have	two	CL	relatively

年轻的	作家：	一	**位**	叫	苏伟真，
niánqīng-de	zuòjiā	yī	**wèi**	jiào	sūwěizhēn
young	writer	one	**CL**	call	Su.Weizhen

一	**位**	叫	简祯。（怀旧 105）
yī	**wèi**	jiào	jiǎnzhēn
one	**CL**	call	Jian.Zhen

'There are two relatively younger writers coming with him, one is called Su Weizhen, and the other is called Jian Zhen.' (*Huáijiù* 105)

(2)
楼下	连带	商店，	有	九	间	店铺，	**七**	**间**
lóuxià	liándài	shāngdiàn	yǒu	jiǔ	jiān	diànpù	**qī**	**jiān**
downstairs	have	shop	have	nine	CL	shop	**seven**	**CL**

经营	电器，	**二**	**间**	经营	五金	生意。（晚上 13）
jīngyíng	diànqì	**èr**	**jiān**	jīngyíng	wǔjīn	shēngyi
operate	appliance	**two**	**CL**	operate	hardware	business

'There are nine shops downstairs, seven dealing in electrical appliances and two in hardware.' (*Wǎnshàng* 13)

(3) 接受   清洗   的   鸟   共有   390   只,
    jiēshòu qīngxǐ de   niǎo gòngyǒu   sānbǎijiǔshí zhī
    accept clean   DE   bird altogether.have three.hundred.and. CL
                                              ninety

    225   只   已   丧生,
    èrbǎièrshíwǔ   zhī   yǐ   sàngshēng
    two.hundred.and.twenty.five   CL   already die

    43   只   已   放回   大自然。（扶轮 70）
    sìshísān   zhī   yǐ   fànghuí   dàzìrán
    forty.three CL   already let.go   nature
    'Of the 390 birds that have been cleaned, 225 have died and 43 have been released back into nature.' (*Fúlún* 70)

(4) 一   美元   换   一万五千   滋洛第。（石头 62）
    yī   měiyuán   huàn   yīwànwǔqiān   zīluòdì
    one   dollar   exchange   fifteen.thousand Zloty
    'One dollar can be exchanged for fifteen thousand Zloty.' (*Shítou* 62)

(5) 八万,   还是   买   贵   了。（撞墙 23）
    bāwàn   hái shì   mǎi   guì   le
    eighty.thousand still SHI   buy   expensive   LE
    'Eighty thousand, the purchase was still too expensive.' (*Zhuàngqiáng* 23)

The subject and the predicate can be both numeral-classifier phrases. The resulting subject-predicate phrases always grammatically denote the meaning of 'every'. For example:

(6)a. 十   元   一   盒。（Δ 天长 15）
       shí   yuán   yī   hé
       ten   CL/yuan   one   CL
       'ten *yuans* for one box' (Δ*Tiāncháng* 15)

   b. 大   减价,   三   件   十   块   啊！（Δ 南风 7）
       dà   jiǎnjià   sān   jiàn   shí   kuài   a
       big   discount   three   CL   ten   CL/yuan   SFP
       'Big sale! Three pieces for ten yuans!'(Δ*Nánfēng* 7)

(7) 一 次 一 个。（梦 149）
    yī   cì   yī   gè
    one   CL   one   CL
    'one at a time' (*Mèng* 149)

It is worth noting that 十元一盒 *shíyuán yīhé* 'ten *yuans* yper box' can also be expressed as 一盒十元 *yīhé shíyuán* 'one box ten *yuans*'. However, the two expressions are different in meaning. For the former, as the numeral-classifier phrase indicating price comes before the one indicating quantity, the whole subject-predicate phrase means that it takes ten *yuans* to buy a box. While for the latter with the reversed order, it means one box costs ten *yuans*.[10]

3   The numeral-classifier phrase can serve as an object. For example:

(8) 连   衣服   也   不   留   一   件。（△ 南风 53）
    lián   yīfú   yě   bù   liú   yī   jiàn
    even clothes also NEG leave one CL
    'Leaving behind not even a piece of clothing' (△*Nánfēng* 53)

(9) 我   忿忿地   说   了   一   句。（太阳 21）
    wǒ   fènfènde   shuō   le   yī   jù
    1SG angrily   say   LE   one CL
    'I said something angrily.' (*Tàiyáng* 21)

(10) 买   了   一   条。（石头 25）
    mǎi   le   yī   tiáo
    buy   LE one   CL
    '(I) bought one.' (*Shítou* 25)

(11) 在   大门   上   轻轻地   扣   了   几   下...（△ 一壶 65）
    zài   dàmén   shàng   qīngqīng-de   kòu   le   jǐ   xià
    at   gate   on   lightly   knock LE several CL
    '(He) lightly knocked at the gate several times.' (△*Yīhú* 65)

(12) 我   赞叹   了   一   声...（独上 70）
    wǒ   zàntàn   le   yī   shēng
    1SG praise   LE   one   CL
    'I let out a sign of praise.' (*Dùshàng* 70)

(13) 前后　　　　　　改嫁　了　三　回。（△ 浮萍 182）
　　 qiánhòu　　　　　 gǎijià　le　sān　huí
　　 from.beginning.to.end　remarry　LE　three　CL
　　 'All in all, she remarried three times.' (△*Fúpíng* 182)

(14) 死　了　十　年　了（风雨 8）
　　 sǐ　le　shí　nián　le
　　 die　LE　ten　year　LE
　　 '(He) has been dead for ten years.' (*Fēngyǔ* 8)

(15) 放映　了　十五　分钟。（华韵 28）
　　 fàngyìng　le　shíwǔ　fēnzhōng
　　 play　LE　fifteen　minute
　　 'have been playing for fifteen minutes.' (*Huáyùn* 28)

(16) 工作　了　二十　天。（短篇 36）
　　 gōngzuò　le　èrshí　tiān
　　 work　LE　twenty　day
　　 'work for twenty days.' (*Duǎnpiān* 36)

　　In examples (8) to (10), the object numeral-classifier phrase contains a nominal classifier, and it is a typical object with a specific reference. In examples (11) to (16), the numeral-classifier phrases in the object position consist of a verbal classifier and a temporal classifier respectively, and they are quasi-objects (see Sections 6.4 and 6.5 in Volume I).

4　In addition, the numeral-classifier phrase can act as predicates. The subject sometimes can be nominal phrases (excluding numerals). For example:

(17) 他　十四　岁。（狮子 68）
　　 tā　shísì　suì
　　 3SG　fourteen　years
　　 'He is fourteen years old.' (*Shīzi* 68)

(18) 焚尸　　　　费　一万　元。（万花筒 34）
　　 fénshī　　　　fèi　yīwàn　yuán
　　 cremate.dead.bodies　fee　ten.thousand　yuan
　　 '(It) costs ten thousand *yuan*s to cremate a body.' (*Wànhuātǒng* 34)

(19)

小品文	一	本,	散文	一	本,	专栏	一	本,
xiǎopǐnwén	yī	běn	sǎnwén	yī	běn	zhuānlán	yī	běn
essay	one	CL	prose	one	CL	column	one	CL

小说	一	本…(△ 天长 176)
xiǎoshuō	yī	ben
novel	one	CL

'One essay, one piece of prose, one column, and one novel.' (△*Tiāncháng* 176)

(20)

新鲜	火腿肉	两	片,	生鸡蛋	两	粒…(石头 48)
xīnxiān	huǒtuǐròu	liǎng	piàn	shēngjīdàn	liǎng	lì
fresh	bacon	two	CL	fresh.egg	two	CL

'two slices of fresh bacon and two fresh eggs.' (*Shítou* 48)

Sometimes the subject can also be numeral-classifier compounds. The resulting subject-predicate phrase has the grammatical meaning of 'every'. For example:

(21)

一	个	人	一	美元	一	人	一	份
yī	gè	rén	yī	měiyuán	yī	rén	yī	fèn
one	CL	person	one	CL/dollar	one	CL/person	one	CL

'One dollar per person' 'One for each person'

(22)

一	种	一	包	一	次	一	个
yī	zhǒng	yī	bāo	yī	cì	yī	gè
one	CL/kind	one	CL/pack	one	CL/time	one	CL

'One pack of each kind' 'One at a time'

5 Furthermore, the numeral-classifier phrase can accept modification of certain adverbs. For example:

(23)

足足	七	个 (△ 一壶 54)
zú-zú	qī	gè
fully	seven	CL

'A full seven of them!' (△*Yīhú* 54)

我	已经	十七	岁	了(华文教材 2A 205)
wǒ	yǐjīng	shíqī	suì	le
1SG	already	seventeen	years	LE

'I'm already seventeen years old.' (*Huáwénjiàocái* 2A, 205)

98 Expressions of Number and Quantity

才　十七　岁（金狮奖（四）22）
cái　shíqī　suì
only　seventeen　years.old

'only seventeen years old' (*Jīnshījiǎng IV*, 22)

It can also be modified by attributes, though they are limited to 的 *de* 'DE' construction. For instance:

(24) 独脚戏，　也　叫　"滑稽"，　也　是　**曲艺**　**的**
*dújiǎoxì　yě　jiào　huájī　yě　shì　**qǔyì**　**de***
monodrama　also　call　comic.talk　also　be　**folk.art**　**DE**

一　种。　（笑眼 139）
yī　zhǒng
one　CL/kind

'Monodrama, also called comic talk, is one of the Chinese folk art forms.' (*Xiàoyǎn* 139)

Sometimes a monosyllabic adjective, most commonly 大 *dà* 'big' and 小 *xiǎo* 'small', can be inserted in numeral-classifier phrases, as shown next:

(25) 闹　了　一　**大**　场　　　一　**大**　群　人
*nào　le　yī　**dà**　chǎng　　yī　**dà**　qún　rén*
quarrel　LE　one　**big**　CL　　one　**big**　CL　person
'Make a terrible scene'　　　　'A large crowd of people'

一　**大**　片　　　　　一　**大**　碗
*yī　**dà**　piàn　　　　yī　**dà**　wǎn*
one　**big**　CL　　　　one　**big**　CL
'a large piece'　　　　　'a large bowl'

一　**大**　笔　钱
*yī　**dà**　bǐ　qián*
one　**big**　CL　money
'a large sum of money'

(26) 一　**小**　碗　菜　　　一　**小**　碟　黑　瓜子
*yī　**xiǎo**　wǎn　cài　　yī　**xiǎo**　dié　hēi　guāzǐ*
one　**small**　CL　food　　one　**small**　CL　black　melon.seeds
'A small bowl of food'　　'A small dish of black melon seeds'

一 小 块 自己 熟悉 的 土壤
yī **xiǎo** kuài zìjǐ shúxī de tǔrǎng
one **small** CL oneself familiar DE earth
'a small piece of familiar earth'

吃 了 几 小 片 年糕
chī le jǐ **xiǎo** piàn niángāo
eat LE several **small** CL rice.cake
'eat several small pieces of rice cake'

(27) 一 长 条
yī **cháng** tiáo
one long CL
'A long strip'

When the numeral is 一 *yī* 'one', the numeral-classifier phrase can be reduplicated. And the whole construction entails the meaning of 'one by one' or 'lots of'. For example:

(28) 发现 家 里 的 东西 一 样 一 样
fāxiàn jiā lǐ de dōngxi yī yàng yī yàng
find home inside DE thing one CL one CL

少 了。（太阳 30）
shǎo le
lose LE
'I found that one by one things in my house were going missing.' (*Tàiyáng* 44)

日子 一 天 一 天 地 飞逝 …（风雨 26）
rìzi yī tiān yī tiān de fēishì
day one CL one CL DE pass.away
'Days are passing away one by one …' (*Fēngyǔ* 26)

(29) 一 盏 一 盏 的 灯 早已 迫不及待地
yī zhǎn yī zhǎn de dēng zǎoyǐ pòbùjídài-de
one CL one CL DE light already can't.wait

亮 起 …（牛车水 15）
liàng qǐ
lighten up
'One by one the lights cannot wait to be lit up.' (*Niúchēshuǐ* 15)

100   *Expressions of Number and Quantity*

搅	出	一	条	一	条	细细长长、	有	韧性、
jiǎo	*chū*	*yī*	*tiáo*	*yī*	*tiáo*	*xìxìchángcháng*	*yǒu*	*rènxìng*
stir	out	**one**	**CL**	**one**	**CL**	thin.and.long	have	tenacity

有	弹性	的	面条	来。（△ 天长 7）
yǒu	*tánxìng*	*de*	*miàntiáo*	*lái*
have	elasticity	DE	noodle	come

'stirring out lots of thin and long noodles with tenacity and elasticity.'
(△*Tiāncháng* 7)

In example (28), the reduplication of the numeral-classifier phrase functions as an adverbial, while in example (29), it serves as an attribute.

1.14.2 Differences in Quantity Expressions Between Singapore Mandarin and Chinese Mandarin

Even though Singapore Mandarin and Chinese Mandarin are basically consistent in quantity expression, differences exist. Three main differences are as follows:

1   If a numeral is greater than one hundred and starts by 一 *yī* 'one', the 一 *yī* 'one' is frequently omitted. For example:

(30)
今年	将	耗资	**亿 2000 万**	元	兴建	一	座
jīnnián	*jiāng*	*hàozī*	***yìliǎngqiānwàn***	*yuán*	*xīngjiàn*	*yī*	*zuò*
this.year	will	spend	**120.million**	yuan	build	one	CL

新的	机场	大厦。（报 1995 年 3 月 2 日 24 版）
xīn-de	*jīchǎng*	*dàshà*
new	airport	building

'A new airport building will be built at a cost of 120 million yuans this year.' (*Bào*, Mar. 2, 1995, Issue no. 24)

In example (30), 亿 2000 万 *yì liǎngqiān wàn* '120 million' is the abbreviated form of 一亿 2000 万 *yīyì liǎngqiān wàn*. Other examples are as follows,

(31)
他	花	了	**百**	**多**	元	买	了
tā	*huā*	*le*	***bǎi***	***duō***	*yuán*	*mǎi*	*le*
3SG	spend	LE	**hundred**	**more**	yuan	buy	LE

一　　双　　　皮鞋。（八方 110）
yī   shuāng   píxié
one   CL   leather.shoes

'He spent over a hundred *yuans* to buy a pair of leather shoes.'
(*Bāfāng* 110)

(32) 目前　　我　　是　　一　　个　　月　　入　　**千**
     mùqián   wǒ   shì   yī   gè   yuè   rù   **qiān**
     now   1SG be   one CL   month earn **thousand**

元　　的　　女　　秘书。（短篇 56）
yuán de   nǚ   mìshū
yuan DE   female secretary

'At present I am a (female) secretary who earns 1,000 *yuans* a month.'
(*Duǎnpiān* 56)

(33) 俱乐部　　设有　　60　　多　　种　　儿童　　班级，　　学生
     jùlèbù   shèyǒu liùshí duō   zhǒng értóng bānjí   xuéshēng
     club   have   60   more CL   children class   student

人数　　　超过　　**千**　　名。（报 1995 年 4 月 19 日 10 版）
rénshù   chāoguò **qiān**   míng
number.   exceed   **thousand** CL
of.people

'The club has more than 60 types of children's classes with more than a thousand students.' (*Bào*, Apr. 19, 1995, Issue no. 10)

In Chinese Mandarin, there is basically no such omission. This kind of abbreviated form can be seen occasionally in the attribute position as in 千人大会 *qiānrén dàhuì* 'Congress of a Thousand People' and 万元户 *wànyuán hù* 'ten-thousand yuan household', with no foreseeable tendency of being used widely. Now, in a Singapore Mandarin newspaper, numerals are generally expressed by Arabic numerals; for example, 千元 *qiānyuán* 'a thousand *yuans*' is written as 1.000 元, 千人 *qiānrén* 'a thousand people' is written as 1,000 人. In this way, we cannot tell whether 一 *yī* 'one' is omitted or not. But in spoken language, 千元 *qiānyuán* 'a thousand *yuans*' and 千人 *qiānrén* 'a thousand people' are still commonly used.

2 When a numeral is used to count money and starts with 一 *yī* 'one', 一 *yī* 'one' is always omitted. For example,

(34) 块　　　　　　三？　你？...
    kuài　　　　 **sān**　 **nǐ**
    CL　　　　　　 three　2SG
    'One yuan and thirty cents? You?...'

    对不起，　我　　身上　　　没有　　零钱。（报 1995
    　　　　　　　　　　　　　　　　　　　　年 4 月 19 日 10 版）
    duìbùqǐ　**wǒ**　**shēnshàng**　**méiyǒu**　**língqián**
    sorry　　 1SG　body　　　 not.have　 change
    'Sorry, I have no change with me.' (*Zàijiàn* 5)

(35) "喂，　老板，　　多少　　钱？"
    wèi　**lǎobǎn**　**duōshǎo**　**qián**
    hello　 boss　　how.much　money
    'Hello, boss, how much is it?'

    "块　　七！"（我有 102）
    kuài　**qī**
    CL　　seven
    'One yuan and seventy cents.' (*Wǒyǒu* 102)

(36) 第四　　天，　"飞力士"　的　　上午　　　行情　　　竟　　 落
    dìsì　**tiān**　**fēilìshì**　**de**　**shàngwǔ**　**hángqíng**　**jìng**　**luò**
    fourth　day　 Felix　　 DE　 morning　 quotation　actually　fall

    毛　　七。（吾土·小说上 92）
    máo　**qī**
    CL　　seven
    'On the fourth day, Felix's quote actually decreased seventeen cents in the morning.' (*Wútǔ Novel I* 92)

(37) 我　　的　　酿豆腐　　　可以　 卖　　角　　 半　　了。（吾土·
    　　　　　　　　　　　　　　　　　　　　　　　　　　　小说上 35）
    wǒ　**de**　**niàngdòufǔ**　**kěyǐ**　**mài**　**jiǎo**　**bàn**　**le**
    1SG　 DE　 stuffed.tofu　　can　　sell　 CL　　half　LE
    'My stuffed tofu can sell at fifteen cents now.' (*Wútǔ Novel I* 35)

There is no such omitted form in Chinese Mandarin either.

Expressions of Number and Quantity 103

3   For numerals which are two-digit and larger than one hundred, the second magnitudinal numeral is often omitted and is followed by classifiers directly. For example,

(38) 有关   公司   被   罚款   九千五
     yǒuguān   gōngsī   bèi   fákuǎn jiǔqiānwǔ
     related   company BEI   fine   nine.thousand.and.five.hundred

元。（报 1995 年 3 月 11 日 12 版）
yuán
yuan

'The related company was fined 9,500 *yuans*.' (*Bào*, Mar. 11, 1995, Issue no. 12)

九千五元 *jiǔqiānwǔyuán* 'nine thousand five hundred *yuans*' is the abbreviated form of 九千五百元 *jiǔqiānwǔbǎiyuán* with the magnitudinal numeral 百 *bǎi* 'hundred' omitted. Other examples are as follows:

(39) 一   妇女   判监   17   个   月,
     yī   fùnǚ   pànjiān   shíqī   gè   yuè
     one   woman   sentence seventeen CL   month

罚   万二   元。（报 1995 年 3 月 11 日 12 版）
fá   wàn'èr   yuán
fine twelve.thousand yuan

'A woman was sentenced to 17 months in prison and fined 12 thousand *yuans*.' (*Bào*, Mar. 11, 1995, Issue no. 12)

(40) 两   人   合   起来   有   千五六
     liǎng   rén   hé   qǐlái   yǒu   qiānwǔliù
     two   person   together   up   have   a.thousand.five.hundred.sixty

块   钱   的   收入。（吾土 · 小说上 71）
kuài   qián   de   shōurù
CL   money   DE   income

'The two of them have a total income of one thousand, five hundred and sixty yuans.' (*Wútǔ Novel I* 71)

(41) 电子厂   化学气体   泄漏,   千五   名
     diànzǐchǎng   huàxuéqìtǐ   xièlòu   qiānwǔ   míng
     electronics.factory chemical.gas leakage   a.thousand.and.   CL
                                                 five.hundred

工友　　紧急　　疏散。（报 1995 年 3 月 11 日 12 版）
gōngyǒu　jǐnjí　　shūsàn
worker　emergent　evacuate

'As there was a chemical gas leakage in the electronics factory, one thousand five hundred workers were evacuated in emergency.' (*Bào*, Mar. 11, 1995, Issue no. 12)

In Chinese Mandarin, for a two-digit numeral greater than one hundred, the second magnitudinal numeral can also be omitted. For example, 二百六十 *èrbǎi liùshí* 'two hundred and sixty' can be abbreviated to 二百六 *èrbǎi liù*, and 三万四千 *sānwàn sìqiān* 'thirty-four thousand' can be substituted by 三万四 *sānwàn sì*. Nevertheless, this abbreviated form cannot be followed by classifiers directly, for example, 二百六十元 *èrbǎi liùshí yuán* 'two hundred and sixty *yuan*s' cannot be expressed as *二百六元 *èrbǎi liù yuán*, that is, the magnitudinal numeral 十 *shí* 'ten' cannot be omitted.

Numeral-classifier phrases all denote numbers, but certain numeral-classifier phrases with nominal classifiers sometimes can have reference functions when being used in pairs, as illustrated by the following examples:

(42)　高空　　与　　深海，　　一　　个　　是　　高不可攀，　　一　　个
　　　gāokōng　yǔ　　shēnhǎi　　yī　　gè　　shì　　gāobùkěpān　　yī　　gè
　　　high.sky　and　deep.sea　　one　CL　be　　unattainable　　one　CL

　　　是　深不可测。（青青 13）
　　　shì　shēnbùkěcè
　　　be　unfathomable

'High sky and deep sea, one is unattainable, and the other is unfathomable.' (*Qīngqīng* 13)

Obviously, in example (42), the former 一个 *yīgè* 'one CL' refers to 高空 *gāokōng* 'high sky', while the latter refers to 深海 *shēnhǎi* 'deep sea'. Another example is as follows:

(43)　看　　你　　两　　位，　　准　　是　　同床异梦，
　　　kàn　nǐ　　liǎng　wèi　　zhǔn　shì　　tóngchuángyìmèng
　　　see　2SG　two　　CL　　must　be　　strange.bedfellows

　　　一　　个　　想　　老婆，　　一　　个　　想　　爱人。（金狮奖 97）
　　　yī　　gè　　xiǎng　lǎopó　　yī　　gè　　xiǎng　àirén
　　　one　CL　miss　wife　　　one　CL　miss　lover

'Look at you two, both must be strange bedfellows: one misses his wife, and the other misses a lover.' (*Jīnshījiǎng* 97)

(44) 跟 他 同 来 的 有 两 位 比较
 gēn tā tóng lái de yǒu liǎng wèi bǐjiào
 with 3SG together come DE have two CL relatively

年轻的 作家： 一 位 叫 苏伟真，
niánqīng-de zuòjiā yī wèi jiào sūwěizhēn
young writer one CL call Su.Weizhen

一 位 叫 简祯。（怀旧 105）
yī wèi jiào jiǎnzhēn
one CL call Jian.Zhen

'There are two relatively younger writers coming with him, one is called Su Weizhen, and the other is called Jian Zhen.' (*Huáijiù* 105)

Notes

1 Translator's note: In English, all the words referring to natural numbers are called cardinals, such as 'one, two, three . . . ten . . . one hundred . . . one thousand . . . ten thousand . . . one hundred thousand . . . one million . . . one billion . . . one trillion'. The words 'ten', 'hundred', 'thousand', 'million', 'billion' and 'trillion' are numerals indicating the increasing of digit numbers in the decimal system. There is no specific word for 'ten thousand' or for 'one hundred million', and thus these two are phrases. In Singapore Mandarin and Chinese Mandarin, there is not a word specifically referring to 'million' or 'billion', but there is a word for 'ten thousand', 万 *wàn*, and 'one hundred million', 亿 *yì*. In English, there is no specific term referring to the words indicating the increasing of digit numbers 'ten', 'hundred', 'thousand', 'million', 'billion' and 'trillion'. However, in Singapore Mandarin and Chinese Mandarin, we have a term called 位数词 *wèishùcí*. Since there is no equivalent term, we translate this term as 'magnitudinal numerals'.
2 The phrase 年过半百 *niánguòbànbǎi* 'over half a hundred years old' is a saying from classical Chinese and has become a fixed expression. We cannot say * 半十 *bànshí* 'half ten', * 半千 *bànqiān* 'half a thousand' or * 半万 *bànwàn* 'half ten thousand' by analogy.
3 See: *The Usage of Punctuation Marks: Explanation on the Usage of Punctuation Marks*, edited by the Revision group, Chinese Press, 1990.
4 These are all multi-category words: both 来 *lái* and 余 *yú* can be a verb and an auxiliary, (来 *lái* 'as a verb means 'come', as an auxiliary means 'about'; 余 *yú* as a verb and as an auxiliary both means 'more') 多 *duō* 'more' can be adjective, verb and auxiliary (the meaning of each is similar), and 左右 *zuǒyòu* 'about' is both a locative word and an auxiliary meaning 'about'.
5 Lü Shuxiang. *Eight Hundred Words of Modern Chinese*, The Commercial Press, 1981.
6 *Dictionary of Functional Words in Modern Chinese,* compiled by language class students of 1955 and 1957 in the Chinese Department of Peking University, The Commercial Press, 1982.
7 In linguistic circles, there are different opinions regarding the syntactic nature of the word 第 *dì*. Some regard it as a prefix, as in *Modern Chinese Grammar* by Ding Shengshu (The Commercial Press, 1961) and *Grammar Handouts* by Zhu Dexi (The

Commercial Press, 1982), while others regard it as an auxiliary, as in *Modern Chinese* by Hu Yushu (Shanghai Educational Publishing House, 1979). In this book, we treat 第 *dì* as an auxiliary.

8 Translator's note: The Chinese style measure words are as follows. We keep the Chinese pinyin as translation of these measure words here.

For length, 1 *lǐ* = 0.5 kilometres; 1 *zhàng* = 10 *chǐ* = 100 *cùn* = 3.333 metres;
For weight, 1 *jīn* = 10 *liǎng* = 0.5 kilogram;
For monetary, 1 *yuán (kuài)* 'Chinese yuan' = 10 *jiǎo (máo)* = 100 *fen*.

9 See Ma Zhen, Yi Jing Jian Ichiro, Yamada Liu Li Zi, Learning Chinese with Teacher Ma, Junhetai Press, 1995, Tokyo.

2 Expressions of Location, Time and Place

2.1 An Overview of Expressions of Location, Time and Place

2.1.1 Localisers

As is implied by the name, a localiser denotes location. It's a subclass of nouns. For example,

(1) 老李　　和　　老张　　　由　　门　　**前**　　经过，　　他们　　的
    lǎolǐ　　*hé*　　*lǎozhāng*　*yóu*　*mén*　***qián***　*jīngguò*　　*tāmen*　*de*
    Lao.Li　and　Lao.Zhang　by　door　**front**　pass.by　　3PL　　DE

   谈话　　　　　声，　　使　　阿兰、　阿英　　停止　　了　　说话，
   tánhuà　　　 *shēng*　*shǐ*　*ālán*　　*āyīng*　*tíngzhǐ*　*le*　*shuōhuà*
   conversation　sound　　make　A.Lan　　A.Ying　stop　　　LE　say

   而　　　注意　　向　　　**外**　　　看。（吾土·戏剧 159）
   ér　　*zhùyì*　*xiàng*　***wài***　　*kàn*
   but　　notice　towards　**outside**　look

   'Lao Li and Lao Zhang passed by the door. The sound of their conversation made A Lan and A Ying stop talking and look out.' (*Wútǔ* (drama) 159)

(2) 朱穆朗　　　　一　　颗　　心　　忐忑不安，　　在　　巴士　　**上**
    zhūmùlǎng　*yī*　*kē*　*xīn*　*tǎntèbùān*　　 *zài*　*bāshì*　***shàng***
    Zhu.Mulang　one　CL　heart　very.upset　　　at　　bus　　**on**

   思前想后。（金狮奖 100）
   sīqiánxiǎnghòu
   ponder.over

   'Zhu Mulang was very upset and was pondering over it on the bus.' (*Jīnshījiǎng* 100)

(3) 她   决定   进   去   店铺   **里**   看看。（跳舞 60）
    tā   juédìng jìn qù diànpù   **lǐ**   kànkàn
    3SG   decide   go   into store   **inside** have.a.look
    'She decided to enter the store and have a look.' (*Tiàowǔ* 60)

(4) **左**   厢   嘛,   就   只   有   两   间   房子,
    zuǒ xiāng   ma   jiù   zhǐ   yǒu   liǎng jiān fángzi
    left wing-building TOP   just only have   two   CL   room

前边   住   着   亚碰   一家人   **后边**   住   的   是
qiánbiān zhù   zhe   yàpèng   yījiārén   **hòubiān** zhù   de   shì
front   live ZHE   Yapeng   family   **back**   live DE   be

虹姑娘。（大喜 5）
hónggūniáng
Miss.Hong

'In the left wing building, there are only two rooms. Yapeng's family lives in the front room, and Miss Hong lives in the back room.' (*Dàxǐ* 5)

(5) 伊班人   死   **后**,   亦   葬   在   森林   的   土地   **里**,
    yībānrén sǐ   **hòu**   yì   zàng   zài   sēnlín de   tǔdì   **lǐ**
    Iban   die   **after** also bury   in   forest DE   soil   **inside**

上面   再   覆盖   了   一   座   低矮的   小屋,   **里面**
shàngmiàn zài fùgài   le   yī   zuò   dīǎide   xiǎowū   **lǐmiàn**
above   again cover   LE   one   CL   low   hut   **inside**

放置   死者   生前   应用   过   的
fàngzhì sǐzhě   shēngqián   yìngyòng guò   de
place   the.dead before.one's.death use   GUO   DE

日用品   及   糯米酒   瓮   等。（南北 31）
rìyòngpǐn   jí   nuòmǐjiǔ   wèng   děng
daily.necessities and   sticky.rice.wine   jar   etc.

'After the Ibans die, they will also buried in the forest, with a low hut above. In the hut, the daily necessities and sticky rice wine jar used by the dead are placed.' (*Nánběi* 31)

The words 前 *qián* 'front', 外 *wài* 'outside', 上 *shàng* 'up', 后 *hòu* 'back', 里 *lǐ* 'inside', 左 *zuǒ* 'left', 前边 *qiánbiān* 'in front', 后边 *hòubiān* 'in back',

里面 *lǐmiàn* 'inside' and 上面 *shàngmiàn* 'above' in examples (1)–(5) are all localisers.

Generally speaking, the use of localisers always requires a reference point. In example (1), 门 *mén* 'door' is the reference point of the localiser 前 *qián* 'front'; in example (2), 巴士 *bāshì* 'bus' is the reference point of the localiser 上 *shàng* 'up'; and in example (3), 店铺 *diànpù* 'store' serves as the reference point of the localiser 里 *lǐ* 'inside'. The same is true of other localisers. It seems that no reference point is available in the case of 外 *wài* 'outside' in (1), but in fact, the reference point is the house A Lan and A Ying were in.

2.1.2 Time Expressions

The concept of time expressions represents more of a semantic classification than a separate word class category.[1] Time expressions, as the name indicates, simply refer to words or phrases denoting time, and they can be classified into two subtypes:

The first subtype includes nouns indicating time. For example,

今天 *jīntiān* 'today'   现在 *xiànzài* 'now'
明年 *míngnián* 'next year'   将来 *jiānglái* 'in the future'
下午 *xiàwǔ* 'afternoon'

The second subtype includes phrases that indicate time. For example,

上个星期 *shànggè xīngqī* 'last week'   五个月 *wǔgè yuè* 'five months'
三年 *sān nián* 'three years'   两个星期 *liǎnggè xīngqī* 'two weeks'
吃饭前 *chīfàn qián* 'before a meal'   放学后 *fàngxué hòu* 'after school'
劳动中 *láodòng zhōng* 'during work'   上课时 *shàngkè shí* 'when having class'
十二点一刻 *shíèr diǎn yī kè* 'a quarter past twelve'

In terms of meaning, time expressions indicate two different kinds of situations related to time. Firstly, they can denote the idea of 'when'. For instance, the following phrases usually indicate a specific time, or in other words, 'point of time'.

星期天 *xīngqītiān* 'Sunday'   后天 *hòutiān* 'the day after tomorrow'
中午 *zhōngwǔ* 'noon'   明年 *míngnián* 'next year'
今天晚上 *jīntiān wǎnshàng* 'tonight'   吃饭前 *chīfàn qián* 'before a meal'
放学后 *fàngxué hòu* 'after school'   劳动中 *láodòng zhōng* 'during work'
上课时 *shàngkè shí* 'when having class'
一九九七年 *yījiǔjiǔqī nián* '1997'

Secondly, time expressions can also denote 'how much time'. As shown by the following phrases, they all indicate the duration of time, or 'period of time'.

三个月 *sāngè yuè* 'three months'   四年 *sì nián* 'four years'
三分钟 *sān fēnzhōng* 'three minutes'   两天 *liǎng tiān* 'two days'
五个晚上 *wǔgè wǎnshàng* 'five nights'

The first subtype of time expressions all denote a 'point of time', while the second subtype of time expressions can denote either a point of time or a period of time, as shown in the following:

Point of time

上个星期 *shànggè xīngqī* 'last week'   中午 *zhōngwǔ* 'noon'
今天晚上 *jīntiān wǎnshàng* 'tonight'   吃饭前 *chīfàn qián* 'before eating'
放学后 *fàngxué hòu* 'after school'   劳动中 *láodòng zhōng* 'during work'
上课时 *shàngkè shí* 'when having class'   一九九七年 *yījiǔjiǔqī nián* '1997'
十二点一刻 *shíèr diǎn yī kè* 'a quarter past twelve'

Period of time

五个月 *wǔgè yuè* 'five months'   三个月 *sāngè yuè* 'three months'
三年 *sān nián* 'three years'   四年 *sì nián* 'four years'
两个星期 *liǎnggè xīngqī* 'two weeks'   两天 *liǎng tiān* 'two days'
三分钟 *sān fēnzhōng* 'three minutes'   五个晚上 *wǔgè wǎnshàng* 'five nights'

It should be noted that a time expression indicating time duration, such as 这两个星期 *zhè liǎnggè xīngqī* 'these two weeks' and 那两天 *nà liǎng tiān* 'those two days', can also express a point of time if it is preceded by a demonstrative pronoun 这 *zhè* 'this' or 那 *nà* 'that', as exemplified by examples (6) and (7),

(6) 看来 **这 三 天** 他们 也 很少
    kànlái **zhè sān tiān** *tāmen yě hěnshǎo*
    it.seems.that **this three day** 3PL also seldom

   在 家。（再见 25）
   zài jiā
   be home
   'It seems that they have seldom been at home these last three days.' (*Zàijiàn* 25)

(7) 约定 相亲 的 **那 一 天，** 九婶 把 九叔
    yuēdìng xiàngqīn de **nà yī tiān,** *jiǔshěn bǎ jiǔshū*
    appoint blind.date DE **that one day** nine-aunt BA nine-uncle

Expressions of Location, Time and Place 111

那	条	"做皮" 的	老款	西装裤	和	发霉的
nà	tiáo	zuòpíde	lǎokuǎn	xīzhuāngkù	hé	fāméide
that	CL	fake.leather	old.style	suit.pants	and	mouldy

白皮鞋	借	给	了	阿秋。	(Δ 断情剪 152)
báipíxié	jiè	gěi	le	āqiū	
white.leather.shoes	lend	give	LE	A.Qiu	

'On the day of the blind date, A Qiu's ninth aunt lent A Qiu his uncle's old fake-leather suit trousers and mouldy white shoes.' (Δ*Duànqíngjiǎn* 152)

The phrases 三天 *sān tiān* 'three days' in example (6) and 一天 *yī tiān* 'one day' in example (7) originally indicate a period of time, and when 这 *zhè* 'this' and 那 *nà* 'that' are added respectively, the resulting phrase 这三天 *zhè sān tiān* 'these three days' and 那一天 *nà yī tiān* 'that day' both denote a point of time. Similarly, adding 前 *qián* 'before' or 后 *hòu* 'later' after a phrase indicating a period of time will also transfer it into a phrase indicating a point of time. For example,

(8)
二十年	前	的	他	与	二十年	后	的	他
èrshínián	qián	de	tā	yǔ	èrshínián	hòu	de	tā
twenty.years	before	DE	3SG	and	twenty.years	after	DE	3SG

怎么	画	上	等号?	(Δ 断情剪 73)
zěnme	huà	shàng	děnghào	
how	draw	up	equal-sign	

'How can one equate him now with the person he was twenty years ago?' (Δ*Duànqíngjiǎn* 73)

The phrase 二十年 *èrshí nián* 'twenty years' in example (8) originally denotes a period of time. After 前 *qián* 'before' and 后 *hòu* 'after' are added, the phrases 二十年前 *èrshí nián qián* 'twenty years ago' and 二十年后 *èrshí nián hòu* 'twenty years later', which are roughly equal to 'the past' and 'the present', both denote a point of time.

It is also necessary to point out that words such as 已经 *yǐjīng* 'already', 曾经 *céngjīng* 'once', 即将 *jíjiāng* 'soon', 将要 *jiāngyào* 'will' and 马上 *mǎshàng* 'immediately' are also related to time. However, they indicate tense rather than time. These are usually called 'temporal adverbs' and do not belong to time expressions. In addition, attention should be paid to the distinction between 刚才 *gāngcái* 'just now', 刚刚 *gānggāng* 'just' and 刚 *gāng* 'just'. They seem to be alike in meaning, yet they are essentially different in nature. 刚才 *gāngcái* 'just now' is a time word, as discussed in this chapter, while 刚刚 *gānggāng* 'just' and 刚 *gāng* 'just' are temporal adverbs.

2.1.3 Place Expressions

Like time expressions, place expressions are not a word class category, either. Place expressions refer to words or phrases that can serve as the object of prepositions 在 *zài* 'in', 到 *dào* 'to', 往 *wǎng* 'towards' and 从 *cóng* 'from' and can be used to respond to questions with 哪儿 *nǎr* 'where'. They denote location and can be replaced by 这儿 *zhèr* 'here' or 那儿 *nàr* 'there', such as 北京 *běijīng* 'Beijing', 新加坡 *xīnjiāpō* 'Singapore', 门口 *ménkǒu* 'doorway' and 桌子上 *zhuōzi shàng* 'on the table'. Place expressions can be divided into the following three subtypes.

The first subtype of place expressions includes nouns that state location directly, as illustrated next.

北京 *běijīng* 'Beijing'   上海 *shànghǎi* 'Shanghai'
纽约 *niǔyuē* 'New York'   东京 *dōngjīng* 'Tokyo'
新加坡 *xīnjiāpō* 'Singapore'   牛车水 *niúchēshuǐ* 'Chinatown'
金文泰 *jīnwéntài* 'Clementi'

The second subtype includes modifier-head phrases composed of nouns and localisers. For example,

门外 *mén wài* 'outside the door'   桌子上 *zhuōzi shàng* 'on the table'
墙上 *qiáng shàng* 'on the wall'   抽屉里 *chōutì lǐ* 'in the drawer'
游泳池旁边 *yóuyǒngchí pángbiān* 'next to the swimming pool'

The third subtype includes nouns indicating organisations, schools, stores and other enterprises and institutions, as well as nouns indicating buildings, halls, facilities and institutes, as shown in the following examples.

教育部 *jiāoyùbù* 'Ministry of Education'
移民局 *yímínjú* 'Immigration Bureau'
华侨银行 *huáqiáo yínháng* 'OCBC Bank'
图书馆 *túshūguǎn* 'Library'
研究所 *yánjiūsuǒ* 'Research Institute'
南洋理工大学 *nányáng lǐgōng dàxué* 'Nanyang Technological University'
华裔馆 *huáyì guǎn* 'Chinese-American Museum'

The first two subtypes are specialised place expressions, while the third subtype can be used both as general noun phrases and place expressions. For example,

(9) 校长岗　　上　建起　了　宏伟的　新　**图书馆**。
　　　　　　　　　　　　　　　　　　　　　　（Δ 母亲 95）
　*xiàozhǎnggǎng　shàng　jiànqǐ　le　hóngwěide　xīn　**túshūguǎn***

| | Principal's.hill | on | build | LE | majestic | new | **library** |

'A magnificent new library has been built on the principal's hill.'
(Δ*Mǔqīn* 95)

(10)	我	在	宿舍	里	便	能	听到	同学们	上
	wǒ	zài	sùshè	lǐ	biàn	néng	tīngdào	tóngxuémen	shàng
	1SG	at	dormitory	inside	thus	can	hear	classmates	go.to

	新	**图书馆**	以及	回去	宿舍	的	脚步声。(Δ 母亲 95)
	xīn	**túshūguǎn**	yǐjí	huíqù	sùshè	de	jiǎobùshēng
	new	**library**	and	return	dorm	DE	footstep.sound

'From my dormitory I could hear the footsteps of my classmates going to the new library and returning.' (Δ*Mǔqīn* 95)

图书馆 *túshūguǎn* 'library' is used as a general noun in example (9), whereas it is used as a place noun in example (10).

2.2 Localisers

2.2.1 Types of Localisers

Localisers can be divided into two types: single localisers and compound localisers.

Translator's note: It should be noted that Localisers is a special type of words in Mandarin and there are many of them as discussed in this section. In English there is no word type as localisers, and in this book we just translate them to prepositions, nouns or adverbs in English according to the meaning expressed.

1. Single Localisers

There are only 16 single localisers, as shown in the following:

上 *shàng* 'up'   下 *xià* 'down'
里 *lǐ* 'inside'   外 *wài* 'outside'
前 *qián* 'front'   后 *hòu* 'back'
东 *dōng* 'east'   南 *nán* 'south'
西 *xī* 'west'   北 *běi* 'north'
左 *zuǒ* 'left'   右 *yòu* 'right'
中 *zhōng* 'middle'   间 *jiān* 'between'
内 *nèi* 'inside'   旁 *páng* 'beside'

For example:

114 Expressions of Location, Time and Place

(1) 我　　向　　**上**　　仰望。（∆ 一壶 10）
　　wǒ　xiàng　**shàng**　yǎngwàng
　　1SG　toward　**up**　look.up
　　'I look up.' (∆*Yīhú* 10)

(2) 一　壁　小　　山崖　　**下**　有　个　池子。（怀旧 30）
　　yī　bì　xiǎo　shānyá　**xià**　yǒu　gè　chízi
　　one　CL　small　cliff　**under**　have　CL　pool
　　'There is a pool under a small cliff.' (*Huáijiù* 30)

(3) 厨房　**里**　　发出　　水壶　　碰击　　的　　声音…（短篇 85）
　　chúfáng　**lǐ**　fāchū　shuǐhú　pèngjī　de　shēngyīn
　　kitchen　**inside**　sound　kettle　clatter　DE　sound
　　'The clattering sound of the kettle comes from the kitchen…'
　　(*Duǎnpiān* 85)

(4) 门　**外**　　来　了　个　白发苍苍的　　　　老头儿…
　　　　　　　　　　　　　　　　　　　　　　　（∆ 大喜 177）
　　mén　**wài**　lái　le　gè　báifācāngcāng-de　lǎotóur
　　door　**outside**　come　LE　CL　hoary-haired　old.man
　　'There was a hoary-haired old man outside the door…' (∆*Dàxǐ* 177)

(5) 站　　在　那　一　列　小食　店　**前**…（∆ 天长 12）
　　zhàn　zài　nà　yī　liè　xiǎoshí　diàn　**qián**
　　stand　at　that　one　row　snack　bar　**front**
　　'Standing in front of that row of snack bars…' (∆*Tiānchǎng* 12)

(6) 一　个　穿　　血红　　丝衫　　的　女郎，
　　yī　gè　chuān　xuèhóng　sīshān　de　nǚláng
　　one　CL　wear　scarlet　silk.blouse　DE　lady

　　在　　车　**后**　帮着　扶　柜。（太阳 38）
　　zài　chē　**hòu**　bāngzhe　fú　guì
　　at　car　**back**　help　hold　cupboard
　　'A lady wearing a scarlet silk blouse was helping to hold the cupboard on the back of the car.' (*Tàiyáng*, 38)

(7) 秦毅民　　来　到　**东**　海岸　一　间　小巧
　　qínyìmín　lái　dào　**dōng**　hǎiàn　yī　jiān　xiǎoqiǎo
　　Qin.YiMin　come　to　**east**　coast　one　CL　small

Expressions of Location, Time and Place

别致的	咖啡座 ...（变调 101）
biézhìde	kāfēizuò
fancy	café

'Qin Yimin came to a small fancy café along the east coast ...' (*Biàndiào* 101)

(8)
清朝	衰亡	的	时候，	随着	家族	携着
qīngcháo	shuāiwáng	de	shíhòu	suízhe	jiāzú	xiézhe
Qing.Dynasty	topple	DE	time	with	family	carry

金银财宝	**南**	下	狮城 ...（青青 18）
jīnyíncáibǎo	**nán**	xià	shīchéng
gold.and.jewellery	**south**	go.down	Singapore

'When the Qing Dynasty fell, (I) went with my family to the south and settled in Singapore with all our possessions and jewellery.' (*Qīngqīng* 18)

(9)
50 年	前	的	报界	前辈，	有的	老成	凋谢，
50nián	qián	de	bàojiè	qiánbèi	yǒude	lǎochéng	diāoxiè
50.years	before	DE	press.circle	senior	some	get.old	wither

驾鹤**西**归。（沦陷 8）
jiàhè**xī** guī

passed.away (literal translation: ride the crane and go back to the **west**)

'Among those seniors who were in the press circle 50 years ago, many are in their dotage and some have passed away.' (*Lúnxiàn* 8)

(10)
车队、	人群、	牛	羊	畜牧，	从	**北**	向
chēduì	rénqún	niú	yáng	xùmù	cóng	**běi**	xiàng
caravan	crowd	cattle	sheep	herds	from	**north**	to

南	在	群山	大地	蠕动 ...（金狮奖 36）
nán	zài	qúnshān	dàdì	rúdòng
south	at	mountains	ground	edge.forward

'The caravan, the crowd, the cattle and sheep all edged from north to south along the mountains on the plain ...' (*Jīnshījiǎng* 36)

(11)
那	刺刀	已	插	在	将军	的	**左**	肩，
nà	cìdāo	yǐ	chā	zài	jiāngjun	de	**zuǒ**	jiān
that	bayonet	already	stab	at	General	DE	**left**	shoulder

血　　　流　　　了　　出来。（金狮奖 23）
xiě　　　liú　　　le　　chūlái
blood　　flow　　LE　　out

'The General was stabbed in the left shoulder with a bayonet, and the blood flowed out.' (*Jīnshījiǎng* 23）

(12) 阿凤　　粗壮的　　　身躯　　　上　　　的　　小　　头颅
　　　āfèng　cūzhuàngde　shēnqū　shàng　de　xiǎo　tóulú
　　　A.Feng　sturdy　　　body　　on　　DE　small　head

习惯性地　　　向　　　**右**　　倾斜 . . .（追云 106）
xíguànxìngde　xiàng　**yòu**　qīngxié
habitually　　towards　**right**　tilt

'A Feng would habitually tilt her small head on her sturdy body to the right . . .' (*Zhuīyún* 106)

(13) 另　　一　　个　　在　　厨房　　　**中**　　　不　　　知
　　　lìng　yī　gè　zài　chúfáng　**zhōng**　bù　zhī
　　　other　one　CL　at　kitchen　**inside**　NEG　know

在　　　忙　　　些　　　什么。（华韵 16）
zài　　máng　xiē　　shénme
in.process　busy　some　what

'The other one was in the kitchen. Who knows what he was busy with.' (*Huáyùn* 16)

(14) 各种　　　建筑　　　　格局　　迥异的　　　农舍　　　分散　　在
　　　gèzhǒng　jiànzhù　　géjú　　jiǒngyì-de　nóngshè　fēnsàn　zài
　　　various　architecture　pattern　different　farmhouse　scatter　at

林荫　　小道　　**间**。（南北 40）
línyīn　xiǎodào　**jiān**
shade　path　　**between**

'Various farmhouses with very different architectural patterns are scattered among the shaded paths.' (*Nánběi* 40)

(15) 你　　报案　　　　说　　是　　在　　裕廊　　A 组
　　　nǐ　　bàoàn　　　　shuō　shì　zài　yùláng　ēi-zǔ
　　　2SG　call.the.police　say　be　at　YuLang　Group.A

Expressions of Location, Time and Place 117

大牌	四号	的	电梯	**内**... (△ 浮萍 7)
dàpái	sìhào	de	diàntī	**nèi**
block	Number.4	DE	elevator	**inside**

'You reported that you were in the elevator of Block 4, Yu Lang Group A...' (△*Fúpíng* 7)

(16) 几 个 收工的 小贩， 围 在 一 张
jǐ gè shōugōng-de xiǎofàn wéi zài yī zhāng
several CL knock.off vendors sit.around at one CL

圆桌 **旁** 聚 赌。（牛车水 24）
yuánzhuō **páng** jù dǔ
round.table **beside** gather gamble

'After work, several vendors gathered around a round table to gamble.' (*Niúchēshuǐ* 24)

2. Compound Localisers

There are three kinds of compound localisers:

The first type is composed of a single localiser and one of these five words: 边 *biān* 'side', 面 *miàn* 'side', 头 *tóu* 'side', 方 *fāng* 'direction', 当 *dāng* 'in'. The possible combinations are listed next:

	边 *biān* 'side'	面 *miàn* 'side'	头 *tóu* 'side'	方 *fāng* 'direction'	当 *dāng* 'in'
上 *shàng* 'up'	上边	上面	上头	上方	—
下 *xià* 'below'	下边	下面	下头	下方	—
里 *lǐ* 'inside'	里边	里面	里头	—	—
外 *wài* 'outside'	外边	外面	外头	—	—
前 *qián* 'front'	前边	前面	前头	前方	—
后 *hòu* 'back'	后边	后面	后头	后方	—
东 *dōng* 'east'	东边	东面	东头	东方	—
西 *xī* 'west'	西边	西面	西头	西方	—
南 *nán* 'south'	南边	南面	南头	南方	—
北 *běi* 'north'	北边	北面	北头	北方	—
左 *zuǒ* 'left'	左边	左面	—	左方	—
右 *yòu* 'right'	右边	右面	—	右方	—
中 *zhōng* 'middle'	—	—	—	—	当中
间 *jiān* 'between'	—	—	—	—	—

内 *nèi* 'inside'　　　　—　　　—　　　—　　　—　　　—
旁 *páng* 'beside'　　旁边　—　　　—　　　—　　　—

The second type consists of a combination of the aforementioned 16 single localisers. The acceptable combinations are listed next:

上下 *shàngxià* 'up and down'　　里外 *lǐwài* 'inside and outside'
前后 *qiánhòu* 'front and back'　　东西 *dōngxī* 'east and west'
东南 *dōngnán* 'southeast'　　东北 *dōngběi* 'northeast'
西南 *xīnán* 'southwest'　　西北 *xīběi* 'northwest'
南北 *nánběi* 'north and south'　　左右 *zuǒyòu* 'left and right'
中间 *zhōngjiān* 'middle'　　内外 *nèiwài* 'inside and outside'
间中 *jiānzhōng* 'in between'　　内中 *nèizhōng* 'within'

Among these combinations, 间中 *jiānzhōng* 'in between' exists only in Singapore Mandarin and is never seen in Chinese Mandarin. The following are some examples:

(17) 左右　　两片，　**间中**　　为　通道。（吾土·戏剧 58）
　　 zuǒyòu　　*liǎngpán*　**jiānzhōng**　*wéi*　*tōngdào*
　　 left.and.right　two.valves　**in.between**　be　pathway
　　 'Left and right are two main valves, in between is the pathway.'
　　 (*Wútǔ* (drama) 58)

(18) 游客　　吸引　了　无数的　　小贩，　多数
　　 yóukè　*xīyǐn*　*le*　*wúshù-de*　*xiǎofàn*　*duōshù*
　　 tourists　attract　LE　countless　vendor　most

　　 是　卖　纪念品　　的，　**间中**　　只有　几　　摊
　　 shì　*mài*　*jìniànpǐn*　*de*　**jiānzhōng**　*zhǐyǒu*　*jǐ*　*tān*
　　 be　sell　souvenirs　DE　**in.between**　only　several　stalls

　　 是　卖　小食品　　的。（石头 25）
　　 shì　*mài*　*xiǎoshípǐn*　*de*
　　 be　sell　snack　DE
　　 'Tourists attracted numerous vendors, most of whom sell souvenirs, with only a few booths in between selling snacks.' (*Shítou* 25)

(19) 只　见　客房　　　以　弧状　　分布　　在　外围，
　　 zhǐ　*jiàn*　*kèfáng*　*yǐ*　*húzhuàng*　*fēnbù*　*zài*　*wàiwéi*
　　 only　see　guestroom　by　arc　distribute　at　peripheral

间中	安插	着	共同的	盥洗室，	至于	接待处、
jiānzhōng	ānchā	zhe	gòngtóngde	guànxǐshì	zhìyú	jiēdàichù
in.between	place	ZHE	shared	washroom	as.for	reception

消闲室	及	餐厅	等	集合	在	中间。（南北 14）
xiāoxiánshì	jí	cāntīng	děng	jíhé	zài	zhōngjiān
recreation.room	and	restaurant	etc.	gather	at	middle

'We can see that arranged in an arc around the periphery are the guest rooms, among which there is a shared bathroom. As for reception, recreation room and the restaurant, they are gathered in the middle.' (*Nánběi* 14)

Here, 间中 *jiānzhōng* 'in between' in example (17) has similar meaning to 中间 *zhōngjiān* 'in the middle'; while the 间中 *jiānzhōng* 'in between' in (18) and (19) means similarly to 其中 *qízhōng* 'among which'.

A third type of compound localisers are trisyllable localisers composed of 东西 *dōngxī* 'east and west', 东南 *dōngnán* 'southeast', 东北 *dōngběi* 'northeast', 西南 *xīnán* 'southwest', 西北 *xīběi* 'northwest' and 南北 *nánběi* 'north and south', plus 方 *fāng* 'direction' 面 *miàn* 'side' or 部 *bù* 'part', as illustrated in the following:

(20)
丹绒峇莱，	位	于	新加坡	的	**西南方** 。（南北 33）
dānróngbālái	wèi	yú	xīnjiāpō	de	**xīnánfāng**
Tanjong.Balai	locate	in	Singapore	DE	southwest

'Tanjong Balai is located in the southwest of Singapore.' (*Nánběi* 33)

(21)
位	于	瑞丽	**西北面**	的	盈江...（南北 90）
wèi	yú	ruìlì	**xīběimiàn**	de	yíngjiāng
locate	at	Ruili	**northwest**	DE	Yingjiang

'Yingjiang, northwest of Ruili...' (*Nánběi* 90)

(22)
位	于	印度	**西北部**	的	拉惹斯坦州...（南北 61）
wèi	yú	yìndù	**xīběibù**	de	lārěsītǎnzhōu
locate	in	India	**northwest**	DE	Rajasthan

'Rajasthan located in the northwest of India...' (*Nánběi* 61)

2.2.2 The Grammatical Functions of Localisers

As a subclass of nouns, localisers have similarities and differences with general nouns in terms of grammatical function. The details are as follows:

120   Expressions of Location, Time and Place

1. On Modifying Nouns and Being Modified by Nouns

A general noun can directly modify the other noun as an attribute (See Sections 3.4 and 8.6 in Volume I respectively). Localisers can also serve as the modifiers of nouns. For instance:

(23) 一   段   日子   后   他们   投诚   **南方**   政府
     yī   duàn   rìzi   hòu   tāmen   tóuchéng   **nánfāng**   zhèngfǔ
     one   CL   day   after   3PL   surrender   **southern**   government

军，   又   开始   了   他们   的   作战   生涯。
                                               （金狮奖 7–8）
jūn   yòu   kāishǐ   le   tāmen   de   zuòzhàn   shēngyá
troops   again   start   LE   3PL   DE   fighting   career

'They surrendered to the Southern Government Army after a few days and started fighting again.' (*Jīnshījiǎng* 7–8)

(24) 小鸭   躲   在   车   底下，   年轻人   在   左边   捉
     xiǎoyā   duǒ   zài   chē   dǐxià   niánqīngrén   zài   zuǒbiān   zhuō
     duckling   hide   at   car   under   youth   at   left   catch

它，   小鸭   却   将   身体   偏移   到   右边。   当
tā   xiǎoyā   què   jiāng   shēntǐ   piānyí   dào   yòubiān   dāng
3SG   duckling   but   BA   body   tilt   to   right   when

右边   那   位   年轻人   伸   手   去   捉   它
yòubiān   nà   wèi   niánqīngrén   shēn   shǒu   qù   zhuō   tā
right   that   CL   youth   stretch   hand   go   catch   3SG

时，   它   又   跑   向   左边。（一心 47）
shí   tā   yòu   pǎo   xiàng   zuǒbiān
when   3SG   again   flee   towards   left

'The duckling hid under the car. The young man tried to catch it on the left but it tilted to the right. When the young man on the right reached out his hand to catch it, it ran to the left again.' (*Yīxīn* 47)

(25) 一   个   不   小心，   **上头**   一   杯   咖啡   受到
     yī   gè   bù   xiǎoxīn   **shàngtou**   yī   bēi   kāfēi   shòudào
     one   CL   NEG   careful   **above**   one   CL   coffee   receive

震颤 而 溢出 少许。（无弦月 7）
zhènchàn ér yìchū shǎoxǔ
shake and spill.out a.little

'The cup of coffee on the top was shaken and spilled out a little because of (his) carelessness.' (*Wúxiányuè* 7)

A single localiser is, however, rarely used to modify a noun, at least not in written language, due to the fact that single localisers are usually accompanied by nouns indicating reference point of location. Very few examples are found in our corpora which consisted of twenty novels, travelogues and collections of essays. As for the following cases, they are better regarded as words rather than phrases.

左手 *zuǒ shǒu* 'left hand'   右手 *yòu shǒu* 'right hand'
左脚 *zuǒ jiǎo* 'left foot'   右脚 *yòu jiǎo* 'right foot'
前门 *qián mén* 'front door'   后门 *hòu mén* 'back door'
里屋 *lǐ wū* 'bedroom'   外衣 *wài yī* 'overcoat'
东半球 *dōng bànqiú* 'the Eastern Hemisphere'
西半球 *xī bànqiú* 'the Western Hemisphere'

On the other hand, it is common practice for localisers to be modified by nouns, and most localisers can accept modification of noun phrases.[2] Let's take a look at some examples:

(26) 然后 分别 装 在 两 个 **塑胶袋** **中**,
ránhòu fēnbié zhuāng zài liǎng ge **sùjiāodài** **zhōng**
then respectively put in two CL plastic.bag inside

提 到 楼下， 塞 进 那 个 黑色的
tí dào lóuxià， sāi jìn nà ge hēisède
take to downstairs stuff in that CL black

大 **垃圾桶** 里。（回忆 28）
dà **lājītǒng** lǐ
big garbage.can inside

'(They) were then stowed in two large plastic bags respectively and taken downstairs to be stuffed into the big black garbage can.' (*Huíyì* 28)

(27) 就 把 巧克力 藏 在 放 衣服 的 **柜子**
jiù bǎ qiǎokèlì cáng zài fàng yīfú de **guìzi**
then BA chocolate hide in place clothes DE wardrobe

里。（报 1995 年 3 月 11 日副刊版）
lǐ
inside

'(She) then hid chocolates in the wardrobe.' (*Bào*, Mar. 11, 1995, supplementary edition)

(28) **箱子　　旁边，**　　蹲　　着　　她　　两　　个　　稚龄的
　　　xiāngzi　pángbiān　dūn　zhe　tā　liǎng　gè　zhìlíng-de
　　　case　　beside　　squat　ZHE　3SG　two　CL　young-aged

孙儿　。（石头 38）
sūnér
grandchild

(29) **山头　　后方**　　被　　燃　　得　　一　　片　　通红 . . .（金狮奖 7）
　　　shāntóu　hòufāng　bèi　rán　dé　yī　piàn　tōnghóng
　　　hill　　back　　BEI　burn　DE　one　CL　extremely.red

'The back of the hill was burning red . . .' (*Jīnshījiǎng* 7)

In examples (26) and (27), it is the single localisers that are modified by nominal phrases, and in examples (28) and (29), it is the compound localisers that are being modified. When localisers are modified by nominal nouns, attention shall be paid to the internal structure of the resulting modifier-head phrases. For instance, example (27) should be analysed as A instead of B.

A　　放衣服的　　柜子　　里　　modifier-head phrase
　　　fàngyīfúde　guìzi　　lǐ
　　　　　1　　　　　2

'inside the clothes cabinet'

B　　放衣服的　　柜子　　里　　modifier-head phrase
　　　fàngyīfúde　guìzi　　lǐ
*　　　　1　　　　　　2

When single localisers are modified by nouns, the attribute cannot take 的 *de* 'DE'. For instance, in example (26), 垃圾桶里 *lājītǒng lǐ* 'inside the garbage can' cannot be changed into *垃圾桶的里 *lājītǒng de lǐ*. When compound localisers are modified by nouns, the attributes generally do not take 的 *de* 'DE', though the addition of 的 *de* 'DE' is also acceptable. For example, 箱子旁边 *xiāngzi pángbiān* 'beside the case' in example (28) can be substituted by 箱子的旁边 *xiāngzi de pángbiān* 'beside the case'. Here is one more example:

(30) 在   城市   的   **北方，**   天   上   被   一阵阵   的
     zài *chéngshì* *de* ***běifāng*** *tiān* *shàng* *bèi* *yīzhènzhèn* *de*
     in   city   DE   **north**   sky   up   BEI   fitful   DE

火光   照   得   炽烈   通红。（金狮奖 33）
huǒguāng *zhào* *dé*   *chìliè*   *tōnghóng*
fire   light   DE   blazing   extremely.red

'In the north of the city, the sky was glowing red with bursts of fire.' (*Jīnshījiǎng* 33)

2. On Being Modified by Numeral-Classifier Phrases

Unlike most general nouns, not all localisers can be modified by numeral-classifier compounds (see Sections 3.4 and 8.9 in Volume I for details). Localisers that can be modified by numeral-classifier compounds include only the following twelve localisers:

Single localisers:

里 *lǐ* 'inside/within'   中 *zhōng* 'middle'
前 *qián* 'front/before/ahead'   后 *hòu* 'behind/after/back'
间 *jiān* 'between'   内 *nèi* 'inside/within'

Compound localisers:

里边 *lǐbiān* 'inside'   里面 *lǐmiàn* 'inside'
里头 *lǐtou* 'inside'   当中 *dāngzhōng* 'within'
中间 *zhōngjiān* 'between'   前后 *qiánhòu* 'before-after'

Among them, 前 *qián* 'before', 后 *hòu* 'after', 间 *jiān* 'between', 内 *nèi* 'within' and 前后 *qiánhòu* 'before-after' are modified only by temporal numeral-classifier compounds. For example,

(31) 写   到   这里，   无意   又   追溯
     xiě *dào* *zhèlǐ*   *wúyì*   *yòu*   *zhuīsù*
     write reach here   unintentionally again   trace.back.to

124   Expressions of Location, Time and Place

五十　年　**前**　　的　　情景。（晚上 39）
wǔshí nián **qián** de qíngjǐng
fifty year **before** DE scene

'Writing on that, I unintentionally traced back to the scene fifty years ago.' (*Wǎnshàng* 39)

(32) 几天　　　　**后**，　我　　曾　　收到　　巫汉明　　的
　　 jǐtiān　　　**hòu**　wǒ　céng　shōudào　wūhànmíng　de
　　 several.days **after** 1SG once receive Wu.Hanming DE

信（Δ 狮城 6）
xìn
letter

'A few days later I received a letter from Wu Hanming.' (Δ*Shīchéng* 6)

(33) 叶时候　　死　于　1945　　　年　　5　　月　　**间**，
　　 yèshíhòu　sǐ　yú　yījiǔsìwǔ　nián　wǔ　yuè　**jiān**
　　 Ye.Shihou die in 1945 year five month **between**

距离　日本　　投降　　　只　　有　　三　　个　　月。（沦陷 12）
jùlí　rìběn　tóuxiáng　zhǐ　yǒu　sān　gè　yuè
from Japan surrender only have three CL month

'Ye Shihou died in May 1945, only three months before Japan surrendered.' (*Lúnxiàn* 12)

(34) 他　　说　　战　　后　　五　　年　　**内**，
　　 tā　shuō　zhàn　hòu　wǔ　nián　**nèi**
　　 3SG say war after five year **within**

很多　　反法西斯主义　　战争，　反殖民地　　的　　作品　　发表，
hěnduō　fǎnfǎxīsīzhǔyì　zhànzhēng　fǎnzhímíndì　de　zuòpǐn　fābiǎo
many anti-fascist war anti-colony DE works publish

这些　都　是 ... （Δ 新华文学 14）
zhèxiē　dōu　shì
these all be

'He said that within the five years after the war, many anti-fascist wars were waged and anti-colonial works were published. These are all ...' (Δ*Xīnhuáwénxué* 14)

(35) 远   在   一九三二   年   **前后**，   已经
     yuǎn zài yījiǔsānèr nián **qiánhòu**   yǐjīng
     far   at   1932   year **before-after** already

在   汕头   的   正报   副刊   《绿茵》
zài   shàntóu de   zhèngbào   fùkān   lǜyīn
in   Shantou DE   Journal.Cheng.Pou   supplementary.edition   Green

与   《活地》   上   发表   作品   了。（△ 狮城 13）
yǔ   huódì   shàng   fābiǎo   zuòpǐn   le
and   Living.Land   on   publish works   LE

'As early as around 1932, (he) was publishing works in supplementary editions *Green* and *Living Land* of Shantou's *Journal Cheng Pou*.' (△*Shīchéng* 13)

The other seven localisers can be modified both by temporal numeral-classifier compounds and other numeral-classifier compounds, as illustrated next.

(36) 两   老   认为   一   年   **中**   最   快乐的   时候
     liǎng   lǎo   rènwéi   yī   nián   **zhōng**   zuì   kuàilè-de   shíhòu
     two   old   think   one   year   **middle** most   happy   time

就   是   儿女   带   着   外孙   回   娘家
jiù   shì   érnǚ   dài   zhe   wàisūn   huí   niángjiā
just   be   children take   ZHE   grandson   return parents'.home

小住   的   那   两   个   星期   了。（风雨 37）
xiǎozhù   de   nà   liǎng   gè   xīngqī   le
live.temporarily DE   that   two   CL   week   LE

'The two elders think that the happiest time in the year is the two weeks when their children take their grandson back home to stay.' (*Fēngyǔ* 37)

(37) 在   这   两   个   月   零   七   天   **里**，
     zài   zhè   liǎng   gè   yuè   líng   qī   tiān   **lǐ**
     at   this two   CL   month   zero   seven   day   **within**

人心惶惶，   谁   也   不   知道   大英帝国
rénxīnhuánghuáng   shuí   yě   bù   zhīdào   dàyīngdìguó
in.panic   who   either   NEG   know   British.empire

126 *Expressions of Location, Time and Place*

的	军事	力量	是否	能	保卫	得
de	*jūnshì*	*lìliàng*	*shìfǒu*	*néng*	*bǎowèi*	*dé*
DE	military	power	whether	can	protect	DE

住　　新加坡。（沦陷 23）
zhù　xīnjiāpō
hold　Singapore

'In these two months and seven days, people were all in panic as no one knew whether the military power of the British Empire was strong enough to safeguard Singapore.' (*Lúnxiàn* 23)

(38)　那时　　住　　的　房子　　也　　很　　破旧，
　　　nàshí　*zhù*　*de*　*fángzi*　*yě*　*hěn*　*pòjiù*
　　　that.time live　DE　house　also　very　old

三　　间　　**中**　　有　　两　　间　　都　　漏　　雨。（沦陷 62）
sān　*jiān*　**zhōng**　*yǒu*　*liǎng*　*jiān*　*dōu*　*lòu*　*yǔ*
three　CL　**middle**　have　two　CL　all　leak　rain

'The house (I) lived in at that time was also very dilapidated and two of the three rooms were leaking.' (*Lúnxiàn* 62)

(39)　现在　的　学生，　十　个　**里**　　有　　四　个　戴
　　　xiànzài　*de*　*xuéshēng*　*shí*　*gè*　**lǐ**　*yǒu*　*sì*　*gè*　*dài*
　　　now　DE　student　ten　CL　**within**　have　four　CL　wear

眼镜。（报 1995 年 3 月 12 日 6 版）
yǎnjìng
glass

'Nowadays four out of ten students wear glasses.' (*Bào*, Mar. 12, 1995, Issue no. 6)

The localisers 中 *zhōng* 'middle' and 里 *lǐ* 'within' are modified by temporal numeral-classifier compounds in examples (36) and (37), while in examples (38) and (39) they are modified by nominal numeral-classifier compounds.

Although the aforementioned twelve localisers can be modified by numeral-classifier compounds, they are different from general nouns in the following aspects:

A　General nouns select classifiers when being modified by numeral-classifier compounds. For example, 书 *shū* 'book' is modified by 本 *běn* 'CL' (三本书 *sān běn shū* 'three books'); 纸 *zhǐ* 'paper' is modified by 张 *zhāng* 'CL' (三张纸 *sān zhāng zhǐ* 'three pieces of paper'), 笔 *bǐ* 'pen' is modified by 支 *zhī* 'CL' (三支笔 *sān zhī bǐ* 'three pens') and 面包 *miànbāo* is modified by 个 *gè* 'CL' (三个面包 *sān gè miànbāo* 'three pieces of bread') and so on. However, when it comes to localisers, there is no such restriction. Taking 里面 'inside' as an example, we can say 三本里面 *sān běn lǐmiàn* 'inside the three (books)', 三张里面 *sān zhāng lǐmiàn* 'inside the three pieces', 三支里面 *sān zhī lǐmiàn* 'inside the three (pens)' or 三个里面 *sān gè lǐmiàn* 'inside the three (ones)'.

B The numeral-classifier compounds can represent the meaning of the whole 'numeral + classifier + noun' phrase in certain contexts. For example, sometimes 三本 *sān běn* 'three-CL' can be used to denote 三本书 *sān běn shū* 'three books'. On the contrary, when localisers are modified by numeral-classifier compounds, in no way can the numeral-classifier compound substitute for the whole modifier-head phrase. For instance, 三本 *sān běn* 'three-CL' can never replace 三本里面 *sān běn lǐmiàn* 'inside the three (books)' in any cases.

C In terms of meaning, when a numeral-classifier compound modifies a general noun, the compound is stating the quantity of the object denoted by the noun it modifies. For example, 三本 *sān běn* in the phrase 三本书 *sān běn shū* 'three books' indicates the quantity of 'books'. On the other hand, the numeral-classifier compound that modifies the localisers indicate not the number of the location, but the range of the things or time represented by the entire phrase. For example, 三本中间 *sān běn zhōngjiān* 'among three (books)' indicates the range of things, while 三年前 *sān nián qián* 'three years ago' indicates the range of time.

3. On Being Subjects

General nouns can serve as subjects without strict constraints. But it is not so for localisers. Generally speaking, compound localisers are relatively free to serve as subjects, as exemplified by the following sentences:

(40) **里面**　　有　　个　　试管婴儿　　呢！（跳舞 152）
   lǐmiàn　*yǒu*　*gè*　*shìguǎnyīngér*　*ne*
   inside　have　CL　test-tube.baby　SFP
   'There is a test-tube baby in it!' (*Tiàowǔ* 152)

(41) 当时，　**后面**　　坐　　着　　一　　位　　印度汉，　我　　坐
   dāngshí　***hòumiàn***　*zuò*　*zhe*　*yī*　*wèi*　*yìndùhàn*　*wǒ*　*zuò*
   at.that.time　**back**　sit　ZHE　one　CL　Indian.man　1SG　sit

   在　　前　　座。（一心 52）
   zài　*qián*　*zuò*
   at　front　seat
   'At that time, there was an Indian man sitting in the back, and I was sitting in the front.' (*Yīxīn* 52)

(42) 右边   是   上楼   的   唯一   楼梯。（扶轮 14）
    yòubiān   shì   shànglóu de   wéiyī   lóutī
    right.side be   go.upstairs DE only   stairway
    'The only stairway up is on the right.' (*Fúlún* 14)

In contrast, single localisers are more restricted in the subject position, which is only occasionally found in contrastive statements. For example,

(43) 前   怕   狼，   后   怕   虎。（华文教材 2A 155）
    qián   pà   láng   **hòu** pà   hǔ
    ahead fear wolf   **behind** fear tiger
    'One hesitates to do something because of fear.' (The literal translation is: 'Fear wolves ahead and tigers behind.') (*Huáwénjiàocái* 2A, 155)

(44) 上   有   天堂，   下   有   苏杭 。（华文教材 2B 77）
    shàng yǒu   tiāntáng **xià** yǒu   sūháng
    up   have   heaven **down** have Suzhou.and.Hangzhou
    'There is heaven above and Suzhou and Hangzhou on earth.'
    (*Huáwénjiàocái* 2B, 77)

(45) （两   座   大   亭   似的   建筑物   分置
    liǎng   zuò   dà   tíng   shìde   jiànzhùwù   fēnzhì
    two   CL   big   pavilion like   building   respectively.stand

    左右，)   左   为   看台，   右   为   舞台。（冰灯 77）
    zuǒyòu   **zuǒ** wéi   kàntái **yòu** wéi   wǔtái
    left.and.right **left** be grandstand **right** be stage
    '(The two large pavilion-like buildings are respectively located on the left and right), the left being the grandstand and the right the stage.' (*Bīngdēng* 77)

4. On Being Objects

There are few restrictions for a general noun to be the object of a verb, but it's rare for a localiser to be in the same position. The following are a few examples:

(46) 好   一阵子，   他   翻   身，   倚   着   树干，
    hǎo   yīzhènzi   tā   fān   shēn   yǐ   zhe   shùgàn
    quite a.while   3SG   turn   body   lean.on ZHE   trunk

Expressions of Location, Time and Place 129

眼	也	不	眨	地	瞪	着	**前方**。（金狮奖 14）
yǎn	yě	bù	zhǎ	de	dèng	zhe	**qiánfāng**
eye	also	NEG	blink	DE	stare	ZHE	**front**

'After quite a while, he turned over, leant on the trunk and stared straight ahead without blinking.' (*Jīnshījiǎng* 14)

(47)
母亲	要	他	去	**东边**,	他	偏偏	去
mǔqīn	yào	tā	qù	**dōngbiān**	tā	piānpiān	qù
mother	want	3SG	go	**the.east.side**	3SG	deliberately	go

西边。（狮子 65）
xībiān
the.west.side

'His mother told him to go to the east side but he deliberately went to the west side.' (*Shīzi* 65)

(48)
我	的	儿子,	他、	他、	他	就	在	**前面**,	撞车
wǒ	de	érzi	tā	tā	tā	jiù	zài	**qiánmiàn**	zhuàngchē
1SG	DE	son	3SG	3SG	3SG	just	in	**ahead**	car.crash

了,	头部	不停地	流血 …… （再见 48）
le	tóubù	bùtíngde	liúxuè
LE	head	constantly	bleed

'My son, he, he, he is just over there, hit by a car and his head is bleeding…' (*Zàijiàn* 48)

It should be noted that single localisers serving as objects of verbs are usually found in contrastive sentences, as illustrated by (49) and (50). The phrase 吃里扒外 *chī lǐ pá wài* 'backstabbing' in (50) has already become an idiomatic expression.

(49)
振强	在	**前**,	振威	在	**后**。	地上	的	影子,
zhènqiáng	zài	**qián**	zhènwēi	zài	**hòu**	dìshàng	de	yǐngzi
Zhenqiang	at	**before**	Zhenwei	at	**behind**	ground	DE	shadow

一	个	长长,	一	个	短短。（狮子 87）
yī	gè	chángcháng	yī	gè	duǎnduǎn
one	CL	rather.long	one	CL	rather.short

'Zhenqiang walks ahead and Zhenwei follows behind. One shadow on the ground is long while the other is short.' (*Shīzi* 87)

(50) 你   这个   吃 **里** 扒 **外**   的   家伙，
      nǐ   zhègè chī**lǐ** pá**wài**   de   jiāhuǒ
      2SG   this   eat-**inside**-help-**outside** DE guy

狼心狗肺，   真   是   狗屎不如！（跳舞 50）
lángxīngǒufèi   zhēn   shì   gǒushǐbùrú
ungrateful.bastard really   be   inferior.to.shit

'You betrayer! You are an ungrateful bastard and you are even worse than shit!' (Literal meaning: live off the inside while secretly help the outside.) (*Tiàowǔ* 50)

Nevertheless, localisers are more frequently used as the objects of prepositions. For example,

(51) 程元   急急忙忙地   往   **前**   走。（金狮奖 29）
      chéngyuán   jíjímángmáng-de   wǎng   **qián**   zǒu
      Cheng.Yuan in.a.rush   towards **ahead** go
      'Cheng Yuan goes ahead in a rush.' (*Jīnshījiǎng* 29)

(52) 他   不由自主地   朝   **后**   退   了   一步。
                                                                      （狮子 68）
      tā   bùyóuzìzhǔde   cháo   **hòu**   tuì   le   yībù
      3SG   unconsciously   towards **back**   move.back   LE   one.step
      'He took a step back involuntarily.' (*Shīzi* 68)

(53) 她   偷偷摸摸地   在   **外头**   借宿   下来。（鞭子 105）
      tā   tōutōumōmō-de   zài   **wàitou** jièsù   xiàlái
      3SG   secretly   in   **outside** lodge   down
      'She secretly borrowed a place to stay outside her home.' (*Biānzǐ* 105)

2.3 The Extensional Meaning of Localisers

Localisers originally denote the location of things, which is closely related to places. Thus, indicating of location or place is the original meaning of localisers.

However, sometimes they can also indicate meanings other than locations or places. In the following example, 前 *qián* 'before' actually represents time.

(1)   新年   **前**   的   那   几   天，   大街小巷
      xīnnián   **qián**   de   nà   jǐ   tiān   dàjiēxiǎoxiàn
      new.year   before   DE   that   several day   high.streets.and.back.lanes

Expressions of Location, Time and Place 131

热闹非常。（华文教材 1A 76）
rènàofēicháng
very.lively
'Everywhere is very lively during the few days before New Year's Eve.'
(*Huáwénjiàocái* 1A, 76)

Also, in the phrase 三本里面 *sān běn lǐmiàn* 'inside the three books', 里面 *lǐmiàn* 'inside' indicates the range of things; in the idiom 欺上瞒下 *qī shàng mán xià* 'deceive one's superiors and subordinates', 上 *shàng* refers to superiors (the leader or senior), and 下 *xià* refers to subordinates (the crowd or junior). These designative meanings other than locations or places are extensional meanings of localisers. More examples follow:

(2) 祖母　　　　走　**后**，　我　　又　　问：…（太阳 21）
　　zǔmǔ　　　 *zǒu* **hòu**　*wǒ*　*yòu*　*wèn*
　　grandmother leave **after** 1SG again ask
　　'When my grandmother left I asked again that …' (*Tàiyáng* 21)

(3) 这个　　仪式　　很　　简单，　**前后**　　只有　　一两　　　分钟，
　　zhège　*yíshì*　*hěn*　*jiǎndān*　**qiánhòu**　*zhǐyǒu*　*yīliǎng*　*fēnzhōng*
　　this　　rite　　very　simple　**before-after**　only　one.or.two　minute

　　便　　大功告成　　　　了。（鞭子）
　　biàn　*dàgōnggàochéng*　*le*
　　then　succeed　　　　　 LE
　　'This ceremony is so simple that it only takes one or two minutes to finish.'
　　(*Biānzi*)

(4) 这个　　字　　　只是　　在　　名字　　**当中**　　用到，…
　　　　　　　　　　　　　　　　　　　　　　　　　　　　（Δ 华语 29）
　　zhège　*zì*　　 *zhǐshì*　*zài*　*míngzi*　**dāngzhōng**　*yòngdào*
　　this　　character only　 in　　name　　**within**　　use
　　'This character is only used in names …' (Δ*Huáyǔ* 29)

(5) 天天　　　在　　风　　**里**、　雨　　**里**、　太阳　　酷晒
　　tiāntiān　*zài*　*fēng* **lǐ**　*yǔ* **lǐ**　*tàiyáng*　*kùshài*
　　everyday　in　　wind **inside** rain **inside** sun　severe.heat

　　里　　挣扎　　　咬牙，　在　　粗茶淡饭　　**里**　　自苦，　日子
　　lǐ　　*zhēngzhá*　*yǎoyá*　*zài*　*cūchádànfàn*　**lǐ**　*zìkǔ*　*rìzi*
　　inside struggle　gnash　　in　　simple.meals　**inside** suffer　day

132 Expressions of Location, Time and Place

很　　难　　挨过　　了。（鞭子 7）
hěn　　nán　　áiguò　　le
very　　hard　　undergo　　LE

'Life becomes very hard to go through when one has to struggle and persist in wind, in rain and in scorching sun, and make do with simple meals.' (*Biānzi* 7)

(6) 阿婵　　有　　个　　哥哥，　　**下面**　　还　　有
āchán　　yǒu　　gè　　gēge　　**xiàmiàn**　　hái　　yǒu
A.Chan　　have　　CL　　elder.brother　　**below**　　also　　have

好　　几　　个　　弟弟　　妹妹。（鞭子 18）
hǎo　　jǐ　　gè　　dìdi　　mèimei
good　　several　　CL　　younger.brother　　younger.sister

'A Chan has an elder brother and several younger brothers and sisters.' (*Biānzi* 18)

In examples (2) and (3), 后 *hòu* 'after' and 前后 *qiánhòu* 'before-after' indicate time; 当中 *dāngzhōng* 'within' in example (4) indicates range; 里 *lǐ* 'inside' refers to condition in example (5); and 下面 *xiàmiàn* 'below' in example (6) expresses ranks of sibling.

2.4 The Collocation of Localisers With 以 *Yǐ* 'YI'/ 之 *Zhī* 'ZHI'

2.4.1 An Overview of ' 以 *Yǐ* 'YI'/ 之 *Zhī* 'ZHI' + Single Localiser'

Most single localisers can combine with 以 *yǐ* 'YI'/ 之 *zhī* 'ZHI'[3] in the form of ' 以 *yǐ* 'YI'/ 之 *zhī* 'ZHI' + localiser'. Details are shown in the following table:

	上 *shàng* 'up'	下 *xià* 'down'	里 *lǐ* 'inside'	外 *wài* 'outside'	前 *qián* 'before'
以 *yǐ* 'YI'	+	+	—	+	+
之 *zhī* 'ZHI'	+	+	—	+	+

	后 *hòu* 'after'	东 *dōng* 'east'	西 *xī* 'west'	南 *nán* 'south'	北 *běi* 'north'
以 *yǐ* 'YI'	+	+	+	+	+
之 *zhī* 'ZHI'	+	+	+	+	+

	左 *zuǒ* 'left'	右 *yòu* 'right'	中 *zhōng* 'amidst'	间 *jiān* 'between'	内 *nèi* 'within'
以 *yǐ* 'YI'	—	—	—	—	+
之 *zhī* 'ZHI'	—	—	+	+	+

('+' indicates that the combination is possible, while '—' stands for the opposite.)

2.4.2 The Classification of the '以 yǐ 'YI'/ 之 zhī 'ZHI' + Single Localiser'

The combination of the '以 yǐ 'YI'/ 之 zhī 'ZHI' + single localiser' can be classified into two groups:

A Some combinations are already lexicalised, which include the following eight compound words:

以上 yǐshàng 'above' 以下 yǐxià 'following'
以外 yǐwài 'except' 以前 yǐqián 'before'
以后 yǐhòu 'after' 以内 yǐnèi 'within'
之前 zhīqián 'before' 之后 zhīhòu 'afterwards'

For instance, 以上 yǐshàng 'above', 以前 yǐqián 'before', 之后 zhīhòu 'afterwards' in the following examples (1)–(3) are all compound words.

(1) 以上   三   个   理由   说明   了   为什么   我   认为
    yǐshàng sān   gè   lǐyóu   shuōmíng le   wéishénme   wǒ   rènwéi
    above   three CL   reason explain   LE   why   1SG   think

   华族   文化   的   前景   是   不   乐观   的。（风筝 11）
   huázú   wénhuà   de   qiánjǐng   shì bù   lèguān   de
   Chinese culture   DE   prospect   be   NEG   optimistic DE

   'The three reasons above explain why I find the prospects of Chinese culture pessimistic.' (*Fēngzhēng* 11)

(2) 它   与   **以前**   出版   的   书目   最大   不同点，
    tā   yǔ   **yǐqián** chūbǎn   de   shūmù   zuìdà   bùtóngdiǎn
    3SG   and   **before** publish   DE   book   the.biggest difference

   在于 ... （Δ 新华文学 77）
   zàiyú
   lie.in

   'Its biggest difference from previous versions lies in...' (Δ*Xīnhuáwénxué* 77)

(3) 再   用   手   搓洗   干净，   **之后，**   再   暴晒
    zài   yòng shǒu   cuōxǐ   gànjìng   **zhīhòu**   zài   bàoshài
    then   use   hand   scrub   clean   **afterwards** then sun.bathing

   至   干   透   为止。   （南北 26）
   zhì   gàn   tòu   wéizhǐ
   until   dry   thorough come.to.an.end

   '... then scrub (it) with your hands and air it in the sun until it gets thoroughly dry.' (*Nánběi* 26)

134 *Expressions of Location, Time and Place*

B Other combinations are not yet lexicalised, and there are fourteen of them.

以东 *yǐdōng* 'the east of'   以西 *yǐxī* 'the west of'
以南 *yǐnán* 'the south of'   以北 *yǐběi* 'the north of'
之上 *zhīshàng* 'above'   之下 *zhīxià* 'below'
之外 *zhīwài* 'beyond'   之东 *zhīdōng* 'the east of'
之西 *zhīxī* 'the west of'   之南 *zhīnán* 'the south of'
之北 *zhīběi* 'the north of'   之中 *zhīzhōng* 'among/middle'
之间 *zhījiān* 'between'   之内 *zhīnèi* 'within'

In most cases, these combination forms always follow other phrases. For example:

(4) 我们   做人,   在   天地   之间,   该
    wǒmen   zuòrén   zài   tiāndì   zhījiān   gāi
    1PL   conduct.oneself   in   sky.and.earth between   should

    做   得   光明磊落,   堂堂正正。（牛车水 55）
    zuò   dé   guāngmínglěiluò   tángtángzhèngzhèng
    behave   DE   frank.and.forthright   dignified.and.imposing
    'As human being in this word we, should be upright and frank.' (*Niúchē-shuǐ* 55)

(5) 如   适   遇   阴天,   一切   陷身   于
    rú   shì   yù   yīntiān   yīqiè   xiànshēn   yú
    if   happen.to   encounter   cloudy.day everything shroud   in

    白茫茫的   云雾   里,   似   坠   入   五   里
    báimángmáng-de   yúnwù   lǐ   sì   zhuì   rù   wǔ   lǐ
    white   mist   in   like   fall   into   five   mile

    云雾   之外。（一心 76）
    yúnwù   zhīwài
    cloud   beyond
    'If it happens to be a cloudy day, everything is enveloped in a white and heavy mist, as if being lost in a thick cloud.' (*Yīxīn* 76)

(6) 长城   像   一   条   巨大的   游龙,   连绵起伏   于
    chángchéng   xiàng   yī   tiáo   jùdà-de   yóulóng   liánmiánqǐfú   yú
    The.Great.   like   one   CL   huge   flying.   rolling   in
    Wall   dragon

Expressions of Location, Time and Place   135

高山	丘陵	之间，	草原	沙漠	之上。（华文教材 2A 174）
gāoshān	qiūlíng	zhījiān	cǎoyuán	shāmò	zhīshàng
mountain	hill	between	prairie	desert	above

'The Great Wall winds its way between rolling mountains and through prairies and deserts as if a huge flying dragon.' (*Huáwénjiàocái* 2A, 174)

2.4.3 The Extensional Meanings of '以 *Yǐ* 'YI'/ 之 *Zhī* 'ZHI' + Single Localiser'

Except for "以 *yǐ* 'YI'/ 之 *zhī* 'ZHI' + 东 *dōng* 'east'/ 南 *nán* 'south'/ 西 *xī* 'west'/ 北 *běi* 'north'", most '以 *yǐ* 'YI'/ 之 *zhī* 'ZHI' + single localiser' combinations have various extensional meanings, among which the most commonly used one indicates time. For example,

(7) 在　　我们　　离开　　**之前，**　　大伙儿　　便　　与　　众　　老人
　　zài　　wǒmen　　líkāi　　**zhīqián**　　dàhuǒer　　biàn　　yǔ　　zhòng　　lǎorén
　　on　　1PL　　leave　　before　　everyone　　then　　with　　all　　the.elderly

　　及　　负责人　　拍照　　留念。（华韵 6）
　　jí　　fùzérén　　pāizhào　　liúniàn
　　and　　manager　　take.photo　　for.remembrance

'Before we left, the group took pictures with the elderly and the manager as a memento of the event.' (*Huáyùn* 6)

(8) 娜尼雅　　未　　来　　**以前，**　　他们　　夫妻　　两人　　便
　　nàníyǎ　　wèi　　lái　　**yǐqián**　　tāmen　　fūqī　　liǎngrén　　biàn
　　Naniya　　NEG　　come　　before　　3PL　　couple　　two people　　then

　　好像　　已经　　有　　了　　裂痕。（跳舞 7）
　　hǎoxiàng　　yǐjīng　　yǒu　　le　　lièhén
　　seem　　already　　have　　LE　　rift

'Before Naniya came, the couple already seemed estranged.' (*Tiàowǔ* 7)

(9) 有　　了　　这次　　惨痛　　经验　　**之后，**　　笔者
　　yǒu　　le　　zhècì　　cǎntòng　　jīngyàn　　**zhīhòu**　　bǐzhě
　　have　　LE　　this　　painstaking　　experience　　after　　writer

　　终于　　大彻大悟 . . .（八方 24）
　　zhōngyú　　dàchèdàwù
　　finally　　have.an.epiphany

'After this painful experience, the author finally had an epiphany . . .' (*Bāfāng* 24)

136 Expressions of Location, Time and Place

(10) （那　　鲜鱼刺身）　　硬生生　　　　吞　　下　　**以后，**
　　　nà　　xiānyúcìshēn　　yìngshēngshēng　tūn　xià　**yǐhòu**
　　　that　sashimi　　　　forcibly　　　　swallow down **after**

　　　好似　　有人　　　在　　　抠　　我　　的　　胃部，
　　　hǎosì　yǒurén　　zài　　　kōu　wǒ　de　　wèibù
　　　seem　someone　in.process　dig　1SG　DE　stomach

　　　有　　呕吐　　的　　恶心感。（△ 天长 47）
　　　yǒu　ǒutù　　de　　ěxīngǎn
　　　have vomit　DE　nausea

'After forcibly swallowing (that sashimi), I felt sick as if somebody was digging at my stomach.' (△*Tiāncháng* 47)

Some combinations imply the range of things or ideas, as shown next:

(11) 她　　在　　他　　身旁　　的　　座位　　坐　　下，　出乎　　他
　　　tā　　zài　tā　　shēnpáng　de　　zuòwèi　zuò　xià　　chūhū　tā
　　　3SG　at　3SG　beside　　DE　　seat　　sit　down　out of　3SG

　　　意料　　**之外**　　地　　以　　一　　句　　纯正的
　　　yìliào　**zhīwài**　de　　yǐ　　yī　　jù　chúnzhèngde
　　　expectation **beyond** DE　with　one　CL　pure

　　　华语　　问　　他…（牛车水 61）
　　　huáyǔ　wèn　tā
　　　Chinese ask　3SG

'She sat down in the seat next to him and, to his surprise, asked him in pure Chinese . . .' (*Niúchēshuǐ* 61)

(12) 在　　破坏公物者　　　　**之中，**　有　　许多　　是　青少年。
　　　　　　　　　　　　　　　　　　　　　　　　　　　　（平心 58）
　　　zài　pòhuàigōngwùzhě　**zhīzhōng**　yǒu　xǔduō　shì qīngshàonián
　　　in　saboteurs　　　　　**among**　　have　many　be　teenagers

'Many of the saboteurs were teenagers.' (*Píngxīn* 58)

And some combinations indicate conditions, for example,

(13) 后来　　在　　卢毕福　　的　　指导　　**之下，**　他　　终于
　　　hòulái　zài　lúbìfú　　　de　　zhǐdǎo　**zhīxià**　tā　　zhōngyú
　　　then　　at　LuBifu　　DE　　guidance **under**　3SG　finally

Expressions of Location, Time and Place 137

发现	了	电离层…（华文教材 4 A 24）
fāxiàn	le	diànlícéng
discover	LE	ionosphere

'Later on, under the guidance of Lu Bifu, he finally discovered the ionosphere . . .' (*Huáwén* textbook 4 A, 24)

Furthermore, 之间 zhījiān 'between' in the following example indicates relations:

(14) 我们　　希望　　建屋局　　与　　居民　　**之间**　　建立
　　　wǒmen　xīwàng　jiànwūjú　yǔ　jūmín　**zhījiān**　jiànlì
　　　1PL　　hope　　HDB　　and　residents　**between**　establish

　　　更　　融洽的　　关系。（平心 27）
　　　gèng　róngqiàde　guānxì
　　　more　harmonious　relation

'We are hoping for a more harmonious relationship between the HDB (Housing & Development Board) and the residents.' (*Píngxīn* 27)

之中 zhīzhōng 'middle' and 之下 zhīxià 'under' in the following examples describes context or circumstance:

(15) 母亲　　仿佛　　陶醉　　在　　那　　一阵　　精神　　的　　胜利
　　　mǔqīn　fǎngfú　táozuì　zài　nà　yīzhèn　jīngshén　de　shènglì
　　　mother　seem　revel　in　that　burst　spiritual　DE　triumph

　　　之中。（短篇 19）
　　　zhīzhōng
　　　middle

'Mother seemed to be revelling in that burst of psychological triumph.' (*Duǎnpiān* 19)

(16) 而且，　　在　　气愤　　**之下，**　　竟　　扬言　　若　　超云　　要
　　　érqiě　　zài　qìfèn　**zhīxià**　jìng　yángyán　ruò　chāoyún　yào
　　　moreover　at　fury　**under**　even　threaten　if　ChaoYun　will

　　　与　　那　　孤女　　结婚，　　就　　要　　脱离　　父子
　　　yǔ　nà　gūnǚ　jiéhūn　jiù　yào　tuōlí　fùzǐ
　　　with　that　orphan.girl　marry　then　will　break.from　father-son

的 关系。（短篇 81）
de guānxì
DE relation

'In fury, he threatened to sever the father-son relationship if Chaoyun should dare to marry that orphan girl.' (*Duǎnpiān* 81)

Also, 以上 *yǐshàng* 'above' and 以下 *yǐxià* 'below' are often used to refer 'what is said above' and 'what will be said in the following' respectively, as exemplified by (17) and (18). They can also be used to indicate boundaries, as illustrated in (19) and (20):

(17) 以上 所 述 揭示 了 现代汉语 中
yǐshàng suǒ shù jiēshì le xiàndàihànyǔ zhōng
above SUO mentioned reveal LE modern.Chinese in

存有 甚多的 文言 成分。（△ 语法修辞 28）
cúnyǒu shènduōde wényán chéngfèn
exist many ancient.Chinese elements

'The above statement reveals the remnants of ancient Chinese in Modern Mandarin.' (△*Yǔfǎxiūcí*, 28)

(18) 以下 所 述 的 分流 所 造成 的
yǐxià suǒ shù de fēnliú suǒ zàochéng de
below SUO mentioned DE diversion SUO result in DE

弊病 是 基于... 而 得到 的 结论。（风筝 76）
bìbìng shì jīyú ér dédào de jiélùn
defect SHI base.on LIG reach DE conclusion

'The following conclusion about the defects of diversion is based on . . .' (*Fēngzhēng* 76)

(19) 人数 是 越多 越好， 至少 也
rénshù shì yuèduō yuèhǎo zhìshǎo yě
the.number.of.people be more better at.least also

必须 有 十 人 以上。（△ 断情剪 6）
bìxū yǒu shí rén **yǐshàng**
must have ten people **above**

'The more people there are, the better. We need at least ten.' (△*Duànqíngjiǎn* 6)

Expressions of Location, Time and Place 139

(20) 十岁 **以下** 的 孩子 都 有 家长 带着。
shísuì **yǐxià** de háizi dōu yǒu jiāzhǎng dàizhe
10.years.old **below** DE kids DOU have parents accompany
'All children under the age of ten are accompanied by their parents.'

2.4.4 'VP + 之 zhī 'ZHI'/ 以前 Yǐqián 'Before' and 'VP + 之 zhī 'ZHI'/ 以后 Yǐhòu 'After' Indicating Time

Both 'VP+ 之 zhī 'ZHI'/ 以前 yǐqián 'before'' and 'VP+ 之 zhī 'ZHI'/ 以后 yǐhòu 'after'' only indicate time as shown in examples (7)–(10). It is necessary to point out that the verbal phrase in the former construction can be either in affirmative or negative form, with basically the same meaning, as illustrated next:

(21) 在 结婚 **之前**， 他们 曾经 很 冷静。（鞭子 77）
zài jiéhūn **zhīqián** tāmen céngjīng hěn lěngjìng
at marry **before** 3PL once very calm
'They used to be calm before they got married.' (*Biānzǐ* 77)

(22) 都 是 发生 在 他 诞生 **以前**。（牛车水 55）
dōu shì fāshēng zài tā dànshēng **yǐqián**
all SHI happen at 3SG born **before**
'It all happened before he was born.' (*Niúchēshuǐ* 55)

(23) 在 未 经 法庭 定罪 **之前** 只 能 是
zài wèi jīng fǎtíng dìngzuì **zhīqián** zhǐ néng shì
at NEG experience court convict **before** only should be

嫌凶、 嫌犯。（Δ 断情剪 36）
xiánxiōng xiánfàn
criminal.suspect criminal.suspect
'Before being convicted by the court, (they) should only be suspects.' (*ΔDuànqíngjiǎn* 36)

(24) 娜尼雅 未 来 **以前**， 他们 夫妻 两 人
nàníyǎ wèi lái **yǐqián** tāmen fūqī liǎng rén
Naniya NEG come **before** 3PL couple two people

就 好像 已经 有 了 裂痕。（跳舞 7）
jiù hǎoxiàng yǐjīng yǒu le lièhén
then seem already have LE rift
'Before Naniya came, the couple already seemed estranged.' (*Tiàowǔ* 7)

140 *Expressions of Location, Time and Place*

In examples (21) and (22), the verbal phrases before 之 *zhī* 'of' / 以前 *yǐqián* 'before' are of affirmative forms, and the meaning will not change if they are converted into negative forms. For comparison:

(25) a. (affirmative form)

在	**结婚**	之前，	他们	曾经	很	冷静。
zài	***jiéhūn***	*zhīqián*	*tāmen*	*céngjīng*	*hěn*	*lěngjìng*
at	**marry**	before	3PL	once	very	calm

'They used to be calm before they got married.'

b. (negative form)

在	**没有**	**结婚**	之前，	他们	曾经	很	冷静。
zài	***méiyǒu***	***jiéhūn***	*zhīqián*	*tāmen*	*céngjīng*	*hěn*	*lěngjìng*
at	**NEG**	**marry**	before	3PL	once	very	calm

'They used to be calm when they were not married.'

(26) a. (affirmative form)

都	是	发生	在	他	**诞生**	以前。
dōu	*shì*	*fāshēng*	*zài*	*tā*	***dànshēng***	*yǐqián*
all	SHI	happen	at	3SG	**born**	before

'It all happened before he was born.'

b. (negative form)

都	是	发生	在	他	**未**	**诞生**	以前。
dōu	*shì*	*fāshēng*	*zài*	*tā*	***wèi***	***dànshēng***	*yǐqián*
all	SHI	happen	at	2SG	**NEG**	**born**	before

'It all happened when he was not born.'

In examples (23) and (24), the verb phrases before 之 *zhī* 'of' / 以前 *yǐqián* 'before' are in negative forms. If it is to be converted to affirmative forms, the meaning will not change, either. Let's compare:

(27) a. (negative form)

在	**未**	**经**	**法庭**	**定罪**	之前	只	能
zài	***wèi***	***jīng***	***fǎtíng***	***dìngzuì***	*zhīqián*	*zhǐ*	*néng*
at	**NEG**	**experience**	**court**	**convict**	before	only	should

是	嫌凶、	嫌犯。
shì	*xiánxiōng*	*xiánfàn*
be	criminal.suspect	criminal.suspect

'Before being convicted by the court, (they) should only be suspects.'

b. (affirmative form)

在	经	法庭	定罪	之前	只	能	是
zài	jīng	fǎtíng	dìngzuì	zhīqián	zhǐ	néng	shì
at	experience	court	convict	before	only	should	be

嫌凶、　　　嫌犯。
xiánxiōng　　xiánfàn
criminal.suspect criminal.suspect

'Before being convicted by the court, (they) should only be suspects.'

(28) a. (negative form)

娜尼雅	未	来	以前,	他们	夫妻	两	人
nàníyǎ	wèi	lái	yǐqián	tāmen	fūqī	liǎng	rén
Naniya	NEG	come	before	3PL	couple	two	people

就	好像	已经	有	了	裂痕。
jiù	hǎoxiàng	yǐjīng	yǒu	le	lièhén
then	seem	already	have	LE	rift

'Before Naniya came, the couple already seemed estranged.'

b. (affirmative form)

娜尼雅	来	以前,	他们	夫妻	两	人	就
nàníyǎ	lái	yǐqián	tāmen	fūqī	liǎng	rén	jiù
Naniya	come	before	3PL	couple	two	people	then

好像	已经	有	了	裂痕 。
hǎoxiàng	yǐjīng	yǒu	le	lièhén
seem	already	have	LE	rift

'Before Naniya came, the couple already seemed estranged.'

Nevertheless, the affirmative form cannot be changed to the negative form if the verb is preceded by 临 *lín* 'about to', as shown in the following examples:

(29)

临	走	之前,	她	又	嘱咐	了	他
lín	zǒu	zhīqián	tā	yòu	zhǔfù	le	tā
about.to	leave	before	3SG	again	advise	LE	3SG

几　　句。（报 1995 年 3 月 18 日副刊 3 版）
jǐ　　jù
several sentence

'Upon departure, she advised him with a few more lines.' (*Bào*, Mar. 18, 1995, Issue no. 3, supplementary edition)

(30) 临   死   之前,   他   看   着   围   在   床边
      lín   sǐ   zhīqián tā   kàn zhe   wéi   zài   chuángbiān
      about.to die before   3SG   look ZHE   gather at   bed.side

  的   儿   女,...（太阳 48）
  de   ér   nǚ
  DE   son   daughter

  'Before dying, he looked at his children who gathered around his bed, and ...' (*Tàiyáng* 48)

The phrase 临走之前 *lín zǒu zhīqián* 'upon departure' in (29) cannot be converted to * 没临走之前 *méi lín zǒu zhīqián* 'not upon departure'. Similarly, in example (30), the phrase 临死之前 *lín sǐ zhīqián* 'upon death' cannot be converted to * 没临死之前 *méi lín sǐ zhīqián* 'not upon death'. On the other hand, the negative form cannot be converted to the affirmative form if the negation is modified by the adverb 还 *hái* 'yet'. For example,

(31) 在   还   没有   坐   飞机   以前,
      zài   hái   méiyǒu   zuò   fēijī   yǐqián
      at   yet   NEG   sit   plane   before

  常常   听到   许多   可怕的   传闻。（八方 10）
  chángcháng tīngdào   xǔduō   kěpà-de   chuánwén
  often   hear   many   horrible   rumours

  'Before I had travelled by plane, I heard many terrible stories.' (*Bāfāng* 10)

The phrase 没有坐飞机以前 *méiyǒu zuò fēijī yǐqián* 'before when not travelling by plane' in (31) cannot be changed into 坐飞机以前 *zuò fēijī yǐqián* 'before travelling by plane' in that the phrase is preceded by the adverb 还 *hái* 'yet'. It is ungrammatical to say * 还坐飞机以前 *hái zuò fēijī yǐqián* 'still before travelling by plane'.

In addition, if the 'VP + 之 *zhī* 'ZHI'/ 以前 *yǐqián* 'before'' construction occur in the attribute position, only the affirmative form is available, as shown in (32).

(32) 我   正在   作   上课   之前   的   准备   。
      wǒ   zhèngzài   zuò   shàngkè   zhīqián   de   zhǔnbèi
      1SG   in.process do   have.class   before   DE   prepare

  'I am preparing for the class.'

上课之前 *shàngkè zhīqián* 'before having the class' cannot be replaced by the negative form of 没上课之前 *méi shàngkè zhīqián* 'not before having the class'; it's ungrammatical for this to be used as the attribute of 准备 *zhǔnbèi* 'prepare'.

2.5 Time Expressions Denoting Point of Time

Before we begin, it is important to give a supplementary explanation about the notion of 'point'. A point can cover an area as small as something not seen with the naked eye and must be observed through a microscope; or as large as Singapore, which can be considered as a point on Earth, and Earth can be regarded as a point in the solar system, and the solar system a point in the galaxy, and the galaxy a point in the universe. Similarly, the range of a point of time can be very small or very big. For example, the time range indicated by 六点 *liùdiǎn* 'six o'clock' is smaller than 刚才 *gāngcái* 'just now', which is smaller than 上午 *shàngwǔ* 'morning', and the list goes on as follows:

六点	<	刚才	<	上午	<	今天	<	这个星期
liù diǎn		*gāngcái*		*shàngwǔ*		*jīntiān*		*zhège xīngqī*
'six o'clock'		'just now'		'morning'		'today'		'this week'

<	五月	<	一九九七年	<	九十年代	<	二十世纪
	wǔyuè		*yījiǔjiǔqī nián*		*jiǔshí niándài*		*èrshí shìjì*
	'May'		'1997'		'the 1990s'		'twentieth century'

2.5.1 Types of Time Expressions Indicating Point of Time

There are five major types of time expressions indicating point of time:

1. Nouns That Indicate Time

These include nouns such as: 今天 *jīntiān* 'today', 刚才 *gāngcái* 'just now', 目前 *mùqián* 'at present', 明晚 *míngwǎn* 'tomorrow evening', 上午 *shàngwǔ* 'morning', 以前 *yǐqián* 'before' and 星期日 *xīngqīrì* 'Sunday'. Sentences for each of these nouns are shown in examples (1)–(7):

(1) 今天　　是　他　女朋友　　的　生日，　他们　已
    jīntiān shì tā nǚpéngyǒu de shēngrì, tāmen yǐ
    today　 be　3SG　girlfriend　 DE　birthday　 3PL　 already

　　准备　　　共　　　度　　　烛光晚餐。（华韵 33）
　　zhǔnbèi　 *gòng*　 *dù*　 *zhúguāngwǎncān*
　　prepare　 together　 spend　 candlelit.dinner

'Today is his girlfriend's birthday, so they are going to have a candlelit dinner together.' (*Huáyùn* 33)

144 *Expressions of Location, Time and Place*

(2) **刚才** 的 不快， 全都 烟消云散 了。（石头 203）
gāngcái de bùkuài quándōu yānxiāoyúnsàn le
just.now DE upset all vanish LE

'All the upset just now vanished.' (*Shítou* 203)

(3) **目前** 她 还 在 警察署 里 等候
mùqián tā hái zài jǐngcháshǔ lǐ děnghòu
at.present 3SG still at police.station inside wait

进一步 的 调查。（Δ 断情剪 39）
jìnyībù de diàochá
further DE investigation

'At present, she is still waiting in the police station for further investigation.' (Δ*Duànqíngjiǎn* 39)

(4) 妈！ 让 我 考虑 一 天， **明晚**
mā ràng wǒ kǎolǜ yī tiān **míngwǎn**
mum let 1SG consider one day **next.evening**

才 说。（微型 98）
cái shuō
only say

'Mum! Let me think over it for a day and settle it tomorrow evening.' (*Wēixíng* 98)

(5) 外子 时常 把 三岁 的 浩儿 在 **上午**
wàizǐ shícháng bǎ sānsuì de hàoér zài **shàngwǔ**
husband often BA three-year-old DE Haoer at **morning**

的 时间 内 带 去 工厂 工地
de shíjiān nèi dài qù gōngchǎng gōngdì
DE time within take go factory construction.site

巡视，...（Δ 含羞草 48–49）
xúnshì
inspect

'My husband often takes three-year-old Haoer with him to inspect the factory's construction site in the morning...' (Δ*Hánxiūcǎo* 48–49)

(6) 现在　　　家　　　中　　　的　　　仙人掌　　　不及　　　以前
　　 xiànzài　*jiā*　*zhōng*　*de*　*xiānrénzhǎng*　*bùjí*　*yǐqián*
　　 now　 family　inside　DE　 cactus　 less.than　before

的　　一半 ...（壁虎 23）
de　*yībàn*
DE　 half

'The cacti at home now are less than half of what they used to be ...'
(*Bìhǔ* 23)

(7) 星期日，　　我　　和　　T　　小两口子，　　　照例　　　提　　了
　　 xīngqīrì　 *wǒ*　*hé*　*tì*　*xiǎoliǎngkǒuzi*　*zhàolì*　*tí*　*le*
　　 Sunday　　1SG　 and　 T　　couple　　　　 as.usual　carry　LE

篮子　　去　　买　　菜。（含羞草 28）
lánzi　*qù*　*mǎi*　*cài*
basket　go　 buy　 vegetable

'On Sunday, T and I, as a couple, took our baskets to buy groceries as usual.' (*Hánxiūcǎo* 28)

The nouns indicating point of time in Singapore Mandarin are basically identical to those in Chinese Mandarin, but there are still some subtle differences between them. In Singapore Mandarin, expressions for days of the week are formed with not only 星期 ... *xīngqī* and 礼拜 ... *lǐbài* (such as 星期一 *xīngqī yī* 'Monday', 星期二 *xīngqī èr* 'Tuesday' and 礼拜一 *lǐbài yī* 'Monday', 礼拜二 *lǐbài èr* 'Tuesday') but also 拜 ... *bài*. For example,

(8) 今天　　　拜六，　　不　　上课，
　　 jīntiān　*bàiliù*　　*bù*　*shàngkè*
　　 today　　Saturday　NEG　have.class

只有　　　课外　　　　　活动。（吾土·戏剧 144）
zhǐyǒu　*kèwài*　　　　*huódòng*
only　 extracurricular　activity

'Today is Saturday. We have no class, only extracurricular activities.'
(*Wútǔ* (drama) 144)

(9) 拜六　　　还　　有　　股票　　交易？（吾土·小说上 95）
　　 bàiliù　 *hái*　*yǒu*　*gǔpiào*　*jiāoyì*
　　 Saturday　still　have　stock　 exchange

'Is there still stock exchange on Saturday?' (*Wútǔ Novel I* 95)

(10) 那　　天，　　**拜三**，　　　好像
　　　nà　　tiān　　**bàisān**　　hǎoxiàng
　　　that　day　　**Wednesday**　seem

　　　是　**拜三**。（苏明美 1995·附录 《会话录音抄录（八）》）
　　　shì　**bàisān**
　　　be　**Wednesday**

　　　'That day was Wednesday. It seems to me that it was Wednesday.' (*Transcription of Conversation Records* VIII (appendix), *Sū Míngměi*, 1995)

This kind of expression is frequently used in both the oral and the written register in Singapore Mandarin. However, no such expression is found in Chinese Mandarin.

Futhermore, in Singapore Mandarin, 礼拜天 *lǐbài tiān* 'Sunday' can be shortened to 礼拜 *lǐbài* 'Sunday'. For instance, 礼拜 *lǐbài* 'Sunday' in (11) is the same as 礼拜天 *lǐbài tiān* 'Sunday'. This abbreviated form is no longer used in Chinese Mandarin.

(11) 不过　　看戏　　　　每次　　都　　要　　等　　到
　　　bùguò　kànxì　　　　měicì　dōu　yào　děng　dào
　　　but　　go.to.the.theatre　every.time　all　need　wait　until

　　　拜六　　**礼拜**。（苏明美 1995·附录 《会话录音抄录（二）》）
　　　bàiliù　**lǐbài**
　　　Saturday　**Sunday**

　　　'But every time I want to go to the theatre, I have to wait until Saturday or Sunday.' (*Transcription of Conversation Records* II (appendix), *Sū Míngměi*, 1995)

2. 'Ordinal + Temporal Classifier' Compounds

The second type is that of 'ordinal + temporal classifier' compounds, such as 一九五九年 *yījiǔwǔjiǔ nián* '1959', 六月 *liù yuè* 'June' and 九时 *jiǔ shí* 'nine o'clock', as in the following sentences:

(12) **一九五九年**　　　摄　于　星洲。（Δ 狮城 12）
　　　yījiǔwǔjiǔnián　shè　yú　xīngzhōu
　　　nineteen.fifty-nine　shot　in　Singapore

　　　'(The photo) was taken in Singapore in 1959.' (Δ*Shīchéng* 12)

(13) **六月**　的　夏　　　夜　　这般　　漫长…（无弦月 11）
　　　liùyuè　de　xià　　ye　　zhèbān　mànzhǎng
　　　June　DE　summer　night　so　　very.long

Expressions of Location, Time and Place 147

'The summer nights in June are so long ...' (*Wúxiányuè* 11)

(14) 我们　　**九时**　　　出发...（怀旧 89）
　　 wǒmen　　**jiǔshí**　　chūfā
　　 1PL　　　**nine.o'clock**　set.out
　　 'We will set out at nine o'clock ...' (*Huáijiù* 89)

In Singapore Mandarin, the minute as a point of time could be expressed with ... 分 *fēn* 'minute'. For example,

　　 十一　　点　　　四十五　　**分**（再见 15）
　　 shíyī　　diǎn　　sìshíwǔ　　**fēn**
　　 eleven　o'clock　forty-five　**minute**
　　 'a quarter to twelve' (*Zàijiàn* 15)

　　 十二　　时　　　五十　　　**分**（青青 81）
　　 shíèr　　shí　　 wǔshí　　 **fēn**
　　 twelve　o'clock　fifty　　　**minute**
　　 'ten minutes to one' (*Qīngqīng* 81)

It could also be expressed with another special word, 个字 *gèzì* 'five minutes'. For instance, 差一个字半十一点 *chà yī gèzì bàn shíyī diǎn* in (15) means 'seven or eight minutes to eleven'. This is quite common in oral Singapore Mandarin but never seen in Chinese Mandarin.

(15) "　差　　一　　**个字**　　　半　　十一　　点。"
　　　 chà　　yī　　**gèzì**　　　 bàn　　shíyī　　diǎn
　　　 short.of　one　**five.minutes**　half　eleven　o'clock

　　　 我　　又　　　看看　　　表。（长哭当歌 53）
　　　 wǒ　　yòu　　kànkàn　　biǎo
　　　 1SG　again　look.at　　watch

　　 '"It's seven or eight minutes to eleven," I glanced at my watch again and said.' (*Chángkūdànggē* 53)

3. Endocentric Phrases

Time words and phrases from the previous two types can be further combined into a big endocentric phrase, which also denotes the point of time. In Chinese Mandarin, such combinations generally conform to the descending order. For example, in 二十世纪九十年代 *èrshí shìjì jiǔshí niándài* 'the nineties of the

20th century', the time range of 二十世纪 èrshí shìjì 'the 20th century' is wider than that of 九十年代 jiǔshí niándài 'the nineties'. The same holds true in 今天下午 jīntiān xiàwǔ 'this afternoon', the order of which cannot be reversed as *下午今天 xiàwǔ jīntiān 'intended meaning: this afternoon'. More examples are as follows:

(16) 去年　　今日... 耳边　　是　你们　的　朗朗　笑语。
　　　　　　　　　　　　　　　　　　　（心情 75）
　　qùnián　jīnrì　ěrbiān　shì　nǐmen　de　lǎnglǎng　xiàoyǔ
　　last.year　today　ear.side　be　2PL　DE　loud　laughter
　　'Your hearty laughter echoed in my ear . . . on this day of last year.'
　　(Xīnqíng 75)

(17) 晚上　　两点　　才　到达。（风筝 187）
　　wǎnshàng　liǎngdiǎn　cái　dàodá
　　evening　two o'clock　just　arrive
　　'(He didn't) arrive until 2 a.m. in the morning.' (Fēngzhēng 187)

(18) 它　在　今天，　在　五月　八日　早上，
　　tā　zài　jīntiān　zài　wǔyuè　bārì　zǎoshàng
　　3SG　on　today　at　May　eighth.day　morning

　　已　　被　　宣判　　为　危楼，...（回忆 17－18）
　　yǐ　　bèi　　xuānpàn　wéi　wēilóu
　　already　BEI　declare　be　dangerous.building
　　'It was declared to be a dangerous building today on the morning of May 8th . . .' (Huíyì 17–18)

(19) 1941 年　　　12 月　　　8 日　　凌晨
　　yījiǔsìyī nián　shí'èryuè　bārì　língchén
　　nineteen.forty.one　December　8th.day　before.dawn

　　12 时　　　45 分　　　在　空军　的
　　shí'èrshí　sìshíwǔfēn　zài　kōngjūn　de
　　12.o'clock　forty.five.minute　at　air.force　DE

　　掩护　下...（沦陷 4）
　　yǎnhù　xià
　　cover　under
　　'At 00:45 a.m. on Dec. 8th, 1941, covered by the air force . . .' (Lúnxiàn 4)

Expressions of Location, Time and Place 149

的 *de* 'DE' can be inserted in between the two time phrases, such as:

星期五　　**的**　　晚上
xīngqīwǔ　*de*　*wǎnshàng*
Friday　　DE　　evening
'on Friday evening'

在　　五月　　八日　　**的**　　傍晚　　　　六点
zài　*wǔyuè*　*bā rì*　*de*　*bàngwǎn*　*liùdiǎn*
on　may　eighth.day　DE　late.afternoon　six.o'clock
'at 6 p.m. in the late afternoon of May 8th'

Due to the influence of English, in written Singapore Mandarin, dates are often expressed in an ascending order, i.e. in the order of 日 *rì* 'day', 月 *yuè* 'month' and 年 *nián* 'year'. For instance,

(20) 《学生》 编辑　　　　 *xuésheng biānjí*　　'Editor of Students'
　　 方叔叔　　　　　　　 *fāng shūshū*　　　　'Uncle Fang'
　　 22.10.1992（小学 6A 6）　'Oct 22nd, 1992'　(*Xiǎoxué* 6A, 6)

(21) 文华　　民众　　联络所　　青年团　　**3-1-1994**（课本 1A 8）
　　 wénhuá　*mínzhòng*　*liánluòsuǒ*　*qīngniántuán*　*sān- yī- yījiǔjiǔsì*
　　 wenhua　people　liaison.office　youth.group　Jan.3rd.1994
　　 'Wenhua People's Liaison Office Youth Group, Jan 3rd, 1994'
　　 (*Kèběn* 1A, 8)

(22) 报案　　日期：**16-8-1988**（华文教材 4B 117）
　　 bàoàn　*rìqī*：*híliù- bā- yījiǔbābā*
　　 report　date　Aug 16th, 1988
　　 'Date of report: Aug 16th, 1988' (*Huáwénjiàocái* 4B, 117)

(23) 翻开　　日记：**25-4-1985**　　　　星期三，
　　 fānkāi　*rìjì*：*èrshíwǔ- sì- yījiǔbāwǔ*　*xīngqīsān*
　　 open　diary　Apr. 25th, 1985　Wednesday

　　 清晨　　　　阵雨，　　阴天。（青青 64）
　　 qīngchén　*zhènyǔ*　*yīntiān*
　　 early.morning　showers　overcast
　　 'Open the diary: April 25th, 1985, Wednesday, early morning showers, overcast.' (*Qīngqīng* 64)

150   *Expressions of Location, Time and Place*

This ascending order applies only to the cases where 年 *nián* 'year', 月 *yuè* 'month' and 日 *rì* 'day' are omitted. Otherwise, the descending order still holds, as in the following example,

(24)   学生   曾华丰   上
      xuéshēng   *Zēnghuáfēng*   *shàng*
      student   Zeng Huafeng   yours.truly

一九八二   年   一月   十日（青青 104）
yījiǔbāèr   *nián*   *yīyuè*   *shírì*
nineteen.eighty.two   year   January   10th.day
'By Student Zeng Huafeng. January 10th, 1982' (*Qīngqīng* 104)

(25)   截止日期： **1994** 年   **2** 月   **2** 日（课本 1A 8）
      jiézhǐrìqī: *yījiǔjiǔsìnián*   *èryuè*   *èrrì*
      deadline   **nineteen.ninety.two** **February** **2nd.day**
'Deadline: February 2, 1992' (*Kèběn* 1A, 8)

(26)   光华   学校   在   **1953**   年
      guānghuá   *xuéxiào*   *zài*   *yījiǔwǔsān*   *nián*
      Kwang Hwa   School   on   **nineteen.fifty.three**   year

1 月   **10** 日   诞生   了。   （薪传 37）
yīyuè   *shírì*   *dànshēng*   *le*
January   10th day   born   LE
'Kwang Hwa School came into being on **January 10, 1953**.' (*Xīnchuán* 37)

In Chinese Mandarin, the expression of dates always follows the order of year, month, day in both spoken or written registers, whether 年 *nián* 'year', 月 *yuè* 'month' and 日 *rì* 'day' are omitted or not.

4. 'X + Localisers' Endocentric Phrases

Localisers that can occur in this construction mainly include: 前 *qián* 'front', 以前 *yǐqián* 'before', 之前 *zhīqián* 'before', 后 *hòu* 'back', 以后 *yǐhòu* 'after' and 之后 *zhīhòu* 'after'. The slot X can be filled by four types of elements. The most commonly seen type is verbs, for example,

(27)   **临**   **走**   **前**,   卿   嘱   我   把   梅花   带
      lín   ***zǒu***   ***qián***   *qīng*   *zhǔ*   *wǒ*   *bǎ*   *méihuā*   *dài*
      about.to **go**   **before**   Qing   ask   1SG   BA   plum.blossom   take

着　　　走。（独上 23）
zhe   zǒu
ZHE   go

'Upon departure, Qing told me to take the plum blossom with me.' (*Dúshàng* 23)

(28) 下车　　以前，　　听到　　P　安慰　　那　位　司机 ...
　　　　　　　　　　　　　　　　　　　　　　　　　（△自然 120）
xiàchē   yǐqián   tīngdào   pì ānwèi   nà   wèi sījī
debus   before   hear   P   console that CL   driver

'Before getting off the bus, (I) heard P consoling the driver...' (△*Zìrán* 120)

(29) 在　**认识　　雪云　　之前，**
　　　zài　**rènshí　xuěyún　zhīqián**
　　　at   meet   Xueyun   before

他　几乎　每　个　周末　往　夜总会　跑。（梦 55）
tā　jīhū　měi　gè　zhōumò　wǎng　yèzǒnghuì　pǎo
3SG almost every CL weekend towards night.club run

'Before meeting Xueyun, he went to the night club almost every weekend.' (*Mèng* 55)

X can also be filled in by numeral-temporal classifier compounds, as shown in the following examples:

(30) 他　绝少　在　**九点钟**　　以前　离开　办公室（金狮奖
　　　　　　　　　　　　　　　　　　　　　　　　　（四）36）
tā　juéshǎo　zài　**jiǔdiǎnzhōng**　yǐqián　líkāi　bàngōngshì
3SG rarely   at   9.o'clock   before leave office

'He rarely leaves the office before nine o'clock.' (*Jīnshījiǎng* (IV), 36)

(31) **一八九五年　　后，**　新　抵达　的　中国　移民　　每年
yībājiǔwǔnián　hòu,　xīn　dǐdá　de　zhōngguó　yímín　měinián
1895   after   new arrive DE Chinese   immigrants yearly

约　　　　　　在　十五万　　到　二十万　　之间。（新华文学 4）
yuē　　　　　zài　shíwǔwàn　dào　èrshíwàn　zhījiān
approximately be 150,000   to   200,000   between

'Since 1895, the number of newly arrived Chinese immigrants has been ranging from 150,000 to 200,000 per year.' (*Xīnhuáwénxué* 4)

152 Expressions of Location, Time and Place

(32) 那 一 道 常 敞开 着、 却 在 三 小时
    nà yī dào cháng chǎngkāi zhe què zài **sān xiǎoshí**
    that one CL often open ZHE yet at **three hour**

前 才 被 锁上 的 门。(回忆 17)
qián cái bèi suǒshàng de mén
before just BEI lock.up DE door

'The gate was often open but had been locked only three hours before.' (*Huíyì* 17)

(33) 三十 年 后， 我 这 一代 人 已经
    sānshí nián hòu wǒ zhè yīdài rén yǐjīng
    thirty year after 1SG this generation people already

长大…（Δ 小小鸟 39）
zhǎngdà
grow.up

'Thirty years later, my generation has already grown up…' (Δ*Xiǎoxiǎoniǎo* 39)

The numeral-classifier compounds in (28) and (29) are composed of ordinals and temporal classifiers. They originally indicate point of time, and still do after adding 前/后 *qián/hòu* 'before/after'. On the other hand, the numeral-classifier compounds in sentences (30) and (31) consisting of cardinals plus temporal classifiers originally indicate time duration, but begin to indicate point of time when followed by 前/后 *qián/hòu* 'before/after'.

Demonstrative pronouns are also found in the X slot, among which 这 'this' is most frequently used as shown below:

(34) 新加坡 在 **这 之前，** 一直 是 海盗 的 窝巢。(Δ 新华文学 4)
    xīnjiāpō zài **zhè zhīqián** yīzhí shì hǎidào de wōcháo
    Singapore at **this before** always be pirate DE lair

'Singapore had always been a den of pirates before this.' (Δ*Xīnhuáwénxué* 4)

(35) **这 以后，** 当 有人 问 我…
    zhè yǐhòu dāng yǒurén wèn wǒ
    this after when someone ask 1SG

'After this, every time someone asked me about…'

(36) 这   之后   我   又   在   毕业典礼   上   见
    zhè   zhīhòu wǒ   yòu   zài   bìyèdiǎnlǐ   shàng jiàn
    this after   1SG   again at   commencement. on   meet
                                    ceremony

    过   鄞碧仪。（变调 25）
    guò   yínbìyí
    GUO   Yin.Biyi

    'After that, I met Yin Biyi again at the commencement ceremony.'
    (Biàndiào 25)

It is also possible for nouns indicating time to fill the X slot, as illustrated below:

(37) 新年   前（华文教材 1A76）
    xīnnián   qián
    New.Year   before

    'before New Year' (Huáwénjiàocái 1A, 76)

    第二次   大战   后（风筝 128）
    dìercì   dàzhàn   hòu
    the.second great.war after

    'after the Second World War' (Fēngzhēng 128)

    午餐   后（追云 59）
    wǔcān   hòu
    lunch   after

    'after lunch' (Zhuīyún 59)

5. Verb Phrases + 时 shí 'Time'

When verb phrases are followed by the word 时 shí 'time', it also indicates point of time, as shown in the following examples:

(38) 当年   买下   这   幢   大   房子   时，   曾经   当
    dāngnián   mǎixià zhè   zhuàng dà   fángzi   shí   céngjīng dāng
    back.then   buy   this   CL   big   house   time   once   face

    着   众   儿女   面前   声明 …（追云 27）
    zhe   zhòng érnǚ   miànqián   shēngmíng
    ZHE   all   children in.front.of declare

    'When this big house was bought, (I) once declared in front of all my children that …' (Zhuīyún 27)

(39) 牵回　　车子　时，　永福桥　　　　上　　的　灯　　都
    qiānhuí　chēzi　shí　yǒngfúqiáo　shàng　de　dēng　dōu
    pull.back　car　time　Yongfu.Bridge　on　DE　lamp　all

    点亮　　了。（寻庙 39）
    diǎnliàng　le
    light.up　LE

    'The lights on the Yongfu Bridge were all lit up when the car was brought back.' (*Xúnmiào* 39)

(40) 我们　冲　　进　　房间　　时，　您　　已　　倒地
    wǒmen　chōng　jìn　fángjiān　shí　nín　yǐ　dǎodì
    1PL　rush　enter　room　time　2SG　already　faint

    不　　醒。（变调 2）
    bù　xǐng
    NEG　awaken

    'When we rushed into the room, you were already lying unconscious on the ground.' (*Biàndiào* 2)

2.5.2 Position of Expressions Indicating the Point of Time in Sentences

Expressions indicating the point of time usually appear before verbal phrases in a sentence. In some cases they are introduced by prepositions as shown in (41) and (42), and in other cases, they are not as in (43) and (44). For example,

(41) 我　　在　　上个　　　月　　被　　调　　　升　　　到
    wǒ　zài　shànggè　yuè　bèi　diào　shēng　dào
    1SG　at　last　month　BEI　transfer　promote　to

    教育部　　　　　　　　　去。
    jiāoyùbù　　　　　　　　　qù
    the.Ministry.of.Education　go

    'I was promoted and transferred to the Ministry of Education last month.'

(42) 在　会考　　来临　　前，　我　　开了不少夜车。（回忆 27）
    zài　huìkǎo　láilín　qián　wǒ　kāi-le-bùshǎo-yèchē
    at　exam　come　before　1SG　stay.up.late.a.lot

    'I stayed up a lot to prepare for the graduation exam.' (*Huíyì* 27)

Expressions of Location, Time and Place 155

(43) 我　**现在**　才　懂得　珍惜　它…（△ 南风 47）
wǒ　**xiànzài**　cái　dǒngdé　zhēnxī　tā
1SG　**now**　just　understand　treasure　3SG
'I didn't realise how precious it was until now…' (△*Nánfēng*, 47)

(44) **刚才**　冯老　跟　你　说　了　些　什么？（金狮奖（四）58）
gāngcái　fénglǎo　gēn　nǐ　shuō　le　xiē　shénme
just.now　Feng.Lao　with　2SG　say　LE　some　what
'What did Mr. Feng say to you just now?' (*Jīnshījiǎng* (IV), 58)

If the time expression is preceded by a preposition, the whole prepositional phrase functions as an adverbial in the sentence, just like the phrases 在上个月 *zài shànggè yuè* 'last month' in (41) and 在会考来临前 *zài huìkǎo láilín qián* 'before the exam' in (42). In cases with no preceding prepositions, the grammatical role that the time expression plays depends on the meaning indicated. When expressing the meaning of 'at the time of…', the time word or phrase functions as the subject, as the 刚才 *gāngcái* 'just now' in example (44). Here are more examples:

(45) **本月**　**七日**　宗乡　会馆　联合　总会　的
　　běnyuè　**qīrì**　zōngxiāng　huìguǎn　liánhé　zǒnghuì　de
　　this.month　**7th.day**　Chinese.clan　association　united　federation　DE

　　章程　已　拟就，　**最近**　即将…（文艺 128）
　　zhāngchéng　yǐ　nǐjiù　　**zuìjìn**　jíjiāng
　　constitution　already　draw.up　**recently**　about.to
'The constitutions of the Singapore Federation of Chinese Clan Associations have been drawn up on the 7th of this month, and will recently…' (*Wényì* 128)

(46) 我　**昨天**　跟　他　打　了　一　场　架…（牛车水 80）
wǒ　**zuótiān**　gēn　tā　dǎ　le　yī　chǎng　jià
1SG　**yesterday**　with　3SG　fight　LE　one　CL　fight
'I had a fight with him yesterday…' (*Niúchēshuǐ* 80)

本月七日 *běnyuè qīrì* 'the 7th day of this month' and 最近 *zuìjìn* 'recently' in (45) and 昨天 *zuótiān* 'yesterday' in (46) are all subjects. Whereas, when the time word means 'until the time of…', it is an adverbial, just like the word 现在 *xiànzài* 'now' illustrated in (43). Another typical example sentence is 明天见 *míngtiān jiàn* 'see you tomorrow', a formulaic sentence people use to bid farewell to each other, in which the word 明天 *míngtiān* 'tomorrow' also serves as an adverbial, meaning 'until tomorrow'. One more example is shown in (47), in which 明天 *míngtiān* 'tomorrow' is also an adverbial:

(47) 平： **明天** 再 说 吧！
     píng ***míngtiān*** *zài* *shuō* *ba*
     Ping **tomorrow** again say SFP

（说 完 关 灯）（金狮奖（四））130
shuō *wán* *guān* *dēng*
say finish close light

'Ping: Let's talk about it tomorrow! (Ping turned off the light after saying this)' (*Jīnshījiǎng* (Ⅳ), 130)

Very rarely, words or phrases indicating point of time occur in the object position of verbs, as shown in the following example:

(48) 掌声 迎来 了 **1988** 年…（科学 171）
     zhǎngshēng *yínglái* *le* ***yījiǔbābā*** *nián*
     applause welcome LE **nineteen.eighty.eight** year

'The year 1988 began among the applause…' (*Kēxué* 171)

It is more of a common practice for them to function as the object of the verb 是 *shì* 'be', as illustrated next:

(49) 大概 **是 去年** 吧。（金狮奖（四）104）
     dàgài ***shì*** ***qùnián*** *ba*
     probably **be** **last.year** SFP

'It was probably last year.' (*Jīnshījiǎng* (Ⅳ) 104)

(50) 今天 **是 星期天**。（△ 南风 73）
     jīntiān ***shì*** ***xīngqītiān***
     today **be** **Sunday**

'It's Sunday today.' (△*Nánfēng*, 73)

Typically, if they are to appear after verbs, there will be a preposition sandwiched between the verb and the time word, as shown in the next example:

(51) 我 生 **于 1917** 年。（沦陷 60）
     wǒ *shēng* ***yú*** ***yījiǔyīqī*** *nián*
     1SG born **in** **nineteen.seventeen** year

'I was born in 1917.' (*Lúnxiàn* 60)

(52) 孟毅   的   《新加坡   华文   文学   作品   选集》
    mèngyì   de   xīnjiāpō huáwén   wénxué   zuòpǐn   xuǎnjí
    Meng.Yi DE   Singapore Chinese Literature Works Anthology

    出版   于   一九七零   年。(△ 新华文学 69)
    chūbǎn   yú   yījiǔqīlíng   nián
    publish   in   nineteen.seventy   year

    'Meng Yi's *Anthology of Singapore Chinese Literature* was published in 1970.' (△*Xīnhuáwénxué* 69)

(53) 书   里   的   文章   大多   写   于
    shū   lǐ   de   wénzhāng dàduō   xiě   yú
    book inside DE   article   mostly   written in

    92   至   93   年。(△ 小小鸟 191)
    jiǔèr   zhì   jiǔsān   nián
    (nineteen).ninety.two to (nineteen).   year
                              ninety.three

    'Most articles in this book were written between 1992 and 1993.' (△*Xiǎoxiǎoniǎo* 191)

2.6 Expressions Indicating a Period of Time

All expressions that indicate a period of time are endocentric phrases rather than words. They can be divided into two subcategories.

1. The numeral-classifier phrases composed of 'cardinals + classifiers'. For example,

    二十年 *èrshí nián* 'twenty years'   三天 *sān tiān* 'three days'
    两小时 *liǎng xiǎoshí* 'two hours'

2. Endocentric phrases composed of 'cardinal + 个 *gè* 'CL' + nouns indicating time'. For example,

    一个月 *yī gè yuè* 'one month'   三个星期 *sān gè xīngqī* 'three weeks'
    五个小时 *wǔ gè xiǎoshí* 'five hours'

Different from time words or phrases indicating a point of time, which are used mainly before verbs in a sentence, those indicating a period of time are used mainly after verbs. For example,

    (1) 走   了   51   天 ... (△ 新华文学 58)
        zǒu   le   wǔshíyī   tiān

walk LE **fifty-one day**
'(He) walked for 51 days . . .' (△*Xīnhuáwénxué* 58)

(2) 灰姑娘　　与　　王子　　结婚　**十八　　年** . . .
　　　　　　　　　　　　　　　　　　　　　　(金狮奖（四）119)
　　*huīgūniáng　yǔ　wángzǐ　jiéhūn　**shíbā　nián***
　　Cinderella　and　prince　marry　**eighteen　year**
　　'Cinderella and the prince have been married for 18 years . . .'
　　(*Jīnshījiǎng* (IV) 119）

Grammatically, time phrases indicating a period of time after the verbs can be treated as objects, and they are a kind of 'quasi-object'. There are differences in meaning between (1) and (2). Example (1) denotes the duration of the action, 走了 51 天 *zǒu le 51 tiān* 'walked for 51 days' means that the action of 'walking' lasted 51 days. Similar examples are as follows:

(3) 我们　　工作　　了　**几十**　　　　年　　了，　在　这里。
　　　　　　　　　　　　　　　　　　　　　　　　　　　（华韵 28）
　　*wǒmen　gōngzuò　le　**jǐshí**　　　nián　le　zài　zhèlǐ*
　　1PL　work　LE　**several.decades**　year　LE　at　here
　　'We have been working here for decades.' (*Huáyùn* 28)

(4) 我　　已经　　注意　　了　**三　　天**。（△自然 71）
　　*wǒ　yǐjīng　zhùyì　le　**sān　tiān***
　　1SG　already　attention　LE　**three　day**
　　'I have been paying attention for three days.' (△*Zìrán* 71)

Example (2) denotes the time span between the completion of the action and the utterance of the sentence. 结婚十八年 *jiéhūn shíbā nián* 'married for eighteen years' means that the time span between the completion of the action 结婚 *jiéhūn* 'marry' and the utterance of the sentence is eighteen years. Similar examples are as follows:

(5) 鲁迅　　逝世　　**50　　年**　了。（△朝雨 102）
　　*lǔxùn　shìshì　**wǔshí　nián**　le*
　　Lu.Xun　pass.away　**fifty　year**　LE
　　'Lu Xun has been dead for 50 years.' (△*Zhāoyǔ*, 102)

(6) 搬　　家　　**三　　年**　了。（壁虎 23）
　　*bān　jiā　**sān　nián**　le*
　　move　home　**three　year**　LE
　　'(It) has been three years since (we) moved.' (*Bìhǔ* 23)

Phrases indicating periods of time are far less frequent, but in a more complicated manner, used before verbs than after verbs. For example,

(7) 一 年 过去 了。（冰灯 16）
yī nián guòqù le
one year pass.by LE
'A year has passed.' (*Bīngdēng* 16)

(8) 十二 年 我 受 的 是 传统 华文
shí'èr nián wǒ shòu de shì chuántǒng huáwén
twelve year 1SG receive DE be traditional Chinese

教育。（梦 16）
jiàoyù
education
'I have been receiving 12 years of traditional Chinese education.' (*Mèng* 16)

(9) 一 个 月 有 二 百 多 元 的 补贴。
（短篇 63）
yī gè yuè yǒu èr bǎi duō yuán de bǔtiē
one CL month have two hundred much yuan DE allowance
'There is a subsidy of more than 200 *yuans* a month.' (*Duǎnpiān* 63)

(10) 三 千 年 你 还 在 吗?（△自然 47）
sān qiān nián nǐ hái zài ma
three thousand year 2SG still be SFP
'Are you still live after 3,000 years?' (△*Zìrán* 47)

(11) 一 天 Y 对 我 说 想 买 一 个
yī tiān Y duì wǒ shuō xiǎng mǎi yī gè
one day Y towards 1SG say want buy one CL

柜子 给 孩子 放 衣服。（梦 154）
guìzi gěi háizi fàng yīfú
cabinet give kid put clothes
'One day, Y told me that he wanted to buy a wardrobe (to put clothes in) for his children.' (*Mèng* 154)

(12) 二十 年 不 算 短 哪！（报 1995 年 3 月 11
日 22 版）
èrshí nián bù suàn duǎn na
twenty year NEG count short SFP

'Twenty years is not short!' (*Bào*, Mar. 11, 1995, Issue no. 22)

(13) 半 天 读 书， 半 天 工作。（Δ 母亲 1）
bàn tiān dú shū bàn tiān gōngzuò
half day read book half day work
'(He) studies half a day and works half a day.' (Δ*Mǔqīn* 1)

Semantically, in (7), 一年 *yī nián* 'a year' refers to the time passed; in (8), 十二年 *shí'èr nián* 'twelve years' actually means 'within the past twelve years'. The time phrase in (9) entails the meaning of 'every', so 一个月 *yī gè yuè* 'one month' actually means 'every month' here. In example (10), 三千年 *sān qiān nián* 'three thousand years' shall be interpreted as 'in three thousand years'. In example (11), 一天 *yī tiān* 'one day' is equivalent to 有一天 *yǒu yītiān* 'one day'. This kind of usage applies only to the numeral 一 *yī* 'one', and the most commonly used phrase is 一天 *yī tiān* 'one day'. Example (12) is a comment on the length of the time 二十年 *èrshí nián* 'twenty years' as a whole. In (13), 半天 *bàn tiān* 'half a day' means 'spend half a day'. Grammatically, these words or phrases indicating periods of time placed before the verbs can all be seen as subjects.

2.7 Place Expressions

In a sentence, a place expression can either follow the verb, as shown in examples (1)–(3), or precede it, as shown in examples (4)–(6):

(1) 那 妇人 带 我们 进入 厅 内。（短篇 21）
nà fūrén dài wǒmen jìnrù tīng nèi
that woman lead 1PL enter hall inside
'That woman led us into the hall.' (*Duǎnpiān* 21)

(2) 离开 了 巴黎 …（再见 94）
líkāi le bālí
leave LE Paris
'Left Paris …' (*Zàijiàn* 94)

(3) 我们 一 伙 人 浩浩荡荡地 沿 着 不是
wǒmen yī huǒ rén hàohàodàngdàng-de yán zhe bùshì
1PL one CL person in.groups along ZHE NEG

很 宽的 楼梯 爬 上 二 楼。（华韵 19）
hěn kuānde lóutī pá shàng èr lóu
very wide stairs climb up second floor

'We went up to the second floor in groups along the narrow stairs.' (*Huáyùn* 19)

(4) 木橱　　　　　　　上　　堆　着　　厚厚的　　　被褥，
　　mùchú　　　　　*shàng*　*duī* *zhe*　*hòuhòu-de*　*bèirù*
　　wooden.wardrobe　on　　pile　ZHE　rather.thick　bedding

　　木桌　　　　　上　　堆　着　　叠叠　　的　　书籍，　木床
　　mùzhuō　　*shàng*　*duī* *zhe*　*diédié*　*de*　*shūjí*　*mùchuáng*
　　wooden.desk　on　　pile　ZHE　stacks　DE　book　　wooden.bed

　　下　　堆　　满　　了　　锻炼　　　身体　　的　　器材。（石头 205）
　　xià　*duī*　*mǎn*　*le*　*duànliàn*　*shēntǐ*　*de*　*qìcái*
　　under　pile　full　LE　exercise　body　DE　equipment

'There is thick bedding piled on the wooden wardrobe, books stacked on the wooden desk and fitness equipment stuffed into the space under the wooden bed.' (*Shítou* 205)

(5) 屋　　外　　　有　　铁丝网，
　　wū　*wài*　　*yǒu*　*tiěsīwǎng*
　　house　outside　have　barbed.wires

　　门　　外　　　有　　人　　　看守。（短篇 99）
　　mén　*wài*　　*yǒu*　*rén*　*kānshǒu*
　　door　outside　have　people　guard

'There are barbed wires outside the house and someone guarding outside the door.' (*Duǎnpiān* 99)

(6) 屋子　　四周　　　前后　　　　　种　　了　　好些
　　wūzi　*sìzhōu*　*qiánhòu*　　　*zhòng*　*le*　*hǎoxiē*
　　house　all.round　front.and.back　plant　LE　many

　　果树　　　花木。（鞭子 94）
　　guǒshù　*huāmù*
　　fruit.tree　flower.and.bush

'There are many fruit trees, flowers and bushes around the house.' (*Biānzi* 94)

The place words or phrases after the verb are the objects. Namely, the words 厅内 *tīng nèi* 'in the hall', 巴黎 *bālí* 'Paris' and 二楼 *èr lóu* 'second floor' in examples (1)–(3) are objects of the verb 进入 *jìn rù* 'enter', 离开了 *lí kāi le* 'have left' and 爬上 *pá shàng* 'climb up' respectively. The place phrases before the verb are generally subjects, which means the phrases 木橱上 *mùchú shàng* 'on the wooden wardrobe', 木桌上 *mùzhuō shàng* 'on the wooden desk', 木床下 *mùchuáng xià* 'under the wooden bed', 屋外 *wū wài* 'outside the house', 门外 *mén wài* 'outside the door' and 屋子四周前后 *wūzi sìzhōu qiánhòu* 'around the house' in examples (4)–(6) are all subjects. Yet place words or phrases may function as adverbials as well. For instance, the phrase 屋里 *wū lǐ* 'inside the house' in the sentence 屋里坐！ *wū lǐ zuò* 'Please take a seat inside.' is an adverbial. Here is another example, in which 前厅 *qiántīng* 'foyer' is an adverbial:

(7) 你们   **前厅**   休息 去   吧。（鞭子 57）
     nǐmen **qiántīng** xiūxī qù   ba
     2PL   **foyer**   rest go   SFP
     'Please take a rest in the foyer.' (*Biānzǐ* 57)

The question that arises is how to decide whether a preverbal place word or phrase is a subject or an adverbial. In general, it depends on the meaning of the place expression in a sentence. If it denotes the same meaning as 'at . . . place', it is a subject. Otherwise, it is an adverbial. All the place expressions in examples (4)–(6) could be explained with this rule. For example, the phrase 木橱上 *mùchú shàng* means 'on the wooden wardrobe', 屋子四周前后 *wūzi sìzhōu qiánhòu* means 'around the house', and the same is true with other examples. Therefore, these phrases are all subjects. However, in example (7), the place word 前厅 *qián tīng* 'foyer' actually means 'go to the foyer', so it acts as an adverbial in the sentence.

A more common usage for a place word or phrase is to act as object of a preposition, as shown in the following examples:

(8) 我们   **在**   云顶高原   停留   了   大半天。（华文教材 1B 10）
     women **zài** yúndǐnggāoyuán   tíngliú le   dàbàntiān
     1PL   **at**   Genting.Highlands   stay   LE   most.of.the.day
     'We stayed in the Genting Highlands for most of the day.' (*Huáwénjiàocái* 1B, 10)

(9) 舅舅   一家三口   **从**   中国   来   探访
     jiùjiu yījiāsānkǒu   **cóng**   zhōngguó   lái   tànfǎng
     uncle   family.of.three **from**   China   come   visit

     我们 。（Δ 好儿童 3B 38）
     women
     1PL

     'My uncle's family of three came to visit us from China.'
     (Δ*Hǎoértóng* 3B, 38)

Expressions of Location, Time and Place

(10) 大哥　　　跟　　着　　大嫂　　**往**　　**厨房**
　　 dàgē　　 gēn　 zhe　 dàsǎo　　**wǎng**　**chúfáng**
　　 elder.brother follow ZHE big.sister-in-law towards kitchen

　　 走　　 去。（鞭子 53）
　　 zǒu　　 qù
　　 walk　 go

　　 '(My) elder brother followed his wife to the kitchen.' (*Biānzǐ* 53)

(11) 雨　　肆意地　　**向**　　**伞**　　**下**　　侵略　着。（撞墙 41）
　　 yǔ　 sìyìde　　**xiàng**　**sǎn**　**xià**　qīnlüè　zhe
　　 rain rampantly towards umbrella under invade ZHE

　　 'The rain swept wantonly under the umbrella.' (*Zhuàngqiáng* 41)

(12) 我　　跌坐　　**在**　**单人**　**床**　　**上**…（撞墙 38）
　　 wǒ　 diēzuò　**zài**　**dānrén**　**chuáng**　**shàng**
　　 1SG slump at single bed up

　　 'I slumped down on the single bed …' (*Zhuàngqiáng* 38)

(13) 这时， 有　 一　 个　 瘦子　　 出现　 了，　双手
　　 zhèshí　yǒu　yī　gè　 shòuzi　　chūxiàn　le　 shuāngshǒu
　　 at.this.time have one CL thin.person appear LE both.hands

　　 直直地　　伸　　**到**　**我**　**面前**　　来，…（石头 1）
　　 zhízhí-de　shēn　**dào**　**wǒ**　**miànqián**　lái
　　 straightly stretch to 1SG front come

　　 'At this time, a thin guy appeared and stretched both his hands out straight towards me …' (*Shítou* 1)

(14) 张金燕　　　是　 粤籍　　人，　 一九零一　　　　年
　　 zhāngjīnyàn　shì　yuèjí　rén，　yījiǔlíngyī　　　　nián
　　 Zhang.Jinyan be Cantonese person nineteen.hundred.and.one year

　　 诞生　　**于**　**中国**。（△ 狮城 23）
　　 dànshēng　**yú**　**zhōngguó**
　　 born　 in　 China

　　 'Zhang Jinyan is a Cantonese person born in China in 1901.' (△*Shīchéng* 23)

(15) 娇小的　　 她　　 今年　　 26 岁，　　　　来　　**自**
　　 jiāoxiǎo-de　tā　 jīnnián　èrshíliùsuì　　lái　**zì**
　　 petite　 3SG this.year twenty.six.years.old come from

中国　　　海南省。（报 1995 年 3 月 10 日 20 版）
zhōngguó　hǎinánshěng
China　　Hainan.province

'The 26-year-old petite girl comes from Hainan Province, China.'
(*Bào*, Mar. 10, 1995, Issue no. 20)

(16) 随着　　世界各国　　　的　　文学　　　走　　向　　　中国，
　　 suízhe　shìjiègèguó　de　wénxué　zǒu　**xiàng**　zhōngguó
　　 as　　　every.country　DE　literature　go　**towards**　China

世界各地　　的　　华文　　　文学　　也　　逐渐　　　　走　　向
shìjiègèdì　de　huáwén　wénxué　yě　zhújiàn　zǒu　**xiàng**
every.place　DE　Chinese　literature　also　gradually　go　**towards**

世界。（△ 新华文学 253）
shìjiè
world

'As the literature of every country in the world is introduced to China, Chinese literature of every place is also gradually spreading to the world.'
(△*Xīnhuáwénxué* 253)

In examples (8)–(11), the prepositional phrases are before the verb phrase, functioning as an adverbial, whereas in examples (12)–(16), they follow the verb phrase, acting as a complement.

In addition, a place expression is also frequently found as an attribute. If the place expression in the attribute position is a noun indicating place names, then it can be either marked with 的 *de* 'DE' or not. For example,

(17) 尼泊尔　　首都 （南北 1）
　　 níbóěr　　shǒudū
　　 Nepal　　capital
　　 'capital of Nepal' (*Nánběi* 1)

(18) 泗水　　的　　交通 （冰灯 67）
　　 sìshuǐ　de　jiāotōng
　　 Surabaya　DE　traffic
　　 'traffic in Surabaya' (*Bīngdēng* 67)

Example (17) can also be expressed as 尼泊尔的首都 *níbóěr de shǒudū* 'capital of Nepal', and example (18) is the same as 泗水交通 *sìshuǐ jiāotōng* 'traffic in

Surabaya'. However, sometimes whether 的 *de* 'DE' appears or not will make a difference in meaning. For instance, 海南鸡饭 *hǎinán jīfàn* 'Hainanese Chicken Rice' is different from 海南的鸡饭 *hǎinán de jīfàn* 'Chicken Rice from Hainan'. For example Singaporeans often say the sentence in (19a), meaning some kind of rice cooked in Hainan style, and it can't be replaced by (19b).

(19) a 我们 去 吃 海南鸡饭
    wǒmen *qù* *chī* *hǎinánjīfàn*
    1PL go eat Hainanese.Chicken.Rice
    'Let's have Hainanese Chicken Rice.'

(19) *b 我们 去 吃 海南 的 鸡饭
    wǒmen *qù* *chī* *hǎinán* *de* *jīfàn*
    1PL go eat Hainan DE chicken.rice
    'Intended meaning: Let's have Hainanese Chicken Rice.'
    'Literal meaning: Let's have Chicken rice from Hainan.'

If the place expression in the attribute position is a modifier-head phrase composed of 'nouns + localisers', 的 *de* 'DE' is usually required as shown by the examples in (20).

(20) **纸盒 里 的** 剩菜剩饭 （△ 好儿童 3B 28）
    zhǐhé **lǐ** **de** *shèngcàishèngfàn*
    paper.box inside DE leftovers
    'leftovers in the paper box' (△*Hǎoértóng* 3B, 28)

房间 外面 的 牌子（痕迹 111）
fángjiān wàimiàn de *páizi*
room outside DE board
'the board outside the room' (*Hénjì*, 111)

屋 后 的 窗（△ 母亲 84）
wū hòu de *chuāng*
house back DE window
'the window at the back of the house' (△*Mǔqīn* 84)

门 前 的 鞭炮 屑（太阳 23）
mén qián de *biānpào* *xiè*
door front DE firecracker scrap
'firecracker scraps in front of the door' (*Tàiyáng* 23)

船　　上　　的　　灯火（寻庙 29）
chuán　shàng　de　dēnghuǒ
boat　　on　　DE　light
'light on the boat' (*Xúnmiào* 29)

However, if the head contains numeral-classifier compounds, demonstrative pronouns or DE construction, then the place phrase in the attribute position will not take 的 *de* 'DE'. For example, we say 桌上的瓷碗 *zhuō shàng de cíwǎn* 'the porcelain bowl on the table' instead of *桌上瓷碗 *zhuō shàng cíwǎn*. Yet, if the head noun 瓷碗 *cíwǎn* 'porcelain bowl' is in a complex form with the elements mentioned earlier, then 的 *de* 'DE' after the place phrase can be omitted, as shown next:

桌　　上　　一　　个　　瓷碗
zhuō　shàng　yī　gè　cíwǎn
table　on　one　CL　porcelain.bowl
'a porcelain bowl on the table'

桌　　上　　那　　瓷碗
zhuō　shàng　nà　cíwǎn
table　on　that　porcelain.bowl
'that porcelain bowl on the table'

桌　　上　　那　　个　　瓷碗
zhuō　shàng　nà　gè　cíwǎn
table　on　that　CL　porcelain.bowl
'that porcelain bowl on the table'

桌　　上　　盛　　了　　菜　　的　　瓷碗
zhuō　shàng　chéng　le　cài　de　cíwǎn
table　up　hold　LE　vegetable　DE　porcelain.bowl
'the porcelain bowl full of food on the table'

Here are more examples:

(21)　**主席台**　上　　几　　位　　学有专长的　　演讲者（怀旧 58）
　　　***zhǔxítái*　shàng　jǐ　wèi　xuéyǒuzhuāncháng-de　yǎnjiǎngzhě**
　　　rostrum　on　several　CL　professional　lecturer
　　　'several professional lecturers on the rostrum' (*Huáijiù* 58)

门　　前　　那　　棵　　树（晚上 119）
mén　qián　nà　kē　shù
door　front　that　CL　tree
'that tree in front of the door' (*Wǎnshàng* 119)

桌　　上　　那　　个　　浅浅的　　碟子（跳舞 20）
zhuō　shàng　nà　gè　qiǎnqiǎn-de　diézi
table　on　that　CL　shallow　saucer
'that shallow saucer on the table' (*Tiàowǔ* 20)

咖啡　　店　　内　　品　　茶　　的　　顾客（一心 46）
kāfēi　diàn　nèi　pǐn　chá　de　gùkè
coffee　shop　inside　taste　tea　DE　customer
'customers who taste tea in the coffee shop' (*Yīxīn* 46)

A place word can modify another place word, and the most typical example is addresses. In such cases, the place words are arranged in descending order. For example, we would use 新加坡牛车水　*xīnjiāpō niúchēshuǐ* 'Singapore, Chinatown' instead of *牛车水新加坡　*niúchēshuǐ xīnjiāpō* 'Chinatown, Singapore'. More examples are as follows:

(22)　香港　　　荷李活　　　道　　92 号　　3 楼　　（华文教材 2B 43）
　　　xiānggǎng　hélǐhuó　　dào　　92hào　　3lóu
　　　Hongkong　Hollywood　avenue　No. 92　the.third.floor
　　　'3F, No. 92 Hollywood Avenue, Hong Kong' (*Huáwénjiàocái* 2B, 43)

(23)　台湾省　　　　台南市　　　东丰路　　　　649　　　　　之
　　　táiwānshěng　tàinánshì　dōngfēnglù　liùsìjiǔ　　zhī
　　　Taiwan.Province　Tainan　Dongfeng.Road　six.four.nine　LIG

　　　二号（报 1995 年 3 月 11 日 10 版）
　　　èrhào
　　　No. 2
　　　'No. 649-2 Dongfeng Road, Tainan City, Taiwan Province' (*Bào*, Mar. 11, 1995, Issue no. 10)

(24)　新加坡　　　惹兰　　苏丹　　二百号　　　布业中心
　　　xīnjiāpō　　rělán　sūdān　èrbǎihào　bùyèzhōngxīn
　　　Singapore　Jalan　Sultan　No. 200　cloth.centre

门牌 　　　零二 / 一八号（报 1995 年 3 月 11 日 14 版）
ménpái　　　língèr　yībāhào
house.number　No. 02　No. 18

'No. 02/18 Cloth Centre, No. 200 Sultan, Jalan, Singapore' (*Bào*, Mar 11, 1995, Issue no. 10)

However, due to the influence of English, words in addresses can also be arranged in ascending order in written Singapore Mandarin. For instance:

(25) 永平大厦　　　　130 号，　永平，　　柔佛州，
　　 yǒngpíngdàshà　130hào　 yǒngpíng　róufózhōu
　　 Yong.Peng.Building　No.130　Yong.Peng　Johor

马来西亚（华文教材 2 A 65）
mǎláixīyà
Malaysia

'No. 130 Yong Peng Building, Yong Peng, Johor, Malaysia' (*Huáwénjiàocái* 2A, 65)

While in spoken language, words in addresses are still expressed according to the descending order.

In Chinese Mandarin, the expression of the address always follows the descending order either in spoken or written genres.

2.8 Place Subject–Verbal Predicate Sentences

If the subject of a sentence is filled with a constituent indicating places, it is called a place subject. If a sentence takes a place constituent as the subject and a verb phrase as the predicate, it is referred as a 'place subject–verbal predicate sentence'. For instance,

(1)　巴黎　是　个　花花世界。（怀旧）
　　 bālí　shì　gè　huāhuāshìjiè
　　 Paris　be　CL　colourful.world
　　 'Paris is a colourful world.' (*Huáijiù*)

(2)　希腊　是　第一　个　基督教　　国家。（南北 49）
　　 xīlà　shì　dìyī　gè　jīdūjiào　guójiā
　　 Greece　be　first　CL　Christian　country
　　 'Greece was the first Christian country.' (*Nánběi* 49)

Expressions of Location, Time and Place   169

(3) 荷兰　　　是　世界　镶造　　钻石　　的　中心。
　　　　　　　　　　　　　　　　　　　　　（△ 天长 20）
    hélán   shì shìjiè xiāngzào zuànshí de zhōngxīn
    Netherlands be world   inlay   diamond DE centre
    'Netherlands is the world centre for inlaying diamonds.' (△*Tiāncháng* 20)

These place subject–verbal predicate sentences are all 是 *shì* 'be' constructions (see Section 5.6 in Volume I), and the subjects are simply nouns denoting places. These sentences are simple and will not be discussed further. What we will demonstrate in the following sections are place subject–verbal predicate sentences, in which the subject positions are filled by 'nouns + localisers' phrases. These sentences can be categorised into three types according to their grammatical meanings expressed.

2.8.1 Place Subject–Verbal Predicate Sentences Indicating 'Existence'

There are four main formats for this type.

1. Format 1: Place Word + 有 *yǒu 'have' + Nominal Phrases*

(4) 身　　上　　有　数不清的　　　细菌。（△ 好儿童 3B 28）
    shēn   shàng yǒu shùbùqīng-de xìjūn
    body   on   have countless   bacteria
    'There are countless bacteria on our bodies.' (*Hǎoértóng* 3B, 28)

(5) 眼　　前　　有　这么好　　的　路。（撞墙 25）
    yǎn   qián   yǒu zhèmehǎo de   lù
    eye   front have so.good   DE   road
    'There is such a good road ahead.' (*Zhuàngqiáng* 25)

(6) 屋　　外　　有　铁丝网。（短篇 99）
    wū   wài   yǒu tiěsīwǎng
    house outside have barbed.wires
    'There is barbed wire outside the house.' (*Duǎnpiān* 99)

In example (4), 身上有数不清的细菌 *shēnshàng yǒu shùbùqīng-de xìjūn* means 'There exist countless bacteria on our body'. The same extensional meaing is true with other examples.

Sometimes 有 *yǒu* 'have' can be followed by 着 *zhe* 'ZHE', as follows:

(7) 面　　前　　有　着　一　个　万丈深渊 （跳舞 42）
    miàn   qián   yǒu zhe yī   gè   wànzhàngshēnyuān

face front have ZHE one CL bottomless.chasm
'There is a bottomless chasm in the front.' (*Tiàowǔ* 42)

Nevertheless, this sentence structure with 着 *zhe* 'ZHE' is seen only occasionally in written Singapore Mandarin.

2. *Format 2: Place Word* + 是 *shì* '*be*' + *Nominal Phrases*

(8) 桌 上 是 凌乱 的 讲义 。
zhuō shàng shì língluàn de jiǎngyì
desk on be messy DE handout
'Handouts cluttered on the desk.'

(9) 他 家 屋 后 是 一 个 花园。（华文教材 1A 106）
tā jiā wū hòu shì yī gè huāyuán
3SG home house behind be one CL garden
'Behind his house is a garden.' (*Huáwénjiàocái* 1A, 106)

(10) 门 内 是 一 间 教室。（回忆 3）
mén nèi shì yī jiān jiàoshì
door inside be one CL classroom
'Behind the door is a classroom.' (*Huíyì* 3)

(11) 湖 的 对面 是 总统 的 标致 别墅。（冰灯 63）
hú de duìmiàn shì zǒngtǒng de biāozhì biéshù
lake DE opposite be president DE pretty villa
'On the opposite side of the lake is the President's fancy villa.' (*Bīngdēng* 63)

(12) 眼 前 是 一 个 很大 很圆 的 坑。（Δ一壶 7）
yǎn qián shì yī gè hěndà hěnyuán-de kēng
eye front be one CL very.big very.round pit
'In front is a very large and round pit.' (Δ*Yīhú* 7)

Both format 1 and format 2 denote existence, but the verbs used are different: In format 1, 有 *yǒu* 'have' is used, and in format 2, 是 *shì* 'be' is used, with a subtle difference in the meaning. The meaning of 是 *shì* 'be' is exclusive, since it indicates that the thing discussed in the sentence is the only thing in the speaker's mind, while 有 *yǒu* 'have' doesn't imply such an exclusive meaning. Let's compare:

(13) a. 书包　　　里　　有　　奶油　　饼干。
　　　　shūbāo　　*lǐ*　　*yǒu*　　*nǎiyóu*　　*bǐnggān*
　　　　schoolbag　**inside**　**have**　**cream**　**biscuit**

   b. 书包　　　里　　是　　奶油　　饼干。
　　　　shūbāo　　*lǐ*　　*shì*　　*nǎiyóu*　　*bǐnggān*
　　　　schoolbag　**inside**　**be**　**cream**　**biscuit**

In sentence (13a), the speaker is certain only of the presence of cream biscuits in the bag. As to other items, no affirmation is made. In contrast, in sentence (13b), the speaker not only affirms the existence of cream biscuits in the bag, but also implies that these are the only things in the bag; even if there are other things, they are not his concern. Since the usage of 是 *shì* 'be' implies an exclusive meaning, it is often modified by the adverb 净 *jìng* 'all', which means 'simply with nothing else'. For example, sentence (13b) can be revised as: 书包里净是奶油饼干 *shūbāo lǐ jìng shì nǎiyóu bǐnggān* 'the school bag is full of nothing but cream biscuits'. This is also illustrated in the following examples:

(14) 海　　边　　**净**　　**是**　　大大小小　　失去　　棱角　　的　　石头。（怀旧 112）
　　　hǎi　*biān*　***jìng***　***shì***　*dàdàxiǎoxiǎo*　*shīqù*　*léngjiǎo*　*de*　*shítou*
　　　ocean　side　**all**　**be**　big.and.small　lose　angle　DE　stone
　　　'The seaside is fully covered with large and small stones that have lost their edges.' (*Huáijiù* 112)

(15) 眼　　前　　**净**　　**是**　　白茫茫的　　浓　　雾。（华文教材 1B10）
　　　yǎn　*qián*　***jìng***　***shì***　*báimángmáng-de*　*nóng*　*wù*
　　　eye　front　**all**　**be**　boundless.white　dense　fog
　　　'A boundless white dense fog spreads before our eyes.'
　　　(*Huáwénjiàocái* 1B, 10)

有 *yǒu* 'have' is never modified by 净 *jìng* 'all', and it's ungrammatical to say *书包里净有奶油饼干 *shūbāo lǐ jìng yǒu nǎiyóu bǐnggān*.

3. Format 3: Place Word + Verb + 着 zhe 'ZHE' + Nominal Phrases (Henceforth Construction X)

(16) 沙发　　上面　　搁　　着　　枕头　　和　　被子。（狮子 41）
　　　shāfā　*shàngmiàn*　*gē*　*zhe*　*zhěntóu*　*hé*　*bèizi*

172   Expressions of Location, Time and Place

    sofa   on   place ZHE pillow and quilt
    'There are pillows and quilts on the sofa.' (*Shīzi* 41)

(17) 海面　　　　上　　停泊　着　多　　艘　巨大的　轮船　。
　　　　　　　　　　　　　　　　　　　　　　　　　　（石头 210）
    hǎimiàn   shàng tíngbó zhe duō sōu jùdà-de lúnchuán
    ocean.surface on   moor   ZHE   many CL   giant   ship
    'There are many huge ships moored on the sea.' (*Shítou* 210)

(18) 高速　　　公路　　的　两旁　　矗立　着　一　　盏盏
    gāosù   gōnglù de   liǎngpáng chùlì zhe yī   zhǎnzhǎn
    high.speed road   DE   two.sides   stand ZHE one CL-CL

    洒　　着　　黄光　　　的　路灯。（青青 83）
    sǎ   zhe   huángguāng de lùdēng
    sprinkle ZHE yellow.light DE street.lamp
    'On both sides of the expressway, there are street lamps shining with yellow light.' (*Qīngqīng* 83)

(19) 书堆　　　　中　夹　着　一　　些　剪报。（短篇 11）
    shūduī   zhōng jiá zhe yī   xiē jiǎnbào
    stack.of.books in   lie ZHE   one CL newspaper.clip
    'There are some newspaper clippings stuck in the pile of books.' (*Duǎnpiān* 11)

(20) 奴隶　塑像　　的　脚下　　坐　着　一　　堆堆　　的
    núlì   sùxiàng de   jiǎoxià   zuò zhe yī   duīduī   de
    slave   statue   DE   foot   sit   ZHE   one CL-CL   DE

    男男　　女女。（怀旧 5）
    nánnán   nǚnǚ
    men   women
    'At the foot of the slave statue sat groups of men and women.' (*Huáijiù* 5)

4. *Format 4: Place Word + Verb +* 满 *mǎn 'Full' +* 了 *le 'LE' + Nominal Phrases*

(21) 马路　两旁　　挤满　　　了　争　　　睹　热闹　的
    mǎlù liǎngpáng jǐmǎn   le   zhēng   dǔ   rènào de
    road two.sides squeeze.full LE struggle.for see bustle DE

人群。（华文教材 1A 62）
rénqún
crowd
'Both sides of the road were crowded with people vying to see the lively scene.' (*Huáwénjiàocái* 1A, 62)

(22) 墙　　　上　　画满　　了　　图案　　花纹。（怀旧 52）
qiáng　shàng　huàmǎn　le　tú'àn　huāwén
wall　on　draw.full　LE　pattern　decoration
'On the walls are painted patterns and floral motifs.' (*Huáijiù* 52)

(23) 礼品店　　里　　摆满　　了　各种各样　　的
lǐpǐndiàn　lǐ　bǎimǎn　le　gèzhǒnggèyàng　de
gift.shop　inside　display.full　LE　all.kinds.of　DE

纪念品。（△ 好儿童 3B 38）
jìniànpǐn
souvenir
'The gift shop is filled with a wide range of souvenirs.' (△*Hǎoértóng* 3B, 38)

(24) 篱外　　沟边　　的　　砖缝　　间　　长满
líwài　gōubiān　de　zhuānfèng　jiān　zhǎngmǎn
hedge.outside　ditch.side　DE　brick.crack　between　grow.full

了　蔓条　杂草。（追云 51）
le　màntiáo　Zácǎo
LE　vine　weeds
'Sprawling weeds grow from the cracks of the bricks at the edge of the ditch outside the hedge.' (*Zhuīyún* 51)

(25) 书桌　　上　　放满　　了　中文　　与　捷克文
shūzhuō　shàng　fàngmǎn　le　zhōngwén　yǔ　jiékèwén
desk　on　put.full　LE　Chinese　and　Czech.language

互译　　　　的　文件。（石头 11）
hùyì　　　　de　wénjiàn
mutually.translated　DE　file
'The desk is covered with bilingual documents in Chinese and Czech.' (*Shítou* 11)

2.8.2 Place Subject–Verbal Predicate Sentences Indicating 'Appearance'

In this case, the predicate may contain either the directional verb 来 *lái* 'come', such as 来 *lái* 'come', 传来 *chuánlái* 'come', and 跑来 *pǎolái* 'run and come' in (26)–(28), or the verb 出 *chū* 'out', such as 出现 *chūxiàn* 'appear', 露出 *lùchū* 'show' and 显出 *xiǎnchū* 'show' in (29)–(31):

(26) 眼前　　　**来**　　了　一　位　中年　的　客人。
　　　　　　　　　　　　　　　　　　　　　　　（追云 55）
　　　yǎnqián　　　**lái**　　le　yī　wèi　zhōngnián　de　kèrén
　　　before.the.eyes　**come**　LE　one　CL　middle-aged　DE　guest
　　　'Here comes a middle-aged guest.' (*Zhuīyún* 55)

(27) 门外　　　**传来**　　了　女佣　的　声音。（狮子 96）
　　　ménwài　　**chuánlái**　le　nǚyòng　de　shēngyīn
　　　outside.the.door　**come**　LE　maid　DE　voice
　　　'The maid's voice came from outside the door.' (*Shīzi* 96)

(28) 那边　　**跑来**　　了　一　个　人。（华文教材 1A 41）
　　　nàbiān　**pǎolái**　le　yī　gè　rén
　　　that.side　**run.come**　LE　one　CL　person
　　　'A man came running from over there.' (*Huáwénjiàocái* 1A, 41)

(29) 高空　　中　**出现**　　三　架　飞机。（华文教材 2B 103）
　　　gāokōng　zhōng　**chūxiàn**　sān　jià　fēijī
　　　high.sky　in　**appear**　three　CL　aircraft
　　　'Three aircraft appeared high in the sky.' (*Huáwénjiàocái* 2B, 103)

(30) 苍白的　　圆脸　　上　**露出**　　了　疲乏　但　却
　　　cāngbái-de　yuánliǎn　shàng　**lùchū**　le　pífá　dàn　què
　　　pale　round.face　on　**show.out**　LE　tired　but　yet

　　　满足的　　笑容。（追云 35）
　　　mǎnzú-de　xiàoróng
　　　content　smile
　　　'A tired but content smile crossed her pale round face.' (*Zhuīyún* 35)

(31) 脸　上　**显出**　　痛苦的　　神情。（华文教材 2A 208）
　　　liǎn　shàng　**xiǎnchū**　tòngkǔ-de　shénqíng
　　　face　on　**show**　painful　expression
　　　'A painful expression appeared on (his) face.' (*Huáwénjiàocái* 2A, 208)

2.8.3 Place Subject–Verbal Predicate Sentences Indicating 'Continuation of a Dynamic Situation'

The format of this type is: place word + verb + 着 *zhe* 'ZHE' + nominal phrases (henceforth we will refer to the format as Construction Y). For example,

(32) 讲堂　　外　　下　　着　　雨。（青青 74）
　　　jiǎngtáng　wài　xià　zhe　yǔ
　　　lecture.hall　outside　fall　ZHE　rain
　　　'It is raining outside the lecture hall.' (*Qīngqīng* 74)

(33) 手　　上　　摇　　着　　手帕。（扶轮 33）
　　　shǒu　shàng　yáo　zhe　shǒupà
　　　hand　on　shake　ZHE　handkerchief
　　　'(Somebody) is waving a handkerchief in his hand.' (*Fúlún* 33)

(34) 大街　　上　　舞　　着　　狮子。
　　　dàjiē　shàng　wǔ　zhe　shīzi
　　　street　on　dance　ZHE　lion
　　　'There is a lion-dance going on in the street.'

(35) 课室　　里　　上　　着　　课。
　　　kèshì　lǐ　shàng　zhe　kè
　　　classroom　in　have　ZHE　class
　　　'There are classes going on in the classroom.'

It should be noted that this Construction Y of a dynamic continuation appears exactly the same as Format 3 of those indicating 'existence' (Construction X), with the same surface order 'place word + verb + 着 *zhe* 'ZHE' + nominal phrases'. However, they are grammatically different mainly in the following two aspects.

First, the nominal phrase in Construction X of existence can be, and often is, modified by a numeral-classifier compound, as shown by 多艘 *duō sōu* 'many (ships)', 一盏盏 *yī zhǎnzhǎn* 'many (lamps)', 一些 *yī xiē* 'some' and 一堆堆 *yī duīduī* 'groups of' in examples (17)–(20). Although no numeral-classifier compounds are included in example (16), it is possible for them to be added as indicated in (16') below, still indicating 'existence'.

(16') 沙发　　上面　　搁　　着　　一　　个　　枕头　　和
　　　shāfā　shàngmiàn　gē　zhe　**yī**　**gè**　zhēntou　hé
　　　sofa　on　place　ZHE　**one**　**CL**　pillow　and
　　　'There are a pillow and two quilts on the sofa.'

两 条 被子。
liǎng tiáo bèizi
two CL quilt

'There are a pillow and two quilts on the sofa.'

However, it is ungrammatical to add numeral-classifier compounds to the nominal phrases of Construction Y of dynamic continuation. For example, sentences (32)–(35) cannot be changed in the following way:

(32)' * 讲堂 外 下 着 一 场 雨。（青青 74）
  jiǎngtáng wài xià zhe yī chǎng yǔ
  lecture.hall outside fall ZHE one CL rain

'Intended meaning: It is raining outside the classroom.' (*Qīngqīng* 74)

(33)' * 手 上 摇 着 两 块 手帕。（扶轮 33）
  shǒu shàng yáo zhe liǎng kuài shǒupà
  hand on shake ZHE two CL handkerchief

'Intended meaning: Somebody is waving two handkerchiefs in (his) hands.' (*Fúlún* 33)

(34)' * 大街 上 舞 着 一 只 狮子。
  dàjiē shàng wǔ zhe yī zhī shīzi
  street on dance ZHE one CL lion

'Intended meaning: A lion-dance is going on in the street.'

(35)' * 课室 里 上 着 一 节 课。
  kèshì lǐ shàng zhe yī jié kè
  classroom inside take ZHE one CL class

'Intended meaning: A class is going on in the classroom.'

Secondly, Construction X can be transformed into the following 'nominal phrases + verb + 在 *zài* 'at' + place word' format, which still indicates 'existence'. For example, examples (16)–(18) can be transformed as follows.

(36) 枕头 和 被子 搁 在 沙发 上面。
  zhěntou hé bèizi gē zài shāfā shàngmiàn
  pillow and quilt place at sofa on

'Pillows and quilts are placed on the sofa.'

(37) 多   艘   巨大的   轮船   停泊   在   海面   上。
    duō   sōu   jùdà-de   lúnchuán tíngbó zài hǎimiàn   shàng
    many CL   giant   ship   moor   at   ocean.surface on
    'Many huge ships are moored on the sea.'

(38) 一   盏盏   洒   着   黄光   的   路灯
    yī   zhǎnzhǎn   sǎ   zhe   huángguāng   de   lùdēng
    one   CL-CL   sprinkle ZHE   yellow.light DE   street.lamp

    矗立   在   高速   公路   的   两旁。
    chùlì   zài   gāosù   gōnglù   de   liǎngpáng
    stand   at   high.speed   road   DE   two.sides
    'Many street lamps with a yellow light are standing on both sides of the highway.'

On the other hand, Construction Y of dynamic continuation can be transformed into another alternative format, 'place word + 正 *zhèng* 'currently' + verb + 着 *zhe* 'ZHE' + nominal phrases + 呢 *ne* 'SFP'' without much change in meaning. For example, examples (32)–(35) can be revised as follows.

(39) 讲堂   外   正   下   着   雨   呢。
    jiǎngtáng   wài   zhèng   xià   zhe   yǔ   ne
    lecture.hall outside   currently   fall   ZHE   rain   SFP
    'It is currently raining outside the classroom.'

(40) 手   上   正   摇   着   手帕   呢。
    shǒu   shàng zhèng   yáo   zhe   shǒupà   ne
    hand   on   currently   shake   ZHE   handkerchief   SFP
    '(Somebody) is waving a handkerchief in his hand.' (*Fúlún* 33)

(41) 大街   上   正   舞   着   狮子   呢。
    dàjiē   shàng   zhèng   wǔ   zhe   shīzi   ne
    street on   currently   dance   ZHE   lion   SFP
    'There is a lion-dance going on right now in the street.'

(42) 课室   里   正   上   着   课   呢。
    kèshì   lǐ   zhèng   shàng   zhe   kè   ne
    classroom   inside   currently   have   ZHE   class   SFP
    'There are classes going on right now in the classroom.'

In contrast, Construction X of existence does not have such an alternative format 'place word + 正 *zhèng* 'currently' + verb + 着 *zhe* 'ZHE' + nominal phrases + 呢 *ne* 'SFP''. That is to say, examples (16)–(18) cannot be revised as:

(16)" *沙发　　上面　　　正　　　　搁　　　着　　　枕头　　　和
　　　shāfā　shàngmiàn　zhèng　　gē　　zhe　　zhěntou　hé
　　　sofa　　on　　　　currently　place　ZHE　pillow　　and

　　　被子　　呢。
　　　bèizi　　ne
　　　quilt　　SFP

　　　'Intended meaning: On the sofa are placed some pillows and quilts.'

(17)" *海面　　　　上　　　正　　　　停泊　　着　　　多　　艘
　　　hǎimiàn　　shàng　zhèng　　tíngbó　zhe　　duō　sōu
　　　ocean.surface　on　　currently　moor　　ZHE　many　CL

　　　巨大的　　　轮船　　　呢。
　　　jùdà-de　　lúnchuán　ne
　　　giant　　　ship　　　SFP

　　　'Intended meaning: There moored many huge ships on the sea.'

(18)" *高速　　　　公路　　的　　两旁　　　　正　　　　矗立　　着　　一
　　　gāosù　　　gōnglù　de　　liǎngpáng　zhèng　　chùlì　　zhe　　yī
　　　high.speed　road　　DE　two.sides　currently　stand　　ZHE　one

　　　盏盏　　　洒　　　着　　黄光　　　　的　　路灯　　　呢。
　　　zhǎnzhǎn　sǎ　　　zhe　　huángguāng　de　　lùdēng　　ne
　　　CL-CL　　sprinkle　ZHE　yellow.light　DE　　street.lamp　SFP

　　　'Intended meaning: On both sides of the expressway, there are street lamps shining with yellow light.'

For similar reasons, Construction Y of dynamic continuation cannot be changed into the 'nominal phrases + verb + 在 *zài* 'at' + place words' format, so examples (32)–(35) cannot be revised as follows:

(32)" *雨　　下　　在　　讲堂　　　　外。
　　　yǔ　　xià　zài　　jiǎngtáng　wài
　　　rain　fall　at　　lecture.hall　outside

　　　'Intended meaning: The rain is falling outside the lecture hall.'

(33)" *手帕　　　摇　　　在　　手　　　上。
　　　 shǒupà　　yáo　　zài　shǒu　shàng
　　　 handkerchief　shake　at　hand　on
　　　 'Intended meaning: The handkerchief is being in the hand.'

(34)" *狮子　　舞　　在　　大街　　上。
　　　 shīzi　　wǔ　　zài　　dàjiē　shàng
　　　 lion　　dance　at　　street　on
　　　 'Intended meaning: A lion is dancing in the street.'

(35)" *课　　上　　在　　课室　　　里。
　　　 kè　　shàng　zài　kèshì　　lǐ
　　　 class　take　at　classroom　inside
　　　 'Intended meaning: The class is taking place in the classroom.'

It is evident from the discussion that Construction X of existence and Construction Y of dynamic continuation share identical surface order, but are totally different from each other both grammatically and semantically. Such a pair of constructions are often called 'homomorphic pattern' in grammar.

Notes

1. Translator's note: In the original book, the term used is 时间词 *shíjiāncí* and the literal translation is 'time words'. But as discussed in the following sections, it not only includes words but also includes phrases. Therefore, we adopt the translation of 'time expressions'. For similar reasons, 处所词 *chùsuǒcí* is translated as 'place expressions' rather than 'place words'.
2. The single localisers 左 *zuǒ* 'left' and 右 *yòu* 'right', as well as compound localisers 间中 *jiānzhōng* 'in between' and 内中 *nèizhōng* 'within', can't be modified by nouns.
3. Translator's note: 以 *yǐ* 'YI'/ 之 *zhī* 'ZHI' are words from ancient Chinese. In some cases they share the same meaning as the auxiliary word 的 *de* 'DE', indicating possessive relations. In other cases they have no meaning at all and is simply used to add one more syllable to form a disyllable word.

3 Composite Sentences

3.1 An Overview of Composite Sentences

Composite sentences are in contrast to simple sentences. Here are a few examples:

(1) 我们　　自己　　要　　　　生活　　　　得　　快乐，
    wǒmen　zìjǐ　　yào　　　shēnghuó　de　　kuàilè
    1PL　　 self　　should　live　　　　DE　　happy

　　也　　　要　　　让　　　别人　　生活　　　　得　　快乐。（伦理·中四91）
　　yě　　 yào　　 ràng　 biérén　shēnghuó　de　　kuàilè
　　also　 should　let　　others　live　　　　DE　　happy
　　'We should live a happy life ourselves, and we should also let others live happily.' (*Lúnlǐ* IV 91)

(2) 你们　　 开　　　多少　　　　价，
    nǐmen　 kāi　　 duōshǎo　　jià
    2PL　　 offer　 how.much　price

　　我　　 就　　　给　　　多少。（回忆44）
　　wǒ　　jiù　　　gěi　　duōshǎo
　　1SG　 just　　give　　how.much
　　'I'll give you whatever price you offer.' (*Huíyì* 44)

(3) 一　　条　　小　　　溪，　　　不分昼夜　　　　地　　向　　　前　　　奔流；
    yī　　tiáo　xiǎo　xī,　　　　bùfēnzhòuyè　　de　　xiàng　qián　bēnliú
    one　CL　 small　stream　　day.and.night　DE　towards　front　run

山谷	里，	总是	响	着	他
shāngǔ	lǐ	zǒngshì	xiǎng	zhe	tā
valley	inside	always	ring	ZHE	3SG

愉快	的	笑声。（华文教材1A36）
yúkuài	de	xiàoshēng
happy	DE	laughter

'A little stream runs forward day and night, with its happy laughter always ringing in the valley.' (*Huáwénjiàocái* 1A, 36)

(4)
现在	国家发展部	又	推行	一	项
xiànzài	guójiāfāzhǎnbù	yòu	tuīxíng	yī	xiàng
now	Ministry.of.National.Development	again	promote	one	CL

别出心裁	的	计划：	在	每年	植树节	那
biéchūxīncái	de	jìhuà	zài	měinián	zhíshùjié	nà
special	DE	plan	on	every.year	Tree.Planting.Day	that

天	展开	"种植	果树	运动"，	由	政府
tiān	zhǎnkāi	zhòngzhí	guǒshù	yùndòng	yóu	zhèngfǔ
day	launch	plant	fruit.tree	campaign	by	government

首长	领导	人民	栽种	果树。（华文教材2A59）
shǒuzhǎng	lǐngdǎo	rénmín	zāizhòng	guǒshù
head	lead	people	plant	fruit.tree

'Now the Ministry of National Development has launched an innovative scheme: on every Tree Planting Day, the Planting Fruit Tree Campaign is launched, in which Government heads will lead the people in planting fruit trees.' (*Huáwénjiàocái* 2A, 59)

(5)
这	绝	不	是	一	小	撮，
zhè	jué	bù	shì	yī	xiǎo	cuō
this	absolutely	NEG	be	one	small	CL

而	是	一	大	群	人	啊！（风筝14）
ér	shì	yī	dà	qún	rén	a
but	be	one	big	crowd	people	SFP

'It's absolutely not a small group of people; it's a crowd!' (*Fēngzhēng* 14)

(6) 既然 读 不 来，
    jìrán dú bù lái
    since read NEG come

    又 何苦 去 读 呢？（追云 30）
    yòu hékǔ qù dú ne
    again why.bother go read SFP
    'Why bother to read it when you can't?' (*Zhuīyún* 30)

(7) 吃， 吃 多 一 点。（狮子 27）
    chī chī duō yī diǎn
    eat eat more one CL
    'Eat it and eat a bit more.' (*Shīzi* 27)

Examples (1)–(7) are all composite sentences.

3.1.1 Generalisations of Composite Sentences

1 Given that a simple sentence is made by a single unit of sentence-building, a complex sentence consists of at least two units of sentence-building. As illustrated by (1), the sentence is compounded by two units of sentence-building, namely, 我们自己要生活得快乐 *wǒmen zìjǐ yào shēnghuó de kuàilè* 'we should live a happy life ourselves' and 也要让别人生活得快乐 *yě yào ràng biérén shēnghuó de kuàilè* 'and also should let others live happily'. In comparison to examples (1)–(3) and (5)–(7), each of which contains two units of sentence building, there are three units in example (4). The unit of sentence-building is referred to as a clause. In some cases, a composite sentence can have several units of sentence-building, i.e. clauses, as manifested in the following sentence (8), which is made up of seven clauses.

(8) 他 年纪 大 了，/
    tā niánjì dà le
    3SG age old LE

    不 能 参加 游击队，/
    bù néng cānjiā yóujīduì
    NEG can join guerrilla

    有 一 天 他 回到 他 被 毁 的
    yǒu yī tiān tā huídào tā bèi huǐ de
    have one day 3SG return 3SG BEI destroy DE

烟店　　　　废墟　堆　中　　　看看，／
yāndiàn　　　fèixū　duī　zhōng　kànkàn
tobacco.shop　ruins　pile　middle　have.a.look

刚好　　附近　　停　　了　一　辆
gānghǎo　fùjìn　　tíng　le　yī　liàng
happen.to　nearby　park　LE　one　CL

满　载　　军火　　　　的　日本　　军车，／
mǎn　zài　jūnhuǒ　　　de　rìběn　jūnchē
full　load　ammunition　DE　Japanese　military.truck

他　用　　火柴　　点燃　　了　车底　　　　　的　汽油，／
tā　yòng　huǒchái　diǎnrán　le　chēdǐ　　　　de　qìyóu
3SG　use　match　　ignite　　LE　under.the.truck　DE　gasoline

把　军车　　　　引爆　　了，／
bǎ　jūnchē　　　yǐnbào　le
BA　military.truck　detonate　LE

他　也　同归于尽。（新华文学 63）
tā　yě　tóngguīyújìn
3SG　also　perish.together

'He was too old to join the guerrillas. One day he returned to the ruins of his destroyed tobacco shop, near which there happened to be a Japanese military vehicle loaded with ammunition. He lit, with a match, the gasoline under the vehicle, detonating the vehicle, and with it sacrificed his own life.' (*Xīnhuáwénxué* 63)

2   The clauses that make up composite sentences are often phrases, as in examples (1) to (6); but they could also be a single word as in (7), in which the first clause contains only one word 吃 *chī* 'eat'. More examples are as follows:

(9)　好，　就　　让　你　　先　　走！（金狮奖 272）
　　hǎo　jiù　　ràng　nǐ　　xiān　zǒu
　　good　then　let　　2SG　first　go
　　'OK, then, you go first!' (*Jīnshījiǎng* 272)

(10) 对，　Miss林　是　选购　衣物　的　专家。（追云 17）
　　　duì　　mīsīlín　shì　xuǎngòu　yīwù　de　zhuānjiā
　　　Yes　　Miss.Lin　be　purchase　clothes　DE　expert
　　　'Yes, Miss Lin is an expert at shopping for clothes.' (*Zhuīyún* 17)

In both of the preceding examples, the first clause is a single word. In cases where the clauses are made of phrases, they can be subject-predicate phrases, as in examples (2) and (3); or predicate-object phrases, as in the second clause of (1) (i.e., 也要 *yě yào* 'also should' being the verb, and 让别人生活得快乐 *ràng biérén shēnghuó de kuàilè* 'let others live happily' being the object); or adverbial-head endocentric phrases, as in the second clause of (6) (i.e., 又 *yòu* 'again' being the modifier and 何苦去读呢 *hékǔ qù dú ne* 'why bother to read' being the head).

3　There must be a pause between clauses, usually represented by a comma (,) as in the preceding examples. In some instances, a semicolon (;) is also applied, as in (3), where a semicolon follows the clause 一条小溪，不分昼夜向前奔流 *yī tiáo xiǎoxī, bù fēn zhòuyè de xiàngqián bēnliú* 'a little stream runs forward day and night'. A similar example is shown in (11):

(11)　国家　　富强，　　　　　人民　　就　　安乐；
　　　guójiā　fùqiáng　　　　　rénmín　jiù　　ānlè
　　　country　rich.and.powerful　people　just　safe.and.happy

　　　国家　　衰弱，　人民　　就　　痛苦。（伦理·中三 99）
　　　guójiā　shuāiruò　rénmín　jiù　　tòngkǔ
　　　country　weak　　people　just　painful

　　　'If the country is prosperous and powerful, the people will be safe and happy, while if the state is weak, the people will suffer.' (*Lúnlǐ* III 99)

In (11), the second clause 人民就安乐 *rénmín jiù ān lè* 'the people will be happy' also ends with a semicolon. Sometimes a colon (:) is also used. As in (4), a colon follows the first clause, 现在国家发展部又推行一项别出心裁的计划 *xiànzài guójiā fāzhǎn bù yòu tuīxíng yī xiàng biéchūxīncái de jìhuà* 'Now the Ministry of National Development has launched an innovative scheme'. One more example is as follows:

(12)　如果　　一切　　　不　　变，
　　　rúguǒ　yīqiè　　　bù　　biàn
　　　if　　　everything　NEG　change

我们	将	会	面对	这么	一	个	困境：
wǒmen	jiāng	huì	miànduì	zhème	yī	gè	kùnjìng
1PL	will	possible	face	such	one	CL	dilemma

我们	的	文坛	依然	会	有	少数	的
wǒmen	de	wéntán	yīrán	huì	yǒu	shǎoshù	de
1PL	DE	literature.altar	still	possible	have	a.few	DE

杰出的	作者，	然而	我们	却	会	缺乏
jiéchūde	zuòzhě	ránér	wǒmen	què	huì	quēfá
outstanding	writer	however	1PL	but	may	lack

足	以	维持	文学	生命	的	读者群。(文艺212)
zú	yǐ	wéichí	wénxué	shēngmìng	de	dúzhěqún
enough	to	maintain	literature	life	DE	reader.group

'If everything stays the same, we will possibly be faced with a dilemma: we may still have a few outstanding writers in the literary world, but we will not have a group of readers that can sustain literary life.' (*Wényì* 212)

We will explain in detail the usage of the semicolon and colon in the follow-up sections about types of composite sentences.

At the end of a composite sentence, there is a long pause. If the whole sentence is a statement, a full stop '。' will be used to indicate such a sentence-final pause, as in examples (1)–(4), (7)–(8) and (10)–(12). If the whole sentence is exclamative, an exclamation mark '!' is used, as in examples (5) and (9) and also:

(13)
我	几乎	认	不	出	我们	的	孩子，
wǒ	jīhū	rèn	bù	chū	wǒmen	de	háizi
1SG	almost	recognise	NEG	out	1PL	DE	child

他	已经	长	这么	大	了！(建屋14)
tā	yǐjīng	zhǎng	zhème	dà	le
3SG	already	grow	so	big	LE

'I could hardly recognise our child; he had grown so much!' (*Jiànwū* 14)

If the whole sentence is interrogative, a question mark '?' is used, as in (6) and (14):

(14)
如果	有	机会，
rúguǒ	yǒu	jīhuì
if	have	chance

你	还	会	回去	家乡	吗？（微型195）
nǐ	hái	huì	huí qù	jiāxiāng	ma
2SG	still	will	return	hometown	SFP

'Would you go back to your hometown if you had the chance?'
(*Wēixíng* 195)

4 The relationship between the clauses of a composite sentence is one of an intimate logical relationship rather than a grammatical one, such as subject-predicate, verb-object, predicate-complement or adverbial-head relationship. For example, the two clauses are of conjunctive relationships as in (1), hypothetical relationship as in (14), progressive relationship as in (7), and causative relationship as in (13). (More discussions on conjunctive, hypothetical, progressive and causative relationships will be in Sections 3.2–3.17). It is worth noting that in (3), two commas and one semicolon are used to divide the composite sentence into four parts, namely, 一条小溪 *yī tiáo xiǎo xī* 'a little stream', 不分昼夜地向前奔流 *bù fēn zhòu yè de xiàng qián bēnliú* 'runs forward day and night', 山谷里 *shāngǔ lǐ* 'in the valley' and 总是响着他愉快的笑声 *zǒngshì xiǎng zhe tā yúkuài de xiào shēng* 'with its happy laughter always ringing'. However, this composite sentence consists of only two clauses: 一条小溪，不分昼夜地向前奔流 *yī tiáo xiǎo xī, bù fēn zhòu yè de xiàng qián bēnliú* 'a little stream runs forward day and night', and 山谷里，总是响着他愉快的笑声 *shāngǔ lǐ, zǒngshì xiǎng zhe tā yúkuài de xiào shēng* 'with its happy laughter always ringing in the valley'. Even though a comma is used after 一条小溪 *yī tiáo xiǎo xī* 'a little stream', it does not form a separate clause, because it is of a 'subject-predicate' relationship rather than a logical relationship with the following constituents 不分昼夜地向前奔流 *bù fēn zhòu yè de xiàng qián bēnliú* 'runs forward day and night'. Similarly, 山谷里 *shāngǔ lǐ* 'in the valley' is not a separate clause either, since it associates with 总是响着他愉快的笑声 *zǒngshì xiǎng zhe tā yúkuài de xiào shēng* 'with its happy laughter always ringing' in a subject-predicate relationship instead of any other logical relation. In summary, clauses in composite sentences are connected by close logical relations.

5 The logical relationship between clauses in a composite sentence is usually presented through connective words. In the previous examples, 也 *yě* 'also' in (1) shows the parallel relationship; 而 *ér* 'but' in (5) shows the adversative relationship; 如果 *rúguǒ* 'if' in (14) shows the hypothetical relationship. The usage of connective words in different types of composite sentences will be detailed in the next section. It is noteworthy that connective words are mandatory in English, as in (15) and (16), but optional in Singapore Mandarin, as in (15)' and (16)'.

(15) **If** it weren't for him, we would have gone astray certainly.
(16) I've got a cold, **so** I'm going to bed.

The English connective words *if* in (15) and *so* in (16) cannot be omitted. Their equivalent Singapore Mandarin translations 如果 *rúguǒ* 'if' and 所以 *suǒyǐ* 'so' are optional as manifested by the contrasting pairs in (15)' and (16)'.

(15)'a. 如果　不　　是　他　(呀)，　我们　　肯定　　　迷路　了。
　　　　rúguǒ　bù　　shì　tā　(ya)　　wǒmen　kěndìng　mílù　le
　　　　if　　　NEG　be　3SG　SFP　　1PL　　certainly　lost　LE
　　　　'If it weren't for him, we would have certainly gone astray.'

　　b.　不　　是　他　(呀)，　我们　　肯定　　　迷路　了。
　　　　bù　　shì　tā　(ya)　　wǒmen　kěndìng　mílù　le
　　　　NEG　be　3SG　SFP　　1PL　　certainly　lost　LE
　　　　'If it weren't for him, we would have certainly gone astray.'

(16)'a. 我　　感冒　　　了，　所以　我　　得　　　　睡觉　　　了。
　　　　wǒ　gǎnmào　le　　suǒyǐ　wǒ　děi　　　shuìjiào　le
　　　　1SG　catch.cold　LE　　so　　1SG　have.to　sleep　　LE
　　　　'I've got a cold, so I'm going to bed.'

　　b.　我　　感冒　　　了，　得　　　　睡觉　　　了。
　　　　wǒ　gǎnmào　le　　děi　　　shuìjiào　le
　　　　1SG　catch.cold　LE　　have.to　sleep　　LE
　　　　'I've got a cold, so I'm going to bed.'

Generally speaking, (15)'b and (16)'b are more commonly used orally. Note that in previous examples of (3), (4) and (7), the connective words do not show up, either. More examples are as follows:

(17)　清晨，　　　　我　　必须　　在　　六点钟　　　　前　　　起身，
　　　qīngchén　　wǒ　bìxū　　zài　liùdiǎnzhōng　qián　qǐshēn
　　　early.morning　1SG　must　at　six.o.'clock　　before　get.up

　　　帮忙　　　　父亲　　准备　　　早餐。(短篇36)
　　　bāngmáng　fùqīn　zhǔnbèi　zǎocān
　　　help　　　　father　prepare　breakfast
　　　'In early morning, I must get up before six o'clock to help my father prepare breakfast.' (*Duǎnpiān* 36)

(18)　叫　　他　多　　在　　家里　　休息，
　　　jiào　tā　duō　zài　jiālǐ　xiūxī
　　　ask　3SG　more　at　home　rest

　　　他　偏　　放不下心。(胜利88)
　　　tā　piān　fàng-bù-xià-xīn

3SG　only　not.feel.relieved

'Although asked to rest more at home, he couldn't set his heart at rest.' (*Shènglì* 88)

(19) 我　　常常　　　去　找　符喜泉　　女士,
   wǒ　*chángcháng*　*qù*　*zhǎo*　*fúxǐquán*　*nǚshì*
   1SG　often　　　　go　find　Fu.Xiquan　lady

   找　　到　　自己　都　　不好意思　　了。(报 1995年 4 月 22日19版)
   zhǎo　*dào*　*zìjǐ*　*dōu*　*bùhǎoyìsi*　*le*
   find　until　oneself　even　embarrassed　LE

   'I visited Ms. Fu Xiquan so often that I myself even felt embarrassed.' (*Bào*, Apr. 22, 1995, Issue no. 9)

(20) 你　　先　　惹　　他　　骂　　他,
   nǐ　*xiān*　*rě*　*tā*　*mà*　*tā*
   2SG　first　offend　3SG　insult　3SG

   是　　你　　不　　对! (今后 11)
   shì　*nǐ*　*bù*　*duì*
   be　2SG　NEG　right

   'It is wrong of you to provoke him and scold him first!' (*Jīnhòu* 11)

(21) 你　　有　　本事,　你　　去　报告　好　　了! (建屋13)
   nǐ　*yǒu*　*běnshì*　*nǐ*　*qù*　*bàogào*　*hǎo*　*le*
   2SG　have　courage　2SG　go　report　good　LE

   'Go report it if you dare!' (*Jiànwū* 13)

The two clauses are of a purposive relationship in (17), an adversative relationship in (18), a progressive relationship in (19), a causative relationship in (20) and an inferential relationship in (21). Connective words are used in none of these composites. In grammar studies, this feature of Singapore Mandarin is usually referred to as parataxis, in which clauses are connected without overt connective words.

3.1.2 Compound Sentences and Complex Sentences

1. Two Types of Composite Sentences

Composite sentences can be roughly divided into two types, namely compound sentences and complex sentences.[1] The clauses in compound sentences are of equal syntactical status or importance. In comparison, the clauses in complex sentences are divided into distinctive primary and secondary clauses as they are unequal in meaning. Compare the following two examples in (22) and (23):

(22) 你 讲 你 的， 我们 讲 我们 的。(风筝137)
nǐ jiǎng nǐ de wǒmen jiǎng wǒmen de
2SG tell 2SG DE 1PL tell 1PL DE
'You tell your story, and we'll tell ours.' (*Fēngzhēng* 137)

(23) 昨晚 我 功课 太 多 做 不 完,
zuówǎn wǒ gōngkè tài duō zuò bù wán
last.night 1SG homework too many do NEG finish

所以 没有 来。（风雨 13）
suǒyǐ méiyǒu lái
so NEG come
'I had too much homework to finish last night, so I didn't come.' (*Fēngyǔ* 13)

In (22), the two clauses are semantically equal. In (23), the first clause states the reason, while the second clause states the result. Thus, the semantic interpretation of the two clauses is asymmetric. The sentence such as (22) is referred to as a compound sentence, whereas (23) is referred to as a complex sentence.

Since there is a primary-secondary contrast between the clauses in a complex sentence, a simple complex sentence minimally contains two clauses. If it includes three or more clauses, these clauses will be in a multilayered binary relation. For example:

(24)a. 只有 守着 这 三 宝 – 老伴、 老本、 老窝,
zhǐyǒu shǒuzhe zhè sān bǎo lǎobàn lǎoběn lǎowō
only.if keep this three treasure old.partner old.capital old.house

b. 银发 生涯 才 能 有 保障,
yínfà shēngyá cái néng yǒu bǎozhàng
grey.hair life then can have guarantee

c. 银发族 也 才 能 过 得 长春、
yínfàzú yě cái néng guò de cháng-chūn
people.with.grey.hair also then can live DE always-young

快乐。（报 1995年6月19日副刊5版）

190 *Composite Sentences*

kuàilè
happy

'Only by keeping these three treasures – the partner, the capital and the house – can the livelihood in old age be guaranteed and the old people can live a happy and prosperous life.' (*Bào*, June 19, 1995, Issue no. 5, supplementary edition)

The conditional complex sentence of (24) includes three clauses, which are of a binary structure as illustrated in (24)'. Obviously, they are at different levels.

(24)' a...   b...   c...
       └──┘   └──────────────────┘
                   └──────┘   └──────┘

In a compound sentence, there is no primary-secondary contrast, and the clauses are on the same level. Thus, a compound sentence usually contains many, rather than two, clauses. For example:

(25)a. 一   扇   扇   小窗   为   你   敞开,
       yī   shàn   shàn   xiǎochuāng   wèi   nǐ   chǎngkāi
       one   CL   CL   small.window for   2SG   open

   b. 一   座   座   心房   以   你   为   帘,
       yī   zuò   zuò   xīnfáng   yǐ   nǐ   wéi   lián
       one   CL   CL   heart   regard 2SG   as   curtain

   c. 一   枚   枚   命运   的   纸牌   因   你   飞动,
       yī   méi   méi   mìngyùn de   zhǐpái   yīn   nǐ   fēidòng
       one   CL   CL   fate   DE   card   because 2SG   fly

   d. 一   束   束   微笑   因   你   甜蜜。(太阳113)
       yī   shù   shù   wēixiào yīn   nǐ   tiánmì
       one   CL   CL   smile   because 2SG   sweet

'Many small windows open for you, and you are the curtain for many hearts; numerous cards of fate are flying because of you, and beams becomes sweet because of you.' (*Tàiyáng* 113)

The compound sentence includes four clauses in (25), which are coordinated equally. Therefore, the sentence is divided into four parts, as illustrated in (25)'.

(25) a. …, b. …, c. …, d. …。

2. Compound Sentences

Generally speaking, the major feature of compound sentences is that the clauses are syntactically equal, without any particular order of importance. However, the semantic relationships between clauses are diversified and can be further divided into seven types, namely, conjunctive, consecutive, contrastive, disjunctive, progressive, annotative and specific-general conjunctive sentences (see Sections 3.2 to 3.8 for details).

3. Complex Sentences

Complex sentences fundamentally consist of two parts: the primary clause that conveys the core meaning and the secondary clause that expresses subsidiary meaning. Based on the different semantic relations between the two clauses, complex sentences are divided into the following subtypes: adversative, hypothetical, conditional, causative, inferential, purposive, temporal and correlative complex sentences.²

The secondary clause usually precedes the primary clause. However, the order may be reversed to emphasise the meaning of the primary clause. As a result, the secondary clause takes only a supplementary position. For example:

(26) 我　　必须　去　闯荡　　　　一　　番,
　　　wǒ　　bìxū　 qù　chuǎngdàng　yī　 fān
　　　1SG　 must　go　venture　　　one　CL

　　　虽然　　未来　　依旧　　茫然　　　不　　可　　测。(寻庙75)
　　　suīrán　wèilái　yījiù　　mángrán　bù　 kě　 cè
　　　though　future　still　　uncertain　NEG　can　measure

　　　'I must take the venture, though the future is still uncertain.' (*Xúnmiào* 75)

(27) 他们　　的　苦难　　　也　　就　　是　　我们　　的　不幸,
　　　tāmen　de　kǔnàn　　 yě　 jiù　 shì　 wǒmen　de　bùxìng
　　　3PL　　DE　suffering　also　just　be　　1PL　　DE　misfortune

　　　因为　　我们　　同样　　　是　　在　　殖民地　　统治
　　　yīnwèi　wǒmen　tóngyàng　shì　 zài　 zhímíndì　tǒngzhì
　　　because　1PL　　too　　　　be　　at　　colony　　rule

　　　下　　的　人民。（沦陷85）
　　　xià　 de　rénmín

under   DE   people

'Their sufferings are also our misfortunes, because we, too, are people under colonial rule.' (*Lúnxiàn* 85)

(28) 距离   是   美   的，
     jùlí   shì   měi   de
     distance be   beautiful   DE

不管   是   时间   的   距离   或者   空间   的   距离。
bùguǎn   shì   shíjiān   de   jùlí   huòzhě   kōngjiān   de   jùlí
whether   be   time   DE   distance or   space   DE   distance

'Distance is beautiful, whether in time or space.'

Example (26) is an adversative complex sentence, the secondary clause expressing adversative meaning being placed after the primary clause. Example (27) is a causative complex sentence, with the secondary clause indicating reason following the primary clause. Example (28) is a conditional complex sentence, and the secondary clause expressing exhaustive condition appears after the primary clause. These reversed secondary clauses all provide complementary meaning. They can all be fronted to the initial position after adding appropriate conjunction words. Here are the revised examples:

(26)' 虽然   未来   依旧   茫然   不   可   测，
      suīrán   wèilái   yījiù   mángrán   bù   kě   cè
      though future   still   uncertain NEG   can   measure

但   我   必须   去   闯荡   一   番。
dàn   wǒ   bìxū   qù   chuǎngdàng   yī   fān
but   1SG   must   go   venture   one   CL

'The future is still unknown, but I must venture.'

(27)' 因为   我们   同样   是   在   殖民地   统治   下   的
      yīnwèi   wǒmen   tóngyàng   shì   zài   zhímíndì   tǒngzhì   xià   de
      because 1PL   same   be   at   colony   rule   under   DE

人民，   所以   他们   的   苦难   也   就   是   我们
rénmín   suǒyǐ   tāmen   de   kǔnán   yě   jiù   shì   wǒmen
people   so   3PL   DE   suffering also   just   be   1PL

的   不幸。
de   bùxìng

DE   misfortune

'Because we are also people under colonial rule, their sufferings are our misfortunes.'

(28)' 不管   是   时间   的   距离,   或者   空间   的   距离,
       bùguǎn   shì   shíjiān   de   jùlí   huòzhě   kōngjiān de   jùlí
       whether be   time   DE   distance or   space   DE   distance

       距离   都   是   美   的。
       jùlí   dōu   shì   měi   de
       distance all   be   beautiful DE

'Whether in time or space, all distance is beautiful.'

It is worth mentioning that in some fixed forms where the primary clause appears before the secondary clause, reversion of the two clauses is not allowed, such as 之所以*zhīsuǒyǐ* 'with such a result that' ...,是因为*shìyīnwèi* 'it is because' ... in causative complex sentences (see Section 3.12 for more details); and ...,以便*yǐbiàn* 'so as to ...,为的是*wèideshì* 'it is in order to'... and ...,以免 *yǐmiǎn* 'lest' ... in purposive complex sentences (see Section 3.14 for more details).

3.2 Conjunctive Compound Sentences

3.2.1 Two Types of Conjunctive Relations

There are two types of conjunctive relations expressed in conjunctive compound sentences as listed in the following.

1   Each clause explains or describes different things or situations, for example:

(1) 我   每时每刻   在   找   她,
     wǒ   měishíměikè   zài   zhǎo   tā
     1SG every.moment   in.process   look.for   3SG

     她   日日夜夜   在   寻   我。(太阳45)
     tā   rìrìyèyè   zài   xún   wǒ
     3SG day.and.night   in.process   look.for   1SG

'I am looking for her all the time, and she is looking for me day and night.' (*Tàiyáng* 45)

(2) 文艺   是   文艺,
     wényì   shì   wényì
     literature.and.art   be   literature.and.art

生意　　　　是　生意。(吾土·小说上 114)
shēngyì　　　shì　shēngyì
business　　　be　business

'Literature and art are literature and art, and business is business.'
(*Wútǔ* Volume I, 114)

2　Each clause explains or describes different aspects of the same thing or the same event, for example:

(3)　我　要　买　大　间　的　房子,
　　　wǒ　yào　mǎi　dà　jiān　de　fángzi
　　　1SG　want　buy　big　CL　DE　house

　　　买　汽车,　去　环球　旅行。(跳舞113)
　　　mǎi　qìchē　qù　huánqiú　lǚxíng
　　　buy　car　go　globe　travel

'I want to buy a big house, buy a car, and travel around the world.'
(*Tiàowǔ* 113)

(4)　这　个　女人　太　阴险,
　　　zhè　gè　nǚrén　tài　yīnxiǎn
　　　this　CL　woman　too　wicked

　　　太　毒辣　了！(有缘17)
　　　tài　dúlà　le
　　　too　sinister　LE

'What a wicked, sinister woman!' (*Yǒuyuán* 17)

3.2.2 Commonly Used Coordinators

No coordinators are used in the examples in Section 3.2.1. However, conjunctive compound sentences often marked by coordinators, as listed next.

1　..., 也 *yě* 'also'... For example:

(5)　丽美　是　我　的　邻居,
　　　lìměi　shì　wǒ　de　línjū
　　　Limei　be　1SG　DE　neighbour

　　　也　是　我　的　玩伴。(好儿童3B49)
　　　yě　shì　wǒ　de　wánbàn

also be 1SG DE playmate
'Limei is my neighbour and playmate.' (*Hǎoértóng* 3B, 49)

Sometimes 也 *yě* 'also' can be added to both clauses, thus forming the construction of 也 *yě* 'also'..., 也 *yě* 'also'..., for example:

(6) 自从　　祖母　　去世　　　后,
    zìcóng　zǔmǔ　qùshì　　hòu
    since　　grandma　pass.away　after

妈妈　　**也**　　不　　再　　　去　　打牌
māma　　yě　　bù　　zài　　qù　　dǎpái
mum　　also　NEG　again　go　play.card

或是　　逛　　　　百货公司　　　　　了,
huòshì　guàng　　bǎihuògōngsī　　le
or　　　shopping　department.store　LE

她　**也**　不　　跟　　　爸爸　　吵架　　　了。(短篇41)
tā　yě　bù　　gēn　　bàba　　chǎojià　le
3SG　also　NEG　with　father　quarrel　LE

'Since grandma passed away, Mum stopped playing cards or going to the department store, and she didn't quarrel with Dad anymore.' (*Duǎnpiān* 41)

In many cases, 既 *jì* 'also' is used in the first clause and the resulting format is 既 *jì* 'also'...,也 *yě* 'also'..., for example:

(7) 她　　**既**　要　　服侍　　　　　公婆,
    tā　　jì　　yào　　fúshì　　　　gōngpó
    3SG　also　should　take.care.of　parents-in-law

也　　要　　服侍　　　　　丈夫。(鞭子167)
yě　　yào　　fúshì　　　　zhàngfu
also　should　take.care.of　husband

'She has to take care of her husband as well as her parents-in-law.' (*Biānzi* 167)

Compound sentences connected by 也 *yě* 'also' always indicate that the two clauses express similar meanings.

2   ..., 又 *yòu* 'also'..., for example:

(8) 田田　　　看看　　　　　爸爸，
    tiántian　 kànkan　　　　bàba
    TianTian　take.a.look.at　father

又　　看看　　　　妈妈。(短篇43)
yòu　 kànkan　　　 māma
also　take.a.look.at　mother
'TianTian looks at his father and then at his mother.' (*Duǎnpiān* 43)

Sometimes 又 *yòu* 'also' are used in both clauses, so that the resulting structure is 又*yòu* 'also'..., 又*yòu* 'also'..., for example:

(9) 小黑狗　　　　像　　 是　 在　　　　　控诉　　 似地　　又
    xiǎohēigǒu　　xiàng　shì　zài　　　　　kòngsù　shì de　yòu
    small.black.dog　seem　be　in.process　complain　seem　also

尽　　　 往　　　　 两　　人　　 的　 怀里　　 乱　　　　　钻，
jìn　　　wǎng　　　liǎng　rén　　de　huái lǐ　luàn　　　　zuān
always　towards　two　　people　DE　arm　　 randomly　get.into

又　　在　　他们　　的　 嘴脸上　　　　　乱　　　　 舔。(追云118–119)
yòu　 zài　tāmen　de　 zuǐ liǎnshàng　luàn　　　　tiǎn
also　at　　3PL　　DE　mouth.and.face　randomly　lick
'The little black dog kept trying to get into their arms and licked their faces, as if making a complaint' (*Zhuīyún* 118–119)

In many cases, 既 *jì* 'also' is employed in the first clause, forming 既*jì* 'also'..., 又*yòu* 'also' ..., for example:

(10) 鄞碧仪　　　既　　 有　　　　风韵，　　　又　　　 有　　　头脑。(变调23)
     yínbìyí　　 jì　　 yǒu　　 fēngyùn，　 yòu　　 yǒu　　 tóunǎo
     Yin.Biyi　 also　have　　charm　　　 also　 have　 wit
'Yin Biyi has both charm and wit.' (*Biàndiào* 23)

A conjunctive compound sentence connected with 又 *yòu* 'also' often entails a grammatical meaning of addition or multiplicity, especially in formats of 又*yòu* 'also'..., 又*yòu* 'also'... and 既*jì* 'also'..., 又*jì* 'also'.... For example:

(11) 他　　这　　 个　　人　　　呀，
     tā　　zhè　　gè　　rén　　　ya
     3SG　this　　CL　　person　TOP

又	喝	酒，	又	抽	烟。
yòu	*hē*	*jiǔ*	*yòu*	*chōu*	*yān*
also	drink	wine	**also**	smoke	cigarettes

'He is a man who both drinks and smokes.'

(12)
她	既	爱	游泳，
tā	***jì***	*ài*	*yóuyǒng*
3SG	**also**	love	swim

又	爱	打	网球，
yòu	*ài*	*dǎ*	*wǎngqiú*
also	love	play	tennis

又	爱	打	乒乓球。
yòu	*ài*	*dǎ*	*pīngpāngqiú*
also	love	play	table.tennis

'She loves swimming and playing tennis, as well as table tennis.'

Example (11) implies that the speaker thinks that 'he' has many bad habits; (12) means that 'she' has various interests in sports. Sometimes the coordinator 还 *hái* 'also' is used to form ..., 还 *hái* 'also'... or 既 *jì* 'also'..., 还 *hái* 'also'... which also expresses grammatical meaning of addition or multiplicity. For example:

(13)
她	会	绘画，	会	做	小	针织品，
tā	*huì*	*huìhuà*	*huì*	*zuò*	*xiǎo*	*zhēnzhīpǐn*
3SG	can	paint	can	do	small	knitwear

还	会	做	小菜。（梦65）
hái	*huì*	*zuò*	*xiǎocài*
also	can	do	small.dish

'She can paint, make small knitwear, and cook small dishes.' (*Mèng* 65)

3   一面 *yīmiàn* 'at the same time'..., 一面 *yīmiàn* 'at the same time'... as shown next:

(14)
爷爷	一面		吃，	一面		看	报纸。
							(风雨25)
yéye	***yīmiàn***		*chī*	***yīmiàn***		*kàn*	*bàozhǐ*
grandpa	**at.the.same.time**		eat	**at.the.same.time**		look	newspaper

'Grandpa read the newspaper as he ate.' (*Fēngyǔ* 25)

(15) 她　　一面　　　　　说，
　　　tā　　yīmiàn　　　　shuō
　　　3SG　at.the.same.time　say

一面　　　　　　展示　　她　　的　　新装。(追云18)
yīmiàn　　　　　zhǎnshì　tā　　de　　xīnzhuāng
at.the.same.time　show　　3SG　DE　　new.clothes

'As she was talking, she showed her new dress.' (*Zhuīyún* 18)

Conjunctive compound sentences connected by 一面 *yīmiàn* 'at the same time' often entail that several actions take place simultaneously. Sometimes, 一边*yībiān*..., 一边*yībiān*... or 边*biān*..., 边*biān*... are used to indicate the same grammatical meaning. For example:

(16) 这　　小子　　　心不在焉　　　地　　一边　　　　　扒　　饭，
　　　zhè　xiǎozi　　xīnbùzàiyān　　de　　yībiān　　　　pá　　fàn
　　　this　small.boy　absent-minded　DE　at.the.same.time　gulp　rice

一边　　　　　　盯　　着　　手　　上　　的　　课本
yībiān　　　　　dīng　zhe　shǒu　shàng　de　kèběn
at.the.same.time　stare　ZHE　hand　up　DE　textbook

不　　放。(有缘51)
bù　　fàng
NEG　let.go

'The boy absent-mindedly gulped his meal and at the same time he kept staring at his textbook' (*Yǒuyuán* 51)

(17) 我　　和　　孩子们　　　边　　　　　　赏月，
　　　wǒ　　hé　　háizimen　　biān　　　　　shǎngyuè
　　　1SG　and　children　　at.the.same.time　enjoy.the.moon

边　　　　　　　观赏　　　孩童　　　提灯　　　　　的　　情趣。
　　　　　　　　　　　　　　　　　　　　　　　　　　　　　(晚上15)
biān　　　　　　guānshǎng　háitóng　tídēng　　　　de　　qíngqù
at.the.same.time　watch　　child　　hold.the.lattern　DE　interest

'The children and I were enjoying the Moon and admiring the interesting view of children playing with lanterns at the same time.' (*Wǎnshàng* 15)

Also, 一手*yīshǒu* 'one hand'...,一手*yīshǒu* 'the other hand'... can be used to connect clauses indicating that the actions happening at the same time are performed with the hands. For example:

(18) 潘展恒　　　**一　手**　　夹　着　　厚厚　的　　宗卷，
　　　pānzhǎnhéng　**yī　shǒu**　jiá　zhe　hòuhòu　de　zōngjuàn
　　　Pan.Zhanheng　**one　hand**　carry　ZHE　thick　DE　dossier

　　　一　手　　提　着　黑皮　　　的　Samsonite　公文箱。
　　　　　　　　　　　　　　　　　　　　　　　　　　　(变调46)
　　　yī　shǒu　tí　zhe　hēipí　　de　Samsonite　gōngwénxiāng
　　　one　hand　lift　ZHE　black.leather　DE　Samsonite　briefcase
　　　'Pan Zhanheng carried a thick dossier in one hand and a black leather Samsonite briefcase in the other.' (*Biàndiào* 46)

Sometimes, 一路*yīlù* 'all the way'..., 一路*yīlù* 'all the way'... is used to connect two actions that take place at the same time while walking, as in (19).

(19) 孩子们　　**一路**　　走，
　　　háizimen　**yīlù**　　zǒu
　　　children　**all.the.way**　walk

　　　一路　　　口手并用　　　　　地　　剥　着
　　　yīlù　　　kǒushǒubìngyòng　de　　bāo　zhe
　　　all.the.way　use.mouth.and.hand.together　DE　peel　ZHE

　　　果壳　　吃　着　红毛丹。(冰灯1)
　　　guǒké　chī　zhe　hóngmáodān
　　　fruit.husk　eat　ZHE　rambutan
　　　'The children were peeling and eating rambutans with their mouths and hands as they were walking.' (*Bīngdēng* 1)

4　"时而*shíér* 'sometimes'..., 时而*shíér* 'sometimes'...", as shown in (20):

(20) 母亲　　　**时而**　　　织　　一　条　裤带，
　　　mǔqīn　　**shíér**　　zhī　yī　tiáo　kùdài
　　　mother　**sometimes**　weave　one　CL　belt

　　　时而　　　　织　　一　块　绸，
　　　shíér　　　zhī　yī　kuài　chóu
　　　sometimes　weave　one　CL　silk

　　　时而　　　　织　　一　段　缎。(晚上27)
　　　shíér　　　zhī　yī　duàn　duàn

sometimes weave one CL satin

'Mother sometimes weaves a trouser belt, sometimes a piece of silk and sometimes a piece of satin.' (*Wǎnshàng* 27)

Sentences connected by 时而*shíér* 'sometimes'...,时而*shíér* 'sometimes'... often indicate alternative actions or events. 一会儿*yīhuìr* 'for a moment'..., 一会儿*yīhuìr* 'for a moment'... and 一忽儿*yīhūer* 'for a moment'..., 一忽儿*yīhūer* 'for a moment' ... have similar function, as in (21):

(21) 他　　**一会儿**　　敲　　冰块，
　　　tā　　**yīhuìr**　　qiāo　　bīngkuài
　　　3SG　**for.a.moment**　knock　ice.cube

一会儿　　捧　　咖啡；　**一忽儿**　　提高　　嗓子　　喊叫：
yīhuìr　　pěng　　kāfēi　　**yīhūer**　　tígāo　　sǎngzi　　hǎnjiào
for.a.moment　hold　coffee　**for.a.moment**　raise　voice　yellshout

"茶　乌，　厚"，　**一忽儿**　　又　　对　　刚　　坐
chá　wū　　hòu　　**yīhūer**　　yòu　　duì　　gāng　　zuò
tea　black　thick　**for.a.moment**　also　towards　just　sit

下　　　　的　　顾客　　问道　　："…。"
xià　　　　de　　gùkè　　wèndào
down　　　DE　　customer　ask

'He knocked the ice cubes for a while, then held the coffee for a while, then raised his voice and shouted: "black tea, thick", and then asked the customer who had just sat down: "…"'

In Singapore Mandarin, 一会子*yīhuìzi* 'for a moment'...,一会子*yīhuìzi* 'for a moment'... can be used to connect clauses, as in (22), but is not used in Chinese Mandarin.

(22) 婆婆　　　　**一会子**　　赞　　房子　　好，　**一会子**　　赞
　　　Pópo　　　**yīhuìzi**　　zàn　　fángzi　　hǎo　　**yīhuìzi**　　zàn
　　　Mother-in-law　**for.a.moment**　praise　house　good　**for.a.moment**　praise

她　　的　　儿子　　与　　媳妇　　　　　　勤劳。(梦134–135)
tā　　de　　érzi　　yǔ　　xífù　　　　　　qínláo
3SG　DE　　son　　and　daughter-in-law　diligent

'The mother-in-law praised the house for being good for a moment, and then praised her son and daughter-in-law for their diligence.' (*Mèng* 134–135)

5   一则 yīzé 'firstly'..., 二则 èrzé 'secondly'...:

(23) 新   媳妇   有 孕   **一则**   意味   着   新的
     xīn   xífù   yǒuyùn   **yīzé** yìwèi zhe   xīnde
     new   daughter-in-law be.pregnant **firstly** mean ZHE   new

     生命   的   孕育,   **二则**   有   望   传递   下去,
     shēngmìng de yùnyù   **èrzé**   yǒu   wàng   chuándì   xiàqù
     life   DE nurture   **secondly** have hope pass   down

     三则   此   乃   天经地义、   最   正常、   最
     sānzé   cǐ   nǎi   tiānjīngdìyì   zuì   zhèngcháng zuì
     thirdly this be   unquestionable most   normal   most

     自然不过   的   生理   现象。(有缘82)
     zìránbùguò   de   shēnglǐ   xiànxiàng
     natural   DE   physiological phenomenon

     'The new daughter in law's pregnancy firstly means the nurturing of a new life; secondly, the expectation that it (the family blood) will be passed on; and thirdly, it is the most normal and natural physiological phenomenon.' (*Yǒuyuán* 82)

一则 yīzé 'firstly'..., 二则 èrzé 'secondly'... often elaborates on two reasons separately when connecting two clauses, and sometimes 一来 yīlái 'firstly'..., 二来 èrlái 'secondly'... is used for the same purpose, as in (24):

(24) 这   **一来**   是   继任   他   父亲   的   缺;
     zhè   **yīlái**   shì   jìrèn   tā   fùqīn   de   quē
     this **firstly** be   succeed 3SG   father   DE   vacancy

     二来   是   希望   仙长   送子   后嗣有人;
     èrlái   shì   xīwàng   xiānzhǎng   sòngzǐ   hòusìyǒurén
     secondly be   hope   fairy   send.child   have.heir

     三来,   使   他   最   感兴趣   的   是...。(追云59)
     sānlái   shǐ   tā   zuì   gǎnxìngqù   de   shì
     thirdly make   3SG   most   interested   DE   be

     'Firstly, he is to fill the vacancy left by his father; secondly, it is hoped that the fairy will send children and heirs; thirdly, what interests him most is ...' (*Zhuīyún* 59)

3.2.3 Representation of Pause Between Clauses

The pause between clauses in a conjunctive compound sentence is often indicated by a comma in writing. But if a comma already exists within a clause indicating a shorter pause, the pause between clauses is represented by a semicolon, as in examples (21) and (24). In (24), a comma is used after 三来 *sānlái* 'thirdly' in the last clause, so semicolons are used between clauses. Another example is shown in (25):

(25) 风， 在 城市 上空 盘旋；
fēng zài chéngshì shàng kōng pánxuán
wind at city sky hover

树， 脱 帽 为 它 送行；
shù tuō mào wèi tā sòngxíng
tree take.off hat for 3SG see.off

街， 成 了 叶 的 舞台；
jiē chéng le yè de wǔtái
street become LE leaf DE stage

人， 瑟缩 在 鸭绒 中 急速 行走。(太阳110)
rén sèsuō zài yāróng zhōng jísù xíngzǒu
people huddle at duck.fluff middle rapidly walk

'A wind is hovering over the city; trees are taking off their hats to say goodbye to it; the street has become the stage for the leaves; and people, huddled in down coats, are walking rapidly.' (*Tàiyáng* 110)

In (25), each of the four clauses is a subject-predicate clause. Since commas are employed to separate subjects and predicates, semicolons are used between clauses.

3.3 Consecutive Compound Sentences

Consecutive compound sentences show a consecutive relationship between events or actions. Therefore, this type of compound sentence always chronologically narrates consecutive events or series of actions. For example:

(1) 他 搓 了 搓 手，
tā cuō le cuō shǒu
3SG rub LE rub hand

端端正正 地 坐 在 椅子 上。(胜利92)
duānduānzhèngzhèng de zuò zài yǐzi shàng
upright DE sit on chair up

'He rubbed his hands and sat upright on the chair.' (*Shènglì* 92)

(2) 小   妮子   笑   着   把   食物   盒   推   过去，
    xiǎo   nīzi   xiào   zhe   bǎ   shíwù hé   tuī   guòqù
    little girl   laugh ZHE   BA   food   box push over

顺手   递   过   一   双   筷子。(金狮奖217)
shùnshǒu   dì   guò   yī   shuāng   kuàizi
by.the.way pass   over   one   pair   chopsticks

'The little girl pushed the food box over with a smile and by the way handed over a pair of chopsticks.' (*Jīnshījiǎng* 217)

Sometimes, the second clause begins with 然后 *ránhòu* 'then' to show the consecutive relationship. For example:

(3) 她   将   落地的   玻璃   窗门
    tā   jiāng   luòdìde   bōli   chuāngmén
    3SG   BA   to.the.ground   glass   window.and.door

都   拉拢   来，   **然后**   回去   厨房。(吾土·戏剧 146)
dōu   lālǒng   lái   **ránhòu**   huíqù   chúfáng
all   pull.close   come   **and.then** return   kitchen

'She closed all the French windows, and then went back to the kitchen.' (*Wútǔ* (drama) 146)

(4) 她   仰头   把   酒性   极   烈   的   廊酒
    tā   yǎngtóu   bǎ   jiǔxìng   jí   liè   de   lángjiǔ
    3SG   raise.head   BA   alcoholic extremely   strong   DE   Benedictine

一   口   喝   干，   **然后**   倒   在   床   上，
yī   kǒu   hē   gān   **ránhòu**   dǎo   zài   chuáng   shàng
one   mouthful   drink   dry   **and.then** fall   on   bed   up

紧   闭   双目。(石头47)
jǐn   bì   shuāngmù
tight   close   eyes

'She flung back her head and drained the extremely strong Benedictine in one gulp. Then she fell back on the bed with her eyes closed.' (*Shítóu* 47)

In Singapore Mandarin, frequently seen formats showing consecutive relationships include 一 *yī* 'as soon as'..., 就 *jiù* 'then'..., 一 *yī* 'as soon as'..., 便 *biàn* 'then'... and 一 *yī* 'as soon as'..., 即 *jí* 'then'.... These formats are used to emphasise that the series of events or actions happen immediately after one another, as shown in (5), (6) and (7) respectively.

(5) 论文　　　一　　　　通过，　　**就**　　马上
　　 lùnwén　　yī　　　　tōngguò　　**jiù**　　mǎshàng
　　 dissertation　as.soon.as　pass　　then　immediately

　　 赶　　回去　　和　　她　　结婚。(金狮奖98)
　　 gǎn　 huí qù　 hé　 tā　 jiéhūn
　　 rush　return　with　3SG　marry

　　 'As soon as the dissertation was passed, (I) rushed back to marry her.'
　　 (*Jīnshījiǎng* 98)

(6) 一　　　　　倒　　下　　去，
　　 yī　　　 dǎo　 xià　 qù
　　 as.soon.as　lie　down　go

　　 便　呼呼入睡。(石头5)
　　 biàn　hūhūrù shuì
　　 then　fall.asleep

　　 'As soon as (he) lay down, (he) fell asleep.' (*Shítóu* 5)

(7) 一　　　　　踏　　进　　家门，　　黄雪嫘　　　**即**
　　 yī　　　 tà　　 jìn　 jiāmén　　huángxuěléi　**jí**
　　 as.soon.as　step　into　house　　Huang.Xuelei　**immediately**

　　 向　　　黄　　　老　　太太　　报讯。(断情剪8)
　　 xiàng　 huáng　 lǎo　 tàitài　 bàoxùn
　　 towards　Huang　old　lady　　report

　　 'As soon as she stepped into the house, Huang Xuelei reported to old lady Huang.' (*Duànqíngjiǎn* 8)

Within a consecutive compound sentence, the pause between clauses is indicated with a comma.

3.4 Contrastive Compound Sentences

Contrastive compound sentences show a contrastive relationship between two clauses. The two clauses either express semantically opposite meanings or list contrastive ideas. The second clause is usually connected with the conjunction 而 *ér* 'while'. For example:

(1) 母亲 要 他 去 东边,
    mǔqīn yào tā qù dōngbiān
    mother want 3SG go east.side

    他 偏偏 去 西边。(狮子 65)
    tā piānpiān qù xībiān
    3SG on.the.contrary go west.side
    'Mother wanted him to go east, however, he chose to go west.' (*Shīzi* 65)

(2) 消费人 应 节制 自己 的 花 钱 方式,
    xiāofèirén yīng jiézhì zìjǐ de huā qián fāngshì
    consumer should control oneself DE spend money method

    而 不 应 太 过 依赖 金融 管理局
    ér *bù yīng tài guò yīlài jīnróng guǎnlíjú*
    while NEG should too over depend finance administration.bureau

    制订 的 保护 措施。(报 1995年3月6日6版)
    zhìdìng de bǎohù cuòshī
    enact DE protect measure
    'Consumers should control the way they spend their money rather than rely too much on the protective measures put in place by the Monetary Authority.' (*Bào*, Mar. 6, 1995, Issue no. 6)

Connective adjunct pairs like 不是*bùshì* 'it is not'…,而是*érshì* 'it is'… or 是*shì* 'it is'…,不是*bùshì* 'it is not'… are frequently used to show this contrastive relationship. Examples for the former are as follows:

(3) 这 绝 **不 是** 一 小 撮,
    *zhè jué **bù shì** yī xiǎo cuō*
    this absolutely **NEG be** one small CL

    而 是 一 大 群 人 啊! (风筝 14)
    ér shì *yī dà qún rén a*
    but be one big crowd people SFP
    'It's absolutely not a handful, but a crowd!' (*Fēngzhēng* 14)

(4) 这　不　是　老人　　联欢会，
　　zhè　bù　shì　lǎorén　　liánhuānhuì
　　this　NEG　be　old.people　get-together.party

　　而　是　老　少　　联欢。(心情33)
　　ér　shì　lǎo　shǎo　liánhuān
　　but　be　old　young　get-together

　　'This is not a party for the elderly, but for both young and old.' (*Xīnqíng* 33)

Examples for the latter are as follows:

(5) 她　是　你　妈，
　　tā　shì　nǐ　mā
　　3SG　be　2SG　mother

　　不　是　我　妈　啊！(撞墙92)
　　bù　shì　wǒ　mā　a
　　NEG　be　1SG　mother　SFP

　　'She's your mother, not my mother!' (*Zhuàngqiáng* 92)

(6) 人们　喜欢　看到　的　是　欢笑，
　　rénmen　xǐhuān　kàndào　de　shì　huānxiào
　　people　like　see　DE　be　laughter

　　而　不　是　悲泣。(独立101)
　　ér　bù　shì　bēiqì
　　while　NEG　be　weep

　　'People like to see laughter, not weeping.' (*Dúlì* 101)

The pause between clauses in a contrastive compound sentence is also indicated with a comma.

3.5 Disjunctive Compound Sentences

Disjunctive sentences show an alternative relationship among the clauses. Each clause states an option to choose respectively. To be more specific, disjunctive sentences can be further divided into three subtypes based on the logical meaning.

3.5.1 Indicating Alternative Choice

Frequently used coordinators indicating alternative choice include 或 *huò* 'or', 或者 *huòzhě* 'or', 或是 *huòshì* 'or', 要么 *yàome* 'either'…,要么 *yàome* 'or'… and 还是 *háishì* 'or', 抑或 *yìhuò* 'or'. For example:

(1) 仿佛   他们   彼此   互   不   认识,
    fǎngfú tāmen   bǐcǐ   hù   bù   rènshi
    seem   3PL   each.other mutual NEG   know

   或   彼此   不   知道   对方   的   存在。(断情剪69)
   huò bǐcǐ   bù   zhīdào   duìfāng   de   cúnzài
   or   each.other NEG   know   opposite.side   DE   exist

   'It seems that they did not know each other or know each other's existence.' (*Duànqíngjiǎn* 69)

(2) 这   个   时期,   就   到   同学   家里   玩   乐,
    zhè   gè   shíqī   jiù   dào   tóngxué   jiālǐ   wánlè
    this CL   period   just   go   classmate   home.inside play

   或者   三五成群   地   去   逛街。(母亲110)
   huòzhě sānwǔchéngqún   de   qù   guàngjiē
   or   be.in.a.group.of.three.or.five   DE   go   shopping

   'During this period, (I) went to my classmates' homes to have fun, or go shopping in groups.' (*Mǔqīn* 110)

(3) **要嘛**,   就   快快乐乐,   地   相聚,
    yàoma   jiù   kuàikuàilèlè   de   xiāngjù
    either   just   happy   DE   get.together

   要嘛,   就   爽爽快快   地   分离。(青青60)
   yàoma   jiù   shuǎngshuǎngkuàikuài   de   fēnlí
   either   just   unhesitatingly   DE   separate

   'It's either to be together happily or to be unhesitatingly separate.' (*Qīngqīng* 60)

(4) 遇上   你   是   我   一生   的   对,   或   错?(想飞63)
    yùshàng   nǐ   shì   wǒ   yīshēng   de   duì   **huò**   cuò
    meet   2SG   be   1SG   life   DE   right   or   wrong

   'Is meeting you the right or wrong choice in my life?' (*Xiǎngfēi* 63)

(5) 巩俐　　答应　　前往，　　究竟　　是　　张艺谋
    gǒnglì dāying qiánwǎng jiūjìng shì zhāngyìmóu
    GongLi agree   go   on.earth be ZhangYimou

    大力　　游说，　**抑或**　是　　上海　　　电影
    dàlì   yóushuì **yìhuò** shì shànghǎi diànyǐng
    hard   lobby   or   be   Shanghai film

    制片厂　　　　的　　要求　　呢？(报 1995年5月16日副刊4版)
    zhìpiànchǎng de   yāoqiú ne
    film.studio   DE   request SFP

'Did Gong Li agree to go because Zhang Yimou lobbied her hard, or because the Shanghai Film Studio asked her to?' (*Bào*, May 16, 1995, Issue no. 4, supplementary edition)

(6) 这　　是　　人生　　　的　　缺陷　　　呢,
    zhè   shì   rénshēng de   quēxiàn   ne
    this be   life   DE   defect   SFP

    还是　社会　　　的　　悲哀？(恶梦8)
    háishì shèhuì de   bēiāi
    or   society DE   sadness

'Is this a defect of life, or a sorrow of society?' (*Èmèng* 8)

The usage of coordinators in Singapore Mandarin differs from those in Chinese Mandarin. Firstly, in Chinese Mandarin, 或者 *huòzhě* 'or' and 或是 *huòshì* 'or' can be used in declaratives but not in interrogatives. In comparison, they can be used in interrogatives in Singapore Mandarin, as in (4), which is obviously influenced by Cantonese and the Min dialect. Secondly, 抑或 *yìhuò* 'or' is a vernacular expression reserved in Singapore Mandarin, and is particularly popular in written form, but in Chinese Mandarin it is rarely used. Thirdly, 或 *huò* 'or' is often used in Singapore Mandarin, but not in Chinese Mandarin, to connect clauses, as in examples (1) and (4).

3.5.2 *Indicating an Either-or Choice*

Correlative coordinators such as 不是 *bùshì* 'if not be'…, 就是 *jiùshì* 'then will be'… and 不是 *bùshì* 'it is not'…, 而是 *érshì* 'but it is'… are used to indicate an either-or choice. For example:

(7) 他　**不是**　静静　　　听　　　老师　　讲课，　**就是**　自己
    tā   **bùshì** jìngjìng tīng   lǎoshī jiǎngkè **jiùshì** zìjǐ
    3SG NEG   quietly   listen.to teacher teach.lesson then   oneself

默默 地 自修。(报1995年3月15日副刊11版)
mòmò de zìxiū
quietly DE self.study
'He either listens quietly to the teacher or studies silently by himself.'
(*Bào*, Mar. 15, 1995, Issue no. 11, supplementary edition)

(8) 许多   中国人   终老   南洋，   **不是**   因为   太
    xǔduō *zhōngguórén* *zhōnglǎo* *nányáng* **bùshì** *yīnwèi* *tài*
    many   Chinese   get.old   Southeast.Asia NEG   because too

穷   无脸回乡，   **便是**   因为   太   富有   舍不得   将
qióng *wúliǎnhuíxiāng*   **biànshì** *yīnwèi* *tài* *fùyǒu* *shěbùdé*   *jiāng*
poor   feel.disgraced.   then   because too   rich   be.reluctant BA
        to.return.home

千辛万苦   建立   起来   的   生意   产业   放弃。(新华
                                                                  文学7)
qiānxīnwànkǔ   *jiànlì*   *qǐlái* *de* *shēngyì* *chǎnyè* *fàngqì*
back-breaking   build   up   DE   business   industry give.up

'Many Chinese ended up in Southeast Asia either because they were too poor and felt too disgraced to return to their homeland or too rich to give up the businesses that they had worked so hard to build.' (*Xīnhuáwénxué* 7)

3.5.3 *Indicating Preference of One Choice Over Another*

Correlative coordinators such as 与其*yǔqí* 'rather than'...,不如*bùrú* 'it is better'... and 与其*yǔqí* 'rather than'...,勿宁*wùnìng* 'it is better'... indicate preference of one choice over another after careful evaluation, as illustrated by the following examples:

(9) **与其**   将来   后悔，
    yǔqí   *jiānglái* *hòuhuǐ*
    rather.than future   regret

倒   **不如**   现在   慎重地   考虑。(狮子116)
dǎo   ***bùrú***   *xiànzài* *shènzhòng*de *kǎolǜ*
instead **it.is.better**   now   discretly   consider

'It is better to consider with discretion now rather than to regret in the future.' (*Shīzi* 116)

(10) 与其 说 我 依然 钟爱 那 一 本
    yǔqí shuō wǒ yīrán zhōng'ài nà yī běn
    rather.than say 1SG still love that one CL

   小说,³ 勿宁 说 我 仍 怀念 着 最初
   xiǎoshuō **wùnìng** shuō wǒ réng huáiniànzhe zuìchū
   novel **it.is.better** say 1SG still miss initial

   看 白话 小说 的 那 一 段 日子。(自然 38)
   kàn báihuà xiǎoshuō de nà yī duàn rìzi
   look vernacular novel DE that one CL day

   'Rather than saying that I still love that novel it is better saying that I still miss the days when I first began to read vernacular novels.' (*Zìrán* 38)

Sometimes, conjunctions like 宁可 *nìngkě* 'would rather' or 宁愿 *nìngyuàn* 'would rather' are used to express similar meanings, which could co-occur with 总 *zǒng* 'always' or 也不 *yěbù* 'also not'. For example:

(11) 宁可 让 人 看做 木头 明哲保身,
    nìngkě ràng rén kàn zuò mùtóu míngzhébǎoshēn
    would.rather let person regard.as wood to.preserve.our.sanity

   总 比 祸从口出 好。(今后 52)
   zǒng bǐ huòcóngkǒuchū hǎo
   always than cause.disaster.from.careless.talk good

   'It's better to be seen as a block of wood to protect yourself than to make trouble with careless talk.' (*Jīnhòu* 52)

(12) 您 宁可 疏远 他们,
    nín **nìngkě** shūyuǎn tāmen
    2SG **would.rather** alienate 3PL

   也 不 愿 趋炎附势。(变调 3)
   yě bù yuàn qūyánfùshì
   also NEG would.like flatter

   'You would rather distance yourself from them than flatter them.' (*Biàndiào* 3)

(13) (若 容 选择,) 我 宁愿 把 花瓶 空置,
    (ruò róng xuǎnzé,) wǒ **nìngyuàn** bǎ huāpíng kōngzhì
    if allow choose 1SG **would.rather** BA vase empty

也	不	希望	在	今天	这	个	情人节
yě	bù	xīwàng	zài	jīntiān	zhè	gè	qíngrénjié
also	NEG	hope	on	today	this	CL	Valentine's.Day

有人	给	我	送	一	支	玫瑰。(有缘 69)
yǒu rén	gěi	wǒ	sòng	yī	zhī	méiguī
someone	give	1SG	send	one	CL	rose

'(If allowed to choose,) I would rather leave the vase empty than have someone send me a rose on this Valentine's Day.' (*Yǒuyuán* 69)

The pause between clauses in a disjunctive sentence is also indicated with a comma.

3.6 Progressive Compound Sentences

Progressive compound sentences show a progressive relationship between the two clauses, with the second clause implying further meanings compared to that of the first clause. This type of sentence can be divided into two subtypes according to the usage of connective words.

3.6.1 Connective Words Attached Only to the Second Clause

The first clause has no connective words, while the second clause is introduced with connective words like 而且 *érqiě* 'but also', 更 *gèng* 'even more', 尤其 *yóuqí* 'especially', 甚至 *shènzhì* 'even', 何况 *hékuàng* 'let alone', 进而 *jìnér* 'and then' and so on to show progressive relation. For example:

(1)
我	考	中	了	四主二副，
wǒ	kǎo	zhòng	le	sìzhǔ-èrfù
1SG	take.exam	win	LE	four.major.course.plus.two.minor.course

而且	还是	四优二良	的	卓越	成绩	呢！
						（短篇3）
érqiě	*háishì*	*sìyōuèrliáng*	de	*zhuóyuè*	*chéngjì*	ne
but.also	also	four.A+.and.two.B	DE	excellent	score	SFP

'I passed the exam for four major courses and two minor courses, and I also got an excellent score with four A+ and two B's!' (*Duǎnpiān* 3)

(2)
他	不	懂得	爱惜	自己，
tā	bù	dǒngdé	àixī	zìjǐ
3SG	NEG	know	love	oneself

	更	不	懂得	照顾		别人。	(梦 45)
	gèng	bù	dǒngé	zhàogù		biérén	
	even.more	NEG	know	take.care.of		others	

'He doesn't know how to love himself, let alone take care of others.' (*Mèng* 45)

(3)
也许,	我	秉承	了	太多	父亲	的	性格,
yéxǔ	wǒ	bǐngchéng	le	tàiduō	fùqīn	de	xìnggé
maybe	1SG	inherit	LE	too.much	father	DE	character

尤其	是	那	一	股	倔强。(青春 116)
yóuqí	shì	nà	yī	gǔ	juéjiàng
especially	be	that	one	CL	stubbornness

'Maybe I have inherited too much of my father's character, especially the stubbornness.' (*Qīngchūn* 116)

(4)
我	看	不	起	他,	**甚至**	恨	他。(太阳 70)
wǒ	kàn	bù	qǐ	tā	**shènzhì**	hèn	tā
1SG	look	NEG	up	3SG	even	hate	3SG

'I looked down on him, even hated him.' (*Tàiyáng* 70)

(5)
他	觉得	一	个	星期	做	两三	小时	的
tā	juéde	yī	gè	xīngqī	zuò	liǎngsān	xiǎoshí	de
3SG	think	one	CL	week	do	two.three	hour	DE

练习	不算	多,	**更何况**	是	自己	感	兴趣
liànxí	bùsuàn	duō	**gènghékuàng**	shì	zìjǐ	gǎn	xìngqù
exercise	NEG	much	let.alone	be	oneself	feel	interest

的	活动。	(报 1995年3月8日7版)
de	huódòng	
DE	activity	

'He doesn't think doing two or three hours of exercise a week is too much, let alone an activity he is interested in.' (*Bào*, Mar. 8, 1995, Issue no. 7)

(6)
它	制造	了	一	股	对	美国	充满	敌意	的
tā	zhìzào	le	yī	gǔ	duì	měiguó	chōngmǎn	díyì	de
3SG	make	LE	one	CL	to	America	fill	hostility	DE

亚洲	联合力量，	也会	把	美国	和	欧洲	分开，
yàzhōu	liánhélìliàng	yěhuì	bǎ	měiguó	hé	ōuzhōu	fēnkāi
Asian	joint.force	also	BA	America	and	Europe	separate

进而	瓦解	整个	世界	贸易	体系。(报 1995年 3月8日7版)
jìnér	wǎjiě	zhěnggè	shìjiè	màoyì	tǐxì
and.then	crumble	entire	world	trade	system

'It creates a united Asian force hostile to the United States, which will also separate the United States from Europe and thus dismantle the entire world trading system.' (*Bào*, Aug. 21, 1995, Issue no. 7)

In rare cases, connective words do not show up in either of the two clauses, as in the following example:

(7)
我	常常	去	找	符喜泉	女士，
wǒ	chángcháng	qù	zhǎo	fúxǐquán	nǚshì
1SG	often	go	find	Fu.Xiquan	lady

找	到	自己	都	不好意思	了。(报 1995年 4月22日19版)
zhǎo	dào	zìjǐ	dōu	bùhǎoyìsi	le
find	until	oneself	even	embarrassed	LE

'I visited Ms. Fu Xiquan so often that I myself even felt embarrassed.' (*Bao*, Apr. 22, 1995, Issue no. 19)

3.6.2 Connective Words Attached to Both Clauses

The first clause is introduced by 不但 *bùdàn* 'not only', 不仅 *bùjǐn* 'not only' or 不只 *bùzhǐ* 'not only', whereas the following clause is introduced by 而且 *érqiě* 'but also', 同时 *tóngshí* 'at the same time', 还 *hái* 'also', 更 *gèng* 'even more', 也 *yě* 'also', 反而 *fǎnér* 'on the contrary' and so on. For example:

(8)
电子	游戏机	**不但**	款式	繁多，
diànzǐ	yóuxìjī	**bùdàn**	kuǎnshì	fánduō
electronic	game.console	**not.only**	style	various

而且	设计	也	十分	精巧。(中学1A110)
érqiě	shèjì	yě	shífēn	jīngqiǎo
but.also	design	also	very	exquisite

'The video game console not only has various styles, but also has exquisite design.' (*Zhōngxué* 1A, 110)

(9) 独立桥 不但 有 它 的 交通 用途，
   dúlìqiáo bùdàn yǒu tā de jiāotōng yòngtú
   Merdeka.Bridge not.only have 3SG DE traffic usage

   同时 有 它 的 历史 价值。（独上 98–99）
   tóngshí *yǒu tā de lìshǐ jiàzhí*
   at.the.same.time have 3SG DE history value

   'Merdeka Bridge is not only used for traffic, but also has its historical value.' (*Dúshàng* 98–99)

(10) 研究 和 出版， 不但 需要 人力、 时间，
   yánjiū hé chūbǎn bùdàn xūyào rénlì shíjiān
   research and publish not.only need human.resource time

   还 须 有 资金 在 背后 支助。（风筝 110）
   hái *xū yǒu zījīn zài bèihòu zhīzhù*
   also need have money at behind support

   'Research and publishing need not only human resources and time, but also the support of money.' (*Fēngzhen*, 110)

(11) 孔子 不但 是 伟大的 教育家， **也** 是 杰出的
   *kóngzǐ bùdàn shì wěidàde jiàoyùjiā **yě** shì jiéchūde*
   Confucius not.only be great educator **also** be excellent

   思想家。（伦理·中三 3）
   sīxiǎngjiā
   thinker

   'Confucius is not only a great educator, but also an excellent thinker.' (*Lúnlǐ* III 3)

(12) 他们 的 儿女 **不仅** 没 来 参加 他们
   *tāmen de ér nǚ **bùjǐn** méi lái cānjiā tāmen*
   3PL DE son daughter **not.only** NEG come attend 3PL

   的 婚礼， **反而** 觉得 父亲 或 母亲 这 种
   *de hūnlǐ, **fǎnér** juéde fùqīn huò mǔqīn zhè zhǒng*
   DE wedding **instead** think father or mother this CL

"老恋"　大大　地　为　自己　丢　了　面子。(太阳 47)
lǎoliàn　dàdà　de　wèi　zìjǐ　diū　le　miànzi
old.love　greatly　DE　for　oneself　lose　LE　face

'Their sons and daughters not only refused to attend their weddings, but even thought the 'old love' of their father or mother greatly dishonours them.' (*Tàiyáng* 47)

(13) 儒家　伦理　**不只**　要　我们　注重　知识，
rújiā　lúnlǐ　**bùzhǐ**　yào　wǒmen　zhùzhòng　zhīshi
Confucian　ethics　**not.only**　require　1PL　pay.attention.to　knowledge

更　要　我们　注重　实践。(伦理·中三 3)
gèng　yào　wǒmen　zhùzhòng　shíjiàn
even.more　require　1SG　pay.attention.to　practice

'Confucian ethics requires us to pay attention to knowledge, and even more to practice.' (*Lúnlǐ* III 3)

Sometimes 尚且 *shàngqiě* 'even'..., 何况 *hékuàng* 'let alone'... is used to connect the two clauses in a progressive compound sentence, implying a much more intensive meaning in the second clause which is often in the form of rhetorical questions. For example:

(14) 蝼蚁　**尚且**　偷生，　**何况**　是　人　呢？(恶梦 63)
lóuyǐ　**shàngqiě**　tōushēng　**hékuàng**　shì　rén　ne
ants　**even**　stay.alive　**let.alone**　be　person　SFP

'Even ants want to stay alive, let alone humans.' (*Èmèng* 63)

(15) 对　事务　**尚且**　如此，　**何况**　对　人？(Δ自然 7)
duì　shìwù　**shàngqiě**　rúcǐ　**hékuàng**　duì　rén
treat　things　**even**　this.way　**let.alone**　treat　people

Even things are treated in this way, let alone people?' (Δ*Zìrán* 7)

The pause between clauses in a progressive compound sentence is represented by a comma.

3.7 Annotative Compound Sentences

Annotative compound sentences refer to sentences in which the second clause provides an annotation to the first clause. For example:

(1) 村镇　　　　的　马路　上　　行人　　十分　稀少，
　　 cūnzhèn　 de　mǎlù　shàng　xíngrén　shífēn　xīshǎo
　　 village.and.town DE road on pedestrian very scarce

只有　几　　个　行走　匆忙　　的　下午　　班
zhǐyǒu jǐ　　gè　xíngzǒu cōngmáng de xiàwǔ　 bān
only several CL walk hastily DE afternoon class

学生。(断情剪185)
xuéshēng
student

'There are few pedestrians on the roads of villages and towns, except a few students from the afternoon class walking in a hurry.' (*Duànqíngjiǎn* 185)

(2) 大海　　和　人　　一样，
　　 dàhǎi　 hé　rén　 yīyàng
　　 sea　　 and person same

都　　是　生命　　的　精灵。(太阳 82)
dōu　 shì shēngmìng de jīnglíng
all　 be　life　　 DE spirit

'The sea, just like people, has a spirit.' (*Tàiyáng* 82)

(3) 村子　里　　的　神庙　　有　　好　几　　间，
　　 cūnzi　 lǐ　 de　shénmiào yǒu　 hǎo jǐ　 jiān
　　 village inside DE temple have quite several CL

关帝庙、　　　　天公坛、　　　　和　包公府
guāndìmiào　　 tiāngōngtán　　　hé　bāogōngfǔ
Temple.of.Guan.Yu Temple.of.Heaven and Temple.of.Baogong

等　　　都　　是。(胜利 37)
děng　　 dōu　 shì
and.so.on all　 be

'There are several temples in the village, like the Temple of Guan Yu, the Temple of Heaven, and the Temple of Baogong and so on.' (*Shènglì* 37)

(4) 征选　　　　空中小姐　　　　的　条件　　非常　　苛刻，
　　 zhēngxuǎn kōngzhōngxiǎojiě de tiáojiàn fēicháng kēkè
　　 recruit　　 stewardess　　　 DE condition very strict

太过   林黛玉   和   楚霸王   的   妹妹
tàiguò líndàiyù   hé   chǔbàwáng   de   mèimèi
too   Lin.Daiyu   and   Chu.King   DE   girl

都   不   适合   担任。(八方 11)
dōu   bù   shìhé   dānrèn
all   NEG   suit   take.up

'The recruiting requirements for stewardess are very strict, and those girls who are too much like Lin Daiyu or Chu King are not suitable.' (*Bāfāng* 11)

(5) 天空，   竟然   已经   消失   了--
    tiānkōng   jìngrán   yǐjīng   xiāoshī   le
    sky   unexpectedly   already   disappear   LE

消失   在   一   片   翁翳   翠绿   之   中。(壁虎 24)
xiāoshī   zài   yī   piàn   wěngyì   cuìlǜ   zhī   zhōng
disappear   at   one   CL   dim   jade.green   LIG   inside

'The sky has unexpectedly disappeared into the dim jade green.' (*Bìhǔ* 24)

(6) 哭   与   笑   都   不能   改变   一   个   事实：
    kū   yǔ   xiào   dōu   bùnéng   gǎibiàn   yī   gè   shìshí
    cry   and   laugh   all   cannot   change   one   CL   fact

蝴蝶   断气   了！(短篇 33–34)
húdié   duànqì   le
butterfly   breathe.one's.last   LE

'crying or laughing, neither can change the fact that the butterfly has died.' (*Duǎnpiān* 33–34)

(7) 它   说明   了   一   个   真理：
    tā   shuōmíng   le   yī   gè   zhēnlǐ
    3SG   demonstrate   LE   one   CL   truth

爱   美   是   人类   的   天性。(文艺 45)
ài   měi   shì   rénlèi   de   tiānxìng
love   beauty   be   human   DE   nature

'It demonstrated a truth that the love of beauty is human nature.' (*Wényì* 45)

218 *Composite Sentences*

In (1), the second clause provides an annotative explanation to the first clause– 马路上行人十分稀少 *mǎlù shàng xíngrén shífēn xīshǎo* 'There are few pedestrians on the roads'. In (2), the second clause also gives further explanation about 大海和人一样 *dàhǎi hé rén yīyàng* 'the sea is just like people' in the first clause. In (3), the second clause – 关帝庙、天公坛和包公府等都是 *guāndìmiào tiāngōngtán hé bāogōngfǔ děng dōu shì* 'like the Temple of Guan Yu, the Temple of Heaven, and the Temple of Baogong and so on' – illustrates the temples mentioned in the first clause – 村子里的神庙有好几间 *cūnzi lǐ de shénmiào yǒu hǎo jǐ jiān* 'there are several temples in the village'. In (4), the second clause details the harsh requirements for the recruitment of stewardesses. In (5), the second clause gives further details about how 'the sky has disappeared'. In (6) and (7), the second clauses describe what is the 事实 *shìshí* 'fact' and 真理 *zhēnlǐ* 'truth' mentioned in the first clauses respectively. The following sentence (8) is another example of an annotative compound sentence:

(8) 子昀　开始　恨　自己，　恨　自己
    zǐyún kāishǐ hèn zìjǐ,   hèn zìjǐ
    Ziyun start   hate oneself hate oneself

　　没　　真正　　下　苦功　　　读书。(金狮奖 165)
　　méi zhēnzhèng xià kǔgōng dúshū
　　NEG really   do   hard.work study

'Ziyun started to hate himself for not really studying hard.' (*Jīnshījiǎng* 165)

In (8), the first clause mentions that Ziyun hates himself, and the second clause further clarifies the reason why Ziyun hates himself.

The pause between the two clauses in an annotative compound sentence could be a comma as in (1) to (4), or a dash as in (5), or a colon as in (6) and (7). Normally, if the second clause gives annotation to the things denoted by the object in the first clause, the pause is usually indicated with a colon.

3.8 Specific-General Compound Sentences

Specific-general compound sentences state the relationship between general statements and specific details. The general statement is usually stated by one clause, and the specific details are usually presented in at least two clauses. The order of clauses with specific details and clauses with general statement comes in two varieties.

1 The general statement precedes the specific details, which is the most frequent order. For example:

(1) 社会　　上　　各种各样　　　的　人　　都　有，
    shèhuì shàng gèzhǒnggèyàng de rén   dōu yǒu
    society up   various   DE person all have

有的	人	道德	休养	高,
yǒude	rén	dàodé	xiūyǎng	gāo
some	person	morality	cultivation	high

有的	人	道德	休养	低,
yǒude	rén	dàodé	xiūyǎng	dī
some	person	morality	cultivation	low

有的	人	甚至	没有	道德。(伦理·中三 38)
yǒude	rén	shènzhì	méiyǒu	dàodé
some	person	even	not.have	morality

'There are all kinds of people in the society: some people have high moral cultivation; some have low moral cultivation; and some don't even have morality.' (*Lúnlǐ* III 38)

(2)
众	姊妹	七手八脚	地	忙	起来	了:
zhòng	zǐmèi	qīshǒubājiǎo	de	máng	qǐlái	le
all	sisters	in.a.bustle	DE	busy	up	LE

有的	去	打	电话	通知	她	的	丈夫	施迪文,
yǒude	qù	dǎ	diànhuà	tōngzhī	tā	de	zhàngfu	shīdíwén
some	go	call	phone	notice	3SG	DE	husband	Steven

有的	扶	送	她	去	医院。(追云 34)
yǒude	fú	sòng	tā	qù	yīyuàn
some	help	send	3SG	go	hospital

'All the sisters got busy in a hurry: some were going to call her husband Steven; others were sending her to the hospital.' (*Zhuīyún* 34)

(3)
香港	最	畅销	的	书	有	两	种,
xiānggǎng	zuì	chàngxiāo	de	shū	yǒu	liǎng	zhǒng
Hong.Kong	most	best-selling	DE	book	have	two	CL

一	是	消闲性	的,	二	是	实用性	的。(心情 175)
yī	shì	xiāoxiánxìng	de	èr	shì	shíyòngxìng	de
one	be	leisure.type	DE	two	be	practical.type	DE

'There are two types of best-selling books in Hong Kong, one being the leisure type, the other being the practical one.' (*Xīnqíng* 175)

2 The specific details precede the general statement. For example:

(4) 做， 要 靠 想 来 指导； 想， 要 靠
    zuò yào kào xiǎng lái zhǐdǎo xiǎng yào kào
    do need rely.on think come guide   think need rely.on

    做 来 证明： 想 和 做 是 紧密地
    zuò lái zhèngmíng xiǎng hé zuò shì jǐnmìde
    do come prove think and do be closely

    结合 在一起 的。 (华文教材 1B 136)
    jiéhé zàiyīqǐ de
    integrate together DE

    'Action must rely on thought for guidance and thought must rely on action for proof, so action and thought are closely integrated.' (*Huáwénjiàocái* 1B, 136)

In a specific-general compound sentence, the pause between the clauses is often indicated by a colon, as in (2) and (4), or sometimes by a comma, as in (1) and (3).

3.9 Adversative Complex Sentences

Adversative complex sentences often indicate an adversative relationship between clauses. More specifically, the primary clause expresses a contradictory or opposite meaning from what the secondary clause expresses. For example:

(1) 他 薪水 比 人家 低，
    tā xīnshuǐ bǐ rénjiā dī
    3SG salary than others low

    工作 却 比 人家 多。(胜利 79)
    gōngzuò què bǐ rénjiā duō
    work yet than others more

    'His salary is lower yet he works more than others.' (*Shènglì* 79)

Example (1) is an adversative complex sentence. The meaning of the second clause is obviously contradictory to that of the first clause.

Adversative complex sentences can be further divided into three types based on the uses of transitional words.

The first type of adversative complex sentences does not include a transitional word in the secondary clause. Sometimes even the primary clause has no transitional words, for example:

(2) 叫   他   多   在   家   里   休息，
    jiào tā   duō   zài   jiā   lǐ   xiūxi
    tell 3SG more at   home inside rest

他   偏   放不下心。(胜利 88)
tā   piān   fàng-bù-xià-xīn
3SG on.the.contrary couldn't.feel.assured

'Although he was told to rest more at home, he couldn't feel assured.' (*Shènglì* 88)

But the more commonly seen pattern is to show adversativity in the primary clause with transitional words like 但（是）*dàn (shì)* 'but', 可（是）*kě (shì)* 'but', 只是 *zhǐshì* 'only', 就是 *jiùshì* 'just', 却 *què* 'but', 然而 *ránér* 'but', 不过 *bùguò* 'but' and 反之 *fǎnzhī* 'whereas'. For example:

(3) 现在   姐姐   已婚，   **但**   婚姻   生活
    xiànzài jiějie   yǐhūn   **dàn** hūnyīn shēnghuó
    now   elder.sister married but   marriage life

并   不   愉快。(华文教材 3A 133)
bìng   bù   yúkuài
but   NEG   happy

'Although married now, my elder sister's marriage life is not happy.' (*Huáwénjiàocái* 3A, 133)

(4) 你   不   一定   需要   相信   什么,   或者   证明
    nǐ   bù   yīdìng   xūyào   xiāngxìn shénme   huòzhě   zhèngmíng
    2SG   NEG   necessary need   believe   something or   prove

什么,   但是   这些   画面   会   让   后人
shénme   dànshì   zhèxiē   huàmiàn   huì   ràng   hòurén
something but   these   image   can   let   later.generation

提供   另一些   思考   的   材料。（报1995年4 月22 日19版）
tígōng   lìngyīxiē   sīkǎo   de   cáiliào
provide   other   think   DE   material

'You don't necessarily need to believe or prove something, but these images will provide the later generation with some materials to think about.' (*Bào*, Apr. 22, 1995, Issue no. 19)

(5) 在　　飞机　　上，　我　的　头，　　千　　　支　　针　　齐
    zài　　fēijī　　shàng　wǒ　de　　tóu　　qiān　　zhī　　zhēn　　qí
    on　　plane　　up　　1SG　DE　head　thousand　CL　needle　together

    扎　　　着　　　似的，　**可**　我　　不敢　　　告诉　　同行
    zhā　　zhe　　shìde　　**kě**　wǒ　bùgǎn　　gàosù　　tóngxíng
    pierce　ZHE　like　　　**but**　1SG　dare.not　tell　travel.together

    的　　人。（再见92）
    de　　rén
    DE　　people

    'On the plane, it seemed that a thousand needles are piercing my head, but I dare not tell my travelling companions.' (*Zàijiàn* 92)

(6) 他　　批评　　　的　　原则　　　和　　立场　　　没有　　改变，
    tā　　pīpíng　　de　　yuánzé　　hé　　lìchǎng　　méiyǒu　gǎibiàn
    3SG　criticise　DE　principle　and　position　NEG　change

    只是　以　　口　　代　　　笔　　而已。（胜利102）
    zhǐshì　yǐ　　kǒu　　dài　　bǐ　　éryǐ
    only　　use　mouth　replace　pen　just

    'The principles and positions of his critics haven't changed. But now he uses his mouth instead of his pen.' (*Shènglì* 102)

(7) 她　　伸　　　出来　　与　　我　　相握　　的　　手，　　是
    tā　　shēn　　chūlái　yǔ　　wǒ　　xiāngwò　de　　shǒu　　shì
    3SG　stretch　out　　with　1SG　shake　　DE　　hand　　be

    冰冷冰冷　　　　　的，　**可是**　手劲　　　　相当　　　有力。（跳舞138）
    bīnglěngbīnglěng　de　　**kěshì**　shǒujìn　　xiāngdāng　yǒulì
    icy　　　　　　　DE　　**but**　　hand.strength　quite　　powerful

    'She stretched out shake hands with me. Her hand is icy, but quite powerful.' (*Tiàowǔ* 138)

(8) 我　　什么　　　都　　肯　　　　　　学，　**就是**　不　　知道
    wǒ　　shénme　　dōu　　kěn　　　　　　xué　　**jiùshì**　bù　　zhīdào
    1SG　anything　all　　be.willing.to　learn　**just**　　NEG　know

    学　　什么　　　才　　好。(微型2)
    xué　shénme　　cái　　hǎo

	learn	what	just	good

'I am willing to learn anything, but I have no idea of what to learn.' (*Wēixíng* 2)

(9) 媚媚　谈　过　她　太　多，**却**　忘　了
　　mèimèi tán guò tā tài duō **què** *wàng le*
　　Meimei talk GUO 3SG too much **but** forget LE

　　告诉　我　她　长　得　如何。(想飞 40)
　　gàosù wǒ tā zhǎng de rúhé
　　tell 1SG 3SG grow DE how

'Meimei had talked about her a lot, but she forgot to tell me how she looked like.' (*Xiǎngfēi* 40)

(10) 人生　常　有　不如意，**不过**　只要　肯
　　rénshēng cháng yǒu bùrúyì **bùguò** *zhǐyào kěn*
　　life often have adversities **but** as.long.as be.willing.to

　　拼　就　一定　会　赢。(扶轮 88)
　　pīn jiù yīdìng huì yíng
　　go.all.out then surly will win

'Life cannot always go as one wishes, but as long as you are willing to go all out in work, you will win.' (*Fúlún* 88)

(11) 我　的　思路　就是　这样地　随着　飘飞的　黄叶
　　wǒ de sīlù jiùshì zhèyàngde suízhe piāofēide huángyè
　　1SG DE thought just this.way with floating yellow.leave

　　和　红叶，天高地阔地　飞驰　着，然而　惊心动魄的
　　hé hóngyè tiāngāodìkuòde fēichí zhe ránér jīngxīndòngpòde
　　and red.leave widely fly ZHE but exciting

　　时刻，终于　到来　了。（壁虎26）
　　shíkè zhōngyú dàolái le
　　moment finally arrive LE

'My thoughts are flying around widely with the floating yellow and red leaves, but the exciting moment finally arrives.' (*Bìhǔ* 26)

Occasionally, the primary clause may include two transitional words to show adversative meaning, for example:

(12) 白人　　　　　　原本　　　就是　白　　的，
　　 báirén　　　　　 yuánběn　 jiùshì bái　 de
　　 the.white.people originally just　 white DE

但是，她　　**却**　比　　一般　　的　　白人
dànshì tā　 **què** bǐ　　yībān　 de　 báirén
but　 3SG **yet** than　average DE　 the.white.people

来　得　　更　　　　白。(大胡子 88)
lái　de　 gèng　　　 bái
come DE even.more　 white

'The white people are originally white, but she is much whiter than the average white people.' (*Dàhúzi* 88)

(13) 在　　微风　　　轻拂　　下，
　　 zài　 wēifēng　　qīngfú　 xià
　　 at　 breeze　　 flick　　down

湖水　　对着　　 青山　　　 细细　低语，**而**　青山
húshuǐ　duìzhe　 qīngshān　　xìxì　dīyǔ　 **ér** qīngshān
lake　　toward　 green.hill　gently whisper **but** green.hill

则　对着　 湖水　　顾影自怜。(石头 115)
zé　duìzhe　húshuǐ　gùyǐngzìlián
yet toward　lake　　lament.oneself.lonely

'Flicked by the breeze, the lake gently whispers to the green hill, while the green hill laments its lonely reflection in the lake.' (*Shítóu* 115)

(14) 崎岖泥泞的　　　　　路途，　　会　　使得　　年轻人　　　　趋向
　　 qíqūnínìngde　　　　 lùtú　　 huì　 shǐdé　 niánqīngrén　　 qūxiàng
　　 rugged.and.muddy　　path　　 can　 cause　 young.people　　become

成熟；**反之**，　　　舒服　　　平稳　　　　　　　　的
chéngshú **fǎnzhī**　　 shūfu　　 píngwěn　　　　　　 de
mature　 **whereas**　 comfortable smooth.and.steady　DE

生活，　　却　　只有　　使　　他们　　浪掷　　青春！(心情 94)
shēnghuó　què　 zhǐyǒu　shǐ　　tāmen　 làngzhì qīngchūn
life　　　yet　 only　　cause 3PL　　 waste　 youth

'A rugged and muddy life path will help young people to gradually become mature. Whereas a comfortable and steady life can only make them waste their youth.' (*Xīnqíng* 94)

The previous sentences all include two connectors in the primary clause, namely 但是 *dànshì* 'but' and 却 *què* 'but' in (12), 而 *ér* 'but' and 则 *zé* 'yet' in (13), and 反之 *fǎnzhī* 'whereas' and 却 *què* 'but' in (14).

Since this type of adversative complex sentences indicate a slight concession, these are also called slight adversative complex sentences.

The second type of adversative complex sentences include both transitional words in the secondary clause, like 虽（然）*suī (rán)* 'although', 虽则 *suīzé* 'although', 尽管 *jǐnguǎn* 'although' and 固然 *gùrán* 'although', and transitional words in the primary clause, like 却 *què* 'but', 但（是）*dàn (shì)* 'but', 可（是）*kě (shì)* 'but', 倒是 *dǎoshì* 'on the contrary' and 就是 *jiùshì* 'just'. Thus, the conjunctives are used in pairs, such as:

虽（然）*suī (rán)* 'although'... 可是*kěshì* 'but'...
虽（然）*suī (rán)* 'although'... 但（是）*dàn (shì)* 'but'...
虽（然）*suī (rán)* 'although'... 却*què* 'but'...
尽管*jǐnguǎn* 'although'... 却*què* 'but'...
and "固然*gùrán* 'although'... 可*kě* 'but'...

This type is often called concessive transitional complex sentence, or adversative complex sentence showing strong transition, as it often entails a more obvious transition. For example:

(15) 花园 中 野草 **虽** 有 请 人 拔除，
huāyuán zhōng yécǎo **suī** *yǒu qǐng rén báchú*
garden inside weed **although** YOU ask people pull.up

可是 却 "春风 吹 又 生"， 奈何它不得。（八方6）
kěshì *què chūnfēng chuī yòu shēng, nàihé-tā-bùdé*
but but spring.wind blow again grow do.nothing.to.it

'Although the weeds in the garden have been pulled up before, they grow again with the spring wind and there is nothing I can do about them.' (*Bāfāng* 6)

(16) 他们 对 人性 **虽然** 有 不同 的 看法，
tāmen duì rénxìng **suīrán** *yǒu bùtóng de kànfǎ*
3PL toward human.nature **although** have different DE opinion

但 都 相信 教育 能 使 人 向上
dàn *dōu xiāngxìn jiàoyù néng shǐ rén xiàngshàng*
but all believe education can cause people to.make.progress

向善。(伦理·中四 94)
xiàngshàn
to.be.good

'Although they held different opinions toward human nature, they all believed that education can help people to be proactive and good.' (*Lúnlǐ* IV 94)

(17) 方法   **虽然**   不同，
    fāngfǎ **suīrán**   bùtóng
    method although   different

目标   和   理想   **却**   是   一致的。(伦理·中三 20)
mùbiāo hé   lǐxiǎng **què** shì   yīzhìde
target and ideal   but   be   same

'Though methods are different, the targets and ideals are the same.' (*Lúnlǐ* III 20)

(18) **虽然**   有些   字儿   看   不   太   懂，
    suīrán   yǒuxiē   zìer   kàn   bù   tài   dǒng
    although   some   word   look NEG   too   understand

图片   **倒是**   很   清楚的。（微型47）
túpiàn **dàoshì**   hěn   qīngchǔde
image   on.the.contrary very   clear

'Although (I) don't understand some words, those images are very clear.' (*Wēixíng* 47)

(19) **虽**   则   多   次   护送   曾楚仪   归   家，
    suī   zé   duō   cì   hùsòng   zēngchǔyí   guī   jiā
    although then   many   time   escort   Zeng.Chuyi back   home

但   从未   踏   入   她   的   家门。（Δ断情剪51）
dàn cóngwèi   tà   rù   tā   de   jiāmén
but   never   step   inside 3SG   DE   door

'Although I escorted Zeng Chuyi back home many times, I have never stepped inside her door.' (Δ*Duànqíng jiǎn* 51)

(20) **尽管**   有人   喜爱   淑女   的   弄姿、
    jǐnguǎn yǒurén   xǐài   shūnǚ   de   nòngzī
    although   some.people like   lady   DE   coquettish

绅士	的	作状，	我	**却**	认为	毫无	掩饰
shēnshì	de	zuòzhuàng	wǒ	**què**	rènwéi	háowú	yǎnshì
gentleman	DE	mannerism	1SG	**but**	think	not.at.all	cover.up

者	的	心胸	更	光明磊落。(文艺 118)
zhě	de	xīnxiōng	gèng	guāngmínglěiluò
person	DE	mind	more	be.open.and.straightforward

'Though some people like the coquettish lady and manneristic gentleman, I prefer people with no disguise, who have a more open and straightforward mind.' (*Wényì* 118)

(21)
勤	学	**固然**	重要，	**但**	更	重要	的
qín	xué	**gùrán**	zhòngyào	**dàn**	gèng	zhòngyào	de
diligent	study	**although**	important	**but**	more	important	DE

还	是	先	要	立志。(伦理·中三 46)
hái	shì	xiān	yào	lìzhì
still	be	first	need	make.resolution

'Studying hard is absolutely important, but it is more important to make resolutions first' (*Lúnlǐ* III 46)

Occasionally the verb 是 *shì* 'be' also implies concession, for example:

(22)
豪华	旅馆	**是**	有	好	几	间，
háohuá	lǚguǎn	**shì**	yǒu	hǎo	jǐ	jiān
luxurious	hotel	**be**	have	quite	several	CL

但	数量	总	不及	小	旅舍	多。(南北 16)
dàn	shùliàng	zǒng	bùjí	xiǎo	lǚshè	duō
but	number	always	less	small	inn	more

'There are several luxury hotels, but not as many small inns.' (*Nánběi* 16)

However, the more commonly seen format with 是 *shì* 'be' indicating concession is A 是 *shì* 'be' A, in which the words before and after 是 *shì* 'be' are identical, as illustrated next:

(23)
这	学生	**好**	**是**	**好**，
zhè	xuéshēng	**hǎo**	**shì**	**hǎo**
this	student	**good**	**be**	**good**

就是　静　了　些。(牛车水 92)
jiùshì　jìng　le　xiē
just　quiet　LE　a.little

'This student is good, but a little bit quiet.' (*Niúchēshuǐ* 92)

The third type of adversative complex sentences expresses hypothetical concession with transitional words such as 即使 *jíshǐ* 'even if' or 就是 *jiùshì* 'even if', 哪怕 *nǎpà* 'even if', 纵（使）*zòng (shǐ)* 'even if', 就算 *jiùsuàn* 'even if', 再 *zài* 'even' and so on in the secondary clause, and 也 *yě* 'also' or 还是 *háishì* 'still' in the primary clause. They are also called "hypothetical adversative complex sentences". For example:

(24) **即使**　是　前途　堪虞，　有　能力　写作　的　人，
 jíshǐ　shì　qiántú　kānyú　yǒu　nénglì　xiězuò　de　rén
 even.if　be　prospect　worrying　have　ability　writing　DE　person

 还是　应该　写　下去　的。(文艺 27)
 háishì　yīnggāi　xiě　xiàqù　de
 still　should　write　on　DE

'People who have the ability to write should keep writing, even though their prospects is not clear.' (*Wényì* 27)

(25) **就是**　去　工厂　当　个　女工，　**也**　强过
 jiùshì　qù　gōngchǎng　dāng　gè　nǔgōng　***yě***　qiángguò
 even.if　go　factory　be.as　CL　female.worker　**also**　better

 做　这般　烦　而　厌、　厌　而　烦
 zuò　zhèbān　fán　ér　yàn　yàn　ér　fán
 do　this.kind　tedious　and　annoying　annoying　and　tedious

 的　杂务。（追云28）
 de　záwù
 DE　chores

'Even going to a factory and becoming a (female) worker is better than doing these kinds of tedious and annoying chores.' (*Zhuīyún* 28)

(26) **哪怕**　你　做牛做马　为　他　服务　一辈子，
 nǎpà　nǐ　zuòniúzuòmǎ　wèi　tā　fúwù　yībèizi
 even.if　2SG　work.hard　for　3SG　serve　lifetime

他　也　未必　会　感激　你。(报 1995年3月 15
　　　　　　　　　　　　　　日副刊11版)
tā　yě　wèibì　huì　gǎnjī　nǐ
3SG also may.not will thank 2SG
'Even if you are at his service for a lifetime, he may not feel grateful to you.' (*Bao*, Mar. 15, 1995, Issue no. 11, supplementary edition)

(27) 我　头上　**纵**　有　再　多　的　名衔，
　　　wǒ　tóushàng　**zòng**　yǒu　zài　duō　de　míngxián
　　　1SG head　even.if have even more DE title

　　　也　换不回　　　青年时　识梦　的　快乐。
　　　　　　　　　　　　　　　　　　　　　（梦77）
　　　yě　huàn-bù-huí　qīngniánshí shímèng de kuàilè
　　　also exchange-NEG-back youth.time dream DE happy
　　　'Though I have so many titles, I can not regain the happiness of dreaming in my youth.' (*Mèng* 77)

(28) **就算**　给　你　伏　在　我　的　肩上　抽泣，
　　　jiùsuàn　gěi　nǐ　fú　zài　wǒ　de　jiānshàng　chōuqì
　　　even.if give 2SG hold at 1SG DE shoulder sob

　　　我　也　说不出　　几　句　安慰的话　来。
　　　　　　　　　　　　　　　　　　　　　(渐行 68)
　　　wǒ　yě　shuō-bù-chū　jǐ　jù　ānwèidehuà　lái
　　　1SG also speak-NEG-out several CL words.of.comfort come
　　　'Even if you bury (your face) on my shoulder and sob, I couldn't say any words of comfort.' (*Jiànxíng* 68)

(29) 美国　**再**　好，　**也**　不　比　家里　好。（金狮奖 117）
　　　měiguó　**zài**　hǎo　**yě**　bù　bǐ　jiālǐ　hǎo
　　　America even good also NEG than home good
　　　'Even though America is good, it is no better than home.' (*Jīnshījiǎng* 117)

3.10 Hypothetical Complex Sentences

Hypothetical complex sentences represent the relationship of assumption and conclusion, with the secondary clause proposing an hypothetical situation and the primary clause spelling out the consequence or conclusion.

Hypothetical complex sentences may involve no connective words in both primary clause and secondary clause, as in (1):

(1) 你　　有　　本事，　　你　　去　　报告　　好　　了。(建屋 13)
　　 nǐ　　yǒu　 běnshì　　nǐ　　qù　　bàogào　hǎo　　le
　　 2SG　have　ablity　　 2SG　go　　report　 good　LE
　　 'Go report it if you dare!' (*Jiànwū* 13)

Also, this relationship of assumption and conclusion can be indicated by explicit use of 就 *jiù* 'then', 便 *biàn* 'then' and 那（么）*nà (me)* 'then' in the primary clause, for example:

(2) 搬　　到　　新居，
　　 bān　　dào　　xīnjū
　　 move　to　　new.residence

　　 就　不　　能　　种　　那么　　多　　仙人掌　　　了。(壁虎 23)
　　 jiù　bù　　néng　zhòng　nàme　duō　xiānrénzhǎng　le
　　 then　NEG　can　　plant　 that　　much　cactus　　　 LE
　　 'When we move to the new residence, we won't be able to grow so many cactus.' (*Bìhǔ* 23)

(3) 尽　　了　　大　　责任，　　　**便**　得　　大　　快乐，
　　 jìn　　le　　dà　　zérèn　　　**biàn**　dé　　dà　　kuàilè
　　 try　　LE　big　 responsibility　**then**　get　 big　　happiness

　　 尽　　得　　小　　责任，　　　**便**　得　　小　　快乐，(含羞草 12)
　　 jìn　　dé　　xiǎo　zérèn　　　**biàn**　dé　　xiǎo　kuàilè
　　 try　　DE　little　responsibility　**then**　get　little　 happiness
　　 'Take on great responsibility, and you will get great happiness; take on little responsibility, and you will get little happiness.' (*Hánxiūcǎo* 12)

(4) 买　　半独立的、　　　　有　　花园　　的　　双层洋房，
　　 mǎi　bàndúlìde　　　　 yǒu　huāyuán　de　　shuāngcéngyángfáng
　　 buy　semi-detached　　have　garden　 DE　　duplex

　　 那就　不会　再　　　给　　楼上　　　芳邻　　　吵到。(吾土·戏剧 128)
　　 nàjiù　bùhuì　zài　　gěi　　lóushàng　fānglín　　chǎodào
　　 then　cannot　again　GEI　upstairs　 neighbour　disturb
　　 'If you buy a semi-detached duplex with a garden, then you won't be bothered by the neighbours upstairs.' (*Wútǔ* (drama) 128)

The more commonly seen pattern is to use conjunctions like 如果 *rúguǒ* 'if', 假如 *jiǎrú* 'if', 假若 *jiǎruò* 'if', 要是 *yàoshì* 'if', 倘若 *tǎngruò* 'if', 一旦 *yīdàn* 'once', 万一 *wànyī* 'if by any chance', 要 *yào* 'if' and 若 *ruò* 'if' in the secondary clause to indicate the assumptive situation. In this case, the primary clause may include no connective words at all. For example:

(5) 如果　　有　　机会，
    rúguǒ　yǒu　jīhuì
    if　　　have　chance

　　你　还　会　回去　家乡　　吗？(微型 195)
　　nǐ　hái　huì　huíqù　jiāxiāng　ma
　　2SG　still　will　return　hometown　SFP
　　'Would you go back to your hometown if you had the chance?' (*Wēixíng* 195)

(6) 要是　　没有　　遇到　　你，　我　　现在　　也　不　　会
    yàoshì　méiyǒu　yùdào　nǐ　wǒ　xiànzài　yě　bù　huì
    if　　　NEG　　　meet　　2SG　1SG　now　　also　NEG　will

　　比　　少梅　　和　若萍　　好。(恶梦 92)
　　bǐ　shàoméi　hé　ruòpíng　hǎo
　　than　Shaomei　and　Ruoping　good
　　'If I hadn't met you, I would not be better than Shaomei and Ruoping.' (*Èmèng* 92)

(7) 倘若　　　看到　　水果摊　　　前　　排　了　长长　　　的
    tǎngruò　kàndào　shuǐguǒtān　qián　pái　le　chángcháng　de
    if　　　　see　　　fruit.stall　　front　line　LE　long　　　　DE

　　人龙，　一定　　是　摊子上　　有　　香蕉　　　出售。(石头 27)
　　rénlóng　yīdìng　shì　tānzishàng　yǒu　xiāngjiāo　chūshòu
　　queue　　must　　be　stall　　　have　banana　　sell
　　'If (you) see a long queue in front of the fruit stall, there must be bananas for sale.' (*Shítou* 27)

(8) 他们　　　一旦　　看透　　　　我，
    tāmen　**yīdàn**　kàntòu　　wǒ
    3PL　　once　　see.through　1SG

他们　会　受不了　　　我　的。(青青 5)
tāmen　huì　shòu-bù-liǎo　wǒ　de
3PL　will　bear-NEG-able　1SG　DE

'Once they see through me, they will not be able to stand me.'
(*Qīngqīng* 5)

(9) **万一**　煤气　越　漏　越　多，
　　　wànyī　méiqì　yuè　lòu　yuè　duō
　　　if　gas　more　leak　more　more

　　　后果　　　　真　　不堪设想。(梦 154)
　　　hòuguǒ　　　zhēn　bùkānshèxiǎng
　　　consequence　really　beyond.imagination

　　　'If by an chance the gas leak got worse and worse, the consequences would be really unimaginable.' (*Mèng* 154)

(10) **要**　保持　　华族　　传统文化　　　　　的　特性，　　　就
　　　yào　bǎochí　huázú　chuántǒngwénhuà　de　tèxìng　　jiù
　　　if　keep　Chinese　traditional.culture　DE　characteristics　then

　　　必须　使　　年轻　　　一代　　扎稳根基。(报 1995
　　　　　　　　　　　　　　　　　　　　　　　年3月5日2版)
　　　bìxū　shǐ　niánqīng　yīdài　zhāwěngēnjī
　　　must　make　young　generation　lay.a.solid.foundation

　　　'To keep the characteristics of Chinese traditional culture, the young generation must lay a solid foundation.' (*Bao*, Mar. 5, 1995, Issue no. 2)

(11) **若**　可能，　再　细　　　研　　　布局。(无臬56)
　　　ruò　kěnéng　zài　xì　yán　bùjú
　　　if　possible　again　carefully　research　layout

　　　'If possible, study the layout more carefully.' (*Wúniè*, 56)

Sometimes, there will be adverbs like就 *jiù* 'then', 那（么）*nà (me)* 'then' or 便 *biàn* 'then' in the primary clause to collocate with the conjunction in the secondary clause. For example:

(12) 你　　**如果**　逼　　我　　回去，
　　　nǐ　**rúguǒ**　bī　wǒ　huíqù
　　　2SG　if　force　1SG　go.back

我	**就**	立刻		飞	回去	澳洲。(大胡子 47)
wǒ	**jiù**	lìkè		fēi	huíqù	àozhōu
1SG	**then**	immediately		fly	return	Australia

'If you force me to go back, I will fly back to Australia immediately.' (*Dàhúzi* 47)

(13)
假如	你	置身	在	这	绿	的	境界，
jiǎrú	nǐ	zhìshēn	zài	zhè	lǜ	de	jìngjiè
if	2SG	stay	at	this	green	DE	realm

那么	你	就	静静	地	坐	一	坐。(独上 81)
nàme	nǐ	jiù	jìngjìng	de	zuò	yī	zuò
then	2SG	just	quiet	DE	sit	one	CL

'If you come to this green realm, then just seat yourself quietly for a while.' (*Dúshàng* 81)

(14)
假若	父亲	聪明	一点	的话，	**就**	应该	悄没声息
jiǎruò	fùqīn	cōngmíng	yīdiǎn	dehuà	**jiù**	yīnggāi	qiāoméishēngxī
if	father	clever	a.little	if	**then**	should	silently

地	转身	从	另	一	个	地方	回家。(太阳 60)
de	zhuǎnshēn	cóng	lìng	yī	gè	dìfāng	huíjiā
DE	turn.around	from	another	one	CL	place	go.home

'If the father had been wiser, he should have silently turned around and gone home from another place.' (*Tàiyáng* 60)

(15)
一旦	认定	我	是	她	爸	的	"传声筒"，
yīdàn	rèndìng	wǒ	shì	tā	bà	de	chuánshēngtǒng
once	affirm	1SG	be	3SG	dad	DE	mouthpiece

她	可能	**便**	会	拂袖而去	了。(石头 40)
tā	kěnéng	**biàn**	huì	fúxiùérqù	le
3SG	maybe	**then**	will	leave.in.a.huff	LE

'Once she takes me as her father's mouthpiece, she may leave in a huff.' (*Shítou* 40)

In some occasions, when conjunctions like 如果 *rúguǒ* 'if' are used in the secondary clause, the auxiliary word 的话 *dehuà* 'if' will be attached to the end of the sentence to reinforce the assumptive situation, as shown in (14), and one more example is shown next:

234 *Composite Sentences*

(16) 如果　要　唱　的话，　可　就　有　令人鼻酸
    rúguǒ yào chàng dehuà kě jiù yǒu lìngrénbísuān
    if   will sing   if   may then have make.people.
                                             choked.up

    的　五十　多　个　感人　的　故事　了。(青青 40)
    de wǔshí duō gè gǎnrén de gùshì le
    DE fifty more CL touching DE story LE
    'If (I) sing, there will be more than fifty touching stories that can make people choked up.' (*Qīngqīng* 40)

3.11 Conditional Complex Sentences

Conditional complex sentences generally express the relationship of condition and result, with the secondary clause stating the condition and the primary clause stating the result. They can be further divided into four subtypes:

3.11.1 Indicating Sufficient Condition

Sufficient conditions are always indicated by a conjunction word 只要 *zhǐyào* 'as long as' in the secondary clause, co-occurring with such adverbs as 就 'then', 便 *biàn* 'then' or 总 *zǒng* 'always' in the primary clause, as illustrated by (1)–(3) respectively:

(1) 一　个　字　只要　差　那么　一点，
    yī gè zì   zhǐyào chà nàme yīdiǎn
    one CL character as.long.as different that a.little

    意义　可　就　大　不　相同　了。(笑眼 62)
    yìyì kě jiù dà bù xiāngtóng le
    meaning may then big NEG same   LE
    'If a Chinese character is changed even slightly, the meaning may change dramatically.' (*Xiàoyǎn* 62)

(2) 只要　学生　有　作答，　他　便　给　分。(胜利 19)
    zhǐyào xuéshēng yǒu zuòdá tā biàn gěi fēn
    as.long.as student have answer 3SG then give point
    'As long as the students wrote some answers, he gave them points.' (*Shènglì* 19)

(3) 只要　有　生　的　希望，
    zhǐyào yǒu shēng de xīwàng
    as.long.as have be.alive DE hope

总　　　好过　　　马革裹尸。(金狮奖 19)
zǒng　　*hǎoguò*　　*mǎgéguǒshī*
always　**better.than**　**die.on.the.battlefield**

'As long as there is hope for survival, it's better than dying on the battlefield.' (*Jīnshījiǎng* 19)

3.11.2 Indicating the Only Condition

Often, the only condition necessary is introduced with a conjunction 只有 *zhǐyǒu* 'only if' in the secondary clause, with an adverb 才 *cái* 'then' pairing with it in the primary clause. For example:

(4)　**只有**　和平共处，　　　人类　　**才**　　能　　自救。(伦理·中四 91)
　　　zhǐyǒu　*hépínggòngchǔ*　*rénlèi*　***cái***　*néng*　*zìjiù*
　　　only.if　coexist.peacefully　human　**then**　able　save.oneself

'Only by living in peace with each other can human beings save themselves.' (*Lúnlǐ* IV 91)

(5)　**只有**　守　　着　　这　　三　　宝　——　老伴、　老本、　老窝，
　　　zhǐyǒu　*shǒu*　*zhe*　*zhè*　*sān*　*bǎo*　　*lǎobàn*　*lǎoběn*　*lǎowō*
　　　only.if　guard　ZHE　this　three　treasure　spouse　capital　house

　　　银发　　生涯　　**才**　　能　　有　　保障。(报 1995年6月19日副刊5版)
　　　yínfà　*shēngyá*　***cái***　*néng*　*yǒu*　*bǎozhàng*
　　　seniors　life　**then**　able　have　guarantee

'Only by keeping the three treasures – spouse, capital, house – can you secure your life when you're old.' (*Bao*, June 19, 1995, Issue no. 5, supplementary edition)

Sometimes, 唯有 *wéiyǒu* 'only if' is used in the secondary clause, as in (6):

(6)　**唯有**　按部就班　　地　　前进，　　唯有　　脚踏实地　　地
　　　wéiyǒu　*ànbùjiùbān*　*de*　*qiánjìn*　*wéiyǒu*　*jiǎotàshídì*　*de*
　　　only.if　step.by.step　DE　move.forward　only.if　down.to.earth　DE

　　　钻研，　**才**　　可以　化　　雄心　　为　　现实。(华文教材 4A 80)
　　　zuānyán　***cái***　*kěyǐ*　*huà*　*xióngxīn*　*wéi*　*xiànshí*
　　　study　**then**　can　make　ambition　into　reality

'Only by moving forward step by step and studying in a down-to-earth manner, can you make your ambition into a reality.' (*Huáwénjiàocái* 4A, 80)

In other cases, conjunctions like 只有 *zhǐyǒu* 'only if' do not show up in the secondary clause, and only an adverb 才 *cái* 'then' is used in the primary clause to express the relationship of sole condition and result between the clauses. For example:

(7) 科学　　知识　　和　　道德　　知识　　这　　两　　方面
    kēxué   zhīshi   hé   dàodé   zhīshi   zhè   liǎng fāngmiàn
    science knowledge and morality knowledge this two   aspects

    的　　知识　　都　　具备　了,　才　　可　　算　　是　　一　　个
    de   zhīshi   dōu   jùbèi   le   cái   kě   suàn   shì   yī   gè
    DE   knowledge all   have   LE   **then** can   consider be   one   CL

    真正　　　　有　　修养　　　　　　的　　人。(伦理·中三 61)
    zhēnzhèng yǒu   xiūyǎng   de   rén
    really   have self-cultivation   DE   person

    'Only when a person possesses both scientific knowledge and moral awareness can they be considered genuinely culltured.' (*Lúnlǐ* III 61)

3.11.3 Indicating Unconditional Conditions

To express unconditional conditionals, the secondary clause is marked by conjunctions like 不管 *bùguǎn* 'no matter', 不论 *bùlùn* 'no matter', 无论 *wúlùn* 'no matter' or 任凭 *rènpíng* 'no matter', and the primary clause is marked by the adverb 都 *dōu* 'all', indicating that the main clause will be true regardless of which option of the conditionals is realized. One example of each conjunction is shown next:

(8) **不管**　　买进　　哪　　一　　只　　股票,　**都**　会　　在
    bùguǎn *mǎijìn   nǎ   yī   zhī   gǔpiào* ***dōu*** *huì   zài*
    no.matter buy.in   which one   CL   stock   **all**   will   in

    三两　　　　天　　里　　就　　　赚　　　了　　几百　　　　　　元。
                                                                    (恶梦 28)
    sānliǎng   tiān   lǐ   jiù   zhuàn   le   jǐbǎi   yuán
    two.or.three day   in   already   earn   LE   several.hundred   yuan

    'Whichever stock (he) bought, (he) would earn several hundred *yuan*s in two or three days.' (*Èmèng* 28)

(9) **不论**　　是　　木雕品、　　瓷制品、　　皮革品,
    bùlùn *shì   mùdiāopǐn   cízhìpǐn   pígépǐn*
    no.matter be   woodcarving porcelain   leather

都 做 得 很 好。(石头206)
dōu zuò de hěn hǎo
all do DE very good

'All products, whether they are woodcarving, porcelain, or leather products, are all well made.' (*Shítou* 206)

(10) 无论 使用 怎样 好 的 洗发乳， 都 必须
wúlùn *shǐyòng zěnyàng hǎo de xǐfàrǔ* **dōu** *bìxū*
no.matter use how good DE shampoo **all** must

将 头发 冲洗 干净。(报 1995年3月15日副刊 2 版)
jiāng tóufa chōngxǐ gānjìng
BA hair wash clean

'No matter how good the shampoo is, you must rinse your hair clean.' (*Bao*, Mar. 15, 1995, Issue no. 2, supplementary edition)

(11) 任凭 他 怎么 花言巧语，
rènpíng *tā zěnme huāyánqiǎoyǔ*
no.matter 3SG how sweet.words

我们 都 不会 上当。(华文教材 1B 60)
wǒmen ***dōu*** *bùhuì shàngdàng*
1PL **all** will.not be.fooled

'No matter what sweet words he spoke, we wouldn't be fooled.' (*Huáwénjiàocái* 1B, 60)

Sometimes, 也好 *yěhǎo* 'also good' or 也罢 *yěbà* 'also good' will be attached to the end of the secondary clause to imply this unconditional meaning. However, these type of secondary clauses have to be used in pairs, as illustrated by the following examples:

(12) 是 舅父 **也好，** 是 爱人 **也好，**
shì jiùfù **yěhǎo** *shì àirén* **yěhǎo**
be uncle **also.good** be spouse **also.good**

总 比 外人 好。(今后 101)
zǒng bǐ wàirén hǎo
always than stranger good

'Be it uncle or spouse, it is all better than a stranger.' (*Jīnhòu* 101)

(13) 青山　　　知　　我　　也罢，　不　　知　　我　　也罢，
　　　qīngshān　zhī　wǒ　yěbà　　bù　zhī　wǒ　yěbà
　　　Qingshan　know　1SG　also.good　NEG　know　1SG　also.good

　　　我　　料　　　　"青山　　　　见　　我　　应
　　　wǒ　liào　　　　qīngshān　　jiàn　wǒ　yīng
　　　1SG　understand　green.mountain　see　1SG　should

　　　如是"　　　的　　要求。(△自然37)
　　　rúshì　　　de　　yāoqiú
　　　this.way　DE　request

'I don't care if the Qingshan understands me or not. I understand his request.'[4] (△*Zìrán* 37)

Occasionally, both conjunctions like 无论 *wúlùn* 'no matter' and auxilary words like 也好 *yěhǎo* 'also good' are found in the same complex sentence, as shown next:

(14) **无论**　　　什么　　　事情，　工作　　　也好，
　　　wúlùn　　shénme　　shìqíng　gōngzuò　yěhǎo
　　　no matter　what　　thing　　job　　also.good

　　　学习　**也好**，　"空想"　　　和　　"盲干"　　都
　　　xuéxí　**yěhǎo**　kōngxiǎng　hé　　mánggàn　dōu
　　　study　**also.good**　daydream　and　blind.try　all

　　　不　　会　　使　　　人　　　进步。(华文教材 1B 135–136)
　　　bù　　huì　shǐ　　rén　　　jìnbù
　　　NEG　will　make　person　progress

'No matter what kind of things they are, be it work or study, daydreaming and rash action won't make people progress.' (*Huáwénjiàocái* 1B, 135–136)

3.11.4 Indicating Excluded Condition

There are three kinds of conditional complex sentence structure indicating an excluded condition:

1 The conjunction 除非 *chúfēi* 'unless' is used in the secondary clause, and the conjunction 否则 *fǒuzé* 'otherwise' is used in the primary

clause, meaning if the condition introduced by 除非 *chúfēi* 'unless' is excluded, then the result will be the one stated in the primary clause. For example:

(15) 除非   政府   明文禁止   香烟   入口，
     chúfēi zhèngfǔ   míngwénjìnzhǐ xiāngyān rùkǒu
     unless government officially.ban cigarette import

   宣布   吸烟   是   非法   的， **否则**   反   烟
   xuānbù   xīyān   shì fēifǎ   de   ***fǒuzé*** fǎn   yān
   announce smoking be   illegal DE   **otherwise** against smoking

   运动   就   难以   奏效   了。(华文教材 4B 10)
   yùndòng   jiù   nányǐ   zòuxiào   le
   movement then   difficult.to take.effect   LE

   'Unless the government officially bans the import of cigarettes and outlaws smoking, the anti-smoking campaign will not have any effect.' (*Huáwénjiàocái* 4B, 10)

In some cases, though quite uncommon, only 除非 *chúfēi* 'unless' remains in the secondary clause, and 否则 *fǒuzé* 'otherwise' in the primary clause is omitted. For example:

(16) 除非   有   子女   陪伴   着，
     chúfēi yǒu   zǐnǚ   péibàn   zhe
     unless   have sons.and.daughters accompany ZHE

   他们   不敢   冒然   去   搭   地铁。(风筝 13)
   tāmen bùgǎn   màorán qù   dā   dìtiě
   3PL   dare.not   rashly go   take   subway

   'They dare not venture to take the subway unless accompanied by their children.' (*Fēngzhēng* 13)

2 The second type of excluded conditional complex sentence contains no 除非 *chúfēi* 'unless' in the secondary clause, only conjunctions like 否则 *fǒuzé* 'otherwise', 不然 *bùrán* 'otherwise' or 要不然 *yàobùrán* 'otherwise' in the primary clause. The meaning expressed is similar to type 1, but the structure of the secondary clauses is slightly different. For example:

(17) 爸爸   要   我们   向   爷爷   道歉，
     bàba   yào   wǒmen   xiàng   yéye   dàoqiàn
     father want   1PL   to   grandfather apologise

否则 圣诞 舞会 就 不准 开 了。(牛车水 78)
fǒuzé shèngdàn wǔhuì jiù bùzhǔn kāi le
otherwise Christmas ball just forbid open LE

'Father required us to apologise to Grandfather, otherwise the Christmas party would not be allowed.' (*Niúchēshuǐ* 78)

(18) 在 机 上 不可 吃 得 太 饱, **不然**,
zài jī shàng bùkě chī de tài bǎo **bùrán**
at plane on cannot eat DE too full otherwise

你 会 变成 沙特 的 一 本 作品: 《呕吐》。(八方 10)
nǐ huì biànchéng shātè de yī běn zuòpǐn ǒutù
2SG will become Sartre DE one CL work Nausea

'Don't overeat on board, otherwise you will be the same as Sartre's *Nausea*.' (*Bāfāng* 10)

(19) 我 得 回去 了, **要不然**,
wǒ děi huíqù le **yàobùrán**
1SG must return LE otherwise

老 太太 又 要 唠叨 个 不停 了。(有缘 91)
lǎo tàitai yòu yào láodao gè bùtíng le
old lady again will chatter CL nonstop LE

'I have to go, otherwise my Mum will be chattering nonstop again.' (*Yǒuyuán* 91)

The condition excluded in (17) is 我们向爷爷道歉 *wǒmen xiàng yéye dàoqiàn* 'we apologise to Grandfather', rather than 爸爸要我们向爷爷道歉 *bàba yào wǒmen xiàng yéye dàoqiàn* 'Father required us to apologise to Grandfather'. If the conjunction 除非 *chúfēi* 'unless' were to be used, the part 爸爸要 *bàba yào* 'Father required us to' should be omitted, as in the following example:

(17)' **除非** 我们 向 爷爷 道歉,
chúfēi wǒmen xiàng yéye dàoqiàn
unless 1PL to grandfather apologise

否则 圣诞 舞会 就 不准 开 了。(牛车水 78)
fǒuzé shèngdàn wǔhuì jiù bùzhǔn kāi le
otherwise Christmas ball just forbid open LE

'Unless we apologise to Grandfather, the Christmas party would not be allowed.' (*Niúchēshuǐ* 78)

3 The third type of excluded conditional complex sentence contains a conjunction 除非 *chúfēi* 'unless' and a correlative adverb 才 *cái* 'then' in the secondary clause and the primary clause respectively. The meaning of this type is different from the first type, meaning that when the condition introduced by 除非 *chúfēi* 'unless' is excluded, the situation discussed in the primary clause will not appear. Therefore, it is very similar to the one showing only condition with 只有 *zhǐyǒu* 'only if' and 才 *cái* 'then', only that the perspective is different. For example:

(20) 除非   以   一   种   关切   旧   的   自己   的   怜悯
     chúfēi *yǐ*   *yī*   *zhǒng* *guānqiè* *jiù* *de*   *zìjǐ*   *de*   *liánmǐn*
     unless with   one   CL   concern old   DE   self   DE   mercy

     来   读   自己   前   几   个   星期   写   的   东西，
     lái   *dú*   *zìjǐ*   *qián*   *jǐ*   *gè*   *xīngqī* *xiě*   *de*   *dōngxī*
     come   read   oneself before several CL   week   write   DE   thing

     才   可以   忍住   笑。(渐行 55)
     cái   *kěyǐ*   *rěnzhù* *xiào*
     then   can   refrain   laugh

     'It is impossible to refrain from laughter unless you read what you have written several weeks ago with a kind of mercy for your old self.' (*Jiànxíng* 55)

(21) 除非   他   亲自   请   我，
     chúfēi *tā*   *qīnzì*   *qǐng*   *wǒ*
     unless 3SG   in.person invite   1SG

     我   才   会   出席。(华文教材 1B 59)
     wǒ   *cái*   *huì*   *chūxí*
     1SG   then   will   be.present

     'I won't be present unless he invites me in person.' (*Huáwénjiàocái* 1B, 59)

In examples (20) and (21), 非 *chúfēi* 'unless' is replaced with 只有 *zhǐyǒu* 'only if'; the meaning is basically the same, as shown next:

(20)' 只有   以   一   种   关切   旧   的   自己   的   怜悯
      zhǐyǒu *yǐ*   *yī*   *zhǒng* *guānqiè* *jiù* *de*   *zìjǐ*   *de*   *liánmǐn*
      only.if with   one   CL   concern old   DE   oneself DE   mercy

      来   读   自己   前   几   个   星期   写   的   东西，
      lái   *dú*   *zìjǐ*   *qián*   *jǐ*   *gè*   *xīngqī* *xiě*   *de*   *dōngxī*
      come   read   oneself before several CL   week   write   DE   thing

才　　可以　　忍住　　笑。
cái　　kěyǐ　　rěnzhù　　xiào
then　can　refrain　laugh

'You can refrain from laughter only if you read what you have written several weeks ago with a kind of mercy for your old self.'

(21)' 只有　他　亲自　请　我，
zhǐyǒu　tā　qīnzì　qǐng　wǒ
only.if　3SG　in.person　invite　1SG

我　才　会　出席。(华文教材 1B 59)
wǒ　cái　huì　chūxí
1SG　then　will　be.present

'I will be present only if he invites me in person.' (*Huáwénjiàocái* 1B, 59)

Examples (20) and (21) state the excluded conditions, while examples (20)' and (21)' emphasise the sole condition.

Conditional complex sentences showing excluded condition actually consist of three parts:

Unless *A*, then *B*, otherwise *C*.

One example containing the three parts is shown next:

(22) 除非　主人　意志　坚定，　才　有　扭转乾坤　的
chúfēi　zhǔrén　yìzhì　jiāndìng　cái　yǒu　niǔzhuǎnqiánkūn　de
unless　master　mind　solid　then　have　totally.change　DE

可能，　否则　消极地　宣传　不可能　收效。
　　　　　　　　　　　　　　　　　　　　　(小小鸟 41)
kěnéng　fǒuzé　xiāojíde　xuānchuán　bùkěnéng　shōuxiào
possibility　otherwise　negatively　advertise　impossible　work

'Negative propaganda will not work unless the master is determined, and only then will the situation be totally changed.' (*Xiǎoxiǎoniǎo* 41)

However, because of the principle of economy, the three parts rarely appear at the same time. Generally, two of them are sufficient. Types 1 and 2 only adopt part A and part C, while Type 3 adopts Part A and Part B. The aforementioned Types 1 and 2 are also called counter-intentional conditional complex sentence by some researchers.[5]

3.12 Causative Complex Sentences

Causative complex sentences express the relationship of cause and result. Sometimes, neither clause involves connective words, as in the following example:

(1) 昨夜　　淫雨绵绵，　　　　所有　的　配备　　都
    zuóyè　　yínyǔmiánmián　　suǒyǒu　de　pèibèi　dōu
    last.night it.rained.continuously all DE equipment all

    已　　　淋湿　　了。
    yǐ　　　línshī　　le
    already　get.wet　LE

    'As it rained continuously last night, all the equipment was wet.'

Particularly, the omission of connective words is very frequent in oral registers, for example:

(2) 我　　很　　累，　我　　先　　睡　　了。(金狮奖 210)
    wǒ　　hěn　　lèi　　wǒ　　xiān　　shuì　　le
    1SG　very　tired　1SG　first　sleep　LE

    'I am very tired, so I will go to bed first.' (*Jīnshījiǎng* 210)

(3) 我　　和　　家人　　　　都　　很　　忙，
    wǒ　　hé　　jiārén　　　　dōu　　hěn　　máng
    1SG　and　family.members　all　　very　busy

    没　　　太多　　　时间　　　看　　电视。(小学6B 6)
    méi　　tàiduō　　shíjiān　　kàn　　diànshì
    not.have too.much　time　　watch　TV

    'My family members and I are all very busy, so we don't have too much time to watch TV.' (*Xiǎoxué* 6B 6)

In conversation, the sentence in (2) will not be expressed with explicit conjunctions:

(2)' 因为　　我　　很　　累，　所以　我　　先　　睡　　了。
     yīnwèi　wǒ　　hěn　　lèi　　suǒyǐ　wǒ　　xiān　　shuì　　le
     because　1SG　very　tired　so　　1SG　first　sleep　LE

     'I am very tired, so I will just go to bed first.'

The same goes with sentence (3). However, in the written register, especially in argumentative writing, connective words are often used in the secondary or primary clause to explicitly show the cause-result relation. There are basically three patterns:

Pattern I: The causative relation is indicated by conjunctions like 因为 *yīnwèi* 'because', 由于 *yóuyú* 'due to' and 因 *yīn* 'because' in the secondary clause, and

所以 *suǒyǐ* 'so', 因此 *yīncǐ* 'therefore', 因而 *yīnér* 'so', 就 *jiù* 'then' and 便 *biàn* 'then' in the primary clause. For example:

(4) **因为** 还 年轻, **所以**, 喜欢 幻想。(扶轮 36)
    yīnwèi   hái   niánqīng   ***suǒyǐ***   xǐhuān   huànxiǎng
    because   still   young   **so**   like   fantasise
    'I like to fantasise because I am still young.' (*Fúlún* 36)

(5) **由于** 性格 内向,
    yóuyú   xìnggé   nèixiàng
    due.to   character   introverted

    因此 她 的 社交 活动 范围 不 广。(无3)
    yīncǐ   tā   de   shèjiāo   huódòng   fànwéi   bù   guǎng
    so   3SG   DE   social   activity   scope   NEG   extensive
    'Being an introvert, she doesn't have a wide range of social activities.' (*Wú* 3)

(6) **由于** 隔岸观火, **就** 难免
    yóuyú   gé'ànguānhuǒ   ***jiù***   nánmiǎn
    due.to   stand.aside.at.other's.trouble   **then**   unavoidable

    无法 掌握 全面 的 资料。(文艺 95)
    wúfǎ   zhǎngwò   quánmiàn   de   zīliào
    not.able.to   grasp   comprehensive   DE   information
    'It's hard for you to grasp all the information because you are indifferent to other people's troubles.' (*Wényì* 95)

Pattern II: Only conjunctions like 因为 *yīnwèi* 'because' and 由于 *yóuyú* 'due to' are used in the secondary clause, but no connective words are used in the primary clause. For example:

(7) **因为** 他们 不 懂 英文, 他们 的 活动
    yīnwèi   tāmen   bù   dǒng   yīngwén   tāmen   de   huódòng
    because   3PL   NEG   understand   English   3PL   DE   activity

    范围 只 限 在 唐人街 内。(风筝 12)
    fànwéi   zhǐ   xiàn   zài   tángrénjiē   nèi
    scope   only   restricted   at   Chinatown   inside
    'Their scope of activity was restricted to Chinatown because they do not understand English.' (*Fēngzheng* 12)

(8) **由于** 玫瑰 的 枝茎 上 长满 了 尖刺，
yóuyú méiguī de zhījīng shàng zhǎngmǎn le jiāncì
due.to rose DE stalk on grow LE sharp.thorns

初 当 采花者， 双手 常常 会
chū dāng cǎihuāzhě shuāngshǒu chángcháng huì
first being flower.picker both.hands often would

被 尖刺 弄 得 鲜血淋漓。(石头 141)
bèi jiāncì nòng de xiānxuèlínlí
BEI sharp.thorns make DE full.of.blood

'Due to the sharp thorns on the stalks of roses, the hands of new flower pickers would often be stabbed by the thorns and bleed.' (*Shítou* 141)

Pattern III: No conjunctions are used in the secondary clause. Only in the primary clause are connective words used, like 所以 *suǒyǐ* 'so', 因此 *yīncǐ* 'therefore' and 因而 *yīnér* 'so', as well as 于是 *yúshì* 'so', 以致 *yǐzhì* 'so as to' and 致使 *zhìshǐ* 'result in', for example:

(9) 我 爱 自己 的 文化， **所以** 当初 抱 着
wǒ ài zìjǐ de wénhuà **suǒyǐ** dāngchū bào zhe
1SG love oneself DE culture **so** at.that.time hold ZHE

不 愿 存 憾 的 心理 去 学 字。(渐行 49)
bù yuàn cún hàn de xīnlǐ qù xué zì
NEG want have regret DE mentality go learn characters

'I love my own culture, so I started my study with the thought that I should not make myself feel regret.' (*Jiànxíng* 49)

(10) 成君 的 诗歌 创作 忽略 了 诗
chéngjūn de shīgē chuàngzuò hūlüè le shī
Cheng Jun DE poem create overlook LE poem

的 独特性， **因而** 出现 像 上述
de dútèxìng **yīnér** chūxiàn xiàng shàngshù
DE uniqueness **therefore** occur like previously.mentioned

两 首 诗 的 缺点。(科学 6)
liǎng shǒu shī de quēdiǎn
two CL poem DE flaws

'Cheng Jun's poetry creation overlooked the uniqueness of poems, and therefore had flaws similar to the two poems mentioned earlier.' (*Kēxué*, 6)

(11) 他   决定   不   吵醒   她， **于是**， 又
    tā   juédìng bù   chǎoxǐng tā   **yúshì** yòu
    3SG decide NEG wake   3SG **so**   again

   轻飘飘地   走   出   了   病室。(断情剪 20)
   qīngpiāopiāode   zǒu   chū   le   bìngshì
   stealthily   walk out   LE   ward

   'He decided not to wake her up, so stealthily, he walked out of the ward again.' (*Duànqíngjiǎn* 20)

(12) 他   这   项   突然   的   声明   使   很多   人
    tā   zhè   xiàng tūrán   de   shēngmíng   shǐ   hěnduō   rén
    3SG this   CL   abrupt DE   statement   cause many   person

   感到   吃惊，   **以致**   引起   舆论   的   强烈
   gǎndào   chījīng   **yǐzhì** yǐnqǐ   yúlùn   de   qiángliè
   feel   surprised **so.as.to** incur public.opinion   DE   strong

   反应。(平心 25)
   fǎnyìng
   response

   'His abrupt statement has surprised many people, and has caused a strong response in public opinion.' (*Píngxīn* 25)

Of these three occasions, patterns I and II are more frequent, and pattern II is comparatively less.

Usually the secondary clause expressing cause appears at the sentence initial position, unless the primary clause needs to be emphasised. In that case, the secondary clause will be placed after the primary clause, adding supplementary information. For example:

(13) 原   文   没有   读到，   **因为**   这   本
    yuán   wén   méiyǒu   dúdào   **yīnwèi** zhè   běn
    original text   NEG   read   **because** this CL

   杂志   并不   公开   发售。(八方 15)
   zázhì   bìngbù   gōngkāi   fāshòu
   magazine NEG   publicly   put.on.sale

   'I have not read the original text, because this magazine is not publicly put on sale.' (*Bāfāng* 15)

Furthermore, there are some conventional patterns with initial result clauses. A most frequent one is 之所以 *zhīsuǒyǐ* 'with such a result'..., 是因为 *shìyīnwèi* 'it is because'..., for example:

(14) 它   **之所以**   能够   吸引   游客,   完全   **是**
     tā   *zhīsuǒyǐ*   *nénggòu* *xīyǐn* *yóukè*   *wánquán* *shì*
     3SG   with.such.a.result   able   attract visitors totally   be

因为   坟场   里   的   "居民"   声名显赫。(石头37)
yīnwèi   *fénchǎng* *lǐ* *de* *jūmín*   *shēngmíngxiǎnhè*
because   graveyard in   DE   residents renowned

'The reason why this graveyard was able to attract visitors was totally because of the fame of the 'residents' there.' (*Shítou* 37)

Sometimes, 之所以 *zhīsuǒyǐ* 'with such a result' is omitted in the primary clause, and only 是因为 *shìyīnwèi* 'it is because' remains in the secondary clause. In this case, the secondary clause has to be placed after the primary clause as well. For example:

(15) 我   恨   他,   **是**   **因为**   我   断定
     wǒ   *hèn*   *tā*   *shì*   *yīnwèi*   *wǒ*   *duàndìng*
     1SG   hate   3SG   be   because   1SG   assert

他   是   一   个   阴谋家。(太阳70)
tā   *shì*   *yī* *gè*   *yīnmóujiā*
3SG   be   one   CL   schemer

'I hate him because I'm sure that he is a schemer.' (*Tàiyáng* 70)

3.13 Inferential Complex Sentences

Inferential complex sentences express an inference, with the secondary clause stating a preexisting fact, and the primary clause stating an inferred conclusion based on the fact. There are two major types of inferential complex sentences:

1   The first type of inferential complex sentences is overtly marked by 既然 *jìrán* 'since' or 既*jì* 'since' in the secondary clause, and 就 *jiù* 'then' in the primary clause. For example:

(1) **既然**   你   要   留   他,
     jìrán   *nǐ*   *yào*   *liú*   *tā*
     since   2SG   want   keep   3SG

我   就   再   给   他   一   个   机会。(风雨 78)
wǒ   jiù   zài   gěi   tā   yī   gè   jīhuì
1SG   then   again   give   3SG   one   CL   chance

'Since you want to keep him, then I will give him another chance.'
(*Fēngyǔ* 78)

(2) 她   既然   说   有,
    tā   jìrán   shuō   yǒu
    3SG   since   say   have

我们   也   就   信   了。(梦 139)
wǒmen   yě   jiù   xìn   le
1PL   also   then   believe LE

'Since she said yes, we believed it.' (*Mèng* 139)

(3) 我们   既   已   得到   了,
    wǒmen   jì   yǐ   dédào   le
    1PL   since   already get   LE

就   应该   感到   满足。(短篇 71)
jiù   yīnggāi   gǎndào   mǎnzú
then   should   feel   satisfied

'We should be satisfied since we have got it.' (*Duǎnpiān* 71)

Sometimes, the primary clause takes the form of a rhetorical question showing the speaker's speculative opinion. Such kind of clauses often contain the adverb 又 *yòu* 'again'. For example:

(4) 既然   读   不   来,
    jìrán   dú   bù   lái
    since   read   NEG   come

又   何苦   去   读   呢?(追云 30)
yòu   hékǔ   qù   dú   ne
again   why.bother   go   read   SFP

'Why bother to read it when you can't?' (*Zhuīyún* 30)

2   The second type of inferential complex sentences use no connective words in the secondary clause, but only 可见 *kějiàn* 'it could be seen that' in the primary clause.

This type has a stronger inferential meaning. For example:

(5) 在 印度， 老鼠 的 数目 比 人口 还 多；
zài yìndù lǎoshǔ de shùmù bǐ rénkǒu hái duō
at India rats DE number than population still more

在 香港， 老鼠 连 人 都 咬； **可见**
zài xiānggǎng lǎoshǔ lián rén dōu yǎo **kějiàn**
at Hong.Kong rats even people all bite it.could.be.seen.that

这 种 动物 狂傲 到 了 人们 不能
zhè zhǒng dòngwù kuángào dào le rénmen bùnéng
this CL animal arrogant to LE people can.not

忍受 的 程度 了。(八方 4)
rěnshòu de chéngdù le
bear DE degree LE

'In India, there are more rats than people; in Hong Kong, rats even bite people; it's evident that this animal has become so arrogant that people are unable to endure it.' (*Bāfāng* 4)

Sometimes, 可见 *kějiàn* 'it could be seen that' can also be used in a more complex form, 由此可见 *yóucǐ kějiàn* 'it could be seen from this that':

(6) 在 先 阶段 政治 人物 眼中， 南大
zài xiān jiēduàn zhèngzhì rénwù yǎnzhōng nándà
at early stage political characters in.one's.view Nanyang.University

精神 是 华族 文化 的 代号； **由此**
jīngshén shì huázú wénhuà de dàihào **yóucǐ**
spirit be Chinese.people culture DE token **from.this**

可见， 政府 所说的 南大 精神
kějiàn zhèngfǔ suǒ-shuō-de nándà jīngshén
it.could. government SUO-talk-DE Nanyang. spirit
be.seen.that Universtiy

更多 时候 涉及 华文 课程 与 活动 如何
gèngduō shíhou shèjí huáwén kèchéng-yǔ-huódòng rúhé
more time involve Chinese curriculum.and.activity how

250 Composite Sentences

在	教育	系统	中	发挥	文化 作用。(小小鸟 111)
zài	jiàoyu	xìtǒng	zhōng	fāhuī	wénhuà-zuòyòng
at	education	system	in	play.a.role	cultural.effect

'In the view of politicians in the early stage, Nanyang University spirit was the symbol of Chinese culture. Therefore, the Nanyang University spirit mentioned by the government more often involved with how the Chinese curriculum and activities play a cultural role in the education system.' (*Xiǎoxiǎoniǎo* 111)

3.14 Purposive Complex Sentences

The secondary clause states the purpose, and the primary clause states the action needed to achieve that purpose. There are two types of purposive complex sentences with different orders between the two clauses:

3.14.1 *The Secondary Clause Preceding the Primary Clause*

When the secondary clause precedes the primary clause, it is usually introduced by 为了 *wèile* 'in order to'…:

(1)
	人们	**为了**	生活	得	更	舒适	更
	rénmen	**wèile**	shēnghuó	de	gèng	shūshì	gèng
	people	**in.order.to**	live	DE	more	comfortable	more

方便,	常常	在	不觉		中,
fāngbiàn	chángcháng	zài	bùjué		zhōng
convenient	often	at	unconsciousness		inside

破坏	了	大	自然	的	秩序。(壁虎 28)
pòhuài	le	dà	zìrán	de	zhìxù
break	LE	big	nature	DE	order

'In order to live more comfortably and conveniently, people often unconsciously break the order of nature.' (*Bìhǔ* 28)

3.14.2 *The Secondary Clause Following the Primary Clause*

With this order, the secondary purposive clause can be either with or without connective words:

1 The secondary purposive clause can contain no connective words, as illustrated by (2) and (3). Nevertheless, it is possible to add 为了 *wèile* 'in order to' to this clause and move it back to its original position at the beginning of the sentence, as illustrated by (2)' and (3)'.

(2) 工会　　　　应　　监督　　顾主，　　使　　他们　　跟
　　gōnghuì　　*yīng*　*jiāndū*　*gùzhǔ*　　*shǐ*　*tāmen*　*gēn*
　　Labour.Union　should　supervise　employer　make　3PL　catch

　　得　　上　　时代　　的　　步伐。(报 1995 年4月 29 日2版)
　　de　*shàng*　*shídài*　*de*　*bùfá*
　　DE　up　　time　DE　step

　　'The Labour Union should supervise the employers and make them keep pace with the time.' (*Bào*, Apr. 29, 1995, Issue no. 2)

(3) 清晨，　　我　　必须　　在　　六点钟　　前　　起身，
　　qīngchén　*wǒ*　*bìxū*　*zài*　*liùdiǎnzhōng*　*qián*　*qǐshēn*
　　early.morning　1SG　must　at　six.o'clock　before　get.up

　　帮忙　　父亲　　准备　　早餐。(短篇 36)
　　bāngmáng　*fùqīn*　*zhǔnbèi*　*zǎocān*
　　help　father　prepare　breakfast

　　'In the early morning, I must get up before six o'clock to help my father prepare breakfast.' (*Duǎnpiān* 36)

(2)' **为了**　　使　　他们　　跟　　得　　上
　　wèile　*shǐ*　*tāmen*　*gēn*　*de*　*shàng*
　　in.order.to　make　3PL　catch　DE　up

　　时代　　的　　步伐，　　工会　　应　　监督　　顾主。
　　shídài　*de*　*bùfá*　*gōnghuì*　*yīng*　*jiāndū*　*gùzhǔ*
　　time　DE　step　Labour.Union　should　supervise　employer

　　'In order to make the employers keep pace with the time, the Labour Union should supervise them.'

(3)' **为了**　　帮忙　　父亲　　准备　　早餐，　　清晨，
　　wèile　*bāngmáng*　*fùqīn*　*zhǔnbèi*　*zǎocān*　*qīngchén*
　　in.order.to　help　father　prepare　breakfast　early.morning

　　我　　必须　　在　　六点钟　　前　　起身。
　　wǒ　*bìxū*　*zài*　*liùdiǎnzhōng*　*qián*　*qǐshēn*
　　1SG　must　at　six.o'clock　before　get.up

　　'In order to help my father prepare breakfast, I must get up before six o'clock in the early morning.'

2 The secondary purposive clause can be overtly marked by some fixed connective words or phrases, such as the following:

Format 1:...,是为了 *shìwèile* 'it is in order to'..., for example:

(4) 许多　　人　　　不远千里　　　　　而　　来，
    xǔduō rén   bùyuǎnqiānlǐ   ér   lái
    many   people despite.a.thousand.miles LIG come

是为了　　　要　　听　　他　　的　　演说。(华文教材 4A 70)
shìwèile　yào　tīng　tā　de　yǎnshuō
it.is.in.order.to want listen 3SG DE speech

'Many people come from far away just in order to listen to his speech.' (*Huáwénjiàocái* 4A, 70)

Format 2:...,为的是 *wèideshì* 'in order that'..., for example:

(5) 他们　　长年累月　　　　地　　工作，　省吃俭用，　　　**为的是**
    tāmen chángniánlěiyuè   de   gōngzuò shěngchījiǎnyòng **wèideshì**
    3PL   year.after.year   DE   work   being.thrifty   **in.order.that**

维持　　唐山　　　的　　父母　　和　　亲人　　　的　　生活。(回忆 4)
wéichí tāngshān de   fùmǔ   hé   qīnrén   de   shēnghuó
sustain Tangshan DE   parent and   relative DE   life

'They worked hard year after year and lived thriftily in order to sustain the lives of their parents and relatives in Tangshan.' (*Huíyì* 4)

Format 3:...,以（便）*yǐ (biàn)* 'so as to'..., for example:

(6) 春节　　　　　前夕，　家庭主妇们　　　　都　　要　　把　　家里
    chūnjié   qiánxī jiātíngzhǔfumen   dōu   yào   bǎ   jiālǐ
    Spring.Festival eve   housewives   all   will BA   house

大　　扫除　　一　　番，　**以便**　除旧迎新。(母亲 120)
dà   sǎochú   yī   fān   **yǐbiàn** chújiùyíngxīn
big clean   one CL   **so.as.to** clear.away.the.old.and.usher.in.the.new

'On Spring Festival Eve, housewives will clean their homes thoroughly in order to clear away the old and usher in the new.' (*Mǔqīn* 120)

Format 4:...,以免 *yǐmiǎn* 'lest'..., for example:

(7) 大多数　　年轻　　　的　　夫妇　　不　　愿意　　太早　　生儿育女，
    dàduōshù　niánqīng　de　　fūfù　　bù　　yuànyì　tài-zǎo　shēngéryùnǚ
    most　　　young　　DE　couple　NEG　willing　too.early　have.a.baby

以免　　个人　　　自由　　受到　　　束缚。(华文教材 4A 11)
yǐmiǎn　gèrén　　zìyóu　　shòudào　shùfù
lest　　　personal　freedom　get　　　bound

'Most young couples are unwilling to have a baby too early, lest their personal freedom should be restricted.' (*Huáwénjiàocái* 4A, 11)

Format 5:..., 免得 *miǎnde* 'so as not to'..., for example:

(8) 没有　　　事　　　　就　　不要　　开开关关　　　　的，
    méiyǒu　　shì　　　jiù　　bùyào　kāikāiguānguān　de
    not.have　business　just　don't　open.and.close　DE

免得　　　　弄坏　　　了　　锁头。(牛车水 111)
miǎnde　　　nònghuài　le　　suǒtóu
so.as.not.to　break　　　LE　lock

'Don't open and close if not necessary, in case you break the lock.' (*Niúchēshuǐ* 111)

Format 6: ..., 目的是 *mùdishì* 'with the purpose of'..., for example:

(9) 哥打巴鲁　　的　　这　　　座　　纪念碑　　　是　　由
    gēdǎbālǔ　　de　　zhè　　zuò　　jìniànbēi　　shì　　yóu
    Kota.Baru　　DE　　this　CL　　monument　　SHI　　by

日本　　出钱　　　兴建　　　　的，　**目的是**　　　　　　"祝愿
rìběn　chūqián　xīngjiàn　　de　　**mùdishì**　　　　　　zhùyuàn
Japan　fund　　establish　DE　　with.the.purpose.of　wish

永远　　　和平　　与　　自由"。(沦陷 6)
yǒngyuǎn　hépíng　yǔ　　zìyóu
forever　　peace　and　freedom

'This monument in Kota Baru was funded by Japan with the wish of having peace and freedom forever.' (*Lúnxiàn* 6)

3.15 Temporal Complex Sentences

In a temporal complex sentence, the secondary adverbial clause specifies the time when the event or action mentioned in the primary clause takes place. The time meaning is not expressed with a noun phrase indicating time; rather, it is indicated by a reference event or situation described by the secondary clause. For example:

(1) 吃　饱　晚饭，　行李　终于　平安　到达。(冰灯 132)
    chī　bǎo　wǎnfàn　xínglǐ　zhōngyú　píngān　dàodá
    eat　full　dinner　luggage　finally　safely　arrive
    'The luggage finally arrived safely after dinner.' (*Bīngdēng* 132)

(2) 赶　到　学校，
    gǎn　dào　xuéxiào
    hurry　arrive　school

    我　已　迟到　约　十五　分钟。(短篇 13)
    wǒ　yǐ　chídào　yuē　shíwǔ　fēnzhōng
    1SG　already　late　about　fifteen　minute
    'When I arrived at school in a hurry, I was about fifteen minutes late.'
    (*Duǎnpiān* 13)

In sentence (1), the first clause 吃饱晚饭 *chībǎo wǎnfàn* 'finished eating dinner' specifies the time when the event described in the second clause takes place, that is, 'the luggage arrived safely'. In sentence (2), the first clause 赶到学校 *gǎndào xuéxiào* 'arrived in school' states the time when the situation described in the second clause occurs, that is 'I was about fifteen minutes late'. The following are more temporal complex sentences:

(3) 过　了　几　分钟，
    guò　le　jǐ　fēnzhōng
    pass　LE　a.few　minute

    乙　和尚　气愤愤　地　跑　进　房　来。(八方 37)
    yǐ　héshang　qìfènfèn　de　pǎo　jìn　fáng　lái
    second　monk　angrily　DE　run　into　house　come
    'After a few minutes, the second monk angrily hurried into the house.'
    (*Bāfāng* 37)

(4) 众人　唱　完，
    zhòngrén　chàng　wán
    everybody　sing　finish

    淑珍　自己　独　唱　了　一　遍。(追云 25)
    shūzhēn　zìjǐ　dú　chàng　le　yī　biàn
    Shuzhen　oneself　alone　sing　LE　one　CL
    'Shuzhen sang the song alone after everybody had sung.' (*Zhuīyún* 25)

(5) 走　　下　　台阶，　　已　　是　　十一点　　左右。(冰灯 40)
　　 zǒu　xià　táijiē　　yǐ　shì　shíyīdiǎn　zuǒyòu
　　 walk down steps　already be eleven.o'clock about
　　 'It was already about eleven o'clock when I walked down the steps.'
　　 (*Bīngdēng* 40)

3.16 Correlative Complex Sentences

In a correlative complex sentence, the meaning of the primary clause changes as the meaning of the secondary clause does. This type of complex sentence is always found with identical constituents in the two clauses to show the semantic connection, for example:

(1) 他们　开　**多少**　价，　我们　就　给　**多少**。(回忆 44)
　　 tāmen　kāi　**duōshǎo**　jià　wǒmen　jiù　gěi　**duōshǎo**
　　 3PL offer **how.much** price 1PL just give **how.much**
　　 'We will pay them whatever price they offer.' (*Huíyì* 44)

In (1) the two clauses correlate with each other with the same phrase 多少 *duōshǎo* 'how much'. This sentence is simply saying that if they offer 60 *yuan*, then we'll pay them 60 *yuan*; if they offer 70 *yuan*, then we'll pay them 70 *yuan*; and if they offer 80 *yuan*, then we'll pay them 80 *yuan*. Anyway the money we pay will change as the price they offer does. One more example is given in (2):

(2) 目的地　**越**　是　靠近，
　　 mùdìdì　**yuè**　shì　kàojìn
　　 destination **more** be close

　　 心情　**越**　是　激荡　紧张。(冰灯 131)
　　 xīnqíng　**yuè**　shì　jīdàng　jǐnzhāng
　　 mood **more** be excited nervous
　　 'The closer the destination is, the more excited and nervous the mood is.'
　　 (*Bīngdēng* 131)

The clauses in (2) are connected through the word 越 *yuè* 'the more'. The whole sentence means that the mood changes as the destination gets closer.

Correlative complex sentences can be divided into two subtypes based on the types of connecting words they use:

In the first type, the two clauses share the same interrogative pronoun as in (1), and also:

256   *Composite Sentences*

(3) 你 爱 呆 **多久**, **就** 呆 **多久**。(报 1995年6月
                                                19日副刊7版)
   nǐ   ài   dāi ***duōjiǔ***   jiù   dāi ***duōjiǔ***
   2SG love stay **how.long** just stay **how.long**
   'Stay as long as you like.' (*Bào*, June 19, 1995, Issue no. 7, supplemental edition)

(4) **哪儿** 请 我, 我 就 到 **哪儿** 去。(牛车水 37)
   nǎer qǐng wǒ   wǒ   jiù dào ***nǎer*** qù
   where invite 1SG 1SG just go **where** go
   'I will go wherever I am invited.' (*Niúchēshuǐ* 37)

In the second type, the two clauses are connected by 越 *yuè* 'the more', as in (2), and also:

(5) 我 **越** 在意, 就 痛 得 **越** 厉害。(天长 94)
   wǒ   ***yuè*** zàiyì   jiù   tòng de   ***yuè*** lìhai
   1SG **more** care   just ache DE **more** terrible
   'The more I care, the more terribly I ache.' (*Tiāncháng* 94)

(6) 人 **越** 有 钱,
   rén ***yuè*** yǒu qián
   people **more** have money

   越 是 空虚 得 可怕。(梦 101)
   yuè shì kōngxū de kěpà
   more be empty DE terrible
   'The richer people are, the more terribly empty they are.' (*Mèng* 101)

3.17 Multi-Layer Complex Sentences

In the previous sections about compound sentences or complex sentences, most examples given include only two clauses. However, whether in oral or written registers, it is relatively common for a complex sentence to include a number of clauses, so as to express more complicated ideas. For example:

(1)a 国 有 国法,   b 校 有 校规,
   guó yǒu guófǎ   xiào yǒu xiàoguī
   country have country.law   school have school.rule

c	今天	请	你	来，	d	是	要	你	为
	jīntiān	qǐng	nǐ	lái		shì	yào	nǐ	wèi
	today	invite	2SG	come		SHI	want	2SG	for

杨仲钦　　　签　一　份　行为　　　保证书。(跳舞 37)
yángzhòngqīn　qiān yī fèn xíngwéi　bǎozhèngshū
Yang.Zhongqin　sign one CL behaviour　guarantee

'A country has its own laws and a school its own regulations. We ask you to come today to sign a behaviour guarantee for Yang Zhongqin.' (*Tiàowǔ* 37)

(2)a 国家　　富强，　　　b 人民　就　安乐；
　　 guójiā　fùqiáng　　　　 rénmín jiù ānlè
　　 country rich.and.powerful people just safe.and.happy

　　c 国家　衰弱，　　　　d 人民　就　痛苦。(伦理·
　　　　　　　　　　　　　　　　　　　　　　　中三99)
　　 guójiā shuāiruò　　　　rénmín jiù tòngkǔ
　　 country weak　　　　　people just painful

'If the country is prosperous and powerful, the people will be safe and happy, while if the state is weak, the people will suffer.' (*Lúnlǐ* III 99)

Sentence (1) comes from a dialogue and sentence (2) comes from an exposition, both being multilayer complex sentences. It's worth noting that the four clauses in each sentence do not belong to the same level syntactically. Sentences (1) and (2) should be respectively analyzed as:

```
         a...,    b...,    c...,    d...
              └─────┘         └─────┘      cause-result relationship
(1)            1                 2
              └───┘  └───┘  └───┘  └───┘   3 and 4: coordinate relationship
               3      4      5      6      5 and 6: purposive relationship


         a...,    b...,    c...,    d...
              └─────┘         └─────┘      coordinate relationship
(2)            1                 2
              └───┘  └───┘  └───┘  └───┘   3 and 4 assumptive relationship
               3      4      5      6      5 and 6 assumptive relationship
```

The following example (3) also includes four clauses:

(3)a 没有　　锣鼓，　　b 没有　　乐队，
　　 méiyǒu　luógǔ　　　　méiyǒu　yuèduì
　　 not.have gongdrum　　not.have band

258 *Composite Sentences*

    c 没有   花圈，   d 没有   纸钱。(太阳 8)
       méiyǒu *huāquān*   *méiyǒu* *zhǐqián*
       not.have wreath   not.have paper.money
       'No gong or drum, no band, no wreath, and no paper money.' (*Tàiyang*, 8)

However, this is not a multilayer complex sentence, because the four clauses are on the same level syntactically. (3) should be analysed as:

(3)   a...,   b...,   c...,   d...
        1   2   3   4   1, 2, 3 and 4: coordinate relationship

It should be clear from these examples that a multilayer complex sentence is made of three or more clauses of different syntactic levels. The following are more such examples of multilayer complex sentences:

(4)a 适婚   女子   找不到   老公,
    shìhūn   *nǚzǐ*   *zhǎobùdào* *lǎogōng*
    marriageable women can.not.find husband

   b 原因   之一   是   太过   保守,
    yuányīn *zhīyī* *shì* *tàiguò* *bǎoshǒu*
    reason one.of be too.much conservative

   c 因此   缺少   社交   机会。(报 1995年3月14日15版)
    yīncǐ *quēshǎo* *shèjiāo* *jīhuì*
    therefore lack socialise opportunity
    'Some women of marriageable age cannot find a partner, one reason for which lies in that they are over conservative, thus lacking social opportunities.' (*Bào*, Mar. 14, 1995, Issue no. 15)

(5)a 他   比   我   先   走,   b 是   他   的   福;
    tā *bǐ* *wǒ* *xiān* *zǒu*   *shì* *tā* *de* *fú*
    3SG than 1SG first leave   be 3SG DE bliss

   c 要是   我   先   走   啊,
    yàoshì *wǒ* *xiān* *zǒu* *a*
    if 1SG first leave SFP

   d 你们   才   惨   呢! (今后152)
    nǐmen *cái* *cǎn* *ne*

	2PL	just	miserable	SFP			

'It is a blessing for him to have left before me. You will be truly miserable if I leave first!' (*Jīnhòu* 152)

(6)a

只要	有人	能	使用	一流	的
zhǐyào	yǒurén	néng	shǐyòng	yīliú	de
as.long.as	someone	can	use	stellar	DE

技巧	与	语言	文字	来	创作,
jìqiǎo	yǔ	yǔyán	wénzì	lái	chuàngzuo
technique	and	language	word	come	create

b

而且	对	自己	的	社会	人民,	甚至	全	世界
érqiě	duì	zìjǐ	de	shèhuì	rénmín	shènzhì	quán	shìjiè
and	to	oneself	DE	society	people	even	all	world

全	人类	有	不平凡	的	认识,
quán	rénlèi	yǒu	bùpíngfán	de	rènshi
all	human	have	extraordinary	DE	knowledge

c

以后	一定	会	有	一流	作家
yǐhòu	yīdìng	huì	yǒu	yīliú	zuòjiā
later	must	will	have	stellar	writer

带	着	伟大	的	作品	出现,
dài	zhe	wěidà	de	zuòpǐn	chūxiàn
bring	ZHE	great	DE	works	appear

d

所以	问题	不	是	客观	的	环境,
suǒyǐ	wèntí	bù	shì	kèguān	de	huánjìng
so	problem	NEG	be	objective	DE	environment

e

而	是	作家	自己。(新华文学274)
ér	shì	zuòjiā	zìjǐ
but	be	writer	oneself

'As long as someone can use stellar skills and language to create, and have an extraordinary understanding of their own society and people, even the entire world and mankind, there will definitely be some stellar writers with their masterpieces. So the problem is not the objective environment, but writers themselves.' (*Xīnhuáwénxué* 274)

(7) a 孟子　　相信　　人性　　　　是　善的，
　　　 mèngzǐ　xiāngxìn　rénxìng　　shì　shànde
　　　 Mencius　believe　human.nature　be　kind

b 所以　要　　人　　发展　　善性，
　 suǒyǐ　yào　rén　fāzhǎn　shànxìng
　 so　　want　people　develop　kindness

c 以　　达到　　至善；
　 yǐ　　dádào　　zhìshàn
　 to　　reach　　the.most.kind

d 荀子　　相信　　人性　　　　是　恶的，
　 xúnzǐ　xiāngxìn　rénxìng　　shì　ède
　 Xunzi　believe　human.nature　be　evil

e 所以　要　　人　　节制　　恶性，
　 suǒyǐ　yào　rén　jiézhì　èxìng
　 so　　want　people　curb　evil

f 以　　由　　恶　　变　　善。(伦理·中三 20)
　 yǐ　　yóu　　è　　biàn　　shàn
　 to　　from　evil　turn　kind

'Mencius believes that human nature is kind, so people should develop this nature to reach the state of perfect kindness. Xunzi believes that human nature is evil, so people should curb their evil nature and turn it into kindness.' (*Lúnlǐ III* 20)

The analysis of the structures of Examples (4) to (7) is shown as follows:

(4)　a ..., b ..., c ...

　　　a...,　　b...,　　c...,
　　　└─1─┘　└─2─┘　　cause-result relationship
　　　　　　└─3─┘└─4─┘　cause-result relationship

　　　a...,　b...;　c...,　d...
(5)　└──1──┘　└──2──┘　coordinate relationship
　　 └3┘└4┘　└5┘└6┘　3 and 4 assumptive relationship
　　　　　　　　　　　　　 5 and 6 assumptive relationship

(6) a ..., b ..., c ..., d ..., e ...,

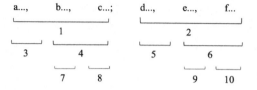

cause-result relationship

3 and 4 conditional relationship;
5 and 6 contrastive relationship
progressive relationship

(7) a ..., b ..., c ..., d ..., e ..., f ...

```
         a...,      b...,     c...;      d...,     e...,     f...
         └──────────┬─────────────┘      └──────────┬─────────────┘
                    1                               2
         ┌─────┐  ┌─────┐      ┌─────┐   ┌─────┐  ┌─────┐
         3        4              5         6        
       ┌───┐  ┌───┐           ┌───┐   ┌───┐
        7      8                9       10
```

coordinate relationship
3 and 4 cause-result relationship;
5 and 6 cause-result relationship
7 and 8 purposive relationship;
9 and 10 purposive relationship

Analyzing multilayer complex sentences is conducive to the understanding of an article. The following three points should be noted.

Firstly, the clauses in a complex sentence are always connected by logical relationships, which, thereby, is the foremost part that needs sufficient attention in the analysis.

Secondly, the clauses are combined hierarchically, an idea which should be kept in mind so as to figure out the structure of the sentence.

Thirdly, the logical relationship between clauses are often flagged by connective words such as 因为 *yīnwèi* 'because', 所以 *suǒyǐ* 'so', 虽然 *suīrán* 'although', 但是 *dànshì* 'but', 不但 *bùdàn* 'not only', 而且 *érqiě* 'but also', 即使 *jíshǐ* 'even if', 也 *yě* 'also' and so on, insomuch that these words could be taken full advantage of in the analysis. For example:

(8)a 由于   石油   大   幅度   涨价，
      yóuyú   *shíyóu* *dà* *fúdù* *zhǎngjià*
      due.to   oil   big   range   increase.price

  b   因此   各国   为了   解决   经济   衰退、   工业
      yīncǐ *gèguó*   *wèile*   *jiějué* *jīngjì* *shuāituì* *gōngyè*
      therefore each.country in.order.to solve economic recess   industry

      生产   萎缩   和   失业率   高   等   难题，
      shēngchǎn *wěisuō* *hé* *shīyèlǜ*   *gāo*   *děng* *nántí*
      production shrink   and   unemployment.rate high etc.   problem

  c   只好   采取   各种   措施，
      zhǐhǎo *cǎiqǔ*   *gèzhǒng* *cuòshī*
      can.only take   various   measure

d 限制　　外国　　货物　　入口，
　xiànzhì　wàiguó　huòwù　rùkǒu
　restrict　foreign　goods　import

e 以　　扶助　　本国的　　　工商业，
　yǐ　　fúzhù　běnguóde　gōngshāngyè
　to　support　domestic　industry.and.commerce

f 于是　　　贸易保护主义　　　　也　　就　　应运而生
　yúshì　màoyìbǎohùzhǔyì　yě　　jiù　yìngyùnérshēng
　therefore　trade.protectionism　also　then　come.into.being

了。(华文教材 4A119)
le
LE

'Due to the soaring oil prices, countries which aspire to solve problems like economic recession, the shrinking of industrial production and high unemployment rates will have to take all kinds of measures to impose restrictions on the import of foreign goods so as to support domestic industry and commerce. Trade protectionism, therefore, comes into being.'
(*Huáwénjiàocái* 4A, 19)

Example (8) includes six clauses complicatedly connected at different levels. Fortunately, we could make use of the connective words – 由于 *yóuyú* 'due to', 因此 *yīncǐ* 'therefore', 为了 *wèile* 'in order to', 只好 *zhǐhǎo* 'can only', 以 *yǐ* 'in order to', 于是 *yúshì* 'so as to' – in some clauses to analyze the whole sentence. Yet, the logical relationship between the clauses is still not evident and needs further analysis. Clause (a) includes a conjunction 由于 *yóuyú* 'due to' indicating cause, and this implies that it will be followed by a result clause; however, this is not easy to decide, since both clause (b) and clause (f) contain result conjunctions, 因此 *yīncǐ* 'therefore' and 于是 *yúshì* 'so as to' respectively. Given that no other clause but (a) comes before clause (b), it could be inferred that the result clause for (a) can only be clause (b). Then the next issue to be addressed is the scope of 因此 *yīncǐ* 'therefore' in clause (b). It is noted that clause (b) also contains another purposive conjunction, 为了 *wèile* 'in order to', which obviously correlates with the connective word 只好 *zhǐhǎo* 'can only' in the follow-up clause (c), the only clause that 只好 *zhǐhǎo* 'can only' covers. Hence, clause (b) and clause (c) are of a purposive relationship. Furthermore, clauses (d) and (e) are related to clause (c) through cyclic purposive relationships, with which they are ultimately connected with clause (b) as well. Clause (d) 限制外国货物入口 *xiànzhì wàiguó huòwù rùkǒu* 'taking various measures to impose restrictions on the import of foreign goods' states the purpose of clause (c) 采取各种措施 *cǎiqǔ gèzhǒng cuòshī* 'taking various measures', while clause (e) 以辅助本国的工商业 *yǐ fúzhù běnguóde gōngshāngyè* states the purpose of clauses (c) and (d) together. That is to say, the resulting clause introduced by 因此 *yīncǐ* 'therefore' is expressed through a purposive complex clause, which is made of clauses (b), (c), (d) and (e). Clause (f), introduced with 于是 *yúshì* 'so as to', describes the final result, and all clauses coming before it serve as its cause. This analysis is shown in the following hierarchical diagram:

(8)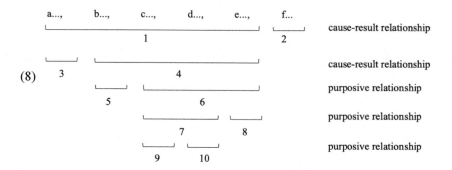

3.18 Connective Words in Composite Sentences

3.18.1 *Connective Words and Conjunctions*

To begin with, connective words and conjunctions are two different concepts. Conjunctions refer to words specifically used to connect words, phrases, clauses or sentences, without taking on any syntactic roles. Connective words refer to words specifically used in composite sentences to connect clauses. Connective words include, but are not restricted to conjunctions.

3.18.2 *Connective Words in Complex Sentences*

1 Conjunctions

Conjunctions are most commonly used connective words, such as 并 *bìng* 'and', 而 *ér* 'but', 并且 *bìngqiě* 'and', 而且 *érqiě* 'but also', 不但 *bùdàn* 'not only', 不仅 *bùjǐn* 'not only', 或者 *huòzhě* 'or', 还是 *háishì* 'still' and 与其 *yǔqí* 'rather than' in compound sentences; 虽然 *suīrán* 'although', 尽管 *jǐnguǎn* 'although', 但是 *dànshì* 'but', 可是 *kěshì* 'but', 即使 *jíshǐ* 'even if', 如果 *rúguǒ* 'if', 假如 *jiǎrú* 'if', 只要 *zhǐyào* 'as long as', 只有 *zhǐyǒu* 'only if', 不论 *bùlùn* 'no matter', 无论 *wúlùn* 'no matter', 因为 *yīnwèi* 'because', 由于 *yóuyú* 'due to', 所以 *suǒyǐ* 'so', 因此 *yīncǐ* 'therefore', 既然 *jìrán* 'since', 为了 *wèile* 'in order to' in complex sentences.

2. Adverbs

Some adverbs are also commonly used as connective words. The most common ones are 也 *yě* 'also', 又 *yòu* 'again', 一 *yī* 'as soon as', 就 *jiù* 'then', 即 *jí* 'then', 便 *biàn* 'then', 更 *gèng* 'even more', 尤其 *yóuqí* 'especially', 还 *hái* 'also', 却 *què* 'but', 才 *cái* 'then', 都 *dōu* 'all', 越 *yuè* 'the more', 再 *zài* 'again' and so on. For example:

(1) 丽美　是　我　的　邻居，
    lìměi　shì　wǒ　de　línjū
    Limei　be　1SG　DE　neighbour

   也　是　我　的　玩伴。(好儿童3B49)
   yě　shì　wǒ　de　wánbàn
   also　be　1SG　DE　playmate

   'Limei is my neighbour and playmate.' (*Hǎoértóng* 3B, 49) (conjunctive compound sentence)

(2) 田田　看看　爸爸，
    tiántian　kànkàn　bàba
    TianTian　look.at　father

   又　看看　妈妈。(短篇 43)
   yòu　kànkàn　mama
   also　look.at　mother

   'TianTian looks at his father and then at his mother.' (*Duǎnpiān* 43) (conjunctive compound sentence)

(3) 学生　一　见　老师　带　了　圣经　来，
    xuésheng　yī　jiàn　lǎoshī　dài　le　shèngjīng　lái
    student　as.soon.as　see　teacher　bring　LE　Bible　come

   就　嚷　着　要　老师　讲　耶稣　的　故事。(梦 40)
   jiù　rǎng　zhe　yào　lǎoshī　jiǎng　yēsū　de　gùshi
   then　clamour　ZHE　want　teacher　tell　Jesus　DE　story

   'As soon as the students saw that teacher had brought the *Bible*, students clamoured for the teacher to tell the story of Jesus.' (*Mèng* 40) (consecutive conjunctive sentence)

(4) 你　如果　逼　我　回去，我　就　立刻
    nǐ　rúguǒ　bī　wǒ　huíqù　wǒ　jiù　lìkè
    2SG　if　force　1SG　go.back　1SG　then　immediately

   飞　回去　澳洲。(大胡子 47)
   fēi　huíqù　àozhōu
   fly　return　Australia

   'If you force me to go back, I will fly back to Australia immediately.' (*Dàhúzi* 47) (hypothetical complex sentence)

(5) 既然   你   要   留   他，
    jìrán nǐ   yào   liú   tā
    since 2SG want.to keep 3SG

    我   就   再   给   他   一   个   机会。(风雨 78)
    wǒ   jiù   zài   gěi   tā   yī   gè   jīhuì
    1SG then again give 3SG one CL   chance

    'Since you want to keep him, then I will give him another chance.' (*Fēngyǔ* 78) (inferential complex sentence)

(6) 一   踏   进   家   门，   黄雪嫘   即
    yī   tà   jìn   jiā   mén   huángxuěléi   jí
    as.soon.as step into home door   Huang Xuelei   immediately

    向   黄老太太   报讯。(断情剪 8)
    xiàng   huánglǎotàitài   bàoxùn
    towards old.lady.huang   report

    'As soon as she stepped into the house, Huang Xuelei reported to old lady Huang immediately.' (*Duànqíngjiǎn* 8) (consecutive conjunctive sentence)

(7) 婆婆   一   啰唆，   她   便   跑   回
    pópo   yī   luōsuō   tā   biàn   pǎo   huí
    mother.in.law as.soon.as blathering 3SG then   run   back

    娘家   去。(追云 34)
    niángjiā   qù
    parents'home go

    'As soon as her mother-in-law started blathering, she ran back to her own parents' house.' (*Zhuīyún* 34) (consecutive conjunctive sentence)

(8) 他   不   懂得   爱惜   自己，
    tā   bù   dǒngdé   àixī   zìjǐ
    3SG NEG know   love   oneself

    更   不   懂得   照顾   别人。(梦 45)
    gèng   bù   dǒngé   zhàogù   biérén
    even.more NEG know   take.care.of others

    'He doesn't know how to love himself, let alone take care of others.' (*Mèng* 45) (progressive conjunctive sentence)

(9) 也许，   我   秉承   了   太多   父亲   的   性格，
    yéxǔ   wǒ   bǐngchéng le   tàiduō   fùqīn   de   xìnggé
    maybe   1SG   inherit   LE   too.much father   DE   character

   尤其   是   那   一   股   倔强。(青春 116)
   yóuqí   shì   nà   yī   gǔ   juéjiàng
   especially be   that   one   CL   stubbornness

   'Maybe I have inherited too much of my father's character, especially the stubbornness.' (*Qīngchūn* 116) (progressive compound sentence)

(10) 研究   和   出版，   不但   需要   人力、   时间，   **还**
     yánjiū   hé   chūbǎn   bùdàn   xūyào   rénlì   shíjiān **hái**
     research and   publish   not.only need   manpower time   **also**

    须   有   资金   在   背后   支助。(风筝 110)
    xū   yǒu   zījīn   zài   bèihòu   zhīzhù
    need   have   capital   at   back   support.and.help

    'Research and publication not only cost manpower and time, but also need to be supported by capital.' (*Fēngzheng* 110) (progressive compound sentence)

(11) 媚媚   谈   过   她   太多，   **却**   忘   了   告诉
     mèimèi tán   guò   tā   tài duō   **què** wàng   le   gàosù
     Meimei talk GUO   3SG   too much **but** forget LE   tell

    我   她   长   得   如何。(想飞 40)
    wǒ   tā   zhǎng   de   rúhé
    1SG   3SG   grow   DE   how

    'Meimei had talked about her too much, but she forgot to tell me how she looked like.' (*Xiǎngfēi* 40) (adversative complex sentence)

(12) 只有   和平共处，   人类   **才**   能   自救。(伦理·中
                                                                    四 91)
     zhǐyǒu   hépíngòngchù   rénlèi   **cái**   néng   zìjiù
     only.if coexist.peacefully human   **just** able   save.oneself

    'Only by living in peace with each other can human beings save themselves.' (*Lúnlǐ* IV 91) (conditional complex sentence)

(13) 不论   是   木雕品、   瓷制品、   皮革品，
     bùlùn   shì   mùdiāopǐn   cízhìpǐn   pígépǐn
     no.matter be   woodcarving   porcelain   leather

都 做 得 很 好。(石头206)
dōu zuò de hěn hǎo
all do DE very good

'All products, whether they are woodcarving, porcelain, or leather products, are all well made.' (*Shítou* 206) (conditional complex sentence)

(14) 我 越 在意， 就 痛 得 越 厉害。(天长 94)
wǒ yuè zàiyì jiù tòng de yuè lìhai
1SG more care just ache DE more terrible

'The more I care, the more terribly I ache.' (*Tiāncháng* 94) (correlative complex sentence)

(15) 外国 再 好， 也 不 比
wàiguó zài hǎo yě bù bǐ
foreign.country no.matter.how good also NEG than

家 里 好。(金狮奖 117)
jiā li hǎo
home inside good

'No matter how good a foreign country is, it is not better than home.' (*Jīnshījiǎng* 117) (adversative complex sentence)

3. Pronouns

Pronouns 那*nà* 'that' and 那么*nàme* 'then' are commonly used as connective words, for example:

(16) 买 半独立的、 有 花园 的 双层洋房，
mǎi bàndúlìde yǒu huāyuán de shuāngcéngyángfáng
buy semi-detached have garden DE duplex

那 就 不会 再 给 楼上 芳邻 吵到。(吾土·戏剧 128)
nà jiù bùhuì zài gěi lóushàng fānglín chǎodào
that then cannot again GEI upstairs neighbour disturb

'If you buy a semi-detached duplex with a garden, then you won't be bothered by the neighbours upstairs.' (*Wútǔ* (drama) 128) (hypothetical complex sentence)

(17) 假如 你 置身 在 这 绿 的 境界， 那么 你
jiǎrú nǐ zhìshēn zài zhè lǜ de jìngjiè nàme nǐ
if 2SG stay at this green DE realm then 2SG

	就	静静	地	坐	一	坐。(独上 81)
	jiù	jìngjìng	de	zuò	yī	zuò
	just	quiet	DE	sit	one	CL/sit

'If you come to this green realm, then you just quietly take a seat for a while.' (*Dúshàng* 81) (hypothetical complex sentence)

4. Fixed Phrases

Connective words can also be fixed phrases, including 一手 *yīshǒu* 'one hand', 一路 *yīlù* 'all the way', 不是 *bùshì* 'it is not', 由此可见 *yóucǐ kějiàn* 'it could be seen from this that', 之所以 *zhī suǒyǐ* 'with such a result', 是因为 *shì yīnwèi* 'it is because', 是为了 *shì wèile* 'it is in order to', 为的是 *wèide shì* 'it is in order to' and 目的是 *mùdi shì* 'the purpose of which is'. See the following examples:

(18)

潘展恒	**一手**	夹	着	厚厚的	宗卷，	**一手**
pānzhǎnhéng	**yīshǒu**	jiá	zhe	hòuhòude	zōngjuàn	**yīshǒu**
PanZhanheng	one.hand	carry	ZHE	thick	dossier	one.hand

提	着	黑皮	的	Samsonite	公文箱。(变调 46)
tí	zhe	hēipí	de	Samsonite	gōngwénxiāng
lift	ZHE	black.leather	DE	Samsonite	briefcase

'Pan Zhanheng carried a thick dossier in one hand and a black leather Samsonite briefcase in the other.' (*Biàndiào* 46) (conjunctive compound sentence)

(19)

孩子们	**一路**	走，
háizimen	**yīlù**	zǒu
children	all.the.way	walk

一路	口手并用		地	剥	着
yīlù	kǒushǒubìngyòng		de	bāo	zhe
all.the.way	use.mouth.hand.simultaneously		DE	peel	ZHE

果壳	吃	着	红毛丹。(冰灯 1)
guǒké	chī	zhe	hóngmáodān
fruit.husk	eat	ZHE	rambutan

'The children were husking and eating rambutans with their mouths and hands as they were walking.' (*Bīngdēng* 1) (conjunctive compound sentence)

(20) 这   不   **是**   老人   联欢会，
    zhè   bù   **shì** lǎorén   liánhuānhuì
    this   NEG   be   old.person get-together.party

    而   **是**   老   少   联欢。(心情33)
    ér   **shì** lǎo   shào   liánhuān
    but   be   old   young   get-together

    'This is not a party for the elderly, but for both young and old.' (*Xīnqíng* 33) (contrastive compound sentence)

(21) 它   **之所以**   能够   吸引   游客，   完全   是
    tā   **zhīsuǒyǐ**   nénggòu   xīyǐn   yóukè   wánquán   shì
    3SG   with.such.a.result   able   attract visitors totally   be

    因为   坟场   里   的   "居民"   声名显赫。(石头37)
    yīnwèi   fénchǎng   lǐ   de   jūmín   shēngmíngxiǎnhè
    because   graveyard   inside DE   residents renowned

    'The reason why this graveyard was able to attract visitors was entirely because of the fame of the 'residents' there.' (*Shítou* 37) (cause-result complex sentence)

(22) 我   恨   他，   **是**   **因为**   我   断定   他   是
    wǒ   hèn   tā   **shì** **yīnwèi** wǒ   duàndìng   tā   shì
    1SG   hate   3SG   be   because   1SG   assert   3SG   be

    一   个   阴谋家。(太阳70)
    yī   gè   yīnmóujiā
    one   CL   schemer

    'I hate him because I'm sure that he is a schemer.' (*Tàiyáng* 70) (causative complex sentence)

(23) 许多   人   不远千里   而   来，   **是**   **为了**
    xǔduō   rén   bùyuǎnqiānlǐ   ér   lái   **shì** **wèile**
    many   people   despite.a.thousand.miles   LIG   come   be   in.order.to

    要   听   他   的   演说。(华文教材 4A 70)
    yào   tīng   tā   de   yǎnshuō
    want   listen 3SG   DE   speech

    'Many people come from far away just in order to listen to his speech.' (*Huáwénjiàocái* 4A, 70) (purposive complex sentence)

5. Verbs

The most commonly used verb as connective word is 是 *shì* 'be', for example:

(24) 她　是　你　妈,
    tā　*shì*　*nǐ*　*mā*
    3SG　be　2SG　mother

    不　是　我　妈　啊！(撞墙92)
    bù　*shì*　*wǒ*　*mā*　*a*
    NEG　be　1SG　mother　SFP

'She's your mother, not my mother!' (*Zhuàngqiáng* 92) (contrastive compound sentence)

3.19 Conjunctions in Singapore Mandarin

3.19.1 Conjunctions in Singapore Mandarin

Conjunctions are functional words specifically used to connect words, phrases, clauses and sentences. The following is a list of conjunctions from the written materials (See appendix 'Sources of Language Materials') and oral materials (TV, radio and my conversation with Singaporeans) I collected during my half-year stay in Singapore (from Feb. 1995 to Aug. 1995)

并*bìng* 'also'	但*dàn* 'but'	而1*ér* 'also'
而2*ér* 'but'	故*gù* 'therefore'	和*hé* 'and'
或*huò* 'or'	及*jí* 'and'	既1*jì* 'also'
既2*jì* 'since'	可*kě* 'but'	且1*qiě* 'also'
且2*qiě* 'but also'	任*rèn* 'no matter'	如*rú* 'if'
若*ruò* 'if'	虽*suī* 'although'	倘*tǎng* 'if'
要*yào* 'if'	以*yǐ* 'so as to'	因*yīn* 'because'
与*yǔ* 'and'	则*zé* 'then'	纵*zòng* 'even if'
并且*bìngqiě* 'and also'	不单*bùdān* 'not only'	不但*bùdàn* 'not only'
不管*bùguǎn* 'no matter'	不过*bùguò* 'but'	不仅*bùjǐn* 'not only'
不论*bùlùn* 'no matter'	不然*bùrán* 'otherwise'	不问*bùwèn* 'regardless'
不只*bùzhǐ* 'not only'	除非*chúfēi* 'unless'	此外*cǐwài* 'besides'
从而*cóng'ér* 'so as to'	但是*dànshì* 'but'	反之*fǎnzhī* 'whereas'
否则*fǒuzé* 'otherwise'	故此*gùcǐ* 'therefore'	固然*gùrán* 'although'

还是 *háishì* 'or'　　　　　　　何况 *hékuàng* 'let alone'　　　或者 *huòzhě* 'or'
即使 *jíshǐ* 'even if'　　　　　既然 *jìrán* 'since'　　　　　　假如 *jiǎrú* 'if'
假若 *jiǎruò* 'if'　　　　　　尽管 *jǐnguǎn* 'although'　　　进而 *jìnér* 'and then'
就是1 *jiùshì* 'just'　　　　　就是2 *jiùshì* 'even if'　　　　就算 *jiùshì* 'even if'
可见 *kějiàn* 'therefore'　　　可是 *kěshì* 'but'　　　　　　况且 *kuàngqiě* 'moreover'
哪怕 *nǎpà* 'even if'　　　　　免得 *miǎnde* 'so as not to'　　乃至 *nǎizhì* 'even'
宁可 *nìngkě* 'would rather'　然而 *ránér* 'but'　　　　　　宁愿 *nìngyuàn* 'would rather'
然后 *ránhòu* 'and then'　　　任凭 *rènpíng* 'no matter'　　如果 *rúguǒ* 'if'
若果 *ruòguǒ* 'if'　　　　　　若是 *ruòshì* 'if'　　　　　　　尚且 *shàngqiě* 'even'
设若 *shèruò* 'if'　　　　　　甚至 *shènzhì* 'even'　　　　　虽然 *suīrán* 'although'
虽说 *suīshuō* 'although'　　虽则 *suīzé* 'although'　　　　所以 *suǒyǐ* 'so'
倘若 *tǎngruò* 'if'　　　　　　万一 *wànyī* 'in case'　　　　　唯有 *wéiyǒu* 'only if'
为了 *wèile* 'in order to'　　无论 *wúlùn* 'no matter'　　　要不 *yàobù* 'otherwise'
要是 *yàoshì* 'if'　　　　　　一旦 *yīdàn* 'once'　　　　　　以便 *yǐbiàn* 'so as to'
以及 *yǐjí* 'and'　　　　　　以免 *yǐmiǎn* 'lest'　　　　　　以至 *yǐzhìyú* 'even'
以致 *yǐzhì* 'so as to'　　　抑或 *yìhuò* 'or'　　　　　　　因此 *yīncǐ* 'therefore'
因而 *yīnér* 'so'　　　　　　因为 *yīnwèi* 'because'　　　　因之 *yīnzhī* 'because of it'
由于 *yóuyú* 'due to'　　　　于是 *yúshì* 'so'　　　　　　　与其 *yǔqí* 'rather than'
再说 *zàishuō* 'besides'　　只要 *zhǐyào* 'as long as'　　只有 *zhǐyǒu* 'only if'
总之 *zǒngzhī* 'in a word'　纵然 *zòngrán* 'even if'　　　纵使 *zòngshǐ* 'even if'
要不然 *yàobùrán* 'otherwise'　要么（嘛）*yàome (ma)* 'or'　以致于 *yǐzhìyú* 'so as to'

The following are some example sentences with conjunctions.

(1) 不但 *bùdàn* 'not only', 而且 *érqiě* 'also'

他	站	起	马步	来，	**不但**	似模似样，
tā	*zhàn*	*qǐ*	*mǎbù*	*lái*	***bùdàn***	*sìmúsìyàng*
3SG	stand	up	horse.stance	come	**not.only**	up.to.the.mark

而且	经久不累。(狮子 3)
érqiě	*jīngjiǔbùlèi*
also	not.tired.after.long.time

When he practices the horse stance, he can not only hold the position up to the mark but also hold it for a long time without getting tired. (*Shīzi* 3)

(2) 不然 *bùrán* 'otherwise', 甚至 *shènzhì* 'even'

不能	预先	想	得	太	多,
bùnéng	yùxiān	xiǎng	de	tài	duō
can.not	in.advance	think	DE	too	much

不然	**甚至**	都	做不成。(梦 4)
bùrán	**shènzhì**	dōu	zuòbùchéng
otherwise	**even**	all	not.able.to.do

'You should not think about it too much beforehand, otherwise you would not be able to do it at all.' (*Mèng* 4)

(3) 况且 *kuàngqiě* 'moreover'

世界	并非	那么	单纯,	**况且**,	又	是	这
shìjiè	bìngfēi	nàme	dānchún	**kuàngqiě**	yòu	shì	zhè
world	NEG	so	pure	**moreover**	again	be	this

与	祖国	一洋之隔	的	南岛。(扶轮 3)
yǔ	zǔguó	yīyángzhīgé	de	nándǎo
with	homeland	separated.by.the.sea	DE	South.Island

'The world is not so simple; moreover, this is the South Island separated from its motherland by the sea.' (*Fúlún* 3)

(4) 纵使 *zòngshǐ* 'even.if'

纵使	在	黑暗	的	夜里,
zòngshǐ	zài	hēiàn	de	yèlǐ
even.if	at	dark	DE	night

仍	有	星光	给	你	照明。(渐行 4)
réng	yǒu	xīngguāng	gěi	nǐ	zhàomíng
still	have	starlight	give	2SG	illuminate

'Even in the dark night, there are still stars to give you illumination.' (*Jiànxíng* 4)

(5) 只要 *zhǐyào* 'as long as'

不管	是	什么	通告,	**只要**	不是	大减价	的
bùguǎn	shì	shénme	tōnggào	**zhǐyào**	bùshì	dàjiǎnjià	de
no.matter	be	what	notice	**as.long.as**	not.be	big.sale	DE

消息， 是 不会 引起 注意 的。（再见65）
xiāoxi shì bùhuì yǐnqǐ zhùyì de
news SHI NEG arouse attention DE

'No matter what notice it is, as long as it is not about a big sale, it is not going to arouse attention.' (*Zàijiàn* 65)

(6) 然而 *ránér* 'but'

我 得到 的 固然 很多， **然而**， 我 所
wǒ dédào de gùrán hěnduō **ránér** wǒ suǒ
1SG get DE although many **but** 1SG SUO

付出 的 代价 更大。（青青56）
fùchū de dàijià gèngdà
pay DE cost bigger

'Although I have got many things, I have paid even more.' (*Qīngqīng* 56)

(7) 还是 *háishì* 'or'

这 是 人生 的 缺陷 呢， **还是** 社会 的 悲哀？（恶梦8）
zhè shì rénshēng de quēxiàn ne **háishì** shèhuì de bēiāi
this be life DE defect SFP **or** society DE sadness

'Is this the defect of life or the sadness of society?' (*Èmèng* 8)

(8) 就是 *jiùshì* 'just'

我 什么 都 肯 学， **就是** 不 知道 学
wǒ shénme dōu kěn xué **jiùshì** bù zhīdào xué
1SG what all be.willing.to learn **just** NEG know learn

什么 才 好。（微型2）
shénme cái hǎo
what only good

'I am willing to learn anything. It's just that I don't know what to learn.' (*Wéixíng* 2)

(9) 但是 *dànshì* 'but'

就算 你 说 重复 着 日子，
jiùsuàn nǐ shuō chóngfù zhe rìzi
even.if 2SG say repeat ZHE day

274 *Composite Sentences*

但是　　岁月　　没有　　重复。（渐行55）
dànshì   suìyuè   méiyǒu   chóngfù
but   life   NEG   repeat

'Even if you say that we are repeating the same days, we are not repeating our lives.' (*Jiànxíng* 55)

(10) 免得 *miǎnde* 'so as not to'

没事　　　　就　　不要　　开开关关　　　　的，　　**免得**
*méishì   jiù   bùyào   kāikāiguānguān   de   **miǎnde**
without.business then   don't   open.and.then.close DE   **so.as.not.to**

弄　　坏　　了　　锁头。（牛车水111）
nòng   huài   le   suǒtóu
get   broke   LE   lock

'Stop playing about with the lock in case you break it.' (*Niúchēshuǐ* 111)

3.19.2 *Correlative Connective Words in Singapore Mandarin*

Apart from the conjunctions listed earlier, there are some conventionally used correlative connective words in Singapore Mandarin. The commonly used ones are as follows:

边 ...边...　　　　　　　　　　　　时而... 时而...
biān ..., biān ...　　　　　　　　　*shíér ..., shíér ...*
at the same time ..., at the same time ...　　sometimes ..., sometimes ...

一边... 一边...　　　　　　　　　　一来... 二来...
yībiān ..., yībiān ...　　　　　　　*yīlái ..., èrlái ...*
at the same time ..., at the same time ...　　firstly ..., secondly ...

一面... 一面...　　　　　　　　　　一则... 一则（二则）...
yīmiàn ..., yīmiàn ...　　　　　　　*yīzé ..., èrzé ...*
at the same time ..., at the same time ...　　on the one hand ..., on the other hand ...(firstly ..., secondly ...)

For example:

(5) 他　　把　　小　　纸张　　　平放　　　在　　掌心　　里，
    tā   bǎ   xiǎo   zhǐzhāng   píngfàng   zài   zhǎngxīn   lǐ
    3SG   BA   small paper   put.flat   at   palm   inside

边		看	边		抄，... (狮子 77)		
biān		*kàn*	*biān*		*chāo*		
at.the.same.time		look	at.the.same.time		transcribe		

'He put a small piece of paper flat in his palm, peeping at it as he transcribed ...' (*Shīzi* 77)

(6)
那	卷	发，	时而	翘起	如	飞，	时而	垂下
nà	*juǎn*	*fà*	*shíér*	*qiàoqǐ*	*rú*	*fēi*	*shíér*	*chuíxià*
that	curly	hair	**sometimes**	tilt	like	fly	**sometimes**	downcast

如	睡，	充分	显示	其	饱满	的	生命力。(无月 61)
rú	*shuì*	*chōngfèn*	*xiǎnshì*	*qí*	*bǎomǎn*	*de*	*shēngmìnglì*
like	sleep	fully	show	its	full	DE	vitality

'That curly hair, sometimes tilted as if it is flying, sometimes hanging down as if it is sleeping, showing its full vitality.' (*Wúyuè*, 61)

(7)
假如	文章	太	长	了，	一来	没有	时间	去	阅读，
jiǎrú	*wénzhāng*	*tài*	*cháng*	*le*	*yīlái*	*méiyǒu*	*shíjiān*	*qù*	*yuèdú*
if	article	too	long	LE	**firstly**	not. have	time	go	read

二来	花费	太	多	精神，	实在	受不了。(一心 10)
èrlái	*huāfèi*	*tài*	*duō*	*jīngshén*	*shízài*	*shòubùliǎo*
secondly	spend	too	much	spirit	really	cannot.bear

'If the article is too long, firstly you do not have time to read it, and secondly it will take you so much energy that you can hardly bear it.' (*Yīxīn* 10)

(8)
父亲	一面	走，
fùqin	*yīmiàn*	*zǒu*
father	**at.the.same.time**	walk

一面	摇	头，	叹气...。(牛车水 17)
yīmiàn	*yáo*	*tóu*	*tànqì*
at.the.same.time	shake	head	sigh

'Father shook his head and sighed as he walked.' (*Niúchēshuǐ* 17)

(9)
房东太太	一边	说	着	一边	溜
fángdōngtàitai	*yībiān*	*shuō*	*zhe*	*yībiān*	*liū*
landlady	**at.the.same.time**	say	ZHE	**at.the.same.time**	slip

着   走开   了。（大喜128）
zhe   zǒukāi   le
ZHE   walk.away LE

'The landlady said something and slipped away.' (*Dàxǐ* 128)

(10) 设立   联络所   的   目的,   一则   可以   发掘   人才、
     shèlì   liáluòsuǒ   de   mùdì   yīzé   kéyǐ   fājué   réncái
     establish contact.base DE   goal   firstly can   discover talent

     铸造   人才,   二则   使   青年人   有   一   个
     zhùzào réncái   èrzé   shǐ   qīngniánrén   yǒu   yī   gè
     create talent   secondly   make   youth   have   one   CL

     理想的   场所。（一心28）
     líxiǎngde   chángsuǒ
     ideal   place

'The purpose of establishing a contact base is first to discover and create talent, and second to provide the youth with an ideal place.' (*Yīxīn* 28)

3.19.3 Elements Connected by Conjunctions

Some conjunctions can be used only to connect words or phrases, not clauses or sentences, such as 和 *hé* 'and', 与 *yǔ* 'and', 及 *jí* 'and', 而 *ér* 'and' and so on; some conjunctions can be used only to connect clauses or sentences, not words or phrases, such as 除非 *chúfēi* 'unless', 固然 *gùrán* 'although', 既然 *jìrán* 'since', 尽管 *jǐnguǎn* 'although', 哪怕 *nǎpà* 'even if', 宁可 *nìngkě* 'would rather' or 宁愿 *nìngyuàn* 'would rather', 任 *rèn* 'no matter', 任凭 *rènpíng* 'no matter', 尚且 *shàngqiě* 'even', 虽然 *suīrán* 'although', 倘 *tǎng* 'if', 万一 *wànyī* 'in case', 要 *yào* 'if' (equals 如果 *rúguǒ* 'if'), 一旦 *yīdàn* 'once', 与其 *yǔqí* 'rather than', 只要 *zhǐyào* 'as long as', 纵 *zòng* 'even if', 纵然 *zòngrán* 'even if', 纵使 *zòngshǐ* 'even if', 不过 *búguò* 'but', 不然 *bùrán* 'otherwise', 此外 *cǐwài* 'besides', 从而 *cóngér* 'so as to', 但是 *dànshì* 'but', 反之 *fǎnzhī* 'whereas', 否则 *fǒuzé* 'otherwise', 故 *gù* 'so' (equals 所以 *suǒyǐ* 'so'), 何况 *hékuàng* 'let alone', 进而 *jìnér* 'and then', 就是2 *jiùshì* 'even if', 可见 *kějiàn* 'therefore', 可是 *kěshì* 'but', 况且 *kuàngqiě* 'moreover', 然而 *ránér* 'but', 然后 *ránhòu* 'and then', 所以 *suǒyǐ* 'so', 要不然 *yàobùrán* 'otherwise', 以 *yǐ* 'in order to', 以便 *yǐbiàn* 'so as to', 以免 *yǐmiǎn* 'lest', 以致 *yǐzhì* 'so as to', 因此 *yīncǐ* 'therefore', 因而 *yīnér* 'so', 于是 *yúshì* 'so', 再说 *zài shuō* 'besides', 只是 *zhǐshì* 'only' and so on. Some conjunctions can be used to connect both words or phrases and clauses, such as 或 *huò* 'or'. Taking the sentences from Liang Wenfu's *zuìhòu de niúchēshuǐ* 'The last Chinatown' and Guanghui's (original name Zeng Zhenguang) essay entitled *yìxīn xiǎng xiě* 'All I want is to write' as examples:

(11) 在 那 蓝色 的 沙漠 上，
zài nà lánsè de shāmò shàng
at that blue DE desert on

星期一 或 星期日 都 一样。(牛车水 50)
xīngqīyī huò xīngqīrì dōu yīyàng
Monday or Sunday all the.same

'In that blue desert, Monday or Sunday would be just the same.' (*Niúchēshuǐ* 50)

(12) 应该 多 方面 组织 **协会** 或 **工会**，
yīnggāi duō fāngmiàn zǔzhī xiéhuì huò gōnghuì
should many field organise association or labour.union

好 让 爱好者 相聚 研究。(一心 21)
hǎo ràng àihàozhě xiāngjù yánjiū
good make enthusiasts gather research

'Associations or labour unions should be organised in many fields, so that enthusiasts can gather together to research.' (*Yīxīn* 21)

(13) 他们 **高兴** **时** **或** **生气** **时**
tāmen gāoxìng shí huò shēngqì shí
3PL happy time or angry time

都 有 如流 的 粗话。(牛车水 49–50)
dōu yǒu rúliú de cūhuà
all have like.stream DE dirty.words

'They curse wildly when happy or angry.' (*Niúchēshuǐ* 49–50)

(14) 仍旧 有 非法者 输入 的 **暴力**
réngjiù yǒu fēifǎzhě shūrù de bàolì
still have illegal.people input DE violent

与 色情 影片 或 非法 录影带。(一心 29)
yǔ sèqíng yǐngpiān huò fēifǎ lùxiàngdài
and porn film or illegal videotape

'There are still violent and pornographic films or illegal videotapes imported by traffickers.' (*Yīxīn* 29)

(15) 一旦   消失   几   个,   或   增添   一些,
yīdàn   xiāoshī   jǐ   gè   huò   zēngtiān   yīxiē
once   disappear several CL   or   add   some

也   不会   有人   特别   留意   的。(牛车水 131)
yě   bùhuì   yǒurén   tèbié   liúyì   de
also will.not someone special pay.attention DE

'Even if several disappear or some are added, no one would pay special attention to that.' (*Niúchēshuǐ* 131)

(16) 有些   学生   在   椰树   下   倾谈,
yǒuxiē   xuéshēng   zài   yēshù   xià   qīngtán
some   student   at   coconut.tree under talk

或   阅读   书籍   和   课文。(一心 6)
huò   yuèdú   shūjí   hé   kèwén
or   read   book   and   text

'Some students are talking under the coconut trees, or reading books and texts.' (*Yīxīn* 6)

The elements connected by 或 *huò* 'or' are words in examples (11) and (12), phrases in (13) and (14) and clauses in (15) and (16).

3.19.4 Classification of Conjunctions in Singapore Mandarin

Conjunctions can be roughly divided into the following fourteen types according to the logical meanings they express:

1 Showing coordinate relationships, such as: 和 *hé* 'and', 与 *yǔ* 'and', 及 *jí* 'and', 以及 *yǐjí* 'and', and 而1 *ér* 'also', 且1 *qiě* 'also', 既1 *jì* 'also' and so on.
2 Showing consecutive relationships, such as 然后 *ránhòu* 'and then'.
3 Showing contrastive relationships, such as 而 *ér* 'while'.
4 Showing disjunctive relationships, such as: 或 *huò* 'or', 或者 *huòzhě* 'or', 抑或 *yìhuò* 'or', 要么（嘛）*yàome (ma)* 'or', 还是 *háishì* 'or', and 与其 *yǔqí* 'rather than', 宁愿 *nìngyuàn* 'would rather', 宁可 *nìngkě* 'would rather' and so on.
5 Showing progressive relationships, such as 不但 *bùdàn* 'not only', 不单 *bùdān* 'not only', 不仅 *bùjǐn* 'not only', 并 *bìng* 'also', 并且 *bìngqiě* 'and also', 而且 *érqiě* 'but also', 且2 *qiě* 'but also', and 甚至 *shènzhì* 'even', 况且 *kuàngqiě* 'moreover', 何况 *hékuàng* 'let alone', 再说 *zài shuō* 'besides' and so on.
6 Showing specific-general relationships, such as 总之 *zǒngzhī* 'in a word'.

7 Showing adversative transitional relationships, including conjunctions indicating concessive relations: 虽 *suī* 'although', 虽然 *suīrán* 'although', 尽管 *jǐnguǎn* 'although' and 固然 *gùrán* 'although', as well as 尚且 *shàngqiě* 'even' and conjunctions indicating transitional relationships: 但 *dàn* 'but', 但是 *dànshì* 'but' as well as 然而 *ránér* 'but', 可 *kě* 'but', 可是 *kěshì* 'but', 而 *ér* 'but', 则 *zé* 'then', 不过 *bùguò* 'but', 只是 *zhǐshì* 'only', 就是2 *jiùshì* 'even if'.
8 Showing hypothetical adversative relationships, such as 即使 *jíshǐ* 'even if', 就是2 *jiùshì* 'even if', 就算 *jiùsuàn* 'even if', 哪怕 *nǎpà* 'even if' and so on.
9 Showing hypothetical relationships, such as 假如 *jiǎrú* 'if', 假若 *jiǎruò* 'if', 如 *rú* 'if', 如果 *rúguǒ* 'if', 若 *ruò* 'if', 若果 *ruòguǒ* 'if', 若是 *ruòshì* 'if', 设若 *shèruò* 'if', 倘 *tǎng* 'if', 倘若 *tǎngruò* 'if', 要 *yào* 'if', 要是 *yàoshì* 'if', 万一 *wànyī* 'in case', 一旦 *yīdàn* 'once', and 纵 *zòng* 'even if', 纵然 *zòngrán* 'even if', 纵使 *zòngshǐ* 'even.if' and so on.
10 Showing conditional relationships, such as 只要 *zhǐyào* 'as long as', 只有 *zhǐyǒu* 'only if', 不管 *bùguǎn* 'no matter', 不论 *bùlùn* 'no matter', 无论 *wúlùn* 'no matter', 任 *rèn* 'no matter', 任凭 *rènpíng* 'no matter' and 除非 *chúfēi* 'unless', as well as 否则 *fǒuzé* 'otherwise', 不然 *bùrán* 'otherwise' or 要不然 *yàobùrán* 'otherwise', 反之 *fǎnzhī* 'whereas' and so on.
11 Showing causative relationships, such as 因 *yīn* 'because', 因为 *yīnwèi* 'because', 由于 *yóuyú* 'due to' showing the reason, and 所以 *suǒyǐ* 'so', 因此 *yīncǐ* 'therefore', 因之 *yīnzhī* 'because of it' 因而 *yīnér* 'so', 故 *gù* 'therefore', 故此 *gùcǐ* 'therefore', 于是 *yúshì* 'so', 以致 *yǐzhì* 'so as to', 以致于 *yǐzhìyú* 'so as to', 从而 *cóngér* 'so as to' and so on.
12 Showing inferential relationships, such as 既2 *jì* 'since', 既然 *jìrán* 'since' and 可见 *kějiàn* 'therefore'.
13 Showing purposive relationships, such as 为了 *wèile* 'in order to', 以便 *yǐbiàn* 'so as to', 以免 *yǐmiǎn* 'lest', 免得 *miǎnde* 'so as not to' and so on.
14 Showing supplementary relationships, such as 此外 *cǐwài* 'besides'.

3.19.5 Differences Between Conjunctions in Singapore Mandarin and Mandarin Chinese

Firstly, some commonly used conjunctions in Mandarin Chinese are not used in Singapore Mandarin. The most obvious examples are conjunctions that show a coordinate relationship – 跟 *gēn* 'with' and 同 *tóng* 'with' (especially 跟 *gēn* 'with'). These words are quite common in Chinese Mandarin, but in Singapore Mandarin, if not absolutely absent, as least they are not found in the written or oral materials I have collected. The following conjunctions seen in Chinese Mandarin do not appear in Singapore Mandarin (listed in alphabetic order): 不独 *bùdú* 'not only', 不光 *bùguāng* 'not only', 不问 *bùwèn* 'disregard', 非但 *fēidàn* 'not only', 跟 *gēn* 'with', 即便 *jíbiàn* 'even if', 假使 *jiǎshǐ* 'if', 如若 *rúruò* 'if', 倘使 *tǎngshǐ* 'if', 同 *tóng* 'with', 以至于 *yǐzhìyú* 'so ... that', 纵令 *zònglìng* 'even if' and so on.

Secondly, some words are hardly or rarely used in Chinese Mandarin but are quite common in Singapore Mandarin. These include conjunctions indicating result in cause-result relationships, such as 故此 *gùcǐ* 'therefore' and 因之 *yīnzhī* 'because of it'; conjunctions indicating hypothetical relationships, such as 若果

ruòguǒ 'if', 设若 *shèruò* 'if', 纵使 *zòngshǐ* 'even if'; conjunctions indicating alternative relationships, like 抑或 *yìhuò* 'or'; conjunctions indicating progressive relationships, like 且 *qiě* 'also' (equals 而且 *érqiě* 'but also').

Thirdly, some conjunctions are relatively common in Chinese Mandarin but are barely used in Singapore Mandarin, and vice versa. Take conjunctions showing an adversative relationship as examples. 但 *dàn* 'but', 但是 *dànshì* 'but', 可 *kě* 'but', 可是 *kěshì* 'but' and 然而 *ránér* 'but' are a group of adversative conjunctions with similar meanings. In Chinese Mandarin, 可 *kě* 'but', 可是 *kěshì* 'but' and 但是 *dànshì* 'but' are used more frequently (可 *kě* 'but' and 可是 *kěshì* 'but' are mainly used especially in the oral genre); and 但 *dàn* 'but' and 然而 *ránér* 'but' are used only occasionally, and only in the written genre. In Singapore Mandarin, on the other hand, 可 *kě* 'but' and 可是 *kěshì* 'but' are rarely seen, while 但 *dàn* 'but' and 然而 *ránér* 'but' are frequently used, both in the written register and oral register. We have counted the usage of these four adversative conjunctions in four representative works – the speech 寻找新加坡本身前进的道路 *xúnzhǎo xīnjiāpō běnshēn qiánjìn de dàolù* 'Seeking Singapore's own path for progress' by Premier Goh Chok Tong addressed to the public assembly on the 30th anniversary of National Day (*Bao*, Aug. 21, 1995, Issue no. 6–7, referred as 总理演说 *zǒnglǐ yǎnshuō*), Liu Huixia's 别做断了线的风筝 *bié zuò duànlexiàn de fēngzheng* 'Don't be the kite without the thread' (referred as *fēngzheng*), Liang Wenfu's 最后的牛车水 *zuìhòu de niúchēshuǐ* 'The last Chinatown' (referred as *niúchēshuǐ*) and Li Yueqing's 南北游踪 *nánběi yóuzōng* 'Travelling Around' (referred as *nánběi*). The usage of the four adversative conjunctions are calculated in the following table:

	总理演说 *zǒnglǐ yǎnshuō*	风筝 *fēngzheng*	牛车水 *niúchēshuǐ*	南北 *nánběi*
但 *dàn* 'but'	37	79	34	83
但是 *dànshì* 'but'	8	13	11	1
可 *kě* 'but'	0	0	0	2
可是 *kěshì* 'but'	2	4	5	4
然而 *ránér* 'but'	3	26	43	2

It is not difficult to see from this table that there is the general tendency to avoid the usage of 可 *kě* 'but' and 可是 *kěshì* 'but' in Singapore Mandarin. This is evident from the examples in the collection of cross-talks 笑眼看人生 *xiàoyǎn kàn rénshēng* 'Look at life with a smile' by famous Singaporean writer Tian Liu, in which 可是 *kěshì* 'but' (34 times) and 可 *kě* 'but' (5 times) are used in cross-talk, but not a single case of 但 *dàn* 'but', 但是 *dànshì* 'but' or 然而 *ránér* 'but' is used; while in the postscript of that book, only 但 *dàn* 'but' and 然而 *ránér* 'but' are used, not 可是 *kěshì* 'but'. The reason is simply because the cross-talks are written with Chinese Mandarin grammar, whereas the postscript is written with Singapore Mandarin grammar. In addition, the hypothetical concessive conjunction word 就是 *jiùshì* 'even if' (equals 即使 *jíshì* 'even if') is common in Chinese Mandarin but seldom used in Singapore Mandarin. On the other hand, 就算 *jiùsuàn* 'even if' (equals 即使 *jíshǐ* 'even if') is very common in Singapore Mandarin and it is even used to annotate the word 即使 *jíshǐ* 'even if' by Professor Lin Wanjing. But in Chinese Mandarin, it is rarely used, and not even included as an entry in the *Dictionary of Functional Words in Modern Chinese* (《现代汉语虚词例释》, compiled by language class students of 1955 and 1957 in the Chinese Department of Peking University, the Commercial Press, 1982, Beijing), which is quite inclusive with regard to the collection of functional words in modern Chinese.

Fourthly, though some conjunctions are commonly used in both Singapore Mandarin and Chinese Mandarin, they are used differently. This is especially true for conjunctions showing coordinate relationships and alternative relationships.

It is impossible to introduce every conjunction in this book. Instead, only some major types and commonly used conjunctions, especially conjunctions with similar meanings but different usage, are selected and explained for reference.

Notes

1 Translator's note: It is necessary to point out that the sentence structure of Chinese and that of English are different. In addition, differerent researchers also have different views on the connotative meaning and the subclassification of each type of sentence. Thus, the compound and complex sentences discussed here in Singapore Mandarin might be different from the subclassification of those in English or in other grammars on Chinese.
2 Listed here are eight types of complex sentences. In fact, the semantic relationship between the primary and secondary clauses are not restricted to the eight types. For example,

他们	踏	着	稳健的	步伐，	英勇地	向前	速步迈进。
							(断情剪113)
tāmen	*tà*	*zhe*	*wěnjiànde*	*bùfá*	*yīngyǒngde*	*xiàngqián*	*sùbùmàijìn*
3PL	tread	ZHE	steady	pace	valiantly	forward	step.quickly

'They tread forward with a steady pace and valiant and quick steps.' (*Duànqíngjiǎn* 176)

In this sentence, the secondary clause describes the manner of the action stated in the primary clause, so it does not belong to any of the eight types listed above.
3 It refers to the novel 家 Jia, written by a famous modern Chinese writer named Pa Chin (1904–2005).
4 Translator's note: In this sentence, the speaker quoted a line from a famous poet Yinqiji of the Song dynasty. The original line is 我见青山多妩媚，料青山见我应如是 'I see that the green mountains are very charming. I guess they should see me in the same way'. The man that the speaker talked about is named Qingshan, which literally means 'green mountain'. That's why the line is quoted.
5 See Ma Zhen. *A Concise Course of Practical Chinese Grammar*, Chapter 7, 2.2, Peking University Press, 1997.

4 Characteristics of Singapore Mandarin Grammar

4.1 Introduction

Grammar characteristics become evident in cross-linguistic comparison. When we discuss the characteristics of Singapore Mandarin grammar, we are comparing it with the grammar of Chinese Mandarin. Singapore Mandarin is the common language among the Chinese ethic race in Singapore, as Chinese Mandarin is in China. They are basically the same as each other. There are, nonetheless, grammatical differences between them due to a variety of reasons. A typical example is the difference in the form of the A-not-A question formed by disyllabic verbs or adjectives. In Chinese Mandarin, we say 参观不参观 *cānguān bù cānguān* 'visit or not' or 干净不干净 *gānjìng bù gānjìng* 'clean or not'. This type of question form is also acceptable in Singapore Mandarin, but it is more likely to be 参不参观 *cān bù cānguān* 'visit or not' or 干不干净 *gān bù gānjìng* 'clean or not' in Singapore Mandarin. Another instance of difference is whether to use 有 *yǒu* 'YOU' in front of a matrix verb or not. Such sentences as 我也有想过 *wǒ yě yǒu xiǎng guò* 'I have also thought about it.' or 你妈妈有在家吗 *nǐ māma yǒu zài jiā ma* 'Is your mum at home?' are conventional usages in Singapore Mandarin, whereas in Chinese Mandarin these sentences are not grammatical and 有 *yǒu* 'YOU' has to be deleted, as in 我也想过 *wǒ yě xiǎng guò* 'I have also thought about it' or 你妈妈在家吗 *nǐ māma zài jiā ma* 'Is your mum at home?'[1]

As Chinese Mandarin is also constantly evolving and absorbing expressive elements from other dialects, several grammatical phenomena in Singapore Mandarin that were influenced by the Min and Cantonese dialects and were formerly deemed unique Singapore Mandarin features are also now quite common in Chinese Mandarin. For example, expressions such as 我小他两岁 *wǒ xiǎo tā liǎng suì* 'I am two years younger than him' and 姐姐大我三岁 *jiějiě dà wǒ sān suì* 'my sister is three years older than me', as well as the use of 来 *lái* 'come' and 去 *qù* 'go' with place objects (e.g. 来新加坡 *lái Xīnjiāpō* 'come to Singapore' and 去上海 *qù Shànghǎi* 'go to Shanghai'), were considered to be features of Singapore Mandarin grammar in the mid-1980s (See the Grammar Section of *Singapore Standard Chinese Language Committee* 1985; Ng 1986). These expressions are, however, extensively employed in Chinese Mandarin currently and thus cannot be considered indicative of Singapore Mandarin grammar.

The characteristics of Singapore Mandarin grammar are detailed in this chapter.

DOI: 10.4324/9781003350248-4

4.2 Double Object Constructions

In Singapore Mandarin, there are two types of double-object constructions.

1 Type I: "V + indirect object + direct object (V for verb)". For example:

(1) 忍着气，　　　　给　了　他　三　块　钱，
    rěnzheqì　　　　 gěi　le　tā　sān　kuài　qián
    holding.back.her.anger give LE 3SG three CL money

   并　嘱咐　他　不　必　再来　了。（追云52）
   bìng zhǔfù tā bù bì zàilái le
   and   tell   3SG NEG need come.again LE
   'Holding back her anger, she gave him three yuan and told him not to come again.' (*Zhuīyún* 52)

(2) 老板，请　给　我　一　盒　双黄　月饼。
                                           （微型16）
    lǎobǎn, qǐng gěi wǒ yī hé shuānghuáng yuèbǐng
    boss   please give 1SG one CL double-yolk mooncake
    'Boss, please give me a box of double-yolk mooncakes.' (*Wēixíng* 16)

(3) 事后，　您　借　了　我　一　本　书，
    shìhòu, nín jiè le wǒ yī běn shū,
    afterwards 2SG lend LE 1SG one CL book

   书名　依稀　是　《怎样　做个　优秀的　领导人》。
                                           （青青103）
   shūmíng yīxī shì zěnyàng zuògè yōuxiùde lǐngdǎorén
   title   vaguely be how   to.be good   leader
   'Afterwards, you lent me a book, the title of which is, I remember vaguely, *How to Be a Good Leader*.' (*Qīngqīng* 103)

(4) 告诉　你　一　个　好　消息。（跳舞107）
    gàosù nǐ yī gè hǎo xiāoxi
    tell   2SG one CL good news
    'Here is a piece of good news for you.' (*Tiàowǔ* 107)

(5) 我　的　邻居　送　了　我　一　只　猫。（报1995年
                                              3月5日副刊11版）
    wǒ de línjū sòng le wǒ yī zhī māo

1SG　DE　neighbour　**give**　**LE**　**me**　**one**　**CL**　**cat**

'My neighbour gave me a cat.' (*Bào*, Mar. 5, 1995, Issue no. 11, supplementary edition)

2　Type II. "V + direct object + indirect object". This format is used mostly in colloquial language. For example:

(6)　我　**给**　**钱**　**他**，　叫　他　去　买　票。
　　　wǒ　**gěi**　**qián**　**tā**，　jiào　tā　qù　mǎi　piào
　　　1SG　**give**　**money**　**3SG**　ask　3SG　go　buy　ticket

'I gave him money and told him to buy a ticket.'

(7)　他　刚才　**给**　这　本　书　我。
　　　tā　gāngcái　**gěi**　zhè　běn　shū　wǒ
　　　3SG　just　**give**　this　CL　book　1SG

'He just gave me this book.'

The use of the Type II form is limited in that it applies only to the verb 给 *gěi* 'give'.

Type I is grammatical in Chinese Mandarin, but not Type II.

4.3 Compound Directional Verbs With Place Objects

In Singapore Mandarin, compound directional verbs can take place objects, whether they are in the main predicate position or the complement position of a predicate-complement phrase. This place object can have two possible positions, as illustrated next.

Position I: The place object can be placed directly after the compound directional verb. For example:

(1)　听　祖父　说，
　　　tīng　zǔfù　shuō,
　　　hear　grandfather　say

他们　已经　**回去**　**印度**　了。（吾土·小说上223）
tāmen　yǐjīng　**huíqù**　**yìndù**　le
3PL　already　**go.back**　**India**　LE

'I heard from my grandfather that they had gone back to India.' (*Wútǔ-xiǎoshuōshàng* 223)

(2) 于是　柯　主任　**回去**　**办公室**,
　　 yúshì　kē　zhǔrèn　**huíqù**　**bàngōngshì**,
　　 so　Ke　director　go.back　office

　　 张石珍　　　也　　道了个歉　　　上课去　　了。（追云15）
　　 zhāngshízhēn　yě　dào-le-gè-qiàn　shàngkèqù　le
　　 Zhang.Shizhen　also　apologise　go.to.class　LE

　　 'So Director Ke went back to his office, and Zhang Shizhen apologised and went to class.' (*Zhuīyún* 15)

(3) 是　　在　　南洋　　　出生　　　的,
　　 shì　zài　nányáng　chūshēng　de,
　　 SHI　in　Southeast.Asia　be.born　DE

　　 她　　没有　　**回去**　过　　**唐山**。（报1995年6月18日副刊9版）
　　 tā　méiyǒu　**huíqù**　guò　**tángshān**
　　 3SG　NEG　go.back　GUO　Tangshan

　　 'She was born in Southeast Asia, and she has never been back to Tangshan.' (*Bào*, June 18, 1995, Issue no. 9, supplementary edition)

(4) 她　　决定　　**进去**　**店铺**　**里**　　看看。（跳舞60）
　　 tā　juédìng　**jìnqù**　**diànpù**　**lǐ**　kànkàn
　　 3SG　decide　enter　store　inside　have.a.look

　　 'She decided to go inside the store to have a look.' (*Tiàowǔ* 60)

(5) 他　　想　　父母亲　　这　一　　去　　就　　永远　　　留在　　唐山,
　　 tā　xiǎng　fùmǔqīn　zhè　yī　qù　jiù　yǒngyuǎn　liúzài　tángshān
　　 3SG　think　parents　this　one　go　then　forever　stay　Tangshan

　　 可能　　不会　　再　　**回来**　　**南洋**。（报1995年6月18日副刊9版）
　　 kěnéng　bùhuì　zài　**huílái**　**nányáng**
　　 maybe　NEG　again　come.back　Southeast.Asia

　　 'He thought that his parents would stay in Tangshan forever and might not come back to Southeast Asia.' (*Bào*, June 18, 1995, Issue no. 9, supplementary edition)

The preceding examples are illustrations of compound directional verb predicates with a direct place object. The following examples demonstrate that the directional verb in the predicate-complement phrase can be followed by a direct place object.

(6) 想不到 过 了 半个钟头 后,
    xiǎngbùdào guò le bàngèzhōngtóu hòu,
    think-NEG-get pass LE half.an.hour after

    同 一 辆 车 又 驾 回来 我们 这里。（风筝186）
    tóng yī liàng chē yòu jià huílái wǒmen zhèlǐ
    same one CL car again drive come.back 1PL here

    'To my surprise, after half-an-hour, the same car came back for us.' (*Fēngzhēng* 186)

(7) 有些人... 还 时常 跑 回来 巴刹 买 东西。（回忆43）
    yǒuxiērén hái shícháng pǎo huílái bāshā mǎi dōngxi
    some.people also often run come.back bazaar buy things

    'Some people .... very often still run back to the bazaar to buy things.' (*Huíyì* 43)

(8) 当初 也 是 你 自己 把 他 带 进来
    dāngchū yě shì nǐ zìjǐ bǎ tā dài jìnlái
    at.first also BE 2SG self BA 3SG bring enter

    这 厂里 的。（吾土·小说上44）
    zhè chǎnglǐ de
    this factory DE

    'In the first place it was you who brought him into the factory.' (*Wútǔ· xiǎoshuō shàng* 44)

(9) 你 如果 逼 我 回去,
    nǐ rúguǒ bī wǒ huíqù,
    2SG if force 1SG go.back

    我 就 立刻 飞 回去 澳洲。（大胡子47）
    wǒ jiù lìkè fēi huíqù àozhōu
    1SG then immediately fly go.back Australia

    'If you force me to go back, I'll fly back to Australia immediately.' (*Dàhúzi* 47)

(10) 没有   想到   他   今天   晚上   就   把   她
     méiyǒu xiǎngdào tā   jīntiān wǎnshàng jiù   bǎ   tā
     NEG   expect   2SG   today   evening   then BA   2SG

    带   过来   我们   家   了。（大胡子25）
    dài   guòlái   wǒmen jiā   le
    bring come.over   1PL   house   LE

'I didn't expect that he would bring her over to our house this evening.' (*Dàhúzi* 25)

Position II. The place object can be placed in the middle of the compound directional verb. For example:

(11) 他   总是   那么   可怜兮兮   的   问   我
     tā   zǒngshì   nàme   kěliánxīxī   de   wèn   wǒ
     2SG always   so   pathetically   DE   ask   1SG

    什么时候   可以   回家去？（风雨38）
    shénmeshíhòu kěyǐ   huí-jiā-qù
    when   can   go.back.home

'He always asks me very pathetically when he can go back home.' (*Fēngyǔ* 38)

(12) 过   了   几分钟，
     guò   le   jǐfēnzhōng,
     pass LE   a.few.minutes

    乙   和尚   气愤愤地   跑   进房来，（八方37）
    yǐ   héshàng   qìfènfènde   pǎo   jìn-fáng-lái
    second monk   angrily   run   into.the.room

'After a few minutes, the second monk angrily ran into the room and ...' (*Bāfāng* 37)

(13) 她   抱   着   录音机，
     tā   bào   zhe   lùyīnjī,
     3SG clutch ZHE   tape.recorder

    几乎是   飞奔   进房里去。（微型68）
    jīhūshì   fēibēn   jìn-fáng-lǐ-qù
    almost   dart   into.the.room

'She clutched the tape recorder and darted into the room.' (*Wēixíng* 68)

(14) 婆婆　　　一　　　噜唆，　她　便　跑　**回娘家去。**（追云34）

　　　 pópo　　　　*yī*　　*lūsuō*　　*tā*　*biàn*　*pǎo*　***huí-niángjiā-qù***
　　　 mother-in-law　once　blather　3SG　then　run　back.to.her.mother's.house

'Once her mother-in-law start blathering, she would run back to her mother's house.' (*Zhuīyún* 34)

The place object in position I is more prevalently seen in Singapore Mandarin. In Chinese Mandarin, however, only position II is available. That is, the place object has to be inserted in the middle of the compound directional verb (Lü 1980; Zhu 1982).

4.4 Numeral-Classifier Phrase as Objects of Reduplicative Verbs

In Singapore Mandarin, the object of reduplicative verbs can be a numeral-classifier phrase, especially phrases with the verbal classifier 一下 *yīxià* 'a little'. For example:

(1) 然后　　找　　一天　　和　　书小姐　　谈　　怎么　　拍照。
　　 ránhòu　*zhǎo*　*yītiān*　*hé*　*shū-xiǎojiě*　*tán*　*zěnme*　*pāizhào*
　　 then　find　a.day　and　Ms.Shu　talk　how　take.photos

谈　　谈　　几　　次，　就　　可以　　约　　她　　去　　拍照。
　　　　　　　　　　　　　　　　　　　　　　　　　　　　　　　（劳达剧作23）
***tán*　*tán*　*jǐ*　*cì*,**　*jiù*　*kěyǐ*　*yuē*　*tā*　*qù*　*pāizhào*
talk　talk　several　times,　then　can　ask　3SG　go　take.photos

'Then one day (you) can talk to Ms Shu about how to take photos. After talking a few times, you can ask her out.' (*Láodájùzuò* 23)

(2) 你　　和　　同学们　　可以　　彼此　　先
　　 nǐ　*hé*　*tóngxuémen*　*kěyǐ*　*bǐcǐ*　*xiān*
　　 2SG　and　classmates　can　each.other　first

认识　　认识　　一下。　　（追云16）
rènshí*　*rènshí*　*yīxià
know　know　a.little

'You and your classmates can get to know each other first.' (*Zhuīyún* 16)

(3) 其实　　给　　父亲　　**骂　　骂　　一下**　又　有
　　 qíshí　*gěi*　*fùqīn*　***mà*　*mà*　*yīxià***　*yòu*　*yǒu*
　　 in.fact　GEI　father　**scold　scold　a.little**　again　have

什么 关系， ... （追云88）
shénme guānxì
what matter

'In fact, it does not matter much if you are scolded by your father, ...' (*Zhuīyún* 88)

In Chinese Mandarin, the reduplicative verbs cannot carry any objects of numeral-classifier phrases (Zhang 1994).

4.5 Predicate-Potential Complement Construction With Objects

In Singapore Mandarin, when the predicate-potential complement construction takes an object, there are two types of word orders for the complement and the object.

Type I. "V 得*de* 'DE'/不*bù* 'NEG' + C + object (V for verb, C for complement)". The object follows the complement. For example:

(1) 那 动辄 千万元 的 合同，
    nà dòngzhé qiānwànyuán de hétóng,
    that easily ten.million.yuan DE contract

他 放得下 心？ （想飞89）
tā fàng-de-xià xīn
3SG put-DE-down heart

'That ten-million-yuan contract, can't he let go of it?' (*Xiǎngfēi* 89)

(2) 我们 斗不过 他们。 （金狮奖18）
    wǒmen dòu-bù-guò tāmen
    1PL fight-NEG-over 3PL

'We can't win the fight over them.' (*Jīnshījiǎng* 18)

(3) 心里 兀自 放不下 那 口 乌气。 （恶梦118）
    xīnlǐ wūzì fang-bù-xià nà kǒu wūqì
    heart still put-NEG-down that CL outrage

'I can't let go of the outrage in my heart.' (*Èmèng* 118)

Type II. "V + object + 不*bù* 'NEG' + C". The object precedes the complement. This is mostly found in colloquial Singapore Mandarin. For example:

(4) 小黑子 向来 就 瞧他不起。 （恶梦37）
    xiǎo-hēizi xiànglái jiù qiáo – tā-bù-qǐ

			Little.Blackie	always	just	**look-3SG-NEG-up**	

'Little Blackie has always looked down on him.' (*Èmèng* 37)

(5)	生活里	的	惊涛骇浪	**击它不碎，**	**砍它不断。（大胡子·序）**
	shēnghuólǐ	*de*	*jīngtāohàilàng*	*jī- tā-bù-suì*	*kǎn-tā-bù-duàn*
	in.life	DE	big.wave	hit-3SG-NEG-break	cut-3SG-NEG-break

'The big waves in life can never break it.' (*Dàhúzi·xù*)

The word order in Type II is applied only to negation sentences with a pronoun in the object position.

Contrasted with the usage in Singapore Mandarin, only Type I usage is available in Chinese Mandarin. Type II usage used to exist in early Chinese vernacular works before 1921, but is no longer seen in modern Chinese Mandarin.

4.6 A Special Extensional Meaning of Directional Complement Verb 回 *Huí* 'back'

In Singapore Mandarin, the meaning of the verb 回*huí* 'back' is more bleached, indicating 'returning to the original state' when it is in the directional complement position. In this case, the predicate verb is no longer limited to a motion verb, but can be a general verb. For example:

(1)	天	冷，	快些	演	好	**穿**	**回**
	tiān	*lěng*	*kuàixiē*	*yǎn*	*hǎo*	*chuān*	*huí*
	weather	cold	fast	act	well.done	**put.on**	**back**

大衣。（报1995年3月22日副刊5版）
dàyī
coat

'It's cold, quickly finish acting and put your coat back on.' (*Bào*, Mar. 22, 1995, Issue no. 24, supplementary edition)

(2)	倘若	电疗，	你	体内的	癌细胞	能	得到
	tǎngruò	*diànliáo*	*nǐ*	*tǐnèide*	*áixìbāo*	*néng*	*dédào*
	if	electrotherapy	2SG	in.your.body	cancer.cell	can	get

良好的	控制，	你	便	能	**得**	**回**	你	曾
liánghǎode	*kòngzhì*	*nǐ*	*biàn*	*néng*	*dé*	*huí*	*nǐ*	*céng*
good	control	2SG	BE	can	**gain**	**back**	2SG	previously

Characteristics of Singapore Mandarin Grammar

一度	失去的	平静	与	安宁。(尘世97)
yīdù	shīqùde	píngjìng	yǔ	ānníng
once	lost	peace	and	tranquillity

'If the cancer cells in your body can be well controlled by electrotherapy, you can regain the peace and tranquillity you once lost.' (*Chénshì* 97)

(3) "快， 快 **给 回** 我！"
kuài kuài **gěi huí** wǒ
come.on hurry **give back** 1SG
'Come on, give it back to me!'

"不 给！"（金狮奖220）
bù gěi
NEG give
'No!' (*Jīnshījiǎng* 220)

(4) 我 爱 人家 多少，
wǒ ài rénjiā duōshǎo
1SG love people how.much

我 一定 要 **得 回** 相等的 爱。（年岁27）
wǒ yīdìng yào **dé huí** xiāngděngde ài
1SG certainly should **gain back** equal love

'I must get back the equal amount of love that I give out to other people.' (*Niánsuì* 27)

(5) **说 回** 德士 司机。 德士 是 旅游业里 重要的
shuō huí déshì sījī déshì shì lǚyóuyè-lǐ zhòngyàode
say back taxi driver taxi BE tourism.industry important

一 环， 对 我国 的 经济 活动
yī huán duì wǒguó de jīngjì huódòng
one part towards our.country DE economic activity

扮演 积极的 角色。（平心73）
bànyǎn jījíde juésè
play active role

'Back to the topic of taxi drivers: Taxis are an important part of the tourism industry and play an active role in our economic activity.' (*Píngxīn* 73)

(6) 连续　　　拍　了　多部　动作片　　　后，
　　 liánxù　　 pāi　le　duōbù　dòngzuòpiàn　hòu,
　　 continuously　shoot　LE　many　action.film　after

　　 她　的　　打女　　　　形象　　越来越　　深入民心，
　　 tā　de　 dǎnǚ　　　xíngxiàng　yuèláiyuè　shēn-rù-mín-xīn
　　 3SG　DE　fighting.women　image　more.and.more　popular

　　 再　　不　离开　　的话，　怕　　难以　　抽身，
　　 zài　bù　líkāi　dehuà,　pà　nányǐ　chōushēn
　　 again　NEG　leave　if　afraid　difficult　leave

　　 做　回　她　　的　　窈窕淑女。（报1995年8月11日副刊6版）
　　 zuò　huí　tā　de　yǎotiǎoshūnǚ
　　 do　back　3SG　DE　fair.lady

'After making many action films, her image as a fighting woman has become more and more popular, and if she does not abandon this image now, she is afraid that it will be difficult for her to go back to being a fair lady.' (*Bào*, Aug. 11, 1995, Issue no. 6, supplementary edition)

This kind of V回*huí* 'back' predicate-complement phrase is very economical and expressive. Some of the phrases can roughly be translated into Chinese Mandarin. For example, the sentences in (2), (3), (4) and (6) can be said as follows in Chinese Mandarin:

(2)' ... 你　　便　　能　　重新　　**得到**　你　　曾　　一度
　　　 nǐ　biàn　néng　chóngxīn　**dédào**　nǐ　céng　yídù
　　　 2SG　BE　can　again　**get**　2SG　once　once

　　　 失去的　　平静　　与　　安宁。
　　　 shīqùde　píngjìng　yǔ　ānníng
　　　 lost　peace　and　tranquillity

'You can regain the peace and tranquillity you once lost.'

(3)' 快，　快　**还给**　我！
　　 kuài,　kuài　**huángěi**　wǒ
　　 hurry　hurry　**return**　1SG

'Hurry up! Give it back to me!'

(4)' 我　　一定　也　要　　从　　人家　那儿　**得到**
　　 wǒ　yīdìng　yě　yào　cóng　rénjiā　nàér　**dédào**

1SG	must	also	want	from	others	there	**get**

'I must get back the equal amount of love that I give out to other people.'

相等的	爱
xiàngděngde	*ài*
equal	love

(6)'	再	成为	窈窕淑女	了。
	zài	*chéngwéi*	*yǎotiǎoshūnǚ*	*le*
	again	become	fair.lady	LE

'To go back to being a fair lady again.'

For the other two sentences in (1) and (5), it is difficult to translate them into a short sentence in Chinese Mandarin. 穿回大衣 *chuān huí dà yī* in (1) means 'to put on the coat one just took off'; 说回德士司机 *shuō huí déshì sījī* in (5) means 'to switch the topic back to taxi driver'.

The directional complement verb 回 *huí* 'back' in Chinese Mandarin does not yet have such an extensional meaning.

4.7 A Special Appositive Modifier Construction N的人 *Derén* 'N-DE-Person'

In Singapore Mandarin, there is a special appositive modifier construction N的人 *derén* 'N-DE-person', which is equivalent to N这个人 *zhègè rén* 'N, this-CL-person' in Chinese Mandarin. N is limited to pronouns or nouns referring to a person. For example:

(1)	你	知道，	**我的人**	一向	是	懒散惯，
	nǐ	*zhīdào*	*wǒ-de-rén*	*yīxiàng*	*shì*	*làisànguàn*
	2SG	know	1SG-DE-person	always	be	lazy.and.slothful

叫	我	做	这种	吃力不讨好	的	事,
jiào	*wǒ*	*zuò*	*zhèzhǒng*	*chīlìbùtǎohǎo*	*de*	*shì*
ask	1SG	do	such	thankless	DE	job

我	才	不。（年岁68）
wǒ	*cái*	*bù*
1SG	actually	NEG

'You know, I'm always lazy and slothful, so I'm not going to do such a thankless job.' (*Niánsuì* 68)

(2)	**你的人**	为什么	这样的	噜嗦。（新马197）
	nǐ-de-rén	*wéishénme*	*zhèyàngde*	*lūsù*

2SG-DE-person   why   such   blathering

'Why are you being so blathering like this?' (*Xīnmǎ* 197)

(3) 你　　哪里　　可以　　这样　　说？
    nǐ   nǎlǐ   kěyǐ   zhèyàng shuō
    2SG   where   can   such   say

院长的人　　　　很　好　的。（木子100）
yuanzhǎng-de-rén hěn hǎo de
dean-DE-person   very nice DE

'Why would you say that? The dean is a very nice person.' (*Mùzǐ* 100)

(4) 与其说   看   阿甘的人   是   为了   满足   好胜心，
    yǔqíshuō   kàn   āgān-de-rén   shì   wéile mǎnzú   hǎoshèngxīn
    rather.than watch Gump-DE-   be   to   satisfy competitive.spirit
                       person

不如说   大家   都   希望   看到   善良   正直
bùrúshuō   dàjiā   dōu   xīwàng   kàndào   shànliáng   zhèngzhí
as.well   people all   wish   see   goodness   justice

得到   伸张。（报1995年4月17日副刊4版）
dédào   shēnzhāng
get   done

'People watch *Forrest Gump* to see goodness and justice be done, rather than to satisfy their competitive spirit.' (*Bào*, Apr. 17, 1995, Issue no. 4, supplementary edition）

In (1) to (4), the appositive phrases 我的人 *wǒ de rén* 'I-DE-person', 你的人 *nǐ de rén* 'you-DE-person', 院长的人 *yuànzhǎng de rén* 'the dean-DE-person' and 阿甘的人 *āgān de rén* 'Gump-DE-Person' are equivalent to 我这个人 *wǒ zhè gè rén* 'I, this person', 你这个人 *nǐ zhè gè rén* 'you, this person', 院长这个人 *yuànzhǎng zhègè rén* 'the dean, this person' and 阿甘这个人 *āgān zhègè rén* 'Forrest Gump, this person'.[2]

There is no such phrase with appositive modifier in Chinese Mandarin.

4.8 A Special 'Adjective + Classifier' Construction

In Chinese Mandarin, an adjective can be placed in the middle of a numeral classifier compound, such as 一大个 *yī dà gè* 'one big piece', 两小粒 *liǎng xiǎo lì* 'two small pieces'. Such usage is also found in Singapore Mandarin. For example:

(1) 这   绝   不   是   一   小   撮,
    zhè jué   bù   shì yī   xiǎo cuō
    this definitely NEG be one small CL

    而   是   一   大   群   人   啊!（风筝14）
    ér   shì yī   dà   qún rén   a
    but be   one big CL   people SFP

    'It's not just a handful, it's a whole bunch of people!' (*Fēngzhēng* 14)

However, the special 'adjective + classifier' construction discussed in this section does not refer to such constructions as shown in (1), in which there is a numeral word before the adjective. What we are referring to is the 'monosyllabic adjective (commonly 大 *dà*) + classifier' construction without a preceding numeral word. In Singapore Mandarin, this type of construction can function as predicates and can be modified by adverbs, particularly degree adverbs. For example:

(2) 咱们   这里   的   刀鱼   顶呱呱,   又   大   条,
    zánmen zhèlǐ   de   dāoyú   dǐngguāguā   yòu   dà   tiáo
    1PL   here   DE   swordfish best   and   big CL

    又   多   肉,...
    yòu   duō   ròu
    and   much   fresh

    'We have the best swordfish here, big and fresh, ...' (*Wúwéicái* 166)

(3) 年轻的   小贩,   把   蛇皮果   摆放   在   竹箩里,
    niánqīngde xiǎofàn bǎ   shépíguǒ   bǎifàng zài zhúluólǐ
    young   vendor   BA   snake-skin.fruit place   in   bamboo.basket

    很   大   粒,   是   爸爸   爱   吃   的   水果。（尘世209）
    hěn   dà   lì   shì   bàba   ài   chī   de   shuǐguǒ
    very big CL   be   father love eat   DE   fruit

    'The young vendor put the very large snake-skin fruits in a bamboo basket. This is the fruit Dad loves.' (*Chénshì* 209)

(4) 可以   买   大   汽车   送   你   上学,
    kěyǐ   mǎi   dà   qìchē   sòng   nǐ   shàngxué
    can   buy   big   car   send   2SG   go.to.school

比 小雯 的 爸爸 的 车 **更 大 辆**,...（再见55）
bǐ xiǎowén de bàba de chē **gèng dà liàng**
than Vivian DE father DE car even big CL

'I can buy a big car to take you to school, bigger than Vivian's father's car ...' (*Zàijiàn* 55)

(5) 他 心里 想: **越 大 只** 的,
tā xīnlǐ xiǎng **yuè dà zhī** de
2SG heart.inside think more big CL DE

颜色 越 漂亮的, 越 好。（胜利8）
yánsè yuè piāoliàngde yuè hǎo
colour more beautiful more better

'He thought to himself, the bigger and more beautiful the colour, the better.' (*Shènglì* 8)

(6) 那件 毛衣, 已 完成 了 三分之二。...
nà jiàn máoyī yǐ wánchéng le sānfēnzhīèr
that sweater already finish LE two.thirds

"钩织 得 真好。" 邓文茵 由衷地 称赞,
gōuzhī de zhēnhǎo dèngwényīn yóuzhōngde chēngzàn,
crochet DE good Deng.Wenyin heartily praise

又 顺口 问道: " 这么 **大 件,** 给 谁
yòu shùnkǒu wèndào zhème **dà jiàn,** gěi shuí
and casually ask such big CL GEI who

钩织 的 呢？ "（跳舞74）
gōuzhī de ne
crochet DE SFP

'Two-thirds of the sweater was done.... It was crocheted very well. Deng Wenyin appreciated it secretly in her heart and then casually asked: Who did you crochet this big one for?' (*Tiàowǔ* 74)

(7) 你 怎么 一个人 住 在 那么 **大 间** 的 旧
nǐ zěnme yīgèrén zhù zài nàme **dà jiān** de jiù
2SG how alone live in such big CL DE old

屋里　　　呢？　　（青青68）
wūlǐ　　*ne*
house　　SFP

'Why do you live alone in such a big old house?' (*Qīngqīng* 68)

The pronouns 这么*zhème* 'such this' and 那么*nàme* 'such that' in (6) and (7) are both adverbials modifying the following "adjective + classifier" predicates. In contrast, such usage is not found in Chinese Mandarin.

4.9 The Functions of Reduplicated Monosyllabic Adjectives

In Singapore Mandarin, 的*de* 'DE' can be attached to the reduplication of a monosyllabic adjective which is used as a predicate, a complement or a modifier. For example:

(1)　我　　看了看　　　姐姐，　　她　　双颊　　**红红的。**（跳舞107）
　　　wǒ　*kànlekàn*　*jiějiě*　　*tā*　*shuāngjiá*　**hónghóngde**
　　　1SG　have.a.look　sister　　3SG　cheeks　　**flushed**

'I looked at my sister, whose cheeks were flushed.' (*Tiàowǔ* 107)

(2)　潮　　也　　退　　得　**远远的，**　　留下　　那座　　大石
　　　cháo　*yě*　*tuì*　*de*　**yuǎnyuǎnde**　*liúxià*　*nàzuò*　*dàshí*
　　　tide　also　recede　DE　**far.away**　　leave　that　big.stone

　　　冷冷地　　　对　　着　　我们。　（水言珠语163）
　　　lěnglěngde　*duì*　*zhe*　*wǒmen*
　　　coldly　　　against　ZHE　1PL

'The tide has already receded, only the big and cold stone remaining there with us.' (*Shuǐyánzhūyǔ* 163)

(3)　车　　拐进　　**长长的**　　　小路，
　　　chē　*guǎijìn*　**chángchángde**　*xiǎolù*
　　　car　turn.into　**long**　　　lane

　　　来到　　一　　个　　**臭臭的**　　地方。(MD 65)
　　　láidào　*yī*　*gè*　**chòuchòude**　*dìfāng*
　　　come.to　a　CL　**stinking**　　place

'The car turned into a long lane and came to a stinking place.' (MD 65)

In (1), 红红的*hónghóngde* 'flushed' is used as a predicate; in (2), 远远的*yuǎnyuǎnde* 'far away' acts as a complement; in (3), 长长的*chángchángde* 'long' and 臭臭的 *chòuchòude* 'stinking' are modifiers. However, 的 *de* 'DE' is not obligatory, as shown by the reduplicated monosyllabic adjective predicates without 的 *de* 'DE' in (4)–(8):

(4) 养病　　　回来，　　少奶奶　　　就　　老　　不高兴，
yǎngbìng　*huílái*　*shàonǎinai*　*jiù*　*lǎo*　*bùgāoxìng*,
recuperation　back　madam　just　very　unhappy

整日　　　**脸　　黑　　黑，**　…（风雨27）
zhěngrì　**liǎn　hēi　hēi**
the.whole.day　face　black　black

'After the recuperation Madam has always been unhappy, pulling a long face all day …' (*Fēngyǔ* 27)

(5) 他　　鼻梁　　**高高，**　嘴唇　　微　　　翘，
tā　*bíliáng*　**gāogāo**　*zuǐchún*　*wēi*　*qiào*,
3SG　nose　high　lips　slightly　curved

像　　一　　尊　　美丽　　高雅的　　石膏像。（吾土·小说上156）
xiàng　*yī*　*zūn*　*měilì*　*gāoyǎde*　*shígāoxiàng*
like　a　CL　beautiful　elegant　plaster.statue

'He has a high nose and slightly curved lips, like a beautiful and elegant plaster statue.' (*Wútǔ·xiǎoshuōshàng* 156)

(6) 她　　眉毛　　弯弯，　双眸　　　**圆圆。**（跳舞120）
tā　*méimáo*　*wānwān*　*shuāngmóu*　**yuányuán**
3SG　eyebrow　arched　eyes　round

'She has arched eyebrows and round eyes.' (*Tiàowǔ* 120)

(7) 女同学　　头　　低低，　男同学　　　脸　　**红红，**
nǚtóngxué　*tóu*　*dīdī*,　*nántóngxué*　*liǎn*　**hónghóng**,
female.students　head　bowed　male.students　face　red

没有　　一　　个　　敢　　出一声。（花雨22）
méiyǒu　*yī*　*gè*　*gǎn*　*chūyīshēng*
not.have　one　CL　dare　make.a.sound

'The female students bowed their heads, the male students' faces flushed, and none of them dared make a sound.' (*Huāyǔ* 22).

(8) 落地长窗　　　外，　　天鹅河　　**狭狭**、　　**长长**、
　　 luòdìchángchuāng　wài,　　tiānéhé　　**xiáxiá**　　**chángcháng**
　　 French.window　　outside　Swan.River　**narrow**　**long**

静静。（大胡子89）
jìngjìng
quiet

'Outside the long French window, the Swan River lay narrow, long and quiet.' (*Dàhúzi* 89)

Reduplicated monosyllabic adjectives without 的 *de* 'DE' can also be used as a complement, as in (9) and (10):

(9) 瞧　啊！　　腊烛　的　　亮光　　　把　　我们　　的　　影子
　　 qiáo　ā!　　làzhú　de　　liàngguāng　bǎ　　wǒmen　de　　yǐngzi
　　 look　ah　　wax　DE　　bright.light　BA　　1PL　　DE　　shadow

拉　　得　**长长**。（风雨17）
lā　　de　**chángcháng**
stretch　DE　**long**

'Look! The bright light of the wax candle elongates our shadows.' (*Fēngyǔ* 17)

(10) 问　他　又　不　答，
　　　wèn　tā　yòu　bù　dá,
　　　ask　2SG　again　NEG　answer

只　把　头　压　得　**低低**。（胜利23）
zhī　bǎ　tóu　yā　de　**dīdī**
only　BA　head　press　DE　**low**

'When asked questions he did not answer, only kept his head down.' (*Shènglì* 23)

They can be used directly as modifiers, as indicated in (11).

(11) 最　　回味的　　　是　　家门前　　　　　　那　　棵　　老树　　下，
　　　zuì　huíwèide　　shì　jiāménqián　　　　　nà　　kē　　lǎoshù　xià,
　　　most　reminiscent　BE　in.front.of.the.house　that　CL　old.tree　under

与　　哥哥　　姐姐　　攀　　**长长**　　　树藤　　荡秋千
yǔ　　gēge　　jiějie　　pān　　**chángcháng**　shùténg　dàngqiūqiān
with　brother　sister　climb　**long**　　　vine　　swing

玩　　森林　王子　　泰山　　游戏　的　　日子...（报1995年
　　　　　　　　　　　　　　　　　　　　　5月3日6版）
wán　sēnlín　wángzǐ　tàishān　yóuxì　de　rìzi
play　forest　prince　Tarzan　game　DE　day

'The most memorable times were the days we spent under the old tree in front of our house, during which we climbed up the long vines to swing and played Prince Tarzan games with my brother and sister ...' (*Bào*, May 3, 1995, p. 6)

According to Zhu (1961), the reduplicated forms of monosyllabic adjectives in Chinese Mandarin can be classified into two groups based on their grammatical roles: Type A and Type B. Type A is adverbial and is used exclusively as adverbial modifiers. For example:

好好：　　　好好　　学习　　　　　　好好　　工作
hǎohǎo　　*hǎohǎo　xuéxí*　　　　*hǎo hǎo　gōng zuò*
hard/well　hard　　study　　　　　hard　　work
　　　　　　'to study hard'　　　　　'to work hard'

　　　　　　*身体　　好好　　　　　　*衣服　　叠　　得　　好好
　　　　　　shēntǐ　hǎohǎo　　　　　*yīfú　dié　de　hǎohǎo*
　　　　　　body　　well　　　　　　clothes　folded　DE　well
　　　　　　Intended: 'The body　　　Intended: 'Clothes are well
　　　　　　is good'　　　　　　　　folded'

　　　　　　*好好　　衣服
　　　　　　hǎohǎo　yīfú
　　　　　　well　　clothes
　　　　　　Intended: 'good clothes'

高高：　　　高高　　举起　　　　　　　　高高　　翘起
gāogāo　*gāogāo　jǔqǐ*　　　　　　　*gāogāo　qiàoqǐ*
high　　　highly　raise　　　　　　　highly　stick.up
　　　　　　'to raise high'　　　　　　　'to stick up high'

　　　　　　*那　　楼房　　　高高　　　　*鸟　　飞　　得　　高高
　　　　　　nà　　lóufáng　gāogāo　　　*niǎo　fēi　de　gāogāo*
　　　　　　that　building　high　　　　bird　fly　DE　highly
　　　　　　Intended: 'That building is high.'　Intended: 'Birds fly high.'

　　　　　　*高高　　宝塔
　　　　　　gāogāo　bǎotǎ

high	pagoda			

Intended: 'a high pagoda'

大大:

大大	大大	提高	生活	水平
dàdà	*dàdà*	*tígāo*	*shēnghuó*	*shuǐpíng*
greatly	greatly	improve	living	standard

'to greatly improve the living standard'

*那	西瓜	大大	*字	写	得	大大
nà	*xī guā*	*dàdà*	*zì*	*xiě*	*de*	*dàdà*
that	melon	greatly	character	write	DE	greatly

Intended: 'that melon is big'   Intended: 'the characters are written large'

*大大	球
dàdà	*qiú*
greatly	ball

Intended meaning: 'big ball'

Other similar reduplicated adjectives include 慢慢*mànmàn* 'slowly', 快快*kuàikuài* 'fast', 远远*yuǎnyuǎn* 'far' and 轻轻 *qīngqīng* 'slightly' among others. In comparison, Type B is a non-word element, i.e. it is not a word and thus does not form a grammatical constituency, such as 热热*rèrè* 'hot', 红红*hónghóng* 'red', 扁扁*biǎnbiǎn* 'flat', 胖胖*pàngpàng* 'fat', 瘦瘦*shòushòu* 'slim' and so on. It is worth mentioning that, regardless of Type A or Type B, the attachment of adjectival suffix *de* (written as 地*de* 'DE' in adverbial position and as 的*de* 'DE' in other positions) will convert it into a stative adjective, which can be employed as an adverbial, a predicate, a complement or a modifier. This is shown in the following pairs of examples.

好好de   **Adverbial**   **Predicate**

hǎohǎo de

好好	地	学习		身体	好好	的
hǎohǎo	*de*	*xuéxí*		*shēntǐ*	*hǎohǎo*	*de*
hard	DE	study		body	fine	DE

'to study hard'   'The body is fine'

                    Complement   **Modifier**

衣服	叠	得	好好	的	好好	的	衣服
yīfú	*dié*	*de*	*hǎohǎo*	*de*	*hǎohǎo*	*de*	*yīfú*
clothes	fold	DE	well	DE	good	DE	clothes

'Clothes are well folded'   'good clothes'

高高de
gāogāo de

Adverbial	**Predicate**
高高 地 举起	那 楼房 高高 的
gāogāo de jǔqǐ	*nà lóufáng gāogāo de*
highly DE raise	that building high DE
'to raise on high'	'That building is tall'
Complement	**Modifier**
鸟 飞 得 高高 的	高高 的 宝塔
niǎo fēi de gāogāo de	*gāogāo de bǎotǎ*
bird fly DE highly DE	tall DE pagoda
'Birds fly high'	'a tall pagoda'

热热de
rèrè de

Adverbial	**Predicate**
热热 地 喝 了 杯 茶	那 茶 热热 的
rèrè de hē le bēi chá	*nà chá rèrè de*
warmly DE drink LE CL tea	that tea hot DE
'to have a warm cup of tea' (Literal translation: to have a cup of tea warmly.)	'The tea is hot'
Complement	**Modifier**
水 烧 得 热热 的	热热 的 咖啡
shuǐ shāo de rèrè de	*rèrè de kāfēi*
water boil DE hot DE	hot DE coffee
'The water is boiled' (Literal translation: The water is boiled very hot.)	'hot coffee'

红红de
hónghóng de

Adverbial

红红 地 抹 了 一脸
hónghóng de mǒ le yīliǎn
red DE paint LE faceful

'painted (one's) face in red' (Literal translation: Redly painted one's face)

Predicate

那 枫叶 红红 的
nà fēngyè hónghóng de
that maple.leaf red DE

'The maple leaves are red'

Complement

炉火	把	她的	脸	映	得	红红	的
lúhuǒ	bǎ	tāde	liǎn	yìng	de	hónghóng	de
fire	BA	her	face	reflect	DE	red	DE

'The red flames reflected off her face' (Literal translation: The fire shines her face in red)

Modifier

红红	的	太阳
hónghóng	de	tàiyáng
red	DE	sun

'the red sun'

In conclusion, the reduplicated form of a monosyllabic adjective in Chinese Mandarin cannot be used as a predicate, a complement, or a modifier directly. It has to be turned into a stative adjective by attaching *de* (written as 的 *de* 'DE' or 地 *de* 'DE'). In contrast, no such requirement is needed in Singapore Mandarin. This is an important point.

4.10 Word Class Shift

4.10.1 Nouns Being Shifted to Adjectives Modified by Degree Adverbs

Consider the following examples:

(1) 他 **很 君子** 地 问: '重不重? 帮
    tā **hěn jūnzǐ** de wèn: zhòngbùzhòng bāng
    3SG **very gentleman** DE ask heavy-NEG-heavy help

你 提上去 好不好？'（想飞54）
nǐ tíshàngqù hǎo-bù-hǎo
2SG lift.up good-NEG-good

'He asked in a very gentlemanly manner, "Is it heavy? Can I help you lift it up?"' (*Xiǎngfēi* 54)

(2) 这 两 个 问题 大概 你 会 **比较 兴趣。**
                                              （金狮奖85）
    zhè liǎng gè wèntí dàgài nǐ huì **bǐjiào xìngqù**
    these two CL question probably 2SG will **more interest**

'These two questions will probably be of more interest to you.' (*Jīnshījiǎng* 85)

(3) 噢，   男人   和   女人， 这   个   课题   大家
    ō   nánrén hé   nǚrén   zhè gè   kètí   dàjiā
    oh   men   and   women   this CL   subject everyone

    一定   会   很   兴趣。（新视第八波道 1995年4月14日早
                                   安，您好！节目）
    yīdìng   huì   **hěn**   **xìngqù**
    definitely will   **very**   **interest**
    'Oh, men and women, this subject will interest everyone.'
    (*Xīnshìdìbābōdào*, Apr. 14, 1995, '*Zǎoān, nínhǎo!*' programme)

(4) "外表   西化，   作风   西化，   但   某些   方面，
    wàibiǎo   xīhuà   zuòfēng   xīhuà   dàn   mǒuxiē   fāngmiàn
    apperance westernised style   westernised but   some   ways

    非常非常的   中国。"   我   指指   头部。（想飞101）
    fēicháng-fēichángde   zhōngguó wǒ   zhǐzhǐ   tóubù
    very-very   China   1SL   point.to   head
    '"Westernised in appearance and in style, but in some ways, very, very Chinese". I pointed to (my) head.' (*Xiǎngfēi* 101)

(5) 我   觉得   爱情   **很**   **贵族**。（年岁17）
    wǒ   juéde   àiqíng   **hěn**   **guìzú**
    1SG   think   love   **very**   **aristocratics**
    'I think love is very noble.' (*Niánsuì* 17)

(6) 一   轮   圆月   像   大   风灯   悬挂   在   天上，
    yī   lún   yuányuè   xiàng   dà   fēng-dēng   xuánguà   zài   tiānshàng
    one   CL   full.moon   like   big   storm.   hung   in   sky
                                                lantern

    非常   **希腊**   的   星空，   打   着   一闪一烁的   密码。
                                                                              （年岁28）
    fēicháng **xīlà**   de   xīngkōng   dǎ   zhe   yīshǎnyīshuòde mìmǎ
    very   **Greek**   DE   starry.sky play   ZHE   flashing   code
    'A full moon hung in the sky like a big storm lantern. The very Greek sky was starry, as if was a flashing code.' (*Niánsuì* 28)

(7) 生疏   冷漠的   气氛   不   适合   谈话，
    shēngshū   lěngmòde   qìfēn   bù   shìhé   tánhuà
    unfamiliar cold   atmosphere NEG   fit   conversation

尤其是　　谈　　一些　**很**　**个人**　　的　　问题。（人生79）
yóuqíshì　tán　yīxiē　**hěn**　**gèrén**　de　wèntí
especially　talk　some　**very**　**personal**　DE　issue

'A unfamiliar and cold atmosphere is not suitable for conversation, especially about some very personal issues.' (*Rénshēng* 79)

(8)　还有　　歌声　　呢！　　多半　　都　　非常　　抒情，
　　　háiyǒu　gēshēng　ne!　duōbàn　dōu　fēicháng　shūqíng
　　　also　　song　　SFP　most　　all　　very　　lyrical

非常　**文艺**，　使　　人　　听　　了　　觉得　　舒服，...（榴43）
fēicháng　**wényì**,　shǐ　rén　tīng　le　juéde　shūfú
very　**artistic**　make　people　hear　LE　feel　comfortable

'And the songs! Most of them are very lyrical and very artistic, making people feel comfortable listening to them....' (*Liú* 43)

(9)　他　驻足　于　池塘边，　把　脸　贴近　那　**非常**
　　　tā　zhùzú　yú　chítángbiān,　bǎ　liǎn　tiējìn　nà　**fēicháng**
　　　3SG　stop　at　pond.side　BA　face　close　that　**very**

玻璃　的　　水　　面，...（木子93）
bōli　de　shuǐ　miàn
glassy　DE　water　surface

'He stopped at the pond and put his face close to the very glassy surface of the water.' (*Mùzǐ* 93)

(10)　阿公　　**真**　**坏蛋**。（胜利7）
　　　āgōng　**zhēn**　**huàidàn**
　　　grandpa　**really**　**badegg**

'Grandpa is really bad.' (*Shènglì* 7)

(11)　（那　顾客）　头　摇　手　摆　地　自圆其说，
　　　nà　gùkè　tóu　yáo　shǒu　bǎi　de　zìyuánqíshuō,
　　　that　customer　head　shake　hand　swing　DE　justify.oneself

可以　想象　　　当时　　　脸部　　表情　　一定
kěyǐ　xiǎngxiàng　dāngshí　　liǎnbù　biǎoqíng　yīdìng
can　image　　　at.that.time　facial　expression　must

非常　　　卡通。
fēicháng　kǎtōng
very　　　cartoon

'(The customer) was shaking his head and swinging his hands to justify himself, and you can imagine how animated his face must have been.' (*Bào*, June 30, 1995, Issue no. 24, supplementary edition)

((12) 蚝　　是　非常　　营养　　　的　食物。
háo　　shì　fēicháng　yíngyǎng　de　shíwù
oyster　be　very　　　nutritious　DE　food

'Oysters are a kind of very nutritious food.' (*Xīnshìdìbābōdào*, May 13, 1995, *zǎoān, nínhǎo!*)

In Chinese Mandarin, there are instances of a noun being temporarily employed as an adjective in comparative sentences with the overt marker 比*bǐ* 'than', such as 他比阿Q还阿Q *tā bǐ ā Q hái ā Q* 'He is even more Ah Q than Ah Q', in which the proper noun 阿Q*ā Q* is temporarily used as an adjective modified by the adverb 还*hái* 'more', indicating a kind of self-deceiving personal character. However, the nouns being modified by degree adverbs in the aforementioned examples, including 君子*jūnzǐ* 'gentleman', 兴趣*xìngqù* 'interest', 中国*Zhōngguó* 'China', 贵族*guìzú* 'aristocratics', 希腊*xīlà* 'Greek', 个人*gèrén* 'person', 文艺*wényì* 'artistic', 玻璃*bōli* 'glass', 坏蛋*huàidàn* 'badass', 卡通*kǎtōng* 'cartoon' and 营养*yíngyǎng* 'nutrition' are not temporary usages. Some of the collocations, such as 比较兴趣*bǐjiào xìngqù* 'more interested', 很兴趣*hěn xìngqù* 'very interested', 很个人*hěn gèrén* 'very personal', 非常抒情*fēicháng shūqíng* 'very lyrical' and 非常营养*fēicháng yíngyǎng* 'very nutritious', among others, have become conventional and fixed expressions. These nouns are not undergoing a word class shift in Chinese Mandarin, and none of them can be modified by degree adverbs.

4.10.2 Nouns Being Used as Adverbs

Consider the following examples:

(13) 他们　　礼貌　　地　向　　他　握手　　　　道谢。
tāmen　lǐmào　de　xiàng　tā　wòshǒu　　dàoxiè
3PL　　polite　DE　to　　3SG　shake.hands　thank

'They politely shook hands and thanked him.' (*Shènglì* 56)

(14) 我　兴趣　　　地　看　　着　他。（青青107）
wǒ　xìngqù　de　kàn　zhe　tā
1SG　interest　DE　look　ZHE　3SG

'I looked at him with interest.' (*Qīngqīng* 107)

(15) 他　　奇迹　　地　　出现，
　　 tā　　qíjì　　de　　chūxiàn,
　　 3SG　miracle　DE　 appear

绅士　　　地　　吻　　她　　的　　手。（报1995年3月5日副刊13版）

shēnshì　de　wěn　tā　de　shǒu
gentleman　DE　kiss　3SG　DE　hand

'He miraculously appeared and kissed her hand like a gentleman.'
(*Bào*, Mar. 5, 1995, Issue no. 13, supplementary edition)

This phenomenon is also found in Chinese Mandarin, such as 我们要历史地看问题 *wǒmen yào lìshǐde kàn wèntí* 'we have to look at things historically', but is not widely used. The nouns 礼貌 *lǐmào* 'politeness', 兴趣 *xìngqù* 'interest', 奇迹 *qíjì* 'wonder' and 绅士 *shēnshì* 'gentleman' in the previous examples cannot be used as adverbs in Chinese Mandarin.

4.10.3 Adjectives Being Used as Transitive Verbs

Consider the following examples:

(16) 用　　外国　　学籍　　和　　地位　　来　　**骄傲**　国人，...
　　　　　　　　　　　　　　　　　　　　　　　　　　　　　（金狮奖76）
　　 yòng　wàiguó　xuéjí　hé　dìwèi　lái　**jiāoào**　guórén
　　 use　 foreign　schooling　and　status　to　**proud**　fellow.countrymen

'Show pride to fellow countrymen with foreign educational experience and status ...' (*Jīnshījiǎng* 76)

(17) 平，　你　　**生气**　妈妈？（新马·剧本 19）
　　 píng,　nǐ　**shēngqì**　māma
　　 Ping　2SG　**angry**　mum

'Ping, are you angry at mum?' (*Xīnmǎ·jùběn* 19)

(18) **亲爱**　父母　　和　　兄弟　　姐妹，
　　 qīnài　fùmǔ　hé　xiōngdì　jiěmèi,
　　 dear　parents　and　brother　sister

就是　仁　　　的　　表现。
jiùshì　rén　de　biǎoxiàn
be　 benevolence　DE　expression

'It is an expression of benevolence to be affectionate to parents, brothers and sisters.' (*Lúnlǐ·zhōngsī* 4)

(19) 佛经   有   一   则   故事,   说   有   一   个   人,
    fó jīng   yǒu   yī   zé   gùshì   shuō yǒu yī   gè rén
    Buddhist. have one CL   story   say   have one CL person
    scriptures

    为了   **恐惧**   自己   会   老死,   便   去   修行。
                                                              （八方142）
    wèile   kǒngjù   zìjǐ   huì   lǎosǐ   biàn qù   xiūxíng
    for   afraid   oneself will   die.of.old.age so   go   practice
    'There is a story in the Buddhist scriptures about a man who went to practice self-cultivation for fear that he would die of old age.' (*Bāfāng* 142)

(20) 我   应该   **恼怒**   你   的   直率,
    wǒ   yīng gāi nǎo nù   nǐ   de   zhíshuài,
    1SG   should   annoy   2SG   DE   bluntness

    抑或   感谢   你   的   提醒?   （牛车水94）
    yìhuò   gǎnxiè   nǐ   de   tíxǐng
    or   thank   2SG   DE   reminding
    'Should I be annoyed at your bluntness, or be thankful for your reminding me?' (*Niúchēshuǐ* 94)

In Chinese Mandarin, adjectives are increasingly being used as transitive verbs in recent years, but such usage is only limited to causative meanings. For example:

方便   顾客   =   使   顾客   方便
fāngbiàn   gùkè   shǐ   gùkè   fāngbiàn
convenient customer   make   customer convenient
Both meaning: 'to make things convenient for customers'

清醒   头脑   =   使   头脑   清醒
qīngxǐng   tóunǎo   shǐ   tóunǎo   qīngxǐng
clear   head   make   head   clear
Both meaning: 'to make one clear-headed'

清洁   环境   =   使   环境   清洁
qīngjié   huánjìng   shǐ   huánjìng   qīngjié
clean   environment   make   environment clean
Both meaning: 'to make the environment clean'

熟练	技术	=	使	技术	熟练
shúliàn	*jìshù*		*shǐ*	*jìshù*	*shúliàn*
skilled	technique		make	technique	skilled

Both meaning: 'to make one skilled in a technique'

None of the examples from (16) to (20) in Singapore Mandarin indicate causative meanings. Specifically, 骄傲国人 *jiāoào guórén* means 'to show one's pride to the fellow countrymen'; 生气妈妈 *shēngqì māma* means 'to be angry at mum'; 亲爱父母和兄弟姐妹 *qīn'ài fùmǔ hé xiōngdì jiěmèi* means 'to be affectionate to parents and siblings'; 恐惧自己会老死 *kǒngjù zìjǐ huì lǎosǐ* means 'for fear at dying of old age'; 恼怒你的直率 *nǎonù nǐde zhíshuài* means 'to be annoyed at your bluntness'. Such usages do not seem to exist in Chinese Mandarin.

4.10.4 Intransitive Verbs Being Used as Transitive Verbs

Consider the following examples:

(21) 不断 的 **修养** 自己。（伦理·中四5）
bùduàn de xiūyǎng zìjǐ
constantly DE **cultivate** oneself
'Constantly cultivate oneself.' (*Lúnlǐ·zhōngsì* 5)

(22) 只 和 他 见了一次面 的 陈 老师，
zhǐ hé tā jiàn-le-yī-cì-miàn de chén lǎoshī
only with 3SG meet.once DE Chen teacher

竟 这么的 关心 他， **帮忙** 他，
jìng zhèmede guānxīn tā bāngmáng tā
actually so concerned 3SG **help** 3SG

他 怎么 不 感动 呢？（噩梦44）
tā zěnme bù gǎndòng ne
3SG how NEG touched SFP

'How could he not be touched by the fact that Mr. Chen, with whom he had only met once, was so concerned and helpful to him?' (*Èmèng* 44)

(23) 你 看看 有 什么 地方 可以 **帮忙** 的，
nǐ kànkàn yǒu shénme dìfāng kěyǐ bāngmáng de
2SG have.a.look have what place can **help** DE

尽量　　帮忙　　　他们。（大胡子67）
jìnliàng　bāngmáng　tāmen
try　　　help　　　3PL

'See if there is anything you can do to help, and try to help them.'
(*Dàhúzi* 67)

(24) 小五　　那　　年　　我　　以为　　自己　　没有　　机会
xiǎowǔ　nà　　nián　wǒ　yǐwéi　　zìjǐ　　méiyǒu　jīhuì
5th.grade that　year　1SG　think　oneself　not.have　chance

参加　　作文　　比赛　　　了，　但　　他　　仍
cānjiā　zuòwén　bǐsài　　le　　dàn　tā　　réng
join　　writing　competition　LE　but　3SG　still

提名　　我。（报1995年6月15日副刊8版）
tímíng　wǒ
nominate　1SG

'I didn't think I would have a chance to participate in the Grade 5 essay contest, but he still nominated me.' (*Bào*, June 15, 1995, Issue no. 8, supplementary edition)

(25) 她　　正　　　忙　　　着　　备战　　本月　　　举行　　的
tā　　zhèng　máng　zhe　bèizhàn　běnyuè　jǔxíng　de
3SG　currently　busy　ZHE　prepare　this.month　hold　DE

全英羽毛球赛　　　　　及　　法国羽毛球公开赛。（报1995
　　　　　　　　　　　　　　　　　　　　　　　年3月2日6版）
quán-yīng-yǔ-máo-qiú-sài　jí　fǎ-guó-yǔ-qiú-gōng-kāi-sài
All.England.Badminton.　and　French.Open.Badminton.
Tournament　　　　　　　　　Tournament

'She is busy preparing for the All England Badminton Tournament and the French Open Badminton Tournament to be held this month.' (*Bào*, March 2, 1995, Issue no. 6)

(26) 让　　顾客　　　拥有　　　七　　天　　的　　时间　　来　　考虑　　是否
ràng　gùkè　　yōngyǒu　qī　　tiān　de　　shíjiān　lái　kǎolǜ　shìfǒu
allow　customer　have　　seven　day　DE　time　　to　consider　if

要　　作废　　已　　签下　　的　　购物　　合约。（报1995
　　　　　　　　　　　　　　　　　　　　　　年3月10日11版）
yào　zuòfèi　yǐ　qiānxià　de　gòuwù　héyuē

| | want | **cancel** | **already** | **sign** | **DE** | **shopping** | **contract** |

'Allow customers seven days to consider whether they want to cancel a signed shopping contract.' (*Bào*, Mar. 10, 1995, Issue no. 11)

(27) 没有　　一　　个　　国家　　愿意　　站出来　　**挑战**
　　*méiyǒu　yī　gè　guójiā　yuànyì　zhànchūlái　**tiǎozhàn***
　　not.have　one　CL　country　willing　stand.up　**challenge**

　　中国　　大陆　　的　　立场，
　　zhōngguó　dàlù　de　lìchǎng
　　China　　mainland　DE　position

　　即使　　美国　　也　　不　　愿意　（报1995年5月1日16版）
　　jíshǐ　měiguó　yě　bù　yuànyì
　　even　America　also　NEG　willing

'No country is willing to stand up and challenge the position of mainland China, not even the United States.' (*Bào*, May 1, 1995, Issue no. 16)

The transtive verbs 修养*xiūyǎng* 'recuperate', 帮忙*bāngmáng* 'help', 提名*tímíng* 'nominate', 挑衅*tiǎoxìn* 'provoke', 备战*bèizhàn* 'prepare', 作废*zuòfèi* 'nullify' and 挑战*tiǎozhàn* 'challenge' in the previous examples are all intransitive and cannot carry objects in Chinese Mandarin.

The fact that intransitive verbs, as well as adjectives, can take objects may be the result of influences from English. For example, the object-taking verb 挑战*tiǎozhàn* 'challenge' is influenced by English, for the English verb '*challenge*' is transitive, as shown in (28).

(28) He challenged me.

Yet the fundamental reason why some intransitive verbs and adjectives are shifting to transitive verbs is because of the economy principle, the demand for concise language expressions. Thus, it is predicted these expressions outlined in this section will remain in active and extensive usage.

4.11 The Particularity of Functional Words (I): Adverbs

4.11.1 Adverb 有*yǒu* 'YOU'

It is known that there are two words 没有*méi yǒu* in modern Chinese: one is the verb 没有*méi yǒu* 'not have', which can be followed by an object noun phrase, such as 没有钱 *méiyǒu qián* 'have no money', 没有房子 *méiyǒu fángzi* 'have no money' or 没有词典 *méiyǒu cídiǎn* 'have no dictionary'; the other is the adverb 没有*méi yǒu* 'NEG', which is used as an adverbial before verbs and adjectives, such as 没有看电视*méiyǒu kàn diànshì* 'have not watched TV', 没有洗干净*méiyǒu xǐ gānjìng* 'have not washed clean', 没有熟 *méiyǒu shú* 'not mature' or 没有亮*méiyǒu liàng* 'not lit up'.

It should be noted that in Singapore Mandarin, there are two 有 *yǒu* as opposed to 没有 *méiyǒu*: one is the verb 有 *yǒu* 'have', which can take an object noun phrase, such as 有许多人 *yǒu xǔduō rén* 'there are many people', 有两个苹果 *yǒu liǎng gè píngguǒ* 'there are two apples', 有五块钱 *yǒu wǔ kuài qián* 'there are five yuans'; the other is the adverb 有 *yǒu* 'YOU', which is mainly used in front of verbal phrases as an adverbial, such as 你有去过吗? *nǐ yǒu qù guò ma* 'Have you been there?' or 我有去过 *wǒ yǒu qù guò* 'I have been there'. In Singapore Mandarin, this adverb 有 *yǒu* 'YOU' is very commonly used. It comes from the Min and Cantonese dialects, whose function is to affirm the existence of an event or action. The following examples from (1) to (6) are of the adverbial usage of 有 *yǒu* 'YOU' in front of verb phrases, whereas (7) and (8) are of the adverbial usage of 有 *yǒu* 'YOU' in front of adjectives.

(1) 学生　　时代　**有**　　读　　过　　一点　　历史。（八方12）
　　*xuéshēng　shídài　**yǒu**　　dú　　guò　　yīdiǎn　　lìshǐ*
　　student　　times　**YOU**　read　GUO　a.little　history
　　'When I was a student I read a little history.' (*Bāfāng* 12)

(2) 我　也　**有**　想　过。（醒醒33）
　　*wǒ　yě　**yǒu**　xiǎng　guò*
　　1SG　also　**YOU**　think　GUO
　　'I've thought about it too.' (*Xǐngxing* 33)

(3) 最近　你　**有**　回　家　吗？（跳舞131）
　　*zuìjìn　nǐ　**yǒu**　huí　jiā　ma*
　　lately　2SG　**YOU**　back　home　SFP
　　'Have you been back home lately?' (*Tiàowǔ* 131)

(4) "这　几天　**有**　下雨　呀！"　我　说。（吾土·小说上127）
　　*zhè　jǐtiān　**yǒu**　xiàyǔ　ya　wǒ　shuō*
　　these　few.days　**YOU**　rain　SFP　1SG　said
　　'"It has rained these past few days!" I said.' (*Wǔtǔ·xiǎoshuōshàng* 127)

(5) 海伦　紧张　地　问："爹地　走　了，
　　hǎilún　jǐnzhāng　di　wèn　diēdi　zǒu　le
　　Helen　nervous　DE　ask　3SG　leave　LE

　　有　骂　我　吗？"（恶梦105）
　　***yǒu**　mà　wǒ　ma*

YOU blame 1SG SFP

'Helen nervously asks, "Has Daddy left, did he scold me?"'
(*Èmèng* 105)

(6) 刚才   有   人   来   捉   贼，
     gāngcái   *yǒu*   *rén*   *lái*   *zhuō*   *zéi*
     just.now   have   someone   come   catch   thief

     有   到   你   家   去   吗？（吾土·戏剧184）
     yǒu   *dào*   *nǐ*   *jiā*   *qù*   *ma*
     YOU   arrive   2SG   home   go   SFP

'Someone has just come to catch a thief, has he come into your house?'
(*Wǔtǔ·xìjù* 184)

(7) 她   哪里   **有**   生气，
     tā   *nǎlǐ*   ***yǒu***   *shēngqì*
     3SG   where   YOU   angry

     她   也   是   在   跟   你   开玩笑   呀，
     tā   *yě*   *shì*   *zài*   *gēn*   *nǐ*   *kāiwánxiào*   *ya*
     3SG   also   in.process.of   be   with   2SG   make.a.joke   SFP

     不   信，   我   去   叫   她   来！（追云111）
     bù   *xìn*   *wǒ*   *qù*   *jiào*   *tā*   *lái*
     NEG   believe   1SG   go   call   2SG   come

'She is not angry. She is just joking with you. If you don't believe me, I will go and ask her to come!' (*Zhuīyún* 111)

(8) "**有**   乖   一点   吗？"
     yǒu   *guāi*   *yīdiǎn*   *ma*
     YOU   behaved   a.little   SFP

     "她   会   乖   一点   就   好   了。"（春风114）
     tā   *huì*   *guāi*   *yīdiǎn*   *jiù*   *hǎo*   *le*
     3SG   could   behaved   a.little   just   good   LE

'"Has she been better behaved?" "It would be good if she could behave herself."' (*Chūnfēng* 114)

The aforementioned sentences are all in realis mood, and 有 *yǒu* 'YOU' can also be used in sentences with irrealis and subjective mood. For example:

(9) 明天　　国庆　　　　大　检阅，　我们　**有**
　　míngtiān　guóqìng　　dà　jiǎnyuè　wǒmen　yǒu
　　tomorrow　National.Day　big　parade　1PL　**YOU**

　　参加　　表演　　　节目。（吾土·戏剧59）
　　cānjiā　biǎoyǎn　　jiémù
　　participate　performance　programme
　　'There will be the National Day Parade tomorrow, and we will participate in the performance.' (*Wǔtǔ·xìjù* 59)

(10) 妈咪，　如果　　今天晚上　　　爹地　　**有**　回　　家
　　māmī　rúguǒ　jīntiānwǎnshàng　diēdì　　yǒu　huí　jiā
　　mummy　if　　tonight　　　　Daddy　**YOU**　back　home

　　的话，　你　　说，　我　　好不好　　　　把　这　个
　　dehuà　nǐ　　shuō　wǒ　hǎo-bù-hǎo　　bǎ　zhè　gè
　　if　　　2SG　say　　1SG　good-NEG-good　BA　this　CL

　　秘密　讲　　给　　爹地　　听？（微型25）
　　mìmi　jiǎng　gěi　diēdì　　tīng
　　secret　tell　give　Daddy　listen
　　'Mummy, if Daddy comes home tonight, do you think I can tell Daddy this secret?' (*Wēixíng* 25)

(11) 今天　　晚上　　　如果　他　**有**　回来，　我　可　得
　　jīntiān　wǎnshàng　rúguǒ　tā　yǒu　huílái　wǒ　kě　děi
　　today　night　　　if　　3SG　**YOU**　back　1SG　may　need

　　要　　好好　　教训　　他　一　　顿。（吾土·小说上120）
　　yào　hǎohǎo　jiàoxùn　tā　yī　　dùn
　　will　carefully　scold　3SG　one　CL
　　'If he comes back tonight, I'll have to teach him a good lesson.' (*Wǔtǔ·xiǎoshuōshàng* 120)

The adverb 有 *yǒu* 'YOU' can also be used alone as a response to questions, just like the adverb 不 *bù* 'NEG' and 没有 *méiyǒu* 'NEG'. For example:

(12) "难道 你 的 公司 没 替 你 投保？"
nándào nǐ de gōngsī méi tì nǐ tóubǎo
does.it 2SG DE company NEG for 2SG insure
"'Doesn't your company buy insurance for you?'"

"有， 不过 那 是 劳工 险，..."（微型 82）
yǒu bùguò nà shì láogōng xiǎn
YOU but that be worker insurance
"'Yes, but that's the workers' compensation insurance.'" (Wēixíng 82)

(13) "他 没有 告诉 你 买 刀 的 意图？"
tā méiyǒu gàosù nǐ mǎi dāo de yìtú
3SG NEG tell 2SG buy knife DE intention
"'Didn't he tell you his intention to buy a knife?'"

"有。"（微型212）
yǒu
YOU
"'Yes.'" (Wēixíng 82)

(14) "刚才 有 听到 什么 声音 吗？"
gāngcái yǒu tīngdào shénme shēngyīn ma
just.now YOU hear what sound SFP
"'Did you hear anything just now?'"

"有。 一 声 猫 叫。"（吾土·戏剧183）
yǒu yī shēng māo jiào
YOU one CL cat cry
"'Yes. A cat's meow.'" (Wǔtǔ·xìjù 183)

(15) "你 上 学期 有 修 柏斯 的 课 吗？"
nǐ shàng xuéqī yǒu xiū bǎisī de kè ma
2SG last semester YOU take Burns DE class SFP

"有。"（金狮奖162）
yǒu
YOU
"'Did you take Burns' class last semester?' 'Yes.'" (Jīnshījiǎng 162)

(16) 访员： 你们 有 雇佣 向导 吗？
　　　fǎngyuán nǐmen yǒu gùyòng xiàngdǎo ma
　　　Interviewer 2PL YOU hire guide SFP
　　　'Interviewer: "Have you hired guides?"'

　　　培雄： 有。（华文教材 1 B 3）
　　　péixióng yǒu
　　　Pui.Hung YOU
　　　'Pui Hung: "Yes."' (*Huáwénjiàocái* 1B, 3)

In Chinese Mandarin, 有 *yǒu* is used only as a verb meaning 'have', not as an adverb. However, due to the influence of the Cantonese dialect, such expressions as 有售 *yǒu shòu* 'on offer' and 有出售 *yǒu chūshòu* 'on offer' also begin to appear in advertisement languages in Chinese Mandarin. But this kind of usage is still rather limited and has not yet spread widely.

4.11.2 Adverb 才*cái* 'Only/then'

In Chinese Mandarin, both 才*cái* 'only/then'[3] and 再*zài* 'again/then' can be used in irrealis marked sentences. For example:

(17) 他 明天 才 走。
　　　tā míngtiān cái zǒu
　　　3SG tomorrow only leave
　　　'He's not leaving until tomorrow.'

(18) 你 唱 得 真 好，
　　　nǐ chàng de zhēn hǎo
　　　2SG sing DE really good

　　　再 给 大家 唱 一 个。
　　　zài gěi dàjiā chàng yī gè
　　　again give everyone sing one CL
　　　'You sing so well, sing one more for everyone.'

(19) 今天 没 买到 电影 票 没 关系，
　　　jīntiān méi mǎidào diànyǐng piào méi guānxi
　　　today NEG buy-get movie ticket not.have problem
　　　'It's okay if you haven't got movie tickets today.'

我们　　明天　　**再**　　看　　好了。
wǒmen　míngtiān　**zài**　kàn　hǎole
1PL　　tomorrow　**then**　watch　ok
'We'll watch it tomorrow.'

However, they indicate different grammatical meanings when being used in irrealis sentences. 才 *cái* 'only/then' indicates that something happens or appears late, as in (17), wheares 再 *zài* 'again/then' indicates repetition, including actual repetition and vacant repetition. The actual repetition means that the action being repeated has been performed before in reality, as in example (18). In comparison, the vacant repetition means that the action being repeated has been planned to be done but actually failed to take place, as in example (19). In Singapore Mandarin, 才 *cái* 'only/then' and 再 *zài* 'again/then' also convey similar grammatical meanings as they are in Chinese Mandarin. The only difference is that 才 *cái* 'only/then' can also refer to repetition, especially the vacant repetition. This usage is quite commonly seen in Singapore Mandarin. For example:

(20) 凯德琳...　站　了　起来，　说道：　"我　要
　　　 kǎidélín　zhàn　le　qǐlái　shuōdào　wǒ　yào
　　　 Caitlin　stand　LE　up　say　1SG　will

走　了，　改　天　**才**　和　你　联络。（大胡子118）
zǒu　le　gǎi　tiān　**cái**　hé　nǐ　liánluò
leave　LE　change　day　**then**　with　2SG　contact

'Caitlin... stood up and said, "I got to go now and I'll contact you some day later."' (*Dàhúzǐ* 118)

(21) 这　个　问题，　我们　等　一　下　**才**　讨论，...（方块93）
　　　 zhè　gè　wèntí　wǒmen　děng　yī　xià　**cái**　tǎolùn
　　　 this　CL　issue　1PL　wait　one　CL　**then**　discuss

'This issue, we will discuss it later...' (*Fāngkuài* 93)

(22) 吃　了　饭　**才**　走　吧！（华文教材 1 A 65）
　　　 chī　le　fàn　**cái**　zǒu　ba
　　　 eat　LE　meal　**then**　go　SFP

'Please eat before (you) go!' (*Huáwénjiàocái* 1A, 65)

(23) 钱　请　你　先　付，　等　你
　　　 qián　qǐng　nǐ　xiān　fù　děng　nǐ
　　　 money　please　2SG　first　pay　wait　2SG

318 *Characteristics of Singapore Mandarin Grammar*

回　　来　　**才**　　奉还。（华文教材 1 B 8）
huí　　lái　　**cái**　　fènghuán
back　come　**then**　return

'Please pay the money (for me) first, and I will return it when you get back.' (*Huáwénjiàocái* 1B, 8)

(24)　天气　　太　　热　　了，　你　　喝　　点　　茶　　**才**
　　　tiānqì　tài　rè　le　　nǐ　hē　diǎn　chá　**cái**
　　　weather　too　hot　LE　2SG　drink　little　tea　**then**

　　　慢慢　　告诉　　我　　你　　要　　写　　些　　什么。（风雨23）
　　　mànmàn　gàosù　wǒ　nǐ　yào　xiě　xiē　shénme
　　　slowly　tell　1SG　2SG　will　write　some　what

'It's so hot, please drink some tea and then slowly tell me what you're going to write.' (*Fēngyǔ* 23)

This usage of 才 *cái* 'only/then' is unique to Singapore Mandarin. 才 *cái* 'only/then' has to be replaced by 再 *zài* 'again' in all these examples in Chinese Mandarin.

4.11.3 Adverb 太过 *tàiguò* 'Too'

In Singapore Mandarin, there is a degree adverb, 太过 *tàiguò* 'too', which is used frequently to express both high degree and excessive meaning. For example:

(25)　那　　也　　未免　　**太过**　　天真　　了。（报1995年3月
　　　　　　　　　　　　　　　　　　　　　　　　14日15版）
　　　nà　yě　wèimiǎn　**tàiguò**　tiānzhēn　le
　　　that　also　rather　**too**　naive　LE

'That would be too naive.' (*Bào*, Mar. 14, 1995, Issue no. 15)

(26)　适婚　　　　女子　　找　　不　　到　　老公，
　　　shìhūn　　　nǚzǐ　　zhǎo　bù　dào　lǎogōng
　　　marriageable　women　find　NEG　get　husband

　　　原因　　之　　一，　　**太过**　　保守，
　　　yuányīn　zhī　yī　　　**tàiguò**　bǎoshǒu
　　　reason　LIG　one　　**too**　conservative

　　　因此　　缺少　　社交　　机会。（报1995年3月
　　　　　　　　　　　　　　　　　　　14日15版）
　　　yīncǐ　quēshǎo　shèjiāo　jīhuì

therefore lack social opportunity
'One of the reasons why marriageable women cannot find a husband is that they are too conservative and therefore lack social interaction opportunities.' (*Bào,* Mar. 14, 1995, Issue no. 15)

(27) 做　　事情　　不　　可　　太过　　野蛮。（新马·剧本23）
　　　zuò　shìqíng　bù　kě　tàiguò　yěmán
　　　do　things　NEG　should　too　rude
　　　'Do not do things too wildly.' (*Xīnmǎ·jùběn* 23)

(28) 一般　　人　　都　　忽略　　了　　精神　　生活，　太过
　　　yībān　rén　dōu　hūluè　le　jīngshén　shēnghuó　tàiguò
　　　general　people　all　neglect　LE　spirit　life　too

　　　重视　　金钱、　地位　　和　　物质　　享受。（伦理·中三2）
　　　zhòngshì　jīnqián　dìwèi　hé　wùzhì　xiǎngshòu
　　　emphasise　money　status　and　material　enjoyment
　　　'People in general neglect their spiritual life and place too much emphasis on money, status and material enjoyment.' (*Lúnlǐ·zhōngsān* 2)

(29) 不要　　太过　　掉以轻心，　　文笔　　　　好　　的　　人
　　　bùyào　tàiguò　diàoyǐqīngxīn　wénbǐ　hǎo　de　rén
　　　do.not　too　underestimate　writing.style　good　DE　people

　　　通常　　历史　　考　　得　　不　　好。（牛车水119）
　　　tōngcháng　lìshǐ　kǎo　de　bù　hǎo
　　　usually　history　test　DE　NEG　well
　　　'Don't take it too lightly, people who write well usually don't do well in history exams.' (*Niúchēshuǐ* 119)

In Chinese Mandarin, there is no such adverb, and 太*tài* 'too' and 过于*guòyú* 'excessively' are used to express similar grammatical meaning.

4.11.4 Adverb 太*Tài* 'So/Too/Very'

In Chinese Mandarin, 太*tài* 'so/too' has two grammatical meanings. First, it is used to express a very high degree of admiration, and in this case it always co-occurs with the sentence final particle 了*le* 'LE'. For example: 这太棒了！ *zhè tài bàng le* 'This is great!' and 这节目太精彩了！ *zhè jiémù tài jīngcǎi le* 'This show is so wonderful!'. Second, it can express a kind of excessive meaning, such as 他太保守了 *tā tài bǎoshǒu le* 'He is too conservative', 这衣服太贵 *zhè yīfú tài guì*

'The clothes are too expensive'. In Singapore Mandarin, 太 tài also has these two grammatical meanings. For example:

(30) 哇！ 香喷喷 的 炸 鸡 翅膀，
wa xiāngpēnpēn de zhà jī chìbǎng
Wow! sizzling DE fry chicken wings

太 好 了。（小学6A 32）
tài hǎo le
so good LE
'Wow! Sizzling fried chicken wings, that's great.' (*Xiǎoxué* 6A, 32)

(31) 有些 司机 把 车子 开 得 太 快，
yǒuxiē sījī bǎ chēzi kāi de **tài** kuài
some drivers BA cars drive DE **too** fast

是 很 危险 的。（小学6A 15）
shì hěn wēixiǎn de
be very dangerous DE
'It is dangerous for some drivers to drive their cars too fast.'
(*Xiǎoxué* 6A, 15)

However, in Singapore Mandarin, 太 tài can also be used to simply indicate a high degree without carrying such stances as exclamative or excessive meanings. In this case, it is equivalent to 很 hěn 'very' and usually modifies the adjective 多 duō 'many/much'. For example:

(32) 也许， 我 秉承 了 **太 多** 父亲 的 性格，
yěxǔ wǒ bǐngchéng le **tài duō** fùqīn de xìnggé
maybe 1SG inherit LE **very much** father DE character

尤其 是 那 一 股 倔强。（青青116）
yóuqí shì nà yī gǔ juèjiàng
especially be that one CL stubbornness
'Perhaps, I carry a lot of my father's character, especially his stubbornness.'
(*Qīngqīng* 116)

(33) 你 有 **太 多** 知识分子 的 缺点。（吾土·戏剧31）
nǐ yǒu **tài duō** zhīshifènzǐ de quēdiǎn

| | 2SG | have | **very** | **many** | intellectual | DE | flaws |
'You have many of the flaws of intellectuals.' (*Wútǔ·xìjù* 31)

(34) 有 **太** **多** 的 感觉 不 是 这些 还 没
yǒu **tài** **duō** de gǎnjué bù shì zhèxiē hái méi
have **very** **many** DE feeling NEG be these still NEG

经历 过 的 人 能够 体会 的。（金狮奖77）
jīnglì guò de rén nénggòu tǐhuì de
experience GUO DE people can feel DE

'There are many feelings that can't be understood by those who haven't experienced them yet.' (*Jīnshījiǎng* 77)

(35) 她 很 早 就 知道 天底下 **太** **多** 事情
tā hěn zǎo jiù zhīdào tiāndǐxià **tài** **duō** shìqíng
3SG very early just know in.this.world **very** **many** things

是 冥冥注定 的。（想飞53）
shì míngmíngzhùdìng de
be predestine DE

'She learned very early on that many things in the world are predestined.' (*Xiǎngfēi* 53)

(36) 目前 有 **太** **多** 因素 影响
mùqián yǒu **tài** **duō** yīnsù yǐngxiǎng
now have **very** **many** factor affect

市场 的 表现。（报1995年3月7日20版）
shìchǎng de biǎoxiàn
market DE performance

'There are many factors affecting the performance of the market at the moment.' (*Bào*, Mar. 7, 1995, Issue no. 20)

The word 太多 *tài duō* 'many' here is equivalent to 很多 *hěn duō* 'many'. Sometimes it is also used to modify other adjectives, for example:

(37) 我 知道 **太** **久** 没 来 这儿 了，
wǒ zhīdào **tài** **jiǔ** méi lái zhèèr le
1SG know **very** **long** NEG come here LE

不然　怎么　会　相见　不　相识　呢？（微型59）
bùrán zěnme huì xiāngjiàn bù xiāngshí ne
otherwise how would meet NEG know SFP
'I know it's been a long time since I've been here, otherwise how could we not meet each other?' (*Wēixíng* 59)

The word 太久 *tài jiǔ* 'very long' here is equivalent to 很久 *hěn jiǔ* 'very long'. This usage is not found in Chinese Mandarin.

4.11.5 Adverb 一般上 *Yībānshàng* 'Generally'

一般上 *yībānshàng* 'generally' is a peculiar adverb that is widely used in Singapore Mandarin. For example:

(38) 一　本　微型　小说　集，　一般上　都　有
yī běn wēixíng xiǎoshuō jí yībānshàng dōu yǒu
one CL miniature novel collection **generally** all have

好　几十　篇　作品。（胜利·序）
hǎo jǐshí piān zuòpǐn
many dozens.of CL works

'A collection of miniature novels usually includes dozens of works.' (*Shènglì·xù*)

(39) 一般上，　"续集"　都　比　"正集"　差劲。（八方27－28）
yībānshàng xùjí dōu bǐ zhèngjí chàjìn
generally sequel all than main.series worse

'Generally speaking, the sequels are worse than the main series.' (*Bāfāng* 27–28)

(40) 一般上　在　一　所　监狱里　工作　几　年　后，
yībānshàng zài yī suǒ jiānyùlǐ gōngzuò jǐ nián hòu
generally at one CL jail work few year after

就　会　被　调到　另　一　所　监狱。（报1995年3月10日2版）
jiù huì bèi diàodào lìng yī suǒ jiānyù
just will BEI transfer.to another one CL jail

Generally speaking, after one has worked in one jail for a few years, one will be transferred to another one.

(41) 自主　　　学校　　的　　师　　　生　　　比例
　　　zìzhǔ　　xuéxiào　de　　shī　　shēng　　bǐlì
　　　independent　school　DE　teacher　student　ratio

一般上　　　较　　　小。（报1995年3月5日1版）
yībānshàng　jiào　　xiǎo
generally　　rather　small

'The teacher-student ratio of independent schools is generally rather small.' (*Bào*, Mar. 5, 1995, Issue no. 1)

(42) **一般上**，　　人　　　对于　　　自己　　感兴趣　　　的　　事，
　　　yībānshàng　rén　　duìyú　　zìjǐ　　gǎnxìngqù　　de　　shì
　　　generally　　people　toward　oneself　interest　　DE　thing

不但　　　会　　自动　　　　去　　做，
bùdàn　　huì　　zìdòng　　　qù　　zuò
not.only　will　automatically　go　　do

而且　　　会　　越　　　做　　越　　　愉快。（伦理·中三30）
érqiě　　huì　　yuè　　zuò　　yuè　　yúkuài
but.also　will　the.more　do　the.more　delighted

'In general, people will not only automatically do what they are interested in, but they will also enjoy doing it more and more.' (*Lúnlǐ·zhōngsān* 30)

一般上 *yībānshàng* 'generally' is roughly equivalent to 一般 *yī bān* 'in general' and 一般说来 *yī bān shuō lái* 'generally speaking' in Chinese Mandarin.

4.12 The Particularity of Functional Words (II): Auxiliaries

4.12.1 Auxiliary 到 Dào 'Until'

In Singapore Mandarin, when a verb or an adjective takes a state complement, it usually needs an auxiliary word 到 *dào* 'until'[4], as shown in the following examples:

(1) 还　　　是　　死　　了　　的　　好。　　真的！
　　hái　　shì　　sǐ　　le　　de　　hǎo　　zhēnde
　　rather　be　　die　LE　　DE　good　　indeed

'It's better to be dead. Indeed!'

	我	做	人	都	做	**到**	厌	了。（吾土·小说上193）
	wǒ	zuò	rén	dōu	zuò	**dào**	yàn	le
	1SG	be	human	even	be	**until**	sick	LE

'I'm sick of being a human being.' (*Wǔtǔ·xiǎoshuōshàng* 193)

(2) "你 今天 玩 **到** 好 高兴 呀！" 小倩
　　 nǐ jīntiān wán **dào** hǎo gāoxìng ya xiǎoqiàn
　　 2SG today play **until** very happy SFP XiaoQian

　　说。（年岁54）
　　shuō
　　say

'"You played so happily today!" Xiao Qian said.' (*Niánsuì* 54)

(3) 他 的 争吵， 闹 **到** 左邻右舍 都 点燃
　　 tā de zhēngchǎo nào **dào** zuǒlínyòushè dōu diǎnrán
　　 3SG DE quarrel stir **until** neighbours all lit

　　烛 火， 出 来 看 个 究竟。（短篇89）
　　zhú huǒ chū lái kàn ge jiūjìng
　　candle fire out come look CL result

'His quarrel was so loud that all the neighbours lit candles and came out to see what was going on.' (*Duǎnpiān* 89)

(4) 他 给 狐狸精 迷 **到** 不 像
　　 tā gěi húlíjīng mí **dào** bù xiàng
　　 3SG GIVE vixen obsess **until** NEG like

　　一 个 人 了，...（吾土·戏剧48）
　　yī gè rén le
　　one CL person LE

'He was so obsessed with this vixen that he didn't behave like a man...' (*Wútǔ·xìjù* 48)

(5) 最后 天 快 黑 了， 温度 转 冷，
　　 zuìhòu tiān kuài hēi le wēndù zhuǎn lěng
　　 finally sky almost dark LE temperature turn cold

　　我们 等 **到** 又 疲倦、 又 口渴。（风筝186）
　　wǒmen děng **dào** yòu píjuàn yòu kǒukě

| | 1PL | wait | **until** | both | tired | | and | thirsty |

'Finally it was almost dark, the temperature turned cold, and we waited until we were tired and thirsty.' (*Fēngzhēng* 186)

(6) 我 常常 去 找 符喜泉 女士， 找 **到**
    wǒ chángcháng qù zhǎo fúxǐquán nǚshì zhǎo **dào**
    1SG often go meet Fu.Xiquan lady find **until**

自己 都 不好意思 了。（报1995年4月22日19版）
zìjǐ dōu bùhǎoyìsi le
oneself even embarrassed LE

'I often went to see Ms. Fu Xiquan, so often that even I myself was embarrassed.' (*Bào*, Mar. 22, 1995, Issue no. 19)

(7) 单单 "理解 与 写作" 这 一 科，
    dāndān lǐjiě yǔ xiězuò zhè yī kē
    only comprehension and writing this one subject

就 搞 **到** 头 很 疼。（年岁45）
jiù gǎo **dào** tóu hěn téng
just do **until** head very ache

'Dealing with the subject of "Comprehension and Writing" alone gives me a headache.' (*Niánsuì* 54)

This auxiliary 到 *dào* 'until' in Singapore Mandarin is equivalent to the auxiliary 得 *de* 'DE' in Chinese Mandarin. Thus, sometimes 得 *de* 'DE' is also found in Singapore Mandarin. For example:

(8) 儒家 重视 仁德， 把 仁德 看 **得**
    rújiā zhòngshì réndé bǎ réndé kàn **de**
    Confucianism value morality BA morality see **DE**

比 生命 还 重要。（伦理·中四6）
bǐ shēngmìng hái zhòngyào
than life still important

'Confucianism values benevolence and morality more than life.' (*Lúnlǐ·zhōngsì* 6)

(9) 他 贴 身 在 垒 壁 上，
    tā tiē shēn zài lěi bì shàng
    3SG close body at bastion wall on

炮火　　　照耀　　　**得**　他　　无处可遁。（金狮奖4）
pàohuǒ　zhàoyào　de　tā　　wúchùkědùn
fire　　　shine　　　DE　3SG　no.where.to.hide

'He put himself close to the bastion wall, and the light of the artillery fire was so bright that he had no place to hide.' (*Jīnshījiǎng* 4)

(10)　学校　　开　　课　　以后，　我　　自己　　忙　　**得**
　　　xuéxiào　kāi　kè　yǐhòu　wǒ　zìjǐ　máng　de
　　　school　start　class　after　1SG　oneself　busy　DE

　　　分身乏术，　　　　　便　　没有　　主动　　地　　去
　　　fēnshēnfáshù　　　biàn　méiyǒu　zhǔdòng　de　qù
　　　hard.to.spare.oneself　so　NEG　　active　　DE　go

　　　联络　　那　一　　对　父女　　　　　　了。（大胡子33）
　　　liánluò　nà　yī　duì　fùnǚ　　　　　le
　　　contact　that　one　pair　father.and.daughter　LE

'After school started, I was so busy that I didn't take the initiative to contact the father and his daughter.' (*Dàhúzǐ* 33)

However, 到 *dào* 'until' is more commonly used than 得 *de* 'DE' in Singapore Mandarin. It can be even used with the causative verb 使 *shǐ* 'make' to get a fixed expression 使到 *shǐdào* 'make', as can be seen in the following examples:

(11)　江浪　　　　笔锋　　　　锐利，　文艺　　理论　　休养　　高，
　　　jiānglàng　　bǐfēng　　　ruìlì　　wényì　　lǐlùn　　xiūyǎng　gāo
　　　Jiang Lang　writing.style　sharp　art　　theory　training　high

　　　为人　　又　　正直，　　敢　　评，　　　敢　　言，　　**使到**
　　　wéirén　yòu　zhèngzhí　gǎn　píng　　gǎn　yán　　shǐdào
　　　character　also　integrated　dare　comment　dare　speak　make

　　　写作　　的　　人　　出书　　时　　都　　战战兢兢。（胜利102）
　　　xiězuò　de　rén　chūshū　shí　dōu　zhànzhànjīngjīng
　　　write　DE　people　publish　when　all　panicked

'Jiang Lang's writing style is very sharp. He has profound theoretical training, moral integrity, and dares to comment and voice his opinions. So the writers tremble with fear when their books are being published.' (*Shènglì* 102)

(12) 多元　　种族　　的　　社会，　不但　　使　　我们　　的
　　　duōyuán　zhǒngzú　de　shèhuì　bùdàn　shǐ　wǒmen　de
　　　diversified　race　DE　society　not.only　make　1PL　DE

　　　饮食　　多样化，　　也　　**使到**　各　　种族　　间　　的
　　　yǐnshí　duōyànghuà　yě　**shǐdào**　gè　zhǒngzú　jiān　de
　　　diet　diversified　also　**make**　each　race　among　DE

　　　来往　　更加　　密切。（小学6A 19）
　　　láiwǎng　gèngjiā　mìqiè
　　　interact　more　close

　　　'A multiracial society has not only diversified our diet, but also makes the interaction between all races more and more close.' (*Xiǎoxué* 6A, 19)

(13) 过去　　一　个　星期，　美元　　连续　　下跌　　了
　　　guòqù　yī　gè　xīngqī　měiyuán　liánxù　xiàdiē　le
　　　past　one　CL　week　dollar　constantly　fall　LE

　　　好　几　天，　**使到**　国际　　金融　　体系　　经历　　了
　　　hǎo　jǐ　tiān　**shǐdào**　guójì　jīnróng　tǐxì　jīnglì　le
　　　fair　few　day　**make**　global　finance　system　undergo　LE

　　　另　一　次　震荡。（报1995年3月11日20版）
　　　lìng　yī　cì　zhèndàng
　　　another　one　CL　shock

　　　'Over the past week, the dollar has been falling for several days, causing the international financial system to experience another shock.' (*Bào*, Mar. 11, 1995, Issue no. 20)

(14) 我　　国　　　环境　　　　部　　　对于　　维持　　及　　改进
　　　wǒ　guó　huánjìng　bù　duìyú　wéichí　jí　gǎijìn
　　　our　country　environment　ministry　for　maintain　and　promote

　　　住宅　　及　　工业　　区　　的　　环境　　　状况
　　　zhùzhái　jí　gōngyè　qū　de　huánjìng　zhuàngkuàng
　　　residence　and　industry　area　DE　environment　condition

　　　向来　　都　　不遗余力，　　这　　**使到**　　新加坡
　　　xiànglái　dōu　bùyíyúlì　zhè　**shǐdào**　xīnjiāpō
　　　always　all　spare.no.effort　this　**make**　Singapore

被　　誉　　为　　一　　个　　花园　　　城市。（报1995年
　　　　　　　　　　　　　　　　　　　　　3月3日17版）
bèi　　yù　　wéi　yī　　gè　　huāyuán　chéngshì
BEI　exalt　as　one　CL　garden　　city

'The Ministry of the Environment has always spared no effort in maintaining and improving the environmental conditions in residential and industrial areas, which has led to Singapore being known as a garden city.' (*Bào*, Mar. 3, 1995, Issue no. 17)

In Chinese Mandarin, only 得*de* 'DE' is used in the structure with the state complement, not 到*dào* 'until'; and there is definitely no such usage as 使到*shǐdào* 'make'.

4.12.2 *Auxiliary Word* 来*Lái* '*Come*'

In Singapore Mandarin, there is a special auxiliary word, 来*lái* 'come', which is particularly attached to the end of the predicate-complement phrase V好*hǎo* 'V good' to form V好来*hǎolái* 'V good-come'. V好来*hǎolái* 'V good-come' is roughly equivalent to V好*hǎo* 'V good' in semantic meanings, but it conveys a stance emphasising the hope of achieving the desired good result. For example:

(15)　他　　又　　想起　　小学　　　　　时候　　的　　那　　位
　　　 tā　　yòu　xiǎngqǐ　xiǎoxué　　　　shíhòu　de　　nà　　wèi
　　　 3SG　again　recall　elementary.school　time　DE　that　CL

　　　 爱　　穿　　旗袍　　的　　女　　老师　　来。是　　她　　教
　　　 ài　　chuān　qípáo　 de　　nǚ　　lǎoshī　lái　　shì　 tā　　jiāo
　　　 love　wear　cheongsam　DE　lady　teacher　come　SHI　3SG　teach

　　　 他　　应该　　怎样　　把　　"人"　　给　　写　　好来。　（机密64）
　　　 tā　　yīnggāi　zěnyàng　bǎ　　rén　　gěi　　xiě　　hǎolái
　　　 3SG　should　how　　BA　human　GEI　write　good-come

'He once again remembered the lady teacher who loved to wear a cheongsam in elementary school. She was the one who taught him how to write the character "人" *rén* "human" well.' (*Jīmì* 64)

(16)　要　　搞　　就　　搞　　好来。
　　　 yào　　gǎo　　jiù　　gǎo　　hǎolái
　　　 want　do　　just　　do　　good-come

　　　 别　　让　　人　　笑话。（牛车水76）
　　　 bié　　ràng　rén　　xiàohua

NEG	let	people	laugh.at	

'It you want to do it, then do it right. Don't make yourself a laughing stock.' (*Niúchēshuǐ* 76)

(17) 坐 好来。 腿 放下 来, 脚 不 可以 摇,
zuò hǎolái *tuǐ fàngxià lái* *jiǎo bù kěyǐ yáo*
sit good-come leg put.down come foot NEG able shake

小孩子 坐 要 有 坐 相,...（水晶集96）
xiǎoháizi zuò yào yǒu zuò xiàng
kid sit need have sit manner

'Sit up, put your legs down, and don't shake your feet. Children should have good manners while sitting down,...' (*Shuǐjīngjí* 96)

4.13 The Particularity of Functional Words (III): Sentence Final Particles and Interjections

4.13.1 Sentence Final Particle 啦 la 'SFP'

In Chinese Mandarin, the sentence final particle 啦 *la* 'SFP' is a sound combination of the two particles: 了 *le* 'SFP' and 啊 *a* 'SFP' (for example: 他回来啦 *tā huílái la* 'He's back' is equivalent to 他回来了啊 *tā huílái le a* 'He's back'). This particle 啦 *la* 'SFP' is also found, though quite rare, in Singapore Mandarin. For example:

(1) 会 啦, 会 啦！ 我 这样 吃 习惯 啦！（吴韦材70）
huì lā huì lā wǒ zhèyàng chī xíguàn lā
can SFP can SFP 1SG this eat accustom SFP

'I can, I can! I'm used to eating like this!' (*Wúwéicái* 70)

(=会 了 啊, 会 了 啊！
huì le a huì le a
can LE SFP can LE SFP

我 这样 吃 习惯 了 啊！
wǒ zhèyàng chī xíguàn le a
1SG this eat accustom LE SFP

'(I can, I can! I'm used to eating like this!)'

In the following sentence, however, 啦 *la* 'SFP' is not a combination of 了 *le* 'SFP' and 啊 *a* 'SFP'.

(2) "不 是 骗 你 的。" 仲钦 的 声音 一本正经：
　　 bù shì piàn nǐ de　　zhòngqīn de shēngyīn yīběnzhèngjīng
　　 NEG be lie 2SG DE　　Zhongqin DE voice serious

　　"不过 呢, 是 哄 你 的 **啦**！"（跳舞24）
　　 bùguò ne shì hǒng nǐ de **lā**
　　 but SFP be coax 2SG DE **SFP**

　　'"I'm not lying to you." Zhongqin's voice was in a serious manner: "But, coaxing you!"' (*Tiàowǔ* 24)

(3) 终于 又 来 找 我 了 是不是？
　　 zhōngyú yòu lái zhǎo wǒ le shìbùshì
　　 finally again come find 1SG LE be-NEG-be
　　 'Finally, you are coming to see me again, aren't you?'

　　我 都 说 过 会 联络 的 **啦**。（吴韦材29）
　　 wǒ dōu shuō guò huì liánluò de **lā**
　　 1SG all say GUO will contact DE **SFP**
　　 'I told you that I would contact you.' (*Wúwéicái* 29)

(4) 他 那 种 人 是 这样 的 **啦**！（木子95）
　　 tā nà zhǒng rén shì zhèyàng de **lā**
　　 2SG that kind person be this.way DE **SFP**
　　 'That kind of person like him acts this way!' (*Mùzǐ* 95)

(5) 我 当然 是 义不容辞 的 **啦**, ...（追云17）
　　 wǒ dāngrán shì yìbùróngcí de **lā**
　　 1SG of.course be obliged DE **SFP**
　　 'Of course, you can count on me,...' (*Zhuīyún* 17)

(6) "那边 的 生意 怎样？"
　　 nàbiān de shēngyì zěnyàng
　　 there DE business how

　　"马马虎虎 **啦**。"（追云56）
　　 mǎmǎhūhū **lā**
　　 so-so **SFP**

　　'"How's business over there?" "Just so so."' (*Zhuīyún* 56)

啦 *la* 'SFP' in the aforementioned examples is actually equivalent to 啊 *a* 'SFP', which is used as a confirmation marker. There is no such a confirming usage of 啦 *la* 'SFP' in Chinese Mandarin.

4.13.2 *Interjection* 嗨 *Hēi 'Hi'*

In Singapore Mandarin, the exclamation word 嗨 *hēi* 'hi' is often used for greeting or getting attention. This is borrowed from the English word 'hi'. For example:

(7) "嗨， 密斯 游。"
    hēi   *mìsī*   *yóu*
    Hi   Miss   You
    "Hi, Ms. You."

    "嗨， 柏斯 教授， 早。"（金狮奖127）
    hēi   *bǎisī*   *jiāoshòu*   *zǎo*
    Hi   Burns   professor   morning
    "Hi, Professor Burns, good morning." (*Jīnshījiǎng* 127)

(8) "嗨， 大家 好。" 柏斯 教授 踏 着 矫健 的
    hēi   *dàjiā*   *hǎo*   *bǎisī*   *jiāoshòu*   *tà*   *zhe*   *jiǎojiàn*   *de*
    Hi   everyone   good   Burns   professor   step   ZHE   vigorous   DE

    步伐， 频频 点 头。（金狮奖118）
    bùfá   *pínpín*   *diǎn*   *tóu*
    pace   frequently   nod   head
    '"Hi, everyone." Professor Burns nodded as he stepped in at a vigorous pace.' (*Jīnshījiǎng* 118)

(9) 杰： 嗨！
    jié   *hēi*
    Jay   Hi
    'Jay: "Hi!"'

    妮： 嗨！
    nī   *hēi*
    Nee   Hi
    Nee: "Hi!"

杰： 一 个 人？
jié yī gè rén
Jay one CL person
Jay: "Alone?"'

妮： 两 个 人。（吾土·戏剧79）
nī liǎng gè rén
Nee two CL person
'Nee: "Two people."' (*Wútǔ·xìjù* 79)

(10) 嗨， 想不想 去 游泳？（青青67）
hēi xiǎngbùxiǎng qù yóuyǒng
Hi want-NEG-want go swim
'Hey, want to go swimming?' (*Qīngqīng* 67)

(11) 嗨！ 阿 X 正 在 隔壁 替 那 家
hēi ā X zhèng zài gébì tì nà jiā
Hi X right at next.door for that CL

新 开张 的 美容院 剪彩 呢。（微型219）
xīn kāizhāng de měiróngyuàn jiǎncǎi ne
new open DE beauty.salon cut.ribbon SFP
'Hi! X is cutting the ribbon for that new beauty salon next door.' (*Wēixíng* 219)

This interjection 嗨*hēi* 'hi' has not yet been used in Chinese Mandarin.

4.13.3 Interjection Word 哇 *Wā* 'Wow'

哇*wā* 'wow', also written as 哗*huā* 'woah/wow', is widely used in spoken Singapore Mandarin to express a compliment or unexpected emotions. 哇*wā* 'wow' comes from the Cantonese dialect. Examples of 哇*wā* 'wow' as a compliment are listed next.

(12) 哇， 九十二 分， 我 的 宝贝，
wā jiǔshíèr fēn wǒ de bǎobèi
wow ninety-two point 1SG DE baby

你 真 行 （胜利82）
nǐ zhēn xíng

2SG   really   good
'Wow! Ninety-two points, my baby, you are really good.' (*Shènglì* 82)

(13) 哇，   这么   好   的   成绩！（短篇4）
      wā   zhème   hǎo   de   chéngjì
      wow   such   good   DE   score
   'Wow, such a good score!' (*Duǎnpiān* 4)

(14) 哇！ 又   有   人   送   花   来   了，
      wā   yòu   yǒu   rén   sòng   huā   lái   le
      wow   again have   someone send   flower come   LE

      爱琳，   还是   你   行！（再见69）
      àilín   háishì nǐ   xíng
      Irene   still   2SG   good
   'Wow! You've got another bunch of flowers. Irene, you're good!' (*Zàijiàn* 69)

(15) 哇！ 香喷喷   的   炸   鸡   翅膀，
      wā   xiāngpēnpēn de   zhà   jī   chìbǎng
      wow! sizzling   DE   fry   chicken wings

      太   好   了。（小学6A 32）
      tài   hǎo   le
      so   good LE
   'Wow! Sizzling fried chicken wings. Great.' (*Xiǎoxué* 6A, 32)

(16) 哗！ 好   美   的   丝带   花   球！（今后86）
      huā hǎo   měi   de   sīdài   huā   qiú
      wow   so   beautiful DE   ribbon flower   ball
   'Wow! What a beautiful ribbon bouquet!' (*Jīnhòu* 86)

(17) 哗！ 太   妙   了。（微型206）
      huā tài   miào   le
      wow   so   fantastic LE
   'Wow! That's fantastic.' (*Wēixíng* 206)

The following are examples of 哇 *wā* 'wow' expressing surprise.

(18) 哇！ 这么   苛刻！（醒醒46）
      wā   zhème   kēkè

wow! so harsh

'Wow! So harsh!' (*Xīngxīng* 46)

(19) **哇，** 如果 不 是 在 这里 碰见 你，
     wā rúguǒ bù shì zài zhèlǐ pèngjiàn nǐ
     wow! if NEG be at here run.into 2SG

     我 真 不 敢 认 你，...（金狮奖131）
     wǒ zhēn bù gǎn rèn nǐ
     1SG really NEG dare say.hello 2SG

     'Wow! If I didn't run into you here, I wouldn't dare to say hello to you...' (*Jīnshījiǎng* 131)

(20) **哇！** 我 国 的 会馆
     wā wǒ guó de huìguǎn
     wow! 1SG country DE hall

     有 一 百 年 的 历史？（小学6A 23）
     yǒu yī bǎi nián de lìshǐ
     have one hundred year DE history

     'Wow! Our Guild Hall is 100 years old?' (*Xiǎoxué* 6A, 23)

(21) **哗！** 一共 有 一 千 一 百
     huā yīgòng yǒu yī qiān yī bǎi
     wow total have one thousand one hundred

     五 十 元 呢！（吾土·小说上27）
     wǔ shí yuan ne
     five ten yuan SFP

     'Wow! That's eleven hundred and fifty yuans in total!' (*Wútǔ·xiǎoshuō-shàng* 27)

(22) **哗，** 想 不 到 几 个 月 不 见，
     huā xiǎng bù dào jǐ gè yuè bù jiàn
     wow think NEG to few CL month NEG meet

     你 倒 发福 了！（恶梦83）
     nǐ dǎo fāfú le

2SG   actually   put.on.weight   LE

'Wow, I didn't expect you've put on so much weight after a few months!' (*Èmèng* 83)

Neither 哇*wā* 'wow' nor 哗*huā* 'wow' is found in Chinese Mandarin.

4.14 The Expressions of Numerals

4.14.1 Omissions in Numeral Expressions

The initial word 一 *yī* 'one' is usually omitted in numeral expressions over a hundred digits. For example:

(1) 谁   愿意   为   了   **千**   **字**   区区   数   十   元
shuí   *yuànyì*   *wèi*   *le*   **qiān**   **zì**   *qūqū*   *shù*   *shí*   *yuán*
who   willing   for   LE   **thousand**   **word**   mere   several   ten   yuan

的   稿费   滥   写   滥   登   呢？（金狮奖115）
de   *gǎofèi*   *làn*   *xiě*   *làn*   *dēng*   *ne*
DE   fee   randomly   write   randomly   publish   SFP

'Who wants to write and publish indiscriminately for a mere tens of yuans per thousand words?' (*Jīnshījiǎng* 115)

(2) 今年   将   耗资   **亿**   **2000**
jīnnián   *jiāng*   *hàozī*   *yì*   *èrqiān*
this.year   will   spend   **hundred.million**   two.thousand

万   元
wàn   *yuan*
ten.thousand   yuan

兴建   一   座   新   的   机场   大厦。（报1995年3月2日24版）
xīngjiàn   *yī*   *zuò*   *xīn*   *de*   *jīchǎng*   *dàshà*
establish   one   CL   new   DE   airport   building

'A new airport building will be built this year at a cost of 120 million yuans.' (*Bào*, Mar. 2, 1995, Issue no. 24)

(3) **万**   套   "花卉"硬币，   ...今   发售。（报1995年4月19日5版）
wàn   *tào*   *huāhuìyìngbì*   *jīn*   *fāshòu*

| | ten. thousand | set | flower.coin | | today | sell |

'10,000 sets of "flower" coins,... ready to sell today.' (*Bào*, Apr. 19, 1995, Issue no. 5)

(4) 俱乐部　设　有　60　多　种　儿童　班级，　学生
    jùlèbù　*shè*　*yǒu*　*liùshí*　*duō*　*zhǒng*　*értóng*　*bānjí*　*xuéshēng*
    club　set　have　60　more　kind　kid　class　student

人数　超过　**千**　名。（报1995年4月19日10版）
rénshù　*chāoguò*　**qiān**　*míng*
number　over　thousand　CL

'The club has more than 60 types of children's classes with more than a thousand students.' (*Bào*, Apr. 19, 1995, Issue no. 10)

(5) 第12　届　亚大　癌症　大会　将　有　各　国
    dì12　*jiè*　*yàdà*　*áizhèng*　*dàhuì*　*jiāng*　*yǒu*　*gè*　*guó*
    12th　CL　ASU　cancer　conference　will　have　each　country

代表　**千**　人　参加。（报1995年4月5日12版）
dàibiǎo　**qiān**　*rén*　*cānjiā*
delegate　thousand　people　attend

'The 12th ASU Cancer Conference will be attended by thousands of delegates from various countries.' (*Bào*, Apr. 19, 1995, Issue no. 12)

In the case of integers, the word 整 *zhěng* 'whole' is often added before the digit word when 一 *yī* 'one' is omitted. For example:

(6) 校　方　在　路　税　上　每　年　可　节省
    xiào　*fāng*　*zài*　*lù*　*shuì*　*shàng*　*měi*　*nián*　*kě*　*jiēshěng*
    school　side　at　road　tax　on　every　year　can　save

整　**千**　元。（报1995年3月5日23版）
zhěng　***qiān***　*yuán*
whole　thousand　yuan

'The university can save a full thousand yuans a year on road taxes.' (*Bào*, Mar. 5, 1995, Issue no. 23)

(7) 富裕　制造　厂　共　有　8　间　工厂，...
    fùyù　*zhìzào*　*chǎng*　*gòng*　*yǒu*　*8*　*jiān*　*gōngchǎng*
    Fuyu　manufacture　plant　total　have　8　CL　factory

员工	大约	有	**整**	**千**	名。（报1995年
yuángōng	dàyuē	yǒu	**zhěng**	**qiān**	míng 3月5日23版）
employee	about	have	**whole**	**thousand**	CL

'In the Fuyu manufacturing plant there are eight factories... about a full thousand employees.' (*Bào*, Mar. 5, 1995, Issue no. 23)

(8)
她	并	没有	令	我们	失望,
tā	bìng	méiyǒu	lìng	wǒmen	shīwàng
3SG	however	NEG	let	1PL	disappoint

两	小	段	**整**	**百**	个	字	的
liǎng	xiǎo	duàn	**zhěng**	**bǎi**	gè	zì	de
two	small	paragraph	**whole**	**hundred**	CL	word	DE

短文	没有	念	错	一	个	字。（机密51）
duǎnwén	méiyǒu	niàn	cuò	yī	gè	zì
short.passage	NEG	read	wrong	one	CL	word

'She did not disappoint us, not mispronouncing a single word in reading a short piece of two small paragraphs of a whole hundred words.' (*Jīmì* 51)

(9)
在	本地	装	刹车	灯,	最便宜	的	25元,
zài	běndì	zhuāng	shāchē	dēng	zuìpiányí	de	25yuán
at	local	install	brake	light	the.cheapest	DE	yuan

最贵	的	要	**整**	**百**	元。	（新视第八波道1995
zuìguì	de	yào	**zhěng**	**bǎi**	yuán	年8月7日晚10点新闻）
dearest	DE	need	**whole**	**hundred**	yuan	

'To install brake lights in local stores will cost at least 25 yuans. The most expensive ones will cost as much as one hundred yuans.' (New TV 8th wave channel, Aug. 7, 1995, 10 p.m. news)

Nowadays, Chinese newspapers in Singapore generally use Arabic numerals. For instance 千元 *qiān yuán* 'a thousand yuans' is written as 1,000元 *yuán* and 千人 *qiān rén* 'a thousand people' is written as 1,000人 *rén*. Thus, the omission of 一 *yī* 'one' is not easily noticed. However, expressions such as 千元 *qiān yuán* 'a thousand yuans' and 千人 *qiān rén* 'a thousand people' are still used in conversations frequently.

In Chinese Mandarin, there is basically no such omission. It is only occasionally found in phrases with a numeral word modifier, such as 千人大会 *qiān rén dàhuì* 'a conference with a thousand people attending' and 万元户 *wàn yuán hù* 'a family with savings of ten thousand yuans'. However, it is not a widespread phenomenon.

The initial numeral word 一yī 'one' is also commonly omitted in phrases expressing prices. For example:

(10) 第四   天，   "飞力士"   的   上午   行情
     dìsì   tiān   fēilìshì   de   shàngwǔ   hángqíng
     the.fourth day   Felix   DE morning   price

     竟   落   了   **毛**   七。（吾土·小说上92）
     jìng   luò   le   **máo**   **qī**
     actually fall LE **ten.cents** **seven**
     'On the fourth day, the morning price of "Felix" actually fell by 17 cents.' (*Wútǔ·xiǎoshuōshàng* 92)

(11) 它   居然   起   到   **块**   **四**   钱，   我   在
     tā   jūrán   qǐ   dào   **kuài**   **sì**   qián   wǒ   zài
     3SG   actually rise to **yuan** **four** money 1SG at

     块   **二**   钱   就   卖掉。   多   可惜，...（吾土·小说上89）
     kuài   **èr**   qián   jiù   màidiào   duō   kěxī
     yuan **two** money just sold so pity
     'It actually rose to 1.4 yuans, I sold it at 1.2 yuans. What a pity, ...' (*Wútǔ·xiǎoshuōshàng* 89)

(12) 我   的   酿   豆腐   可以   卖
     wǒ   de   niàng   dòufu   kěyǐ   mài
     1SG   DE   stuffed tofu could sell

     角   **半**   了。（吾土·小说上35）
     jiǎo   **bàn**   le
     ten.cents **half** LE
     'I can sell my stuffed tofu for 15 cents.' (*Wútǔ·xiǎoshuōshàng* 35)

(13) "**块**   **三**?   你?   ...   对不起，   我   身   上
     kuài   **sān**   nǐ   duìbùqǐ   wǒ   shēn   shàng
     yuan **three** 2SG sorry 1SG body on

     没有   零钱。"（再见5）
     méiyǒu   língqián

not.have   change

'1.3 yuan? You?... Sorry, I don't have any change on me.' (*Zàijiàn* 5)

(14)   "喂，   老板，   多少钱？"
      wèi   *lǎobǎn*   *duōshǎoqián*
      Hey   boss   how.much

"块   七！"（我有102）
kuài   *qī*
yuan   seven

'Hey, boss, how much is it?' '1.7 yuans!' (*wǒyǒu* 102)

There is also no such omission in Chinese Mandarin.

Two-digit numerals over a hundred can be followed by a classifier with the lower digit word omitted. For example:

(15)   有关   代理   公司   被   罚款
      yǒuguān *dàilǐ* *gōngsī* *bèi* *fákuǎn*
      related   agent   corporation BEI fine

九千五   元。（报1995年3月11日12版）
jiǔqiānwǔ   *yuán*
nine.thousand.five.hundred yuan

'The agent concerned was fined nine thousand five hundred yuans.' (*Bào*, Mar. 11, 1995, Issue no. 12)

Here 九千五元 *jiǔ qiān wǔ yuán* refers to 九千五百元 *jiǔ qiān wǔ bǎi yuán* 'nine thousand and five hundred yuan', where the digit word 百 *bǎi* 'hundred' is omitted. Other examples are as follows.

(16)   一   妇女   判监   17   个   月，
      yī   *fùnǚ*   *pànjiān* *shíqī* *gè* *yuè*
      one women sentence seventeen CL month

罚   万二   元。（报1995年3月11日12版）
fá   *wàn'èr*   *yuán*
fine twelve.thousand yuan

'A woman was sentenced to 17 months in prison and fined 12,000 yuans.' (*Bào*, Mar. 11, 1995, Issue no. 12)

(17) 电缆   电视   本   月   23日   起   进入
    diànlǎn diànshì běn   yuè   èrshísānrì   qǐ   jìnrù
    cable   TV   this   month twenty-third start   enter

    淡滨尼   万五   户   人家。（报1995年6月8日1版）
    dànbīnní wàn-wǔ   hù   rénjiā
    Tampines fifteen.thousand   CL   home

    'Cable TV will enter 15,000 homes in Tampines from the 23rd of this month.' (*Bào*, June 8, 1995, Issue no. 1)

(18) 两   人   合   起来   有   千五六
    liǎng   rén   hé   qǐlái   yǒu   qiān-wǔ-liù
    two   people together up   have   one.thousand.five.or.six.hundred

    块   钱   的   收入。（吾土·小说上71）
    kuài   qián   de   shōurù
    yuan   money   DE   income

    'The two of them together have fifteen or one thousand and five or six hundred yuans' worth of income.' (*Wútǔ·xiǎoshuōshàng* 71)

In Chinese Mandarin, two-digit numerals over a hundred can also be followed by a classifier with the lower digit word omitted. For example: 二百六十 *èr bǎi liù shí* 'two hundred and sixty' can be said as 两百六 *liǎng bǎi liù*; 三万四千 *sān wàn sì qiān* 'thirty-four thousand' can be said as 三万四 *sān wàn sì*. However, this form of omission cannot be directly followed by a classifier referring to money. For instance, 两百六十元 *liǎng bǎi liù shí yuán* 'two hundred and sixty yuans' cannot be expressed as 两百六元 *liǎng bǎi liù yuán*, where the digit 十 *shí* 'ten' is omitted.

4.14.2 Percentage Expressions

In Singapore Mandarin, there are three ways to express percentages.

First, they can be expressed by Arabic numerals with "%". This is used only in written registers and mostly found in newspapers. For example:

(19) 根据   估计，   到   公元   2030   年，
    gēnjù   gūjì   dào   gōngyuán   èrlíngsānlíng   nián
    according.to estimation until   AD   twenty.thirty   year

    我国   的   老人   将   达   八十二万，
    wǒguó   de   lǎorén   jiāng   dá   bāshíèrwàn
    our.country DE   elderly   will   reach   eight.hundred.and.twenty.thousand

	占	总	人口	的	**22%**。（华文教材2A 143）
	zhàn	zǒng	rénkǒu	de	*bǎifēnzhī-èrshí 'èr*
	make.up	gross	population	DE	**twenty.two.percent**

It is estimated that by 2030, the number of elderly people in China will reach 82 million, accounting for 22% of the total population. (*Huáwénjiàocái* 2A, 143)

(20)
公积金	局	从	7月1日	起，	调整
gōngjījīn	jú	cóng	qīyuèyīrì	qǐ	tiáozhěng
CPF	bureau	from	July 1st	start	adjust

公积金	会员	的	存款	利率，	从	目前	的
gōngjījīn	huìyuán	de	cúnkuǎn	lìlǜ	cóng	mùqián	de
CPF	member	DE	deposit	interest	from	now	DE

3.1%		调高	到	**3.82%**。	（报1995年 5月13日3版）
bǎifēnzhī-sāndiǎnyī		tiáogāo	dào	***bǎifēnzhī-sāndiǎnbā'èr***	
three.point.one.percent		raise	to	**three.point.eight.two.percent**	

'The CPF Board decided that the deposit rate for CPF members will be adjusted from the current 3.1% to 3.82% since July 1st.' (*Bào*, May 13, 1995, Issue no. 3)

(21)
佳果	联营	冷仓	有限	公司	的
jiāguǒ	liányíng	lěngcāng	yǒuxiàn	gōngsī	de
Jaguar	united	warehouse	limited	corporation	DE

佳果	冷藏	大厦	租用	率	已
jiāguǒ	lěngcáng	dàshà	zūyòng	lǜ	yǐ
Jaguar	cold.storage	building	rent	rate	already

达	**100%**。（报1995年5月5日19版）
dá	***bǎifēnzhī-bǎi***
reach	**hundred.percent**

'The occupancy rate of the Jaguar Cold Storage Building of the Jaguar United Cold Storage Co reached 100%.' (*Bào*, May 5, 1995, Issue no. 19)

Second, it can be expressed with 百分之 *bǎi fēn zhī* 'percent'. This expression is mostly used in broadcasting and occasionally found in writing. For example:

(22) 路　　税　　又　　高涨　　了，　　调高　　**百分之三十。**（胜利83）
　　　lù　　shuì　yòu　gāozhǎng　le　　tiáogāo　**bǎifēnzhī-sānshí**
　　　road　tax　again　soar　　　LE　　raise　　**thirty.percent**
　　　'The road tax was raised again, by 30 percent.' (*Shènglì* 83)

(23) 新加坡　　来　　的　　新闻　　工作者　　有的　　说　　听懂
　　　xīnjiāpō　lái　　de　　xīnwén　gōngzuòzhě　yǒude　shuō　tīngdǒng
　　　Singapore　come　DE　news　　journalist　　some　say　understand

　　　百分之十，　　有的　　说　　**百分之六十，**...（平心116）
　　　bǎifēnzhī-shí　yǒude　shuō　**bǎifēnzhī-liùshí**
　　　ten.percent　some　say　**sixty.percent**
　　　'Some journalists from Singapore say they understand 10 percent, some say 60 percent...' (*Píngxīn* 116)

Third, it can be expressed by numerals with 巴仙 *bāxiān* 'percent'. 巴仙 *bāxiān* is the transliteration of the English word 'percent', an expression that is commonly used in both spoken and written Singapore Mandarin. Numerals in both Chinese characters and Arabic forms are found in written language. For example:

(24) 当初　　　新　　厂　　　合　　股，...　自己　　只　　占
　　　dāngchū　xīn　chǎng　hé　　gǔ　　　zìjǐ　　zhǐ　zhàn
　　　back.then　new　factory　joint　stock　oneself　only　own

　　　四十五　　**巴仙**　　的　　股份。（吾土·小说上41）
　　　sìshíwǔ　　**bāxiān**　de　　gǔfèn
　　　forty-five　**percent**　DE　share
　　　'When the new factory formed a partnership ... they only possessed 45 percent of the shares.' (*Wútǔ·xiǎoshuōshàng* 41)

(25) 你们　　不是　　加　　了　　**五**　　**巴仙**　　薪水　　喽？（吾土·小说上31）
　　　nǐmen　bùshì　jiā　le　　**wǔ**　　**bāxiān**　xīnshuǐ　lou
　　　2PL　　NEG　　raise　LE　**five**　**percent**　salary　SFP
　　　'You didn't get the 5 percent pay rise?' (*Wútǔ·xiǎoshuōshàng* 31)

(26) 马来西亚　　的　　胡椒　　产量　　　居　　世界　　第4　　位，
　　　mǎláixīyà　de　　hújiāo　chǎnliàng　jū　　shìjiè　　dì 4　　wèi
　　　Malaysia　　DE　pepper　production　rank　world　　No.4　　CL

Characteristics of Singapore Mandarin Grammar 343

砂越 就 占 了 其中 的 **95** 巴仙。
（南北26）
*shāyuè jiù zhàn le qízhōng de **jiǔshíwǔ bāxiān***
Sarawak just make.up LE among DE **ninety.five percent**

'Malaysia ranks 4th in the world for pepper production, and Sarawak alone accounts for 95 percent of the total.' (*Nánběi* 26)

(27) "电脑 医生" 的 效率 很 高, 以 心脏病
diànnǎo yīshēng de xiàolǜ hěn gāo yǐ xīnzàngbìng
computer doctor DE efficiency very high for heart.attack

来说, 已 证实 有 **90** 巴仙 的 准确性。
（华文教材2A 97）
*láishuō yǐ zhèngshí yǒu **jiǔshí bāxiān** de zhǔnquèxìng*
to.say already prove have **ninety percent** DE accuracy

'The "computer doctor" is very efficient and has been proven to be 90 percent accurate for heart disease.' (*Huáwénjiàocái* 2A, 97)

In Chinese Mandarin, only the first two examples, but not 巴仙 *bāxiān* 'percent', are used to express percentages.

4.14.3 The Expression of Numerals Larger Than Ten Thousand

In Singapore Mandarin, there are two strategies to express numbers over ten thousand.

First, it can be expressed by 万 *wàn* 'ten thousand'. For example:

(28) 至少 一万二！ （再见87）
zhìshǎo yīwàn'èr
at.least twelve.thousand

'At least 12,000 dollars!' (*Zàijiàn* 87)

(29) 可口可乐 有限 公司 以及 亚洲 乳酪品 私人 有限
kěkǒukělè yǒuxiàn gōngsī yǐjí yàzhōu rǔlàopǐn sīrén yǒuxiàn
Coca-Cola limited company and Asian dairy private limited

公司 各 捐 **2** 万 5000
*gōngsī gè juān **èr** wàn wǔqiān*
company each donate **two** ten.thousand five.thousand

元 （报1995年3月12日1版）
yuán
dollar

'The Coca-Cola Company Limited and the Asian Dairy Products Pte Ltd. each donated 25,000 yuans.' (*Bào*, Mar. 12, 1995, Issue no. 1)

(30) 预料　　在　　今　　年　　完成　　的　　私人　　房地产　　有
yùliào　zài　jīn　nián　wánchéng　de　sīrén　fángdìchǎn　yǒu
expect　at　this　year　accomplish　DE　private　real.estate　have

8200　　　　　　　个　单位，　明年　　　有
bāqiānèrbǎi　　　gè　dānwèi　míngnián　yǒu
eight.thousand.two.hundred　CL　unit　next.year　have

1　万　　　　　6400　　　　　　　　个　单位，
yī　wàn　　　liùqiānsìbǎi　　　　　gè　dānwèi
one　ten.thousand　six.thousand.four.hundred　CL　unit

后年　　　有　1　万　　　　5700
hòunián　yǒu　yī　wàn　　wǔqiānqībǎi
the.year.after　have　one　ten.thousand　five.thousand.seven.hundred

个　单位。　（报1995年3月7日3版）
gè　dānwèi
CL　unit

'It is expected that 8,200 units of private real estate will be completed this year, 16,400 units next year and 15,700 units the year after.' (*Bào*, Mar. 7, 1995, Issue no. 3)

Second, it can be expressed by 千 *qiān* 'thousand'. This is an expression influenced by English. For example:

(31) "多少？"
duōshǎo
how.much
'How much?'

"好象　　是　二十千　　　的　税务　　回扣。"（生命141）
*hǎoxiàng　shì　**èrshí-qiān**　de　shuìwù　huíkòu*

likely be **twenty.thousand** DE tax rebate

'It seems that there is a tax rebate of twenty thousand dollars.' (*Shēngmìng* 141)

(32) 小全　　　上　　礼拜　　赌　　马　　输　　了
　　 xiǎoquán　shàng　lǐbài　dǔ　mǎ　shū　le
　　 Xiaoquan　last　week　gamble　horse　lose　LE

　　 二十　　几　　千，...（吾土·小说上14）
　　 èrshí　jǐ　qiān
　　 twenty　several　thousand

'Xiaoquan lost more than twenty thousand last week gambling on horses...' (*Wútǔ·xiǎoshuōshàng* 14)

(33) 准备　　一　　炫　　　　自己　　这　　装修　　了
　　 zhǔnbèi　yī　xuàn　　　zìjǐ　　zhè　zhuāngxiū　le
　　 prepare　once　show.off　oneself　this　renovate　LE

　　 数十千　　　　元　　的　　华　　　屋。（再见83）
　　 shù-shí-qiān　yuán　de　huá　wū
　　 several-ten-thousand　yuan　DE　luxurious　house

'Prepare to show off the flashy house that has been renovated for tens of thousands of yuans.' (*Zàijiàn* 83)

(34) 我　　看　　他　　这　　一　　次　　输　　了　　**几十千**，
　　 wǒ　kàn　tā　zhè　yī　cì　shū　le　**jǐshíqiān**
　　 1SG　look　3SG　this　one　time　lose　LE　**tens.of.thousands**

　　 大概　　是　　跑掉　　了　　吧！（新马199）
　　 dàgài　shì　pǎodiào　le　ba
　　 probably　be　run.away　LE　SFP

'I think he lost tens of thousands of dollars this time, so he probably has run away!' (*Xīnmǎ* 199)

(35) 3房　　　估价：　　新元　　　　　**25千**　　　　　　到
　　 sānfáng　gūjià　xīnyuán　　　　**èrshíwǔqiān**　　dào
　　 3rooms　valuation　Singapore.dollar　**twenty.five.thousand**　to

　　 50千，　　　　　　现金。（豪丰产业广告）
　　 wǔshíqiān　　　　xiànjīn

fifty.thousand cash

'valuation of three rooms: twenty-five thousand to fifty thousand, cash.' (*Háofēng* Industrial Advertisement)

In Chinese Mandarin, only the first kind of expression 万 *wàn* 'ten thousand' is employed for numerals larger than ten thousand.

4.14.4 Expression of Approximate Numbers

In Chinese Mandarin, approximate numbers are expressed by using two adjacent numbers, such as 七八个 *qībāgè* 'seven or eight', 五六个 *wǔliùgè* 'five or six' and so on. This kind of expression is also found in Singapore Mandarin, for example:

(36) 我　　一　　天　　**两、三**　　块　　的　　收入，
   wǒ *yī* *tiān* ***liǎngsān*** *kuài* *de* *shōurù*
   1SG one day two.or.three yuan DE income

   怎么　　应付　　得　　了　　每日　　的　　生活　　费用
   zěnme *yìngfù* *de* *liǎo* *měirì* *de* *shēnghuó* *fèiyòng*
   how handle DE able daily DE life expense

   及　　父亲　　的　　医药　　费？（短篇36）
   jí *fùqīn* *de* *yīyào* *fèi*
   and father DE medical expense

'With an income of two or three yuans a day, how can I afford to pay for my daily living expenses and my father's medical expenses?' (*Duǎnpiān* 36)

(37) 那　　时候，　　有　　个　　**五六十**　　岁　　的　　老头，
   nà *shíhòu* *yǒu* *gè* ***wǔliùshí*** *suì* *de* *lǎotóu*
   that time have CL fifty.or.sixty age DE old.man

   常　　划　　着　　艘　　小　　舢舨　　在
   cháng *huá* *zhe* *sōu* *xiǎo* *shānbǎn* *zài*
   often row ZHE CL small sampan at

   河　　中　　来来往往。（金狮奖352）
   hé *zhōng* *láiláiwǎngwǎng*
   river middle come.and.go

'At that time, there was an old man in his fifties or sixties who used to row a small sampan back and forth on the river.' (*Jīnshījiǎng* 352)

(38) 我　一　日　的　收入　仅　得
　　　wǒ　yī　rì　de　shōurù　jǐn　dé
　　　1SG one day DE income only get

　　　一、两　　元　　而已。（短篇35）
　　　yīliǎng　　yuán　　éryǐ
　　　one.or.two yuan　only

　　　'My daily income is only one or two yuans.' (*Duǎnpiān* 35)

But a more commonly used expressions is "classifier (or magnitudal numbers) +多 *duō* 'more' + 两 *liǎng* 'two' + classifier (or magnitudal numbers)", the meaning of which is the same with the approximate number expression of 一两 *yī liǎng*... 'one or two ...'. For example:

(39) 所　花　也　不过　**块**　**多**　**两**　**块**　钱（风雨88）
　　　suǒ　huā　yě　bùguò　**kuài**　**duō**　**liǎng**　**kuài**　qián
　　　SUO cost also just **CL** **more** **two** **CL** money
　　　'The cost is only one or two yuans.' (*Fēngyǔ* 88)

(40) "一　套　多少　钱？这么　小看　我。"
　　　yī　tào　duōshǎo　qián　zhème　xiǎokàn　wǒ
　　　one set how.much money this belittle 1SG
　　　'How much is a set? You are belittling me.'

　　　"千　　多　　两千　　块！"（蓝天50）
　　　qiān　　duō　　liǎngqiān　　kuài
　　　thousand more two.thousand CL
　　　'A thousand or two thousand yuans!' (*Lántiān* 50)

(41) 家才，这　个　地方，你　也　住　了　**十**　**多**
　　　jiācái　zhè　gè　dìfāng　nǐ　yě　zhù　le　**shí**　**duō**
　　　Jia.Cai this CL place 2SG also live LE **ten** **more**

　　　二十　年　了，就　这么　一　句　话，
　　　èrshí　**nián**　le　jiù　zhème　yī　jù　huà
　　　twenty **year** LE just this one CL sentence

　　　说　走　就　走？（华文教材4B 59）
　　　shuō　zǒu　jiù　zǒu

say   leave just leave

'Jia Cai, you've lived in this place for more than ten or twenty years, so you just say that and leave?' (*Huáwénjiàocái* 4B, 59)

(42) （电话　卡）　只　　买　了　**百**　　**多**
　　　diànhuà　kǎ　　zhǐ　mǎi　le　**bǎi**　**duō**
　　　phone　　card　only　buy　LE　**hundred**　**more**

　　　二　　百　　　块。（新视第八波道1995年8月25日晚10点新闻）
　　　èr　　bǎi　　kuài
　　　two　hundred　CL

'(Phone cards) only sold for about one hundred or two hundred yuans.' (New TV Channel 8, August 25, 1995, 10:00 p.m. News)

In these examples, 块多两块钱 *kuài duō liǎng kuài qián* is equivalent to 一两块钱 *yī liǎng kuài qián* 'one or two yuans'; 千多两千块 *qiān duō liǎng qiān kuài* is equivalent to 一两千块钱 *yī liǎng qiān kuài* 'one or two thousand yuans'; 十多二十年 *shí duō èr shí nián* is equivalent to 一二十年 *yī èr shí nián* 'one or two decades'; 百多二百块 *bǎi duō èr bǎi kuài* is equivalent to 一二百块 *yī èr bǎi kuài* 'one or two hundred yuans'. There are no such expressions in Chinese Mandarin.

4.14.5 Expressions for Asking Age

In Singapore Mandarin, the expression 几岁 *jǐsuì* 'how old' can be used for enquiring about the age of a child, an adult or an elderly person. For example:

(43) 您　　今年　　　几岁　　　啊?⁵
　　　nín　jīnnián　　jǐsuì　　　a
　　　2SG　this.year　how.old　SFP
　　　How old are you?

(45) 凤娇　　　今年　　　才　　几岁?
　　　fèngjiāo　jīnnián　　cái　　jǐsuì
　　　Fengjiao　this.year　just　how.old
　　　'How old is Feng Jiao this year?'

(45) 不　　满　　　十六岁。(吾土·小说上120)
　　　bù　　mǎn　　shíliùsuì
　　　NEG　full　　sixteen.year.old
　　　'Not yet sixteen.' (*Wútǔ·xiǎoshuōshàng* 120)

(46) 小熊， 你 几岁 了？
xiǎoxióng nǐ jǐsuì le
Little Bear 2SL how.old LE
'Little Bear, how old are you?'

二十。 (金狮奖208)
èrshí
twenty
'Twenty.' (*Jīnshījiǎng* 208)

(47) "你 知道 我 今年 几岁 了？"
nǐ zhīdào wǒ jīnnián jǐsuì le?
2SG know 1SG this.year how.old LE
'Do you know how old I am?'

"你 还 年青。"
nǐ hái niánqīng。
2SG still young
'You are still young.'

"快 三十七 了。" （吾土·小说上107）
kuài sānshíqī le
almost thirty-seven LE
'(I'm) almost thirty-seven.'

"你 看来 才 二十七。"
nǐ kànlái cái èrshíqī。
2SG seem only twenty-seven
'You seem to be only twenty-seven'. (*Wútǔ·xiǎoshuōshàng* 107)

In Chinese Mandarin, 几岁 *jǐ suì* 'how old', of which the literal translation is 'several years', can be used only to ask for a child's age. Usually 多大 *duō dà* 'how old', 多大年纪 *duōdà niánjì* 'how many years old' or 多大岁数 *duōdà suìshù* 'how many years old' are used when the person being asked is an adult or an elderly person.

4.14.6 Time Expressions

1. Date Expressions

In spoken Singapore Mandarin, dates are expressed from year to day. For example: 1995年*nián* 5月*yuè* 8日*rì* 'May 8, 1995'. There are two ways to express time in written Singapore Mandarin.

The first method is to express dates from year to day when the words 年 *nián* 'year', 月 *yuè* 'month' and 日 *rì* 'day' are all spelled out, and the specific date can be written in either Chinese characters or Arabic numerals. For example:

(48) 学生　　　曾华丰　　　　上
　　 xuéshēng　zēnghuáfēng　　shàng
　　 student　　Zeng.Huafeng　yours.truly

　　 一九八二　　　　年　　一月　　十日　　（青青104）
　　 yījiǔbāèr　　　　nián　　yīyuè　　shí rì
　　 nineteen.eighty.two　year　January　tenth.day

'Your Student Zeng Huafeng. January 10th, 1982' (*Qīngqīng* 104)

(49) 截止日期：　1994　　　　　　年　　2月　　2日（课本1A 8）
　　 jiézhǐrìqī　　yījiǔjiǔsì　　　　nián　　èryuè　　èrrì
　　 deadline　　nineteen.ninety.four　year　February　second.day

'Deadline: February 2, 1994' (*Kèběn* 1A, 8)

(50) 光华　　　学校　　在　1953　　　　　　年
　　 guānghuá　xuéxiào　zài　yījiǔwǔsān　　nián
　　 Kwang Hwa　School　on　nineteen.fifty.three　year

　　 1月　　10日　　诞生　　了。　（薪传37）
　　 yīyuè　　shírì　　dànshēng　le
　　 January　tenth.day　born　　　LE

'Kwang Hwa School was established on January 10, 1953.' (*Xīnchuán* 37)

The second approach is to write in the order from day to year, which is adopted when the Chinese characters 年 *nián* 'year', 月 *yuè* 'month' and 日 *rì* 'day' are not spelled out. This is influenced by English. For example:

(51) 《学生》编辑　　　　　*xuéshēng biānjí*　　'Editor of Students'
　　 方叔叔　　　　　　　*fāng shūshū*　　　　'Uncle Fang'
　　 22.10.1992（小学6A 6）　　'Oct 22nd, 1992'　(*Xiǎoxué* 6A, 6)

(52) 文华　　民众　　联络　　所　　青年团　　3-1-1994（课本1A 8）
　　 wénhuá　mínzhòng　liánluò　suǒ　qīngniántuán　sānrì yīyuè yījiǔjiǔsìnián
　　 Wenhua　people　　liaison　office　youth.group　Jan.3rd, 1994

'Wenhua People's Liaison Office Youth Group, Jan 3rd, 1994' (*Kèběn* 1A, 8)

(53) 报案　　日期：　　**16-8-1988**（华文教材4B 117）
　　　bàoàn　　rìqī:　　shíliùrì bāyuè yījiǔbābānián
　　　report　　date　　Aug.16th, 1988
　　'Date of report: Aug 16th, 1988.' (*Huáwénjiàocái* 4B, 117)

(54) 翻开　　日记：　　**25-4-1985**　　　　　　　　星期三，
　　　fānkāi　　rìjì　　èrshíwǔrì sìyuè yījiǔbāwǔnián　　xīngqīsān
　　　open　　diary　　Apr. 25th, 1985　　　　　　　Wednesday

　　清晨　　　阵雨，　　阴天。（青青64）
　　qīngchén　zhènyǔ　　yīntiān
　　early.morning　showers　overcast
　　'Open the diary: April 25th, 1985, Wednesday, early morning showers, overcast.' (*Qīngqīng* 64)

　　In Chinese Mandarin, dates are expressed from year to day, regardless of the style (written or spoken) and the occurrence of 年*nián* 'year', 月*yuè* 'month' and 日*rì* 'day'. The second approach presented here is not found in Chinese Mandarin.

2. Expressions for Weeks

In Singapore Mandarin, the expressions for the week include not only 星期*xīngqī* ... or 礼拜*lǐbài* ... (such as 星期一*xīngqī yī* 'Monday' or 星期二*xīngqī èr* 'Tuesday', 礼拜一 *lǐbài yī* 'Monday' or 礼拜二*lǐbài èr* 'Tuesday', etc.), but also 拜*bài* ..., for example:

(55) 今天　　**拜六，**　　不　　上课，
　　　jīntiān　　**bàiliù**　　bù　　shàngkè
　　　today　　**Saturday**　　NGE　　have.class

　　只有　　课外　　　　活动。　　（吾土·戏剧144）
　　zhǐyǒu　　kèwài　　　　huódòng
　　only　　extracurricular　activity
　　'Today is Saturday. There will be no classes, only extracurricular activities.' (*Wútǔ·xìjù* 144)

(56) **拜六**　　还　　有　　股票　　交易？（吾土·小说上95）
　　　bàiliù　　hái　　yǒu　　gǔpiào　　jiāoyì
　　　Saturday　also　have　stock　　trading
　　'There is still stock trading on Saturday?' (*Wútǔ·xiǎoshuōshàng* 95)

(57) 那　　天，　　**拜三，**
　　　nà　　tiān，　　**bàisān，**
　　　that　day　　**Wednesday**

　　　好象　　　是　　**拜三。**（苏明美1995附录《会话录音抄
　　　　　　　　　　　　　　　　　录（八）》）
　　　hǎoxiàng　shì　**bàisān**
　　　seem　　be　　**Wednesday**

　　　'That day is Wednesday. It seems to be Wednesday.' (*Sūmíngměi 1995 fùlù<huì huàlùyīnchāolù (VIII)>*)

This kind of expression is frequently used in both spoken and written Singapore Mandarin, but never found in Chinese Mandarin.

Additionally, 礼拜天 *lǐbàitiān* 'Sunday' can be abbreviated to 礼拜 *lǐbài* 'Sunday' in Singapore Mandarin, as illustrated in the following example:

(58) 不过　　看　　戏　　每次　　都　　要　　等到　　**拜六**
　　　bùguò　kàn　xì　měicì　dōu　yào　děngdào　**bàiliù**
　　　but　　watch　play　each.time　all　will　wait　**Saturday**

　　　礼拜。　　（苏明美1995附录《会话录音抄录（二）》）
　　　lǐbài
　　　Sunday

　　　'However, we have to wait until Saturday or Sunday each time to watch the play.' (*Sūmíngměi 1995 fùlù<huì huàlùyīnchāolù(II)>*)

Here 礼拜 *lǐ bài* is equivalent to 礼拜天 *lǐ bài tiān* 'Sunday'. This is no longer used in Chinese Mandarin.

3. Expressions for Minutes

In Singapore Mandarin, minutes are expressed by 分 *fēn* 'minute', as shown in the following:

(59) 十一　　点　　四十五　　**分，**　　主人　　的
　　　shíyī　diǎn　sìshíwǔ　**fēn，**　zhǔrén　de
　　　eleven　hour　forty-five　**minute**　master　DE

　　　车笛　叫　门　了！　（再见15）
　　　chēdí　jiào　mén　le
　　　siren　call　door　LE

　　　'Eleven forty-five, the master is hooting the car horn outside the door!' (*Zàijiàn* 15)

(60) 下意识地　　看一看　　　表，　　十二　时　　五十　**分，**
　　　*xiàyìshíde　　kànyīkàn　　biǎo　　shíèr　shí　　wǔshí　**fēn***
　　　subconsciously　have.a.look　watch　twelve　hour　fifty　**minute**
　　　'(He/she) subconsciously took a look at the watch, and it was twelve fifty.'
　　　(*Qīngqīng* 81)

In addition, another special word, 字*zì*, is used to represent five minutes. For example:

(61) 差　　一　　个　　**字**　　　　　半　　十一点。
　　　chà　yī　　gè　　zì　　　　　bàn　　shíyīdiǎn
　　　less　one　CL　**five.minutes**　half　eleven.o'clock

　　　我　　又　　　看看　　　表。
　　　wǒ　　yòu　　kànkàn　　biǎo
　　　1SG　again　look.at　　watch
　　　'I look at my watch again and it's seven or eight minutes to eleven o'clock.' (*Chángkūdānggē,* 53)

The expression 差一个字半十一点 *chà yī gè zì bàn shíyī diǎn* in the aforementioned example has the same meaning as 差七八分钟十一点 *chà qī bā fēnzhōng shíyī diǎn* 'seven or eight minutes to eleven o'clock'. There are no such expressions in Chinese Mandarin.

4.15 Classifiers

Most of the classifiers in Singapore Mandarin are the same as those in Chinese Mandarin, but there are also some differences, notably the wide use of the classifier 粒*lì* 'CL' and 间*jiān* 'CL'.

4.15.1 粒 *Lì 'CL'*

In Singapore Mandarin, the classifier 粒*lì* 'CL', which is used with high frequency, can be used either for objects of very small grains, such as 一粒米*yī lì mǐ* 'a grain of rice' and 一粒芝麻*yī lì zhīmá* 'a grain of sesame', or for large, round things, such as apples, eggs, watermelons, basketballs and so on. For example:

(1) 他　　到　　水果摊　　　去　　买　　了　　**几**　　**粒**　　小桃...
　　*tā　　dào　　shuǐguǒtān　qù　　mǎi　le　　**jǐ**　　**lì**　　xiǎotáo*
　　3SG　go　　fruit.stand　　go　　buy　LE　**several**　**CL**　small.peache
　　'He went to the fruit stand and bought a few small peaches...' (*Èmèng* 30)

(2) 我   拉开   了   抽屉， 翻出   一把   小刀，
    wǒ   lākāi   le   chōutì fānchū   yībǎ   xiǎodāo
    1SG   open   LE   drawer rummage one   pocket.knife

    还有   一   粒   苹果。(微型39)
    háiyǒu   yī   lì   píngguǒ
    also   one   CL   apple

    'I pulled open the drawer and rummaged around, found a pocket knife and an apple.' (*Wēixíng* 39)

(3) 国才   两手   各   挽   着   一   粒
    Guócái   liǎngshǒu   gè   wǎn   zhe   yī   lì
    Guocai   two.hands   each   held   ZHE   one   CL

    重重的   西瓜。
    zhòngzhòngde   xīguā
    heavy   watermelon

    'Guocai held a heavy watermelon in each hand.' (*Duǎnpiān* 16)

(4) 老福   也   吓了一跳，   掉了   一   粒   鱼丸。（吾土·小
                                                              说上34）
    lǎofú   yè   xiàleyītiào   diàole   yī   lì   yúwán
    Lao.Fu also startled   drop   one   CL   fish.ball

    'Lao Fu was also startled and dropped a fish ball.' (*Wútǔ·xiǎoshuōshàng* 34)

(5) 一个   幼儿   一个   星期   至少   应该   吃   三   次   鱼
    yīgè   yòuér   yīgè   xīngqī   zhìshǎo   yīnggāi   chī   sān   cì   yú
    one   child   one   week   at.least should   eat   three   CL   fish

    和   不超过   五   粒   鸡蛋。(报1995年3月5日14版)
    hé   bùchāoguò   wǔ   lì   jīdàn
    and no.more.than five   CL   egg

    'A child should eat fish and no more than five eggs at least three times a week.' (*Bào*, Mar. 5, 1995, Issue no. 14)

(6) 前排的   老人   握着   筷子，   从   纸盘里
    qiánpáide   lǎorén   wòzhe   kuàizi   cóng   zhǐpánlǐ
    in.the.front.row   old.man   hold   chopsticks   from   paper.plate

    夹起   一   粒   乒乓球，...（青青107）
    jiáqǐ   yī   lì   pīngpāngqiú

pick.up one CL ping.pong.ball

'The old man in the front row held up chopsticks and picked up a ping pong ball from a paper plate…' (*Qīngqīng* 107)

In each of these examples, 粒*lì* 'CL' will be replaced by 个*gè* 'CL' in Chinese Mandarin.

4.15.2 间 *Jiān*

In Singapore Mandarin, 间 *jiān* 'CL' is used for any commercial, cultural and educational establishments or premises related to housing. For example:

两	间	公司		一	间	制衣厂
liǎng	*jiān*	*gōngsī*		*yī*	*jiān*	*zhìyīchǎng*
two	CL	company		one	CL	garment.factory
'two companies'				'a/one garment factory'		

这	间	银行		一	间	饭庄
zhè	*jiān*	*yínháng*		*yī*	*jiān*	*fànzhuāng*
this	CL	bank		one	CL	restaurant
'this bank'				'a/one restaurant'		

一	间	健身院		一	间	学院
yī	*jiān*	*jiànshēnyuàn*		*yī*	*jiān*	*xuéyuàn*
one	CL	fitness.club		one	CL	academy
'a/one fitness club'				'an/one academy'		

哪	间	学校		几十	间	幼稚园
nǎ	*jiān*	*xuéxiào*		*yī*	*jiān*	*yòuzhìyuán*
which	CL	school		tens.of	CL	kindergarten
'which school'				'dozens of kindergartens'		

15	间	小学		有	课室	5	间
shíwǔ	*jiān*	*xiǎoxué*		*yǒu*	*kèshì*	*wǔ*	*jiān*
fifteen	CL	primary.school		have	classroom	five	CL
'15 primary schools'				'There are five classrooms.'			

一	间	商店		一	间	独立式	洋房
yī	*jiān*	*shāngdiàn*		*yī*	*jiān*	*dúlìshì*	*yángfáng*
one	CL	shop		one	CL	separate	villa
'a/one shop'				'a/one detached villa'			

某	间	中学		8	间	工厂
mǒu	**jiān**	zhōngxué		bā	**jiān**	gōngchǎng
certain	**CL**	middle.school		eight	**CL**	factory
'certain middle school'				'eight factories'		

142	间	公寓		416	间	托儿所
yībǎisìshíèr	**jiān**	gōngyù		sìbǎiyīshíliù	**jiān**	tuōérsuǒ
one.hundred.forty.two	**CL**	apartment		four.hundred.sixteen	**CL**	nursery
'142 apartments'				'416 nurseries'		

神庙	有	好几	间
shénmiào	yǒu	hǎojǐ	**jiān**
shrine	have	several	**CL**
'There are several shrines.'			

In Chinese Mandarin, 个 *gè* 'CL' and 家 *jiā* 'CL' are generally used for industrial and commercial organisations, for example:

一	个/家	公司		一	个/家	工厂
yī	**gè/jiā**	gōngsī		yī	**gè/jiā**	gōngchǎng
one	**CL/CL**	company		one	**CL/CL**	factory
a/one company				a/one factory		

一	个/家	银行		一	个/家	商店
yī	**gè/jiā**	yínháng		yī	**gè/jiā**	shāngdiàn
one	**CL/CL**	bank		one	**CL/CL**	shop
a/one bank				a/one store		

一	个/家	饭店
yī	**gè/jiā**	fàndiàn
one	**CL/CL**	restaurant
a/one restaurant		

The institutions of education and culture are generally expressed as 个 *gè* 'CL' or 所 *suǒ* 'CL', for example:

一	个/所	小学		一	个/所	中学
yī	**gè/suǒ**	xiǎoxué		yī	**gè/suǒ**	zhōngxué
one	**CL/CL**	primary.school		one	**CL/CL**	middle.school
a/one elementary school				a/one middle school		

一	个/所	大学		一	个	托儿所
yī	*gè /suǒ*	*dàxué*		*yī*	*gè*	*tuōérsuǒ*
one	CL/CL	university		one	CL	nursery
a/one university				a/one nusery		

一	个/所	学校		一	个/所	学院
yī	*gè /suǒ*	*xuéxiào*		*yī*	*gè /suǒ*	*xuéyuàn*
one	CL/CL	school		one	CL/CL	college
a/one school				a/one college		

For places related to housing, 个*gè* 'CL' or other classifiers are usually used. 间*jiān* 'CL' is only used for 屋子*wūzi* 'room', 卧室*wòshì* 'bedroom' and 客房*kèfáng* 'guest room', and even for these few words, there is a tendency to use 个*gè* 'CL'. For example:

一	个	课室	一	个	仓库	一	个	大厅
yī	*gè*	*kèshì*	*yī*	*gè*	*cāngkù*	*yī*	*gè*	*dàtīng*
one	CL	classroom	one	CL	warehouse	one	CL	hall
a/one classroom			a/one warehouse			a/one hall		

一	个/座	公寓	一	个/幢	洋房	一	个/座	庙
yī	*gè /zuò*	*gōngyù*	*yī*	*gè/zhuàng*	*yángfáng*	*yī*	*gè /zuò*	*miào*
one	CL/CL	apartment	one	CL/CL	villa	one	CL/CL	temple
an/one apartment			a/one villa			a/one temple		

4.16 Features of Interrogative Sentences (I): VP-NEG Questions

4.16.1 VP-NEG Questions With 没有*Méiyǒu* 'NEG'

In Chinese Mandarin, VP-NEG questions are in the form of "VP + 没有*méiyǒu* 'NEG'" (VP stands for predicate), such as 你吃了没有*nǐ chī le méiyǒu* 'Have you eaten yet?', 他来了没有*tā lái le méiyǒu* 'Is he here yet?' and 昨天你们看电影没有*zuó tiān nǐ men kàn diàn yǐng méiyǒu* 'Did you watch the movie yesterday?'. This question form is also attested in Singapore Mandarin, as illustrated next:

(1) 国才， 你 吃 过 午饭 了 **没有**?
    guócái *nǐ* *chī* *guò* *wǔfàn* *le* ***méiyǒu***?
    Guocai 2SG eat GUO lunch LE **NEG**

门外 传来 母亲 对 他 关怀的 呼唤。(短篇11)
ménwài *chuánlái* *mǔqīn* *duì* *tā* *guānhuáide* *hūhuàn*

outside   come   mother to   3SG   caring   call

'"Guocai, have you had lunch yet?" The call of his caring mother came from outside the door.' (*Duǎnpiān* 11)

(2) 论文 大纲 拟 好 了 **没有？**（金狮奖87）
   lùnwén *dàgāng* *nǐ* *hǎo* *le* ***méiyǒu***
   paper outline prepare good LE **NEG**
   'Have you prepared the outline of the paper yet?' (*Jīnshījiǎng* 87)

(3) 怎样？ 问 清楚 了 **没有**？ 在 哪一班？（追云45）
   zěnyàng *wèn* *qīngchǔ* *le* ***méiyǒu*** *zài* *nǎyībān*
   how.is.it ask clear LE **NEG** in which.class
   'How is it? Are you clear? In which class?' (*Zhuīyún* 45)

However, the more common form in Singapore Mandarin is "有没有 *yǒu-méi-yǒu* 'YOU-NEG' + VP". For example:

(4) 我 这次 访 英，
   wǒ *zhècì* *fǎng* *yīng*
   1SG this.time visit Britain

   有没有 得到 新的 心得？ （风筝194）
   yǒu-méi-yǒu *dédào* *xīnde* *xīndé*
   YOU-NEG gain new insight
   'Did I gain any new insights from my visit to Britain?' (*Fēngzhēng* 194)

(5) "你 **有没有** 跟 他 谈谈？"
   nǐ ***yǒu-méi-yǒu*** *gēn* *tā* *tántán*
   2SG **YOU-NEG** with 3SG talk
   'Did you talk to him?'

   "有， 我 跟 他 谈 过 不知
   yǒu *wǒ* *gēn* *tā* *tán* *guò* *bùzhī*
   YOU 1SG with 3SG talk GUO don't.know

   多少 次。"（醒醒96）
   duōshǎo *cì*

	how.many	times

'Yes, I've talked to him I don't know how many times.' (*Xīngxīng* 96)

(6) 幺七， 你 **有没有** 做 梦 啊？（金狮奖194）
　　 yāoqī 　 *nǐ* 　 ***yǒu-méi-yǒu*** 　 *zuò* 　 *mèng* 　 *a*
　　 Yaoqi 　 2SG 　 YOU-NEG 　 make 　 dream 　 SFP
'Yaoqi, did you have a dream?' (*Jīnshījiǎng* 194)

(7) 爸爸 **有没有** 买 东西 给 珍珠
　　 bàba 　 ***yǒu-méi-yǒu*** 　 *mǎi* 　 *dōngxī* 　 *gěi* 　 *zhēnzhū*
　　 dad 　 YOU-NEG 　 buy 　 things 　 give 　 Pearl

吃 呀？ （吾土·小说上199）
chī 　 *ya*
eat 　 SFP

'Did Dad buy anything for Pearl to eat?' (*Wútǔ·xiǎoshuōshàng* 199)

(8) **有没有** 给 医生 看 呀？（恶梦125）
　　 yǒu-méi-yǒu 　 *gěi* 　 *yīshēng* 　 *kàn* 　 *ya*
　　 YOU-NEG 　 give 　 doctor 　 see 　 SFP
'Did you see the doctor?' (*Èmèng* 125)

(9) 调查人员 问 卡南：" 王 **有没有** 拿
　　 diàochárényuán 　 *wèn* 　 *kǎnán* 　 　 *wáng* 　 ***yǒu-méi-yǒu*** 　 *ná*
　　 investigator 　 ask 　 Kanan 　 　 Wang 　 YOU-NEG 　 take

那 笔 钱？" 卡南 说 有。（报1995年3月14日13版）
nà 　 *bǐ* 　 *qián* 　 *kǎnán* 　 *shuō* 　 *yǒu*
that 　 CL 　 money 　 Kanan 　 say 　 YOU

'The investigator asked Kana "Did Wang take the money?" Kanan said yes.' (*Bào*, Mar. 14, 1995, Issue no. 13)

In Chinese Mandarin, though the form of "VP + 没有 *méiyǒu* 'NEG'" is dominant, the form of "有没有 *yǒu-méi-yǒu* 'HAVE-NEG' + VP" has also begun to appear due to the increasing influence of Cantonese as the rapid economic development of Guangzhou, Shenzhen, Zhuhai and other regions are having more influence over the economy of the whole nation, but it is not being widely used yet (Chen 1984; Xing 1989).

In Chinese Mandarin, another form of VP-NEG question with 没有 *méiyǒu* 'NEG' is "V 没(有) *méi(yǒu)* 'NEG' V",[6] as demonstrated in the following examples:

(10) 你　　昨天　　**看没（有）看**　　电影？
　　　 nǐ　　*zuótiān*　　**kàn-méi(yǒu)-kàn**　　*diànyǐng*
　　　 2SG　yesterday　**watch-NEG-watch**　movie
　　　 'Did you watch a movie yesterday?'

(11) 他　　上礼拜　　**见没（有）见**　　过　　汪先生？
　　　 tā　　*shànglǐbài*　　**jiàn-méi(yǒu)-jiàn**　　*guò*　　*wāngxiānshēng*
　　　 3SG　last.week　**see-NEG-see**　GUO　Mr. Wang
　　　 'Did he see Mr. Wang last week?'

We have not found this type of questioning in Singapore Mandarin.

4.16.2 VP-NEG Questions With 不 *Bù* 'NEG'

In Singapore Mandarin, VP-NEG questions formed by a monosyllabic verb or adjective and 不 *bū* 'NEG' is in the form of "X 不 *bū* 'NEG' X" (where X stands for a monosyllabic verb or adjective), which is the same as that in Chinese Mandarin. For example:

(12) 外面　　打雷　　他　　**怕不怕**？（吾土·戏剧147）
　　　 wàimiàn　　*dǎléi*　　*tā*　　**pà-bù-pà**
　　　 outside　thunder　3SG　**afraid-NEG-afraid**
　　　 'Is he afraid of the thunder outside or not?' (*Wútǔ·xìjù* 147)

(13) 小萱，　听说　她　在　谈恋爱，　**是不是**？（梦91）
　　　 xiǎoxuān　*tīngshuō*　*tā*　*zài*　*tánliànài*　**shì-bù-shì**
　　　 Xiao.Xuan　hear　3SG　in　love　**be-NEG-be**
　　　 'Xiao Xuan, I heard that she's in love, right?' (*Mèng* 91)

(14) 女姐，　　**去不去**　　买　　菜？（梦152）
　　　 nǚjiě　　**qù-bù-qù**　　*mǎi*　　*cài*
　　　 sister　**go-NEG-go**　buy　vegetable
　　　 'Sister, are you going to buy vegetables or not?' (*Mèng* 152)

(15) 妈妈，　您　说　**对不对**？（今后68）
　　　 māma　*nín*　*shuō*　**duì-bù-duì**
　　　 mum　2SG　say　**right-NEG-right**

'Mum, don't you think so?' (*Jīnhòu* 68)

However, VP-NEG questions formed by a disyllabic verb or adjective and 不 *bù* 'NEG' in Singapore Mandarin is different from that in Chinese Mandarin. Singapore Mandarin allows the following two forms:

Form I. XY不*bū* 'NEG' XY (where XY stands for a two-syllable verb or adjective). For example:

(16) 你　　知道不知道，
　　 nǐ　　zhīdào-bù-zhīdào,
　　 2SG　know-NEG-know

　　 我　　是　　未来的　　跑车　　冠军　　哪！（跳舞30）
　　 wǒ　　shì　　wèiláide　　pǎochē　　guànjūn　　na
　　 1SG　be　　future　　sports.car　champion　SFP
　　 'Did you know that I am a future sports car champion?' (*Tiàowǔ* 30)

Form II. X 不 *bū* 'NEG' XY (where XY stands for a two-syllable verb or adjective and X stands for the first syllable of XY). For example:

(17) 记不记得　　　　　　你　　以前　　曾经　　把　　婚姻
　　 jì-bù-jìdé　　　　　 nǐ　　yǐqián　　céngjīng　bǎ　　hūnyīn
　　 remember-NEG-remember　2SG　before　　ever　　BA　marriage

　　 比作　　　　　框子？（大胡子116）
　　 bǐzuò　　　　 kuàngzi
　　 be.compared.to　frame
　　 'Do you remember that you used to compare marriage to a frame?' (*Dàhúzi* 116)

(18) 沈先生，　　　 你　　可不可以　　　长话短说　　　　　呀？（吾土·戏剧68）
　　 shěnxiānshēng　nǐ　　kě-bù-kěyǐ　　 chánghuàduǎnshuō　ya
　　 Mr.Shen　　　　2SG　can-NEG-can　make.it.short　　　　SFP
　　 'Mr. Shen, can you make it short?' (*Wútǔ·xìjù* 68)

(19) 他　　问　　我　　到底　　信不信任　　　他　　办理　　买卖契约。
　　　　　　　　　　　　　　　　　　　　　　　　　　　　　　　　（今后32）
　　 tā　　wèn　wǒ　　dàodǐ　　xìn-bù-xìnrèn　tā　　bànlǐ　　mǎimàiqìyuē
　　 3SG　ask　1SG　on.earth　trust-not-trust　3SG　handle　sale.contract
　　 'He asked me if I trusted him to handle the sale deed or not.' (*Jīnhòu* 32)

(20) 现在   是   工人   决定   到   哪里   工作，   而
    xiànzài shì gōngrén juédìng dào nǎlǐ gōngzuò ér
    now   SHI worker   decide   go   where work   but

    不   是   公司   决定   **聘不聘请**   工人。（报 1995年
                                                     3月3日8版）
    bù   shì gōngsī juédìng pìn-bù-pìnqǐng gōngrén
    NEG SHI company decide   hire-NEG-hire   worker
    'Now it is the worker who decides where to work, not the company that decides whether to hire workers or not.' (*Bào*, Mar. 3 1995, Issue no. 8)

(21) 你   怎么   啦？   **要不要紧**？（恶梦125）
    nǐ   zěnme   lā?   yào-bù-yàojǐn?
    2SG   how   SFP   okay-NEG-okay
    'What's wrong with you? Are you okay?' (*Èmèng* 125)

(22) 到底   他   的   话   **可不可信**？（吾土·小说上152）
    dàodǐ   tā   de   huà   kě-bù-kěxìn
    whether 2SG   DE   words trust-NEG-trust
    'Can his words be trusted or not?' (*Wútǔ·xiǎoshuōshàng* 152)

(23) 同学们，   这样的   指甲   **好不好看**？（胜利24）
    tóngxuémen   zhèyàngde   zhǐjiǎ   hǎo-bù-hǎokàn
    students   this.kind.of nail   good-NEG-good
    'Everyone, do these kind of nails look good?' (*Shènglì* 24)

(24) 究竟   这种   说法   **正不正确**？（报1995年3月
                                                      15日副刊2版）
    jiūjìng   zhèzhǒng   shuōfǎ   zhèng-bù-zhèngquè
    on.earth this.kind.of view   right-NEG-right
    'Is this kind of view correct or not?' (*Bào*, Mar. 15, 1995, Issue no. 2, supplementary edition)

Form II, namely "X不*bù* 'NEG' XY", is more commonly seen in Singapore Mandarin. In contrast, Form I, "XY 不*bù* 'NEG' XY", is employed in Chinese Mandarin (Ma 1991). Form II is also found in many Chinese dialects and is finding its way to Chinese Mandarin (Chen 1984), yet it is still not widely accepted.

Accordingly, in Singapore Mandarin Form II is adopted for VP-NEG questions of the potential complement phrases, i.e. "V 不*bù* 'NEG' V 得*de* 'DE' C?" (where V stands for verb, and C for complement). For example:

(25) 明日　　也　　不　　知　　见不见得着　　　　你。(想飞55)
　　　míngrì　yě　bù　zhī　jiàn-bù-jiàn-de-zhao　nǐ
　　　tomorrow also NEG know see-NEG-see-DE-reach 2SG
　　　'I don't know if I'll see you tomorrow.' (*Xiǎngfēi* 55)

(26) 对于　　任何　　理论　　或　　建议，我　　只　　问　　一件　事，
　　　duìyú　rènhé　lǐlùn　huò　jiànyì　wǒ　zhǐ　wèn　yījiàn　shì
　　　for　any　theory　or　proposal 1SG only ask　one　thing

　　　就是　行不行得通？（报1995年5月1日6版）
　　　jiùshì　xíng-bù-xíng-de-tōng
　　　just.be　work-NEG-work-DE-through
　　　'For any theory or proposal, I only ask one thing: Does it work?'
　　　(*Bào*, May 1, 1995, Issue no. 6)

In Chinese Mandarin, the two previous sentences would have to be said in the form of "V 得 *de* 'DE' C + V 不 *bù* 'NEG' C".

(25)' 明日　　也不知　　见得着　　　见不着　　　你。
　　　míngrì　yěbùzhī　jiàn-de-zháo　jiàn-bù-zháo　nǐ
　　　tomorrow don't.know see-DE-reach see-NEG-reach 2SG
　　　'I don't know if I'll see you tomorrow.'

(26)' 我　　只　　问　　一件　事，就是　行得通　　　行不通？
　　　wǒ　zhǐ　wèn　yījiàn　shì　jiùshì　xíng-de-tōng　xíng-bù-tōng
　　　1SG only ask one thing be　　　work-DE-reach work-NEG-reach
　　　'I only ask one thing, is it workable or not?'

In Chinese Mandarin, there is another kind of VP-NEG question with 不 *bù* 'NEG' in the form of "VP + 不 *bù* 'NEG'", which occurs with high frequency as well. For example:

(27) 羊肉　　你　　吃不？
　　　yángròu　nǐ　chī-bù
　　　lamb　2SG　eat-NEG
　　　'Do you eat lamb?'

(28) 今晚上　　　你　　还　　回来不？
　　　jīnwǎnshàng　nǐ　hái　huílái-bù

tonight   2SG   also come.back-NEG
'Are you coming back tonight?'

But this question form is rarely seen in Singapore Mandarin. We found only two examples.

(29) 昨晚   她   穿   得   很   漂亮，   **是不？**
      zuówǎn   tā   chuān   de   hěn   piàoliàng **shìbù?**
      last.night 3SG dress   DE   very   beautiful   be-NEG

      那   是   我   给   她   打扮   的，...（大树下102）
      nà   shì   wǒ   gěi   tā   dǎbàn   de
      that SHI   1SG   for   3SG   dress   DE

      'She dressed up prettily last night, didn't she? It was me who dressed her up...' (*Dàshùxià* 102)

(30) 一起   去   吃个饭   **好不？**
      yīqí   qù   chīgèfàn   **hǎo-bù?**
      together go   have.dinner ok-NEG

      我们   总不能   一直   站   在   这里。（想飞63）
      wǒmen   zǒngbùnéng yīzhí   zhàn   zài   zhèlǐ
      1PL   can't   always   stand   at   here

      'Let's go have dinner together, shall we? We can't just stand here.' (*Xiǎngfēi* 63)

4.17 Features of Interrogative Sentences (II): Alternative Questions

In Singapore Mandarin, there are three types of conjunctive words that can be used within an alternative question.

4.17.1 还是 *Háishì* '*Or*'

The first conjunctive word is 还是 *háishì* 'or', and alternative questions connected by this word are in the form of "..., 还是 *háishì* 'or' ..."

(1)   这   是   人生   的   缺陷   呢，
      zhè   shì   rénshēng   de   quēxiàn   ne
      this be   life   DE   flaw   SFP

还是		社会	的	悲哀？	（恶梦8）
háishì		shèhuì	de	bēiāi	
or		society	DE	woe	

'Is this the flaw of life, or the sadness of society?' (*Èmèng* 8)

4.17.2 抑或 *Yìhuò* 'Or'

The second conjunctive word is 抑或*yìhuò* 'or', and alternative questions connected by this word take the form of "... 抑或*yìhuò* 'or' ...?". This is found in written Singapore Mandarin.

(2)
消息	到底	是	真实
xiāoxi	dàodǐ	shì	zhēnshí
news	on.earth	be	true

抑或	炒家	在	故弄玄虚？	（吾土·小说上74）
yìhuò	chǎojiā	zài	gùnòngxuánxū	
or	speculator	in.process	play.tricks	

'Is the news true or is it that the speculators are playing tricks?' (*Wútǔ· xiǎoshuōshàng* 74)

(3)
这	对	瑞宁	是	好	抑或	是	坏？
zhè	duì	ruìníng	shì	hǎo	yìhuò	shì	huài?
this	for	Ruining	be	good	or	be	bad

是	力量	抑或	是	勇气？	我	有点	迷惑。	（人生77）
shì	lìliàng	yìhuò	shì	yǒngqì	wǒ	yǒudiǎn	míhuò	
be	strength	or	be	courage	1SG	a.little	confused	

'Is this good or bad for Ruining? Is it strength or courage? I'm a little confused.' (*Rénshēng* 77)

(4)
对方	是	何许人	啊？	男的	抑或	女的？	（第一8）
duìfāng	shì	héxǔrén	a	nánde	yìhuò	nǚde	
others	be	who	SFP	male	or	female	

'Who is the other person? Male or female?' (*Dìyī* 8)

(5)
它	是	在	苦求？	抑或	是	在	忏悔？	——
tā	shì	zài	kǔqiú?	yìhuò	shì	zài	chànhuǐ	
3SG	be	at	bitter.plea	or	be	at	repentance	

谁　　　也　　说不上来。（追云12）
shuí　　yě　　shuō-bù-shànglái
who　　also　unable.to.say

'Is it a bitter plea? Or is it in repentance? No one can say.' (*Zhuīyún* 12)

(6) 巩俐　　　答应　　前往，　　究竟　　是　　张艺谋　　大力　　　游说，
　　 gǒnglì　　dāyìng　qiánwǎng　jiūjìng　shì　zhāngyìmóu　dàlì　　yóushuì
　　 Gong.Li　agree　　come　　on.earth　be　Zhang.　　　intense　lobby
　　　　　　　　　　　　　　　　　　　　　　Yimou

抑或　　是　　上海　电影　　　　制片厂　　　的　　要求
yìhuò　shì　shànghǎidiànyǐng　zhìpiànchǎng　de　yàoqiú
or　　be　Shanghai.Film　　　Studio　　　DE　request

呢？（报1995年5月16日副刊4版）
ne
SFP

'Was Gong Li's agreement to go there the result of intense lobbying by Zhang Yimou, or was it at the request of the Shanghai Film Studio?' (*Bào*, May 16, 1995, Issue no. 4, supplementary edition)

(7) 他们　　是　　认为　　　自己　　还　　没有　　　喊累　　　的　　资格？
　　 tāmen　shì　rènwéi　zìjǐ　　hái　méiyǒu　hǎnlèi　　de　zīgé?
　　 3PL　　SHI　think　　oneself　yet　not.have　claim.tired　DE　right

抑或　　上述　　问题　　在　　他们　看来　　　根本
yìhuò　shàngshù　wèntí　zài　tāmen　kànlái　gēnběn
or　　above　　question　to　3PL　　see-come　at.all

都　　不　　像　　是　　问题？（报1995年3月12日副刊9版）
dōu　bù　xiàng　shì　wèntí
all　NEG　like　be　question

'Do they think they have no right to complain about being tired? Or do they think that none of the above problems are problems at all?' (*Bào*, Mar. 12, 1995, Issue no. 12, supplementary edition)

4.17.3 或 *Huò* 'Or'/或者 *Huòzhě* 'Or'/或是 *Huòshì* 'Or'

The third type of conjunctive words includes three similar words 或 *huò* 'or', 或者 *huòzhě* 'or' and 或是 *huòshì* 'or', which can be in the form of "..., 或 *huò*/或者 *huòzhě*/或是 *huòshì* ...?" as shown next:

(8) 遇上   你   是   我   一生   的   对,   **或**   错?（想飞63）
    yùshàng nǐ   shì   wǒ   yīshēng de   duì   **huò** cuò
    meet   2SG be   1SG life   DE   right   or   wrong
    'Is meeting you the right or wrong thing in my life?' (*Xiǎngfēi* 63)

(9) 他们   是   真的   没有   丝毫不舍?   **或者**   是   那   份
    tāmen shì   zhēnde méiyǒu sīháobùshě? **huòzhě** shì   nà   fèn
    3PL   be   really   not.have a.bit.sadness or   be   that CL

    憾然的   别情   已经   被   瀚然的   人潮   冲淡   了,
    hànránde biéqíng yǐjīng   bèi   hànránde réncháo chōngdàn le
    regretful farewell already BEI   vast   people   wash.away LE

    淹没   了?（牛车水15）
    yānmò   le
    submerge   LE
    'Did they really not feel the least bit of sadness? Or was the regretful farewell washed away in the vast tide of people?' (*Niúchēshuǐ* 15)

(10) 此时   该   是   得意?   **或是**   羞愧?（吾土·
                                                小说上146）
     cǐshí   gāi   shì   déyì   **huòshì** xiūkuì
     at.this.point should be proud   or   ashamed
     'Should I be proud or ashamed of myself at this point?'
     (*Wútǔ·xiǎoshuōshàng* 146)

(11) 现在   究竟   是   回到   了   乡下   **或是**   被
     xiànzài jiūjìng   shì   huídào le   xiāngxià **huòshì** bèi
     now   on.earth be   return   LE   countryside or   BEI

     卡在   半路,   还   不   知道。（报1995年6月3日副刊21版）
     kǎzài   bànlù   hái   bù   zhīdào
     stuck   halfway yet   NEG know
     'Now it is not known whether he has returned to the countryside or is stuck halfway.' (*Bào*, June 3, 1995, Issue no. 21, supplementary edition)

4.17.4 Mixed Use of 还是 *Háishì* 'Or' and 或（是）*Huò(shì)* 'Or'

(12) 到底   是   沟通   渠道   出   了   问题,
     dàodǐ   shì   gōutōng   qúdào   chū   le   wèntí
     indeed be   communicate channel have LE   problem

368　*Characteristics of Singapore Mandarin Grammar*

还是	政策	决定者	未能	把握	民意，
háishì	*zhèngcè*	*juédìngzhě*	*wèinéng*	*bǎwò*	*mínyì*
or	policy	maker	fail	grasp	public.opinion

或	二者兼有？（风筝170－171）
huò	*èrzhějiānyǒu*
or	have.both

'Is it a problem with communication channels, or is it the failure of policy makers to grasp public opinion, or both?' (*Fēngzhēng* 170–171)

In Chinese Mandarin, only 还是*háishì* 'or' is found in alternative questions, not 抑或 *yìhuò* 'or' or 或*huò*/或者 *huòzhě*/或是 *huòshì* 'or'. 抑或*yìhuò* is a written vernacular term that is no longer used in Chinese Mandarin. 或*huò*/或者*huòzhě*/或是*huòshì* is used in Chinese Mandarin only for declarative sentences, not for alternative questions.

4.18 Comparative Sentences

There are mainly three types of comparative constructions in Singapore Mandarin to express the comparison of two items.

4.18.1 X比*bǐ* 'Than' Y ...

The first type of construction is in the form of 'X比*bǐ* 'than' Y ...', where X and Y stand for the items to be compared, as shown next:

(1)

他	在	工作单位	里，	薪水	比	人家	低，
tā	*zài*	*gōngzuòdānwèi*	*lǐ*	*xīnshuǐ*	*bǐ*	*rénjiā*	*dī*
3SG	at	workplace	inside	payment	than	others	less

工作	却	比	人家	多。（胜利79）
gōngzuò	*què*	*bǐ*	*rénjiā*	*duō*
work	but	than	others	more

'He is paid less than others in his workplace, but works more than others.' (*Shènglì* 79)

(2)

在	你	的	心目中，
zài	*nǐ*	*de*	*xīnmùzhōng*
in	2SG	DE	heart

我	比	你	儿子	重要？	（吾土·戏剧25）
wǒ	*bǐ*	*nǐ*	*érzi*	*zhòngyào*	

| 1SG | | than | 2SG | son | important |

'In your mind, am I more important than your son?' (*Wútǔ·xìjù* 25)

(3) 中四　　　是　　会考班，
　　zhōngsì　shì　huìkǎobān
　　grade 4　be　GCE.class

　　功课　　　比　　中三　　　更多、　　更繁、　　更重。（跳舞76）
　　gōngkè　　bǐ　　zhōngsān　gèngduō　gèngfán　gèngzhòng
　　homework　**than**　grade.3　　more　　　heavier　more.demanding

'Grade 4 is the GCE class, and the homework is more complicated and more demanding than that of Grade 3.' (*Tiàowǔ* 76)

This construction is very similar to the 比 *bǐ* 'than' comparative construction in Chinese Mandarin, but with a slight difference. In Singapore Mandarin, there is often a fixed element, 来得 *láide* 'come-DE', between the item Y and the adjective that follows. For instance:

(4) 自己　　　承认　　　总　　　　比　　人家　　审问
　　zìjǐ　　　chéngrèn　zǒng　　　bǐ　　rénjiā　　shěnwèn
　　oneself　admit　　　always　　than　others　interrogate

　　来得　　干净利落。（吾土·戏剧38）
　　láide　　gànjìnglìluò
　　come-DE　efficient

'It's better to admit it yourself than to be interrogated.' (*Wútǔ·xìjù* 38)

(5) 他　　比　　谁　　都　　**来得**　　沉默、　　安静。（金狮奖69）
　　tā　　bǐ　　shuí　dōu　**láide**　　chénmò　　ānjìng
　　3SG　than　who　all　**come-DE**　silent　　　quiet

'He is more silent and quiet than anyone else.' (*Jīnshīijiǎng* 69)

(6) 不论　　②句　　　　　　或　　③句，
　　bùlùn　èr-jù　　　　　　huò　sān-jù
　　either　sentence-two　or　sentence-three

　　都　　比　　①句　　　　　　**来得**　　生动。（华文教材2A 150）
　　dōu　bǐ　　yī-jù　　　　　　**láide**　　shēngdòng
　　all　than　sentence-one　**come-DE**　vivid

'Either sentence 2 or sentence 3 is more vivid than sentence 1.' (*Huáwénjiàocái* 2A, 150)

(7) 《海峡时报》 的 一 项 调查 显示：
    hǎixiáshíbào *de* *yī* *xiàng* *diàochá* *xiǎnshì*
    The.Straits.Times DE one CL survey show

    电子游戏机 的 噪音， 比 车辆 发出 的
    diànzǐyóuxìjī *de* *zàoyīn* *bǐ* *chēliàng* *fāchū* *de*
    video.games DE noise than vehicle make DE

    还 **来得** 强烈。（中学1A 111）
    hái ***láide*** *qiángliè*
    yet **come-DE** intense

    'A survey by *The Straits Times* shows that the noise from video games is more intense than that from vehicles.' (*Zhōngxué* 1A, 111)

(8) 白人 原本 就是 白的， 但是， 她
    báirén *yuánběn* *jiùshì* *báide* *dànshì* *tā*
    white.people originally be white but 3SG

    却 比 一般的 白人 **来得** 更 白。（大胡子88）
    què *bǐ* *yībānde* *báirén* ***láide*** *gèng* *bái*
    yet than average white.people **come-DE** more white

    'White people are originally white, but she came to be whiter than the average white person.' (*Dàhúzi* 88)

(9) 所以 在 我 脑子里 的 小说 永远 比
    suǒyǐ *zài* *wǒ* *nǎozilǐ* *de* *xiǎoshuō* *yǒngyuǎn* *bǐ*
    so in 1SG brain DE novel always than

    我 写 在 稿纸上 的 小说 **来得** 多。（木子129）
    wǒ *xiě* *zài* *gǎozhǐshàng* *de* *xiǎoshuō* ***láide*** *duō*
    1SG write at paper DE novel **come-DE** more

    'Therefore there will always be more novels in my head than there are written on manuscript.' (*Mùzǐ* 129)

(10) 我国 今年 的 预算案 比 香港
     wǒguó *jīnnián* *de* *yùsuànàn* *bǐ* *xiānggǎng*
     our.country this.year DE budget than Hong Kong

	来得	慷慨得	多。	（报1995年3月3日10版）
	láide	*kāngkǎi-de*	*duō*	
	come-DE	generous-DE	more	

'Our budget this year is much more generous than that of Hong Kong.'
(*Bào*, Mar. 3, 1995, Issue no. 10)

This expression is not generally found in Chinese Mandarin.

4.18.2 XAY + Numeral-Classifier Compound

The second type of construction is in the form of 'XAY + numeral-classifier compound', in which X and Y stand for the items to be compared and A stands for adjective.

(11) 我 父亲 虽然 只 小 他 四岁， 但…（新马255）
wǒ fùqīn suīrán zhǐ xiǎo tā sìsuì dàn
1SG father although only young 2SG four.years but
'My father is only four years younger than him, but …'
(*Xīnmǎ* 255)

(12) 男的 大 女的 三岁。（胜利64）
nánde dà nǚde sānsuì
the.male old female three.years
'The man is three years older than the woman.' (*Shènglì* 64)

This kind of expression is also prevalent in Chinese Mandarin.

4.18.3 XA过*Guò* 'Than' Y

The third type of comparative construction is 'XA过*guò* 'than' Y',[8] in which X and Y stand for the items to be compared and A stands for adjective.

(13) 和 邻居 和睦相处，
hé línjū hémùxiāngchǔ
with neighbours get.along.with

总 **好** 过 正面冲突。（吾土·戏剧149）
zǒng hǎo guò zhèngmiànchōngtū
always good than head-on.confrontation
'It is better to get along with your neighbours than to have a head-on confrontation.' (*Wútǔ·xìjù* 149)

(14) 小时候，   他   跟   别的   孩子   打架，
     xiǎoshíhòu tā   gēn   biéde   háizi   dǎjià
     childhood   3SG   with other   chidren fight

   伤   了   些儿， 我   心里   痛   过   他   百倍。（金
                                                              狮奖287）
   shāng le   xiēér   wǒ   xīnlǐ   tòng   guò   tā   bǎibèi
   hurt LE   a.bit   1SG   heart   pained than   3SG   hundred.times

   'In his childhood, when he fought with other children and got hurt, I felt a hundred times more pained than he did.' (*Jīnshījiǎng* 287)

(15) 它   自己   所   订   的   公务员   起薪
     tā   zìjǐ   suǒ   dìng   de   gōngwùyuán   qǐxīn
     3SG   oneself SUO   make   DE   civil.servant starting.salary

   却   低   过   最低   生活费。（报1995年3月9日26版）
   què   dī   guò   zuìdī   shēnghuófèi
   but   low   than   lowest cost.of.living

   'The starting salary for civil servants is lower than the minimum cost of living.' (*Bào*, Mar. 9, 1995, Issue no. 26)

(16) 曾经   在   病中   被   逼   看   土产电视剧，
     céngjīng zài   bìngzhōng   bèi   bī   kàn   tǔchǎndiànshìjù
     once   in   sick   BEI   forced watch   local.TV.drama

   其   难受   程度   惨   过   吃药。（报1995年3月22日副
                                                           刊5版）
   qí   nánshòu   chéngdù   cǎn   guò   chīyào
   this   suffering degree   bad   than   taking.medicine

   '(I) was once forced to watch a local TV drama while (I) was sick, and the degree of suffering was worse than taking medicine.' (*Bào*, Mar. 22, 1995, Issue no. 5, supplementary edition)

Adjectives that may appear in this comparative construction are generally monosyllabic. There is no such usage in Chinese Mandarin.

4.19 Europeanised Sentence Patterns

Due to the influence of English, there are more Europeanised sentences in Singapore Mandarin than in Chinese Mandarin, especially in the written language.

4.19.1 Pronouns Preceded by Modifiers

Pronouns preceded by modifiers are commonly seen in Singapore Mandarin. For example:

(1) 火车　　最终　　还是　　走　　了，　泪眼模糊　　中，
　　 huǒchē　zuìzhōng　háishì　zǒu　le　　lèiyǎnmóhú　zhōng
　　 train　　finally　　still　　leave　LE　a.blur.of.tears　in

　　 我　向　下　　　了　车、　在　　月台上
　　 wǒ　xiàng　xià　le　chē　zài　yuètáishàng
　　 1SG　to　get.off　LE　train　at　platform.on

　　 的　你　挥手。（青青56）
　　 de　nǐ　huīshǒu
　　 DE　2SG　wave

　　 'The train finally left, and in a blur of tears, I waved to you, who had got off the train and on to the platform.' (*Qīngqīng* 56)

(2) 饿　　得　　肚子　　呱呱叫　　的　他，
　　 è　　de　　dùzi　　guāguājiào　de　tā
　　 hungry　DE　stomach　croak　　　DE　3SG

　　 只　那么　几　口　就　吃完　了。（恶梦121）
　　 zhǐ　nàme　jǐ　kǒu　jiù　chīwán　le
　　 only　those　several　CL　then　eat-finish　LE

　　 'He was so hungry that his stomach rumbled and he finished eating in just a few bites.' (*Èmèng* 121)

(3) 目前　　育有　　一　个　3　岁　　女儿
　　 mùqián　yùyǒu　yī　gè　sān　suì　nǚér
　　 currently　have　one　CL　three　year.old　daughter

　　 的　他　说：…（报1995年3月10日6版）
　　 de　tā　shuō
　　 DE　3SG　say

　　 'He, who currently has a 3-year-old daughter, says: …' (*Bào*, Mar. 10, 1995, Issue no. 6)

(4) 作为   义顺中组屋区   居民   的   我， 向   这些
    zuòwéi yìshùnzhōngzǔwūqū   jūmín   de   wǒ   xiàng zhèxiē
    as   Yishun.Central.HDB. resident DE 1SG   to   these
            area

    荣获   最佳   安全   住家   称号   的   住户
    rónghuò zuìjiā ānquán zhùjiā   chēnghào de   zhùhù
    win   best   safe   house   title   DE   resident

    表示   敬意。（报1995年4月19日8版）
    biǎoshì   jìngyì
    show   respect

    'As a resident of the Yishun Central HDB area, I would like to pay tribute to these tenants who were awarded the title of the best safe house.' (*Bào*, April 19, 1995, Issue no. 8)

(5) 比   他   年轻   了   将近   十   岁   的   她，
    bǐ   tā   niánqīng le   jiāngjìn   shí   suì   de   tā
    than 3SG   young   LE   nearly   ten   year   DE   3SG

    看   起来   却   分明   像   他   的   姐姐。
    kàn   qǐlái què   fēnmíng   xiàng   tā   de   jiějiě
    look   up   but   distinctly like   3SG   DE   sister

    'She, who is nearly ten years younger than him, looks very much like his older sister.'

(6) 身为   主办国   的   我们，   将来   就
    shēnwéi zhǔbànguó   de   wǒmen   jiānglái   jiù
    as   host.country DE   1PL   future   then

    永   没   机会   争取   到   冠军   和   亚军
    yǒng   méi   jīhuì   zhēngqǔ   dào   guànjūn   hé   yàjūn
    forever not.have   chance   fight   get   champion   and   runner-up

    的   荣誉   了。（风筝53）
    de   róngyù   le
    DE   honor   LE

    'As the host country, we will never have the chance to fight for the honour of the championship and the runner-up in the future.' (*Fēngzhēng* 53)

(7) 那   个   蹲着   看   蚂蚁   的   小孩，
    nà   gè   dūnzhe   kàn   mǎyǐ   de   xiǎohái
    that CL   squat   wtch ant   DE   child

   童心未泯地   端详着   将   自己   忙碌   成
   tóngxīnwèimǐnde   duānxiángzhe   jiāng   zìjǐ   mánglù   chéng
   a.childish.manner   watch   BA   oneself busy   become

   蚂蚁   的   我们。（牛车水109）
   mǎyǐ   de   women
   ant   DE   1PL

   'The child who squatted and looked at the ants looked at us, who were busy turning ourselves into ants, with a childlike innocence' (*Niúchēshuǐ* 109)

(8) 对于   这样的   事实，   跟   他们   呼吸   同一种   空气
    duìyú   zhèyàngde   shìshí   gēn   tāmen   hūxī   tóngyīzhǒng   kōngqì
    about   such   fact   with   3PL   breathe   same   air

   的   我们，   会   有   什么   感想   呢？（华文教材2B 165）
   de   wǒmen   huì   yǒu   shénme   gǎnxiǎng   ne
   DE   1PL   would   have   what   feeling   SFP

   'What do we, who breathe the same air as they do, think about such a fact?' (*Huáwénjiàocái* 2B, 165)

Such Europeanised expressions are occasionally found in Chinese Mandarin, particularly in translated works.

4.19.2 Unstressed 是 *shì* 'be' With Adjective-Predicated Sentences

In Singapore Mandarin, the unstressed copular verb 是*shì* 'be' can be used in the adjective-predicated sentences. There is no such Europeanised usage in Chinese Mandarin, in which the adjective can serve as the predicates directly.

(9) 本地   手工艺品，   如   贝壳   纪念品、   手织
    běndì   shǒugōngyìpǐn   rú   bèiké   jìniànpǐn   shǒuzhī
    local   handicraft   such.as   shell   souvenir   hand-knitted

   帕子、   大理石   日用品、   等，   都   是
   pàzi   dàlǐshí   rìyòngpǐn   děng   dōu   shì
   handkerchief   marble   daily.goods   and.so.on   all   be

价廉　　　物美。（风筝190）
jiàlián　　wùměi
inexpensive　good.value

'Local handicrafts, such as shell souvenirs, hand-knitted handkerchieves, and marble daily goods, are inexpensive and with good value.' (*Fēngzhēng* 190)

(10) 五、六十年代，　市区中心　　的　房屋，　一般上　　**是**
　　　wǔliùshíniándài　shìqūzhōngxīn　de　fángwū　yībānshàng　**shì**
　　　the.1950s.and.1960s　downtown.center　DE　house　generally　**be**

　　　拥挤、　杂乱　　和　陈旧。（风筝139）
　　　yōngjǐ　záluàn　hé　chénjiù
　　　crowded　cluttered　and　old-fashioned

'In the 1950s and 1960s, the houses in downtown centers were generally crowded, cluttered and old-fashioned.' (*Fēngzhēng* 139)

(11) 银行　　的　业务　　一直　　**是**　蒸蒸日上。（雾锁10）
　　　yínháng　de　yèwù　　yīzhí　**shì**　zhēngzhēngrìshàng
　　　bank　DE　business　always　**be**　booming

'The bank's business is always booming.' (*Wùsuǒ*, 10)

(12) 没有人　　知道　他　**是**　痛苦　　到　　什么　程度。（新马183）
　　　méiyǒurén　zhīdào　tā　**shì**　tòngkǔ　dào　shénme　chéngdù
　　　nobody　know　3SG　**be**　painful　reach　what　extent

'No one knows to what extent he is suffering.' (*Xīnmǎ* 183)

(13) 我　认为　　这　**是**　很　　不公平。（报1995年4月5日18版）
　　　wǒ　rènwéi　zhè　**shì**　hěn　bùgōngpíng
　　　1SG　think　this　**be**　very　unfair

'I think this is very unfair.' (*Bào*, Apr. 5, 1995, Issue no. 18)

4.19.3 Extensive Use of 被 *bèi* BEI Sentences

Because of the influence of English, the word 被*bèi* 'BEI' is widely used in Singapore Mandarin, not particularly restricted to translated works, as shown next. 被*bèi* 'BEI' in the following sentences has to be deleted if they are to be accepted in Chinese Mandarin.

(14) 信　　已　　**被**　　投入　　了　邮筒。（都市1）
　　　xìn　yǐ　**bèi**　tóurù　le　yóutǒng

letter already **BEI** put.into LE mailbox

'The letter has been put into the mailbox.' (*Dūshì*, 1)

(15) 君子 抛弃 了 仁德，
jūnzǐ pāoqì le réndé
gentleman abandon LE benevolence

怎么 还能 **被** 称为 君子 呢？（伦理·中四5）
zěnme háinéng **bèi** chēngwéi jūnzǐ ne
how can **BEI** call gentleman SFP

'How can a gentleman be called a gentleman when he has abandoned benevolence?' (*Lúnlǐ·zhōngsì* 5)

(16) 这 件 事， 立刻 流传开去， 成 了 美谈，
zhè jiàn shì lìkè liúchuánkāiqù chéng le měitán
this CL thing immediately spread.over become LE beautiful.story

一直 到 今天， 还 **被** 传诵 着。（伦理·中四37）
yīzhí dào jīntiān hái **bèi** chuánsòng zhe
until at today still **BEI** widely.read ZHE

'This incident was immediately spread and became a beautiful story, and is still circulated to this day.' (*Lúnlǐ·zhōngsì* 37)

(17) 你 可以 看见 爱华小学 四 个 无限 豪气
nǐ kěyǐ kànjiàn àihuáxiǎoxué sì gè wúxiàn háoqì
2SL can see Aihua.Elementary.School four CL infinite pride

的 字， **被** 悬挂 在 礼堂 的 墙上。（新马248）
de zì **bèi** xuánguà zài lǐtáng de qiángshàng
DE word **BEI** hang at auditorium DE wall

'You can see the four characters 爱华小学 *àihuáxiǎoxué* 'Aihua Elementary School' proudly hanging on the wall of the auditorium.' (*Xīnmǎ* 248)

(18) 大厦 附近 6 条 街 的 居民 都 已
dàshà fùjìn liù tiáo jiē de jūmín dōu yǐ
building nearby six CL street DE resident all already

378　*Characteristics of Singapore Mandarin Grammar*

被	撤离一空。（新明日报1995年4月20日26版）
bèi	**chèlíyīkōng**
BEI	evacuate

'All the residents of the six streets near the building have been evacuated.'
(*Xīnmíngrìbào*, April 20, 1995, Issue no.26)

4.20 Subsidiary Word Formation

4.20.1 Prefix 阿 ā 'Ah' and 老 Lǎo 'Old'

1. Prefix 阿 ā 'Ah'

In Singapore Mandarin, the prefix 阿 ā 'ah' is frequently used, usually to derive nouns referring to people. It is often added to the front of monosyllabic names. For example:

(1) 你们　　阿宝　　也　　该　　买　　些　　背心、
　　nǐmen　**ābǎo**　yě　gāi　mǎi　xiē　bèixīn
　　2PL　**Ah.Bao**　also　should　buy　some　vest

　　裤子　的　了。（金狮奖279）
　　kùzi　de　le
　　trousers　DE　LE

'Your Ah Bao should also buy some vests and trousers.' (*Jīnshījiǎng* 279)

(2) 他们　的　谈话　　　声，　使　　阿兰、　阿英　　停止
　　tāmen　de　tánhuà　shēng　shǐ　**ālán**　**āyīng**　tíngzhǐ
　　3PL　DE　conversation　sound　make　**Ah.Lan**　**Ah.Ying**　stop

　　了　说话，　而　注意　向外　　看。（吾土·戏剧159）
　　le　shuōhuà　ér　zhùyì　xiàngwài　kàn
　　LE　talk　and　focus　outward　look

'The sound of their conversation caused Ah Lan and Ah Ying to stop talking and focus on looking out.' (*Wútǔ·xìjù* 159)

(3) 阿音！　快快　　　请　　先生　　　进来！（今后46）
　　āyīn　kuàikuài　qǐng　xiānshēng　jìnlái
　　Ah.Yin　hurry.up　invite　gentleman　come.in

'Ah Yin! Hurry up and invite the gentleman in!' (*Jīnhòu* 46)

(4) 阿芋！ 做人 要 自量！（今后77）
    āyù   zuòrén yào   zìliàng
    Ah.Yu be.a.man should estimate.oneself
    'Ayu! As a man you should estimate your own ability!' (*Jīnhòu* 77)

(5) 阿娇 是 新来 的 红头巾。（课本2A 56）
    ājiāo shì xīnlái   de hóngtóujīn
    Ah.Jiao be newly.come DE red.kerchief
    'Ah Jiao is the new red kerchief.'[9] (*Kèběn* 2A, 56)

阿 *ā* 'ah' can also be prefixed to monosyllabic kinship appellation nouns, as in the following:

(6) 进门 后， **阿妈** 帮 我 把 行李 搬进
    jìnmén hòu **āmā** bāng wǒ bǎ xínglǐ bānjìn
    enter.door after **ah.mum** help 1SG BA luggage carry.into

    房子……（微型13）
    fángzi
    house
    'When I entered the house, my Mum helped me carry my luggage in.' (*Wēixíng* 13)

(7) 嫂： **阿婆**！
    sǎo   **āpó**
    sister-in-law **ah.grandma**
    'Sister-in-law: Grandma!'

    婆： 哦， 是 林嫂 啊！（吾土·戏剧179）
    pó   ò   shì línsǎo a
    grandma Oh be Mrs.Lin SFP
    'Grandma: Oh, it's Mrs. Lin!' (*Wútǔ·xìjù* 179)

(8) **阿伯**， 你 对 潮乐 很 有
    ābó   nǐ duì cháoyuè hěn yǒu
    ah.uncle 2SG about Chiu.Chow.music very have

    研究 吗？（青青106）
    yánjiū ma

　　　　　　　　study　SFP
　　　　'Uncle, do you know a lot about Chiu Chow music?' (*Qīngqīng* 106)

(9)　给　　你　　**阿爸**　　打！（今后136）
　　　gěi　　nǐ　　**ābà**　　dǎ
　　　GEI　 2SG　**ah.dad**　phone
　　'(You're gonna) get beat up by your dad!' (*Jīnhòu* 136)

(10)　对呀！　　**阿嫂，**　　　　你　　的　　话　　很　　对！（恶梦126）
　　　duìya　　**āsǎo**　　　　　nǐ　　de　　huà　　hěn　　duì
　　　right　　**ah.sister.in.law**　2SG　DE　words　very　right
　　'That's right! Sister-in-law, your words are right!' (*Èmèng* 126)

(11)　新视　　　　**阿姐**　　郑惠玉　　　也　　有　　一　　人　　演
　　　xīnshì　　 **ājiě**　　zhènghuìyù　yě　 yǒu　yī　rén　yǎn
　　　New.Vision　**ah.sister**　Zheng.Huiyu　also　have　one　person　act

　　　两　　人　　的　　经验。（报1995年6月15日副刊1版）
　　　liǎng　rén　de　jīngyàn
　　　two　people　DE　experience
　　'New Vision's Sister Zheng Huiyu also has the experience of acting two roles by herself.' (*Bào*, June 15, 1995, Issue no. 1, supplementary edition)

(12)　**阿妹！**　　你　　爸爸　　在　　家　　么？（今后45）
　　　āmèi　　nǐ　　bàba　　zài　　jiā　　me
　　　ah.sister　2SG　dad　　be　　home　SFP
　　Sister! Is your father at home? (*Jīnhòu* 45)

It can also be prefixed to nouns indicating last name. For example:

(13)　**阿宋，**　　怎么　　不　　回来　　看看　　我们　　住　　过
　　　āsòng　　zěnme　bù　　huílái　　kànkàn　wǒmen　zhù　guò
　　　Ah.Song　how　　NEG　come.back　see　　1PL　　live　GUO

　　　的　　宿舍，　　工作　　忙　　走不开　　　　吧？（牛车水126）
　　　de　　sùshè　　gōngzuò　máng　zǒu-bù-kāi　　ba
　　　DE　dormitory　work　　busy　walk-NEG-leave　SFP
　　'Ah Song, why don't you come back to see the dormitory where we lived before? You couldn't take time off due to your busy work, could you?' (*Niúchēshuǐ* 126)

(14) 被告   的   朋友   **阿张**   告诉   被告   说，
    bèigào   de   péngyou   **āzhāng**   gàosù   bèigào   shuō
    defendant DE friend   **Ah.Zhang** tell   defendant say

    他   要   用   股票   作   抵押，
    tā   yào   yòng   gǔpiào   zuò   dǐyā
    3SG want   use   stock   as   collateral

    向   人家   借钱。（报1995年5月20日4版）
    xiàng   rénjiā   jièqián
    to   others   borrow.money

    'The defendant's friend, Ah Zhang, told the defendant that he was going to use the stock as collateral and borrow money from others.' (*Bào*, May 20, 1995, Issue no. 4)

It can also be added to the front of other morphemes referring to a person, as evidenced in the following example in which 阿*ā* 'ah' is prefixed to the word 兵*bīng* 'soldier':

(15) 也   有   结党成群   的   **阿兵哥**。（吾土·小说上65）
    yě   yǒu   jiédǎngchéngqún   de   **ābīnggē**
    also have   gang.up   DE   **ah-soldier-brother**

    'There are also gangs of soldiers.' (*Wútǔ·xiǎoshuōshàng* 65)

This prefix 阿*ā* 'ah' does not exist in Chinese Mandarin.

2. Prefix 老*Lǎo* 'Old'

In Singapore Mandarin, the prefix 老*lǎo* may have four usages.[10]

A   It can be added to a morpheme referring to an animal, such as 老虎*lǎohǔ* 'tiger', 老鼠*lǎoshǔ* 'mouse', 老鹰*lǎoyīng* 'eagle', etc.
B   It can be prefixed to a morpheme that refers to the ranking of a person (such as: 大*dà* 'first', 二*èr* 'second', 三*sān* 'third', etc.), as shown next:

(16) 他   是   黄家   的   **老二，**   律师。（胜利88）
    tā   shì   huángjiā   de   **lǎoèr**   lùshī
    3SG be   Huang.family DE   **the.second**   lawyer

    'He, a lawyer, is the second son of the Huang family.' (*Shènglì* 88)

(17) 黄卫民   在   家   排行   **老大**。
    huángwèimín   zài   jiā   páiháng   **lǎodà**

            Huang.Weimin   at   home   rank   **the.eldest**

            'Huang Weimin is the eldest child in the family.' (*Bào*, Mar. 7, 1995, Issue no. 2, supplementary edition)

C   It can be prefixed to monosyllabic morphemes of surnames, as in (18) and (19):

(18)   喂，   **老李，**   怎样？   巨人   跑   第几？（追云62）
        wèi   **lǎolǐ**   zěnyàng   jùrén   pǎo   dìjǐ
        Hey   **old.Li**   how.is.it   Giant run   which.rank

        'Hey, old Li, How's it going? What place was Giant in the running race?' (*Zhuīyún* 62)

(19)   我   必须   关照   **老刘，**   从   今天起，
        wǒ   bìxū   guānzhào **lǎoliú**   cóng   jīntiānqǐ
        1SG   must   take.care.of **old.Liu**   from   today

        更   要   特别   呵护   这   座   不幸的
        gèng yào   tèbié   hēhù   zhè   zuò   bùxìngde
        more should special   care   this   CL   unfortunate

        可怜的   城   啊。（回忆21）
        kěliánde chéng a
        poor   city   SFP

        'I must take care of old Liu, and from today onwards, take special care of this unfortunate poor city.' (*Huíyì* 21)

D   It can be added to the front of the morpheme referring to kinship expressions. For example:

(20)   给   **老爸**   买   电视？   算了   吧！（再见73）
        gěi   **lǎobà**   mǎi   diànshì suànle   ba
        give **dad**   buy   TV   forget   SFP

        'Buy a TV for Dad? Forget about it!' (*Zàijiàn* 73)

(21)   **老爸**   叫   我   回家   吃饭。（报1995年3月5日9版）
        lǎobà   jiào   wǒ   huíjiā   chīfàn
        dad   ask   1SG   go.home eat.dinner

        'Dad called me home for dinner.' (*Bào*, March 5, 1995, Issue no. 9)

(22)   我   **老爹**   便   是   其中   的   一   个。（金狮奖113）
        wǒ   **lǎodiē** biàn   shì   qízhōng de   yī   gè

| | 1SG | **dad** | then | be | among | DE | one | CL |

'My dad is one of them.' (*Jīnshījiǎng* 113)

Two points are worth noting about the prefix 老*lǎo* 'old'. First, the C usage is rare in Singapore Mandarin, but quite common in Chinese Mandarin. Second, for the D usage, only 老兄 *lǎo xiōng* 'brother' and 老弟*lǎo dì* 'brother' – not 老爸*lǎo bà* 'dad', 老爹*lǎo diē* 'father' or 老妈*lǎo mā* 'mum' – are used in Chinese Mandarin. Whether 老*lǎo* in 老兄*lǎo xiōng* 'brother' and 老弟*lǎo dì* 'brother' is of the same grammatical level as 老*lǎo* in 老爸*lǎo bà* 'dad' or 老妈*lǎo mā* 'mum' still needs to be studied further. In addition, in Singapore Mandarin there are also such expressions as老姑*lǎo gū* and 老姨*lǎo yí*, in which 老*lǎo* functions at another level. Here老姑*lǎo gū* refers not to 'aunt' but to 'father's aunt', and老姨*lǎo yí* refers not to 'mother's sister', but to 'grandmother's sister'.[11] There are no such expressions in Chinese Mandarin, either.

4.20.2 *Suffix* 佬*Lǎo,* 仔*Zǎi and* 族*Zú*

1. Suffix佬Lǎo 'Guy'

The nouns suffixed by 佬*lǎo* 'guy' refer to a person (especially an adult man) with some sort of contemptuous meaning. This suffix is also found in Chinese Mandarin with only a few words, including 阔佬*kuòlǎo* 'fat cat rich guy', 美国佬*měiguó lǎo* 'Yankee', or 英国佬*yīngguólǎo* 'Limey'. However, it is very commonly used in Singapore Mandarin. For example:

(23) 对 他 一 瞪眼， 骂道： **衰佬。**（金狮奖182）
duì tā yī dèngyǎn màdào **shuāilǎo**
at 3SG one glare curse **bad.'guy'**
'(She) glared at him and cursed: bad guy'. (*Jīnshījiǎng* 182)

(24) 亨！ 这 个 **碧眼佬**！（今后28）
hēng zhè gè **bìyǎnlǎo**
hum this CL **blue-eyed.guy**
'Hum! This blue-eyed guy!' '(*Jīnhòu* 28)

(25) 老细 是 个 老于世故 的 **生意佬。**（写作人23）
lǎoxì shì gè lǎoyúshìgù de **shēngyìlǎo**
Old.Tiny be CL sophisticate DE **businessman**
'Old Tiny is a sophisticated businessman.' (*Xiězuòrén,* 23)

(26) 喏， 刚刚 找到 这 个 **肥佬，** 你 来得
nuò gānggāng zhǎodào zhè gè **féilǎo** nǐ láide
well just find this CL **fat.guy** 2SG come-DE

正好，	让	我们	趁机		喝	个	饱，
zhènghǎo	ràng	wǒmen	chènjī		hē	gè	bǎo
in.time	let	1PL	take.the.opportunity		drink	CL	full

享受	一	番	吧？（追云114）
xiǎngshòu	yī	fān	ba
enjoy	one	CL	SFP

'Well, I just found this fat guy, you're just in time, let's take the opportunity to have a drink and enjoy?' (*Zhuīyún* 114)

(27)
她	叫	我们	不要	理采	爸爸，
tā	jiào	wǒmen	bùyào	lǐcǎi	bàba
3SG	let	1PL	don't	pay.attention.to	dad

说	爸爸	是	**神经佬**。（短篇64）
shuō	bàba	shì	**shénjīnglǎo**
say	dad	be	**psycho**

'She told us to ignore papa, saying that he was a psycho.' (*Duǎnpiān* 64)

(28)
本来，	我	是	要	下坡	找	**写信佬**
běnlái	wǒ	shì	yào	xiàpō	zhǎo	**xiěxìnlǎo**
originally	1SG	SHI	want	go.downhill	find	**letter.writer**

写	的，	不过，...（风雨23）
xiě	de	bùguò
write	DE	but

'Originally, I wanted to go downhill to find a letter writer to write, but, ...' (*Fēngyǔ* 23)

(29)
三	年	前	老伴	决别而去，
sān	nián	qián	lǎobàn	juébiéérqù
three	years	ago	partner	leave

他	成	了	伶仃仃	的	**寡佬**。（MD 37）
tā	chéng	le	língdīngdīng	de	**guǎlǎo**
3SG	become	LE	lonely	DE	**widower**

'Three years ago, his partner left him and he became a widower.'(MD 37)

Sometimes it is used to address a close friend, in which case there is even a sense of affection. For example:

(30) 喂， **近视佬，** 这 封 什么 信？（梦28）
    wèi **jìnshìlǎo** zhè fēng shénme xìn
    hey **myopic.guy** this CL what letter
    'Hey, myopic guy, what kind of letter is this?' (*Mèng* 28)

None of the above expressions are found in Chinese Mandarin.

2. Suffix 仔 *Zǎi* 'Baby'

仔 *zǎi* 'baby' is widely used in Singapore Mandarin, usually being suffixed to nouns refering to little animals. For example:

(31) 我们 吃饭 的 时候， 你 就 爬上
    wǒmen chīfàn de shíhòu nǐ jiù páshàng
    1PL have.dinner DE time 2SG then climb.up

    椅子， 跟 爸爸 讨 **江鱼仔** 吃。 给 了
    yǐzi gēn bàba tǎo **jiāngyúzǎi** chī gěi le
    chair with dad ask **baby.fish** eat give LE

    一 条， 跑去 阳台 站 一 下， 又 跑回来
    yī tiáo pǎoqù yángtái zhàn yī xià yòu pǎohuílái
    one CL run.to balcony stand one CL again run.back

    嚷嚷： 我 要 **江鱼仔，** **江鱼仔**！（金狮奖306）
    rǎngrǎng wǒ yào **jiāngyúzǎi** **jiāngyúzǎi**
    yell 1SG want **baby.fish** **baby.fish**

'When we were having dinner, you climbed up on the chair and asked your father for baby fish. After you were given one, you went to the balcony and stood there for a while, and then came back and yelled again, "I want to eat the baby fish, the baby fish!"' (*Jīnshījiǎng* 306)

Nevertheless, more frequently, 仔 *zǎi* 'baby' is used in nouns refering to children. For example:

(32) 黄老头 又 带着 那 活泼的 小孙儿
    huánglǎotóu yòu dàizhe nà huópōde xiǎosūnér
    old.man.Huang again bring that lively little.grandson

    明仔 在 散步 了。（恶梦9）
    míngzǎi zài sànbù le

Ming   in.process walk LE
'Old man Huang is walking again with his lively little grandson, Ming.' (Èmèng 9)

(33) 小狗仔！ 我 的 爸爸 要 卖 榴莲 了！（恶梦120）
xiǎogǒuzǎi wǒ de bàba yào mài liúlián le
little.puppy 1SG DE dad will sell durian LE
'Little Puppy! My dad is going to sell durians!' (Èmèng 120)

(34) "你 的 物理科 得分 多少？" "90分。"
nǐ de wùlǐkē défēn duōshǎo jiǔshífēn
2SG DE physics score how.many 90.points

"这 一 个 肥妹仔 呢？"（微型216）
zhè yī gè **féimèizǎi** ne
this one CL **fat.girl** SFP

'What was your score in Physics?' '90 points.' 'What about this overweight girl?' (Wēixíng 216)

(35) 你 看 这 个 小鬼，
nǐ kàn zhè gè xiǎoguǐ
2SG see this CL little.devil

公然 在 簿子上 画 公仔。（胜利19）
gōngrán zài bùzishàng huà **gōngzǎi**
openly at book draw **doll**

'Look at this little devil! He is openly drawing dolls in the book.' (Shènglì 19)

(36) 这 夭寿仔 交 给 你。（今后1）
zhè **yāoshòuzǎi** jiāo gěi nǐ
this **damned.boy** hand give 2SG
'This damned boy is handed over to you.' (Jīnhòu 1)

仔zǎi 'baby' can be even used to address old people by their elderly parents or relatives, for the younger generation will always be seen as children in the eyes of the elderly, although they are very old. For example:

(37) "爸、 妈、 妹妹， 我 回来 了"。
bà mā mèimei wǒ huílái le

	dad	mum	sister	1SG	come.back	LE

'Dad, mum, sister, I'm back.'

"成仔	啊，	几年	不	见	了，
chéngzǎi	a	jǐnián	bù	jiàn	le
Cheng	SFP	a.few.years	NEG	meet	LE

长	得	还	结实	啊。"
zhǎng	de	hái	jiēshí	a
grow	DE	still	strong	SFP

'Cheng, I haven't seen you for a few years. You've grown strong.'

杨成	的	母亲	拉着	他，	打量	个
yángchéng	de	mǔqīn	lāzhe	tā	dǎliang	gè
Yang.Cheng	DE	mum	pull	3SG	look	GE

不	停。（梦64）
bù	tíng
NEG	stop

'Yang Cheng's mother held his hands and sized him up.' (*Mèng* 64)

(38)
吉仔!	你	回来	啦!	妈	以为，
jízǎi	nǐ	huílái	lā	mā	yǐwéi
Ji	2SG	come.back	SFP	mum	think

今生今世	再也	见不到	你	啦!（浊流220）
jīnshēngjīnshì	zàiyě	jiàn-bù-dào	nǐ	lā
in.this.life	again	can't.see	2SG	SFP

'Ji! You're back! I thought I'd never see you again in all my life!' (*Zhuóliú*, 220)

(39)
喂!	**德仔，**	好久不见，	你	不会	是	来
wèi	**dézǎi**	hǎojiǔbùjiàn	nǐ	bùhuì	shì	lái
hey	Tak	long.time.no.see	2SG	seem.not	SHI	come

补鞋	吧?（浊流221）
bǔxié	ba
mend.shoes	SFP

'Hey! Tak, long time no see. You're not here to mend shoes, are you?' (*Zhuóliú*, 221)

The suffix 仔*zǎi* 'baby' is also attested in Chinese Mandarin. However, nouns with this suffix refer only to little animals rather than people, such as 猪仔*zhūzǎi* 'piggy' and 猫仔*māozǎi* 'kitty'.

3. Suffix 族*Zú* 'Group'

族*zú* 'group' is an emerging suffix being employed to derive collective nouns referring to persons. Originated from Japanese, 族*zú* 'group' was first borrowed by Taiwan Mandarin before being introduced into Singapore Mandarin (Wang 1995). The most commonly seen expression with 族*zú* 'group' in written Singapore Mandarin is 上班族*shàngbān zú* 'commuter (working people)'. For example:

(40) 她　　感到　　懊恼，　　**上班族**　　的　　懊恼。（胜利76）
　　　tā　　*gǎndào*　*àonǎo*　　***shàngbānzú***　*de*　*àonǎo*
　　　3SG　feel　　chagrin　　**commuter**　DE　chagrin
　　'She felt chagrin, the chagrin of the commuters.' (*Shènglì* 76)

(41) 家里　　光　　我们　　两　　个　　**上班族**。（想飞39）
　　　jiālǐ　*guāng*　*wǒmen*　*liǎng*　*gè*　***shàngbānzú***
　　　family　only　　1PL　　two　　CL　**commuter**
　　'We are the only two working people in the family.' (*Xiǎngfēi* 39)

(42) 我　　于是　　厚着脸皮　　走向　　正　　拾级而上　　的
　　　wǒ　*yúshì*　*hòuzheliǎnpí*　*zǒuxiàng*　*zhèng*　*shèjí'érshàng*　*de*
　　　1SG　then　　brazenly　　walk.towards　current　walk.up.stairs　DE

　　　一　　位　　**上班族**　　小姐。（再见5）
　　　yī　*wèi*　***shàngbānzú***　*xiǎojiě*
　　　one　CL　**commuter**　　lady
　　'I then brazenly walked up to a working lady who was walking up the stairs.' (*Zàijiàn* 5)

(43) 我们　　每天　　乘　　地铁　　的　　千千万万　　的
　　　wǒmen　*měitiān*　*chéng*　*dìtiě*　*de*　*qiānqiānwànwàn*　*de*
　　　1PL　　everyday　take　subway　DE　millions.of　　　DE

　　　上班族，　有　　多少　　人　　能　　注意到
　　　shàngbānzú　*yǒu*　*duōshǎo*　*rén*　*néng*　*zhùyìdào*
　　　commuters　have　how.many　people　can　notice

礼让？（风筝166）
lǐràng
courtesy

'How many of the millions of commuters who take the subway every day are aware of this courtesy?' (*Fēngzhēng* 166)

(44) 有   一   群   **上班族**   以   独特   的   方式   来
     yǒu *yī* *qún* ***shàngbānzú*** *yǐ* *dútè* *de* *fāngshì* *lái*
     have one   CL   **commuter**   use   unique DE   way   come

度过   他们   每   一   个   珍贵   的   周末
dùguò *tāmen* *měi* *yī* *gè* *zhēnguì* *de* *zhōumò*
spend   3PL   every one   CL   precious   DE   weekend

傍晚。(报1995年3月8日7版)
bàngwǎn
evening

'There is a group of working people who spend every precious weekend evening in a unique way.' (*Bào*, Mar. 8, 1995, Issue no. 7)

The use of the suffix 族*zú* 'group' is currently spreading widely, especially in newspapers. For example:

(45) 一   上台   总是   脸   臭臭、   脾气   很   坏、
     yī *shàngtái* *zǒngshì* *liǎn* *chòuchòu* *píqì* *hěn* *huài*
     once on.stage   always   face   bad   temper very   bad

口   出   恶   言   的，   通常   给   归入
kǒu   *chū*   *è*   *yán*   *de*   *tōngcháng* *gěi* *guīrù*
mouth   speak   bad   word   DE   usually   GEI   classified.as

坏人族， 如...； 样子   比较   正直、   上镜的、
huàirénzú *rú*   *yàngzi*   *bǐjiào* *zhèngzhí* *shàngjìngde*
bad.guys   such.as appearance rather   upright   photogenic

不时   有   点   亲善举动   的，   则
bùshí   *yǒu* *diǎn*   *shànjǔdòng*   *de*   *zé*
sometimes   have   a.little act.of.kindness   DE   in.contrast

会　　 给　　 归入　　 **好人族，**　　 如...（报1995年6月14日副刊1版）
huì　　 gěi　　 guīrù　　 **hǎorénzú**　　 rú
will　　 GEI　 classify　 **good.guys**　 for.example

'Those who always have bad faces, bad tempers and bad words on stage are usually classified as bad guys, such as ...; those who are more upright and photogenic, and who have act of kindness from time to time, are classified as good guys. Good guys, such as ...' (*Bào*, June 14, 1995, Issue no. 1, supplementary edition)

(46)　只有　　 守着　　 这　　 三宝 – –　　 老伴、　　 老本、　　 老窝，
　　　 zhǐyǒu　 shǒuzhe　 zhè　 sānbǎo　　　 lǎobàn　　 lǎoběn　　 lǎowō
　　　 only　　 keep　　 this　 three.treasures　 partner　　 money　　 home

银发　　 生涯　　 才能　　 有　　 保障，　　 **银发族**
yínfà　　 shēngyá　 cáinéng　 yǒu　 bǎozhàng　 **yínfàzú**
silver-hair　 life　　 can　　 have　 guarantee　 **the.silver-haired.people**

也　　 才能　　 过　 得　　 长春、　　 快活。　　（报1995年6月19日副刊5版）
yě　　 cáinéng　 guò　 de　　 chángchūn　 kuàihuo
also　 can　　 live　 DE　 long　　　　 happy

'Only by keeping these three treasures – the old companion, the old capital and the old nest – can the livelihood in old age be guaranteed and the silver-haired people can live a long and happy life.' (*Bào*, June 19, 1995, Issue no. 8, supplementary edition)

(47)　中国人　　　　 喝酒　　 少说　　 也　　 已经　　 有
　　　 zhōngguórén　 hējiǔ　　 shǎoshuō　 yě　 yǐjīng　 yǒu
　　　 Chinese.people　 drink　 at.least　 also　 already　 have

六七千　　　　　　　 年　　 的　 历史　　 了，　古往今来
liùqīqiān　　　　　　 nián　 de　 lìshǐ　　 le　　 gǔwǎngjīnlái
six.to.seven.thousand　 year　 DE　 history　 LE　 throughout.the.ages

的　 **喝酒族**　　　　 累积　　 了　 许多　 喝酒　 时
de　 **hējiǔzú**　　　　 lěijī　　 le　 xǔduō　 hējiǔ　 shí
DE　 **drinking.people**　 accumulate　 LE　 many　 drink　 time

的　 禁忌。 （报1995年8月8日副刊7版）
de　 jìnjì

DE   taboo

'Chinese people have been drinking for at least 6,000 to 7,000 years, and throughout the ages the drinking community has accumulated many taboos related to drinking.' (*Bào*, Aug. 8, 1995, Issue no. 7, supplementary edition)

There are more detailed peculiar features about Singapore Mandarin grammar. For instance, the adverb 乱 *luàn* 'messily' and 硬 *yìng* 'hard' can be reduplicated; 像极了 *xiàng jíle* 'extremely resemble' can take an object; and the classifiers 只 *zhī* and 支 *zhī* are used differently from those in Chinese Mandarin. The descriptions in this chapter are not intended to encompass all distinguishing features; rather, we have only highlighted the most salient ones.

Every feature of Singapore Mandarin grammar has its origins, which are not touched upon in this chapter. There are some related discussions in prior works; however, most of them are not verified. We chose to skip this issue rather than provide some general quotations.

Notes

1 Translator's note: The original book contains several more paragraphs discussing reasons for differences between Singapore Mandarin and Chinese Mandarin, and analysing the nature of various differences between the two varieties of Mandarin. The author also repeats these discussions in Chapter 5 Volume II for emphasis. In the translated version, with the author's consent, the relevant discussions are deleted here and are kept only in Chapter 5, Volume II.
2 Translator's note: Expressions like 我这个人 *wǒ zhè gè rén* 'I, this person' is a well-accepted appositive phrase in Chinese Mandarin, which means 'I myself ...' or 'I am the person who ...'.
3 Translator's note: This adverb convey a kind of stance indicating that something happens late. In some contexts it can be roughly translated into 'then', 'only' or 'until' in English and in some other contexts there is no corresponding word in English.
4 Translator's note: The original meaning of this word 到 *dào is* 'reach' or 'arrive'.
5 The host of the programme *Good Morning* on Channel 8 asked Mr. Yu Chonghao about his age on April 3, 1995.
6 Translator's note: The parentheses here means that the word inside 有 *yǒu* is optional.
7 Translator's note: 'Ruining' is the name of a person.
8 Translator's note: the original meaning of the word 过 *guò* is 'pass'.
9 Translator's note: Red kerchief refers to the group of poorly educated women immigrants from Guangdong Province in China who came to Singapore in the 1920s, usually working at the construction sites for long hours and low pay.
10 Translator's note: In Singapore Mandarin, the literal meaning of the word 老 *lǎo* is 'old'. However, when it is used as a prefix, apart from adding another syllable, it does not convey any meaning of 'old'.
11 Translator's note: In both Singapore Mandarin and Chinese Mandarin, the word 姑 *gū* means 'aunt on the father's side' and 姨 *yí* means 'aunt on the mother's side'.

5 The Standardisation of Singapore Mandarin

5.1 Reasons for the Differences Between Singapore Mandarin and Chinese Mandarin

In previous chapters we have discussed the features of Singapore Mandarin grammar. Singapore Mandarin and Chinese Mandarin share the same origins. However, why are they so dissimilar? Prior to responding to this question, a rigorous identification is needed to ascertain the grammatical distinctions between Singapore Mandarin and Chinese Mandarin. We cannot presume that any grammatical features we see or hear that are different from Chinese Mandarin are peculiar to Singapore Mandarin and label them as characteristics of this language.

What we read in books and newspapers published in Singapore, or what we hear from a native Singaporean may differ from the Chinese Mandarin. However, these differences are of different nature.

First, some differences are indeed unique syntactic features of Singapore Mandarin. For example, the comparative sentence is in the form of 'XA 过 *guò* 'than' Y' (where X and Y represent the items to be compared respectively, and A stands for adjective) as shown in (1).

(1)a 乌敏岛   的   维修费   **高**   **过**   我   国
      wūmǐndǎo *de* *wéixiūfèi*   *gāo*   *guò* *wǒ* *guó*
      Pulau Ubin DE   maintenance.cost high   than   1SG   country

本岛 。(报 1995 年 3 月 5 日 8 版)
běn-dǎo
main.island

'The maintenance cost of Pulau Ubin is higher than our own main island' (*Bào*, March 5, 1995, Ed. 8)

Such constructions are not found in Chinese Mandarin, where the construction of "X 比 *bǐ* 'than' YA" is used. So example (1) needs to be spoken in the following way:

(1)b 乌敏岛   的   维修费   比   我   国   本岛
     wūmǐndǎo de   wéixiūfèi   bǐ   wǒ   guó běndǎo
     Umin.Island DE maintenance.cost than 1SG country main.island

高   （报1995年3月5日8版）
gāo
high

'The maintenance cost of Umin Island is higher than our own main island' (*Bào*, March 5, 1995, Ed. 8)

Second, some differences actually represent dialectic elements that have not yet been absorbed by Singapore Mandarin. For example, the reduplicated form of the monosyllabic adjective 'AAAA' is a form of expression influenced by the Min dialect.

(2) 今晚   的   星空   很   漂亮，   小小小小   的
    jīnwǎn   de   xīngkōng hěn   piàoliàng xiǎoxiǎoxiǎoxiǎo   de
    tonight   DE   starry.sky very beautiful little   DE

白点   缀满   整个   黑色的   天幕，…（金狮奖 206）
báidiǎn   zhuìmǎn   zhěnggè hēisède   tiānmù
white.dots decorate entire   black   sky

'The starry sky tonight is so beautiful and tiny little white dots decorate the entire black sky …' (*Jīnshījiǎng* 206)

This reduplicated form of 'AAAA' is certainly not found in Chinese Mandarin, and it has not yet been incorporated into Singapore Mandarin, either.

Third, some differences are indeed grammatical errors rather than unique features of Singapore Mandarin. For example, the use of the sentence final particle 吗 *ma* 'SFP' in VP-Neg question, as in (3), is, in fact, ungrammatical.

(3) *林东海   这   位   后卫   是否   能   再   攀上
     líndōnghǎi   zhè wèi   hòuwèi   shìfǒu   néng zài   pānshàng
     Lin Donghai this CL   defender whether can   again climb

另一个   高峰   吗 ？（报 1995 年 3 月 7 日 24 版）
lìngyīgè   gāofēng   ma?
another   peak   SFP

Intended meaning: 'Can Lin Donghai, the defender, climb to another peak of his career?' (*Bào*, March 7, 1995, Issue no. 24)

There are de facto differences between Singapore Mandarin and Chinese Mandarin, as have been discussed in Chapter 4 of this volume. The task arising is to explore why such distinctions exist. We hold the view that the reasons are threefold.

Firstly, Singapore is an independent country which differs from China in terms of social system as well as economic and cultural development. It had been isolated from China for almost forty years, which is quite a long period of time during which it had little or no contact with mainland China. Due to the fact that languages are always evolving, the growth of Singapore Mandarin and Chinese Mandarin in two independent countries would inevitably result in variances, including grammatical differences.

Secondly, the common language is under the constant influence of various dialects. The vast majority of Singaporean Chinese are descended from people Fujian and Guangdong, and they are native speakers of southern Chinese dialects such as Min, Cantonese and Hakka. Therefore, these dialects have significantly larger influences on Singapore Mandarin than Chinese Mandarin does. Not surprisingly, this will lead to distinctions between Singapore Mandarin and Chinese Mandarin as well.

Thirdly, Singapore is a multi-ethnic country that implements a bilingual system, with English being the official language or primary medium language. Singaporean Chinese are generally bilingual, speaking English and their native tongue. In such conditions, Singapore Mandarin is inevitably influenced in numerous ways, including grammar, by English and other ethnic languages. This is another reason why Singapore Mandarin differs from Chinese Mandarin.

The aforementioned factors contributed to the existing traits of the Singapore Mandarin language, and the task of linguists is to discover and describe such traits, setting the basis for the standardisation of the Singapore Mandarin language. Furthermore, the investigation concerning the cause of distinctions between the two varieties of Mandarin will help to clarify some of the issues concerning Singapore Mandarin standardisation.

5.2 The Standardisation of Singapore Mandarin

The vast majority of Singaporean Chinese originate in Guangdong and Fujian provinces in China, with relatively few from northern China (and even fewer from Beijing), where northern dialects are spoken. However, since the establishment of the Singapore Mandarin Girls' School in 1917, the lingua franca of modern Chinese nationals (also known as Standard Chinese 标准华语 *biāozhǔn huáyǔ*) has been embraced as the medium language in education, particularly in writing. Moreover, social interaction and communication also require a common language. Thus, despite the fact that the majority of Singaporean Chinese are not native Mandarin speakers, Mandarin has gradually become the common language in Singapore that transcends dialects.

Singapore Mandarin has a history of at least 70 to 80 years. Following Singapore's independence in 1965, the government instituted a bilingual (English and native language) policy, mandating all Singaporeans to learn English as their first language. Meanwhile, the Chinese community actively promoted Singapore

Mandarin as a common language. Singaporean Chinese typically speak their own dialect at home and with relatives and friends. However, they will speak and write Singapore Mandarin in social activities and formal settings, though many of them would incorporate many dialectal elements into their speaking and writing.

Although the term Singapore Mandarin has a variety of interpretations, the fact that it is a "modern standard common language, with both spoken and written form, for Chinese nationalities in Singapore" (Lu 1984) is universally acknowledged. Meanwhile, we cannot deny the fact that due to its unique historical context and social setting, there are numerous dialectic components and traits of foreign language influences in Singapore Mandarin, particularly in the spoken language, as many scholars have noted. Standard and authentic Mandarin has been promoted in Chinese language education by the Singapore Ministry of Education, in Chinese language programmes broadcasting on television and radio, and the promotion has been in full swing since 1979. Despite all these efforts, spoken Singapore Mandarin has not yet reached the phase of maturation as a common language for Singaporeans. Written Singapore Mandarin has developed into a common language for Singaporean Chinese people. Nevertheless, it still retains numerous dialectic components and features of foreign linguistic influences. In this sense, standardisation of Singapore Mandarin Chinese is a challenge in the current context.

5.3 Main Challenges and Suggestions in Regulating Singapore Mandarin Grammar

The primary challenges to regulating Singapore Mandarin grammar are influences from dialects and foreign language.

5.3.1 Tackling Influences of Dialects

To determine whether a certain dialectic feature should be assimilated into standard Singapore Mandarin or not, we should take the following two factors into consideration.

The first factor to evaluate is universality. That is, whether a certain grammatical phenomenon in the dialect is acceptable to Singapore Mandarin speakers in general. For example, 有没有 *yǒuméiyǒu* 'YOU+NEG' + VP (e.g., 你有没有看电影 *nǐ yǒuméiyǒu kàn diànyǐng* 'Have you seen the movie?') has been overwhelmingly accepted by Singaporean Chinese, and thus could be regarded as a syntactic feature of Singapore Mandarin. However, the following expressions do not seem to be widely accepted by Singaporean Chinese, at least in written registers.

A   V + 看看 *kànkàn* 'see-see' (V for verb)

吃	看看	穿	看看
chī	*kànkàn*	*chuān*	*kànkàn*
eat	see-see	wear	see-see
'try eating'		'try wearing'	

B V + AA (AA for monosyllabic adjectives in the reduplicated form)
   跑　　快快　　　　讲　　好好
   pǎo　kuàikuài　　jiǎng　hǎohǎo
   run　fast-fast　　speak　well-well
   'run fast'　　　　'speak well'

C quantity + 出 chū 'out'
   三千　　　　出　　就　　可以　了
   sānqiān　　chū　jiù　　kěyǐ　le
   three.thousand　out　just　ok　SFP
   'Over three thousand will make it'

   我　　来　　了　　新加坡　　四年　　　出
   wǒ　lái　le　　xīnjiāpō　sìnián　chū
   1SG　come　LE　Singapore　four.year　out
   'I've been in Singapore over four years'.

D V + 有 yǒu 'YOU' / 没有 méiyǒu 'NEG'
   我　　听　　有　　　　我　　找　　　　没有
   wǒ　tīng　yǒu　　　wǒ　zhǎo　　méiyǒu
   1SG　hear　YOU　　1SG　look.for　NEG
   'I've heard'　　　　'I didn't find it'

E VV + complement (VV stands for monosyllabic verb reduplication)
   吃吃　　掉　　　　做做　　完
   chīchī　diào　　　zuòzuò　wán
   eat-eat　over　　do-do　complete
   'eat over'　　　　'have done (something)'

F V + 输 shū 'lose' + 过 guò 'than'/ 给 gěi 'give' + object
   他　　跑　　输　　过 / 给　　我
   tā　pǎo　shū　guò /gěi　wǒ
   3SG　run　lose　than/give　1SG
   'He lost to me in the running race.'

   他　　游　　输　　过 / 给　　我
   tā　yóu　shū　guò /gěi　wǒ
   3SG　swim　lose　than/give　1SG
   'He lost to me in the swimming race.'

G V + 到 *dào* 'until' + C (C for complement)

输	到	光		吃	到	饱
shū	*dào*	*guāng*		*chī*	*dào*	*bǎo*
lose	until	bare		eat	until	full
'lose totally'				'eat fully'		

H V (O) + 了 (*liǎo*) + 了 (*le*) (O represents the object)

学费	已经	交	了	了
xuéfèi	*yǐjīng*	*jiāo*	*liǎo*	*le*
tuition	already	pay	finish	LE

'The tuition has been paid'

我	已经	问	他	了	了
wǒ	*yǐjīng*	*wèn*	*tā*	*liǎo*	*le*
1SG	already	ask	3SG	finish	LE

'I have asked him (about it)'

The various expressions from A to H are basically not found in written registers. Therefore, it is not appropriate to treat these syntactic constructions as parts of Singapore Mandarin grammar at the moment.

The second factor is systematicity. Whether certain grammatical phenomena from dialects are accepted or not as features of the common language should be assessed from the perspective of Singapore Mandarin grammar as a whole. If the language phenomena does not impair the systematicity of Singapore Mandarin grammar and has a certain degree of universality, it may be considered for assimilation; otherwise, we should adopt a prudent attitude and avoid the assimilation of such features into common language grammar. For example, in the Cantonese dialect, the adverb 先 *xiān* 'first' follows the verb phrase it modifies, as in 你行先 *nǐ xíng xiān* 'you go first'. Due to the influence of Cantonese, many Singaporean Chinese also say 你走先 *nǐ zǒu xiān* 'you go first'. Whether to accept this usage as the feature of Singapore Mandarin is a question. As we all know, in modern Mandarin, adverbs frequently precede the verbs or adjectives they modify, and this undoubtedly is the case in Singapore Mandarin grammar. Given the fact that the expression "VP + 先 *xiān* 'first'" goes against the pre-existing norm and a language system cannot have two conflicting rules, it should not be regarded as Singapore Mandarin grammar. Regarding the written data we have observed, numerous examples of '先 + VP' are found. For example:

(1) 好, 就 让 你 **先** 走！（金狮奖 272）
*hǎo jiù ràng nǐ **xiān** zǒu*
okay just let 2SG **first** go

'Okay, I'll let you go first!' (*Jīnshījiǎng* 272)

(2) 小孩子　　　　先　　回。（微型 7）
    xiǎoháizi　　　xiān　huí
    little.children　first　return
    'The children go back first.' (*Wēixíng* 7)

(3) "饭　　好了，　要　　吃　吗？"
    fàn　　hǎole　　yào　　chī　ma
    dinner　ready　　want　eat　SFP

    "你　　先　　吃　吧。"（金狮奖 204）
    nǐ　　xiān　　chī　ba
    2SG　first　　eat　SFP
    '"The meal is ready, want to eat?" "You eat first."' (*Jīnshījiǎng* 204)

(4) 我　　先　　走　了。（胜利 90）
    wǒ　　xiān　　zǒu　le
    1SG　first　　go　　LE
    'I'll go first.' (*Shènglì* 90)

(5) 阿婆，　　你　　先　　坐下。（再见 44）
    āpó　　　nǐ　　xiān　zuòxià
    grandma　2SG　first　sit.down
    'Grandma, please take a seat first.' (*Zàijiàn* 44)

(6) 你　　先　　喝　　杯　咖啡。（吾土·戏剧 153）
    nǐ　　xiān　hē　　bēi　kāfēi
    2SG　first　drink　CL　coffee
    'Have a cup of coffee first.' (*Wútǔ·xìjù* 153)

(7) 我　要　　先　　吃　嘛！（恶梦 102）
    wǒ　yào　xiān　chī　ma
    1SG　want　first　eat　SFP
    'I want to eat first!' (*Èmèng* 102)

(8) 你　　先　　坐下，　我　去　倒　杯　水　　来。（风雨 23）
    nǐ　　xiān　zuòxià　wǒ　qù　dào　bēi　shuǐ　lái
    2SG　first　sit.down　1SG　go　pour　CL　water　come
    'Take a seat, I'll get a glass of water.' (*Fēngyǔ* 23)

(9) 先　　去　问问，　看　谁　　肯　　让　　你　参加？（今后 5）
    xiān　qù　wènwèn　kàn　shuí　kěn　ràng　nǐ　cānjiā

| | first | go | ask | | see | who | will | let | 2SG | join |

'Go ask first and see who will let you participate.' (*Jīnhòu* 5)

(10) 先　　回去，　　我们　　　以后　　会　　　通知　　　再
　　　xiān　huíqù　　wǒmen　　yǐhòu　　huì　　tōngzhī　　zài
　　　first　go.back　　1PL　　　later　　will　　notice　　again

来　　的。（吾土・小说上 142）
lái　　de
come　DE

'Go back first, we will inform you when to come back later.'
(*Wútǔ·xiǎoshuōshàng* 142)

(11) 刚　　　吃饱　　　　了，　　怎可能　　　马上　　　做　　　功课　　　哩，
　　　gāng　chībǎo　　　le　　　zěnkěnéng　mǎshàng　zuò　gōngkè　li
　　　just　eat.enough　LE　　how.can　　right.away　do　homework　SFP

也该　　**先**　　休息　　一　　下　　嘛。（短篇 11）
yěgāi　***xiān***　xiūxī　yī　xià　ma
should　**first**　rest　one　CL　SFP

'How can one do the homework right away after eating. It's better to take a rest first.' (*Duǎnpiān* 11)

The usage of "VP + 先 *xiān* 'first'" is also found, but very rarely, as illustrated by the following example:

(12) 给　　你　　尝　　**先**。（金狮奖 267）
　　　gěi　nǐ　cháng　***xiān***
　　　GEI　2SG　taste　**first**

'You have a taste first.' (*Jīnshījiǎng* 267)

It is evident that the majority of Singapore Mandarin speakers do not consider this to be standard usage. Thus, it is inappropriate to include the expression "VP + 先 *xiān* 'first'" into Singapore Mandarin grammar.

Of the two factors, universality comes first, and systematicity is ultimately subordinated to universality. This is because linguistic variation is an absolute phenomenon, which will inevitably contradict with linguistic systematicity. Meanwhile, language is authorised by usage. Whether a linguistic component (phonological, lexical or grammatical) has legitimacy in a language depends mainly on whether it is spoken, used or acknowledged by all the members in the community. Thus, universality is the first factor to be considered in language standardisation. However, systematicity is not dispensable, either. As a language evolves, there are two sorts of variation. One sort of variation is compatible with the original language system. In other words, the variation does not go beyond or run into conflicts with the original language system.

For example, over the last two decades, adjectives in Chinese Mandarin have undergone noticeable changes in that an increasing number of them begin to take causative objects, such as 方便顾客 *fāngbiàn gùkè* 'make things convenient for customers', 清洁城市 *qīngjié chéngshì* 'make the city clean', 繁荣市场 *fánróng shìchǎng* 'make markets prosperous', 清醒头脑 *qīngxǐng tóunǎo* 'make one's mind alert', 温暖人心 *wēnnuǎn rénxīn* 'make one's heart warm' and 满意群众 *mǎnyì qúnzhòng* 'make people satisfied'. In Chinese Mandarin, the phenomenon that adjectives take a causative object is not new (For example, 丰富我们的精神生活 *fēngfù wǒmen de jīngshén shēnghuó* 'enrich our spiritual life', 健全组织 *jiànquán zǔzhī* 'strengthen organisations'), so this variation is easily assimilated by Chinese Mandarin.

The other sort of variation is the one that is incompatible with the original system of the language. Generally speaking, the first sort of variation is easily assimilated, whereas the second sort will encounter great resistance unless it has unique expressive power, in which case systematicity has an important role to play. In either case, universality is the ultimate deciding factor for the language variations to be assimilated as part of the language system.

5.3.2 Tackling Influences From Foreign Languages

To deal with the influence of foreign languages in the standardisation of Singapore Mandarin, the fundamental principle is the same as that in dealing with dialectic components: universality and systematicity.

In terms of syntax, the following evidence of English influence are observed.

A Percentage numerals are expressed as 'classifiers + 巴仙 *bāxiān*'.
B Apart from 万 *wàn* 'ten thousand', 千 *qiān* 'thousand' is also used to express numerals over ten thousand.
C In writing, dates are expressed from day to year.
D A personal pronoun can be preceded by a definite article.
E 是 *shì* 'be' is used in adjective-predicated sentences.
F The word 被 *bèi* 'BEI' is widely used.

Of all these syntactic features, phenomenon D is not only found in translated works but also being frequently used by Singaporean Chinese people themselves, and thus there should be no doubt that it could be incorporated as part of Singapore Mandarin grammar. Phenomenon C, however, is found only in written language, and it is inconsistent with the time and location expression rules of modern Mandarin in genearal, which always follows the principle of going from large to small. Hence, we predict that phenomenon C will not survive in Singapore Mandarin. As for the remaining four phenomena (i.e., A, B, E and F), whether or not they will become features of Singapore Mandarin is largely a matter of universality, since there is no contradiction with the grammatical system of the Singapore Mandarin language. Further observation and extensive investigation are required before a conclusion can be made.

In short, there is no doubt that the errors found in books and newspapers should be amended. But words or grammatical features from dialects or foreign languages should be treated with caution. Whether they are accepted or not, or how many of them can be accepted, all depend on the universality of the expressions and systematicity of the language as a whole.

5.4 Should the Regulation of Singapore Mandarin be Constrained by the Standard of Chinese Mandarin?

In the discussion about Singapore Mandarin standardisation, some argue that it should maintain alignment with Chinese Mandarin; others believe that Singapore Mandarin can refer to the Chinese Mandarin standard but does not have to be fully constrained by it. What kind of perspective we should take on this issue is the question we will address in this section.

Singapore Mandarin, like Chinese Mandarin, also takes the phonological system of Beijing Mandarin as its norm of pronunciation and the Northern dialect as its foundation dialect. Thus, in the standardisation of Singapore Mandarin, it should stay as close to Chinese Mandarin as practicable as possible. For example, as we have previously mentioned, the expression "VP + 先 xiān 'first'" is slightly more prevalent in spoken language, while " 先 xiān 'first' + VP" is more dominated in written language. Given that in both Chinese Mandarin and Singapore Mandarin it is more universal for adverbs to precede verbs or adjectives, Singapore Mandarin should be in line with Chinese Mandarin in taking "先 xiān 'first' +VP" as a standard expression rather than "VP+ 先 xiān 'first'", so as to conform to the grammatical rule of the modern common language of Chinese.

However, in my belief, the standardisation of Singapore Mandarin does not have to be entirely bounded by Chinese Mandarin standards. It is well recognised that language evolves continuously with the development of society and that language usage is established by conventions. As Singapore is an independent country, its historical background and living environment are distinct from China; consequently, it is impossible for Singapore Mandarin to evolve concurrently with Chinese Mandarin. This is an objective reality independent of human will. Thus, there is no room for sentimentality when discussing Singapore Mandarin standardisation; rather, we should come down to the language reality and make serious considerations. As for components from dialects or foreign languages, they can be accepted and integrated into the Singapore Mandarin language if they are expressive and would not undermine the standard language. For instance, as discussed in the previous chapter, in Singapore Mandarin a compound directional verb can be followed by a place object (for example, 回去家里 huíqù jiālǐ 'go back home', or 跑出来教室 pǎo chūlái jiàoshì 'run out of the classroom'). Although they originate from dialects, they are extensively used in Singapore Mandarin. Thus, they can be acknowledged as a typical grammatical feature of this language rather than being regarded as nonstandard simply because they are not yet widely accepted in Chinese Mandarin.

Some people may have the concern that Chinese people in Singapore will be unable to communicate with Chinese people in China in the future if Singapore

Mandarin is not standardised according to standards of Chinese Mandarin. This concern is completely unfounded.

First, it must be stated unequivocally that Singapore Mandarin cannot and will not develop concurrently with Chinese Mandarin. As previously stated, language evolves alongside the development of society, and it is a conventional phenomenon. Singapore is a sovereign state with a distinct historical background and way of life from China. Therefore, the features of Singapore Mandarin cannot be the same as those of Chinese Mandarin. On the other hand, it's worth noting that Singapore Mandarin is basically identical to Chinese Mandarin in terms of phonology, vocabulary and grammar. The similarities are primary and dominant, whereas the differences are secondary. This will continue to be the case in the future.

Second, languages will mutually influence each other, particularly between common languages of the same ethnic group. With the growing economic, political, technological and cultural ties between Singapore and China, contact between Singaporean Chinese and Chinese people in China will become increasingly frequent. Following this development trajectory, the reciprocal influence between Singapore Mandarin and Chinese Mandarin is definitely growing, and will eventually reach a phase in which the two languages are mutually integrated. Indeed, since the establishment of diplomatic relations between Singapore and China, and particularly since China's opening up in the last decades, to meet various communication demands Chinese Mandarin has already absorbed numerous elements from Singapore Mandarin, as well as Hong Kong Mandarin and Taiwan Mandarin.

In 1995, when I was conducting research on the characteristics of Singapore Mandarin in Singapore, the interrogative form of 'X 不 *bù*/ 没 *méi* 'NEG' XY' (e.g. 参不 / 没参观科技展览会 *cān bù/méi cānguān kējì zhǎnlǎnhuì* 'Did you visit the technology exhibition?') peculiar to Singapore Mandarin was not found in Chinese Mandarin. However, after five or six years, as Hong Kong, Shenzhen and Guangzhou's economic influence on mainland China grew, communication and exchange between Singapore and China became more frequent, and this interrogative form gradually permeated Chinese Mandarin and became prevalent in newspapers and literary works, since it is quite expressive and conforms to the economy principle.

Third, language has a self-adjusting mechanism. Though the common language of a single ethnic group varies amongst communities due to different historical backgrounds and living environment, it will adjust itself as the interaction between members of different community increases. This self-adjustment mechanism works in such a way that when speakers from a different speaking community communicate with one another, they will consciously or unconsciously absorb new linguistic elements from each other. They discard old linguistic elements of their own, gradually increasing the similarities and decreasing the differences so as to achieve smooth communication.

On the basis of the foregoing, I concur with the idea that Singapore Mandarin standardisation does not have to be constrained by the Chinese Mandarin standard. Meanwhile, it is necessary to reemphasise that even in doing so, there is absolutely no need for us to worry that Chinese Singaporeans will be unable to converse with Chinese people in China in the future.

Postscript

At the end of 1994, I received a letter from Professor Chew Ching Hai, Director of the Nanyang Technological University's Centre for Chinese Language and Culture, inviting me to conduct research on Singapore Mandarin grammar as a visiting professor. I was delighted to accept the invitation. From February 25 to August 31, 1995, I stayed at Nanyang Technological University's Chinese Language and Culture Centre. The objective of the visit was quite clear: To conduct a comparative study of Singapore Mandarin and modern standard Chinese Mandarin, specifically to submit to the centre a report on the characteristics of Singapore Mandarin grammar by the end of my visit.

I met Professor Chew in 1985 at the First International Symposium on Chinese Language Teaching held at the Fragrant Hill Hotel in Beijing. I was told that Professor Chew was the only professor of Chinese language and grammatology in Singapore and had served as Prime Minister Lee Kuan Yew's Chinese language teacher. On meeting him, I found him extremely knowledgeable, and he had a firm grasp of grammatical principles. Having spent only a few days in Beijing, he immediately noticed that Chinese Mandarin was different from Singapore Mandarin. He knew that I was primarily focused on the study of modern Chinese grammar, so he shared with me his insights and said, "I'm not sure how much difference there is." I responded to him casually "I'm afraid this needs some research to ascertain the peculiarities of Singapore Mandarin and compare them with Chinese Mandarin." Apparently, Professor Chew kept my words in mind. In 1994, shortly after the establishment of the Centre for Chinese Language and Culture at Nanyang Technological University, he invited me to conduct the comparative study.

Given the short duration of my visit to the centre, Professor Chew invited Mr. Zhang Chuhao from Singapore and Ms. Qian Ping, a visiting scholar from Kunming, China, to collect materials and collaborate with me. Thus, a research team was formed to ensure the research report was completed by the end of my visit.

We started the research by focusing on both written and spoken Mandarin in Singapore. However, after about a month, it became clear that spoken Singapore Mandarin had not yet matured into a common language for Singaporean Chinese. On the other hand, written Mandarin in Singapore had developed into a common language, despite the presence of dialectic and foreign language influences. Therefore, we chose to focus exclusively on written resources. We borrowed nearly all the literary works from the Nanyang Technological University library, and some literary works and textbooks from the libraries of the National University of Singapore and several secondary schools. After ascertaining that the works were written by Singaporeans, we leafed through each book, making notes on cards as we went. Although Professor Chew was preoccupied with his work, he attended each lecture and provided us with numerous useful comments. We benefited from his insights and assistance throughout the process of data gathering, inquiry, analysis, research and writing.

There is one interesting episode about my first day at the centre. After showing me around the entire Chinese Language and Culture Centre, Professor Chew accompanied me to my research room, where he pointed to a computer and said to me, "This is your computer." I instantly responded, "I have no idea how to use a computer, and I don't need it." Professor Chew grinned and added, "If you're not clear how to use it, you can learn. At the end of your visit you are expected to submit a research report to the centre. This cannot be a handwritten manuscript, but a printed one and an electronic copy. You have to learn it since nobody will type it for you. You know that labour costs in Singapore are extremely high." Then, he contacted the secretary of the centre and told her to teach me how to use the computer. It was during that time that I slowly learned to use a computer. Now I use it every day and cannot work without it. Writing by hand cannot bring about any inspiration or thoughts at all.

Throughout the research process, I felt that if I were to grasp the peculiarities of Singapore Mandarin grammar, I had to have a comprehensive understanding of it first. Thus, in addition to fulfilling the assigned duty, reflecting and formulating specific ideas about the characteristics of Singapore Mandarin grammar over those three months, I decided to write a compact grammar book about Singapore Mandarin. During that time apart from normal working hours, I worked on evenings, weekends and holidays. The hard work paid off. On June 16, 1995, at the invitation of the *Lianhe Zaobao,* I wrote an article entitled "The Standardization of Chinese Language in Singapore," which was warmly appreciated by Singapore's Chinese-language community. One week ahead of the end of my visit, I completed a study report entitled "Characteristics of Singapore Mandarin Grammar," and it was also published in the inaugural issue of the *Journal of Chinese Language and Culture, NTU* (1996), a journal founded by Nanyang Technological University's Centre for Chinese Language and Culture. Nonetheless, for the planned grammar book, before leaving Singapore I managed to finish only the part on the syntax of Singapore grammar, whereas the parts on morphology and functional words were not completed. All the materials were kept at the Chinese Language and Culture Centre since I couldn't take all the books and newspapers with me upon my departure. So I could not continue the work after I came back, leaving only the draft on Singapore Mandarin syntax on my computer.

Professor Chew is a scholar with a worldwide perspective and an international outlook who is passionate about Chinese language instruction. He has not only advocated for the compilation of the *Global Chinese Dictionary* and the *Great*

Global Chinese Dictionary (both published by the Commercial Press) since the turn of the 20th century, but has also promoted the study of Global Chinese Grammar, a research project lead by Prof. Xing Fuyi of the Central China Normal University, a portion of whose findings would be published by the Commercial Press.

Being inspired by the idea of global Chinese grammar, I began to reflect on what I had written on Singapore Mandarin grammar. Even though my original manuscript discussed only syntax, and as for the writing of this book, 20 years has already passed since I wrote the original text the abundance and authenticity of the examples would make it a historical marker for Singapore Mandarin grammar if it were to be published. My idea was strongly supported by Professor Chew, who promised to write a foreword for the book. The original plan was to publish in Singapore, and Professor Chew also assisted me in contacting a publisher. However, after taking into consideration the number of readers, I contacted Zhou Hongbo, Editor-in-Chief of the Commercial Press, to see if it was worth publication in China. After hearing about the introduction, Zhou instantly agreed to publish the book, as it would echo perfectly with Mr. Xing Fuyi's upcoming series of *Global Chinese Grammar*. Professor Chew was also overjoyed at the news and sent me the foreword within a few days. His preamble is unique, written in straightforward language and brimming with intellectual, authentic, and emotional depth. Professor Chew's introduction, which is a piece of academic work by an expert, surely adds colour to my works.

From the introduction, it is clear that though the title of the book is *Singapore Mandarin Grammar*, it only includes syntax, and it is a descriptive grammar without detailed explanation. There are inevitable missing points and inaccuracies in our examination and description of Singapore Mandarin grammar and we hope that our readers will evaluate and amend our research while reading in the future.

Finally, I would like to summarise two points.

First, language, as the primary means of human communication, is continually evolving as society develops. One of the primary motivations for language change is the language contact between different languages, dialects and communities. Chinese Mandarin in mainland China gradually spread to the world following China's Reform and Opening-up policy in the late 1970s. Meanwhile, Chinese Mandarin is also influenced by other varieties of Mandarin in Taiwan and Hong Kong, Singapore, Malaysia and Thailand. Thus, through language contact, numerous patterns formerly considered to be distinctive features of Singapore Mandarin in the 1990s have gradually been assimilated into Chinese Mandarin. The prominent examples include: (1) 有没有 *yǒuméiyǒu* 'have not have' VP? (such as 有没有做梦？ *yǒuméiyǒu zuòmèng* 'Did you dream?'; 有没有拿那笔钱？ *yǒuméiyǒu ná nà bǐ qián* 'Did you get that money?'); (2) the question forms of 干不干净 *gān bù gānjìng* 'Is it clean?' or 学不学习 *xué bù xuéxí* 'learn or not?'; (3) 很 *hěn* 'very' + N (such as 很贵族 *hěn guìzú* 'very aristocratic' or 很希腊 *hěn xīlà* 'very Greek'); (4) the interjection word 哗 *huā* 'wow'; (5) words with the prefix 老 *lǎo* 'old', like 老爸 *lǎo bà* 'dad' *or* 老爹 *lǎo diē* 'dad'; (6) words with the suffix 族 *zú* 'group' as in 上班族 *shàngbān zú* 'commuter (working people)' 银发族 *yínfàzú* 'silver-haired people'). Such expressions are also widely used in Chinese Mandarin now. From this perspective of language change, the book's portrayal of Singapore Mandarin grammar is historically significant.

Second, at the beginning of Chapter 5 of Volume II, it is mentioned that while there is a need to explore the characteristics of Singapore Mandarin grammar, we cannot presume that anything we see or hear in Singapore Mandarin is grammatically different from Chinese Mandarin. Numerous variables contribute to the disparities. Among those differences, we originally mentioned one type of 'deliberately coined' words in Singapore Mandarin. The example we cited is 有者 *yǒuzhě* 'someone/something/some phenomena'. Neither of my two collaborators disputed this at that time. It was not until I participated in the compilation of the *Global Chinese Dictionary* edited by Professor Li Yuming that I discovered that 有者 *yǒuzhě* 'someone/something/some phenomena' was not a deliberately coined word. Later, I read Khoo Khee Wee's paper "An Analysis of the Lexical Description of 有者 *yǒuzhě* in Malaysian Chinese" (*Overseas Chinese Teaching*, No. 4, 2016) and I knew that the appearance of the word 有者 *yǒuzhě* 'someone/something/some phenomena' is not very late. Actually, it had already been frequently used in Malaysian newspapers as early as the 1920s, indicating meanings equivalent to 有的人 *yǒuderén* 'someone', 有的东西 *yǒude dōngxi* 'something' and 有的现象 *yǒude xiànxiàng* 'some phenomena'. Therefore, we deleted the original discussions on this matter in Chapter 4, Volume II.

I'd like to express my heartfelt gratitude to Professor Chew Ching Hai and Editor-in-Chief Zhou Hongbo for making this book available to readers. I would not have authored this book had it not been for Professor Chew's request to conduct the research, and my manuscript would not have been resurrected from the computer had it not for their diligent assistance.

Appendix 1
English-Chinese Term List

Terms in English	Terms in Chinese
abstract noun	抽象名词
accusative object	受事宾语
act as complement	充任补语
action	行为动作
action-patient	动作-受事
activity verb	动作动词
actor	动作者
actual discourse	实际话语
adjectival predicate sentence	形容词谓语句
adjective phrase	形容词性词语
adverbial	状语
adverbial-head	状语-中心语
adverbial-head endocentric phrase	状中偏正词组
adversative complex sentence	转折复句
adversative conjunction	转折连词
adversative relation	转折关系
affected object	对象宾语
affiliated relation	隶属关系
affiliation	隶属
agent	施事
agent of the predicate verb	述语动词施事
agentive object	施事宾语
agent-subject sentence	施事主语句
alternative question	选择问句
ancient Chinese	古代汉语
annotative conjunctive sentence	注解复句
annotative relation	注释关系
answer	答话
appositive modifier-head construction	同位性偏正结构
appositive relation	同位关系
approximate number	约数
approximation	概数
aspect auxiliary	状态助词
assertion	陈述性说明
hypothetical complex sentence	假设复句
hypothetical concession	假设让步

(Continued)

(Continued)

Terms in English	Terms in Chinese
hypothetical concessive sentence	假设让步转折复句
attribute	定语
attribute-head phrase	定中偏正词组
auxiliary	助词
auxiliary structure	助词结构
BA construction/sentence	把字句
BEI construction/sentence	被字句
binary	一分为二
cardinal	基数词
categorical nominal classifier	种类名量词
categorical relation	类别关系
causative object	致使宾语
causative verb	使令意义的动词
causative complex sentence	因果复句
cause-result relation	因果关系
character	字
Chinese Mandarin	普通话
classifier	量词（个、只）
clause	分句
collective nominal classifier	集合名量词
companion	伴随者
comparative construction	比较句式
comparative relation	比况关系
comparative sentence	比较句
complement	补语
complement of time and place	时地补语
complex predicate phrase	复谓词组
complex sentence	复句
compound and complex sentence/composite sentence	复句
compound cardinal	系位结构
compound directional verb	复合趋向动词
compound nominal classifier	复合名量词
concession	让步
concessive transitional complex sentence	让步转折复句
concrete noun	具体名词
conditional complex sentence	条件复句
conjunction	连词
connective word	关联词语
consecutive actions	前后连贯的行为动作
consecutive compound sentence	连贯复句
construction	格式
content word	实词
continuation of dynamic situation	动态状况持续义
contracted correlative phrase	连锁词组
contrastive	对举
contrastive compound sentence	对立复句
compound sentence	联合复句
conjunctive compound sentence	并列复句
coordinate phrase	联合词组
coordinate relation	并列关系

Terms in English	Terms in Chinese
copula verb	判断动词
correlative complex sentence	倚变复句
dative object	与事宾语
DE construction	"的"字结构
decimal	小数
declarative mood	陈述语气
declarative sentence	陈述句
definite	有定
degree adverb	程度副词
degree complement	程度补语
demonstrative classifier compound	指量词
demonstrative pronoun	指示代词
dependency relations	倚变关系
direct object	直接宾语
directional complement	趋向补语
directional verb	趋向动词
discourse linguistics	话语语言学
disjunctive	或此或彼
disjunctive sentence	选择复句
displacement	位移
disposal	处置
distinguishing word	区别词
distributive subject sentence	周遍性主语句
disyllabic verb	双音节动词
disyllable	双音节
ditransitive construction	带双宾语的述宾词组
dominating grammatical relation	支配关系
double object construction	双宾结构
dynamic auxiliary	动态助词
entity to be compared with	比较项
erhua, rhotacisation	儿化
Europeanised sentences	欧化句式
exclamative mood	感叹语气
exclamative sentence	感叹句
excluded conditional complex sentence	排除条件的条件复句
exhaustive conditional complex sentence	无条件复句
existential meaning	存在义
existential verb	存在动词
extensional meaning	引申意义
fixed phrase	固定词组
forming relationship	组成关系
fraction	分数
functional word	虚词
general classifier	一般量词
grammar study	语法学
grammatical construction	语法结构
grammatical function	语法功能
grammatical unit	语法单位
grammaticalised from verbs	从动词虚化而来
head	中心语

(*Continued*)

(Continued)

Terms in English	Terms in Chinese
Hierarchical Analysis	层次分析法
high level tone	阴平调
homomorphic pattern/construction	同形句式
idiom	成语
Immediate Constituent Analysis (IC analysis)	直接成分分析法
imperative sentence	祈使句
indefinite nominal classifier	不定名量词
indefinite temporal classifier	不定时量词
indirect object	间接宾语
individual nominal classifier	个体名量词
instrument	工具
instrument object	工具宾语
integer	整数
interrogative mood	疑问语气
interrogative pronoun	疑问代词
interrogative sentence	问话
intonation	句调
intransitive verb	不及物动词
irrealis	未然
kinship relation	亲属关系
kinship term	亲属称谓的名词
lingua franca of the Han people	现代汉民族共同语
linked object	表称宾语，系事宾语
localiser	方位词
magnitude number	位数词
major subject	大主语
maker of adverseness	"不如意"的标志
manner object	方式宾语
material relation	质料关系
matrix clause	主句
meaning of appearance	出现义
measure word	度量名量词
minor subject	小主语
modal verb	能愿动词
modern Singapore Mandarin	现代华语
modern standard common language	华族共同语
modifier	修饰语
modifier-head	定语-中心语
modifier-head phrase	偏正词组
monosyllabic adjective	单音节形容词
monosyllabic verb	单音节动词
monosyllable	单音节
mood	语气
morpheme	语素
morphological marker	形态标记
morphological transformation	形态变化
multi-category	兼类
multi-category word	兼类词
multilayer embedded attribute	定语多层套叠
multilayered complex sentence	多重复句

Terms in English	Terms in Chinese
multiple	倍数
multi-syllable	多音节
mutually exclusive	非此即彼
natural stress	自然重音
necessary conditional complex sentence	唯一条件的条件复句
negative adverb	否定副词
neutral tone	轻音
nominal classifier	名量词
nominal object	体词性宾语
nominal phrase	名词性词语
nominal predicate	体词性谓语
nominal predicate sentence	名词谓语句
nominal pronoun	体词性代词
nominal subject	体词性主语
nominal verb	名动词
nominal word	体词
non-subject-predicate sentence	非主谓句
non-word	非词
numeral	数词
numeral-classifier compound	数量词
numeral-classifier phrase/compound	数量词词组（如，三个）
numeral-classifier-noun object	"数 量 名"宾语
object	宾语
numeral-classifier phrase as objects	数量宾语
numeral-nominal classifier phrase as object	名量宾语
numeral-temporal classifier phrase as object	时量宾语
one-word sentence	独词句
onomatopoeia	拟声词
ordinal	序数词
parataxis	意合法
passive marker	被动标志
passive voice	被动式
passivity	被动性
patient	受事
patient of the predicate verb	述语动词受事
patient-subject sentence	受事主语句
personal pronoun	人称代词
phonological principle	语音规则
phrase	词组
pivotal phrase	递系词组
place object	处所宾语
place words	处所词
polyfunctionality	多重性
possession relationship	领有关系
potential complement	可能补语
pragmatic principle	语用规则
predicate	述语，谓语
predicate word	谓词
predicate-complement	述语-补语
predicate-complement construction	述补结构

(*Continued*)

(Continued)

Terms in English	Terms in Chinese
predicate-complement phrase	述补词组
predicate-object construction	述宾结构
predicate-object phrase	述宾词组
predicative object	谓词性宾语
predicative-object-taking verbs	真谓宾动词
prefix	前缀
preposition	介词
preposition-object structure	介宾结构
primary-subordinate	主次
progressive compound sentence	递进复句
progressive relation	递进关系
pronoun	代词
proper noun	专有名词
psychological verb	心理感受动词
purpose relation	目的关系
purposive complex sentence	目的复句
purposive relation	目的关系
quadrisyllabic unit	四字格
quantifier	量词（例如，每，些）
quasi-directional complement	准趋向补语
quasi-predicate-object-taking verb	准谓宾动词
quasi-object	准宾语
realis	已然
realising relationship	实现关系
recipient	与事
reduplication	重叠式
reduplication of adjective	形容词重叠式
reduplication of verb	动词重叠式
referent	所指
referential relation	称代关系
result object	结果宾语
resultative complement	结果补语
rhotacisation of syllable final	儿化韵
rising tone	上声声调
sample survey	抽样调查
semantic orientation	语义指向
semantic principle	语义规则
semantic relation	语义关系
sentence-final particle	语气词
sentence-final pause	句末停顿
sentence-making unit	造句单位
serial predicate phrase	连谓词组
shape of characters	字形
simple adjective	单个形容词
simple sentence	单句
Singapore Mandarin	新加坡华语
single cardinal	系数词
slight adversative complex sentence	轻转的转折复句
slight-pause mark	顿号
sound combination	合音

Terms in English	Terms in Chinese
specialised temporal classifier	专用时量词
specialised verbal classifier	专用动量词
specific-general compound sentence	分合复句
inferential complex sentence	推论复句
standard Chinese	标准华语
state complement	状态补语
stative adjective	状态形容词
stative word	状态词
stative word-predicate sentence	状态词谓语句
stroke order of characters	笔顺
strong adversative complex sentence	重转的转折复句
structural auxiliary	结构助词
subject-predicate construction	主谓关系
subject-predicate phrase	主谓词组
subject-predicate predicate sentence	主谓谓语句
subjunctive sentence	假设句
subsidiary word formation	附带说构词
sufficient conditional complex sentence	充足条件的条件复句
suffix	后缀
supplement	追加
supplementary relation	追加补充关系
systematicity	系统性
temporal classifiers	时量词
temporal complex sentence	时间复句
temporary nominal classifier	借用名量词
time word	时间词
topic	话题
transitive verb	及物动词
transliterated word	音译词
unit(s) of sound and meaning	音义结合体
universality	普遍性
verbal classifier	动量词
verb phrase	动词性词语
verbal predicate sentence	动词谓语句
verb-object construction	动宾结构
verbs taking nominal object	体宾动词
verbs taking predicative object	谓宾动词
vernacular	白话
vocative sentence	呼应句
VP-Neg question	反复问
word class	词类
word class shift	词性转移
word of overlapping classes	一词多类
word order	词序

Appendix 2
Translation of Examples and Glossary

There are abundant Singapore Mandarin examples in the book, and they are translated into two ways depending on their length and location in the text. For the examples in the main text or short-phrase examples on separate lines, the translation version includes the Chinese characters, Chinese Pinyin with tones and English translations. For the sentences or long phrase examples on separate lines, the translation version has four lines, showing, respectively, the Chinese characters, Chinese Pinyin, word glossaries and translations.

In the original book the author has cited numerous authentic examples from various resources to demonstrate that the language phenomena discussed are quite common in the Singapore Mandarin language. In the translated version, all the original examples discussed in the main text are kept and translated, and, if it is a long sentence, the example is put in a separate line with a number. However, owing to space limitations, long sentence examples appearing on separate lines with numbers are not all translated and are omitted with the author's consent under the condition that the omission will not affect the main discussion. Therefore, the number of examples in the translated version is different from that in the original version.

The glossary words that indicate distinctive grammatical functions in the examples are listed below in alphabetical order:

Glossary	Grammatical Meaning	Singapore Mandarin
1PL	First person plural	我们
1SG	First person singular	我
2PL	Second person plural	你们
2SG	Second person singular	你
3PL	Third person plural	他们、她们、它们
3SG	Third person singular	他、她、它
AM	Agent marker	叫、让
BA	Disposal marker	把、将
BEI	Adverseness marker	被
DE	Postverbal auxiliary word	的, 得, 地
GE	Postverbal auxiliary word taking state complement	个 (例 "看个清楚")

(Continued)

Glossary	Grammatical Meaning	Singapore Mandarin
GEI	Grammaticalised form of verb give	给
GUO	Postverbal auxiliary word indicating the experienced aspect	过
LE	Postverbal auxiliary word indicating the perfective aspect; Auxiliary word at sentence final position	了
LIG	Ligature	而, 之
NEG	Negative adverb	不、没、没有、不是
SFP	Sentence final particle	吗、吧、呢等
SHI	Focus marker	是
SUO	Preverbal auxiliary word	所
TOP	Topic marker	呀、啦、呢
YOU	Adverb before verbs and adjectives	有
ZHE	Postverbal auxiliary word indicating durative and progressive aspect	着

Appendix 3
The Sources of Examples

The examples in this book are adapted from the following works, which are listed alphabetically under the authors' names

Ai, Hua. (1993). *Kēxué yŭ shīde huìhé* [The incorporation of science and poetry]. Sinoforeign Translation Book Press [Lēxué][1].

Bai, He. (1981). *Dúshànggāolóu Xīnjiāpō huáwén zhōngxué jiàoshīhuì* [Alone on tall buildings, Singapore Chinese Secondary School Teachers Association]. [Dúshàng].

Bai, He. (1989). *Fēngyŭ gùrén lái* [Old friends come]. Shengyou Bookstore [Fēngyŭ].

Chen, Huashu. (1988). *Zhuī yúnyuè* [Chasing the cloud and the moon]. Shengyou Bookstore, Singapore Writers Association [Zhuīyún].

Chen, Huashu. (1994). *Bīngdēng huīyìng de wănshàng* [The night of the ice lantern]. Singapore Chaozhou Bayi Hall [Bīngdēng].

Chen, Miaohua. (1995). *Héshàng fēngyún* [Storms on the River]. Favorite Publishing Service Press [Héshàng].

Dìèrjiè shīchéng fúlúnwénxuéjiăng déjiăngzuòpĭnjí [The 2nd Lion City Rotary Literature Award Winning Works Collection]. (1990). Rotary Club of Lion City, Chinese Society of Huachu Alumni Association [Fúlún].

Ding, Zhiping. (1977). *Èyútánbiān de èmèng* [The nightmare by the Crocodile Pond]. Education Press [Èmèng].

Duănpiān xiăoshuō chuàngzuò bĭsài jiāzuòtèjí [Short story writing competition·Excellent Works Special]. (1997). Education Press [Duănpiān].

Editorial Board of xinsha New Chinese Literature Department. (1971). *Xīnmă huáwén wénxué dàxì: jùbĕn* [Chinese Literature in Singapore and Malaysia: the scripts]. Education Press [Xīnmă·jùbĕn].

Fei, Xin. (1990). *Jiànxíngjiànyuăn* [Drifting away]. Huazhong Junior College [Jiànxíng].

Feng, Bingzhang. (1992). *Xīnlíng zhī yăn* [The eye of the mind]. Dot Line Press [Xīnlíng].

Feng, Huanhao. (1989). *Bù diāowĕi de huíyì* [Memories unfaded]. Sino-foreign Translation Book Press [Huíyì].

Feng, Shayan. (1993). *Wényì xùyŭ jí* [Collections of Literary Talks]. Sino-foreign Translation Book Press [Wényì].

Guang, Hui. (1991). *Méiyŏu diàndēng de wănshàng* [Nights without lights]. Shengyou Bookstore [Wănshàng].

Guang, Hui. (1994). *Yīxīnxiăngxiĕ* [Writing heart and soul]. Shengyou Bookstore [Yīxīn].

Guo, Baokun. (1969). *Wèi xĭngxĭng* [Hey! Wake up]. Performing Arts Publishing Press [Xĭngxĭng].

Guo, Yi. (1983). *Chūnfēnghuàyǔ* [Breeze and rain in spring: the beneficial influence of education]. Education Press Pte Ltd. [Chūnfēng].
Guo, Yongxiu. (1989). *Bìhǔ zhī liàn* [Gecko love]. Publishing Group, Cultural and Educational Committee of Bayi Guild Hall, Singapore [Bìhǔ].
Han, Laoda. (1986). *Láodá jùzuò* [Lauda's plays]. Publishing Group, Cultural and Educational Committee of Bayi Guild Hall, Singapore [Láodájùzuò].
He, Naiqiang. (1987). *Értóng bìngfáng* [Children's Ward]. Sino-foreign Translation Book Press [értóng].
Hong, Youhe. (1995). *Huàjù biǎoyǎn xùnliàn bǎilì* [One hundred cases of drama performance training]. Cultural Publishing Press [Huàjù].
Hu, Yuebao. (1993). *Zhuàngqiáng* [Hitting the wall]. Huazhong Junior College [Zhuàngqiáng].
Hu, Yuebao. (1994). *Yǒuyuán zàijiàn* [Goodbye by fate]. Singapore Authors Association, Dadi Cultural Enterprise Co., Ltd. [Zàijiàn].
Hua, Zhifeng. (1988). *Wǔtái èrjuàn* [Stage of two volums]. Publishing Group, Cultural and Educational Committee of Bayi Guild Hall, Singapore [Wǔtái].
Huai, Ying, Zhang, Hui, Hong, Di, Tian, Liu. (1989). *Lántiān zài xuánzhuǎn* [The spinning blue sky]. New Cultural Institution, Shin Min Daily [Lántiān].
Huang, Mengwen. (1982). *Xiězuòrén xiǎoshuōxuǎn* [Selected stories of writers]. World Bookstore [Xiězuòrén].
Huáyùn·dìshíbāqī [Huayun·Eighteenth issue]. (1993). Huazhong Junior College [Huáyùn].
Jīnshījiǎng huòjiǎngzuòpǐnjí·dìyījiè 1981–1982 [The First Golden Lion Award winning works 1981–1982). (1982). Nanyang Commercial Daily, Sin Chew Daily [Jīnshījiǎng].
Jīnshījiǎng huòjiǎngzuòpǐnjí·dìsìjiè1990 [The forth Golden Lion Award winning works 1990). (1990). Lianhe Zaobao, Education Publishing Private Limited [Jīnshījiǎngsì].
Ke, Siren. (1988). *Xúnmiào* [Finding the temple]. Singapore Junior College [Xúnmiào].
Li, Guo. (1984). *Fénchéngjì* [The story of burning the city]. Education Press [Fénchéngjì].
Li, Jian. (1990). *Shānchéng gùshì* [Tales of the mountain city]. Shengyou Bookstore [Shānchéng].
Li, Jian. (1991). *Fàngxià nǐ de biānzǐ* [Put down your whip]. Mountain View Publishing House [Biānzǐ].
Li, Yixiang, Xu, Fuji, Zeng, Jifeng. (1991). *Xīnqíng dié zài qīngqīng de rìjìlǐ* [Moods folded in Qingqing's diary]. Mood Studio [Xīnqíng].
Li, Yueqing. (1993). *Nánběi yóuzōng* [North-South Journey]. Pisces Advertising Design Pte Ltd, U.S. China Printing Pte Ltd [Nánběi].
Liang, Wenfu. (1988). *Zuìhòu de Niú chēshuǐ* [The last Niu Cheshui]. Guanhe Production Publishing House [Niúchēshuǐ].
Liánhézǎobào.1995.2.–1995.8. [Lianhezaobao 1995.2–1995.8). [Bào].
Lin, Chen. (1961). *Jiànwū gōngdìshàng* [On the building site of the house]. Nanyang Literature and Art Publishing House [Jiànwū].
Lin, Jin. (1990). *Wǒ búyào shènglì* [I don't want victory]. New Asia Publishing House [Shènglì].
Lin, Kang. (1986). *Chǎnggēdàngkū* [The song of cry]. Publishing Group, Cultural and Educational Committee of Bayi Guild Hall, Singapore [Chǎnggēdàngkū].
Lin, Kang. (1988). *Xièhòu yītiáo hēigǒu* [Encountering with a black dog]. Cactus Press [Xièhòu].
Lin, Qiuxia. (1993). *Xiǎngfēi* [Wanna fly]. Dot Line Press [Xiǎngfēi].
Ling, Xi. (1989). *Huāyǔzhōng de mèng* [Dreams in the rain of flowers]. Wanli Bookstore [Huāyǔ].

Liu, Huixia. (1992). *Bié zuò duànlexiàn de fēngzhēng* [Don't be a kite with a broken string]. Mountain View Publishing House [fēngzhēng].

Liu, Jun. (1987). *Zhuóliú* [Turbid flow]. Publishing Group, Cultural and Educational Committee of Bayi Guild Hall, Singapore [Zhuóliú].

Liu, Shun. (1987). *MD shì zhèyàng xuǎnchūlái de* [This is how MD is selected]. Cactus Press [MD].

Liu, Su. (1991). *Rénshēng shì huā* [Life is a flower]. Life is a flower [Rénshēng].

Liu, Wenzhu. (1989). *Huànbìng de tàiyáng* [The sick sun]. Singapore Writers Association [Huànbìng].

Lu, Tao. (1989). *Hénjì* [Trace]. Mountain View Publishing House [Hénjì].

Meng, Zi. (1988). *Jīnhòu wǒ shì zhēnde* [I'm sure from now on]. Shengyou Bookstore, Singapore Writers Association [Jīnhòu].

Mu, Zi. (1990). *Mùzǐ xiǎoshuō* [Muzi's Novels]. Xinhua Cultural Enterprise [New]. Co., Ltd. [Mùzǐ].

Mu, Zi. (1990). *Wǒ yǒu huà yào shuō* [I have something to say]. Shengyou Bookstore [Wǒyǒu].

Mu, Zi. (1993). *Wǒ hái yǒu huà yào shuō* [I still have something to say]. Shengyou Bookstore [Wǒháiyǒu].

Nan, Zi. (1985). *Bāfāngfēngyǔ* [Floating all the directions]. Literature Bookstore [Bāfāng].

Nan, Zi. (1987). *Niánsuì de chǐhén* [The marks of years]. Publishing Group, Cultural and Educational Committee of Bayi Guild Hall, Singapore [Niánsuì].

Nanyang University Academic Staff Association. (1986). *Xīngmǎ xiǎoshuō jiāzuò xuǎnjí* [Selected works of Xingma novels]. Education Press [Xīngmǎ].

Peng, Zhifeng. (1989). *Xīnjiāpō wēixíng xiǎoshuōxuǎn* [A selection of Singapore mini stories]. Aljunied Literary Creation and Translation Society Publishing Press [Wēixíng].

Qu, Rubai. (1993). *Lúnxiàn suìyuè* [Colonised years]. Shengyou Bookstore [Lúnxiàn].

Singapore class development board. (1988). *Rújiālǐlùn·zhōngsìkèběn* [Confucian theory: Textbook of the fourth year of middle school]. Education Publishing Private Limited [Lúlǐ·zhōngsì].

Singapore class development board. (1994). *Zhōngxué huáwén kèběn* [Middle school Chinese textbook 1A]. Education Publishing Private Limited [Zhōngxué 1A].

Singapore class development board. (1984). *Zhōngxué huáwén jiāocái* [Middle school Chinese textbook 1A]. Education Publishing Private Limited [Huáwénjiàocái 1A].

Singapore class development board. (1985). *Zhōngxué huáwén jiāocái* [Middle school Chinese textbook 2A]. Education Publishing Private Limited [Huáwénjiàocái 2A].

Singapore class development board. (1986). *Zhōngxué huáwén jiāocái* [Middle school Chinese textbook 3A]. Education Publishing Private Limited [Huáwénjiàocái 3A].

Singapore class development board. (1987). *Zhōngxué huáwén jiāocái* [Middle school Chinese textbook 4A]. Education Publishing Private Limited [Huáwénjiàocái 4A].

Singapore class development board. (1988). *Rújiālǐlùn·zhōngsānkèběn* [Confucian theory: Textbook of the third year of middle school]. Education Publishing Private Limited [Lúlǐ·zhōngsān].

Singapore class development board. (1989). *Zhōngxué huáwén jiāocái* [Middle school Chinese textbook 1B]. Education Publishing Private Limited [Huáwénjiàocái 1B].

Singapore class development board. (1989). *Zhōngxué huáwén jiāocái* [Middle school Chinese textbook 2B]. Education Publishing Private Limited [Huáwénjiàocái 2B].

Singapore class development board. (1990). *Zhōngxué huáwén jiāocái* [Middle school Chinese textbook 3B]. Education Publishing Private Limited [Huáwénjiàocái 3B].

Singapore class development board. (1992). *Xiǎoxué huáwén jiāocái* [Primary school Chinese textbook 6A]. Education Publishing Private Limited [Xiǎoxué 6A].
Singapore class development board. (1992). *Zhōngxué huáwén jiāocái* [Middle school Chinese textbook 4B]. Education Publishing Private Limited [Huáwénjiàocái 4B].
Singapore class development board. (1993). *Shíyòng huáwén kèběn* [Practical Chinese textbook 1A]. Education Publishing Private Limited [Kèběn 1A].
Singapore class development board. (1993). *Xiǎoxué huáwén jiāocái* [Primary school Chinese textbook 6B]. Education Publishing Private Limited [Xiǎoxué 6B].
Singapore class development board. (1994). *Shíyòng huáwén kèběn* [Practical Chinese textbook 2A]. Education Publishing Private Limited [Kèběn 2A].
Singapore class development board. (1994). *Shíyòng huáwén kèběn* [Practical Chinese textbook 1B]. Education Publishing Private Limited [Kèběn 1B].
Sun, Ailing. (1988). *Bìluó shílǐ xiāng* [The aroma of green tea]. Singapore Art Research Association [Bìluó].
Sun, Ailing. (1993). *Shuǐjīng jí* [The crystal collection]. Shengyou Bookstore [Shuǐjīngjí].
Tian, Liu. (1980). *Xīnmǎ xiǎoshuō xuǎnjí* [Selected Malaysian and Singaporean stories]. Dadi Cultural Enterprise Co., Ltd. [Xīnmǎ].
Tian, Liu. (1989). *Xiàoyǎn kàn rénshēng* [A glimpse of life with a smile]. Shengyou Bookstore [Xiàoyǎn].
Wu, Cisu. (1986). *Mèng* [Dream]. Wanli Bookstore [Mèng].
Wu, Mu. (1989). *Wúxiányuè* [Moon without a quarter]. Seven Oceans Publishing House [Wúxiányuè].
Wu, Mu. (1993). *Zhìxìng de yíqíng* [The empathy of the supreme nature]. Publishing Group, Cultural and Educational Committee of Bayi Guild Hall, Singapore [Zhìxìng].
Wu, Weicai. (1989). *Wú Wěicái guàitán* [Wu Weicai's odd tales]. Pan Pacific Press Pte Ltd [Wú Wěicái].
Wu, Yuanhua. (1991). *Píngxīnérlùn* [A fair discission]. Victory Publishing Pte Ltd [Píngxīn].
Wútǔwúmín chuàngzuòxuǎn xìjù [Selected literature of Wutuwumin·play]. (1982). Nanyang Commercial Daily [Wútǔ·xìjù].
Wútǔwúmín chuàngzuòxuǎn·xiǎoshuōshàng [Selected literature of Wutuwumin·novel]. (1982). Nanyang Commercial Daily [Wútǔ·xiǎoshuōshàng].
Xi, Nier. (1992). *Shēngmìnglǐ nányǐchéngshòu de zhòng* [The unbearable weight of life]. Publishing Group, Cultural and Educational Committee of Bayi Guild Hall, Singapore [Shēngmìng].
Xiao, Xin. (1991). *Nǚér huílái le* [The return of the daughter]. South Asia Press [Nǚér].
Xie, Qing. (1988). *Shuǐyánzhūyǔ* [The words of water drops]. Publishing Group, Cultural and Educational Committee of Bayi Guild Hall, Singapore [Shuǐyánzhūyǔ].
Xie, Zewen. (1994). *Xīnjiāpō huáwén jiàoxué lùnwénjí* [Collected essays of Singapore Chinese teaching]. Beijing Language Institute Press [Huáwén].
Xin, Zhu. (1992). *Dìyīgèmèng* [First dream]. Shengyou Bookstore [Dìyī].
Xīnchuán guānghuáxuéxiào sìshí zhōunián jìniàn tèkān [Xinchuan-Guanghua School's 40th anniversary special issue]. (1990). Victory Publishing Pte Ltd. [Xīnchuán].
Xīnjiāpō diànshìjīgòu dìbābōdào.1995.3.–1995.8. Some Chinese programs on the 8th channel of Singapore television from March 1995 to August 1995. [Xīnshìdìbābōdào].
Xu, Fuji. Li, Yixiang. Zeng, Jifeng. (1987). *Qīngchūn zhī lǚ* [The journey of youth]. People's Bookstore [Qīngchūn].
Yao, Zi. (1988). *Jiǔyuè de yuányě* [September's wilderness]. Chen Longyue [Jiǔyuè].

Yi, Fan. (1990). *Dàshùxià liănggè lăorén* [Two old people under the big tree]. Pan Pacific Press Pte Ltd [Dàshùxià].
Ying, Peian. (1988). *Gūjì de liăn* [The face of solitude]. Grassroots Press [Gūjì].
You, Jin. (1988). *Tàiyáng bù kĕn huíjiāqù* [The sun won't go home]. Dongsheng Publishing House [Tàiyáng].
You, Jin. (1989). *Dàhúzi de chūn yŭ dōng* [The spring and winter of the bearded man]. New Asia Publishing Press [Dàhúzi].
You, Jin. (1989). *Rénjiān lètŭ* [Paradise on earth]. New Asia Publishing Press [Rénjiān].
You, Jin. (1990). *Chénshì fúdiāo* [Earthly relief]. Success Press [Chénshì].
You, Jin. (1990). *Ránshāo de shīzi* [The burning lion]. Education Publishing House Private Limited [Shīzi].
You, Jin. (1991). *Ránshāo de shīzi* [The burning lion]. Education Publishing House Private Limited [Ránshāo].
You, Jin. (1992). *Shítouchéng* [The city of stone]. New Asia Publishing Press [Shítou].
You, Jin. (1992). *Tiàowŭ de xiàngrìkuí* [The dancing sunflower]. Education Publishing House Private Limited [Tiàowŭ].
Yun, Kai. (1984). *Wù suŏ nányáng* [Fog covered Nanyang]. Singapore Broadcasting Bureau [Wùsuŏ].
Zhang, Hui. (1990). *45·45Huìyì jīmì* [45·45 Meeting confidential]. Singapore Authors Association [jīmì].
Zhang, Hui. (1992). *Shí mèng lù* [Records of ten dreams]. Singapore Authors Association [Shímènglù].
Zhang, Xina. (1990). *Biàndiào* [Tone change]. Grassroots Library [iàndiào].
Zhou, Can. (1980). *Liúliánshùxià* [Under the durian tree]. Pan Pacific Book Pte Ltd [Liúlián].
Zhou, Can. (1983). *Fāngkuài wénzhāng* [A cubic article]. Book Publishing Department, Singapore Press and Publishing Co., Ltd. [Fāngkuài].
Zhou, Can. (1988). *Dūshì de liăn* [The urban face]. Shengyou Bookstore [Dūshì].
Zhou, Can. (1988). *Èmó zhī yè* [A devil night]. Dongsheng Publishing Press, Tropical Press [èmó].
Zhou, Can. (1990). *Mílù de tóngnián* [The lost childhood]. Success Press [Mílù].
Zhou, Can. (1991). *Cíhuàrén* [The magnetized man]. Shengyou Bookstore [Cíhuàrén].
Zhou, Can. (1994). *Wànhuātŏng* [Kaleidoscope]. Singapore Writers Association, Dadi Cultural Enterprise Co., Ltd. [Wànhuātŏng].
Zhuang, Xin. (1993). *Yĕ shì huáijiù* [Also nostalgic]. Intellectual Publishing House [Huáijiù].

Note

1 The content in brackets are the abbreviations shown in texts.

References

Chen, C. (1994). Minnanhua he Putonghua "You" Zi Yongfa de Bijiao [A Comparison of '有 you' in Southern Min and Putonghua]. In *Shuangyu Shuang Fangyan III* [Bilingual and Dual Dialects III]. Shenzhen: Hanxue Press.

Chen, C-Y. (1993). Xinjiapo Huayu Yufa yu Cihui Tezheng [The Grammatical and Lexical Features of Singapore Mandarin]. In *Huayu Yanjiu Lunwenji* [Essays on Chinese Studies]. Singapore: National University of Singapore Mandarin Language Research Centre (Note: This paper was first published as a separate paper by the Centre for Chinese Studies, National University of Singapore in 1981. Parts of its contents was published under the title of Features of Singaporean Chinese Grammar on the first issue of Yuyan Yanjiu [Language Studies], 1986).

Chen, E. (1990). Shi Lun Yueyu Zai Zhongguo Yuyan Shenghuo Zhong de Diwei [On the Status of Cantonese in Chinese Language Life]. In *Di Er Jie Yuefangyan Yantaohui Lunwenji* [Proceedings of the Second Conference on Cantonese Dialects]. Guangzhou: Jinan University Press.

Chen, J. (1984). *Hanyu Kouyu* [Spoken Chinese]. Beijing: Beijing Press.

Cheng, R.L. (1990). Cong Taiwan Dangdai Xiaoshuo Kan Hanyu Yufa Yanbian [Chinese Grammatical Change from the Perspective of Taiwan Contemporary Novels]. In *Xinjiapo Shijie Huawen Jiaoxue Yantaohui Lunwenji* [Selected Papers of International Symposium of Chinese Teaching, Singapore]. Singapore: Singapore Society of Culture Studies.

Chow, C. (1994). Yufa Yanjiu yu Yufa Jiaoxue [Grammar Studies and Grammar Teaching]. In *Xinjiapo Huawen Jiaoxue Lunwenji* [Essays of Singapore Mandarin Teaching]. Beijing: Beijing Language and Culture Press.

Ding, S. (1961). *Xiandai Hanyu Yufa Jianghua* [Speeches on Modern Chinese Grammar]. Beijing: Commercial Press.

Gao, H. (1980). *Guangzhou Fangyan Yanjiu* [The Study of Guangzhou Dialect]. Hong Kong: Commercial Press.

Goh, N.W. (1978). *Xinjiapo de Shehui Yuyan* [The Social Languages of Singapore]. Singapore: Educational Publishing.

Goh, Y.S. (1986). *Xinjiapo Huayu Yufa Yanjiu* [Studies on Singapore Mandarin Grammar]. Singapore: Singapore Society of Culture Studies.

Goh, Y.S. (1990). *Cong Xinjiapo Huayu Jufa Shikuang Diaocha Taolun Huayu Jufa Guifanhua Wenti* [The Standardization of Chinese from the Fact-finding Investigation of Singapore Mandarin Syntax]. Singapore: Singapore Society of Culture Studies.

The Grammar Section of Singapore Standard Chinese Committee. (1985). *Huayu Yufa Yanjiu Baogao Cifa he Jufa* [Reports on Chinese Grammar Studies: Lexicology and Syntax]. Singapore: Singapore Standard Chinese Committee.

Hsieh, Y-F. (1976). Huayu de Biaozhun Wenti [On the Standardization of Singapore Mandarin]. In *Huayu Yanjiu Zhongxin Xueshu Jiangyan Huilu* [Proceedings of Academic Speeches of Chinese Research Center]. Singapore: Chinese Research Center of Nanyang University.

Huang, G. (1988). *Taiwan Dangdai Xiaoshuo de Cihui Yufa Tedian* [Lexical and Syntactical Features of Contemporary Taiwan Novels]. Zhongguo Yuwen [Chinese Linguistics], 3, 194–201.

Kuo, E. CY. (1976). Cong Shehuixue de Guandian Lun Xinjiapo de Yuyan [On the Languages of Singapore from the Perspective of Sociology]. In *Huayu Yanjiu Zhongxin Xueshu Jiangyan Huilu* [Proceedings of Academic Speeches of Chinese Research Centre]. Singapore: Chinese Research Centre of Nanyang University.

Kuo, E. CY. (1985). *Xinjiapo de Yuyan yu Shehui* [The Languages and Society of Singapore]. Taipei: Cheng Chung Book.

Lee, S.G. (Ed.). (1989). *Tuiguang Huayu Yundong Kaimu Yanjiang Zhuanji 1979–1989* [Lectures on the Opening of Promoting Mandarin Movements 1979–1989]. Singapore: Promote Mandarin Council Secretariat of Ministry of of Communications and Information.

Li, R. (1986). Minnanhua de "u4" and "mo2" ['有 u4' and '无 mo2' in Southern Min]. *Journal of Fujian Normal University*, 6, 76–83.

Li, Y-C. (1988). Huayu Yufa Biaozhun Wenti de Tantao [Discussions on Chinese Standardization]. *Di Er Jie Shijie Huayuwen Jiaoxue Yantaohui Lunwenji: Jiaoxue yu Yingyong Pian (Shang Ce)* [Proceedings of the 2nd International Symposium of Chinese Teaching: Teaching and Application I]. Taipei: Global Chinese Press.

Lü, S. (Ed) (1980). *Xiandai Hanyu Babai Ci* [800 Words in Modern Chinese]. Beijing: Commercial Press.

Lu, S. (1984). *Huayu Lunji* [Selected Papers on Chinese]. Singapore: Jin Chang Press.

Ma, Z. (1991). Nanchonghua Li de Fanfu Wenju yu "Meide" He "Meiyou" [VP-Neg Interrogatives and 'Meide' and 'Meiyou' in Nanchong Dialect]. *Yuyanxue Luncong* [Essays on Linguistics], 16, 99–111.

Modern Chinese, Department of Chinese, Peking University, 1993, Modern Chinese. The Commercial Press, Beijing, China.

Section of Modern Chinese, Department of Chinese, Peking University. (1993). *Xiandai Hanyu* [Modern Chinese]. Beijing: Commercial Press.

Su, M. (1995). *Xinjiapo Huayu Zhong Yantan Biaozhi Yanjiu* [A Study of Speech Markers in Singapore Mandarin]. BA(Hons) Thesis. Singapore: Chinese Language Department, National University of Singapore.

Tian, H. (1994). Haiwai Huayu yu Xiandai Hanyu de Yitong [Similarities and Differences between Overseas Chinese and Modern Chinese]. *Journal of Hubei University (Philosophy and Social Science Edition)*, 4, 73–79.

Wang, H. (1995). ×× Zu [××Family]. In *Shicheng Yuwen Xiantan* [Language Talk of Singapore Mandarin]. Singapore: Federal Publications.

Wu, Y. (1989). Xianggang Hanyu yu Dalu Hanyu de Cihui Yufa Chayi [The Lexical and Grammatical Differences of Chinese between Hong Kong and Mainland China]. In E. Chen (Ed.), *Shuangyu Shuang Fangyan* [Bilingual and Dual Dialects]. Guangzhou: Sun Yat-sen University Press.

Xing, F. (1989). "Youmeiyou VP" Yiwen Jushi [Interrogative Construction of 'Youmeiyou VP']. In E. Chen (Ed.), *Shuangyu Shuang Fangyan* [Bilingual and Dual Dialects]. Guangzhou: Sun Yat-sen University Press.

Yuan, J. (1960). *Hanyu Fangyan Gaiyao* [Outline of Chinese Dialects]. Beijing: Wenzi Gaige Press.

Zhang, X. (1994). Shilun Chongdieshi Dongci de Yufa Gongneng [On the Grammatical Functions of Reduplicated Forms of Verbs]. *Yuyan Yanjiu* [Language Studies], 1, 21–29.

Zhou, X. (1989). Xinjiapo Huayu Xiaoshuo de Yufa Tedian [Grammatical Features of Singapore Chinese Novels]. In E. Chen (Ed.), *Shuangyu Shuang Fangyan* [Bilingual and Dual Dialects]. Guangzhou: Sun Yat-sen University Press.

Zhu, D. (1961). Shuo "de" [On *de*]. *Zhongguo Yuwen* [Chinese Linguistics], 12.

Zhu, D. (1982). *Yufa Jiangyi* [Lectures on Grammar]. Beijing: Commercial Press.

Index

action 57, 66, 75–78, 81, 158, 198–200, 202, 204, 220, 238, 250, 253, 281, 292, 312, 317
adverbial 100, 155–156, 162, 164, 184, 186, 253, 297, 300–302, 312; -head 184, 186; -head endocentric phrase 184
adversative conjunction 280
agent 339
alternative question 364–365, 368
ancient Chinese 138, 179
answer 59, 299
approximate number 25, 346–347
approximation 6, 8, 20, 23–24, 26, 28, 30–31, 33–36
attribute 57, 61, 92, 98, 100–101, 119, 122, 142–143, 164–166
auxiliary 30–34, 42, 47, 51–53, 55, 105–106, 179, 233, 323, 325, 328

binary 189–190

cardinal 1–6, 8–11, 15, 18, 20, 23–24, 28, 30–31, 33, 42, 44, 105, 152, 157; compound 8–10, 23, 30–31, 33; single 1–6, 8–9, 15, 18, 23–24, 28
causative: complex sentence 242; object 400; verb 326
character 17, 44, 47, 131, 212, 234, 244–245, 249, 266, 301, 320–321, 328, 342, 350, 377
Chinese Mandarin 15, 18, 25, 31, 34, 36–37, 72, 74, 91, 100–102 104–105, 118, 145–147, 150, 168, 200, 208, 279–282, 284, 288–290, 292–294, 297, 300, 303, 306–309, 312, 316–320, 322–323, 325, 328–329, 331–332, 335, 337, 339–340, 343, 346, 348–349, 351–353, 355–357, 360–361, 363, 368–369, 371–372, 375–376, 381, 383, 385, 388, 391–394, 400–403, 405–406

classifier 1–3, 6, 10, 28, 30, 32–33, 35–38, 57, 60–61, 64, 66–72, 75–79, 81–83, 87–90, 92–100, 102, 104, 123, 125–127, 146, 151–152, 157, 166, 175–176, 288–289, 294–295, 297, 339–340, 347, 353, 357, 371, 391, 400; categorical nominal 67; collective nominal 64; indefinite nominal 68; indefinite temporal 83, 90; individual nominal 61;nominal 57, 61, 64, 67–72, 96, 104; numeral- 3, 79, 87, 92–100; numeral-compound 30, 32–33, 57, 88–89, 92, 97, 123, 125–127, 152, 166, 175–176, 371; specialised temporal 83, 87; temporal 57, 61, 83, 87, 89–90, 152; temporary nominal 68–69, 71; verbal 57, 75–79, 81–82, 90, 96, 288
clause 182–184, 186, 188–196, 198, 200–206, 208, 211, 213, 215, 218, 220–221, 223, 225, 228–229, 241–248, 250, 252–258, 261–263, 270, 276, 278, 281
companion 390
comparative: construction 368–369, 371–373; sentence 306, 368, 392
complement 164, 186, 284, 286, 289–290, 292–293, 297, 299, 301–303, 323, 328, 363, 396; directional 290, 293; potential 289, 363; predicate- 186, 286, 328; state 323, 328
complex sentence 182, 188–193, 220–221, 225, 228–230, 234, 238–239, 241–242, 247–248, 250, 253–258, 261, 263–269, 281; adversative 192, 220–221, 225, 228, 266–267; causative 242; cause-result 269; compound and 281; concessive transitional 225; conditional 190, 192, 234, 238–239, 241–242, 266–267; correlative 191, 255, 267; hypothetical 229–230, 268; inferential 247–248; purposive 193, 250, 269; slight adversative 225; temporal 253–254

Index 425

composite sentence 182, 186, 188–189, 263
compound: cardinal 8–10, 23, 30–31, 33; conjunctive 193–194, 196, 202, 264, 268; contrastive 204, 206, 269–270; directional verb 284–285, 287–288, 401; nominal classifier 71; sentence 188–191, 193–196, 198, 202, 204, 206, 211, 215, 218, 220, 256, 263–264, 266, 268–270
concession 225, 227–228
conjunction 192, 205, 210, 231–236, 238–241, 243–245, 262–263, 270–271, 274, 276, 278–281
connective word 186–188, 211, 213, 230–231, 242–245, 248, 250, 252, 261–263, 267–268, 270, 274
consecutive conjunctive sentence 264–265
construction 35–36, 60, 92, 98–99, 139, 142, 144, 150, 166, 169, 171, 175–179, 195, 283, 289, 293–295, 368–369, 371–372, 391–392, 397; appositive modifier-head 293; comparative 368–369, 371–373; DE 98, 166; double object 283
contrastive 128–129, 191, 204–206, 269–270, 278
copula verb 41

decimal 6, 8, 11–12, 19, 105
declarative sentence 368
definite 400
degree adverb 295, 303, 306, 318
demonstrative pronoun 57, 110, 166
directional verb 174, 284–288, 401
disjunctive 191, 206, 211, 278; sentence 206, 211
disyllable 179; verb 282, 361

Europeanised sentence 372
extensional meaning 130–131, 135, 290, 293

fraction 6, 8, 15, 18–19
functional word 105, 270, 281, 312, 323, 329, 404

grammar study 188, 380
grammatical function 57, 92, 119

head 8, 57, 64, 92–93, 112, 116, 122, 127, 129, 165–166, 181, 184, 186, 203, 229, 275, 293–294, 298–299, 304, 306, 309, 331, 370–371
homomorphic pattern 179
hypothetical concession 228

idiom 131
instrument 62, 77–78
integer 6, 8–12, 19, 38, 42, 336
interrogative: pronoun 4, 57, 255; sentence 357, 364
intransitive verb 309, 312
irrealis 314, 316–317

localiser 107, 109, 112–113, 117, 119, 121–123, 125–132, 135, 150, 165, 169, 179

measure word 66, 93, 106
modern standard common language 394
modifier 8, 38–39, 112, 119, 122, 127, 165, 184, 293–294, 297–303, 337, 373
modifier-head 8, 112, 122, 127, 165, 293–294
monosyllable 79; monosyllabic adjective 93, 98, 295, 297–300, 303, 393, 395; monosyllabic verb 360, 396
mood 255, 314
morpheme 57, 381–382
multi-category: word 105
multiple 6, 8, 37, 39

non-word 301
numeral 1–4, 6, 8–9, 12, 15, 17, 19, 23–24, 30–33, 35, 37, 56–57, 60, 68, 75, 79, 81–82, 87–90, 92–105, 123, 125–127, 151–152, 157, 160, 166, 175–176, 288–289, 294–295, 335, 337–340, 342–343, 346, 350, 371, 400

object 37, 41, 68, 75–76, 79, 95–96, 112, 127–130, 156, 158, 162, 184, 186, 218, 282–290, 312, 353, 391, 396–397, 400–401; causative 400; direct 283–284; indirect 283–284; numeral-classifier phrase as 288; place 282, 284–288, 401; predicate- phrase 184; quasi- 75–76, 79, 96, 158
ordinal 1, 29, 38–39, 41–42, 44, 47, 51–53, 55–57, 146, 152

parataxis 188
personal pronoun 400
phrase 1 3, 8–9, 24, 28–30, 57, 79, 87–88, 92–100, 104–105, 109, 111–112, 121–123, 127, 129, 131, 134, 139–140, 142, 147, 149–150, 153–158, 160, 162, 164–166, 168–172, 175–179, 183–184, 252, 254–255, 263, 268, 270, 276, 278, 284, 286, 288–289, 292, 294, 312, 328, 337–338, 363, 391, 397; adverbial-head

426 *Index*

endocentric 184; coordinate 9, 29; fixed 268; modifier-head 8, 112, 122, 127, 165, 294; nominal 96, 122, 169–172, 175–178; numeral-classifier 3, 79, 87, 92–100, 104, 123, 157, 288–289; numeral-classifier as objects 288; predicate-complement 286, 328; predicate-object 184; subject-predicate 94–95, 97, 184; verb 140, 153, 164, 168, 312, 397
place words 162, 167, 178–179
predicate 41, 79, 93–97, 168–169, 174–175, 184, 186, 202, 284–286, 289–290, 292, 295, 297–298, 301–303, 328, 357, 375
prefix 105, 378, 381, 383, 391, 405
preposition 112, 130, 154–156, 162
progressive: conjunctive sentence 265; relation 211
pronoun 4, 57, 110, 152, 166, 255, 267, 290, 293, 297, 306, 373, 400

realis 314
reduplication 100, 297, 396
rhotacisation 91

semantic relation 191
sentence-final pause 185
simple sentence 180, 182
Singapore Mandarin 2, 8, 11–12, 15, 18, 25, 28, 31, 35–36, 38, 45, 60, 67–68, 72, 91, 100–101 105, 118, 145–147, 149, 157, 159, 168, 170, 186, 188, 200, 204, 208, 270, 274, 278–290, 297, 303, 309, 312, 317–318, 320, 322–323, 325–326, 328, 331–332, 340, 343, 346, 348, 351–353, 355, 357–358, 360–364, 368–369, 372–373, 375–376, 378, 381, 383, 385, 391, 395, 397, 400–401, 406
slight-pause mark 25–26, 28, 41
sound combination 329
specific-general conjunctive sentence 191
standard Chinese 282, 394, 403
stative adjective 301, 303
subsidiary word formation 378
suffix 301, 383, 385, 388–389, 405
systematicity 397, 399–401

time word 111, 147, 155–157, 179
topic 81, 291, 293
transitive verb 307–309, 312

universality 395, 397, 399–401

verbal predicate sentence 168–169, 174–175
vernacular 208, 210, 290, 368
VP-Neg question 357, 360–361, 363, 393

word class 109, 112, 303, 306; shift 303, 306
word order 289–290